AFT

MW00579364

THE
WARNING
TO
2038

BRUCE CYR

Front Cover

The theme of the front cover reflects scenes from the overall fulfillment of the scriptures of Joel 3: 1-4 reiterated in Acts 2: 16-21. These scriptures are the same events as the three secrets or events revealed in the early 1960s at Garabandal, Spain by Mary, Mother of Jesus. Then in the 1980s, Mary reveals more details, at Medjugorje, Bosnia Herzegovina, of 10 secrets or events that are about to unfold.

This front cover depicts the first event, called the Warning, when all humanity will see Jesus Christ on the Cross [1] and experience an assessment of their lives or a correction of conscience, like a judgment before the Lord. On the third day, all humanity will experience a second event, an Outpouring of the Holy Spirit.

The last events, the great and terrible day of the Lord, God's Chastisements, with the sun [2] as black as sackcloth, with the moon and the clouds blood red, during the time of the passing comet in 2038. This is not the end of the earth or people on it. A remnant of the Church (humanity) will continue.

1 Blessed Anne Catherine Emmerich saw in her visions, the sky obscured by a lurid reddish fog during the crucifixion.
2 On the cover, the light ellipse, fading to black, represents the sun.

ISBN: 978-0-9936196-2-5 (Book-paperback)
Copyright © 2017 by Bruce A. Cyr

Web: **www.AfterTheWarningTo2038.com**

Published by: Bruce A. Cyr
Okotoks, Alberta
Canada

Printed in Canada

1st Printing- November 2014– under the title: After The Warning 2016
2nd Printing-September, 2016– under the title: After The Warning 2016
1st Printing- January, 2017–under the new title: After The Warning To 2038
2nd Printing- update January, 2018–under the title: After The Warning To 2038
3rd Printing- update August, 2018–under the title: After The Warning To 2038
4th Printing- update February, 2019–under the title: After The Warning To 2038
5th Printing- update June, 2019–under the title: After The Warning To 2038

6th Printing- update **January**, **2020**–under the title: **After The Warning To 2038**
This latest book is generally the same information with revisions and updates.

All Biblical quotations are taken from: The New American Bible, 1970, Catholic
Publishers Inc., 1971, a division of Thomas Nelson Publishers, Inc., New York, unless
otherwise stated. The Catholic Biblical Association of America translated this Bible
from the original languages with critical use of all the Ancient sources.

DECLARATION

Since October 1966, Pope Paul VI has authorized that books and other communications
no longer require a Nihil Obstat or Imprimatur. The laity or faithful are free to read,
discuss and record private revelations, from and through books, and other
communications; obtained from the Bible, early Church Fathers, Doctors of the
Church, venerable, blessed, or canonized saints, those considered mystics including
stigmatists, priests and religious, ordinary men and women of notable discernible
credibility; including those witnessing Marian apparitions, who may have received
revelation through apparitions, visions, miracles, locutions, or prophecies; even though,
the events may still be under investigation. It is our right, our privilege, and our duty to
be informed and aware of these experiences and messages but it is imperative to ensure,
they do not contradict faith and morals.

The author accepts the final conclusions of the Holy Roman Catholic Church in regards
to apparitions that are under investigation by the authority of the Holy See in Rome.

"Extinguish not the Spirit. Despise not prophecies. But prove all things; hold fast to that
which is good." 1-Thessalonians 5: 19-21

DEDICATION

TO

SAINT BRIDGET OF SWEDEN

AND

SAINT THERESE OF LISIEUX

TABLE OF CONTENTS

Author's Preface xi
Introduction xii

Section I

    An Awakening xiv
1 Beginnings 1
2 Saint Bridget of Sweden 3
3 Prophecies of Saint Bridget 5
4 Prophecies of Catholic Saints... 8
5 Holzhauser's Prophecies and the Seven Church Ages 10
    Seven Church Ages - Venerable Holzhauser (summary) 11
    Holzhauser's Prophecies 13
6 Birth Pangs 15
7 The Fifth Church Age (1520 to 2038) 17
    Marian Apparitions 18
    Marian Apparitions (summary) 20
    Mystery of Iniquity.. 23

Section II

    The Fifth Church Age Begins... 24
8 The Downward Spiral 25
    Pope Leo X... 25
    Reign of Charles V 25
    Martin Luther... 26
    King Henry VIII... 30
    The Council of Trent 30
9 The Woman Clothed with the Sun.. 31
    Our Lady of Guadalupe... 31
    Battle of Lepanto.. 34
    Our Lady of Good Success 34
    Mary of Agreda 37
    Margaret Mary Alacoque 38
10 Secret Sects-Freemasonry and Conspiracies 39
    Age of Enlightenment 44
    The French Revolution (1789-1802)..45
    Napoleon and the Republic 51
11 Our Lady's Call for Prayer Warriors....................................... 52
    St. Louis De Montfort 52
    Anne Catherine Emmerich.. 52
    Our Lady of the Miraculous Medal 53
    Our Lady of La Salette 55
12 The Illusion of Karl Marx... 59
13 Our Lady of Lourdes (1858).. 62
14 Demons Unloosed From Hell.. 73
    Pope Leo XIII–Vision of God and Satan 74

Section III

    Satan's Extended Reign... 76

15 The Twentieth Century Begins... 77

    The Deception of Communism... 78

    Shadow Government Above Governments 79

    Council on Foreign Relations 80

    The Federal Reserve... 81

    World War I.. 82

16 Our Lady of Fatima (1917) 83

17 Fruit of the Federal Reserve and Wall Street 91

    Who Financed the Rise of Communism?............................... 91

    Roaring '20s, Crash of '29 and Dirty '30s Depression 93

18 Divine Mercy.. 95

    Saint Faustina Kowalska... 95

    Therese Neumann.. 97

19 War is Big Business.. 98

    World War II 98

    Hitler.. 99

20 The Great Deception (1945– 2021)...................................... 101

    "Fifty or Sixty Years Before the Year 2000" 101

    United Nations 102

    Literal Fulfillment of Old Testament Prophecies 103

    Rise of Suburbia 106

    The Seton Prophecy.. 107

    The Deception of Television 108

21 Our Lady of Garabandal (1961-1965)............................... 110

    Mary's First Message to the World 110

    The Warning.. 111

    The Miracle Sign 112

    All Those Present Will be Healed.. 113

    The Chastisement 113

    Three More Popes Prophecy 114

    Unusual Blessings 115

    The Second Message to the World 115

22 A Changing Church.. 116

    Vatican II... 116

    The Charismatic Renewal.. 117

23 1960's Revolution and Rebellion 119

    Holzhauser's Prophecies... 119

    Politics and Greed... 120

24 Freemasonry in the Church.. 123

    Communist Infiltration in the Church................................. 124

    Prophecies Connecting the Secret Sect 125

    Persecution of Pope Paul VI.. 126

    The Smoke of Satan has Entered the Church 127

    Implementation of Vatican II Gone Awry 127

    Prophecies of Marie-Julie Jahenny 129

    Prophecies at Akita... 130

25 "The Wicked Shall Prevail" (1980(s) 131

26 Our Lady of Medjugorje (1981 to ?) 133

    Father Jozo Zovko.. 139

Ten Secrets of Medjugorje 141
Defeat of the Soviet Union 143
Heaven, Hell, and Purgatory 144
27 John Paul II Consecrates Russia 147
Significance of Marian Feast Days 147
Understanding the True Face of Communism 150
28 Tears of the Virgin Mary 151
Our Lady of Kibeho, Rwanda 152
Our Lady of Peace to Pedro Regis at Anguera, Brazil 154
29 Earthly Concerns 158
Global Dimming 158
Decreased Pan Evaporation 159
Global Weather Extremes 159
Extreme Ocean Changes 160
Ocean Pollution 160
Destruction of Coral Reefs and Fisheries 161
Industrial Pollution Affecting People, Land, Water, and Air 161
Agricultural Pollution 161
Global Resource Depletion 162
Wild Mammals and Birds Endangered 162
Wakeup Call to Genetically Modified Foods 163
Bees Vanishing 163
Blaming Everything but the Sin of Mankind 164
30 The World, Temptation, and the Devil 165
Declining Demographics in the Western World 165
Same Sins of Civilizations Past 166
The World Has Become Desolate 166
My Beloved Ones, I Plead With You 168
In Hell, It's Too Late 169

Section IV
The Great Tribulation 172
31 Forty Years of Tribulation (2000-2040) 174
Prophecies of Saint Malachy 176
"I Did Not Come from Heaven for Your Amusement" 178
32 The Secret Sect's New World Order 179
The Bilderberg Group 181
The Trilateral Commission 181
Controlling the Media for World Domination 181
World Bank and International Monetary Fund 182
The Bohemian Grove 182
Major Changes Not Seen 182
Prophecies Pointing to Grave Changes 184
9-11: 'Who Dun It?' 185
Prophecies Expose Mohammedans, Tyrants, and Heretics 186
33 The Second Revolution (2020) 188
"Upheaval of a Region of the World" (2020 or 2021) 190
"When Conditions Are at Their Worst" (2020 or 2021) 191
34 Divine Intervention (2020 or 2021) 193
Divine Justice Approaches 193
Three Admonitions from God 194
The Worldwide Warning (2020 or 2021) 195

Enlightenment from God's Admonitions...199
John Paul II the Mystical 201
Opening of the First Seal of Revelation (2020 or 2021)...................202
Outpouring of the Holy Spirit Upon All Mankind (2020 or 2021)............ 204

35 Decrees of Punishments (2021–2038)...206
Opening of the Second Seal of Revelation (2020 or 2021)...............209
New York, New York (2021)...210
Major War and Worldwide Civil Chaos (2021)..............................214
Hope During the Great Storm...215
War Will Take Place (2021)..217
Remain Where God has Placed Us..218
To Stock Up Food, Water, and Other Necessities.............................219
A Step-Down Decree...222
Prophecies of Worldwide Chaos 223
The Mohammedans Will Rise Up..224
Chaos in the Church..225

36 Sorrowful Events Upon the Earth 226
Canada..226
United States of America...227
The Land of Santa Cruz (USA?)..227
Central America 228
South America...228
England 229
Europe..229
Eastern Europe 230
Middle East...230
Africa 230
Southeast Asia..231
Unusually Interesting..231

37 The Rescue by Our Lady of the Immaculate Conception.................233
The Rescue from the Storm..233
The Triumph of Mary's Immaculate Heart..234
Optimistic Messages of Medjugorje...235
Our Lady as Co-Redemptrix, Mediatrix, and Advocate....................236
"I Will Pour Out My Spirit on All Mankind".....................................238
Day of the Miracle and Miracle Signs (2021)...................................240
Miracle Signs at Credible Marian Apparition Sites...........................241
Miracle Sign on "Martyr of the Eucharist" Feast Day........................242
Restoration from God's Three Admonitions. 243
A Time of Evangelization...244
Spiritual Direction 245
"Will Have Little Time to Convert"...246

38 Decrees of Punishments Will Continue. 247
Opening of the Third Seal of Revelation (Fifth secret of Medjugorje?).. 247
Prophecies of Famine 249
Opening of the Fourth Seal of Revelation (Sixth secret of Medjugorje?)..........250
Spiritual Abandonment Reflects Catastrophic Events 251
Shift of the Magnetic Field..251
Earthquakes..252
Shift of the Earth's Axis..253
Gravitational Changes..253
Changes in Nature..253
Fire...254

Severe Weather Extremes 254
Mountains 255
Volcanos 255
Extreme Explosions 256
Tsunamis 256
Stones and Boulders 256
Genetic and Technological Destruction 256
Plagues Without a Solution 257
Death 259
39   Back to the Future (2020s and 2030s) 260
     After Oil 261
     Look to the Amish 263
40   The "Fatal Event," Chaos in the Church (Seventh secret)(Late 2020s) 266
     The Vengeance of Hell Against the Church 266
     Schism 269
     An Apostasy 270
     Antichrists Will Rise Up 271
     Visible Break Down of the Church 272
     How Many Popes? 273
41   Opening of the Fifth Seal of Revelation (Eighth secret of Medjugorje?) 274
     Prophecies of Persecution and Martyrdom 275
42   Opening of the Sixth Seal of Revelation (Very late 2020s to 2038) 278
     A Collision in the Universe (Very late 2020s or early 2030s) 279
     Worldwide Destruction of the Electrical Grids 280
     The Trumpets 281
     The First Angel's Trumpet 282
     Rapid Melting of Polar Caps & Glaciers 284
     Sunlight Will Become Perceptibly Weaker (2030s) 284
     Four Years of War Before the Comet (2033-June 2037) 285
     The End of an Age 285
43   Great Catholic Monarch (2030s) 286
     Charles of Austria to the Great Catholic Monarch 287
     Prophecies of the Great Catholic Monarch 288
     The Counter-Revolution Begins 291
     Battles of the Great Catholic Monarch (2033-2037) 292
     He Will Push Back the Mohammedans 293
     Birch Tree Country Prophecies 294
44   The Gates of Hell Shall Not Prevail Against His Church. 296
     Imminent Invasion of the Vatican 296
     The Russians Are Coming 297
     Pope Flees Rome and is Martyred (2033-2035) 298
     No Pope in Rome 299
     Rome and the Vatican Destroyed 300
45   God's Chastisements (2030-2038). 302
     "The Whole World Shall Cry, Woe!" 302
     The Second Angel's Trumpet 305
     The Third Angel's Trumpet 305
     Just Before the Comet Comes (July 2037- April 2038) 306

The Fourth Angel's Trumpet... 307
Answering the Cry of the Poor.. 308
Two Days of Darkness Before the Three Days of Darkness (March 2038)..... 309
The Comet (April 2038) 310
Prophecies of the Comet 312
Three Days of Darkness (2038) 315
The Angels Will Help 316
Prophecies of Three Days of Darkness... 316
46   The Aftermath on Earth 323
A Remnant Shall Be Saved... 324
The Comet Fertilizes the Earth 326
A Great Sign Appears in the Sky... 326
Definitive Triumph of Mary's Immaculate Heart 327

Section V
The Sixth Church Age 328
47   Age of Peace (2038-2383?)... 329
Satan Will Be Bound... 329
Reign of the Sacred Heart of Jesus and the Immaculate Heart of Mary 330
"A Period of Peace" (2038-2383?) 330
A Transformed Earth... 331
Like a Garden... 332
48   The Powerful Monarch and the Holy Pope... 333
The Holy Pope and the Cross-on His Forehead (2038-?) 334
Prophecies of the Holy Pope 335
Revival of the Holy Roman Empire 337
Reign of the Powerful Monarch (2038-?) 338
49   Time of Faith and Order.. 340
Unusual Prophecies During the Sixth Church Age 341
A Spiritual Transformation.. 342
Ecumenical Council in the Sixth Church Age.................................... 343
All Nations Will Become Catholic 344
50   The End of the Sixth Church Age 345
As the Sixth Church Age Progresses.. 345
Seventy-Weeks of Years 346
The False Prophet... 348
The Antichrist... 349
The Antichrist Will Be Coming... 351

Section VI
The Seventh Church Age (2383? -3383 or longer?)............................. 353
51   The Final Tribulation of the Gentile Church...................................... 354
The Birth of Antichrist.. 355
He Will Be Possessed by Satan... 356
He Will Deceive the Jewish People.. 356
Rebuilding of the Jewish Temple (3rd)... 357
He Will Deceive Christians 357
The Abomination of Desolation 358
The Image of the Beast 359
The Mark of the Beast.. 359
Three and One-Half Years... 359
Wondering Where The Lions Are?.. 360

The Two Witnesses 361
The Ark of the Covenant Revealed by the Two Witnesses 365
Conversion of the Jews to the Messiah–Jesus Christ 365
The Seven Bowls of Plagues 365
The End of Antichrist 367
The Two Harvests of God 368
52   Christ Comes Again 369
The Fullness of the Gentile (Bride) Church 371
In the Twinkling of an Eye 371
The First Resurrection 373
The Messiah is Coming 373
Understanding the Differences 374
The Seven Kingdoms of Daniel 7 & Revelation 17 374
53   The Thousand Years 377
A Utopia During the Seventh Church Age 377
Like the Sands of the Sea 378

Section VII
His Reign Will be Forever 380
54   After the Thousand Years 381
The Last Judgment 382
A New Heavens and a New Earth 383

Epilogue 385
St. Therese of Lisieux 385

Bibliography 386
Acknowledgements & References 390

AUTHOR'S PREFACE

To receive the revelations in this book, our hearts and minds must be open to the Holy Spirit, to awaken us to His predestined plan. A logical and rational person, unknowingly surrendering to the prevailing pseudo-logic, of the present world, may not be able to understand what God is saying, and what He will do. This work awakens us, to the truth about past events. It looks at some of the spiritual events of good and evil that have not been understood nor revealed by the mainstream media of this world. But surprisingly, the truth about our past and present will reflect on our future in accordance with God's will.

Revealed are **many words from Heaven** of future events, given to us by the Holy Spirit, taken from the Bible, the Early Church Fathers, Doctors of the Church, and Catholic saints, including notable saints of discernible credibility and from visionaries who have seen Mary, Mother of Jesus; all placed in a chronological order. This book may lead to denial of some of its contents, and without praying for humility and wisdom, a person may not find the road less traveled... I do not say this lightly.

INTRODUCTION

" **S**hould there be a prophet among you, in visions will I reveal myself to him, in dreams will I speak to him. Not so, with my servant Moses, throughout my house he bears my trust, face to face. I speak to him; plainly and **not in riddles**." (Numbers 12: 6-8)

Historically, God has spoken to us in fragmentary and varied ways. Disclosures from God, were given like puzzle pieces over the centuries to prophets, accumulated in both the Old and New Testament. Jesus made it clear when He spoke about the Holy Spirit, just before His ascension, that the Holy Spirit would be sent, to give us more information about the future.

The Book of Revelation is an example of what the Holy Spirit reveals. More prophetic information has continued to come to us in fragments, throughout the last 2000 years, influenced by the Holy Spirit, mainly through the Early Church Fathers, Doctors of the Church, Catholic Saints, through visionaries of Mary, Mother of Jesus, and from Jesus, our Lord, through visions and locutions, translated into books and journals, and passed on from generation to generation within the Church. All true prophecies continue to come to us through the Holy Spirit. Some Christians say that the Bible is the main source of spiritual authority and understanding, but the Holy Spirit is the one true source of all true information that goes beyond the written word, in the Bible, by expanding that information, revealing to us many things unknown. This has become part of our Catholic Church tradition and is handed down to us, to help us to be aware of the things to come. In the last 200 years, information has accelerated, giving rise to an abundance of prophecies, foretelling incredible changes ahead of us.

To **understand the topics in this work** and of **how** the prophecies come to us, an **explanation** on the **Holy Spirit** is **paramount**. The Holy Spirit is a person or personality, making up part of the Holy Trinity and is the arm or extension of the Father and the Son, Jesus Christ, and is the "another" in John 14:16 that Jesus asked the Father to send. The Holy Spirit is like the wind; we know it is there, by its effects. The best way to understand the Holy Spirit is **to experience the presence** of the Holy Spirit. God wants us to take the first step though, by talking to Him, as if talking to a friend. **This friendship** comes with hours of connecting, called prayer, or in every day language, talking to a friend. He desires this of us, each day, so it will become a real relationship, an intimate experience.

Jesus explains the imminent workings of the Holy Spirit, in two chapters, from the Gospel of John, clarifying **how** the Holy Spirit will inform us.

In **John 14**: 25-26, Jesus tells His Apostles: "This much I have told you, while I was still with you; the Holy Spirit, whom I will send in my name, will **instruct you in everything.**" That is, He will relate everything to us, when we are in need of understanding. This is more information than Jesus gave when He was still on the earth and is more information than what is chronicled in the Bible. **In John 16**: 12-13, when Jesus was continuing with his last discourse, He said to the Apostles, "I have (so) much to tell you, but you cannot bear it now. When He (Holy Spirit) comes…He will guide you to **all truth**… and **will announce to you the things to come.**"

The Holy Spirit has revealed to us many **future events** in the Bible and will continue to expound on those events, not fully described in the Bible. He also reveals, **unknown future events** that are not described in the Bible. How does the Holy Spirit reveal all truths and the things to come? After Jesus ascended to Heaven, the Holy Spirit was poured out upon the Apostles; many gifts were evident and continue to be poured out to this very day. Recorded in Acts of the Apostles, Peter reiterates the prophecy of Joel 3: 1-4. "Your sons and daughters **shall prophecy**, your young men shall **see visions**, and your old men shall **dream dreams.**" Over the centuries, many saints had visions and dreams, revealing to them what God wanted to convey. Many people are very ordinary people, not recognized saints, but God gives His revelations just the same. In Ecclesiasticus or Sirach 34:5-6, it says: "Dreams are frivolous and chasing of the wind, unless they are **from emissaries, from on High.**" We can discern, if it is from God.

St. Paul speaks of Charism gifts, such as the gift of Wisdom, the gift of Knowledge, the gift of Prophecy, and many others. These gifts are **not of the natural gifts**, of our normal lives, but are extraordinary or **supernatural** gifts, that the Holy Spirit bestows upon certain people from time to time; to reveal information to a doubting world, for ourselves and for those around us.

The gift of Prophecy, in simple terms, is **God speaking to us**. You may hear God speaking to you interiorly (in your mind or in your thoughts) or through locution (hearing an audible voice) to provide instruction, guidance, or direction. St. Paul says: "**above all** the gifts, **desire** the gift of **Prophecy.**" "Extinguish not the Spirit. Despise not prophecies, but prove all things; hold fast to that which is good…"

In Isaiah 46: 9-12, God **speaks in advance**: "I am God, there is no other… at the beginning, **I**, foretell the outcome, in advance, things not yet done. **I** say that my plan shall stand… Yes, **I** have spoken, **I** will accomplish it; **I** have planned it, and **I** will do it. Listen to me, you fainthearted, you who seem far from the victory… **I am bringing on my Justice, it is not far off…**"

Section I

An Awakening

Our civilization as we know it, is running out of time, but most fail to see **the sudden destruction,** soon to fall upon us. Before this destruction, a Warning will come directly from God and few people are aware of the hour. This can be calculated accurately based upon scores of prophecies available to us, through Catholic saints, inspired by the Holy Spirit. An awakening is coming to all mankind, but that will not spare everyone. In the end, only a remnant of people will be left to continue on this earth. The destruction to the world, as we know it, will be worldwide.

The first seven chapters provide an overview of **prophecies** and **events** that have unfolded, those that are unfolding, and those that will unfold, in chronological order. The first three chapters, detail why I became personally involved in this work, leading to many years collecting and studying prophecies, including four plus years writing, while pleading with our Lord for the truth. This has led to understanding, somewhat, threatening organizations in high places, on this earth, and events directly from God who will counter this threat that I did not see coming.

CHAPTER I

BEGINNINGS

My first conscious memories of God came from visits with my grandmother, who would talk about Jesus as if she knew Him. She taught us words to pray and always prayed the rosary, even when pulling dandelions out of her lawn. When answering the door, she would have a prayer book in one hand and a rosary in the other. I often heard her use the phrase "if God is willing." She was very gracious to others, with her words and in her concern for those on her street, reputed to not believe in God; she prayed for them.

At the age of 11 years old, I practiced skating at the arena, in town, on Sunday afternoons. We went to church, in town, on Sunday mornings and I would ask if I could stay at Grandma's house to go skating. Otherwise, on Sundays she generally came to the farm where we lived, to spend the day.

One of those times when I was waiting to go skating, I sat in a rocking chair on one side of the living room, and she sat in the other rocking chair by the window. This was her favorite place to sit, so she could watch through the window and observe the passersby on the sidewalk. As noonday approached, she decided to pray her usual, Sunday noonday prayers and asked me if I wanted to pray. I shrugged my shoulders indifferently, as I had just gone to church. She responded, "I'm going to pray for you." She continued on praying, and then, all of a sudden, she moved up to the edge of her rocking chair and exclaimed, "Oh dear me! God just told me something about you." I said: "He did? I didn't hear anything? How did you hear Him? What did he say?" She said, "I hear Him in my head, in my thoughts." "What did He say?" "He said, you would be a preacher some day." After that she always thought I would become a priest, I would say to her, I want to be a rancher. She shrugged her shoulders, her trust in the Lord unwavering.

My grandmother died a few years later, and since then, I gradually came to realize my grandmother possessed the gift of prophecy, that is, the Lord would speak to her. She also had the gift of anointing, in that, she experienced the presence of God, to teach her and guide her. The anointing is experienced initially in Baptism, but the anointing is the presence of the Holy Spirit that continues to be active in our lives if we are open.

My next spiritual experience came at the age of 11 or 12. I didn't really understand what was happening at the time. I was out playing by an old hay stacker that was used with horses, in earlier days on the farm. I started singing in a different language, though I did not understand the words; the song just seemed to flow from me in a natural way. I then felt a presence around me and thought, "Is this God?" I looked up into the blue sky but saw and heard nothing. Yet, looking back, I am certain, of having experienced the presence of God. As Psalm 27 says: "Your presence, O Lord, I seek." 1-John 2:24-27 talks about the anointing or presence of the Holy Spirit, manifest in people's lives. Singing in various tongues or languages is one of the major gifts of the Holy Spirit, recorded in 1-Corinthians 12: 4-11. I had been confirmed at the age of 10 years but did not understand these particular gifts of the Holy Spirit. I was not taught about these kinds of experiences from my Baltimore Catechism!

At the age of 16, my next experience of God's presence came while I was walking in knee-deep snow in the foothills of the Rocky Mountains of Southern Alberta, checking a trap-line of beaver traps in late winter. I had forgotten my snowshoes. It was cold, (-10 F) early in the morning. I was walking through the trees and breaking through hard-packed snowdrifts up to my knees. I continued down a long hill through thick willow brush and headed towards a clearing. When I finally reached the clearing, I realized to my relief that the snow had been blown away by the west wind on earlier days. I had been thinking, God must be preparing me for some real hardships in my life, to allow me to struggle, through such pain and perseverance on my own accord.

At that moment, a strong gust of warm west wind, rushed through the clearing, unexpectedly, as the west winds do from time to time, the famous Chinook winds of Western Canada! The temperature rose quickly, and at that very moment, God's presence came upon me in a distinct way, confirming what I was just thinking. In the next moment, I spotted an eagle circling majestically in the sky above me. I walked farther and saw the blue glazed ice pond ahead, and to my surprise a beaver was lying dead, on the ground, upside down. I skinned the hide off this large beaver and carried the fur pelt home. As a young entrepreneur, I had been collecting fur pelts to sell. Receiving the fur pelt was a direct gift from God that was not recognized at the time. I am still awed to this day by that experience, so far back in the high country, where the valleys and the foothills gently slope away from the Rocky Mountains of Southwestern Alberta.

CHAPTER 2

SAINT BRIDGET OF SWEDEN

In February of 1992, our ninth and last child was born to my wife and me. In the spring of that year, I experienced a vision in the night. I saw a very wise older-looking woman, beautiful and serious-looking, dressed in clothes that were worn in centuries past. An abundance of **wisdom radiated from her face**, though I cannot explain how I could see this depth of wisdom emanating from her. She seemed to be inside an old hotel lobby with a TV above her. I could see the TV screen from the side, and the man on that television, I recognized with all of my soul and spirit as the Antichrist. I had studied prophecies of the Antichrist, so I was quite familiar with the subject. The despicable pride, reflecting from the face of this deceiver, frightened me deep within. The beautiful, wise-looking lady said, "**Protect your children from the Antichrist,**" and then she was gone.

I didn't know who the lady was at first; I thought it might be Mary, the Mother of Jesus, but the woman didn't seem like Mary. I just waited and prayed to understand. Four years passed before I found the answer, in a book called, *The Final Hour*, which described that some people who went to Medjugorje would see visions of Mary, saints, or prophets such as Elijah. I was led to discover that it was likely St. Bridget of Sweden. After my discovery, I searched for more information on St. Bridget; confirming that she was the saint who had appeared to me. Inspired one evening to find St. Bridget's feast day, I went down stairs and looked at the Catholic calendar. This particular evening was July 23, her feast day. I was surprised and in wonder.

My search for more information on St. Bridget led to *The Holy Shroud and Four Visions*, a great little book on St. Bridget, Anne Catherine Emmerich, Mary of Agreda, and Therese Neumann. Each had detailed accounts of the passion of Jesus Christ through visions, for hours on end, as well as visions of the lives of others, who were part of the life of Christ.

St. Bridget, who lived in the 1300s, was the first one whose visions of the Passion of Christ were recorded; she saw the whole process for many hours at a time and observed detailed moments of suffering that our Lord went through. She had visions of the last days, of the Great Catholic Monarch, and of the Antichrist. In my research, this opened the possibilities of **other** canonized **saints having visions** 'of the things to come.'

Many prophecies have been revealed throughout the last 2000 years, to early Church Fathers, Doctors of the Church, many venerable, blessed, and canonized saints, and other exceptional followers of Christ. Prophecies also come from visionaries through Marian apparitions or those who see Mary, Mother of Jesus. Marian apparitions always come through the Holy Spirit.

To understand the message that St. Bridget related, was at first very confusing. I believed it should be taken literally, that the Antichrist, whom St. Paul, early Church Fathers, Doctors of the Church, and many other prophesying Catholic saints talk about, was about to arrive in our time. But as time passed, after an anointing or confirmation from the Holy Spirit, St. Bridget's statement was not to be taken literally. I realized the needed to pray for my children, grandchildren, and great grandchildren, and to inform them of what is going to take place, and to realize that the Antichrist spirit (Satan) is trying to seduce our society towards a culture of death. In fact, **Satan wants to destroy** all of **mankind** and is getting very close **to this reality**. Immoral attitudes are portrayed by modern media communications through sitcoms and advertisements, slowly and subtly leading us away from the truth about the direction our lives should take.

CHAPTER 3

PROPHECIES
OF SAINT BRIDGET

In the 1970s and 1980s, I spent many hours reading and studying the Bible and protestant/evangelical speculation of eschatological (end times) themes. I always knew in my heart that this civilization was cold and self-gratifying, not what my parents and grandparents had lived in. When watching TV and hearing the non-Catholic televangelists, preaching the end to this world and the second coming of Christ, it sparked an acute interest in non-Catholic writings on end-time's scriptures. Shortly thereafter, I was prayed with, for personal direction in a Catholic charismatic prayer group and received a word from the Lord, through a member with the gift of prophecy. The Lord said: "My time is coming, but I will come in my time, not in your time." After hearing this, I was disappointed, but was convinced, that Jesus' second coming is not at this time. I stopped listening to the end times thinking and just went on with my life. Twelve years later, in 1992, I received that vision of St. Bridget, I related to.

After reading St. Bridget's prophecies, I read many prophecies of Catholic saints. At first, as I read many of the prophecies, they didn't make much sense. As I continued to read and reread the prophecies, they were like picture puzzle pieces; some of the pieces started to connect. I would reread and reread the prophecies, with more and more pieces fitting together. I started to see a picture of **what God has been doing in history** and **what is going to take place.**

St. Bridget was born in Sweden and lived from 1303 to 1373. Bridget's mother nearly drowned just before Bridget was born. An angel appeared to Bridget's mother and told her she was saved because of the child, to be born to her. The angel added: "Nourish (her) with the love of God because it is God who has given (her) to you."[1] St. Bridget was from a wealthy family, and her father was a governor in Sweden. Bridget had visions from childhood. She had a vision of Christ who said to her, "You shall be my bride and my channel... shall give countless nations **wisdom to drink**."[2] She received revelations at an early age, but being ridiculed by those whom she waited on and worked for, she decided these revelations, were not from God. Later, however, a priest confirmed one of her revelations, and he asked that she write them all down.

Her prophecies about secular and worldly affairs of her day, eventually came true.

Her mother died when she was eleven, and by the age of 13, her father chose Ulf, an 18-year-old who was 'rich, noble, and wise', to be her husband. She took that as God's will, and they had eight children in 28 years of marriage. One of her children, Catherine, was venerated as a saint. In 1335, Bridget was lady in waiting to the King and Queen of Sweden and became very close to them. Ulf died, after a journey and return trip from a pilgrimage to Santiago de Compostela in Spain in 1341. Afterwards, she established a double monastery for men and women, with the help of the King of Sweden. She established religious orders of men and women and called it the 'Order of the Most Holy Savior'. They became known as the Bridgettines.

In 1349, amidst the plague sweeping Europe, Bridget went to Rome; she would never return to Sweden. There, she continued to establish her religious order in Rome and took care of Swedish pilgrims, looking after the poor. At the same time, she continued to have revelations from the Holy Spirit and guided the King of Sweden in worldly affairs. When in Rome, she was led by God to warn, encourage, and correct Church leaders. Bridget continued to suffer ridicule because of her prophecies and revelations to Church leaders. With inspiration from the Holy Spirit, she encouraged the Pope to leave Avignon, France and to come back to Rome. Four years after Bridget's death, Pope Gregory returned to the Vatican.

St. Bridget was an exceptional woman of the Church, a patron saint of her country, and was given formal status as co-patroness of Europe with St. Catherine of Sienna and St. Teresa Benedicta of the Cross-, by Pope John Paul II. She was described as "kind and meek to every creature and had a laughing face." [3] She was a mystic, and yet, raised a family going through all the trials of ordinary life. Bridget had visions of Jesus' life of suffering and passion on the cross, and of Mary, His Mother. In 1371, she undertook a pilgrimage to the Holy Land. She died July 23, 1373 and was canonized a saint not long after in 1391.

St. Bridget provides **two** prophecies **with dates attached**, or clues to certain time-frames. One foretold the darkness of 1980s and the other, for 2038 pertinent to our time. Part of the **first prophecy** goes like this: "The time of this Antichrist well known to me, will come when iniquity and impiety shall above measure abound, when injustice shall have filled the measure to over flowing, and wickedness shall have grown to immeasurable proportions... Hence, when many Christians will be lovers of heresies and wicked men will persecute the clergy and trample spirituality and justice underfoot, this will be the sign that Antichrist shall come without delay... He will reign during three years, and shall have dominion over the whole earth...**in the year 1980**(s) **the wicked shall prevail**..." [4]

It sounds like the time of the Antichrist starts in the late 20th century. It will become apparent that this is not the time for this Man of Iniquity, whom St. Paul talks about, although our time, the fifth Church age, is certainly a time where the spirit of antichrist (Satan) is coming against Christ and has power on the earth. The rise of the Antichrist that St. Paul speaks about does not arrive on the earth until after the age of peace, the sixth Church age. In this **fifth Church age**, we will examine and **witness Mary**, Mother of Jesus accomplishing **a victory** against this 'iniquity of evil' that brings **Satan's influence** on this earth **to a standstill**. [5]

The **second prophecy** of St. Bridget with dates on it, is a riddle: "When the **Feast** of **St. Mark** shall fall on **Easter;** the Feast of **St. Anthony** on **Pentecost;** and that of **St. John** on **Corpus Christi;** the whole world will cry, Woe!"[6] Now, St. Mark's feast day is **April 25;** St. Anthony's (Padua) is **June 13;** and St. John the Baptist is **June 24.** Since St. Bridget's birth, Easter has fallen on April 25 in the Julian calendar in 1451, 1546, and in the Gregorian calendar in 1666, 1734, 1886, 1943, and will coincide **in the year 2038,** then not again until 2190.

CHAPTER 4

PROPHECIES OF CATHOLIC SAINTS

S t. Bridget is not the only one to assign specific time frames to prophecies. Throughout this work, prophecies of Anne Catherine Emmerich who lived in the 1800s, Therese Neumann 1900s, St. Hildegard Bingen 1100s, Bartholomew Holzhauser 1600s, Bishop Christianos Agreda 1200s, and Mother Mariana de Jesus Torres 1600s, predicted events pertinent to the 20th and 21st century. Here are some interesting prophecies, pertinent to our times:

St. Anthony of the Desert (born 251, died 356): "Men will **surrender to the spirit of the age**. They will say that if they had lived in our day, faith would be simple and easy. But in their day, they say, things are complex; the church must be brought up to date and made meaningful to the day's problems. When the Church and the world are one, then those days are at hand." [1]

St. Senanus (b 488 to d 560): "Falsehood will characterize that class of men who will sit in judgment to pass sentence according to the law; between the father and his son, litigations will subsist. The clergy of the Holy Church will be addicted to pride and injustice... **Women** will abandon feelings of delicacy and **cohabit with men** out of wedlock. They will follow those practices without secrecy, and such habits will become almost insuppressible. All will rush into iniquity, against the will of the Son of the Blessed Virgin Mary." [2]

St. Columba or Columbkille (d 597): "Harken...I relate things that shall come to pass, in the latter age of the world. Great wars shall be made, justice shall be outraged...many unjust laws will be administered...they will employ themselves at reading and writing...(but) will scoff at acts of humanity...at irreproachable humility...Neither justice nor covenant will be observed by any one-people, of the race of Adam...will become hardhearted and penurious...devoid of piety. The clergy will become fosterer's, in consequence of the tidings of wretchedness, churches shall be held in bondage, by all powerful men of the day...Excellent men shall be steeped in poverty...people will become inhospitable...The professors of science shall not be rewarded, amiability shall not characterize the people, prosperity and hospitality shall not exist...The **changes of seasons** (weather) **shall produce** only **half their verdure**, the regular festivals of the Church will not be observed, all classes of men shall be filled with hatred and enmity towards each other...**The clergy shall be led into error** by the **misinterpretation of their readings,** the relics of the saints will be considered powerless...Young women will become unblushing...aged men will be of irascible temper...The possessors of abundance shall fall through the multiplicity of their falsehoods...their arrogance will know no bounds. Between mother and daughter, anger and bitter sarcasms shall continually exist, neighbors will become treacherous, cold and false-hearted towards each other...blood relations will become cool towards each other. Church (property) will become lay property." [3]

St. Hildegard of Bingen-Doctor of the Church (b 1098- d 1179): "The time is coming when princes and peoples will reject the authority of the Pope. Some countries will prefer their own Church rulers to the Pope. The German empire will be divided. Church property will be secularized. Priests will be persecuted." [4]

Ven. Anne de la Foi (birth and death unknown): "There will be discord within the Catholic Church. In those days, men will wear women's clothes, and women will put on men's clothes." [5]

Bishop Christianos Ageda (d 1204): "**In the 20th century there will** be wars and fury that will last a long time; whole provinces shall be emptied of their inhabitants, and kingdoms shall be thrown into confusion. In many places, the land shall be left untilled, and there shall be great slaughters of the upper class. The right hand of the world shall fear the left, and the north shall prevail over the south." [6]

Our Lady of Good Success to **Venerable Mother Mariana de Jesus Torres in Quito,** Ecuador (d 1634): "Moreover, in these unhappy times, **there will be unbridled luxury** which acting thus to snare the rest into sin, will conquer innumerable frivolous souls who will be lost. Innocence will almost no longer be found in children, nor modesty in women, and in this supreme moment of need in the Church, those who should speak, will fall silent."[7] **"When your name is made known in the 20th century,** there will be many who will not believe, claiming that this devotion is not pleasing to God."[8] "Our Heavenly Father communicates His secrets to the simple of heart and not to those whose hearts are inflated with pride, pretending to know what they do not, or self-satisfied with empty knowledge." [9]

Blessed Bernardt Rembordt (1689-1793): "God will punish the world when men have **devised marvelous inventions that will lead them to forgetting God.** They will have **horseless carriages**, and they **will fly like birds.** But they will laugh at the idea of God, thinking that they are 'very clever.' There will be signs from heaven, but men, in their pride, will laugh them off. Men will indulge in voluptuousness, and lewd fashions will be seen." [10]

CHAPTER 5

HOLZHAUSER'S PROPHECIES AND THE SEVEN CHURCH AGES

Venerable Father Bartholomew Holzhauser was born in Laugna, Germany in 1613. He grew up in a pious and honest family, his father a shoemaker. He read many books at an early age and desired to join the priesthood. After studies, was ordained and was sought after as a confessor for advice. He had many gifts of the Holy Spirit; many miraculous healings occurred, experienced visions of the future, and received the gift of Prophecy. He foresaw the execution of Charles I of England, a total banishment of the Holy Sacrifice of the Mass in England for 120 years. He saw that England will be converted and will do more for religion, than after its first conversion.

Venerable Holzhauser authored extraordinary works, about the future, for education, for seminarians, and for disciples under trials that were used extensively for the next two centuries. Works written on the various visions that he experienced, served as valuable teaching. He wrote a book explaining parts of Revelation, from the visions, from information circulating in the Middle Ages, and from Blessed Abbot Merlin Joachim of Fiore of Italy, who died in 1202; that can be interpreted in short, as follows: "the seven stars and the seven candlesticks **seen by St. John, signify seven periods** [1] (of time), **of the history of the Church,** from its foundation to its consummation at the final judgment. To these **periods,** correspond the seven churches of Asia Minor, the seven days of the Mosaic record of creation, the seven ages before Christ, and the seven gifts of the Holy Ghost. Since, he says, all life is developed in seven stages, so God has fixed seven periods for regeneration."[2] This regeneration is in an order, to discharge Satan and his influence from this earth and to provide the opportunity for peoples of nations, to receive eternal redemption, during these seven Church ages.

Holzhauser's "*Interpretation of the Apocalypse of St. John*" includes an in-depth interpretation of the seven Church ages, particularly the fifth, and the sixth Church ages. The **fifth Church age that** started about 1520 with a pope, will end with **a Strong Ruler** and **a Holy Pope** that awakens us to major changes in the near future. Most of this work will describe pertinent events of **the fifth Church age**, the age of affliction in the Latin Western or Roman Catholic, calling attention to events that are weakening the Church.

At the same time and as a result, the world is turning away from God. After this age of affliction is over, and with God's intervention towards the end of this fifth Church age, only a remnant Church will survive, leading us into a real period of Peace, in the sixth Church age starting in 2038. The seventh Church age, many hundreds of years from now, will begin with the birth and rise of the Antichrist that awakens the Jewish people to the true Messiah, described in the Old Testament who is Jesus Christ.

Seven Church Ages - Venerable Holzhauser

Summary [3]

The seven Church ages described, are a correlation to the seven churches from Revelation in Chapters 2 and 3. Although, these seven churches, reflect a variety of meanings, each church also reflects a period of years, unfolding in a chronological order, of Church history to its completion. This information is based largely on Venerable Holzhauser's visions:

First Church Age	Christ & Apostles to Pope Linus & Emperor Nero[4]	4 BC to 79 AD
Second Church Age	The Days of Persecution	79 AD to 314 AD
Third Church Age	Pope Sylvester to Pope Leo III	314 AD to 795 AD
Fourth Church Age	Pope Leo III to Leo X	795 AD to 1520 AD
Fifth Church Age	Pope Leo X to a **Strong Ruler** and **Holy Pope**	1520 to 2038

This is the **present** Church age of **Sardis** coming to a close.

Mary reveals 10 Secrets (events) to unfold:	2020 or 2021 to 2038
First 2 events are admonitions from God	2020 or 2021
The 3rd event is an admonition from God	2021
Next 5 are punishments, a recoil of our sins upon us	2021 to 2038
Last 2 are Chastisements directly from God	early 2030s to 2038

The Great Catholic Monarch (Strong Ruler) rises up taking back Europe in the 2030s. The Holy Pope with a sign of redemption on his forehead will reign in 2038 and afterwards. St. Bridget exclaims: " the whole world will cry, Woe ! " in the year 2038.

Sixth Church Age

"A **Strong Ruler** and **a Holy Pope** to **Birth of Antichrist**"–2038 to 2383?
This is the **future** Church age of **Philadelphia.**

After the 10 events, Mary claims a '**certain period of peace**'on earth.
Reign of the Sacred Heart of Jesus and the Immaculate Heart of Mary.
Holzhauser says - All Nations will be **united** in the Catholic Faith.

Under the protection of the Great Monarch and his successors.
He will submit everything to his authority.
The Great Monarch will break the empire of the Mohammedans.
He will show great zeal for the true Church and the Holy Pope.

Seventh Church Age

"**Birth of Antichrist** [4] to **End of the world**"– 2383 ? to 3483 ?
This is the **last** Church age of **Laodicea.**

The **Reign** of Antichrist for seven years.
The Two Witnesses, Elijah, and Enoch will be sent back to earth.
The Coming of Christ on the clouds & taking up of the Bride.
The completion of the Bride, Gentile Church.

Last Church age is 1000 years of peace or longer.
A time for the **Jewish people** in the last Church age.
Final coming of Christ after the 1000 years.

[4]Author anointed–Our Lord confirmed this summary in two places. Note: The Holy Spirit has confirmed to me some of the prophecies, events, and information that are being placed in this work. This happens when a person experiences the presence of the Holy Spirit for a moment. Then, that person knows, particular information is true, by the action of the Holy Spirit, assuring that person that it is true. This is one of the major gifts of the Holy Spirit mentioned in 1-Corinthians 12.

Holzhauser's Prophecies

This is a detailed description of some of Venerable Bartholomew Holzhauser's prophecies for the fifth Church age. His works were found in several manuscripts at Bamberg, Ratisbon, and Vienna. Some of these prophecies are separate observations and from separate sources, for different times in history. Some are recorded here and others are recorded later in this work.

Holzhauser describes some sobering details. He writes: "The fifth epoch of time, dates from the reign of Charles V, until the reign of the Great Catholic Monarch…" [5] (1519-2030s).

"The fifth period is **one of affliction, desolation, humiliation,** and **poverty** for the (Catholic) Church. Jesus Christ will purify His people through cruel wars, famines, plagues, epidemics, and other horrible calamities. He will also **afflict** the **Latin Church** with many heresies. It is a **period of defections, calamities,** and **exterminations.** Those Christians who survive the sword, plague, and famines will be few on earth. Nations will fight against nations, and will be decimated by internecine (characterized by great slaughter) dissensions…Are we not to fear during this period that the Mohammedans will come again, working out their sinister schemes against the Latin Church?" "During the fifth period, we see only calamities, devastation, and oppression of Catholics by tyrants and heretics, executions of kings, and conspiracies to set up republics."[6] **"A great lament** will come over all mankind and only a small batch will survive the storm, the pestilence and horror." [7]

This next prophecy is a **cross section of both ages** that Holzhauser saw; the end of the fifth Church age, just before 2038, and the glorious time of the sixth Church age, until the end of that age: "When everything has been ruined by war, when Catholics are hard pressed by **traitorous co-religionists,** and **heretics,** when the Church and her servants are denied their rights, monarchies have been abolished , and rulers murdered…"

"Then the Hand of Almighty God will work a marvelous change, something apparently impossible according to human understanding. There **will rise up, a valiant monarch anointed by God.** He will be Catholic. He will rule supreme in temporal matters. The Pope will rule supreme in spiritual matters, at the same time. Persecution will cease, and justice shall reign. Religion seems to be oppressed, but by the changes of entire kingdoms, it will be made firmer…He will **root out false doctrines** and **destroy** the **rule** of **Muslimism.** His dominion will extend from the East to the West. All nations will adore God, their Lord, according to the Catholic teaching. There will be many wise and just men. The people will love justice, and peace will reign over the whole earth, for divine power will bind Satan for many years…" [8]

Of the **sixth Church age**: "The Powerful Monarch, who will be sent by God, will uproot every republic. He will submit everything to his authority, and he will show great zeal for the true Church of Christ. The empire of the Mohammedans will be broken up, and this Monarch will reign in the East, as well as in the West. All nations will come to worship God in the true Catholic and Roman faith. There will be many Saints and Doctors of the Church on earth. Peace will reign over the whole earth because God will bind Satan for a number of years, until the days of the Son of Perdition (Antichrist). No one will be able to pervert the word of God, since, during the sixth period, there will be an Ecumenical council which will be the greatest of all councils. By the grace of God, the power of the Great Monarch, the authority of the Holy pontiff, and the union of all the most devout princes, atheism and every heresy will be banished from the earth. The Council will define the true sense of Holy Scripture, and this will be believed and accepted by everyone." [9] "The Great Monarch of the world will create new laws for the new mankind and will cause **a new age to begin**. There will be only one flock and one Shepherd, and **peace will be of long, long duration**, for the glory of God in heaven and earth…" [10]

The sixth Church age is a time of a genuine '**Period of Peace**' that Mary, Mother of Jesus speaks about at Fatima. The Early Church Fathers, Doctors of the Church, Venerable Holzhauser, and other saints speak of this age of Peace as well. **After,** the end of the sixth Church age, the Antichrist rises up for a short time.

Holzhauser states the **seventh Church age** will start with: "Birth of Antichrist to the end of the world." [11] After Antichrist, this age will last a thousand years or more.

CHAPTER 6

BIRTH PANGS

T o understand the Church ages' beginning and ending, and how Christ and his Church will increase, while Satan and evil will decrease, we must reflect on the **birth pangs** recorded in Revelation 12:2 and on Mary, Mother of Jesus, that parallels the painful unfolding of the Church: "She was with child, she wailed aloud in pain, as she labored to give birth."

Jesus relates to **birth pangs** as he was seated on the Mount of Olives with his apostles, who were asking him: "What will be the sign of your coming and the end of the world?" In Matthew Chapter 24 verse 3-8, Jesus replies, "See that no one deceives you. For many will come in my name, saying, "I am the Messiah," and they will deceive many, you will hear of wars and rumors of wars, see that you are not alarmed, for these things must happen, but it will not be the end. Nation will rise against nation, and kingdom against kingdom, there will be famines, pestilence, and earthquakes in various places, **all these are the beginnings of the birth pangs**... And because of the increase of evil, the love of most, will grow cold. The one who holds out to the end, will see salvation. This gospel of the Kingdom will be preached throughout the whole world as a witness to all nations. Then the end will come."

Among mothers, birth pangs are a complex experience; an intensity of pain and suffering mixed with the hope and promise of new life. Jesus refers to the kingdom of God coming in this way. As a baby starts down through the birth canal, the birth in its fullness gets closer. These are the early stages of birth pangs. Then, the birth pangs come closer together and with greater intensity, letting off for a moment, to let the body of the mother and child, rest and recuperate.

During the first four Church ages, birth pangs, over each age, continued to grow in intensity. The **most intense birth pangs**, the longest ones, and the hardest ones, is **this fifth Church age** that we live in. This age started around 1520. We are getting close to the end of this age, around 2038.

Soon, during the Illumination of all men's consciences, we will see Christ's face, when he intervenes in human history for a second time. In a surprise appearance, all the peoples of the world will see him on the cross in his passionate suffering. This event will awaken the whole human race, to Christ, at this time in history.

16

The **next birth pangs** get easier but still intense, with the main body coming through, during the **sixth Church age** after 2038. It will be the literal preaching of the gospel, throughout the whole world and a period of peace on the earth. This is the age of the building up of the body of Christ until the body, that is, the Bride, Gentile Church will have reached its fullness. Just after the end of this sixth Church age, will culminate the completion of the Bride, affirmed in Revelation 19: 7-9, where the full number will have entered in. St. Paul states to the Romans 11: 25: "I do not want you to be unaware of the mystery... a hardening has come upon Israel... until the full number of Gentles have entered in." Just after this age closes, Jesus Christ will come on the clouds to meet his Bride. Christ will still remain at the right hand of the Father at that time.

The **last birth pangs** start about four hundred years from now, as the remaining part of the body comes through **during the seventh Church age;** this will be a time of utopia and peace on the earth. It will be the time for the Jewish people, the last nation to hear the gospels, culminating the fulfillment of many of the prophecies of the Bible that are promised in God's word. For example, Zachariah 8:23 states: "In those days, ten men of every nationality... will take hold of a Jew by the edge of his garment, and say, let us go with you, for we have heard that God is with you." That is in a future time. At the end of this age, after 1000 years or more, Christ will come back to the earth and land at the Mount of Olives, as the angels stated to the apostles, recorded in Acts 1:11. Then will come the final Judgment.

Romans 8: 22 reveals: "We know that all creation is groaning in **labor pains,** even until now... we so groan, within ourselves, as we wait for... redemption." The **birth pangs** of the fifth Church age are the most intense and alarming long-term period of all the Church ages that will come to pass.[1]

Understanding birth pangs or labor pains **will help** to **relate** to the ways that the events of **God's decrees will unfold** in the future, in these last Church ages.

CHAPTER 7

THE FIFTH CHURCH AGE

1520 to 2038

An outstanding, long-term antagonism is building to a crescendo at the end of this fifth Church age. From the beginning of this age, Mary, Mother of Jesus, sent by the Holy Spirit, increases her efforts of intercession. Mary appeared at Guadalupe, Mexico to Juan Diego in 1531 and will continue to **do battle** throughout this age, until after the unfolding of the ten secrets (events) of Medjugorje where she will have accomplish her greatest work by 2038. She has been commissioned by her Son to defeat Satan on this earth, as recorded in Revelation 12.

In the 20th century, the Holy Spirit also reveals through Mary at Medjugorje and other apparition sites, **knowledge of a decisive battle to defeat Satan at this time**. Many prophecies reveal to us what she will do at this time. Mary has said, when she is finished appearing at Medjugorje: "This is the last time, I am on this earth, in this way." [1] The birth pangs are lessened, as a fuller kingdom comes on the earth, as it is in Heaven. This brings about a lesser influence of evil on earth, accomplishing a more complete defeat of Satan, by Mary and the Church on this earth. This will eventually lead to an age of genuine peace on this earth in the sixth Church age.

God allows the mystery of iniquity to ensnare the Church, engendering divisions, starting with Martin Luther. Freemasonry and other dark, powerful organizations intertwine their diabolical, unseen influence, continuing to subvert the Church and the world. This influence through Satan's extended reign in the 20th century and part of the 21st century is about to destroy the Church from within, and in fact all of mankind. Mary is commissioned to intervene, defeating Satan when the Church is weakened.

This work will reflect on the two adversaries: Mary and Satan throughout this present fifth Church age. **Marian Apparitions** (Mary) are listed in a summary and are revealed in a chronological order throughout this work. The **Mystery of Iniquity** (Satan) is also revealed in a chronological order, through out this work. During this fifth Church age, **God counteracts** the **Mystery of Iniquity,** through **Marian influence** during her apparitions, appealing for prayer and other reparations, **preventing the demise of the human race.**

Marian Apparitions

To understand Marian apparitions, God commissions Mary, Mother of Jesus, to engage against Satan on this earth. In Genesis 3:15, it is recorded, Adam and Eve disobeyed God in the garden, and even though they had sinned, God considers Satan the guilty party. God is speaking to Satan: "I will put **enmity** between **you** and the **Woman**," asserting that the battle will be "between your **offspring and hers**." Now Satan's offspring is the progeny of evil produced in this world. The woman's offspring is Jesus and all those who are born into new life, becoming part of the body of Christ or the Church. Mary is **the "Woman."** A **poignant theme** of **the Woman** exists **from Genesis** to **Revelation**. Many in error think this is Eve, but Eve was defeated and lost her power in the garden to defeat Satan at that time; this includes all her children throughout the generations to come. But uniquely a daughter of Eve will be blessed, chosen by God. Isaiah 7:14 prophesies a **young woman** (virgin) to give birth. There are clues in the New Testament where Jesus does not refer to Mary as his mother in public but in fact calls her **Woman**. Before the miracle at the wedding of Cana, he refers to her as, "Woman...my hour has not come." At the cross He says to her: "Woman, there is your son." In Revelation 12:1-3, the **battle** is reiterated: "A great sign appeared in the sky, a Woman clothed with the sun, with the moon under her feetand upon her head a crown of twelve stars.... She was with child... (and) she labored to give birth."

"Then another sign appeared in the sky: It was a huge dragon, flaming red, with seven heads and with ten horns." Revelation 12: 7-9 states: "War broke out in heaven...**He (Satan) was hurled down to earth**, and his minions with him." Revelation 12: 13-17 states: "When the dragon realized that he had been cast down to the earth, he pursued **the woman who gave birth** to **the boy**... the dragon went off to make war on the rest of her off-spring." This distinctly refers to Mary, Mother of Jesus.

Mary, the humblest of all creatures, is commissioned by the Holy Trinity to accomplish a work, of defeating Satan in a decisive battle on earth, for the sake of her children, the body of Christ in the Seven Church ages. This is central to our understanding of Mary; her work on earth is to protect her children (offspring) from immediate harm and eternal damnation.

A brief history of Mary's work, started about 40 A. D. Mary was sent by the Holy Spirit to Saragossa, Spain to encourage St. James to build a Church over a Pillar with a small statue of Mary on it that was made by angels. Whether she came to him through a vision or by angels, we do not know, but Mary was still on the earth at that time. In 352, Our Lady of the Snows requested a church to be built on Esquilline Hill, in Rome, at a place where snow fell on a hot summer night. Today that Church is well known as the Basilica of St. Mary Major. In 1061, Our Lady appeared at Walsingham in Norfolk, England, where a woman was instructed to construct a shrine of the Annunciation. The first apparitions of Mary, in the first thousand years, are traditionally accepted. As time passed, she requested churches to be built in many places throughout the world; despite persecutions, the Church continues to grow.

The number of apparitions of Mary increased during the **second millennium** and particularly after the 1200s. Around this time, begins preparation for battle. Our Lady of the Rosary was attributed to Mary appearing to a priest, St. Dominic, in 1214. St. Dominic struggled to convert the Albigensians who persisted in their heresy. Within a forest near Toulouse, France, he prayed for three days and nights. Suddenly, Mary, Mother of Jesus appeared to him with three angels and said: "Dear Dominic, do you know **which weapon,** the **Blessed Trinity wants to use,** to reform the world?" Dominic at the time did not know. Mary replied, "I want you to know that **in this kind** of **warfare,** the battering ram has always been **the Angelic Psalter,** which is the foundation stone of the New Testament."[2] The Angelic Psalter is referring to the words that the angel Gabriel proclaimed, from the Father in Heaven, recorded in Luke 1:26-38. The Angelic Psalter and Elizabeth's greeting for the **Woman,** are said with the rosary, to obtain fulfillment of many requests and to do battle against Satan.

Our Lady of Mount Carmel (Mary) in 1251, visits St. Simon Stock offering a brown Scapular cloth, hung around the neck as a sign of protection and graces. By the 1300s, rebellion in the Church and mainstream society became widespread. God spoke to saints and warned the world of chastisement to come. Soon thereafter, plague broke out, throughout Europe, and many people lost their lives, at different intervals of time, to this pestilence, over the next two centuries. Towards the end of the fourth Church age, on August 2, 1492, on the feast of our Lady of the Angels, Christopher Columbus set out to find the 'New World' and the promise of new beginnings. He consecrated his voyage to Our Lady and prayed that he would find land by October 12, 1492, or he would return to Spain. On that very feast day of Our Lady of the Pillar, he spotted land to the west.

From the 1500s onwards, the Church officially began to approve apparitions of Mary in a systematic way. Only the **Marian apparitions that speak to the whole world** will be explained in this work because of the importance and gravity of the messages, and how they line up with many other prophecies of the saints, including Biblical prophecies.

Although, apparitions are all private revelation, they are of great importance to the public, and the messages are relevant to all people. According to *The Last Secret,* by Michael H. Brown, at least eight thousand significant apparitions of the Virgin Mary have taken place since the beginning of the Church. Some three hundred cases of apparitions to children are recorded in one research.

According to Fr. Johann G. Roten, of the International Marian Research Institute: "Close to a thousand major, minor, and related apparitions have occurred between 1830 and 1981." [3]

When Pope Benedict XVI was still cardinal, he stated in The Ratzinger Report, "one of the signs of our times is the announcement of Marian apparitions multiplying all over the world." [4] After the 1980s, the Vatican has continued to investigate so many contemporary events, and caution must be taken in some of these so-called events. In the second millennium, credible details of approved apparitions, in the order of occurrence awakens and begs the question: what is going on, now and in the future?

As the Church became more organized, and its activities more thoroughly documented, the actual first approved apparition by the Church was decided after 1531, when Our Lady of Guadalupe appeared to Juan Diego reflecting a similar image of Revelation 12. Apparitions that will follow, **show a pattern of ever increasing urgency towards the concern for mankind,** particularly after the French Revolution.

Included in this work are three apparitions of Mary appearing at Garabandal, Spain; Medjugorje, Bosnia-Herzegovina; and Anguera, Brazil that have some validation but not fully approved by the Roman Catholic Church. Fulfillment may still take over 20 years from the estimated times of the prophecies to be fulfilled, keeping in mind traditionally, apparitions are normally not considered for approval or disapproval until the apparitions have ended. Interestingly, Pope Benedict XVI, formed a Vatican commission in 2010, investigating the Medjugorje apparitions until May of 2017 and recognizing the supernatural nature of the first ten days and first seven visions.

The urgency of the messages from Garabandal, Medjugorje, and Anguera need to be addressed immediately, due to the future plight of mankind. **These messages** bring us to **a fuller understanding** of what is **going to take place** in the near future. [5]

Marian Apparitions

Summary

The major apparitions of Mary, Mother of Jesus during the fifth Church age from 1531 to 2038, concert Mary and the Church's **battle against Satan,** reaching **a decisive victory, on this earth,** corresponding to Revelation 12.

Our Lady of **Guadalupe** to Juan Diego, 1531 at Guadalupe, Mexico: Our Lady appeared in a similar image as in Revelation 12: "A great sign appeared in the sky, a woman clothed with the sun, with the moon under her feet, and on her head, a crown of twelve stars." Nine million Aztecs, a visual people, came to Christ in a short time by visual observance of the Tilma of Our Lady of Guadalupe without a word preached.

Our Lady of Good Success to Mother Mariana de Jesus Torres, 1600s, at Quito, Ecuador: Prophecies of Freemasonry from the 1600s are found in the latter part of the 20th century, as the prophecies were being fulfilled.

Our Lady of the Miraculous Medal to Catherine Laboure in 1830s at Rue de Bac, Paris, France: She is asked to strike a medal. Those who wear this medal will receive great graces and protection. Our Lady awakens the Church to a fifth Marian title of recourse to her.

Our Lady of La Salette to Melanie Calvat and Maximin Giraud in 1846 in the high French Alps: Words of warning are heard that our world is 'on the edge of the abyss.' In 1864, many demons will be unloosed from Hell.

Our Lady of Lourdes appears to St. Bernadette in 1858 at Lourdes, France, at a grotto across the river. Our Lady appeared to Bernadette in the Morning and gave her secrets, but they were never revealed. Called to Penance, Penance, Penance. Our Lady stated: "I am the Immaculate Conception," [6] a statement that confirms a central Church dogma.

Our Lady of Fatima came to Lucia, Francisco, Jacinta, in 1917 at Fatima, Portugal and appeared at High Noon on the 13th, of May, June, July, August, September, and October. On her last visit, Mary appeared as **Our Lady of Mount Carmel.**

Our Lady gave three secrets:
1   Vision of Hell.
2   **Predicts**-end of World War I.
     Russia and communism will rise up.
     Mary asks the Holy Father to consecrate Russia to Mary's
     Immaculate Heart, if not, Russia will spread her errors
     throughout the world.
     A Great light will appear in the sky before Second World War.
     Second World War.
     A Miracle of the sun will occur in October 1917.
3   Third secret revealed by Pope John Paul II in the year 2000.

Our Lady of Garabandal appears to four young girls, Conchita, Mari Loli, Jacinta, and Mari Cruz, between 1961-1965 at Garabandal, Spain at 6 p.m. in the evening. On her first visit, Mary appears as Our Lady of Mount Carmel. Called to Penance, Penance, Penance. "Many Cardinals, Bishops, and Priests are on the road to Perdition and are taking many souls with them." [7]

Our Lady reveals three secrets:
    The Warning
    The Miracle and Miracle sign
    The Chastisement (conditional at that time)

After 2000 apparitions, Mary said the world was not listening to her. St. Michael came the last time to convey a message to the world. For the first time in Church history, Mary discontinues a mission of apparitions.

Our Lady of Akita, Japan appears to Sister Agnes Sasagawa in 1973-1979 dire warnings to the clergy: "The work of the devil will infiltrate even into the Church, in such a way, that one will see **cardinals opposing cardinals, bishops against bishops...**" "If men do not repent and better themselves, the Father will inflict a terrible punishment on all humanity. It will be a punishment greater than the deluge, such as one, will never have seen before. Fire will fall from the sky and will wipe out a great portion of humanity, the good, as well as the bad, sparing neither priests nor faithful." This apparition was approved by the local Bishop, diocese of Niigata, Japan in 1984 after consultation with the Holy see.

Our Lady of Medjugorje appears to five teenagers and one eleven-year-old from June 24, 1981 to end of apparitions at Medjugorje, Bosnia-Herzegovina at **6:40 in the evening.** She appears clothed in gray and blue (working clothes) with a rosary in her left hand, with 12 stars around her head. Called to **Pray, Pray, Pray.** Appears to only three visionaries now.

Our Lady gives 10 secrets to the visionaries and consists of:
Three Admonitions:
> The Warning (also called) Illumination or Correction of conscience
> A Day of Outpouring of the Holy Spirit
> The visible Miracle sign and healings

Five Punishments:
> War, world civil chaos (New York)
> Droughts and famine,
> Malnourishment, sickness, disease, plague, and death
> Church breakdown (Rome and Vatican)
> Persecution and Death

Two Chastisements from God:
> Comet and other celestial events come to the earth (not conditional)
> Three Days of Darkness (not conditional)

This will be the last time that Mary appears on earth in this way.

Our Lady of Peace has appeared to **Pedro Regis**, since September 29, 1987 to an unknown time in the future, at Anguera, Bahia, Brazil. Mary is commissioned to **speak publicly and directly for the first time about future events**: "Never before have I revealed in any of my apparitions in the world, what I have revealed here. Only in this land **has God permitted me to speak to you about future events.** God has chosen the land of the Holy Cross (Brazil) **to announce what is to come to the world.**" [8]

Mystery of Iniquity

The 'Mystery of Iniquity' is the **darkness of evil** to which mankind yields to, during this fifth Church age. It is hard to understand why God allows Satan to afflict mankind even after Jesus Christ has conquered sin and death at the cross.

In Acts 2:35, God the Father has said to Jesus, **"sit at my right hand**, until I make **your enemies your foot stool**." St. Paul explains in 1-Corinthians 15: 20-26, how this is taking place: "Christ is now risen from the dead... so in Christ, all will come to life again but each in proper order; after having destroyed every sovereignty, authority, and power. He will hand over the kingdom to God the Father. Christ must sit at the right hand, until God the Father has put all enemies under his feet, the last enemy to be destroyed is death." 1-John 5:19 states: "We know that we belong to God, while the world is under the evil one."

The **real work** of conquering Satan and the world powers continues, convincing every man, woman, and child to undergo a process of trial and error, in order to be convinced that the only true way of being governed and guided is through Jesus Christ. We need to experience this process through the free will that God allows us. God wants us to know that all forms of government – independent governing, self-governing, republics, democracies, communism, socialism, monarchical – will ultimately fail. Monarchical governing with God in mind may be the most, long-term effective way with kings and kingdoms. God's prophetic word signifies **kingship** in Christ as the promise of long-term governing. But at this moment, this is not the way of the world, nor of its thinking. The unveiled truth reveals, a world listening to the dark side and is coming with a price.

This Mystery of Iniquity reveals the most outstanding **events and plots of evil** coming against the Church and the world throughout **the fifth Church age.** As it says in Ephesians 6:12: "For our wrestling is not against flesh and blood but against principalities and powers, against the rulers of this world of this (present) darkness, against the spirits of wickedness in high places."

SECTION II

THE FIFTH
CHURCH AGE BEGINS

CHAPTER 8

THE DOWNWARD SPIRAL

The fifth Church age starts in the early 1500s; Pope Leo X, King Charles V of the Holy Roman Empire, Martin Luther, and King Henry VIII, come together in leadership but lose their direction to fulfill God's will. This collision of forces and events, that Venerable Holzhauser saw, thrusts the world into an unholy, downward spiral, bringing affliction, desolation, humiliation, and poverty to the Catholic Church.

Pope Leo X

In 1513, Pope Leo X was the last non-priest to be elected pope, at the age of 38. He had a love for pleasure, music, theatre, art, poetry, and experienced all forms of entertainment including owning an elephant and many other pleasures, not all of good standing. The papal palace became a theater. Plenary indulgences were promoted by alms giving and used in the rebuilding of St. Peter's Basilica. He helped shore up Rome's status as a center of culture called, 'the Eternal City.'

It was said Pope Leo did not realize the seriousness of Martin Luther's opposition and abuses, nor the seriousness of the division in the Church. Although, Pope Leo excommunicated Luther for many of his teachings, no steps were taken to stop the abuse from Rome. In 1521, Pope Leo died suddenly at age 46. In the end, it was said, he used up the finances of three Popes including the one after him.

Reign of Charles V

In 1520, Charles V would be the last emperor of the Holy Roman Empire to be crowned and blessed by a Pope. He was also the King of Spain and presided over Spanish territories opening in the 'new world,' in Central America through Cortez and Pizarro. Charles saw himself as leader of the Christian world. He was the most visible Monarch, being the third monarch in the Habsburg Dynasty, and traveled the Holy Roman Empire extensively during his time.

Charles allowed Martin Luther to come to the Diet (general assembly of the estates) of the city of Worms in 1521. Charles did not realize the alarming influence that Martin Luther's writ at Wittenberg had on the German people. Rebellion of peasants in Germany, and formal Lutheran organizations brought about revolt, starting the breakdown in north and eastern parts of Charles's Empire. He later put a price on Luther's head but recanted after a year. Charles was fearful of the papacy gaining more power and wanted to leave Luther as a rival against the Church. He was preoccupied with holding back the Muslims of the Ottoman Empire, advancing into his empire of Europe particularly from the eastern countries. He continued to battle against France and the problems that existed there. Because his campaigns were taking a financial toll, he ignored the rise up of Protestantism, considering it secondary to maintaining his empire.

Martin Luther

Martin Luther was born at Eisleben, Germany in 1483, the oldest son of a miner who was reputed to be stern and irritable, possessing an uncontrollable rage. Before Martin was born, it was circulating that his Father had taken a heavy horse bridle and killed a man in a rage, forcing him and his wife to leave Mohra, the family township, to escape punishment. People to this day still point to the place where this murder took place. Martin's mother was considered modest, with fear of the Lord and prayerfulness. Two accounts of punishment from Martin himself are recorded; one from his mother who beat him until the blood flowed, and his father beating him mercilessly, embittering him, causing him to run away from home, for a time. He suffered many punishments at school as well. This grieved Martin's deep inner soul. He could not find forgiveness or healing that led him to bouts of depression and melancholy. Eventually, the confusion sown by his inner wounds flared into anger and rebellion.

Little is known about his early monastic life, but he is quoted, upon seeing the Bible at Erfurt Monastery: "I had as yet never seen a Bible and I alone in the Erfurt Monastery read the Bible." [1] It seems improbable that he was the only one that read the Bible in a monastery when, in fact the Augustinian rule stresses, "Read the Scriptures assiduously, hear it devoutly, and learn it fervently."[2] There were certainly not many Bibles at the time, although, Johannes Gutenberg had invented the printing press, in 1439, in Germany, and by the late 1400s, printing had been established throughout Europe.

He was ordained as a Priest in 1507, and continued in the monastic life, eventually being sent to the University of Wittenberg, teaching philosophy and dialectics, though continuing theological studies.

In 1510 or 11, he was sent on a mission to Rome, some say because of difficulties in his monastic life. Luther himself said, that it was a pilgrimage to fulfill a vow of going to confession in the Eternal city of Rome. Martin climbed the Scala Santa stairs. These stairs were brought to Rome by St. Helena, the mother of Emperor Constantine. Jesus walked up these stairs, to stand before Pontius Pilate. As Martin Luther was climbing these stairs on his knees, a powerful thought flashed through his mind: "**The just man shall live by faith.**" [3] He immediately left the stairs and returned to Wittenberg in 1512, appointed sub prior and was lecturer on the Bible. It was well recorded; he was a man far from the road of disciplined direction, instead trusting in himself, breaching rules and practices, including neglect of reciting the daily office for weeks, lack of study habits, with disregard for the counsels of confessors, instead, responding to his wounded emotions, building a reputation for his own decisions.

He relied on his own rationale, in this perverse spiritual progress, reveal-ing a defect of pride, and once said: "Be a sinner and sin on bravely, but have stronger faith and rejoice in Christ, who is the victor of sin, and death, and the world. Do not for a moment imagine that this life is the abiding place of justice; sin must be committed... the sin cannot tear you away from him, even though you commit adultery a hundred times a day and commit as many murders." [4]

By 1516-17, Martin Luther sees fewer people going to confession. He is told, that in towns not far from Wittenberg, they provide, the selling of indulgences, for the remission of their sins, eliminating the need for confession. Other confusion arises, in the misinterpretation of the selling of indulgences, for the souls in purgatory, and the sale of indulgences for future sins committed. Whether it was the misunderstanding of uneducated listeners, giving inaccurate information to Luther, or, did Luther not understand the correct information, is still to this day questionable. Everyone was going to the towns to hear the great orator Johann Tetzel, a Dominican friar, and papal commissioner for indulgences who was sent to Germany to preach: understanding the grace of receiving indulgences, to mitigate temporal punishment due to sin, by performing good works; one option includes almsgiving. Luther denied temporal punishment for sin.

Archbishop Albert, who proceeded with the authorization of the original intent of an indulgence that Tetzel preached, made it clear and lucid for the character and provisions of the indulgence, in a long document. He points out the spiritual benefits offered; is a plenary indulgence that provides the fulfillment of temporal punishment due to sin, by which the pains of purgatory are alleviated. He also laid out the conditions for gaining the indulgence. He also stated the grace of God, obtained by making a contrite confession. The indulgence was of the same instruction, as is prescribed in our day.

Martin Luther's original declaration of his Ninety-five Theses is nailed to the Castle Church door in Wittenberg on October 31, 1517, the Day of the Hallowed Eve, before All Saints Day. That evening, is normally an evening, where the parish Church community, celebrates in anticipation of the import-ant holiday. The original intent of the theses, was to spur on banter, as was the usual case in those days, with differences of opinion. But this thesis had a completely different reaction. Nobody responded. What was in this thesis? One non-Catholic writer stated: "The 95 sledge-hammer strokes delivered at the grossest ecclesiastical abuse of the age, terrified no one and emphasized the boldness and rashness of their author, attacking the doctrines of the Catholic Church." [5]

Another non-Catholic author states: "They impress the reader as thrown together, somewhat in haste, rather than showing carefully, digested thought and deliberate theological intention; they bear him out, one moment into the audacity of rebellion, and then carry him back to the of conformity." [6] Many of the theses were leveled at the abuse of the papal indulgences, on the doctrine of indulgences, and the authority of the Pope. By 1521, he countered that priests and monks should be able to marry, demanded all pictures and statues be remo-ved from the church, made public protest against the reservation of the Blessed Sacrament, argued for no elevation of the host at Mass, denounced the withholding of the Chalice, called for a cessation of prayers for the dead and demanded Mass be said in German.

By 1521, the Church in Rome asked him to recant his statement, but he refuses. Over the next ten years, eight million people leave the Catholic Church. In1521, rebellion within the monastery and towns around were rampant, with Martin Luther inciting other religious leaders, to a call to religious denouncement of Church practices. He was preaching that all men are of a universal priesthood, which authorizes every man to preach, offering full access to the sacraments, rejecting infant Baptism and preaching a treatise 'On Free Will'. This precipitated a period of unrest that grew excessive, with individuals abandoning guilds, industry, and trade.

When the storm of discontent was out of control, Luther called for an "exhortation of peace" on one hand but contradicted that by calling "upon the princes to slaughter the offending peasants like mad dogs, to stab, strangle, and slay as best one can, and hold out as a reward the promise of heaven." [7] "The encounters were more in the character of massacres, than battles. The undisciplined peasants, with their rude farming implements as weapons, were slaughtered like cattle in the shambles. More than 1000 monasteries and castles were leveled to the ground, hundreds of villages were reduced to ashes, the harvests of the nation were destroyed, and 100,000 were killed. The fact that one commander alone boasted that 'he hanged forty evangelical preachers and executed 11,000 revolutionists and heretics,' and that history, with hardly a dissenting voice, fastens the origin of this war on Luther, shows where its source and responsibility lay." [8]

By 1526, his bitterness and brutality of his words, in phrases fit for barnyard use only, his innuendos of men, to money, to women and to scriptures, started to compel the upright and conscientious, to revive their allegiance to the Old Church. Those in political affairs were recognizing the growing religious anarchy, the rise up of German peasantry, and at the source

was: the heresy of Wittenberg. Luther opposed every doctrine of the time but his own innovation. "This anarchy in faith," resulted in, "**the whole reformation, was a triumph of the temporal power over the spiritual.** [9] Luther himself, to escape anarchy, placed all authority in the hands of the princes." [10] They accepted the new opinions and were given possession of these temporal powers, introducing them as a territorial religion. "Freedom of religion became the monopoly of the ruling princes," with "as many new churches as there were principalities or republics." [11] Carlstadt, one of the 'princes' gave treatises on the Eucharist, flatly rejecting the words 'this is my Body,' although Luther himself rejected this. Zwingli, a Swiss reformer confirmed Carlstadt's doctrines for the most part. With Luther's credibility waning, he still had accustomed choice words for the 'adversaries,' as "doctrine to the devil." [12] The masses of people were turning from Wittenberg to Zurich, confirming the frivolous and artful machinations of the demon. Luther thus having two wings of reform, rejected any attempt to compromise.

After 12 years, in 1534, Martin Luther completed his translation of the Bible to German. That same year, Pope Paul III' s accession, encouraged a meeting, but the protestant estates refused, exhibiting the first public renunciation of the Papacy. The internal controversies continued with Swiss Protestantism rejected, the incurable wounds of the new church, the ceaseless quarrels of the preachers, the dictatorial temporal powers, the growing contempt for the clergy, and the servility to the princes. Luther's advice of double marriage, the intervention of Luther in domestic affairs of Wittenberg, blasting his country neighbors, the pamphlets printed, and condemning in grotesque manners, his perverted opinion; contrary to all that is good.

Luther's health was declining in his later years, feeling a sense of abandonment, from supporters in the past who expressed, "hardly one of us can escape Luther's anger and his public scourging." [13] Carlstadt had left in 1522, Melanchthon confessing: "humiliation of his ignoble servitude." [14] Meanwhile, Luther engaged in blasphemous speech, including, encouraging sins of the flesh, and calling down Christ himself. Some of the protestant biographers concluded that Luther was a shameful example of leadership in the reformation.

Luther's last days brought torturing assaults of the devil, with "no rest for even a single day."[15] At night, he encounters demonic attacks, "exhausted, and martyred to an intensity that he was barely able to gasp or take breath." [16] Even in that time, he continued to speak out in printed form, "against the Jews and their lies," and his prayed for, last passionate act: "Against the papacy established by the devil." [17]

Luther died February 18, 1546, leaving a disjointed unity within Germany. Over the next 475 years, other professed venues have arisen, to fulfill every spiritual deficiency on the planet, until 40,000 plus churches, all claim to uphold what they think is right, 'according to the Bible' but misunderstand the complete source of guidance, the Holy Spirit.

King Henry VIII

King Henry VIII was trained in Church affairs at a young age and wrote a book on the Church's dogmatic teachings, regarding the sacraments and the Mass, and strengthening the position of the Roman Church against Martin Luther. Pope Leo X conferred upon him, Defender of the Faith that remains with the English crown to this day. Sir Thomas More saw him as keeper of the faith.

In his personal life, Henry tried in vain to get a divorce through proper procedures. He took it into his own hands to eliminate subjection to the papacy, making himself supreme head of the Church of England. New laws were passed in the parliament, to suit his domestic needs, thus forcing the Church and state into submission for all clergy and statesmen. Pope Clement VII, excommunicated Henry, declaring his divorce and remarriage not binding. All payments to Rome were abolished. Those few who refused to follow the changes, in all of England, were sent to prison, and then the axe. After his death, Mary, his daughter, reigned as a strong Catholic known as bloody Mary that 'rid' her of many, contrary to the faith, ruling until 1558. Elizabeth became queen, reigning until 1603; being raised as a protestant, outlawed the Mass, issuing fines to those who did not attend the protestant way, enforcing reformation in England.

The Council of Trent

The Council of Trent in response to the challenges encountered by the Church, took place in Trent, Italy, during three separate meetings between 1545 and 1563; representing the first concrete response to the Protestant reformations. The doctrines of the Roman Catholic Church were in need of reaffirmation in light of the reforms by Luther and those ministers who followed him. They started with the Bible, listing all the books approved by the Holy Ghost, and that printing of the text must be as close to the original Vulgate edition. Subjects of concern included: Adam and Eve, the consequence of sin, justification of Christ's grace through faith, the vain confidence of heretics, the matter of predestination, the gift of perseverance, on the merits of good works, and the nature of merits. Canon laws were formed and decrees on reformation were cited. Canon laws on the sacraments were set in place, along with many clarifications on Holy Eucharist, including transubstantiation and veneration. Safety was stressed for Protestants.

Understanding of Purgatory, indulgences, fasting, and regulatory conduct of all ministers in the Church were addressed. These measures were long overdue and brought the Church into a more mature, organized institution; an overhaul it would need, in order to muster the strength to survive the Masonic and Communist infiltration in the centuries ahead.

CHAPTER 9

THE WOMAN CLOTHED
WITH THE SUN

In the year 1531, at the beginning of the fifth Church age, enters the Woman clothed with the Sun, with the moon under her feet; an image depicted in part by the **Woman** in Revelation 12:1. Since the beginning of the Church and particularly in this fifth Church age, Jesus has commissioned His Mother to come against the Red Dragon, as it is stated in Revelation 12:3. The woman in Revelation symbolizes the Church as well. Sister Lucia of the Fatima apparitions states: the Woman in Revelation is 'Mary, the Mother of Jesus' who is the Mother of the Body of Christ or the Church. The Church is comprised of three parts, the Church Triumphant, the Church Suffering, and the Church Militant. That means those in Heaven, those in Purgatory, and those who are on the earth in spiritual warfare, are all part of the Church.

Scripturally, Mary has been in battle for over 2000 years, starting with her 'yes' to the angel Gabriel's request of the conception of Jesus in her womb. She continued in action, along side the apostles, after Jesus ascended to Heaven. After her assumption into Heaven, she continues to plead for the Church before the throne of God and is sent by the Holy Spirit throughout the Church ages, requesting churches to be built in different places in the world, often on pagan sites, in order to bring to an end the worship of false gods. She appeared before and during wars in various countries of Europe, to obtain a win and rout out the Muslim and pagan religions, resulting in strengthening Christian peoples. Mary has continued to appear throughout the centuries in well-known apparitions, to rescue humanity, right up to the present day.

Our Lady of Guadalupe

Columbus's 'discovery' of the Americas, in 1492, paved the way for an influx of Catholic missionaries, especially to the Aztecs, in Mesoamerica, but they struggled to bring the people to the faith of Jesus Christ. The people were under strong, demonic delusion, sacrificing adults and babies to the serpent god Quetzalcoatl. Mary, Mother of Jesus, intervened at this time, starting down a path, procuring **a decisive battle** against Satan, in this fifth Church age, by inspiring a prodigious prayer army of native/Spanish descent even to this day.

Juan Diego, a 57-year-old Aztec, peasant farmer who had converted to Catholic faith, was walking to an early Saturday morning Mass on Dec 9, 1531. On the way, he passed by the hill, called Tepeyac, where the shrine of the goddess Tonantzin, had been worshiped in the winter solstice for centuries. It was at that time of the year when he heard celestial music and the sound of beating wings. He moved up the hill, where he saw a lovely, young woman with cinnamon skin, dressed in the attire of an Aztec princess. Instantly overcome, he fell to his knees. She asks him where he is going. He responds, that he was heading to the celebration of the Mass, not far from there. She says: "You must know and be very certain in your heart, my son, that I am truly the perpetual and perfect Virgin Mary, holy Mother of the True God…I…desire that in this place my sanctuary be erected…. You must go to the house of the Bishop of Mexico, and tell him that I sent you, and that it is my desire to have a sanctuary built here." [1]

Juan Diego hurried to the Bishop's house but wasn't taken seriously. He went to meet the Virgin on the hill that evening, where he pleaded with her to send someone else. But Mary convinced him, he was chosen by her.

On Sunday, Juan approached the bishop once again, and this time he was more receptive, but requested proof from this Lady who claimed to be the Mother of God. At sunset, Juan Diego met the Lady at the hill, and she promised to give him, the sign that the Bishop was looking for. But that night when Juan went home, his Uncle Juan Bernardino was very ill. The next day, Juan did not go to the hill but stayed with his uncle, thinking he was going to die.

So on Tuesday morning, Dec 12, 1531, Juan Diego went to get a priest to anoint him. He tried to avoid the hill at Tepeyac, out of fear and embarrassment, for not fulfilling the promise to the Virgin. Accordingly, Mary met him on the side of the hill and asked him where he was going. As he explained the situation about his uncle, she assured him that his uncle would be well.

She asked him to go to the top of the hill, pick the flowers blooming and bring them to her. It was winter, and the hill was covered with thorns, thistles, and cactus. When he reached the top, "beautiful Castilian roses touched with dew, of exquisite fragrance," were gathered and given to Mary. "Mary took them from him, as he gathered them, arranged them with her own hands and put them in his cloak, or Tilma, made from the fiber of the Maguey cactus. She tied a knot in it, behind his neck, to hold the roses in place." She instructed him: "This is the sign that you must take to the Lord Bishop. In my name, tell him that with this, he will see and recognize my will, and that he must do what I ask; and you are my ambassador, worthy of my confidence…tell him all that you have seen, so that you will persuade the Lord Bishop, and he will see that the church is built, for which I ask." [2]

After Juan Diego told the Bishop all that had happened, he opened his cloak. The roses flowed out on to the floor. To the great astonishment of everyone in the room, the Tilma revealed a full image of the Mother of God.

To this day, the Image of Holy Mary of Guadalupe remains in perfect condition. Although the fiber material of the Maguey cactus should have only lasted 30 years, it has been miraculously preserved for 486 years and hangs in the Basilica of Guadalupe in Mexico City.

She appeared this way on the Tilma to communicate to the Aztec people whom she was. The Aztecs were a **highly visual people** with an "elaborate, coherent symbolic system for making sense of their lives. When this was destroyed by the Spaniards, something new was needed to fill the void and make sense of the New Spain." [3] She stood in front of the sun, in other words, the sun stood behind her, the Aztecs saw her as greater than the dreaded sun god. Her feet rested on the crescent moon, a symbol of a goddess, and the sister of the major Aztec sun and war god, showing Mary as above, this light of the moon. The blue-green, hue-like jade on her mantle was the color worn by Aztec Royalty, therefore, she was seen as a Queen. Jade was also the stone that allowed the soul to reach the gods. They eventually realized that she was one who would lead them to the true God.

The stars strewn across her mantle, told the Aztecs that she was greater than the stars of heaven, which they worshipped as gods. Miraculously, the constellation of stars on her mantle resemble the position of the stars in the sky on Dec. 12, 1531, in reverse; that is from Heaven looking down to the earth.

The gold border on her mantle and on the edge of her robe and embroidered cuffs signifies her royal dignity. The rose colored robe is symbolic of earth, blood, and life. The lined white ermine seen as white feathers to the Aztecs, symbolizes closeness to gods. Stylized leaf and rosette design on her robe, symbolize hills and mountains. At her waist is fastened a cingulum, a girdle–like band around her waist that is worn by unmarried women and removed only upon marriage. It is a symbol of Perfect Virginity. Yet, Mary is visibly pregnant. Revelation 12:2 says, "… She was with child…" The four-petal flower over her womb was a symbol of plenitude, representing the four directions of the earth, originating from the circle in the center. Here heaven and the underworld vertically encountered the earth in the center. Placed over Mary's womb, the four-petal flower announced that even though their fifth sun had died, the sixth sun was to be born of Mary of Guadalupe, her son Jesus Christ. The angels' red, white, and green–feathered wings were seen as eagle's wings, supporting the woman. The eagle was the bird that represented the sun, the greatest of all gods. She comes riding on eagle's wings; therefore, she comes riding on wings of absolute truth. She could not be God herself, since her hands were joined in prayer, and her head was bowed in reverence, clearly to one greater than her. Her eyes are looking downward, not forward, as they would if she was a goddess.

Finally, the black-cross displayed on the gold brooch at her neck was identical to the one emblazoned on the banners and helmets of the Spaniards, as if telling the Aztecs to embrace the religion of their conquerors. The Virgin's head is inclined gracefully to the right, evading the center seam which would otherwise disfigure her face.

In a very short period, nine million Aztecs who observed this Tilma, came to Jesus Christ without a word being preached. This reflects a counter-moment in history, in which Mary helped replenish souls that Martin Luther took out by his divisiveness.

Another discovery on the Tilma is the reflected images on the cornea of the eyes. The reflection in Our Lady's eyes, reveal, who are believed to be: Juan Diego, Juan Gonzales the interpreter and Bishop Zumarraga. With the aid of digital imaging, one can also see a family with children and a baby who occupy the center of the pupil of the eye. One ophthalmologist noted the eyes seemed alive when examined. [4]

The Battle of Lepanto

Mary continued to engage in battles, particularly at Lepanto, against the Moslem's trying to enter into Europe again, after the crusades. On October 7, 1571, the **Turkish Muslims** of the Ottoman Empire, entered into the Bay of Lepanto, off the coast of Cyprus, to destroy the Christian fleet of the Mediterranean and to open all of Europe to invasion and dominance by Muslim religious control. They had galley ships that held Christian prisoners, to man the oars of their fleet of over 220 ships, to destroy the 206 ships of the fleet of the Holy League although the men in battle were around 30,000 each. Pope Pius V realized the future of Christian Europe was being threatened, ordered public prayers, leading the people of Rome in vigils and **processions in prayer with rosaries to Our Lady.** It was considered the bloodiest battle in history, and thousands prayed that day as the sea became red with blood. Two thirds of the fleet of the Turkish Muslims was destroyed. That night, **the pope realized by the knowledge of the Holy Spirit**, before a message was given to him by courier, that they had won the battle. His words were: "This is not a moment for business; make haste to thank God, because our fleet this moment has won a victory over the Turks." [5] Pius established October 7th, as the feast of **Our Lady of the Rosary,** joyfully recognizing through petitions to her, that the battle was won. October became the month of the Most Holy Rosary.

Our Lady of Good Success

This is a little known apparition of Venerable Mother Mariana de Jesus Torres. Her prophecies **would not be revealed to the world until the end of the 20th century** when in fact that did occur.

There is a history of Our Lady of Good Success in Spain and in Rome, but in 1577, when Sister Mariana, a 13-year-old, went to Quito, Ecuador with four other sisters to start the first convent, she experiences something unusual. In 1582, she **dies** for the **first time**, standing before the judgment seat and was rewarded with Heaven, but was given a choice of staying or going back to suffer for the sins of the 20th century, which she did. A few years later in 1588, she experienced on Good Friday, visions of the horrible abuses and heresies that would exist in the Church in the 20th century and **died again,** remaining in death for 2 days until Easter Sunday. [6]

In 1594, Mary appears to Mariana stating, "I am Mary of Good Success, the Queen of Heaven and Earth." [7] She describes her role, to prolong as long as she can, by interceding in people's lives, extending the time of the Church; consequently restraining, "...the hand of Divine Justice, always so ready to chastise this unhappy and criminal world."[8] In 1599, Mary appears, requesting a statue in her likeness.

On January 21, 1610, Mary appears a third time, confiding to Mariana, secrets of the future and other information for Marian devotion, in the convent of the Immaculate Conception. Mary continues: "Thus, I make it known to you that from the end of the 19th century and from **shortly after the middle of the 20th century**...passions will erupt, and there will be a total corruption of customs, for **Satan will reign** almost completely, **by means of the masonic sects.** They will focus principally on children (education, in order to sustain this general corruption. Woe to the children of these times! It will be difficult to receive the sacrament of Baptism and that of Confir-mation. They will receive the sacrament of Confession, only if they remain in Catholic schools, for the Devil will make a great effort to destroy it, through persons in positions of authority. The same thing will happen with Holy Communion. Alas! How deeply I grieve to manifest to you, the many enormous sacrileges, both public as well as secret that will occur from profanations of the Holy Eucharist." [9]

"This battle will reach its most acute stage because of some irresponsible religious, under the appearance of virtue and with bad-intentioned zeal, will undermine **the existence of their Mother**. The Sacrament of **Extreme Unction** will be little valued. Many will die without receiving it...Others, incited by the Devil, will rebel against the spirit of the Catholic Church and will deprive countless souls of innumerable graces, consolations, and the strength they need, to make that great leap from time to eternity."

"As the Sacrament of **Matrimony**, which symbolizes the union of Christ with His Church, it will be attacked and deeply profaned. **Freemasonry**, which **will then be in power**, will enact iniquitous laws, with the aim of doing away with this Sacrament, making it easy for everyone to live in sin and **encouraging** the **procreation** of **illegitimate children**, born without the blessing of the Church. The Catholic spirit will rapidly decay; the precious light of Faith will gradually be extinguished, until there will be an almost total and general corruption of customs. Added to this, will be the effects of secular education, which will be one reason for the dearth of priestly and religious vocations."

"The Sacrament of **Holy Orders** will be ridiculed...the devil will try **to persecute the ministers**...with cruel and subtle astuteness **to deviate them** from the spirit of their vocation and will corrupt many of them. These depraved priests, who will scandalize the Christian people, will result in hatred, towards bad Catholics. The enemies of the Roman Catholic and Apostolic Church will come against all priests...This apparent triumph of Satan will bring enormous sufferings to good priests, and the Vicar of Christ on earth, who is a prisoner in the Vatican, will shed secret and bitter tears, in the presence of his God and Lord, beseeching light, sanctity, and perfection for all the clergy of the world..." [10]

"For this knowledge will only be known to the general public, in the 20th century. During this epoch, the Church will find herself attacked by terrible **hordes of the Masonic sect**...the corruption of customs, unbridled luxury, the impious press, and secular education. The vices of impurity, blasphemy, and sacrilege will dominate in this time of depraved desolation... will ensnare the rest into sin and conquer innumerable frivolous souls who will be lost. Innocence will almost no longer be found in children, nor modesty in women. In this supreme moment of need of the Church, **the one who should speak will fall silent.**" "Know, beloved daughter, that when **your name will become known in the 20th century**, there will be many who will not believe, claiming that this devotion is not pleasing to God." [11]

On February 2, 1634, Mother Mariana the only remaining founding member towards the end of her life, was praying before the Blessed Sacrament when **the Sanctuary lamp went out.** She was given prophecies by Our Lady of Good Success that reiterate, clarify, and add to what was said earlier. She states: "The sanctuary light burning before the altar that **you saw extinguished, has many meanings.** At the end of the 19th century and advancing into a large part of the 20th century, **various heresies will spread.** As they come to dominate, the precious light of faith will be extinguished in souls, by the almost total corruption of customs. During this period, there will be great physical and moral catastrophes, both public and private... How many authentic vocations will perish because of the lack of discretion, discernment, and prudence...they should be souls of prayer and well learned in the varied spiritual ways. Woe to the souls who return to **the Babylon of the world**...the Spirit of impurity will saturate the atmosphere (TV and computers) in those times. Like a filthy ocean, it will inundate the streets, squares, and public places with an astonishing liberty. There will be almost no virgins in the world. Without virginity, **it would be necessary for the fire of heaven to fall upon these lands** to purify them."

"The **Masonic sect**, having infiltrated all the social classes, will **be so subtle** as to introduce itself into domestic ambiances (TV), in order to corrupt the children. In this epoch, the secular clergy will leave much to be desired because priests will become careless in their sacred duties. Losing **the divine compass** (Holy Spirit), they will stray from the road traced by God, for the priestly ministry, and they will become attached to wealth and riches, which they will unduly strive to attain. **How the Church will suffer on that occasion; the dark night of the lack of a Prelate** and a Father to watch over them... **many priests will lose their spirit, placing their souls in great danger.**"

"Pray insistently without tiring... imploring our celestial Father that... he might take pity on His ministers and bring to an end, those ominous times, **sending to this Church**, the prelate (Angelic Pastor /Pope) **who will restore the spirit** of **its priests.**"[12]"Know moreover, that Divine Justice releases terrible chastisements on entire nations, not only for the sins of the people, but for those of priests and religious persons." [13]

In January 1635, Mariana, died on the ground imitating St. Francis with her community around her. Her body remained flexible with a smile on her face. At her funeral, a miracle of healing took place when a blind girl could see again after a flower, from around Mariana's head, touched the young girl.

In 1906, her tomb was opened during the process of remodeling the convent. There, they discovered her body whole and incorrupt, after three centuries, complete with her habit and articles of penance intact. An aroma of lilies emanated from her body; another outward sign from God.

Mary of Agreda

Mary of Agreda's visions in the 1600s of Jesus, Heaven, and the mysteries of the life of Mary are recorded in four volumes called, The Mystical City of God. She also had the unusual gift of bilocation, (of being in two places at the same time) although, she never left her convent in Agreda, Spain. She was called to evangelize from her convent. She was sent by Our Lord, over 500 times to teach the faith to some 10,000 Jumano natives, on the great desert plains of the future states of Arizona, New Mexico, and parts of Texas, missed by the missionaries of that time. The historical archives of these states, document a lady in blue, the nun of Agreda, teaching the Jumano natives the faith of Jesus Christ. She described the topography of the land and points of interest in those particular states of America, and of the relationships with the Jumano natives. She is one of the visionaries, having seen the Passion of Christ, including the life events of his mother Mary. Her body, too, is incorrupt.

Margaret Mary Alacoque

At the end of these first two centuries of the fifth Church age, Jesus appears to Margaret Mary to reignite an early Church veneration; the devotion to the Sacred Heart of Jesus. In the 1600s, the faith of people had been badly shaken amidst the rise of Protestantism and the spread of heresies of Jansenism. Margaret Mary received visions of Jesus, reminding her of the devotion that had been around since the beginning of the Church **to His Sacred Heart**. "He opened His heart for the first time" to her, stating: "My Divine Heart so passionately loves all men and you in particular, that no longer am I able, to contain the flame of its burning charity [love]; it has to pour forth through you, and it must manifest itself to them, to enrich them with its precious treasures, which I am revealing to you, and which contains the sanctifying and salutary graces, necessary to snatch them from the abyss of perdition." [14] The month of June is appointed for this devotion, and since 1929, has been one of the most popular devotions. Margaret Mary's body is incorrupt, confirming Christ's intervention in her life, relating a message for all of us to respond to.

CHAPTER 10

SECRET SECTS–FREEMASONRY AND CONSPIRACIES

Most people are unfamiliar with the secret sects of Freemasonry and Illuminati even though these nefarious, shadowy networks hold many nations in a diabolical stranglehold. Those who affect the world the most, are not easily seen, in fact, their agendas are hidden, but often their accomplishments are in plain sight.

This brief warning does not even begin to describe the intensity and the forcefulness of a plot to bring the world under control, by a financially powerful few; in pursuit of a new world order, one, they themselves do not realize, **the true conspiracy: Satan's ultimate goal of world destruction.**

Most people are not aware of how they have infiltrated the Catholic Church in this fifth Church age and want to destroy it. This **would sound preposterous** if not for the prophecies of the canonized saints and the Popes who have spoken out against it, through various statements of clarification, called encyclicals. In 1738, Pope Clement XII was the first to condemn Freemasonry: "The peculiar…naturalistic character of Freemasonry, by which theoretically and practically, **it undermines the Catholic and Christian faith,** first in its members and through them, in the rest of society, creating religious indifferentism and contempt for orthodoxy and ecclesiastical authority…. The inscrutable secrecy and **fallacious ever-changing disguise** of the **Masonic association** and **of its 'work',** by which "men of this sort" break as thieves into the house…**perverting** the hearts of the simple, ruining their spiritual and temporal welfare."

"The **oaths of secrecy and of fidelity to Masonry and Masonic work**… cannot be justified in their scope, their object, or their form…. The oaths are condemnable…and the candidate in most cases is ignorant of the…extent of the obligation which he takes upon himself."

"The danger (of) such societies…would be nevertheless contrary to public order because by their very existence, as secret societies, based on the Masonic principles…encourage and promote the foundation of other really dangerous secret societies and render difficult, if not impossible, efficacious action (against) the civil and ecclesiastical authorities." [1]

The first Masons were originally, ordinary men who constructed buildings with stone. The earliest known mason guilds existed in Scotland, around 1057 and then in England about 1220. They were allowed to travel from country to country, including France and most of Europe, at a time when travel was intensely restricted. Stonemasons were highly sought after, for their valuable building skills and expertise in their craft. There were three major levels of stonemasons: hard-hewers digging and cutting stones, rough masons building walls, and with instruction from master masons. The 'master freestone masons,' as it is recorded in a statute of authorization of payment, in 1350, who had knowledge of geometry, mathematics and the ability to read, were given higher wages. They worked either within or outside the trade guilds. This may have given them special privileges, such as free travel. A system of signs and passwords were eventually established to recognize their competent skills.

Traditionally, mason guilds were used historically to build many churches and estates of Europe. The oldest manuscripts of freemasonry disciplines, were written in 1390, 1450, and revised in 1723, as the earliest genuine records from England. A coat of arms of three castles and compasses were incorporated in 1473. Such tools as the square, level, plumb, compass, and trowel are used for ceremonial use and symbols.

Around 1540, English guilds started accepting non-skilled members into the existing guilds. After 1646, the desire of non-stone masons to be included, increased membership and started to transform Masonic meetings into club-like affairs, characterized by lively discussion of morals and science in an underground flavor. English lodges copied the Scottish rite structure but set up their own form of Freemasonry; the York rite, which maintained the symbolism, gravitated towards modern progressiveness in science, business, and 'enlightened thinking'. By 1717, four London lodges, formed into a premier Grand Lodge of England and increased into three levels or three degrees of a fraternity membership. In 1728, the Grand Lodge of London, formed the first French, Masonic body. In the late 1700s, schisms resulted in two major groups. One of 'Antients' with a four-degree system, wanting to revert to an operative ritual, while the 'Moderns' with a three-degree system wanted to continue in a progressive fashion. Their popularity grew throughout the United Kingdom and Europe. In 1731, the first American Grand lodge formed in Pennsylvania. By 1772, a part of the Grande Lodge of France that was of the Scottish rite, separated into a new organization called, 'Grande Orient of France' that followed a 'Modern way.

According to Nesta Webster, the Grand Orient of France:"...was an undeniably subversive body, and by a coalition with the Grand Chapter, in 1786, acquired a far more dangerous character. For whilst 'the spirit of the Grand Orient was frankly democratic, the spirit of the Grand Chapter (members) was revolutionary, but the revolution was to be accomplished, above all, for the benefit of the upper class[bourgeoisie], with the people as its instrument." [2]

How did Freemasonry transform from three or four levels **to 33 levels?** It is necessary to look at the exploitation by the Illuminati. In 1770, **Adam Weishaupt**, a trained priest under the Jesuits, who studied Catholic Canon law at the University of Ingolstodt, Bavaria, Germany, became dissatisfied with the rigors of the ascetic journey, eventually lured by the Enlightened philosophers, doctrines of the Manicheans, occult secrets of the Rosicrucians, Egyptian occultism, and Freemasonry. The Academy of Science at Munich became an anti-ecclesiastical influence, leaning towards a view of 'Rationalism' and 'Enlightenment' that brought regression to the process of the Jesuit influence in Germany. Adam Weishaupt believed in humanism, which taught a person's power came from one's self (atheism). He had a knack for languages, studied ancient manuscripts, and delved into the occult of satanic worship. This influenced the **Order of Illuminati,** meaning enlightened or light bearers, whose machinations were designed to take control and rule the world.

Weishaupt spent five years developing a scheme to transform the human race **through revolutions**, with the employment of ancient diabolical sources, fashioning this organization into a pyramid structure. On May 1, 1776, he established **a Constitution** that he called the 'Novus Ordo Seclorum' or **'New World Order'** (the same words are now on the back of the Federal Reserve (American) dollar bill at the bottom of the Pyramid). The **Constitution** had six major **goals** at the time:

"1 The abolition of Monarchies and all ordered governments.

2 Abolition of private property.

3 Abolition of inheritance.

4 Abolition of patriotism.

5 Abolition of marriage, the family, all morality, and the institution of communal education for children.

6 The abolition of all religion." [3]

Historian Nesta Webster confirms: "As we shall see, the plan of Illuminism, as codified by the above points, has continued up to the present day, to form the exact programme of the World Revolution. How can we doubt that the whole movement originated with the Illuminati or with secret influences at work behind them?" [4] This programme continues to manifest itself in present-day events. Especially since the NAFTA agreement, these goals are increasingly taking shape in North America and beyond, reinforcing the control, the Globalists wield over the world's political and monetary systems.

Abbe Augustin Barruel, a Jesuit priest who personally knew Weishupt, referred to him as 'a human devil,' studied the primary documents of his dark intentions, and extensively researched and documented the clandestine goings-on of the Illuminati. Discoveries by the Bavarian police in Germany, during that period, confirmed the existence of these agendas.

Abbe Barruel quotes Weishaupt: "The greatest of our mysteries must be the novelty of our order. The fewer persons, there are in the secret, the better we shall thrive." [5] Nesta H. Webster states: "Secrecy being thus the great principle of his system, Weishaupt had not been slow to perceive the advantages, offered by an alliance with Freemasonry. During this period when he was thinking out his plan, the real aims of masonry were unknown to him." [6] He adds: "He only knew that the Freemasons held secret meetings, he saw them united by a mysterious link that recognized each other as brothers, by certain signs and certain words, to whatever nation they belonged; he therefore conceived a new combination, of which the result, was to be a society adopting for its methods –as far as it suited him- the regime of the Jesuits and the mysterious silence, the obscure existence of the Masons…" [7]

Weishaupt adopted part of the Jesuits' organizational system for his own sinister goals. In 1777, Weishaupt joined Freemasonry at Munich for the sole purpose of discovering their secrets. In 1780, Baron Von Knigge, a Freemason, was received into the Illuminati. These two revealed and discussed their ideas, to promote world revolutionary goals. Weishaupt made incriminating statements that plied together, the organizations of Freemasonry and Illuminati. He referred to Knigge as: "(He) is the master from whom to take lessons; give me six men of his stamp, and with them I will change the face of the Universe." [8]

The congress of Wilhelmsbad in Germany, as one researcher put it: "At the grand convention of Masonry held at Wilhelmsbad in 1782, the order of the Strict Observance was suspended, and Von Knigge disclosed the scheme of Weishaupt to the assembled representatives of the Masonic and mystical fraternities. Then and there, disciples of… as well as the statesmen, scientists, magicians, and magistrates of all countries, were converted to Illuminism." [9] Nesta H. Webster states from a freemason's account: "What passed at this terrible Congress will never be revealed to the outside world. The term 'tragic secrets' mentioned, and the quote…. I can only tell you that all this, is more serious than you think. The conspiracy being woven is so well thought out that it will be, so to speak, impossible for the Monarchy and the Church to escape from." [10]

After the congress of Wilhelmsbad, new members were told that the order was part of the Church, and that the first advocator of Illumunism was Christ, whose secret mission, they said, was to restore original liberty and equality to men and to prepare the world for doing away with property ownership. Weishaupt told his right hand man and lawyer Zwack: "The most admirable thing of all, is that great protestant and reformed theologians [Lutherans and Calvinists] who belong to our Order, really believe they see in it the true genuine mind of the Christian religion."[11] When members reached the highest degrees, it was revealed to them: "Behold our secret…in order to destroy all Christianity, all religion, we have pretended to have the sole true religion…to deliver one day, the human race from all religion."[12] "One must speak sometimes in one way, sometimes in another, so that our real purpose should remain impenetrable to our inferiors."[13] When commenting on promoting unsuspecting new people to the organization, Weishaupt states: "These good people swell our numbers and fill our money box. Set yourselves to work; these gentlemen must be made to nibble at our bait… but let us beware of telling them our secrets, this sort of people must be made to believe that the grade (level) they have reached is the last."[14, 15]

Nesta H. Webster continues: "At the masonic congress of Wilhelms-bad…. Jews should no longer be excluded from the lodges. At the same time it was decided to move the headquarters of the Illuminized Freemasonry to Frankfurt, which was the stronghold of Jewish finance, controlled at this date, by such leading members of the race as **Rothschild** (means Redshield), Mayer Amschel–later to become Rothschild also Oppenheimer, Wertheimer, Shuster, Speyer, Stern, and others." [16] The admission of Jewish people into the organization at this later date, tells us, **true Jewish people** did not start this organization. It is clear that Jews who have joined this diabolical organization, cease to be true Jewish people of God. People with Jewish last names for generations, exist in this organization to this very day but the authenticity of an ongoing undertone of World Revolution, as an international Jewish plot is not credible.

There are 33 degrees (levels) in Freemasonry, each replete with its own cryptic oaths, symbols, and iconography; all characteristic of the dark side. This organization appropriates many symbols of ordinary stonemason work, such as the trowel, apron, compass, and square. Symbols for the Illuminati at higher levels are borrowed from the ruins of the ancient civilizations of Egypt, Babylon, Greek, Phoenician, and city of Tyre, whose denizens worshiped false or mythical deities connected to devil worship. The Illuminati (Satanic) membership remains in the shadows in the higher degrees, hidden within Freemasonry's outer structure but taking it to 33 degrees. Former members have written their experiences in reaching the highest degrees after exiting this diabolical organization, with the threat of death always in front of them. Their exposs have been invaluable in revealing this evil for what it is. Among them are Jim Shaw of New York, who wrote *The Deadly Deception*, and John Salza, who penned *Masonry Unmasked*.

Secret societies, that at least **13 popes have spoken out against**, that saints have recognized through visions from the Holy Spirit, and by those who have defected from the highest 'degrees,' recognizing the deception of the Illuminati within Freemasonry. Although not always called Illuminati in our day, they exist in part within the framework of the 'innocent store front' secret societies of the so-called benevolent Freemasons, to deceive in an ambiguous way, 'the direction to the light.'

Sister Jeanne Le Royer (1731- 1798 received this vision during that same period as the **constitution of the Illuminati** was established in secret: "God has manifested to me the malice of Lucifer and the perverse and diabolical intentions of **his henchmen** against the Holy Church of Jesus Christ. At the command of their master, these wicked men have crossed the world like furies to prepare the way and place for the Antichrist, whose reign (beginning of seventh Church age is approaching. Through the corrupt breath of their proud spirit, they have poisoned the minds of men. Like persons infected with pestilence, they have communicated the evil to each other, and the contagion has become general. The storm began in France, and France shall be the first theatre of its ravages, after having been its cradle. The Church in Council shall one day strike with anathemas, pull down and destroy the evil principles of that criminal constitution..."[17] The prohibition by the Catholic Church, of the constitution of the order of Illuminati, will not take place until the sixth Church age of peace.

Age of Enlightenment

The so-called European age of Enlightenment, concentrated in France and Germany and reaching all the way to Russia, developed as a set of ideas but even more as a set of values. It was an age of reasoning or rationalism, the age of freedom of men, to use their own thoughts, while embracing the arrogant and false doctrine, 'God is dead...Man is God.' Many European writers and philosophers of the era, such as Voltaire, Rousseau, Hume, Berkley, Bacon, Pascal, and Galileo, revolutionized continental thinking. These new ideas, debated at length in coffee houses, salons and clubs throughout Europe, stirred great social change. Thoughts of **turning away from** religious authority, gild-based economic systems, censorship of ideas, divine rights of kings and kingdoms, **to** self-governments, republics, natural law and liberty, individual rights, scientific discovery, electro-magnetism, and numerous inventions permeated the masses. Even though there was a need for changes, towards individual rights, and concern for those around us, God was being left out. The wisdom of dependence on God, as our best source for answers and direction was left out. This greater darkness started to raise its evil head when the ways of the Church were not taken seriously. It reached into the middle upper class, the bourgeoisie, entertained by so-called enlightened ideas for many years to come.

The French Revolution
1789-1802

A second revolution is about to explode on a worldwide basis, according to prophecies of the saints in the Catholic Church. This work on the French Revolution is necessary to understand the format, of what is about to happen across the world.

The significance of the French Revolution extends far beyond France. It only started there. What the history books leave out of the French Revolution was the beginning of an unforeseen campaign to abolish monarchies and all individual rights for peoples of nations. [18] This was the first manifestation of communism. This includes the abolition of religion, particularly against the Catholic faith. Those in high places, orchestrate change and control of a nation, without peoples' awareness, by convincing individuals that the purpose of change, is truly for the good of the individual. It was deceivingly procured as, for the people by the people. The true purpose of this change was to shift control of the monetary systems, to those with the greatest financial possession. This also took place in the Bolshevik Revolution in Russia.

The spreading of propaganda through speeches, paper, and discussion at clubs, salons, and coffee houses served to convince the masses of a need for change. This avalanche of rumors and lies against governing bodies, provoked the common people, to rebellion, initially forcing the overthrow of the governing systems in two, three or more rounds of revolutionary change, within a short period of time. Many people lose their lives during the rounds of crises. Through chaos, people fall into their [19] plans of rescued platforms ultimately leading people into directions, for the purposes of the wealthy. The plan evolves governing systems into the hands of private individuals, by forming committees and organizations, to surrender the control of a country, into the hands of those unseen. These were and are the secret societies, originally called Illuminati.

Evidence suggests that the Rothschilds and other wealthy families out of Germany and France were behind this political scheme. Although, they were not recognized at the time, they lived in the same area as the Illuminati's major headquarters in Frankfurt. The Jacobins were another name or tentacle of the darkness of Illuminati /Freemasonry. This ultimate darkness of the Jacobins in the history of the French Revolution, was that duplicitous voice of the strongest persuasion, by any means for their purposes.

Nesta H. Webster stated: "If then, it is said that the [French] Revolution was prepared in the lodges of Freemasons–and many French Masons have boasted of the fact–let it be added, that it was Illuminized Freemasonry that made the Revolution, and that the Masons who acclaim it, are Illuminized masons, inheritors of the same tradition, introduced into the lodges of France, (1787) by the disciples of Weishaupt, patriarch of the Jacobins." [20]

A. Ralph Epperson, who researched the subject for over 50 years, states: "The invisible hand that guided the entire French Revolution was the Illuminati; only 13 years in existence, yet powerful enough to cause a revolution in one of the major countries of the world." [21]

The **first round of revolutionary change**, saw the radical Jacobins, insidiously arouse the National Constituent Assembly that would start to make decisions for the country. King Louis XVI, increased troops around Paris. On **June 19, 1789,** about half of the First Estate comprised of Clergy, joined the National Assembly. Nobles of the Second Estate began to join the National Assembly. The King had lost popularity and tried to present new far-reaching reforms but contradictions brought pandemonium.

William Bramley stated: "During the first French Revolution, a key rebel leader was the Duke of Orleans, who was grand master of French Masonry, before his resignation at the height of the Revolution. Marquis de Lafayette, who had been initiated into the Masonic fraternity, by George Washington, also played an important role in the French Revolutionary cause. The Jacobin Club was the radical nucleus of the French revolutionary movement that was founded by prominent Freemasons."

"It was the Duke of Orleans, grand master of the Grand Orient Lodge of Freemasons, who reportedly bought all the grain in 1789 and either sold it abroad or hid it away, thus creating near starvation among commoners. Gallart de Montjoie, a contemporary, blamed the Revolution almost solely on the Duke of Orleans, adding, (he) was moved by that invisible hand, which seemed to have created all the events of our revolution, in order to lead us towards a goal that we do not see at present." [22]

Nesta H. Webster contends: "The plan of Weishaupt was always to make use of princes' to further their own ends...wherewith as the Revolution proceeded he replenished his coffers...from the funds of the Illuminati in those places..." [23] "In the French Revolution, we see for the first time that **plan in operation** which **has been carried on right up to the present moment;** the **systematic attempt** to **create grievances,** in order to **exploit** them (**the people).**" [24][25]

On July 14, 1789, the Bastille, the prison fortress, was stormed, looted, and torn down. The Kings soldiers were ordered to leave Paris, and the King knew he had lost Royal power. Sovereignty was now in the hands of the people, the **National Constituent Assembly.**

Nesta H. Webster states: "All the revolutionaries of the Constituent Assembly were initiated into the third degree." Jim Marrs asserts they were, "...of Illuminized Masonry, including revolutionary leaders such as the Duke of Orleans, Valance, Lafayette, Mirabeau, Garat, Rabaud, Marat, Robespierre, Danton, and Desmoulins." [26]

Nesta H. Webster remarks: "the extraordinary incident known to history as, '**The Great Fear**' when on the same day, **July 22, 1789,** and almost at the same hour, in towns and villages all over France, a panic was created by the announcement that brigands were approaching, and therefore that all good citizens must take up arms. The messengers who brought the news post, hastened on horseback...bearing the words, the King orders all chateaux (houses) to be burnt down; he only wishes to keep his own!" [27]

Fear, panic, and destruction ensued. "The object of the conspirators was thus achieved; **arming of the populace** against law and order, a device which, **ever since 1789, has always formed the first item in the programme of the social revolution.**" [28] Nesta H. Webster continues: "Brigands from the south were deliberately enticed to Paris in 1789, employed and paid by the revolutionary leaders, is a fact confirmed by authorities, too numerous to quote at length...In other words, the importation of the contingent of hired brigands, conclusively refutes the theory that the Revolution was an irrepressible rising of the people." [29]

By August 26, 1789, decisions were made to abolish the feudal system. A Declaration of the Rights of Man and the citizen were implemented. Louis XVI does not ratify the Declaration. Then, a Paris mob forms on October 6, 1789, and women march to Versailles storming the Palace. Louis XVI ratifies the Declaration. Church property is nationalized and expropriated. By 1790 monastic vows are banned, nobility is abolished and the clergy must swear an oath to the constitution, which is condemned by the Pope.

Meanwhile, the Jacobins were a growing influence on the people. In 1791, the Jacobins continued to push the National Assembly to extreme exploits. Gabriel Mirabeau was elected first president of the National Assembly. He stated privately: "We must flatter the people by gratuitous justice, promise them great diminution in taxes and a more equal division, more extension in fortunes, and less humiliation. These fantasies will fanaticize the people, who will flatten all resistance." [30] But in this same year Mirabeau dies. The King accepts the new Constitution and swears allegiance to it but defends the clergy who do not comply. On September 30, the National Assembly is dissolved.

On October 1, the **second round** of **revolutionary change**, the Legislative Assembly meets, with all new and mostly inexperienced young men. This is a new twist to the revolution prepared far in advance of October 1.

Jim Marrs states: "Mirabeau called for the overthrow of all order, all laws, and all power to 'leave the people in anarchy.' He said the public must be promised 'Power to the people' and lower taxes but never given real power. 'For people as legislators are very dangerous [as] they only establish laws which coincide with their passions.' He said, the clergy should be destroyed by 'ridiculing religion.' " Mirabeau ended with: "What matters the means as long as one arrives at the end." [31]

In 1792, the Holy Roman Emperor Francis II, is against the Constitution and Revolution. The Holy Roman Empire is threatened. A call goes out to resist the Jacobin's violent push to Revolutionary change. Confusion and fear were everywhere, the people did not knowing which way to turn.

In the **third round of the revolutionary change**, the Jacobins forced the **Legislative Assembly** to be replaced with a **National Convention**. A stronger call was heard to **overthrow the Monarchy**. France is named a Republic, and the people wonder what to do with the King. A trial takes place for Louis XVI and **the Terror** begins.

On January 21, 1793, King Louis XVI is executed by Guillotine. France declares war on supportive nations. Three hundred thousand men are called to defend the Republic. Food riots explode in Paris. A **Revolutionary Tribunal** is created. Armies and committees are created. Robespierre, leader of the Jacobins heads the Committee of Public Safety. The government is declared revolutionary. By September, terror by government was the norm. A Law of Suspects is passed. Having price controls on grain and other necessary goods is proclaimed by the **National Convention** to feed those in the cities and to prevent hoarding. The devastation of the industrial and manufacturing towns, and the ruin of many merchants is senseless. The burning of libraries, destruction of art, literature, opposition to science were examples of the **elimination of education**. To abolish luxury trades as parasitic trades. Bloody measures were taken, over nonconformist and suspects of any kind mostly priests, nobility and resistant Catholics, with over sixteen thousand people going to the guillotine. Many guillotined were of the upper class at that time.

Nesta H. Webster states one real intention is **to control education:** "The attacks on civilization carried out in the summer of 1793, the burning of libraries and the destruction of treasures of art and literature, were all part of the scheme of Weishaupt, but they were also perfectly consistent with the Socialistic theory of the 'Sovereignty of the people.' For if one considers that in the least educated portion of the community, all wisdom and all virtue reside, the only logical thing to do is burn the libraries and close the schools. Of what avail is it to train the intellectual faculties of a child, if **manual labor** alone is to be held honorable?" [32]

In 1794, many continue to be guillotined, including **Mass killings** with whatever means at their disposal. At Vendee, one hundred and seventy thousand **French Catholics** rebelled against the Revolution because of their priests being **killed**, eventually slaughtered themselves. The **National Convention** through Robespierre established the Cult of the Supreme Being. The **Revolutionary Tribunal** executed many without proof of witnesses. Eventually Robespierre is arrested, and guillotined along with the rest of the Committee of Public Safety. By the end of July, the Reign of Terror ceases. France is in bankruptcy. The Jacobins were successful in their destructive intentions although the revolution was not completely successful. The Jacobin clubs were closed, ending the Jacobin influence.

Nesta H. Webster states: "Behind the Conventions, behind the clubs, behind the **Revolutionary Tribunal**, there existed **that most secret convention** which directed everything…an occult and terrible power of which the other convention became the slave, and which was composed of the prime initiates of Illuminism." [33] Lord John Dalberg Acton comments: "The appalling thing in the French Revolution is not the tumult but the design. Through all the fire and smoke, we perceived the evidence of a calculating organization. The managers remain studiously concealed and masked; but there is no doubt about their presence from the first." [34]

The **last round,** after the exhaustion of all resources of the nation, allows **the secret prime initiates** to take over the nation. In 1795, the **National Convention** is dissolved, and from 1795-1799, the **Executive Directory** is established consisting of five directors, elected by the **Council of Ancients** (Illuminati), numbering five hundred. The Ancients were against Christianity, the Church, and the State. They wanted the expulsion of all priests from France. Many non-conforming priests were celebrating Mass again. But a new socialist conspiracy was discovered that was more important to squelch. Napoleon who was given command of the French army gave honor to the Pope. The expulsion of priests was abandoned.

Afterwards, observers were dismayed at the result of the so-called revolution. "France was demoralized," writes Louis M. Madelin. "She was exhausted, this is the last trait of this country in ruins. There is no longer any public opinion, or rather this opinion is made up only of hatred. They hate the Directors, and they hate the deputies; they hate the terrorists, and they hate the [royalist]; they hate the rich, and they hate the anarchists; they hate the revolution, and the counter revolution... But where hatred reaches paroxysm, **is in the newly rich.**

"Of all the ruins found and increased by the Directory–ruins of parties... power...national representation...churches...finances...homes...consciences... intellects...there is nothing more pitiable than this: the ruin of the national character." [35]

Henry Redhead Yorke comments, "The Revolution, which was brought about ostensibly for the benefit of the lower classes of society, has sunk them to a degree of degradation and misfortune to which they never were reduced under the ancient monarchy. They have been disinherited, stripped, and **deprived of every resource for existence...** For what and for whom are all this havoc and desolation?" [36] Louis-Marie Prudhomme gave remarkable, on the scene, illustrations (drawings of events of the French Revolution for the French Revolutionary Newspaper from July 1789 to 1794 and states: "In what sort of epilepsy, into which France had fallen, not only of the revolutionary nobles, set themselves by preference; against nobles, priests against priests, merchants against merchants, rich against rich, but even the (common people, once they themselves became judges, did not any more spare the (common people, who had remained amongst the crowd of citizens. **How could the people have suspected the system of universal depopulation?** Until then, it had not been heard of in history.

This great doctrine, however, was not chimerical, **it existed**, it was visible, the leaders of opinion, only wished to reign over deserts."[37] Whether depopulation was in the origins of the Illuminati constitution, it was part of the agenda in France. This was certainly the case in the Russian Revolution, Hitler in Germany, Khmer Rouge in Cambodia, China, and other countries in similar ways. Depopulation is in the language of our present day Globalist.

Nesta H. Webster: "Revelations on the real facts of the terror…describing the First French Revolution as a 'bourgeois movement'…has been the case in every outbreak of World Revolution…but in the French 'Terror' as in Russia…**the bourgeoisie were also the victims.**" [38]

The French Revolution was just the beginning; taking over the monetary systems, by a self-appointed cabal, has since become a worldwide phenomenon. In the last fifty years, it is accomplished, in more subtle and secretive ways. Those who accomplish the monetary takeovers, today, are the Globalists, the richest of the rich, exploiting most nations, monetarily. In 2014, a prime example of a monetary takeover **to central banking** is the charade of the Ukraine fiasco. Loans are then issued from the globalist bankers, charging interest, resulting in more taxation for nations. It is solicited to the people, procuring protection for nations, from wars and terrorism, and for people's so-called economic gains. This protection is about convincing the people, through fear of an enemy, and is imminently calling for the need, to change the governmental systems or laws of a country, so the wealthiest men of the day, can deceiving reap inclusively from nations. Since the French Revolution, this system is designed for taking everything they can, from common people, through interest and taxation of a nation, and calling it foreign policy. This still leaves people in serfdom, just in a new way.

It is also about taking God out of the affairs of mankind and bringing in secular humanist schemes, including destroying the credibility of the Catholic Church. It has been more offensive than most realize. This change of the governing systems continued throughout Europe, and they would never be the same again, nor much of the world. Surprisingly, these sweeping changes are foretold in prophecy; the signs are already there, for those who are wise enough to see it.

Venerable Holzhauser states: "During the fifth period, we saw only calamities and devastation; oppression of Catholics by tyrants and heretics; executions of Kings and **conspiracies to set up republics…**" [39]

This again comes from **Sister Jeanne Le Royer** who experienced the French Revolution towards the end of her life and foretold of the execution of King Louis XVI, including other incites through the Holy Spirit: "One day I heard a voice which said: The **New Constitution** will appear to many, **other** than what it really is. They will bless it as a gift from Heaven; Where as, **it is in fact** sent **from Hell** and permitted by God, in His just wrath. It will only be by its effects that people will be led **to recognize the Dragon** who wanted to destroy all and devour all." [40]

In addition, **Venerable Magdalene Porsat** states: "The year 1789 upset France only; **that which is coming**, shall cause the **revolution of the whole world**." [41]

Napoleon and the Republic

A republic is a form of government without a monarch. The word republic from the Latin translation becomes a 'public affair.' Republics first were seen in Greece and then Rome, given to representation by peoples and governing bodies in a state. At first glance, this would seem like a better way of governing, but is it?

After Napoleon Bonaparte's rise to power in the late eighteenth century, and with his Grande Arme, created a new constitution, managing to bring a close to the wars of France and crowned himself Emperor of France, the Republic. Napoleon was aware of how the system now worked in France with this comment: "When a government is dependent for money upon the bankers, **they**, not the leaders of the government, control the situation, since the hand that gives, is above the hand that takes,... financiers are without patriotism and without decency..." [42]

He reformed the economy, Church, military, education, and legal system with the Napoleonic Code that has stood the test of time. The code: sought to uphold accessible law, not favoring privileges by birth, religion, or superstition, nor based on local customs, exemptions, or feudal Lords. Under the penal code, only true crimes, not phony offenses were outlawed. A code of civil procedure, a commercial code, a code of Criminal instructions was published, declaring the rights of citizens presumed innocent until declared guilty. It is one of the few positive documents to have influence on the rule of law to this day.

CHAPTER 11

OUR LADY'S CALL FOR PRAYER WARRIORS

God is conferring on Mary, Mother of Jesus, the grace well earned, through her sufferings, at beholding her Son on the cross, **to build up an army in secret,** through **prayer with a rosary,** fasting, and penance, calling followers to protect the Church from the imminent danger approaching humanity. She intercedes to warn the body of Christ: to save many from temptation, abandonment of the faith, and eternal damnation. She reaches out to save those who are foreign to the faith and who have not acknowledged God.

Mary of Agreda in the 1600s prophesied: "It was revealed to me through the intercession of the Mother of God, all heresies will disappear. Christ, for His Blessed Mother, has reserved the victory over all heresies. Mary, more than ever, must shine in mercy and grace, in order to bring unbelievers into the Catholic faith. The power of Mary in the latter days will be very conspicuous. Mary will extend the reign of Christ over the heathens and the Mohammedans, and it will be a time of great joy when Mary is enthroned as mistress and Queen of hearts." [1]

St. Louis De Montfort

In the late 1700s, a humble priest, looked down upon by his fellow priests, was sent to the poorest parish in France, after which many miracles took place. "The **power of Mary** over all devils will be particularly outstanding in the last period of time," he declared. "She will extend the Kingdom of Christ **over the idolaters** and **Muslims,** and there will come a **glorious era** when **Mary is the Ruler and Queen of hearts.**" [2] This relates to the future period of peace in the sixth Church age.

Anne Catherine Emmerich

Anne Catherine Emmerich was born in Westphalia, Germany, and for years experienced hours-long, detailed visions of the Passion of Christ, observing events all the way back to the fall of the Angels. She also saw Mary's Assumption into Heaven. She was an Augustinian nun who suffered stigmata, and related all of her visions to a poet, Clemens Brentano who sat by her bedside listening and recording her visions which became his life's work.

Anne Catherine Emmerich was given extensive information on various subjects. In her visions, she observed how demons operate in this world: **"Some** (demons) **are let loose now** in our own day, and **others** will be freed **shortly after our time."** [3] This confirms the increase of demons unloosed in the 1800s and later in the 20th century. In the early 1800s, after the French Revolution, at a time when mankind is imperiled by many worldly doctrines, luring mankind from the truth, God is giving us precise in-depth information of the events of Jesus' life and others around him **that are not recorded in the Bible**. These recorded visions give us more evidence and proof of what He did. Some of her visions were fulfilled in the 20th century. John Paul II beatified Anne Catherine Emmerich in 2004.

Our Lady of the Miraculous Medal

Our Lady of the Miraculous Medal appeared to Catherine Laboure, in 1830, in Paris, to offer graces and protection that seemed unusual. Catherine was born ninth of eleven children. After receiving her first communion, she woke up daily at 4 a.m. and walked several miles to assist at Mass and to pray. One night she dreamt of an old priest saying Mass. After Mass, the priest beckoned to her, but she withdrew from him. The vision continued into a room for the sick, again seeing the same priest, he said to her: "My daughter, it is good to care for the sick. You may be running away from me now, but one day you will be happy to come to me. God has designs on you. Do not forget it." [4]

Some years later, she was visiting a hospital of the daughters of Charity. She saw a picture on the wall of the same priest as in her dream, and asked who he was. She was told, "That is our holy founder Saint Vincent De Paul." [5] In January 1830, Catherine entered the hospice and later, the seminary of the Mother House of the Daughters of Charity on Rue De Bac (Baker Street in Paris. She was given many visions of the heart of Saint Vincent and of Jesus Christ, while in front of the Blessed Sacrament in different ways according to the liturgy of the day.

On July 19, the eve of the feast of Saint Vincent de Paul, she was awakened in her curtained bed by her guardian angel who seemed like a child and said, "Sister Laboure, come to the Chapel, the Blessed Virgin awaits you." Catherine replied, "We shall be discovered." The angel smiled, "Do not be uneasy, it is half past eleven, everyone is sleeping. Come, I am waiting for you." After she dressed, she was amazed; the hall lights were all on. As they walked, the chapel door opened at the touch of the angel. The chapel lights were brightly lit, and as they moved towards the sanctuary, she could hear the rustle of silk and saw the most beautiful Lady walking towards her. She wore an ivory, colored dress with a bright, blue mantle and a white veil. She sat down in the director's chair.

The angel told Catherine, "This is the Blessed Virgin." [7] In the sanctuary, Catherine knelt beside the Blessed Mother and laid her hands on Her lap. Mary said, "God wishes to charge you with a mission. You will be contradicted, but do not fear; you will have the grace. Tell with confidence all that passes within you. The times are very evil.... Sorrows will come upon France. The whole world will be upset by miseries of every kind." A look of pain touched the Virgin's face. She continued, "Come to the foot of the Altar. Graces will be shed on all, great and little, especially upon those who ask for them...the protection of God, and St. Vincent will protect you...." [8] "The cross will be treated with contempt, they will hurl it to the ground...blood will flow." [9] After a long conversation, the Lady faded away. The angel took Catherine back to her bed as the clock struck two.

On November 27, of that same year, she went to the Chapel in the evening, again heard the faint swish of the silk dress and immediately raised her head to see the Beautiful Lady dressed in white standing on a globe. She held in her hands to the height of her shoulders, a golden ball that represented the world, with her eyes raised to Heaven. Then, rays of light flowing down to the globe, symbolized graces asked for and given to humanity. The jewels on her fingers, giving no rays, are the graces that were not asked for.

Next, Mary changed in appearance, now dressed in white with a blue mantle, with a white veil opening the scene. She requested, the imprint on 'a medal to be struck.' She was standing on the globe, with one foot on the head of the serpent that was under her feet. The year '1830' was imprinted on the globe. Her arms and hands were pointed downwards to the globe, shining rays towards the globe. An oval frame formed around the Blessed Virgin. Written around the frame in gold was: "O Mary, conceived without sin, pray for us who have recourse to you." [10] On the reverse side of the medal, was a cross with a bar at its feet, with which was intertwined an 'M' under the hearts of Jesus and Mary, both surmounted by flames of love, one having a crown of thorns, and other pierced with a sword. Encircling all of this were twelve stars around the oval frame.

Mary insisted: "Have a medal struck after this model. All who wear it will receive great graces, they should wear it around the neck." [11] Mary continued six more times over the next year to show Catherine this same image until she was confident in her ability to fulfill her mission for the world. This is the only time that Mary ever requested the formation of a medal in her combat for souls. The wearing of this medal is for special protection and graces. Today, Catherine's body lies incorrupt, in a reliquary at Rue de Bac in Paris.

Our Lady of La Salette

Our Lady appeared to Melanie Calvat, 15, and Maximin Giraud, 11, near La Salette, France on Saturday September 19, 1846, the feast of Our Lady of Sorrows. This time, Mary **ignites the battle against communism** before anyone knows it is happening. Mary uses harsh words and takes a firm tone that is unusual, almost desperate, knowing people must respond. Her clothing and appearance are highly disturbing. The words to her priests are very revealing of their conduct.

On this occasion, Melanie and Maximin were tending their cows in the morning, near the tiny village, in the southeastern French Alps. They had only met the day before, so this day, they played while they watched their cows. Melanie and Maximin gathered flowers of various colors for their 'paradise,' to make with stones, into a little house, comprised of two floors. Above the ground floor, a single large flat stone, already in the hillside, would be decorated with different colors of flowers, with garlands hanging from the flower stalks. When they finished, they sat down, looked at their paradise, and fell asleep on the grass a little ways off. When they awoke, mid-afternoon, Melanie could not see the cows, so she ran up the hill and spotted the cows placidly chewing their cud. As she was going down the hill, Maximin was coming up. Just then, Melanie saw a beautiful light shining more brightly than the sun, close to their 'paradise.'

Melanie describes the encounter: "At the same moment, I dropped the stick I was holding, something inconceivably delicious passed through me in that moment, and I felt myself being drawn. I felt a great respect, full of love, and my heart would have wished to run faster than myself. I kept my eyes firmly fixed on this light, which was motionless, and, as if it had opened up, I caught sight of another, much more brilliant light which was moving. In this light, I saw a most beautiful lady, sitting on top of our 'paradise,' with her head in her hands." [12] This tall, beautiful lady stood up and crossed her arms into her pearl studded sleeves. Her unusual attire displayed a white shawl, laced with a garland of roses, on the outer edge and with a heavy chain above it, alongside the roses. A tiara of light shone upwards from her head; with roses around the lower part.

Hanging with heavy chain from her neck was a crucifix, with a brilliantly, shining figure of Christ on it; adorned with a hammer and pinchers. Around her shoulders, heavy chain hung down towards her waist. The heavy chains signify the bondage of mankind's sin weighing heavily on Mary. The hammer, symbolizes the sins of humankind, which drove the nails into Jesus' hands and feet. The open pinchers, recall how these nails are mercifully removed and remind us of our obligation to repent of our sins and become reconciled with Christ, her son. The whole effect was as if she was made of light. Then she said, "Come, my children, fear not, I am here to proclaim great news to you."

Melanie states: "These soft and sweet words made me fly to her, and my heart desired to attach itself to her, forever. When I was up close to the beautiful lady, in front of her, to her right, she began to speak and from her beautiful eyes, tears also started to flow."

Our Lady states: "If my people do not wish to submit themselves, I am forced to let go of the hand of my Son...a great famine will come. Before the famine comes, children under the age of seven will begin to tremble and die in the arms of those who hold them. The others will do penance through hunger..." "At this point," Melanie explains further, "the beautiful lady, who was entrancing me, for a moment, did not make herself heard... At this moment, Maximin was receiving his secret. Then, turning to me, the most Holy Virgin spoke to me and gave me a secret in French." [13]

The original secrets were given to Pope Pius IX in 1851 and only discovered in the Vatican archives in 1999, but are shorter. It is also known that Maximin wrote brief versions about the secrets at three different times. His brief secret, repeats some of Melanie's and will not be mentioned here. Melanie wrote down information five times, including a lengthy detailed text, in 1879, that received an imprimatur by Bishop Zola of Leece, Italy. [14] Copies of this version have been reprinted for well over a hundred years. This is a portion of the 1879 copy, placed in a more chronological order:

"Melanie, what I am going to tell you now, will not always be a secret; you can publish it in 1858. The priests, ministers of my Son, priests, by their wicked lives, by their irreverence and their impiety in the celebration of the holy mysteries, by their love of money, their love of honors and pleasures, the priests, have become cesspools of impurity. Yes, the priests, are asking for vengeance, and vengeance is hanging over their heads. Woe, to the priests, and to those dedicated to God, who by their infidelity and their wicked lives, are crucifying My Son, again! The sins of those consecrated to God, cry towards Heaven and call for vengeance, and now vengeance is at their door, for there is no one left to beg mercy and forgiveness for the people. There are no more generous souls, there is no one left worthy of offering the spotless sacrifice to the Eternal, on behalf of the world..."

"In the year **1864, Lucifer** together **with a large number of demons will be unloosed from hell;** they will put an end to faith, little by little, even in those dedicated to God. They will blind them, in such a way, that, unless they are blessed with a special grace, these people will take on the spirit of these angels of hell; several religious institutions will lose all faith and will lose many souls..."

"In the year 1865, there will be desecration of holy places. In convents, the flowers of the Church will decompose and the devil will make himself, like the king of all hearts. May those in charge of religious communities be on their guard against the people they must receive, for the devil will resort to all his evil tricks, to introduce sinners into religious orders, for disorder and the love of carnal pleasures will be spread all over the earth."

"May the Pope guard against the performers of miracles. For the time has come when the most astonishing wonders will take place on the earth and in the air...In all places, there will be extraordinary wonders, because true faith has died, and false light shines on the world. Woe to the Princes of the Church, whose only occupation will be to heap wealth upon wealth, and to preserve their authority and proud domination!"

"My Son's Vicar will have much to suffer because for a time, the Church will be handed over to great persecutions; it will be the time of darkness; the Church will undergo a frightful crisis. With God's holy faith forgotten, each individual will want to direct himself and rise above his peers. Civil and ecclesiastical authority will be abolished, all order and justice will be trampled underfoot. Only murders, hatred, jealousy, lying and discord will be seen, with no love of country or family."

"The Holy Father will suffer greatly. I will be by his side until the end to receive his sacrifice. The wicked will make several attempts on his life, but they cannot harm him. Neither he nor his successor will see the triumph of the Church of God."

"All the civil governments will have one and the same plan, which will be to abolish and do away with every religious principal to make way for materialism, atheism, spiritism and vice of all kinds."

"Italy will be punished for her ambition, in wanting to shake off the yoke of the Lord of Lords. And so, she will be left to fight a war; blood will flow on all sides. Churches will be locked up or desecrated. Priests and religious orders will be hunted down and made to die a cruel death. Many will abandon the faith, and a great number of priests and members of religious orders, will break away from the true religion; among these people, there will even be bishops..."

"France, Italy, Spain, and England will be at war. Blood will flow in the streets. Frenchman will fight Frenchman. Italian will fight Italian. A general war will follow, which will be appalling. For a time, God will cease to remember France and Italy because the Gospel of Jesus Christ has been forgotten. The wicked will make use of all their evil ways. Men will kill each other; massacre each other, even in their homes..."

"God will strike in an unparalleled manner. Woe to the inhabitants of the earth! God will exhaust His anger, and no one will be able to escape so many evils at once. The heads, the leaders of the people of God, have neglected prayer and penance, and the devil has darkened their minds; they have become those wandering stars, which the ancient devil will drag with his tail to destruction. God will permit the ancient serpent to sow divisions among rulers, in all societies and in all families, both physical and moral punishments will be suffered. **God will abandon men to themselves and will send chastisements, one after the other for over 35 years...**The society of men is on the eve of the most terrible scourges and of gravest events. Mankind must expect to be ruled with an iron rod and to drink from the chalice of the wrath of God…"

"At the first blow of His thundering sword, the mountains and all nature will tremble in terror, for the disorders and crimes of men have pierced the vault of the heavens. Paris will burn, and Marseilles will be engulfed. Several cities will be shaken down and swallowed up by earthquakes. People will believe that all is lost. Nothing will be seen but murder, nothing will be heard but the clash of arms and blasphemy."

"The righteous will suffer greatly. Their prayers, their penances, and their tears will rise up to Heaven, and all of God's people will beg for forgiveness and mercy and will plead for my help and intercession. And then, Jesus Christ, in an act of His justice and His great mercy, will command His Angels to have all His enemies put to death. Suddenly, the persecutors of the Church of Jesus Christ and all those given over to sin, will perish and the earth will become desert-like…" [15, 16] Our Lady then, slowly walked up the hill, she turned and gazed in the direction of Rome and before disappearing reminded them: "And so my children, **you will pass this on to my people.**" [17] The first part of this prophecy refers to the 1800s and 1900s, but the last part will transpire by 2038.

Our Lady of La Salette, speaks of **a darkness** that **is rising up**, addressing **the actions** of **priests** and **religious** who respond to the spirit of the world, causing the loss of many souls and much disorder. It mentions the **great punishments** and **chastisements** that are **coming to mankind**. Other parts of her message refer to the sixth and seventh Church age and are recorded later in this work, in the appropriate time frame. The bishop appointed a commission and approved the apparitions. Miraculous cures took place and pilgrimages began and declared the Virgin Mary as Our Lady of La Salette.

In 1848, a similar European Revolution took place, as in the French Revolution. **Nesta H. Webster** states: "The 1848 Revolution, was thus the second great attempt of the Illuminized Freemasonry, to bring about world conflagration (holocaust)." [18]

Meanwhile, at this time, a cruel scheme called Communism, began to emerge, although, hardly anyone was aware of it. Members of the Illuminizied Freemasonry and those of the same conspiratorial goals, developed the **Communist Manifesto from 1844 to 1848.** Consequently, Mary appears at La Salette **in 1846,** and is wearing harsh-looking apparel to get our attention. Heaven is taking action against the evils that are slowly and subtly eroding the thinking of mankind. No one will be left on the earth, without an intervention of God in the future.

CHAPTER 12

THE ILLUSION
OF KARL MARX

What was the source of his thinking? Karl Marx was born in 1818, in Triera, Eastern Germany. His Christian family was a well to do bourgeois family, his father being a lawyer. He entered the universities of Bonn and Berlin majoring in history and philosophy becoming involved with a group of left wing Hegelians, misled into rationalism, resulting in atheistic and revolutionary conclusions.

But a darker side is not revealed in many of the history books, nor is it taught in the propaganda of communism throughout the world. Revelations come from Richard Wurmbrand, a Christian minister who spent 14 years in two communist prisons in Romania, where he endured horrific tortures. After prison, he moved to the United States, studying communism, spreading literature and writing books about the atrocities of the regime. In his books, he looks deeply at Karl Marx, who is considered the father of communism and finds poems and letters written by Marx to his father.

Marx had studied the Bible and was quite familiar with it. In high school, he had a love for Christ. He wrote: "Union with Christ could give an inner elevation, comfort in sorrow, calm trust, and a heart susceptible to human love, to everything noble and great, not for the sake of ambition and glory but only for the sake of Christ."[1] But something changed after high school.

In Wurmbrand's book, *Marx and Satan*, the author quotes a poem attributed to Marx: "I wish to avenge myself against one who rules above...." "At an age, when most young men have beautiful dreams of doing good to others and preparing a career for themselves, the young Marx wrote the following lines in his poem:"[2]

> "So a god has snatched from me, my all,
> in the curse and rack of destiny.
> All his worlds are gone, beyond recall!
> Nothing but revenge is left to me.
> I shall build my throne high overhead,
> Cold, tremendous, shall its summit be.
> For its bulwark, superstitious, dread. For
> its Marshall-blackest agony."[3]

Here he is speaking the same words as Lucifer that are recorded in Isaiah 14:13, "I will ascend into heaven, I will exalt my throne above the stars of God." [4] Marx states many cursed-lines that will not be placed here. He goes on,

"Yet I have power within my youthful arms,
To clench and crush you [i.e., personified humanity]
with tempestuous force,
While for us, both, the abyss yawns in darkness. You
will sink down and I shall follow laughing,
whispering in your ears, 'Descend,
come with me, friend.'" [5]

Wurmbrand states: "The Bible, which Marx had studied in his high school years, and which he knew quite well in his mature years, says, that the devil will be bound by an angel and cast into the bottomless pit (Rev 20:3). **Marx desires to draw the whole of mankind into this pit** reserved for the Devil and his angels. Who speaks through Marx in this drama? Is it reasonable to expect of a young student, to entertain as his life's dream, the vision of mankind entering into the abyss of darkness [outer darkness is a biblical expression for hell] and of himself, laughing as he follows those he has led to unbelief? Nowhere in the world is this ideal cultivated, except in the initiation rites of the Satanist church, at its highest degrees." [6] Marx continues:

"If there is something which devours,
I'll leap within it, though I bring the
world to ruins–
The world that bulks between me and
the abyss,
I will smash to pieces with my
enduring curses." [7]

"Marx does what the Devil does; he consigns the entire human race to damnation," [8] Wurmbrand states, "He had no vision of serving mankind, the proletariat, or socialism. He merely wished to bring the world to ruin, to build for himself, a throne whose bulwark would be human fear." [9]

Letters written between Karl Marx and his father expose cryptic passages. The son writes: "A curtain has fallen. My holy of holies was rent asunder, and new gods had to be installed." [10] The father replies, "I refrained from insisting upon an explanation about a very mysterious matter although it seemed highly dubious." Four months later Marx's father writes his son: "Your advancement, the dear hope of seeing your name, someday of great repute, and your earthly well-being, are not the only desires of my heart. These are illusions I have had a long time, but I can assure you that their fulfillment would not have made me happy. Only if your heart remains pure and beats humanly, and if **no demon** is able to alienate your heart from better feelings, only then will I be happy." [11]

Wurmbrand asks: "What made a father suddenly express the fear of demonic influence upon a young son, who until then had been a confessed Christian? Was it the poems he received as a present, from his son for his fifty-fifth birthday?" A quote from Marx's poem, "On Hegel:"

"Words I teach all mixed up, into a devilish muddle. Thus, anyone may think just what he chooses to think." [12]

Marx was involved with a Satanist church during the years at the university of Bonn and Berlin. In 1841, he was turned down for a teaching position because of his revolutionary activities. He studied economics in Paris and learned about French communism but was expelled for revolutionary reasons.

"In 1844, he wrote the book, *A World Without Jews* even though he was Jewish and (at the time) met German philosopher Fredrick Engels." [13] Engels, who was also a 32nd degree (Illuminati) Mason, commented that Marx was, "the monster possessed by 10,000 devils." [14] "In 1848, Marx published the Communist Manifesto...worked on from 1830-47. It was based on a draft by Engels...an extension of Engel's 'Confessions of a Communist'...borrowed heavily from Clinton Roosevelt's Book, 'The Science of Government Founded on Natural Law' which in turn echoed Weishaupt. The Communist League in London commissioned the Manifesto. Formerly known as the League of the Just...evolved from the Jacobin movement...by Illuminati members ...made up of rich and powerful men from different countries." [15] These were the dark elements that **produced the Communist Manifesto** called, "The Charter of Freedom of the Workers of the World." [16]

This **revolutionary plan for socialism** was a call to the workers, that is, the proletariat, to revolt against those in power and seize control of the state and their means of production, distributing goods to all in need and as needed. However, **this has been the deceptive scheme**, seducing the working class and reducing them into submission and control, witnessed throughout various parts of the world since the French Revolution.

"When Marx died in 1883, only six people attended his funeral. He never supported his wife and six children. Three of his offspring died of starvation in infancy and two others committed suicide. Engels supported Marx with income from his father's cotton mills in England." [17]

CHAPTER 13

OUR LADY OF LOURDES

1858

Lourdes, a small town at that time, of 4500 people, in the foothills of the Pyrenees Mountains of southwestern France, was home to Bernadette Soubrious, who was the oldest of six children, born to a family that lost its milling business after the French Revolution. This chaotic breakdown, resulted in hardship, losing their house, a shortage of food, and resorting to living at a former jail house, called a cachot. Malnourished, she contracted cholera, in addition to suffering from high fevers and asthma for the rest of her life, on top of the emotional toll of living in poverty.

But Bernadette was blessed in other ways. She received eighteen apparitions of Mary, Mother of Jesus over six months. Bernadette experienced the **first apparition** on Thursday, February 11, 1858, just before Ash Wednesday. It was a school holiday. That particular day was cold, and her mother wanted more firewood. Jeanne Abadie, a friend, showed up and went with Bernadette and her sister Marie-Toinette to gather dry branches down by the river. Bernadette took another basket to collect bones, to sell at the Ragpicker's. Her mother was concerned about them falling into the River Gave but finally let them go. Nearly opposite the grotto of Massabielle, they passed by the mill, near the river. The current of the canal, for the mill, was moving slowly, with the mill shut down that day for repairs. Jeanne and Marie-Toinette crossed the millstream, but Bernadette was hesitant. After gathering some wood and bones, the pair walked farther down, along the river Gave and could not be seen. Bernadette had just pulled off a stocking when suddenly she heard the sound of wind, as in a storm. She turned towards the meadow, but the trees were not moving. She took off her other stocking and stepped into the cold stream.

At a glance, she noticed the branches under the top opening of the grotto moving. She saw, what she thought was a girl of her age, with her arms out slightly and a rosary over her right arm. Frightened at first, she rubbed her eyes and then saw her smile. This young woman had an oval face and blue eyes of whom Bernadette had never seen before, standing at the entrance of the opening, above the rose bush. She wore a white dress; a veil covered her head and came over her shoulders and arms almost to the bottom of her dress. A yellow rose was visible on each foot. The sash of her dress was blue down to her knees. The chain of the rosary was golden with large white beads widely spaced. A golden cloud seemed in front of her.

She looked directly at Bernadette and smiled, signaling to come closer. Bernadette felt no fear, as if she was in an eternal state. She now felt she knew who was present. She **took her rosary in her hands** and went to her knees. The Lady affirmed her approval and **took into her hands, the rosary** from her right arm. Bernadette attempted to say the rosary but could not move her hand to her forehead. It was only after the Lady had signed herself that Bernadette could do the same. The Lady let Bernadette say the 'Hail Marys,' as the Lady passed the beads of her rosary between her fingers, saying nothing. At the end of each decade, she would say the 'Glory Be' with Bernadette. After the Rosary was finished, the Lady moved to the interior of the rock and disappeared. Jeanne and Marie-Toinette returned and found Bernadette on her knees, but they could not get her attention at first. They wondered why she was praying.

As she went back, Bernadette felt comfortable crossing the stream, as the water now seemed warm to her. Bernadette asked Jeanne and Marie-Toinette if they had noticed anything at the grotto. They answered, "No, and you, what did you see?" "Nothing then," she replied. [1] But before they got to the house, Bernadette told Marie-Toinette of the visitation of the Lady at the grotto, asking her to keep it a secret.

But on reaching home, Marie-Toinette could not contain herself and blurted it out. Her mother asked for details and responded, "Your eyes must have been playing you tricks. You must have seen some white stone." "No," replied Bernadette firmly, "She has a lovely face." [2] Her mother left it alone. That evening during family prayers, Bernadette began to cry. Her mother asked more questions but to no avail. They went to bed, but the face of the Lady, so lovingly and gracious, remained alive in her memory.

Just before the **second apparition**, Bernadette's mother insisted that this was an illusion. On Sunday, February 14, she heard within her soul a summons to meet the Lady at the Grotto. Finally, with reluctant permission of Bernadette's father, Bernadette reached the grotto and fell to her knees to pray. The Lady appeared. One of Bernadette's friends, armed with a vial of holy water, told her to throw the holy water at the apparition. Bernadette stated the Lady was not angry and was smiling at them. The girls knelt beside her. At that moment, Bernadette fell into ecstasy; her face completely transfigured and radiated happiness. Her eyes were fixed on the niche, for some time, motionless.

After a time the girls around her, thought something was not right. They were crying. Their cries could be heard at the mill, bringing women and a young man from the mill. Seeing the ecstatic child, they called to her, tried to move her, and covered her eyes. The young man later said he had never seen a more marvelous sight. He felt it was useless for him to deny what he saw, and felt it was not worth disturbing the child. The young man urged by his mother, gently pulled Bernadette away, though her eyes were still fixed in front and a little above her.

Walking to the mill, Bernadette gradually became conscience of her physical surroundings. She related that she prayed the rosary accompanied by the Lady, who moved her lips only at each 'Glory Be' and who had again disappeared at the conclusion of the prayers. Bernadette's mother Louise was summoned and was crying, thinking her daughter was dead. She was angry when she saw Bernadette telling what happened. "What do you mean by making everyone run after you?" Bernadette returned in a subdued voice, "But Mamma, I never told anyone to follow me." [3] Louise was about to strike her, but one of the women stopped her from hitting the child, saying, "Louise what are you doing? Why strike her? Your daughter is an angel from Heaven!" [4] Frustrated and overcome by emotion, Bernadette's mother burst into tears. She then led the young girl home. Bernadette looked back at the grotto as she was taken home. The girls told people in the town of the extraordinary events but few took them seriously. However, two women who were interested in the apparitions, came to hear Bernadette's description of the beautiful Lady. This brought tears to one of the ladies who convinced Louise to take Bernadette to the grotto.

In the early morning of the **third apparition** on Thursday, February 18, Mademoiselle Antoinette Peyret took with her pen and paper. Madame Millet went with a candle in hand used for special feasts arriving at the cachot to collect Bernadette. Following Mass, the three headed for the grotto. Bernadette ran ahead and reached the grotto first, **kneeling with her rosary in her hand**, waiting. Madame Millet lit her candle, and the two women knelt. Suddenly, Bernadette exclaimed, "There she is!" [5]

The two women could not see anything, but they could see that Bernadette was entranced by something visible to her. She was happy, smiling and would bow her head in affirmation. After finishing the rosary, Antoinette gave the pen and paper to Bernadette to give to the Lady, asking if she would write anything she wishes to tell them. Bernadette moved towards the Lady, signing to the two ladies to stay back. She reached up to the Lady, then appeared to be listening to the Lady; she lowered her arms, made a deep bow and returned to her place. Antoinette asked what the Lady had replied. Bernadette stated, the Lady began to laugh replying, "There is no need for me to write down what I have to say to you." [6]

The Lady also asked Bernadette, **"Would you have the kindness to come here for fifteen days?"** [7] She agreed. Madame Millet asked why this request. Bernadette did not know, and said she did not say. Madame Millet asked why they had to stay back. Bernadette said this was done in obedience to the Lady. Madame Millet was distressed and wanted to know if they were disturbing the

Lady. Bernadette asked and the Lady replied, "There is nothing to keep you from coming." As they continued to pray, there seemed to be conversation between Bernadette and the invisible Lady. Bernadette related one part afterwards: "I do not promise to make you happy in this world, but in the next." [8] Antoinette asked Bernadette: "Since the Lady consents to speak to you, why do you not ask her for her name? Bernadette replied that she had already done so. The women asked what her name was, to which Bernadette replied: "I do not know, she lowered her head with a smile, but she did not answer." [9]

Returning home with the two women, Bernadette related everything to her parents. Instead of reacting with joy, they became distressed, not believing their lowly daughter could be chosen to receive this privilege from the Queen of Heaven–and why would the Queen of Heaven appear at the grotto, where cattle sheltered themselves during storms, an unholy site, used to dump refuse? Or was this a soul from Purgatory? A demon from hell? Why would she give no name?

Aunt Bernarde, her godmother, was considered wise, and opined: "If the vision is of heavenly nature, we have nothing to fear. If it is some trickery of the devil, it is not possible that the Virgin should allow a child who trusts her, with such innocence of heart to be deceived. Moreover, we ourselves have done wrong in not going to Massabielle with her, to see what is really taking place there. This, we must do, before anything else, and then we shall be able to form an opinion, based upon the facts themselves and decide upon a future line of action." [10]

The **fourth apparition** on Friday, February 19, started fifteen days of apparitions. Bernadette left before dawn with her parents, and her Aunt Bernarde, trying not to be seen although eight others who saw them walking, came to the grotto as well. Bernadette knelt and **began the rosary**, her face glowed of light beyond this world, but still Louise found it hard to accept that her child was experiencing this. After 30 minutes in ecstasy, she appeared happy. As she walked home, she related that the Lady was pleased with her commitment to the fifteen days, and that she would relate secrets to her. Bernadette also related that during the vision she heard a loud uproar of quarreling voices colliding with each other that seemed to be rising out of the river, telling her to escape. The Lady heard the voices. She simply raised her eyes in the direction of the voices, which were then seized with fear and began to disperse, finally fading away altogether.

After the reports spread throughout Lourdes, several hundred attended for the **fifth apparition,** on Saturday the 20th. She approached the grotto at 6:30 in the morning with her mother. Bernadette knelt upon a small rock as usual and after the vision, the Lady taught her a private prayer for her own personal use and private personal needs. She prayed this prayer until her death never revealing the prayer.

On the 21st, the first Sunday of Lent, in the early morning, the wind felt very cold. Bernadette, accompanied by her mother and aunt for the **sixth apparition**, walked through a larger crowd than ever. Dr. Dozous, who was not a religious man, was nonetheless intrigued by what he heard and came to investigate being in science. He wrote: "As soon as she was in front of the grotto, Bernadette knelt down, took her rosary out of her pocket and began to pray... Her face underwent a transformation, noticed by everyone near her, showing that she was in touch with her Apparition. While her beads were moving with her right hand, she held in her left hand, a lighted candle, which was blown out by the very strong breeze along the Gave; but she handed it each time, to the person nearest her, to be immediately relighted." [11]

"I asked her, when she had finished her prayers, and the mysterious being had disappeared, what had passed within her during this long station. She answered: 'The Lady, looking away from me for a moment, directed her glance afar, above my head. Then, looking down upon me again, for I had asked her what had saddened her, she replied, 'Pray for the sinners.' I was very quickly reassured by the expression of goodness and sweetness which I saw return to her face, and immediately she disappeared.' In leaving this place, where her emotion had been so great, Bernadette retired, as she always did, in the most simple and modest attitude." [12]

The next day, a Monday, would be different. Bernadette's parents ordered hero not to go to the grotto but instead to go to school. The police commissioner terrified them because of his position. After lunch, she returned to school, but she felt an invisible barrier holding her from going on to school. Bernadette relates later that she tried more than once but could not move ahead. Then she felt the interior call. The two policemen saw her heading for the Grotto. They followed her and stood a little ways off. Bernadette knelt and **prayed the rosary** for a long time, waiting for the Lady. She finally got up. The police asked her if she saw the Lady. Bernadette said she did not.

On the **seventh apparition**, February 23, over two hundred people from the town and country were already there, before Bernadette arrived. She went to the niche as usual and began to pray the rosary. A gentleman, Jean Estrade stood beside her, along with his sister and the parish priest. He comments as the apparition begins: "She gave a start of amazement...her eyes lighted up and sparkled...the visionary's soul seemed to be striving to show itself outwardly...we men...uncovered our heads and bent our knees like the humblest...the visionary took up the attitude of a listener...when the conversation was broken off, then the child would resume the rosary...The ecstasy lasted for about an hour...It was the most solemn hour of my life...had been permitted to come so close to the Queen of Heaven...a great change was being brought in us; our prejudices were collapsing...giving free rein to our emotions..."[13] She was confided three secrets that were never revealed.

At this point, the events taking place were mostly for Bernadette's spiritual improvement and understanding, but it also exerted an enormous impact on the surrounding community, transforming many. Four to five hundred people came during the **eighth apparition** of the Lady. The light of grace shone upon Bernadette's face, but after a few minutes, Bernadette faced the crowd and asked, who shook the briar, referring to the rose bush below the niche. A girl was trying to get closer to the vision. The Lady from Heaven moved to the lower hollow, at the base of the Grotto, resuming communication with Bernadette. Then, Bernadette's face was distraught and tears flowed down her face. Turning to the crowd she cried out: **"Penance...Penance... Penance!"** [14] This was the first message for the people of Lourdes and the world.

This **ninth day**, the 25th, the Lady offered a gift for the whole world, though it was not understood on this day. Mademoiselle Elfrida Lacrampe, whose parents owned a hotel, claimed about four hundred people were in front of the grotto and under the rock near the Gave River. Approaching her place, Bernadette raised her dress a little so as not to muddy it, then knelt down. The child had not recited a decade of her beads. The Lady said to her: **"Go and drink at the spring and wash yourself in it."** [15]

Then all of a sudden, she set off on her knees and began to climb up the slope that led to the interior of the grotto. When reaching the entrance to the vault, she gently and without pausing, pushed aside the branches that hung down from the rock. From there, she went on towards the back of the grotto. The crowd was pressing close behind her. When she reached the back of the grotto, Bernadette turned about and came back, still on her knees, down the same slope. Then she was seen advancing but turned, as though she was hearing something and came back to the left side of the base of the grotto.

She looked towards the niche and with a puzzled look, listening to the Lady. She dug into the dirt. Muddy water surfaced, after three scoops, and she drank the fourth scoop of water and washed her face. The crowd looked at Bernadette's muddy face and thought she had gone mad. Their distress heightened when Bernadette eat some of the herbs that the Lady had shown her to eat. Everyone seeing the actions of Bernadette could not explain them. Many of the onlookers felt insulted that a child had duped them. By afternoon the water channeled into a small stream flowing towards the Gave.

The next morning, Bernadette knelt and prayed for a long time, feeling sad and distressed. The Lady did not arrive. The crowd was in awe at the stream of water that flowed from the spring at the base of the Grotto revealed by the Lady.

On Saturday the 27th, Bernadette held her lit candle along with many others and would see the Lady at her usual place for the **tenth apparition.** On several occasions, she bowed low to the ground, weeping and sometimes smiling. She was asked to kiss the ground in penance for sinners. Towards the end of the vision, she was told to tell the priests, the Lady is requesting to have a chapel built there. As she left, she drank from the spring. Despite her fears of the priest, she headed directly to the rectory. She approached the priest while praying his divine office prayers. His reception did not seem very cordial, and Bernadette was very timid in his presence, yet most people knew him as a warm and friendly priest.

Father Peyramale wanted to know what she wanted. She replied, "The Lady of the grotto has ordered me to tell the priests that she wishes **a chapel to be built** at **Massabielle** and that is why I have come." The priest remained unmoved. "Who is this lady of whom you speak?" "She is a very beautiful lady who appeared to me on the Massabielle rock." Still Father Peyramale gave away nothing of his feelings. "But who is she? Is she from Lourdes? Do you know her?" Bernadette replied that she did not. "And yet you undertake to carry a message like the one you have just given me, from a person who you do not know?" he enquired coldly. "Oh, but Monsieur, the Lady who sends me, is not like other ladies." Asked to explain, she continued, "I mean that she is as beautiful as they are in Heaven, I would think."

By now the priest was finding it difficult to control his emotion, touched by the obvious sincerity of the girl standing before him. He asked if Bernadette had ever inquired of the Lady's name. "Yes, but when I ask her, she bows her head slightly, smiles and gives me no answer." Peyramale asked if the Lady was then dumb. "No, because she talks to me every day. If she were dumb, she would not have been able to tell me to come to you." Father Peyramale asked Bernadette to describe the events, which had taken place so far. He pointed to a chair and she sat. He sat opposite her and listened.

Within a few minutes, the priest lost all his doubts, although he declined to make the child aware of this fact. "You imagine that a lady who has no name, who takes up her abode on a rock and has bare feet, deserves to be taken seriously. My child, there is one thing I do fear, and that you are the victim of an illusion." Bernadette hung her head but did not reply. Then the priest spoke once more. "Tell the lady who has sent you, that the parish priest of Lourdes is not in the habit of dealing with people whom he does not know. Say that before anything else, he demands to know her name and that she must prove that this name belongs to her. If this lady has the right to a chapel, she will understand the meaning of my words to you, if she does not understand, tell her that she need not trouble to send me any more messages." [16] Bernadette courteously left.

On Sunday February 28, approximately two thousand people were there after seven in the morning for the **eleventh apparition**. Bernadette had a difficult time getting through and performing her penances on her knees, kissing the ground at intervals, moving towards the apparition at the niche and back again.

On Monday, Bernadette arrived with her parents at 7:00 a.m. for the **twelfth apparition**. An unusual fervor took place that day. Kneeling down again, she took her beads out, then the Lady said something to her. She held up her beads as high as her little arm would allow, there was a moment's pause, and she placed the beads back into her pocket. She showed the Lady a different pair, waving it as high as she could. The Lady was satisfied, so she continued her rosary. "With a spontaneous movement, everyone took out their rosaries and waved them. Then they shouted, "VIVE MARIE," went down on their knees, and prayed with tears in their eyes." [17] Bernadette explained later on, that a seamstress asked her that morning to use her rosary, so she could have a memento of the apparitions.

The **thirteenth apparition** on March 2, took place **with the rosary prayed**, candles lit, and with Bernadette's acts of penance. After the end of the apparition, Bernadette was upset and anxious with the request from the Lady, to ask the priest again to build a chapel at Massabielle. Bernadette asked her aunts to go with her, for she was so afraid of the parish priest. In a loud, dominant voice, he responded, "It is high time for me to get out of the imbroglio, in which the Lady and you seek to entangle me. Tell her that with the priest of Lourdes, she must speak clearly and concisely. She wants a chapel. What right has she to these honors, which she claims? Who is she? Where does she come from? What has she done to deserve our homage? Don't let us beat about the bush, if your Lady is she, whom you suggest, I will show her a means of obtaining recognition and giving authority to her messages. You tell me she stations herself in a niche, above a wild rose bush. Well ask her from me, to make the rose bush burst into flower suddenly, in the presence of the assembled multitude. The morning, when you come, to tell that this prodigy has occurred, I will believe your word, and I will promise to go with you to Massabielle!" [18]

Bernadette was so terrified of this man that she forgot to ask the second part of the request. She realized she had to go back and asked her aunts and parents but they said no, as they were equally terrified of the priest as well. Finally, after asking a neighbor, she was before the priest once again on the same day. She again requested: "The Lady has ordered me, to tell you, that she wishes to have a chapel at Massabielle, and now she adds, **I wish people to come here in procession.**"

The priest responded with skepticism, calling it a "trap...not very cleverly laid." Bernadette replied, "But sir, the Lady did not tell me that she wanted a procession to come to the grotto immediately. She only said, 'I wish people to come here in procession.' And if I understand her rightly, she was speaking of the future and not of the present." The priest counters, "We'll do better than that, we shall give you a torch, and you shall have a procession all to yourself. You have many followers; you have no need of any priests!" In turn, she responded, "But Monsieur Le Cure, I never say anything to anyone. I don't ask them to come with me to the grotto." [19]

Father Peyramale hesitated for a minute, "Ask the Lady her name once more, and when we know her name, we will build her a chapel. And it won't be a little one, I tell you; it will be a very big one." [20] Bernadette left smiling.

The next morning March 3, on the **fourteenth apparition,** three thousand people were present, and Bernadette began the rosary and waited, but the Lady did not appear. Bernadette felt she had not satisfied the Lady's request with the priest and was so forlorn. A relative that owned the cachot where she lived, encouraged her to go back to the grotto after nine and when most of the large crowd had left, as some had stayed all night. The Lady appeared and again requested to ask the priest to build the chapel. This time, the priest was more submissive to the Lady's appeal. "She smiled when I told her that you were asking her to work a miracle. I told her to make the rose bush, which was near her, bloom; she smiled once more. But she wants the chapel." [21] The priest asked Bernadette if she had the money for this chapel, replying she did not. In turn, the priest said he did not and asked her to ask the Lady to give her some. Later that day a relative asked why the Lady did not appear. Bernadette said she had. The Lady said, "You did not see me this morning because there were some people there, who wanted to see what you looked like, in my presence and they were unworthy of it, they spent the night at the grotto and they dishonored it." [22]

The **fifteenth apparition** was about to take place. By now, approximately 20,000 pilgrims were present, having come from all over France. In the early morning March 4, Bernadette attended Mass, and after communion, felt compelled to go to the grotto. The police had to make way for her to get there. A cousin of hers, Jeanne Vedere observes: "Holding a candle in one hand and **her rosary** in the other, Bernadette recited her beads without a pause, as far as the third (Hail Mary) of the second decade, her eyes fixed all the time on the niche and the (rose bush. At that moment, a marvelous change came over her face, and everyone cried out, 'now she can see her!' They fell to their knees. I experienced at that moment, such intense feelings of joy and happiness, as I could never express; I felt the presence of a supernatural being, but though I looked hard, I could see nothing..." [23] The rosary had been said three times that morning. The vision continued for a long time. Then, without saying goodbye the Lady departed.

Bernadette continued to go to the grotto but in the late afternoons, hidden in the darker part of the crypt, and contemplated the beautiful Lady, praying for long periods. This continued for 21 days until March 25, 1858, the Feast of the Annunciation. The night before she told her parents that she was being called again by an interior pulse, which she experienced many times before an apparition.

She could not sleep that night and was at the grotto at first light. There were many people, eager to see something miraculous, since it was the day of the feast. Bernadette arrived at five in the morning with her parents and her candle in hand. As she reached Massabielle from a distance, she could see the light starting to glow in the niche. Bernadette relates: "She was there tranquil and smiling and watching the crowd, just as a fond mother watches her children. When I knelt down before her, I begged her pardon for coming late. Still kindly towards me, she made a sign with her head that I had no need to apologize. Then I told her of all my love and regard for her and how happy I was to see her again. And after pouring out my heart to her, I took up my beads." [24]

The Lady moved to the base of the grotto where Bernadette had prayed for the last many days, and continued to talk to her. Bernadette relates: "Whilst I was praying, the thought of asking her name, came to my mind…At last, under an irresistible impulse, the words fell from my mouth, and I begged the Lady to tell me whom she was. The Lady did as she had always done before, she bowed her head and smiled, but she did not reply. I cannot say why, but I felt myself bolder, and asked her again to graciously tell her name, however, she only smiled and bowed, as before, remaining silent. Then once more, for the third time, clasping my hands and confessing myself unworthy of the great favor I was asking of her, I again made my request…At my third request, her face became very serious and she seemed to bow in an attitude of humility. Then she joined her hands and raised them to her breast. She looked up to Heaven. Then slowly opening her hands and leaning towards me, she said to me in a voice vibrating with emotion, **"I am the Immaculate Conception."** She smiled again, spoke no more, and disappeared, smiling." [25]

Bernadette left the candle she was holding and placed it in front of the niche. She repeated the name of the Immaculate Conception all the way to the priest's residence; on hearing the child he asked, "What's that you say?" "I am the Immaculate Conception. It is the Lady, who has just said these words to me." He asked her if she understood what that meant. She said she did not know what that meant. "How can you say things that you do not understand?" "All the way from the grotto I have been repeating, 'I am the Immaculate Conception' for fear I would forget them." "Good, I shall consider what is to be done." [26] He left her and went inside overcome and amazed at this statement by little Bernadette.

Not until Easter week on April 7, was the splendor and transfiguration seen on her face again. Over those next months, many good and evil events took place. A pool for the water from the spring was made with tile so people could wash, bath, and collect water in containers. The local workers built expansions of walkways. Sick and invalids of all kinds were placed into the pool and many (though not all were healed). There was opposition to the place being open. The authorities of Lourdes boarded up the place until the water was tested and fit for consumption and bathing. More sinisterly, demonic manifestations took place with frightful experiences by some, during and after the apparitions. It is revealed in Genesis that God would allow opposition by Satan, "I will put enmity between you and the woman."

Finally, on July 16, **the Feast of Our Lady of Mount Carmel** was the last time that Bernadette would see her on earth. Bernadette spent her remaining years at the convent of St. Gildard at Nevers, France, suffering much harassment from some members in her convent, from theologians' interrogations, from asthma, bone cancer, other complications, including tuberculosis that ended her life in 1879, at the age of 35. Her body is incorrupt, still supple, as though she is sleeping and can be seen in a reliquary at the convent at Nevers, France.

Mary was sent to Lourdes to persuade people to pray throughout the world, for countering the next set of evil events unfolding, the rise up of communism and greed in the 20th century by those given into Satan and his cohort. Many even to this day, continue to join the request to pray rosaries on a daily basis. Mary continues to gather **prayer warriors** requesting solidarity in prayer that will defeat Satan's power in the 20th and 21st century ending in 2038. Mary asked Melanie at La Salette to reveal her secrets in 1858, the same year as the apparitions of Lourdes.

CHAPTER 14

DEMONS UNLOOSED
FROM HELL

In 1846, when Melanie Calvat and Maximum Giraud received an apparition at La Salette, France, part of the message was clear: "In the year 1864, Lucifer, together with a great number of demons, will be unloosed from hell; they will put an end to faith little by little, even in those dedicated to God. They will blind them in such a way… these people will take on the spirit of these angels of Hell; several religious institutions will lose all faith and will lose many souls." [1] Anne Catherine Emmerich states: "Some other demons are to be freed before Lucifer, in order to chastise and tempt mankind." [2] This took place during and after the 1820s.

In **1864,** Karl Marx, began the first International Working Men's Association in London, consisting of English, French, German, Italian, Swiss, and Polish Socialists, at which time, he issued the first address, resolutions, and manifestos, without God in mind, to unite the working class, who struggled against abuse of workers, at the beginning of the industrial age.

However,the **Communist Manifesto** was put into place by an unrecognized force; of **demons unloosed from Hell**. Since the inception of Freemasonry and in the aftermath of the French Revolution, the Communist Manifesto became another vehicle, to drive their goals to fruition, particularly infiltrating the workers labor movements in the industrial age, destroying faith little by little, in the workplace. The corruption of thought continued into education and religious formation.

Meanwhile, socialist political parties increased rapidly throughout Europe, serving only the powerful financial elite. This system, although distinct from the Soviet Union version, has infiltrated all civilized society, including Canada and the United States and the very foundations of the Catholic Church and the family, the bases for all Christian life.

This also confirms the time, seen by a Bernardine Sister: "In 1863, (I) was shown in spirit, the vast desolation caused by the Devil throughout the world. At the same time, she heard the Blessed Virgin telling her, it was true, **Hell had been let loose upon the earth,** and that the time had come to pray to her as Queen of Angels and to ask of her the assistance, of the Heavenly Legions, to fight against these deadly foes of God and men. "But, my good Mother," she replied, "you who are so kind, could you not send them without our asking?" "No," Our Lady answered, "because **prayer is one of the conditions** required by God himself, **for obtaining favors**." [3]

Pope Leo XIII - Vision of God and Satan

On October 13, 1884, Pope Leo XIII was attending a thanksgiving Mass in his private Vatican chapel after celebrating morning Mass. Attended by a few Cardinals and Vatican staff, Pope Leo suddenly stared motionlessly at something, without movement of eye. His expression was one of horror and awe, and his face went ashen white. He was seeing and hearing something unusual and grave.

He explained afterwards, "What a horrible picture, I was permitted to see!" He could hear two voices, one was kind and gentle, and the other was guttural and harsh. They seemed to come from near the tabernacle. The guttural voice of Satan in his pride, boasted to our Lord, "**I can destroy your Church**." The gentle voice said, "You can, then go ahead and do so." Satan said, "To do so, **I will need more time** and **more power**." Our Lord said, "How much time? How much power? Satan said, "**100 years**, and **a greater power over those who will give themselves** over to my service." Our Lord said, "You have the time, you will have the power. Do with them what you will." [4]

According to his private secretary, Pope Leo also saw a vision of demonic spirits congregating in Rome, the Eternal City. "He saw what was going to happen in the future, the misleading powers and the ravings of the devils, against the Church in all countries." [5]

Then he seemed to be back to himself, immediately left the chapel, and went to his office where he was writing for about half an hour. He had it reprinted and sent to all the churches through the world, requesting that it be said at the end of every Mass. It was **the St. Michael's Prayer**. He instructed: To kneel when reciting this prayer and to say the Salve Regina to the Holy Queen of Heaven. The prayer is as follows: "*St. Michael the Archangel, defend us in this day of battle, be our safeguard against the wickedness and snares of the devil; may God rebuke him, we humbly pray and do thou, O Prince of the heavenly host, by the power of God, cast into hell Satan and all the evil spirits who prowl through the world seeking the ruin of souls. Amen.*" [6]

This practice continued from 1886 until after Vatican II, when the conciliar reforms took place in 1964. **The first wave of reverent prayers was slashed from the Mass.** Freemasonry by now had infiltrated the Church reforms. By 1968, the St. Michael prayer and the last gospel were eliminated from the Mass, making the Mass shorter as Blessed Anne Catherine Emmerich saw in her visions for the future.

It is sad that this prayer was eliminated in the 1960s from the end of the Mass when it was most needed in the Church and in the world. We now understand that demons are not only unloosed from hell in 1864, but Satan will have an **extended reign** of 100 years, for most of the 20th century and into part of the 21st century. The beginning and ending of this extended reign will be realized clearly at the unfolding of the first secrets (events) of Medjugorje.

Fr. Gabriele Amorth, Rome's exorcist for many years, has commented: "As we can see, the popes remind us often of the terrible presence of Satan among us, Pius XI, (one of the popes since Leo XIII), recommended directives to strike at **the false doctrines** that are so prevalent in our (20th) century and continue **to poison the lives not only of theologians** but of **all people**. The fact that the directives of Pius XI were not followed, is the fault of those whose task it was to implement them." [7]

SECTION III

SATAN'S EXTENDED REIGN

In this 20th century, Satan is allowed the opportunity to accomplish his greatest challenge since the beginning of mankind. The power of darkness has been increasing for many years since the rise of Freemasonry/Illuminati. Beginning in 1917, God allows Satan **an extended reign** of **one hundred years**, allowing **more time** and **more power** to destroy the Church. God has given great graces to humanity in creative accomplishments at this time, but will keep humanity in check, particularly of those opposed to God, who deceive themselves as their own creators. Self-pride in these accomplishments will eventually lead to self-destruction. This will be the time of the greatest decisive battle, between Mary, Mother of Jesus, and Satan. The hundred years of extended power will end in 2017, but Satan will still be able to influence mankind for while longer.

CHAPTER 15

THE TWENTIETH CENTURY BEGINS

I n light of the prophecies for the 20th century, it becomes alarmingly clear that what is in the history books, newspapers, and magazines is far from the truth. The truth has been distorted and manipulated by those who have controlled most of the world events for financial gain. This regime, started in the 1700s and has continued to spread insidiously, through the 1800s, amidst the revolutions of change, towards a socialist deception with an agenda not recognized.

In the 20th century, lifelong researcher Dr. Carroll Quigley who was a professor of history at the foreign school of Georgetown University, wrote a 1,300 page book called *Tragedy and Hope,* exposing a powerful network of elite, whose secret operations control the political and financial world, for the purpose of world domination. Dr. Quigley claims to be one of the 'insiders' and supports the 'network,' claiming, "I know of the operations of this network because I have studied it for twenty years and was permitted for two years, in the early 1960s, to examine its papers and secret records. I have no aversion to it or to most of its aims, and have for much of my life, been close to it and to many of its instruments. I have objected, both in the past and recently, to a few of its policies…but in general, my chief difference of opinion is that: **It wishes to remain unknown**, and I believe its role in history is significant enough to be known." [1] In response to Quigley's tome, W. Cleon Skousen asserted, **"that there actually exists a relatively small but powerful group which has succeeded in acquiring a choke hold on the affairs of practically the entire human race."** [2]

The start of the 20th century, witnessed the increased destruction of mankind against itself. There were more wars and more deaths in the 20th century than in all other centuries combined, which has been called the 'Century of Genocide.' R.J. Rummel studied 'Democides,' by including death by government regimes. Before the 20th century, it is estimated that 133,147,000 people have died unnaturally in wars for all the centuries past. In the 20th century alone, the estimates are around 174,000,000 unnatural deaths. Certainly there are larger populations today and we could rationalize these numbers away, but could population growth alone account for such staggering figures in such a short period?

The Deception of Communism

When reflecting on the messages related by Mary at La Salette, Mary's words are harsh and blunt; not characteristic of her apparitions. She knows that the conspiracy is from Satan: seducing the Freemasonry/Illuminati/Satanic worshippers, influencing the Marxist/Communist manifesto doctrines, defining the socialist/communist plots to infiltrate countries; to gain monetary and governmental control, to manipulate the educational systems towards atheism, spreading errors to all nations, including subtle infiltration of errors into priests and lay peoples minds, weakening the Catholic faith in the world.

This is the Red Dragon that Mary, the Woman of Revelation, is in battle against. At the turn of the 20th century, she again reveals to us, her distress and sorrow for her children, who are plunging into Hell. Mary, in direct, concise words is **complaining; her priests could have halted this plot if they had responded to her pleadings.**

On Sept 19, 1901, **Mary** speaks to **Marie-Julie Jahenny**, who lived from 1850 to 1941 in La Fraudais, France, a stigmatist with many visitations from Mary and Jesus. Mary is still reflecting on her La Salette apparitions when speaking to Marie-Julie: "I wanted to bring my children the good news if they converted, but sad news, if they continued with their iniquities.... **They take little notice of what I revealed**... now is the time that these great promises (would) be accomplished, that **the Church authorities have despised**... Pain oppresses my heart at this moment...."

"It is **to see** the **pastors detaching themselves** from **the Sacred Bond** (Holy Spirit) that directs and governs Holy Church... when I brought my warnings to the Holy Mountain (La Salette), to the threatened world (from Communism); **when I remember the harsh reception of my words!** They despised them, and most of them refused their confidence.... **False apostles,** under the appearance of honeyed words and false promises, tell lies, soliciting my dear children to save their lives...flee from the very shadow of these men who are none other than the enemies of my Divine Son. I see pastors at the head of the Holy Church... this irreparable outrage... a disaster for my dear people... my sorrow is immense. Pray for those pastors, whose weakness will cause the loss of a multitude of souls." [3]

Jesus speaks to **Marie-Julie Jahenny** (1903): "(My) words were rebuffed by those who should have propagated them, listened to them and increased the grace of love. The missions that (My Mother) fulfilled on earth have not been known. No notice was taken of her solemn words. There was a revolt against her revelations... from those who should have spread these words..." [4]

Our Lady of Good Success to Mother Mariana de Jesus Torres (1600s): "The devil will take advantage of **the century of lights** to spread his evil, with the almost general corruption of customs, bringing about the loss of many souls. He will avail himself of imprudent men who will fall into his clutches and **divert various intelligent men from the truth**, robbing God of many minds; had they continued in the truth of the Roman Catholic and Apostolic Church, would have sustained it in those impious times..." [5]

A German monk (1600s): "The 20th century will be a period of terror and misery...everything evil and disagreeable that can be imagined will happen. In many countries, princes will rise against their fathers, the citizens against authority, the children against their parents, the pagans against God, entire peoples against the established order. A civil war will breakout in which almost all the world will be turned upside down (Russia). Financial disasters and ruin of property will cause many tears to fall. Men will be without mind and without piety. Poisoned clouds and rays which can burn more deeply than the equatorial sun, iron armies marching, flying vessels full of terrible bombs and of arrow, fatal flying stars and sulfuric fire destroying great cities. This century will be the most perverse of all, because men will raise themselves up and destroy each other mutually." [6]

Bishop Christianos Ageda (d 1204): "In the 20th century, France's union with England will prove to be utter destruction, for there will be great shedding of blood by the people of the Kingdom. There will be wars and fury which will last long; provinces divested of their people and kingdoms in confusion; many strongholds and noble houses shall be destroyed, and their cities and towns shall be forsaken of their inhabitants; in divers places, the ground shall be untilled, and there shall be a great slaughter of the nobility; their sun shall be darkened and never shine again, for France shall be desolate and her leader destroyed (kings). There shall be great mutations and changes of kings and rulers; for the right hand of the world shall fear the left and the north prevail over the south." [7]

Shadow Government Above Governments

The last 200 years have seen the emergence of international governing bodies, craftily organized by people in high places, capable of financial domination and control, formulating agreements like a cancer to nations. The agreements have placed a stranglehold, on the people of those nations and of the governing bodies to pay as much as they can bear, in interest payments for all the loans, programs, and so called foreign policy, with the delusion of giving protection, increasing taxation, unknowingly payable to a monster that exists above governments, serving only to enrich the global elite.

Before the world wars, taxation only existed on land owned. After the wars, however, taxation was incurred on revenues earned as well as myriad other nefarious schemes. The United States of America, being the largest and strongest economy for so long, is the most obvious example of a country supposedly for the people by the people that not only has lost control of its own destiny as a country but also remains unaware of the oppression that exists in their own backyard. One of the saddest realities of the 20th century is the manipulation of peoples and of nations, into all the wars of the 20th century, seduced by the global elite for economic gains. Many of these financiers were in fact, financing both sides of the war effort, in all of the wars of the 20th century; mostly from America's Wall Street and England's Banking Square interests.

Council on Foreign Relations

The Council on Foreign Relations (CFR had its beginnings in the 1830s as a secret round table discussion by British loyalists, including George Peabody, JP Morgan, Andrew Carnegie, Nicholas M. Butler, and Col. Edward House. Cecil Rhodes of South Africa connected with Rothschild, Morgan, Carnegie, and Rockefeller as another separate round table secret group, manipulating the affairs of countries in business. According to Dr. Stanley Monteith, author of *'Brotherhood of Darkness,'* which exposes these groups and its connection to dark spiritual elements; were robber barons trading in goods exclusively for governments, large companies, and many rich individuals, extending into the United States during and after the American Civil War, eventually controlling all of the steel industry and the 'war machine.' Carnegie sought an unholy alliance between the United States and Europe, with the eventual goal of a unification of the whole human race, an objective that seems to be on course. At the turn of the 20th century, the Carnegie trustees concluded that the most effective way to alter the life of a country or people **was to create wars**. They decided to find a way to involve the United States in a war; seizing control of diplomatic bodies and the mass media, thus starting the greatest genocide in the 20th century, greater than all the centuries past. In pursuit of profit, they persuaded President Woodrow Wilson, not to end the First World War too quickly.

House, who was influenced by the old British Fabian society and by Marxism, wrote a fictional book in 1911-12 called *Philip Dru: Administrator*, consisting of a plan for conquest of America by gaining control of both the Republican and Democratic parties; **using them** to create **a socialist world government**, based upon a graduated federal income tax system with a central bank to circumvent financial direction, away from different states. It also called for no candidate to be nominated unless their views were similar to a socialist world government.

After World War I, 270 members attended secret meetings at the time of the Versailles Treaty talks. The British Round Table group formed an above ground organization called **the Royal Institute of International Affairs** that was directly linked to the **Council of Foreign Relations** with its **head quarters in New York,** established in 1921. Superficially and unsuspectingly, the American people saw it as a separate foreign affairs organization, though in fact, **was the same** round table of secret members.

The members were the **same group who established the Federal Reserve** in America, **privately owned by the same members** for the most part.

The purported charitable foundations of "Rockefeller, Ford and Carnegie have been... instruments of covert U.S. foreign policy... (and as agents of U.S. intelligence." [8] The foundations are non-taxable institutions, but they pursue business ventures and profits by mass manipulation, by donating large sums of money, to the media and to public education. A quoted observation: "The CFR has been the preeminent intermediary, between **the world of high finance**, big oil, corporate elitism, **and** the U.S. government. Its members slide smoothly into cabinet–level jobs in Republican and Democratic administrations. The policies, promulgated in its quarterly journal, once stated: "Foreign Affairs, becomes U.S. policy." [9] "Members of the CFR when accused of being involved in a conspiracy have protested to the contrary and by and large are right, wrote conspiracy researcher and author Antony C. Sutton. Most CFR members are not involved in a conspiracy and have no knowledge of any conspiracy... However, there **is a group within** the Council on Foreign Relations which belong to a secret society, sworn to secrecy, and which more or less control the CFR."[10]The CFR has control over the government of the United States, including domestic and foreign policy for personal investment interests.

The Federal Reserve

One would think, **the Federal Reserve** in the United States is an organization, for the people by the people, but this is not so. By 1901, Morgan and Rockefeller were the major financiers of a staggering 22 billion dollars in assets. In 1910, eight financiers including the two aforementioned, met at Jekyll Island, off the coast of Georgia, 'to shoot ducks' and drafted the scheme of "the Federal Reserve System as **a fount of credit**, not of capital." This means to receive loans, a borrower must be backed up, with precious metals or commodities or real-estate but the reserve note from the Feds is only numbers on 'paper' at interest, lending to industry and commerce, without any back up what so-ever. This credit scheme has continued over the 20th century and beyond, in foreign policy schemes for two world wars, a pseudo cold war with the former Soviet Union, and now a so-called war on terror. One senator stated: "The **Federal Reserve Board** is the most gigantic financial power in the world. Instead of using this great power as the **Federal Reserve Act** intended, the board delegated this power (over to the banks."[11] Antony Sutton concludes: "The Federal Reserve System is a legal private monopoly of money credit, operated for the benefit of the few, **under the guise** of protecting and promoting the public interest." [12]

In 1912, Woodrow Wilson is elected President of the U.S. and reads the book, written by Col. Edward M. House, *Philip Dru: Administrator*, while on vacation. It was understood that, "Colonel House was able to control the men who led the world between 1912 and 1938 because he had the ability to 'ooze' thoughts into people's minds." [13] Researchers more than once commented on his mystical ability, and within two years, Wilson reorganized the financial structure, with the same theme of House's book, for directives, for the United States government. The foremost regret that even Woodrow Wilson would have, one for which he apologized to the nation, at the end of his life, was the passing of the Federal Reserve Bill in 1913. He admitted that he was bilked.

Similarly, the IRS in the United States is a private corporation, to collect taxes for the private Federal Reserve System that receives taxes paid, fulfilling interest payment for 'the Fed'. It has reached the point, not all interest can be paid by taxpayers, so the Federal Reserve receives IOUs from the government of the United States with interest.

The Federal Reserve dollar has succeeded as the currency of trade throughout the world, but in fact, it has become a tool of the multinational corporations and their connected banking systems. Most of the world today is still under the illusion that the American dollar, that is the Federal Reserve dollar belongs to the United States, for the people by the people, but it is in fact, a private money system of the Global Elite. Antony Sutton wrote in *The Federal Reserve Conspiracy*: "Quietly, without fanfare and with the vast bulk of **citizens unaware**, the world bankers have been building an international money machine; an international Federal Reserve System with power to control the world's financial and economic system." [14]

World War I

In 1914, Archduke Francis Ferdinand was assassinated, causing nations to go to war. In 1915, the ocean liner, the Lusitania, was sunk in the English Channel. These stories appeared in the many newspapers that J.P. Morgan owned across the country of the United States, changing public opinion to intervene into the war. The deliberate sinking was found out only after the war but was hushed up quickly. In the end, the war was a great financial success for the 'war machine' and the profiteers who oversaw it, lining the pockets of the rich, at the expense of the 16 million war dead and 21 million victims and wounded, plus all of the devastation of property. Moreover, this gave opportunity for the financial banking empires to cash in on reconstruction work for many years afterwards. It helped thrust America into the Roaring Twenties era, of success, fortune, and manipulated failure.

CHAPTER 16

OUR LADY OF FATIMA

1917

This is the beginning of the **ultimate battle** between Satan and the Woman, the Blessed Virgin Mary. It was at this time in 1917 that Satan was given an extended reign by Our Lord. He has been given **more time** consisting of one hundred years and has been given **more power** to subdue those who will give themselves over to his service; to defeat and destroy the Church and in fact all mankind. Fatima is the second place where Mary is requesting **prayer warriors** and pleading with many, for prayer with the rosary.

Fatima is a small village in lower mid-western Portugal. In the spring of 1916, about one year before the apparitions of Mary, an angel appears to three children Lucia Santos, nine years, and her two cousins Jacinta and Francisco Marti, six and eight, who were grazing sheep on a hill. A strong wind suddenly came up shaking the trees. What looked like a young man of 15, shining as bright as the sun, knelt on the earth saying: "Do not fear! I am the **Angel of Peace**. Pray with me." [1] He taught them a prayer to have faith, hope, and charity, and to pray for those who do not, repeating it three times. Then the angel was gone. They felt the presence of the Lord in this supernatural event for days afterwards. In the summer of that same year, they were playing by a well, and the angel suddenly appeared and asked, "What are you doing?" and asked them to, "Pray, pray a great deal! The Hearts of Jesus and Mary have designs of mercy on you. Offer unceasingly, prayers, and sacrifice yourselves to the most High…Make a sacrifice of everything that you can and offer it to the Lord, as an act of reparation, for the sins by which He is offended and in supplication for the conversion of sinners. This will bring peace upon your country. I am the Guardian Angel, the Angel of Portugal." [2] The Angel explained many other things as well.

In the fall of that same year, the Angel appeared this time, with the chalice and the host suspended in the air in which drops of blood fell into the chalice. Leaving the Chalice and the Host suspended in the air, he prostrated himself on the ground, near the children, and repeated three times a prayer to the Trinity: "Most Holy Trinity, Father, Son, and Holy Ghost, I adore You profoundly, and I offer you the most precious Body, Blood, Soul and Divinity of Jesus Christ, present in the tabernacles of the world, in reparation for the outrages, sacrileges, and indifferences by which He, Himself is offended. And I draw upon the infinite merits of the Most Sacred Heart of Jesus and of the Immaculate Heart of Mary that you might convert sinners." [3] Then getting up, he gave Lucia Communion and Francisco and Jacinta the Blood from the chalice. Then they repeated the same prayer, three times, prostrated on the ground, and the Angel disappeared.

After Sunday Mass on **May 13, 1917**, the children took the sheep to a field, called Cova da Iria, and after having lunch **at noon** and praying the rosary, they began to play. A sudden burst of what looked like lightning, compelled them to head home, but they encountered another flash part way down the hill. At that moment, appeared a beautiful lady dressed in white, not that tall, on a small cloud, just above a holm-oak tree. "She was more brilliant than the sun and radiated a light more clear and intense, than a crystal glass filled with sparkling water when the rays of the burning sun shone through it." They stopped, finding themselves in the light of the vision. The Lady said: "Do not be afraid. I will do you no harm." Lucia asks: "Where are you from?" "I am from Heaven." "What do you want of me?" "I have come to ask you, to come here for six months in succession, on the 13th day, at this same hour. Later on, I will tell you who I am and what I want. Afterwards, I will return here yet a seventh time."

Lucia asked: "Will I go to Heaven?" Mary says, "Yes you will." "And Jacinta?" "Also." "And Francisco?" "Also, but he will have to say many rosaries." Lucy then asked about two girls that had died recently. "Is Maria das Neves already in Heaven?" "Yes she is." "And Amelia?" "She will be in purgatory until the end of the world." Mary asks if they were willing to suffer, as an act of reparation for sins and for the conversion of sinners. They said they were, and then Mary spoke, "The grace of God will be your comfort." An intense light emanated from her hands, allowing the children to see themselves in God. They fell to their knees, repeating the prayer to the Holy Trinity that the angel had taught them. At the end of that first apparition, Mary asked them to **recite the Rosary every day,** to obtain peace for the world and for an end to the World War. Then she could be seen rising serenely, going towards the east and disappearing in the distance of the sky.

Lucia explained, when Our Lady came, it plunged them into a supernatural presence but much milder than the apparition of the Angel that voluntarily surrendered their actions in prostration to the Divine. [4]

On **June 13**, 1917, the children went to the Cova da Iria with several dozen people gathered from other hamlets. At **noon**, the crowd said the rosary, and Lucia announced to the crowd, the lightning, but no one heard or saw anything. Lucia explains: "The flashes of lightning were not really lightning but the reflected rays of light, which was approaching. It was because we saw the light that we sometimes said, we saw Our Lady coming, but properly speaking, we only perceived Our Lady in that light when she was already on the holm oak tree." One woman claimed to see the branches of the tree pushed down, on the whole top of the small tree, indicating a presence on the treetop, and some observed the noonday sun was unusually dim. Lucia asked: "What do you want of me? Mary replied, "I wish you to come here on the 13th of next month, to pray the rosary every day, and to learn how to read. Later, I will tell you what I want." Lucia asked to cure a sick person where Mary replied, that he be converted first. Lucia asked if they could be taken to Heaven, and Mary replied that Jacinta and Francisco would be coming soon, but that Lucia would have to stay longer on earth, to help to establish a devotion to my Immaculate Heart. They saw the light reflect from Mary's hands, submerging them into divine explanation of themselves and God's purpose for the three children. They also saw in the palm of Our Lady's right hand, a heart surrounded by thorns that seemed to be pierced; in pain from the sins of humanity. As Our Lady was leaving, the crowd noticed a small cloud lifting up from the tree and disappearing to the east.[5]

On Friday **July 13**, 1917, over 5000 people were praying the rosary. At noon, Lucia looked to the east and saw a flash of light, realizing the arrival of the Lady. Lucia asks, "What do you want of me?" Our Lady replies: "I want you to come here on the 13th of next month, to continue **to pray** the **Rosary, everyday**, in honor of '**Our Lady of the Rosary** ' in order to **obtain peace** for the world, and the **end** of **the war** because only she can help you." She said, "In October, I will tell you who I am and what I want, and I will perform a miracle for all to see and believe…Sacrifice yourselves for sinners, and say many times, especially whenever you make some sacrifice: O Jesus, it is for love of you, for the conversion of sinners and in reparation for the sins committed against the Immaculate Heart of Mary."

As Our Lady spoke these words, she opened her hands and light penetrated the earth. The children seemed to be looking deep inside the middle of the earth. **"We saw as it were a sea of fire. Plunged in this fire were demons and souls in human form,** like transparent burning embers, all blackened or burnished bronze, floating about in the conflagration, now raised into the air by the flames that issued from within themselves, together with great clouds of smoke, now falling back on every side like sparks in huge fires, without weight or equilibrium, amid shrieks and groans of pain and despair, which horrified us and made us tremble with fear. [It must have been this sight, which caused me to cry out, as people say they heard me.] The demons could be distinguished by their terrifying and repellent likeness to frightful animals, black and transparent like burning coals. Terrified and as if to plead for succor, we looked up at Our Lady, who said to us, so kindly and so sadly: " You have seen hell where the souls of poor sinners go. To save them from falling into hell, God wishes to establish in the world, devotion to my Immaculate Heart. If what I say to you is done, many souls will be saved, and there will be peace."

"The war is going to end; but if people do not cease offending God, a worse one will break out during the reign of Pius XI. When you see a night illuminated by an unknown light, know that God is about to punish the world for its crimes by means of war, famine, and persecutions of the Church and of the Holy Father...To prevent this, I shall come to ask for the consecration of Russia to my Immaculate Heart and the Communion of Reparation on the First Saturdays. If my requests are heeded, Russia will be converted, and there will be peace; if not, she will spread her errors throughout the world, causing wars and persecutions of the Church. The good will be martyred, the Holy Father will have much to suffer, and various nations will be annihilated. In the end, My Immaculate Heart will triumph." "The Holy Father will consecrate Russia to me, and she will be converted, and a period of peace will be granted to the world. In Portugal, the dogma of the faith will always be preserved... Do not tell this to anybody. Francisco, yes, you may tell him."

"When you **pray the Rosary**, say after each mystery: "O my Jesus, forgive us our sins, save us from the fires of hell. Lead all souls to heaven, especially those who are most in need of thy mercy." After this, there was a moment of silence. Lucia asks, "Is there anything more that you want of me?" "No, I do not want anything more of you today." Our Lady began to ascend towards the east until she finally disappeared in the immense distance of the firmament. [6]

On **August 13**, 1917, 15,000 to 20,000 people gathered at the Cova da Iria. The three children were taken prisoner. A well-known Freemason tried for two days to get the children to deny the events. The threat of boiling with oil and other means only made them more steadfast to rejoice that they were getting close to going to Heaven. The Freemason was not successful and let them go after the apparition. Mary came anyway, to the Cova da Iria with the telltale signs of her presence. The people heard the clap of thunder and saw the lightning and then a small white cloud that hovered at the holm oak tree. During the apparition, the faces of the peoples were all colors of the rainbow. The trees seemed to have flowers on them, and the ground was covered with squares of different colors. Their clothes were of the rainbow. Then the cloud rose up and disappeared in the same manner as before.

On **August 19,** the children were taking the sheep to a pasture when Mary appeared to them and asked them to come again to the Cova da Iria on the 13th and to **pray the rosary,** saying that she would perform a miracle on the last month. She says an unusual thing to them: "If they had not taken you to the town, the miracle **would have been better known.**" "Pray, pray very much," as her beautiful features take on a look of great sadness, "and make sacrifices for sinners, for many souls go to Hell because they have no one to make sacrifices and to pray for them." [7]

On **September 13**, 1917, at noon almost 30,000 had travelled to Cova da

Iria. "The sun loses its customary glow, the atmosphere assumes the same golden tint seen on previous occasions. The people gaze in silent wonder as the sun grows dimmer and dimmer, fading to such a degree that some actually see the moon and the stars." [8]

As Lucia exclaims: "There she is! I see her!" The crowd is overwhelmed as they see "a globe of light which advances from east to west, gliding slowly and gracefully down the valley. As it floats majestically along, this globe shines brightly with a most pleasing light... it is going towards the bottom of the hollow...the luminous globe comes to settle over the mutilated Carrasqueira (holm oak) tree." Many people pulled branches off as spiritual tokens. Lucia responds to the Lady again with, "What do you want of me?" [9] Mary tells the children: "Continue to **pray the rosary** in order to obtain the end of the war. In October, Our Lord will come as well as Our Lady of Dolours (Sorrows) and Our Lady of Mount Carmel. Saint Joseph will appear with the Child Jesus to bless the world. God is pleased with your sacrifices. He does not want you to sleep with the rope on, but only wear it during the daytime."[10] Lucia asked again that people would be cured. Mary said she would cure some, but she said others would not be because Our Lord knows they have not converted to Him. Lucia asked what was to be done with the money that was donated. Mary said to use some to build a chapel here.

October 13, 1917, 70,000 people came, many the night before. A cold rain fell on those who were there. The area was muddy, and when Our Lady appeared, Lucia asked to close their umbrellas. Lucia asked, "What do you want of me?" "I want a chapel built here in honor of the Lady of the Rosary. Continue without fail to say the beads (**pray the rosary)** every day. The war is going to end, and the soldiers will soon return to their homes." Lucia asks: "Will you tell me what your name is?" "I am the Lady of the Rosary." Lucia continues: "I have many favors to ask. Many people seek cures and conversions." Our Lady says, "I will grant some of the requests but not all of them. They must amend their lives and ask forgiveness for their sins." Looking more saddened Our Lady said: People must not offend the Lord, Our God anymore, for He is already greatly offended!"

Our Lady slowly ascends eastward as though towards the sun. Then Lucia exclaims: "Look at the sun!" [11] All the people turn around towards the sun that was in the opposite direction of the tree and where the apparition took place. The rain suddenly stops, and the clouds open up. They could see the sun, like a clear disc, with its sharp edge that did not hurt the eyes, its light continued but seemed to be spinning like a wheel on a gaming table. It looked like a plate of brightly shining silver, shaking and trembling with fire on the outside and taking on the colors of the rainbow that reflected onto the faces of the people and their clothes. Then cries and moans erupted from the entire crowd as the fiery sun continued its rapid rotation, suddenly freeing itself as if dancing, turning blood red, plunging down towards the standing crowd, as the crowd was thrown into panic. Just as suddenly, the sun is back to normal in a clear blue sky, then repeating the same prodigy of events, twice more, for almost ten minutes. The crowd was shouting for joy, with renewed vigor after the events. Their clothes were instantly dried and clean, after the mud and rain of that morning. No one had ever seen the sun in this way. They could look at the sun without it hurting their eyes. Through this, they felt peace, comfort, and love in a profound way.

As the whole crowd witnessed the 'miracle of the sun', the children saw other events. Lucy states: "After Our Lady had disappeared in the immense distance of the firmament, we beheld, Saint Joseph with the child Jesus and Our Lady robed in white with a blue mantle beside the sun. Saint Joseph and the child Jesus appeared to bless the world; they traced the sign of the cross with their hands." "When a little later, this apparition disappeared, I saw Our Lord and Our Lady, it seemed like it was Our Lady of Dolours (Sorrows. Our Lord appeared to bless the world in the manner as Saint Joseph had done. This apparition also vanished, and I saw Our Lady once more, this time as **Our Lady of Mount Carmel**."[12] This last appearance as of Our Lady of Mount Carmel is a visual sign connecting to the next major apparition in which Mary appears at Garabandal in northern Spain, in the early 1960s, uniquely as Our Lady of Mount Carmel, and as Our Lady of Garabandal.

There are three secrets of information that are not immediately revealed; in fact, the first and second secrets apparently were not revealed publicly until 1943. The **First secret** is the **vision of Hell** given in the July apparition. Mary says, "God wishes to establish in the world a devotion to my Immaculate Heart," to save many souls from Hell and to bring peace to the world. The **Second secret is a multiple prophecy:** "The **war is going to end, but** if people do not cease offending God, a worse one will breakout during the reign of Pius XI." [13]

Just after October 13, 1917, Satan's 100 years of extended reign begins, with regimes of darkness, the likes that have never been seen on the earth before. In November 1917, the Bolshevik party led by Vladimir Lenin along with the workers' Soviets, overthrow the provisional government in Petrograd in the October Revolution. The Russian people were in the Julian calendar; October 25 corresponds with the Gregorian November 7, 1917, in the west. At that time, little was known, if anything, about the power of the cruel socialist regime that was to emerge. Even more hidden is the revelation, with the spilling of the blood of millions of people by this red regime is a direct link to the symbol, "Red" of the Red Dragon spoken of in Revelation 12. Mary is commissioned, to come against the rise up and spreading of the errors world-wide, of this Red Communist regime that would take over the world, placing all in bondage or bring about the destruction of most of the world through a major exchange of nuclear weapons accomplishing Satan's total annihilation of the human race. But the humble intervention of the unexpected Lady from Heaven will change the course of history. On November 11, 1918, the First World War ended.

On June 13, 1929, the Virgin Mary speaks to Lucia at Tuy, Spain: "The moment has come in which God asks the Holy Father in union with all the bishops of the world to make the consecration of Russia to my Immaculate Heart, promising to save it by this means." [14] After some time, Jesus appears to Lucia and states: "They did not heed my request. Like the king of France, they will repent and do so, but it will be late. Russia will already have spread her errors throughout the world, causing wars and persecutions of the Church. The Holy Father will have much to suffer." [15]

Mary states to Lucia: "When you see a night, illumined by an unknown light, know that this is the great sign given you by God that he is about to punish the world for its crimes, by means of war, famine, and persecu-tions against the Church and the Holy Father."[16] On the night of January 25/26, 1938, an unexplainable light predicted by Mary, is seen all over the northern hemisphere in all the countries that would be involved in the Second World War.

The Third Secret was revealed to the children on July 13, 1917, as well. It was written down by the order of the Bishop of Leiria, Portugal in 1941. Our Lady continued to speak and guide Sister Lucia over the years. The Third secret was given to the Vatican office of Pope Pius XII in April 1957 and was to be revealed to the public after 1960. Pope John XXIII opened the envelope given to him in August 1959, with prayer and hesitation decided not to reveal it. Pope Paul VI in March 1965 read it and decided not to publish it. It wasn't until after John Paul II was shot in Vatican square that he asked for the secret and all other pertinent information. He responded to the call of the Blessed Mother. The third secret was revealed in 2000: "After the two parts which I have already explained, at the left of Our Lady and a little above, we saw an angel with a flaming sword in his left hand, flashing, it gave out flames that looked as though they would set the world on fire; but they died out in contact with the splendor that Our Lady radiated towards him from her right hand, pointing to the earth with his right hand, the Angel cried out in a loud voice: Penance, Penance, Penance! And we saw in an immense light that is God; something similar to how people appear in a mirror when they pass in front of it, a Bishop dressed in white; we had the impression that it was the Holy Father.

Other bishops, priests, men and women religious went up a steep moun-tain, at the top of which there was a big cross of rough–hewn trunks as of a cork-tree with the bark; before reaching there, the Holy Father passed through a big city, half in ruins and half trembling with halting step, afflicted with pain and sorrow, he prayed for the souls of the corpses he met on his way; having reached the top of the mountain, on his knees at the foot of the big cross, he was killed by a group of soldiers who fired bullets and arrows at him, and in the same way there, died one after another, the other bishops, priests, men and women religious, and various lay people of different ranks and positions. Beneath the two arms of the cross, there were two Angels, each with a Crystal aspersorium in his hand in which they gathered up the blood of the Martyrs and with it, sprinkled the souls that were making their way to God." [16]

What is the interpretation of the third secret? Then–Cardinal Ratzinger concluded that it involved Pope John Paul II and humanity, and is completed, although later, he has inferred that there is more to it in content.

A Catholic prophet **Charles Johnston** of our time who has had visions of the Pope and other calamities to come states his understanding like this: "The assassination attempt against John Paul II and its timing identify him as the Pope of Fatima, but it is not the point of this secret. The ascent up the hill represents this Pope's particular mission. The city which lies half in ruins is Christianity, half of which no longer believes in God but says Jesus was a good moral teacher. The corpses, the Pope meets and prays for on his way are those who, though they breathe, are spiritually dead. The cross at the top of the hill is the end of the Pope's mission on earth. It represents both his triumph and his death to this world. He kneels before it, offering **his work** to Christ. **It is after this triumph that the terror begins. It is the body of the Pope's work, which the soldiers fire at.** These are the legions (Freemasonry), which have given themselves over to Satan. But the Pope has his legions as well. They are priests, bishops, religious, and laity who join them to him and followed him on his way. They will be true champions for Christ as the battle is joined. Prominent among them will be some of the dead souls (the corpses), reborn to spiritual life through the popes prayers." [17]

The third secret is about an apostasy of the faith for a time, with specific reference to John Paul II, first of all but continuing with Pope Benedict XVI. Also, Pope Francis I, is **the continuation** of **that work** and is **also the completion of this secret.** During the time of Pope Francis I, many trials and tribulations will occur. The work of these three popes has been and is to steer the Church in the most difficult time in the history of the Church. It is their work that will be destroyed from a visible point of view, by an organized effort, but not for long, the Church will be reborn into poverty of a simple, humble, and loving Church after members suffer much trial, tribulation, and persecution.

Mary offers a promise of hope: "But in the end my Immaculate Heart will triumph. The Holy Father will consecrate Russia to me, and she will be converted, and the world will enjoy a period of peace. In Portugal the faith will always be preserved." [18]

CHAPTER 17

FRUIT OF THE FEDERAL RESERVE AND WALL STREET

The book, *'Brotherhood of Darkness'* by Dr. Stanley Monteith, an orthopedic surgeon in South Africa, recorded the connections of the Global Elite or Secret Sect's monopoly on the financial direction of nations, deeply rooted and influenced by the Freemasonry/Illuminati brotherhood that follow odious principles of dark secret societies, including satanic worship, all influenced by Satan. He documents a vast body of evidence, gathered over forty years, that reveals the truth **about what really happens in world affairs,** and **how it is kept from us, by those who have control of the media.** Much of this research awakens us to the degree of darkness that exists in high places in the United States, Britain, and Europe conspiring to transform Russia and China into villainous regimes never seen on the earth before.

Who Financed the Rise of Communism?

In the first half of the 20th century, Dr. Bella Dodd, a leader of the Communist Party in America, brings to light very unusual information in the early 1950s; **the organization for communism throughout the world was controlled from America.** As W. Cleon Skousen stated: "Dr. Dodd said, she first became **aware of some mysterious super-leadership** right after World War II when the U. S. Communist Party had difficulty getting instructions from Moscow, on several vital matters, requiring immediate attention. The American Communist hierarchy was told that any time they had an emergency of this kind, they should contact any one of three designated persons at the Waldorf Towers (in New York City). Dr. Dodd noted that whenever the party obtained instructions from any of these three men, Moscow always ratified them. What puzzled Dr. Dodd was the fact that not one of these three contacts was a Russian. Nor were any of them communist. In fact, all three were **extremely wealthy American capitalist!"** She said: "I think **the communist conspiracy is merely a branch of a much bigger conspiracy!"** [1]

Those in high places in Britain and America **financed the rise of communism.** Antony Sutton's book, *Wall Street and the Bolshevik Revolution,* exposes how John D. Rockefeller and other American capitalists financed the

Bolshevik Revolution in Russia. He also noted that no information was found in the press or by any other means, but financial business connections of banking and other operational links between the original Bolshevik Revolution, the Soviets, and Rockefeller's empire left no doubt of collusion.

One of the goals was to bring about socialist regimes under the guise of a so-called frightening adversary of communism. The American State Department has released documents exposing British and American financiers' patronage of the Bolsheviks. There were two revolutions in Russia, one after the other. The first, replaced the czar with Kerensky who wanted to continue the war but then was replaced by Lenin, a professional revolutionary, who was brought in from Switzerland. Trotsky who was trained in upstate New York as a revolutionary was brought in from the United States through Canada and Switzerland. These two, started the counterrevolution in Russia towards hard-core communism. This is hard to believe, but members of the Federal Reserve, J.P. Morgan and others in control, were part of Bolshevik Executive meetings. It was found that Lenin nationalized every bank in Russia except for the Rockefeller-controlled National City Bank in Russia, which remained open and continued to provide funds for the communist regime in Russia, for most of the 20th century until it ceased funding to Russia due to failing returns in the 1980s.

State Department documents reveal the following about the American Relief Mission after World War I, in a letter to President Wilson in 1919: "As a result of the Bolshevik economic conceptions, the people of Russia are dying of hunger and disease at the rate of some hundreds of thousands monthly in a country that formerly supplied food to a large part of the world.... The Bolsheviki has resorted to terror, bloodshed and murder, to a degree, long since abandoned, even amongst reactionary tyrannies." [2] Lenin and Stalin murdered over 60 million people.

The catalogued distribution of food and medical supplies from the United States sent to Russia at the time of the revolution and afterwards reveals:

"Food and clothing and medical supplies:
27,588 tons sent to the areas controlled by the anti-communists.
740,571 tons sent to the areas controlled by the Bolsheviks.
Charities from the United States:
$ 332,508 was sent to areas controlled by the anti–communists.
$55,994,588 was sent to areas controlled by the Bolsheviks." [3]

Researchers now know that communism was controlled from the United States and have pointed to the fact that Nikita Khrushchev, the most powerful man in the USSR, was deposed shortly after Rockefeller visited Russia in 1964. Researchers asked: "Who had the power to fire the dictator of the USSR ?" [4]

In 1973, David Rockefeller, commenting on communism and the extermination of 40 to 60 million people in China, claimed: "Whatever the price... The social experiment in China under Mao's leadership is one of the most important and successful in history." [5]

Roaring '20s, Crash of '29, and Dirty '30s Depression

After the First World War, radio, movies, electric refrigerators, automobiles, indoor plumbing, and other modern conveniences provided more time and leisure for the public. Amidst this burst of consumer spending, the 'high life' was emphasized, and a rush to prosperity was encouraged with the promise that it would never end. In the same way, the Federal Reserve lent money far in excess of its true reserves because of the great profits it had been making.

During that era, competition of the largest oil companies after World War I brought depressed oil prices. Rockefeller reached an agreement with, "The seven major companies in the cartel, known as the Seven Sisters, were: Esso... Mobil...Gulf Oil, Texaco, Chevron, and the two British companies, Royal Dutch Shell and the Anglo-Persian Oil Company [later named British Petroleum]. These...**remain today the real cartel,** and not the squabbling Arabs in OPEC. They agreed to purchase, or deal even more inhospitably with, any company outside the cartel, if it got big enough to be of concern." [6] By 1928, the Federal Reserve met in Europe with central banks and was anticipating triggering a major crash. "...the Governor of the Bank of England, and without doubt, the world's most influential banker, precipitated the United States stock market crash by his secret request to...the Governor of the New York **Federal Reserve** Bank, to end the American post-war inflation, by raising U.S. interest rates and restricting credit." [7]

In February 1929, the Governor of the Bank of England met in the United States with the Secretary of the Treasury who "had only one formula: liquidate labor, liquidate stocks, liquidate the farmers, liquidate real estate. He insisted that when the people get an inflation brainstorm, the only way to get it out of their blood is to let it collapse, and held that even a panic was not altogether a bad thing, claiming it will purge the rottenness out of the system. High costs of living and high living will come down..." [8]

By March 1929, many insider investors were selling out their stocks and investments while prices were high. On August 9, 1929, the Federal Reserve increased bank rates and sold securities on the open market reducing money supply.

By October 1929, the stock market crashed, and over $40 billion dollars ceased to exist over the course of the next year. Hundreds of banks failed because private investors wanted their cash money, but the Federal Reserve, legally responsible as the lender of last resort, failed to lend money to the smaller banking institutions. This was to the Federal Reserve's advantage. About 12,000 banks out of 25,000 banks were eliminated or taken over, thus allowing more room for the Federal Reserve to become an upfront lender in the future, consolidating its power and expanding its revenue from interest. Those in high government, officially blamed the Federal Reserve for not following policy. This sequence of events brought major failure for private individuals and small family business ventures into the 1930s. This allowed a vast amount of real estate wealth to be bought up for next to nothing, starting a trend for those in high places, to own vast amounts of properties in towns, cities, and rural land for industrial and agricultural purposes, and reinforcing the cycle of exploitation.

Chapter 18

Divine Mercy

God does intervene in our lives to remind us of his great graces that have been given to us for all time. At this time, he reminds us of his unfathomable Divine Mercy. We can always come back to him, no matter what we have done in life. He will bring deliverance and healing to our body and soul, all we need to do is ask.

Saint Faustina Kowalska

Sister Mary Faustina Kowalska was born on August 25, 1905, in west-central Poland to a poor religious family of peasants. The third of ten children, she was baptized as Helena and was very aware of her first communion, to the presence of **the Divine guest within her soul**. At sixteen, she went to work as a housekeeper. At 20 years on August 1, 1925, she saw the Suffering Christ in a mystical experience and then entered the Congregation of the Sisters of Our Lady of Mercy; over time, lived in three different convents. She had extraordinary gifts of revelation, visions, hidden stigmata, participation in the passion of the Lord, the gift of bilocation, the reading of human souls, the gift of Prophecy, and the rare gift of mystical engagement and marriage. She had encounters in mystical visions of the Blessed Virgin Mary, the angels and saints, encounters with souls in purgatory, was led by an angel to Hell, to relate her experience to the world, and suffered trials from spiritual darkness. She knew well, that all of this did not constitute sanctity. In one revelation, she experienced the **illumination of her soul** and saw her soul as God saw her. She made the comment: **"Once I was summoned to the Judgment seat of God.** I stood alone before the Lord. Jesus appeared such, as we know him during His passion. After a moment, His wounds disappeared except for five, those in His hands, His feet, and His side. Suddenly, I saw the complete condition of my soul as God sees it. I could see clearly all that was displeasing to God. **I did not know that even the smallest transgressions would have to be accounted for."** [1]

In the most impressive vision, Jesus showed her the **image of His Divine Mercy:** "In the evening, when I was in my cell, I saw the Lord Jesus clothed in a white garment. One hand rose in the gesture of blessings, the other was touching the garment at the breast. From beneath the garment, slightly drawn aside at the breast, there were emanating two large rays, one red, the other pale. In silence, I kept my gaze fixed on the Lord; my soul was struck with awe but also with great joy. After a while, Jesus said to me, 'Paint an image according to the pattern you see, with the signature: **"Jesus, I trust in you."** I desire that this image be venerated, first in your chapel, and (afterwards) throughout the world. I promise that the soul that will venerate this image will not perish. I also promise victory over enemies already here on earth, especially at the hour of death. I myself will defend it (your soul) as My own glory." [2] This image shows Jesus' right hand issuing a blessing and at the same time, His left hand is near His heart where water and blood are flowing from His heart. As it says in 1-John 5: 6: "Jesus Christ... came through the water and blood.... It is the spirit who testifies to this.... God gave us eternal life, and this life comes through the Son. **Whoever possesses the Son possesses life**; whoever does not possess the Son of God does not possess life."

Jesus revealed to her, prayers of Divine Mercy that can be recited any time and is recited as a novena, nine days, before Divine Mercy Sunday. The powerful prayer, Chaplet of Divine Mercy is a daily request of Jesus for everyone. Sister Faustina wrote everything down that Jesus told her, and it was compiled into 697 pages in a diary called, Divine Mercy in My Soul. Sister Faustina died of tuberculosis in Krakow on October 5, 1938.

These apparitions began at St. Faustina's convent in Krakow, near where Karol Woytila (John Paul II) lived and worked. Pope John Paul II beatified her in 1993, canonized her in the year 2000, and established Divine Mercy Sunday, the first Sunday after Easter. In his homily, he said: "It is important that **we accept the whole message** that comes to us from the word of God on this Second Sunday of Easter (first Sunday after Easter)... from now on throughout the Church, will be called Divine Mercy Sunday." [3] To receive this special grace, we are called to: Celebration of the feast, have repentance of our sins, have complete trust in Jesus, in a state of grace from confession, receive communion, **venerate the Image of Divine Mercy** and perform works of mercy .

Messages of Jesus that are pertinent to our times: "Before the **Day of Justice,**I am sending the day of Mercy."[4]**"I am prolonging the time of Mercy for the sake of sinners**. But woe to them, if they do not recognize this time of My Visitation."[5] "Tell souls about this great Mercy of Mine because the awful day, the day of My Justice, is near."[6] **"He who refuses to pass through the door of My Mercy must pass through My Divine Justice."**[7] "Speak to the world about My mercy... it is a sign for the end times; after it, **will come the Day of Justice."** [8]

Therese Neumann

Therese Neumann was born in Konnersreuth, Bavaria in southern Germany and became an unusual mystic. In addition to experiencing stigmata, she did not eat, or drink, or sleep, or have bodily functions for 40 years. It is claimed that she eat no earthly food but lived on Holy Communion from 1922 and took no water from 1926 until her death in 1962. She is one of the visionaries that experienced Christ's passion for hours on end and experienced many other visions of Christ's life as well. She had mystical experiences with St. Therese of Lisieux and other various saints. Moreover, she had unusual comprehension of many languages and was more versed than the experts that questioned her. Many healings took place and she had gifts of knowledge, prophecy, and bilocation.

Her most unusual suffering was the stigmata that she suffered on Fridays. She received the first stigmata in March 1926, on the first Friday of lent. It continued largely, each Friday, until she was experiencing the sufferings from Holy Thursday until 3 p.m. on Good Friday; the visible bleeding of the wounds of Jesus Christ on her body. She suffered from visible wounds, of **the Longinus lance** just above the heart on the left side. From her hands and her feet, blood flowed profusely. Blood from her eyes, rolled down both cheeks, collecting about her throat and chest.

She received nine wounds on her forehead, reflecting the crown of thorns, and had bleeding on the shoulders and back from the wood of the cross. It is estimated that she suffered from about 45 wounds that never disappeared; even in her death, the wounds remained visible. **Over those 36 years, these phenomenal sufferings took place at the same time of day and in exact conformity to the liturgical calendar of the Catholic Church.** It is understood that she suffered about 50% of the Fridays in any given year. During an ecstasy, she seemed to be unaware of her surroundings and was usually immersed in a vision, seeing the passion or other events of saints suffering.

Therese Neumann suffered in the years during some of the most conflicting years of Germany's existence with the rise of the fascist movement of Hitler and the rise of Nazism.

It is interesting to reflect on what God does at certain times in history. During her time in Germany, Therese Neumann was, in her suffering, a spiritual contradiction to Hitler and all that was evil. At the same time, Hitler was a contradiction to all that was good. After World War II, it was reported that over half a million GI's went to visit Therese Neumann, until her death in 1962.

Therese had prophecies for some who visited and was well known and respected. She claimed that America would never be invaded or destroyed but would suffer economical destruction at the end of the 20th century.

CHAPTER 19

WAR IS BIG BUSINESS

(Fr.) **Pere Lamy** (1855-1931) states, "I will not tell you a tenth part [of what I know of the future]. Some things would not be well, to say even in 40 years' time... Penance, penance, penance–terrible times are coming..." [1] "Peace will be given back to the world, but I will not see it and other things will come to pass of which I do not personally see the end...War is Big Business." [2]

Antony Sutton's, *"Wall Street and the Rise of Hitler,"* proved that many American financial institutions provided Adolf Hitler with military equipment and armaments as well as financial assistance during the Second World War. He claims, I. G. Farben, the largest chemical company in the world at that time, in Germany, was financed by American holdings that transferred funds through a Swiss holding company. I.G. Farben produced the Zyklon B gas used in the concentration camps. I G. Farben was in fact part of the same company with the same directors, as the American I.G. Company; who were also members of the Federal Reserve, Ford Motor Co., Bank of Manhattan, and Standard Oil. This same company produced all the synthetic rubber, methanol, lubricating oil, and the majority of nickel, plastics, magnesium, explosives, gunpowder, and high-octane gasoline. It is also known that these particular plants were off limits to American planes bombing Germany.

World War II

The events of World War II, from 1939-1945, killed 60 to 70 million people, including innocent victims of the war. This we know from history books. What is less known, are the individuals who instigated this vast war for the true purposes; financial gain. The direction came from those above the governments of Britain and America. This series of wars could have been prevented or shortened, but were in fact encouraged by money placed into the hands of mad men with an agenda, that could be manipulated to continue the war. Eventually, the working force was depleting at 'home,' and the call at 'home' to bring war to an end was demanded. America was given the grace of success in that war, because of the Atomic bomb, holding power for many decades.

Hitler

Hitler's involvement in the occult was revealed in the newspapers shortly after World War II was over. News of this, abruptly stopped, with no one admitting or wanting to talk about it, as was prevalent with the controlled news media. In the latter part of the 20th century, many things have come to light.

Hitler had meager beginnings as the fourth child of six. His father was very abusive to him, and he rebelled against everything his father believed in. His father died when he was 14 years, and his mother died when he was 18 years. Hitler became an embittered young man, angry towards God and the miserable life that he had been given.

He remained in unforgiveness, choosing to reach to the dark side, instead of choosing God's healing graces. Consequently, he spent much time in the Vienna library, studying the history of the occult, eastern religions, yoga, hypnosis, astrology, dark mysteries of Nordic and Teutonic mythology and folklore. At the Habsburg Treasure House, lay the treasure of an ancient spear, believed to be the spear that pierced the side of Jesus Christ by the soldier Longinus. He heard a guide mention: "There is a legend associated with this spear that whoever claims it, and solves its secret, holds the destiny of the world in his hands for good or evil." [3,4] Hitler claimed these words changed his life. He believed it had secret occult power.

Walter Stein recounts once observing Hitler, gazing at the spear: "Adolf Hitler stood beside [me] like a man in a trance, a man over whom some dreadful magic spell had been cast. His face was flushed, and his brooding eyes shone with an alien emanation. He was swaying on his feet as though caught in some totally inexplicable euphoria. The very space around him seemed enlivened with some subtle irradiation, a kind of ghostly ectoplasmic light. His whole facial physiognomy and stance appeared transformed, as if some mighty spirit now inhabited his very soul, creating within and around him, a kind of evil transformation of its own nature and power." [5] Hitler continued to search for direction from the occult, finding Echardt, a true Satanist, who had reached levels of demonic powers. He translated to Hitler that his mission was to prepare a leader for Antichrist. Hitler believed he was that man. Hitler changed from a shy, timid speaker to a most powerful spellbinding orator who could mesmerize his audiences. By 1921, at age 33, he was preparing to take over the National Socialist Party.

Amidst the worldwide depression of the 1930s, Hitler rose up quickly, taking advantage of the hardships of the time and convincing the masses that he was the 'Savior' chosen to make a strong Germany, by eliminating the weak, 'the Jews', and reviving ancient Nordic and pan Germanic mysticism, in the desired Aryan nation of supremacy, eventually going so far as to indoctrinate school children, to say the Lord's prayer with Hitler as God.

His sadistic ambitions, led him to accomplish his goals of mass extermination of 'lesser peoples,' at any cost, during the war.

CHAPTER 20

THE GREAT DECEPTION

1945 to 2021

The latter part of 20th century has affected us, with a sense of experiencing the greatest civilization that has ever occurred. The truth about this period is not apparent. Something is certainly wrong, and much has drastically changed. Satan is being given his greatest power and strength, during the latter part of the designated 100 years of extended reign.

"Fifty or Sixty Years Before the Year 2000"

These prophecies refer in part to the strength and power that Lucifer has over nations, abetted by the Global Elite who formed the United Nations. They control events of nations for their purposes, but unknowingly, have set up the ultimate destruction of all nations, by Lucifer and those who follow him; as you will see at the close of this fifth Church age.

Blessed Anne Catherine Emmerich 1820s a German mystic gives us information that is very sobering for the last half of the 20th century: "When Jesus gave up His soul on the cross...I saw Him as a luminous figure... penetrating the earth at the foot of the Holy Cross...going into hell.... In the center was an abyss of darkness. Lucifer was cast into it, chained...this took place by Divine decree. **I heard** that **Lucifer will be freed again**, for a while, **fifty or sixty years before the year 2000.**" [1]

Sister Lucy of Fatima to Father Augustin Fuentes on December 26, 1957: "Father, the **devil** is in the mood for **engaging in a decisive battle against** the **Blessed Virgin.** And the devil knows, what it is that offends God the most, and which, in a short space of time, will gain for him the greatest number of souls. Thus, the devil does everything to overcome souls, consecrated to God, because in this way, the devil will succeed, in leaving souls of the faithful, abandoned by their leaders, thereby, the more easily will he seize them."

"That which afflicts the Immaculate Heart of Mary and the (Sacred) Heart of Jesus is the fall of religious and priestly souls. The devil knows that religious and priests who fall away from their beautiful vocation, drag numerous souls to hell.... The devil wishes to take possession of consecrated souls. He tries to corrupt them in order to lull to sleep, the souls of laypeople and thereby lead them to final impenitence..." [2]

Centuries before, **Our Lady of Good Success** said to Mother Mariana of Quito, Ecuador, 1610: "Thus I make it known to you that from the end of the 19th century and from **shortly after the middle of the 20th century...**passions will erupt, and there will be a total corruption of customs, for **Satan will reign** almost completely **by means of the masonic sects...** How deeply I grieve to manifest to you, the many enormous sacrileges, both public as well as secret that will occur from profanations of the Holy Eucharist. Often during this epoch, the enemies of Jesus Christ, instigated by the devil, will steal consecrated hosts from the churches so that they might profane the Eucharistic Species. My Most Holy Son will see Himself cast on the ground and trampled upon by filthy feet." [3]

United Nations

The United Nations, replaced the failed League of Nations to bring nations of financial concern together. After the devastation of the Second World War, the United Nations was formed in 1946. In 1947, it commits to help Israel gain their original homeland back. Israeli people, accept this offer in 1948, displacing the Palestinian people in various regions of their lands. This seems a wonderful gesture at that time for the Jewish people returning to Israel, but the real reasons for forming this alliance and bringing Israel to nationhood, involves political and financial progress. It was to have a conduit, to enter the Middle East at any time, protecting the nation of Israel, but to ultimately have, options to control areas of the Middle East and have access to the major oil reserves, after World War II. In this juxtaposition, God's predicted promise for Israel, becoming a nation again, is fulfilled.

There have been conflicting reports over the years about what the real purposes of the United Nations is. It is not all it claims to be, as the seemingly benevolent organization. Some contemporary prophecies and statements have revealed a perverse image of the United Nations and are worth reflecting on. John Paul II's biography written by Carl Bernstein and Marco Politi stated: "**John Paul II** had decided to declare his own state of war against the United Nations." [4] **Josyp Terelya** who was tortured in the gulag, in the former Soviet Union, and was kept alive by the Blessed Virgin, who said to him: "It is Satan himself who speaks through the false prophet of the organization of the United Nations, using the dead corpse of the organization of the United Nations to deceive mankind."[5] In 1993, **Zdenko 'Jim' Singer**, a Canadian who claimed apparitions of Jesus, was told: "Out of His mercy and grace, the Father has gifted you the Queen of Peace, yet nations prostitute themselves to this **dead head**, which now lives again in that city by the ocean." [6]

The United Nations was in the beginning, perceived as humanitarian for mankind and to bring us closer together. They have a neutral U.N. army to keep the peace in many war torn areas, but investigation of the real reasons for some of the wars, suggests otherwise. In the last 40 years, the agendas of those who use the U.N. as a platform, to move into strategic areas, are far from benevolent purposes; namely to take hold of a nations' productivity, including illegal productivity throughout the world by big business.

Literal Fulfillment of Old Testament Prophecies

Some scriptures, that God decreed for the Jewish people, must be contemplated. The Jewish people, who lived in the last 900 years before Christ were worshiping false gods or false idols; to the greatest extent by sacrificing their children to false gods. They were warned by many of the Old Testament prophets to repent. By continuing in their practices, God allowed them to be captured, and they were exiled to Babylon for seventy years, according to Jeremiah. After the seventy years, they were allowed to come back but continued to suffer in their own land, eventually suffering under Antiochus Epiphanies. **Daniel questioned God**, in his prayer, about the seventy years and why was the punishment continuing. The suffering seemed to be extended.

In order to understand what was actually happening, the punishment would be measured upon them to the full, according to the law of Moses in Leviticus 26:14-46, that states in short form here: "If you reject my precepts and spurn my decrees refusing to obey all my commandments and breaking my covenants, I will, in turn, give you your deserts.... If even after this you do not obey, I will increase the chastisement for your sins **sevenfold**... till your population dwindles... if defiant...**another sevenfold**,... continue to defy me... smite you **seven times harder**... still persist... **seven fold fiercer**..., until you eat the flesh of your own sons and daughters... lay waste your cities... cast your corpses... scatter you among the nations... with country side desolate... faint hearted... fleeing with no one pursuing them... lost among the Gentiles... wasted away from their fathers' guilt..."

Other prophecies of Exodus, explained the continual punishment of the Jewish people. In Exodus 20, after God gives the first commandment stressing the sin of worshipping false idols, He states: "I am a jealous God inflicting **punishment for their fathers' sins, on the children** of those who hate me, **down to the third and fourth generation**." It is reiterated to the Israelites in Exodus 34: 7: "The Lord... forgiving wickedness, crime, and sin; yet **not declaring the guilty guiltless**, but **punishing** children and grandchildren **to the third and fourth generation** for their fathers' wickedness!" They continued to receive punishment and persecution until the Messiah. When Jesus was born and appears before them, they, still in their sinful blindness, **rejected the Messiah**, subsequently **exiled into all nations**, spurring on suffering, seven times, more than once, just as God had stated was possible, recorded in Leviticus 26.

God goes on: "Thus **they will have to confess** that they and their fathers were guilty, of having rebelled against me and having defied me... When their... uncircumcised hearts are humbled and they **make amends for** their **guilt**... make up its lost Sabbaths and make good the debt of their guilt... I will not reject or spurn them... nor wipe them out... I will remember them because of the covenant I made with their forefathers."

The consequences continued, for more than 1800 years after Christ, before they were weakened enough and suffered the dwindling of their population, persevering through persecution and ridicule by Christians, Muslims, and all nations on the earth, as documented in the Bible. The Jewish people were as Ezekiel 36:3-4 states: **"made the subject of people's talk and gossip...that they have become the laughing stock of all the surrounding nations."** People assume that the Jews are finished, as God's people, rejected by God, because they rejected the Messiah, Jesus. They have been dispersed into many nations all over the earth and many think that God will not fulfill the prophecies literally. In fact, some claim the prophecies, now have only allegorical meaning for the Church. **Is that what God is saying in His word?** In Ezekiel 36:16-19, God's charge against them: "Son of Man, the members of the House of Israel lived in their own land, but they defiled it by their conduct and actions; to Me their conduct was unclean as a women's menstruation. I then discharged my fury at them because of the blood they shed in their land.... (ultimately Jesus' blood) I scattered them among the nations and dispersed them in foreign lands."

When Jesus stood before Pontius Pilate and the Jewish people, Pilate washed his hands and said, "**I am innocent of the blood of this man**," while the Jewish crowd said: "**Let the blood be upon us and upon our children.**" The chosen people of God have suffered for that decision. They were dispersed into all nations of the world after the destruction of Jerusalem as Jesus had predicted.

God's word promises a return to their homeland, never to leave it again. Ezekiel 36:24 states: "I am going to **take you from all the nations** and **gather you together** from all the foreign lands and **bring you home** to your own land." Ezekiel 39:22,23,27 confirms: "From that day forward the house of Israel shall know that I am the Lord their God. The nations shall know that because of its sins, the house of Israel went into exile; for they transgressed against me, and I hid my face...**I will gather them, from the lands of their enemies, and I will prove my Holiness through them, in the sight of many nations.**" The return of Israel gaining back their homeland is the most significant prophecy **to be fulfilled literally** in the 20th century.

Other Old Testament prophecies of Israel's dispersal and then gathered up again from all nations, confirms this same prediction:

Jeremiah 29:13-15: "When you look for me, you will find me with you, says the Lord, and I will change your lot, I will gather you together, **from all the nations** and all the places that I have banished you, says the Lord and bring you back to the place, that I have exiled you."

Amos 9:14-15: "I will bring about the restoration of my people Israel, **they shall rebuild and inhabit their ruined cities**, plant vineyards and drink the wine, set out gardens and eat the fruit. I will plant them upon their own ground, **never again** shall they be plucked from the land I have given them, say I, the Lord, your God." Some saints confirm the same promise, such as :

(Fr.) **Pere Lamy** (d 1931) "The Jews are scattered all over the world, but they will not be abandoned. God never forsakes His own." [7]

On November 29, 1947, the United Nations forms a general assembly resolution for a separate state for the Jewish and Arab peoples. On May 14, 1948, Israel proclaims their Declaration of Independence. This is "**the utterance of the word**" for Israel "that Jerusalem was to be rebuilt" according to Daniel 9:25.

Looking back in history, Israel was forced to leave the land of Canaan (Israel after Abraham's time. The **beginning of the nation** of Israel started when the twelve sons of Jacob were forced down to Egypt during a severe drought and famine. Eventually, subtly caught up into slavery. After many years, God took the people of Israel out of Egypt into the desert. Moses was informed at that time and prophesied that **Israel would be dispersed twice**, out of their homeland, because of their abandonment of their true God. They were **taken captive to Babylon**, after moving into the cities and towns of the Promised Land and intermixing in marriage with the peoples of the land at that time, taking on some of their traditions, including worshipping false idols. This false worship resulted in the loss of their protection by God and allowed their capture and exile from the Promised Land. After 70 years in Babylon, they were able to come back to their homeland.

After the crucifixion of Jesus, from about 66 AD, Greek and Jewish religious differences continued, but Roman suppression brought them together. This brought about uprisings and revolts, until the Jewish people took control of the city of Jerusalem from the Romans. The Romans surrounded the city of Jerusalem not allowing anyone to leave, crucifying thousands as they tried to escape. Eventually, the Romans breached the walls and as the prophecy of Jesus was fulfilled, for the most part, as recorded in Mark 13:2: "not one stone will be left upon another." Revolts continued until about 135 A.D. but were successfully quelled by the Romans. It was at this time that the Jewish people **went into hiding, dispersed widely throughout the world**. The establishment of Israel's nationhood in the 20th century is a spectacular event! It fulfills incredible prophecies that were spoken by prophets, recorded in the Old Testament from about 1000 B.C. to about 400 B.C. It was fulfilled literally in the 20th century and begs the question: **Is God, still, going to literally fulfill the rest of His promises,** recorded in the Old Testament to the Jewish people? Why was the 'return to their homeland' prophecies fulfilled in the 20th century? There are promises for the Jewish people at the beginning of the seventh Church age.

Rise of Suburbia

After World War II, Canada and the U.S.A., emerged strong and self-assured as victors. They were confident of peace with the use of atomic weaponry, feeling safe to raise families and rightfully so. What would be called, the 'Baby Boomer' generation from 1946 until the late 1960s, gave birth to many children, stimulating an economy that prospered until around the year 2000. This prosperity was unprecedented, with the continued expansion of so many inventions and discoveries. Ingenuity flourished during the Second World War out of necessity. That stimulus continued, bringing about improvements for the home and businesses such as natural gas heating, refrigerators, electric stoves, deep freezers, many electrical appliances, and television in the late '40s, '50s and '60s. This ingenuity continued at a phenomenal rate in the 1980s and onward with computers, electronics, and many devices of communication and convenience to this present time.

In 1946, with government stimulus packages and an awakening through radio and television advertising, brought unrealistic promises by construction companies selling **the suburban dream**. They were buying up farmland, sub-dividing it into lots, creating suburbs **across the USA and Canada**. Eventually, other places in the world experienced the promise of a beautiful dream. **The promise** that you can live out in the country but still have close proximity to all city shopping amenities, living in affordable places with spacious property and great views, with neighbors at a distance, and the use of automobiles, using cheap oil and gas to get you to work and back, is the life!

However, **this is one of the major deceptions of the latter part of the 20th century** and into the beginning of this 21st century. In the very near future it will become apparent, living in houses side by side, depending on monetary equivalent, will not supply our needs. The new option, will necessitate growing the bulk of our foods in a self sustaining manner. Our lifestyle today is a delusion of incalculable proportions that will precipitate the loss of millions upon millions of lives in the future.

A video called, *End of Suburbia*, looks at the inevitable result of a planet that is running out of oil and other natural resources. James Howard Kunstler says, of the glamor of suburbia: "It is the greatest misallocation of resources in the history of the world. America took all of its post war wealth and **has invested it in a living arrangement that has no future**." [8] This is, not only in America and is only part of the problem. This lack of awareness of what is really evolving in our so-called lifestyle, is leading us onto a dead end road.

This arrangement is affecting our society today, exhibiting greed, a self-centered lifestyle, and environmental disregard to name a few. Many resources are depleting. Fish stocks will be virtually gone from the oceans by the 2030s. Bees are dying in many areas from pollution in their environment. We are running out of gasoline and oil according to the known reserves and are using up our resources of metals and timber creating a future crisis. Furthermore, the beguilement of agricultural conglomerates, are aggressively dominating agriculture to the point of controlling the selling of seed with breeder's rights. They have produced genetically modified seed, so that it does not reproduce as seed, restricting producers growing food plants, and forcing them to buy seed each year from multi-national agricultural corporations. Heritage seed companies are being bought up and original heritage seed stocks are restricted from the public. Heritage seed is also destroyed by cross-pollination by aggressive genetically modified varieties.

The causes for pollution, loss of ozone protection, extreme weather changes and record temperatures to our planet, global dimming of the sun's rays on the earth, melting of the polar north, the depletion and extinction of animals and birds caused from a lack of a safe environment continue to be denied.

Then, we think we will get our pensions, medical care, and dental treatment with a smaller working force to provide for the larger retired population. Positive demographics for our western societies to stimulate our economy is just not there anymore. Last but not least, we still foolishly believe, all around us that everything is all right, and that this 'good life' is going to last for generations to come. This **apathy of our present lifestyle** demands the greatest outcry in the history of the world.

The Seton Prophecy

St. Elizabeth Ann Seton (1774-1821) was born in the United States, married at nineteen to a wealthy businessman and had five children. Her husband went bankrupt, became sick and not too long after died. Elizabeth spent time with a family that was Catholic and eventually became Catholic. She lost support of her friends and family. She established a school community in Emmitsburg, Maryland, for the poor children, the first free school in America.

She founded the Sisters of Charity Girls School, and the society for the relief of widows with small children, in New York. She spent much time in prayer believing that **one should pray unceasingly**. She died at age 46. Elizabeth Ann Seton had a vision in the early 1800s. She saw in the future what would enter: "**Every American would have a black box in their home, through which the devil would enter.**" [9] **Television** comes out 50 to 60 years before the year 2000. This is what Blessed Anne Catherine Emmerich and St. Bridget are trying to tell us! **Satan subtly** conveys denial of the truth about the future. What's on television has desensitized us to violence and sexual immorality, to right and wrong, to what is real and not real, to a deception that has grown to immense proportions, causing us to believe in a world that tells us we are number one. The world promises us everything but is fleeting and leaves us with nothing in the long term. It has brought us to a realm of make believe, thinking it is real life. To think that we can sit in front of a TV and not be affected by it, is **the greatest of all deceptions**. We wonder what is happening to the children of this age, when the television serves as baby-sitting, with both parents working. How is it that the things seen on television were abominations for all generations in the past? Our response today is, 'It's alright, were adults!'

In the 1950s and early '60s, television portrayed '**father knows best**', in the family, but by the 1980s, sitcoms, portrayed the father/husband image as the 'idiot'. This order of the father/husband **as head** and **decision maker** is being destroyed through television, destroying the strength and the structure that God has placed for mankind in the family. The mother or wife is the **homemaker** and the **heart of the family**. This is deceivingly denied through television.

The Deception of Television

Researcher Herbert Krugman discovered what happens to the brain of a person watching television. Monitoring subjects' brain waves repeatedly, he found within 30 seconds the beta waves, which assert alert and conscious attention, change to alpha waves, lacking focus and attention. The state of aimless fantasy and daydreaming is below the state of consciousness. When given something to read, beta waves reappeared. What surprised Krugman was how rapidly the alpha state emerged. Surprisingly, more research proved just as astounding: "The left side of the brain is the side that accepted the step you just read about. It processes the information and critically analyzes it. The right side of the brain forms the images of what you think or see, receiving information emotionally, and does not critically analyze it, leaving that job to the left side. The right side is where images are formed. It perceives the world in terms of moods, sensations, and feelings and starts to form an image dependent on the left side to analyze and logically help it, to form the image. Krugman concluded, 'the brain responds to the medium of television, not the content difference.' In other words, the 'medium' the 'thing' causes the left side (beta) of the brain, which defends your thoughts, your values, to tune out, bypassing your logical reasoning process, going straight to the right side (alpha) which contains all the feelings and sensations to implant, prompt, stamp, or mark an image in your mind and which can be made use of in temptations. [10] Krugman, along with other researchers, have found that watching television tends to shut down the left side, thereby disengaging the information processing of this area of the brain. Krugman concluded: 'What you receive on TV is not thought about at the time you see it.'" [11]

Comments by those hearing the Holy Spirit:

Padre Pio said: "The devil is in it," and was disgusted by television, realizing that it would destroy family life, telling everyone not to buy one. [12]

Pope Pius XII is quoted: "Everyone knows well that very often children can avoid the transient of attack of a disease outside their home, but cannot escape it when it lurks in the home itself. It is wrong to introduce risk in any form into the sanctity of the home surroundings." [13]

Fr. Jozo said, "Listen to God, give yourself time to read His words... the television, **especially commercials**, is the most destructive thing that has ever come against man." [14]

Mary, Mother of Jesus at Medjugorie has stated: **"Avoid Television...**start from this moment. **Turn off the television** and renounce various things that are of no value." "If you look at the programs, if you look at the newspapers, your heads are filled with news, then there is no longer any place for me in your hearts." "It would be a good thing to **give up television**, because after seeing some programs, you are distracted and unable to pray. You can give up alcohol, cigarettes, and other pleasures. You yourselves know what you have to do." Our Lady then profoundly kneels down, serious with Her hands extended. She prays to Jesus: "My beloved Son, I beseech you to be willing to forgive the world **its great sin through which it offends you.**" [15]

CHAPTER 21

Our Lady of Garabandal

1961-1965

This important apparition gives much information for future events but is not well known and is a forerunner of Mary appearing at Medjugorje. On June 18, 1961, Mary appeared to Conchita Gonzales, Mari Loli Mazon, Jacinta Gonzales, and Mari Cruz Gonzales, in San Sebastian de Garabandal, a small village of three hundred people in the beautiful Cantabrian Mountains of northern Spain in the Diocese of Santander. Apparitions continued until Saturday, November 13, 1965.

It began at an apple tree. The three 12-year-old girls and one 11-year-old Mari Cruz were eating apples. They heard thunder and saw a beautiful angel, the Archangel Michael. He did not speak to them and then disappeared. The girls ran to the village church and told everyone about the occurrence. He made eight silent appearances, and on July 1, 1961, announced, that Mary would appear to them. Sunday July 2, at **six in the evening** the girls went to the place where the angel had appeared and saw Mary, accompanied by two angels, one being Michael the Archangel. They described her, dressed in a white robe with a blue mantle and a crown of 12 golden stars, with a brown Scapular on her right arm**, appearing as our Lady of Mount Carmel.** This is a visible sign of the connection between this apparition and the last time Mary appeared at Fatima. She appeared as our Lady of Mount Carmel in the last moments during the Miracle of the Sun to the three children. It is the continuation of Our Blessed Mother's purpose, given to her by her Son, fulfilling more of Revelation 12.

Mary's First Message to the World

Mary announces on July 4, 1961, a first message will be given to the world on October 18, 1961: "**We must make many sacrifices, perform much penance, and visit the Blessed Sacrament frequently.** But first, we must lead good lives. If we do not, a chastisement will befall us. The cup is already filling up and if **we do not change, a very great Chastisement will come upon us.**" [1]

The Warning

Mary tells the children of events that are coming, because of the accumulated sin of the world. She speaks to them of a '**Worldwide Warning**.' This is the first time this message is heard from Mary, although this Warning was revealed to some Catholic saints in past centuries. It is recorded in the Old Testament by some of the prophets and is predicted in the New Testament but is somewhat hidden within other associated events.

Conchita states: "Our Lady said, that a Warning would be given to the entire world, before the Miracle, in order that the world might amend itself. It will come directly from God and will be visible throughout the entire world." [2] "This Warning, like the chastisement, is a fearful thing, for the good as well as for the wicked. It will draw the good closer to God and warn the wicked that the end of time is coming. And that these are the last warnings." [3] She goes on to say, it's "like two stars...that crash and make a lot of noise, and a lot of light...but they don't fall. It's not going to hurt us but we're going to see it, and, in that moment, we're going to see our consciences." [4]

"**They will find themselves alone in the world** no matter where they are at the time, **alone with their conscience right before God. They will see all of their sins** and **what their sins have caused**. We will all feel it differently because it will depend on our conscience. The Warning will be very personal; therefore, we will all act differently to it. The most important thing will be, to recognize our own sins and the bad consequences of them. You will have a different view of the Warning, than me, because your sins are different from mine...but will horrify us because at that very moment, we will see our souls and the harm we have done. **It will be as though we are in agony, but we will not die by its effects,** but perhaps we will die of fright, or of shock, to see ourselves...No one will have doubts of it being from God, and of it, not being human. We must always be prepared with our souls in peace and not tie ourselves down so much to this world." [5]

"In whatever place anyone might be...**will be a revelation of our sins**, and it will be seen and experienced equally by believers and nonbelievers and people of any religion whatsoever." It will be like a purification before the Miracle and "is sort of a catastrophe. It will make us think of the dead, that is, we would prefer to be dead than to experience the Warning." The Warning will not be explained by science...but will be both seen and felt. "The most important thing about that day, is that everyone in the world will see a sign, a grace, or a punishment within themselves, in other words, a warning." [6] "...It will be visible all over the world. I don't know if people will die. They could only die from the emotional shock of seeing it... The Warning will **be a correction of conscience** of the world." [7]

Jacinta: "The Warning is something that is first seen in the air, everywhere in the world, and immediately is transmitted into the interior of our souls. It will last for a very little time, but it will seem a very long time, because of its effects within us. It will be good for our souls, in order to see in ourselves, our conscience…the good that we have failed to do and the bad that we have done. Then, we will feel a great love, towards our heavenly parents and ask forgiveness for all our offenses. The Warning is for everybody because God wants our salvation. The Warning is for us, to draw closer to Him and to increase our faith. Therefore, one should prepare for that day but not await it with fear. God does not send things for the sake of fear but rather with justice and love. He does it for the good of all His children, so they might enjoy eternal happiness and not be lost." [8] "The Virgin said that the Warning will come when conditions are at their worst." [9]

The Miracle Sign

Based upon interviews with Conchita, the Miracle sign will be from God and will be like a pillar of smoke or a pillar of light that will convince atheists to come to God.

Conchita in 1973, stated: "I will tell you all that I can, just as the Virgin told it to me. She told me that God was going to perform a great Miracle, and that there would be no doubt about the fact that it was a miracle. It will come directly from God with no human intervention. A day will come, and she told me the day, the month, and the year so I know the exact date." [10]

"It will take place on or **between the eighth and sixteenth** of March, April, or May. It will not happen in February or June." [11] "I am the only one to whom the Blessed Virgin spoke of the Miracle. She forbade me to say what it will consist of. I can't announce the date either, **until eight days before** it is due to occur. What I can reveal is that it **will coincide with an event** in the Church and with the feast of a saint, **martyr of the Eucharist**; that it will take place **at 8:30 on a Thursday evening**; that it **will be visible to all** those who are in **the village** and **surrounding mountains**; that the sick who are present will **be cured** and the incredulous will believe. It will be the greatest miracle that Jesus will have performed for the world. There won't be the slightest doubt that it comes from God, and that it is for the good of mankind. A **sign of the Miracle**…which it will be possible to film or televise, will remain forever…at the pines." [12]

"The sick who are there will be cured, no matter what their disease or religion."[13] "It will last **about fifteen minutes**."[14] After about fifteen minutes, **the perpetual "sign** will remain…at the pines after the Miracle is over."[15] "This sign that will remain **forever at the pines**, is something that we will be able to photograph, televise, and see, but not touch. It will be evident that it is not a thing of this world but from God." [16]

Conchita says, **the Pope will see the Miracle wherever he is in the world. It will take place on a regular feast day in the Church.** In the Old Testament, similar signs took place. In the book of Exodus, the Israelites followed a pillar of cloud by day and a pillar of fire by night. When the pillar of fire stopped, the one and a half million people would stop and camp for the night. Whenever Moses went into the tent of the tabernacle to talk to God, the pillar of fire or cloud would descend at the door of the tent of the Tabernacle, and all the Israelites saw it. When God was finished speaking with Moses, the pillar of cloud or fire would go back up from the tent.

All Those Present Will be Healed

Conchita stated the Miracle sign, "will be visible to all those who are in the village and surrounding mountains; that the sick **who are present will be cured** and the incredulous will believe. It will be the greatest miracle that Jesus has performed for the world. There won't be the slightest doubt that it comes from God, and it is for the good of mankind."[17]

The Chastisement

On June 19 and 20, 1962, before the Feast of Corpus Christi, Conchita, Mari Loli, Jacinta, and Mari Cruz were shown visions of the Chastisement that **was conditional in the 1960s.** "The Chastisement is conditional and depends on whether or not mankind heeds the messages of the Blessed Virgin Mary and the Miracle," Conchita stated. "I have seen the Chastisement. I can assure you that if it comes, it is worse than being enveloped in fire, worse than having fire above and beneath you…" [18] "It will be a result of a direct intervention of God, which makes it more fearful than anything we can imagine." [19]

The most unusual events seen, took place during the evenings of the visions of the Chastisement. It has been called 'the Nights of Screams.' Father Valentin witnessed on June 18, 1962: "In the evening, Mari Cruz went to the cuadro (square) and fell into ecstasy and afterwards went through the village. A little later, Jacinta and Mari Loli went outside. They also went to the cuadro and fell into ecstasy. They said they saw the Angel."[20] St. Michael appeared again, exactly one year after the first apparition of the angel. The angel told them that the Virgin would come later, but the people should stay at a distance that no one should pass beyond the last house in the village where the children were seeing the vision.

Father Valentin stated: "At 10:30 p.m. Jacinta, Mari Loli, and Mari Cruz were in the cuadro." Conchita was not with them because of a bad knee. Her mother would not let her go, but it is recorded that she picked up a piece of paper, and holding it by the bottom edge in the air, she began to write on it with her pen. Then she went back to her room and continued to write.

Someone came to the house and asked, "Did you hear the screams of the girls.... They were horrible." Mari Loli wrote afterwards: "The Chastisement, I write with a capital, so no one will interpret it to be an ordinary chastisement, announced in the first message of October 18 that is inexorably going to come. The reason for this, is that only penitential reform can save us from it, and instead of this, what is happening in the world today, is a rapid progression down the road of the filthiest deviations. Only those who prepare themselves by a sincere return to God, together with constant prayer and vigilance, will be in the proper state, to face the terrible test." [21] After that first night of screams when the girls came to the people, they were in tears and had incoherent speech. The village was unable to sleep peacefully that night.

The next evening on the vigil of the feast of Corpus Christi, Father Valentin states: "the girls let out terrifying screams, and they said, wait wait...everyone should confess! Oh! Oh!" The people began to pray and to ask pardon publicly.... The priest, who was very excited, prayed in a loud voice, and we all prayed with him. When he (momentarily stopped) the girls cried and screamed again in a very anguished manner. They calmed down again when the prayer restarted." [22]

They all spent the night in prayer. The people stayed where they were and prayed rosaries the rest of the night. The next morning, the whole village went to confession.

Three More Popes Prophecy

Pope John XXIII died on June 3, 1963. Amidst the melodic peal of the toll bells, Conchita's mother Aniceta asserted: "It's for the Pope." Conchita remarked: "Certainly...Now only three remain," referring to three more popes. Aniceta was shocked, and asked: "What are you saying?" "What I heard, that only three popes remain." "And where did you pick that up?" "I didn't pick that up; the Virgin told it to me." [23] Aniceta responded after a moment: "Then, you mean that the end of the world is coming?" Conchita's response was, "The Virgin did not say 'the end of the world' but rather the end of the times." "Aren't they the same?" "I don't know." [24] Conchita had spoken of this, at least four other recorded times, including to a priest professor at a pontifical university and to her head mistress at a school she attended.

To realize the fulfillment of this prophecy, the three popes, Paul VI, John Paul I, and John Paul II have passed on. The events of the Warning and the Miracle sign must unfold, **during the lifetime** of Pope Emeritus Benedict XVI, even though Pope Francis I is reigning.

Unusual Blessings

St. Padre Pio, a stigmatist priest and staunch believer in the apparitions of Garabandal, is said to have seen the Miracle sign before his death.

Fr. Luis Andreu, a 38-year-old Jesuit priest, on August 8, 1961, saw the Miracle in advance, at Garabandal and cried out, "Miracle, Miracle, Miracle... What a favor the Blessed Virgin has bestowed on me!" [25] He left Garabandal by car and on the way back, he lowered his head and died. His body will be found incorrupt on the day of Miracles.

The Second Message to the World

Mary appeared approximately 2000 times to the children of Garabandal. On January 1, 1965, Our Lady appeared to Conchita and said that on June 18, 1965, she would be given a **second message** for the world. But when the time came, surprisingly, **St. Michael, the archangel appeared** and gave this message from Our Lady: "As my message of October 18 (1961 has not been complied with and has not been made known to the world, I am advising you that **this is the last one.** Before, the cup was filling up. Now it is flowing over. **Many cardinals, many bishops,** and **many priests are on the road to perdition** and **are taking many souls with them**. Less and less importance is being given to the Eucharist. You should turn the wrath of God away from yourselves by your efforts. If you ask His forgiveness with sincere hearts, He will pardon you. I, your Mother, through the intercession of Saint Michael the Archangel, ask you to amend your lives. You are now receiving the last warnings. I love you much and do not want your condemnation. Pray to us with sincerity, and we will grant your requests. You should make more sacrifices. Think about the passion of Jesus." [26]

This is the first time in the history of Marian apparitions that Mary has 'abandoned' appearing. 'No one' is listening. By 1965, the conciliar reforms were advancing, by cardinals, bishops and priests on the road to perdition. The chastisement was conditional in the 1960s, but by the 1980s the chastisement coming from God will no longer be conditional. It will eventually take place.

CHAPTER 22

A CHANGING CHURCH

Vatican II

When Pope John XXIII called leaders of the Roman Catholic Church to the Vatican II Council in October 1962, many reforms were expected. Moreover, for the first time non-Catholic churches including Pentecostal representation, were asked to participate, for input and dialogue. After World War II, amidst increasingly empty churches, particularly in Europe as well as the United States and other countries, reform was imperative. Some of the reforms looked at were: the Liturgy of the Mass, changing from Latin to English or of the country's native language. The schema of Revelation of the two sources of revelation: the written word of Biblical Scriptures and the traditional teachings inspired by the Holy Spirit to the early Church Fathers, Doctors of the Church, and credible saints throughout the last two thousand years, including the words and apparitions of Mary, Mother of Jesus that are considered historical and eternal, were discussed.

Sixteen major documents were promulgated for the Church, including Sacred Liturgy, Social Communication, a Dogmatic Constitution on the Church, on Catholic Churches of the Eastern Rite, Ecumenism, Pastoral Office of Bishops in the Church, Renewal of Religious Life, Priestly Training, Christian Education, Relation of the Church to Non-Christian Religions, Dogmatic Constitution on Divine Revelation, Apostolate of the Laity, Religious Freedom, Mission Activity of the Church, Ministry and Life of Priests, and Pastoral Constitution on the Church in the Modern World.

Before Pope John XXIII passed on, he prayed for a 'new Pentecost' in the Church, a prayer that was answered with a renewal movement that ignited around the world, called the Charismatic Renewal.

The Charismatic Renewal

Pope Leo XIII, after experiencing the vision of God and the devil in 1884, and realizing how communism and Freemasonry were taking hold of the world, he prayed on Jan 1, 1901 for a fresh outpouring of the Holy Spirit for the 20th century. Pope John XXIII prayed for a New Pentecost in the 1960s.

In 1967, a group of students from Duquesne University, in Pittsburgh, Pennsylvania were on a retreat weekend where the Holy Spirit started to answer the prayers of the Popes; igniting a spiritual awakening in the Catholic Church that has continued to this day. Students and professors experienced a **'Baptism in the Holy Spirit'**; an **immersion into God's presence,** that is not easily understood until a person experiences this presence themselves, in the body, soul, and spirit. It is receiving a personal renewed relation ship with a personal Jesus, in our lives.

Some people experience what is called, **'Slain in the Spirit'** in which God blesses a person by enabling a person to feel enveloped in the loving presence of God. They feel an immersion in love, like floating on air, but on a spiritual, not merely physical level.

After 'Baptism in the Holy Spirit', a person can receive different supernatural gifts of the Holy Spirit called Charisms that are useful in a person's life. Receiving the gift of Prophecy is one where a person hears the Lord speaking to them. St. Paul said above all the gifts, desire the gift of Prophecy.

The **gifts of healing** offer us other ways to receive healing other than through the seven sacraments because the Holy Spirit heals many, **where they are at,** in their lives. He heals us body, soul, and spirit that is physically, emotionally, and spiritually. Many people cannot relate to healing within the sacraments so God meets them where they are at, in their walk towards God.

The **gift of discernment** allows certain people to recognize evil, and they may be called to deliver those in bondage from evil. Other gifts of Wisdom and Knowledge are revealed in a supernatural way as well. These gifts are for the building up of the Church. Unfortunately, many teachers of our day have missed these events entirely and have missed the experiences of these special blessings. This renewal is a **movement** or action **of the Holy Spirit** in the Church and is not an organization.

Pope Paul VI supported the Charismatic Renewal in 1975 when he said to the 10,000 participants in Rome; "Nothing is more necessary to this more and more secularized world, than the witness of the Spiritual renewal that we see the Holy Spirit evoking in the most diverse regions and milieux (culture)..."[1]

John Paul II in 1998, stated: "Open yourselves docilely to the gifts of your (the) Spirit. Accept gratefully and obediently, the charisms which the Spirit never ceases to bestow on us; do not forget that every charism is given for the common good, that is, for the benefit of the whole Church."[2]   Cardinal Ratzinger, who later became Pope Benedict XVI, stated: "to those responsible for the ecclesiastical ministry, from parish Priests to Bishops, **let not the renewal pass them by**, but to welcome it fully; and to members of the renewal, to cherish and to maintain their link with the whole Church and the charisms of their pastors." [3]

When 'people of renewal' gather together in prayer groups, it is always in a joyful, enthusiastic, praising the Lord, singing and clapping hands with their main purpose of giving glory to God through Jesus Christ with the benefits of the Holy Spirit pouring out on individuals, at each happening.

Prayer meetings take place all over the world and are particularly encouraged by Mary in her monthly messages at Medjugorje, where prayer groups flourish and are encouraged. **Mary spoke** to one of the visionaries: "Today I call you to open yourselves to prayer. May prayer become joy for you. Renew prayer in your families and **form prayer groups**. In this way, you will experience joy in prayer and togetherness. All those who pray and are members of prayer groups are open to God's will in their hearts and joyfully witness God's love." [4] "**Prayer groups** are powerful, and through them I can see, little children, that the Holy Spirit is at work in the world." [5] Father Gabrielle Amorth, a former exorcist of Rome, emphasized especially, frequent participation at prayer meetings, as part of the practice of the faith, to keep demonic influences at bay .

Since 1967, more than 120 million people in 220 countries have experienced renewal and refreshment. The **tools** of the Holy Spirit **are being offered** to this generation, who **will need this deep connection** in order to pass through the difficult years ahead of us. I recall thought-provoking words, through which God spoke to us directly, through prophecies at prayer meetings: "**I am preparing a people...**" [6]

CHAPTER 23

1960's REVOLUTION AND REBELLION

By the 1960s almost every family owned a television. Watching sinful acts of real violence, real sex, anger, and the rebellion brought unprecedented changes in attitudes among the public. Attitudes like: 'It's ok to sin, everybody is doing it!' 'If it feels good do it.' 'I'm here for a good time not a long time,' were some of the clichés that were heard at that time. Rock bands replaced choirs. Songs to the devil brought moral decay in society. Attractive melodies with words that changed our thinking were reflective of modern music for the times. Pot smoking, drugs, free sex, down with the establishment, flower power, new age movement, men and women indistinguishable in features, long-haired hippies, same jeans and same shirts tie dyed were topics of the day. Rock bands were dedicating their music and bands to Satan himself.

In 1969, Woodstock brought a public display of 400,000 people in a farmer's field in upstate New York where anything goes, listening to the music of the times, 'they are a changing.'

Sexuality, homosexual, bisexual, monogamous, polygamous relationships were talked about and embraced under the motto: it's ok, as long as, 'it is right for me and it's done with love and no one gets hurt by it.' We were hearing about women's freedoms, burning the bra and the right to abortion. There was a 'population explosion,' having more than 1.2 children was frowned upon.

Holzhauser's Prophecies

Venerable Holzhauser (1600s) had foreseen all of this: "After a great war (world war II), will come **a new period** in which two mighty ones will face each other. The wrangle between these two will begin in the second half of the twentieth century. It will overthrow mountains and silt up rivers. A great change will come to pass, such as no mortal man will have expected. Heaven and Hell will confront each other in this struggle, old states will perish and light and darkness will be pitted against each other with swords, but it will be swords of a different fashion. With these swords, it will be possible to cut up the skies and split the earth. Neither of the two adversaries (Khrushchev/

Kennedy) will conquer nor be vanquished. Both mighty ones will **lie on the ground,** and a **new mankind will come into existence**. God possesses the key to everything. Blessed is he who will then be able to praise Him, having obeyed all His Commandments." [1]

"During this period, many men will abuse the freedom of conscience conceded to them. It is of such men that Jude the apostle spoke, when he said, "these men blaspheme whatever they do not understand, and they corrupt whatever they know naturally, as irrational animals do. They feast together without restraint, feeding themselves, grumbling mummers, walking according to their lusts; their mouths speaking proud things, they admire people for the sake of gain; they bring about division, sensual men, having not the spirit." [2]

"**During this unhappy period** there will be laxity in divine and human precepts. Discipline will suffer. The Holy Canons will be completely disregarded, and **the Clergy** will not respect the laws of the Church. Everyone will get carried away and be led to believe in what he fancies, **according to the manner of the flesh**." [3] "They will ridicule Christian simplicity; they will call it folly and nonsense. They will have the highest regard for advanced knowledge and for the skill by which the axioms of the law exist, but the precepts of morality, the holy canons, and religious dogmas are clouded by senseless questions and elaborate arguments. As a result, no principle at all, however holy, authentic, ancient, and certain it may be, will remain free of censure, criticism, false interpretation, modification, and delimitation by man." [4]

Politics and Greed

In the early 1960s, the Cold War was at its height. When Kennedy became president of the United States, a wonderful promise of a mythical Camelot stirred the hearts and minds of his supporters. On January 20, 1961, his inaugural speech famously called on Americans to: "Ask not what your country can do for you – ask what you can do for your country." [5]

The Bay of Pigs invasion, a government plot to spark revolt in Cuba, was a disaster for the administration. It wasn't long after, on April 27, 1961, Kennedy gave an address to the media, to convey to the American people, that **not all is true, as it seems**. Only parts of this speech will be repeated, to help us recognize that the 'clear and present danger' is from the secret societies that control the country from a higher position than visible government. Although many presumed he was referring to communism only, he is in fact, alluding to the ones who financed communism, and who control the banking systems throughout most of the western financial world; the Global elite, above the government of America.

Kennedy directs this speech to the media and starts with a bit of humor, reflecting with them, that if a certain publisher, Horace Greeley, (a member of Freemasonry/Illuminati) for the New York Herald Tribune in 1851, had paid a foreign correspondent, Karl Marx ('Father' of Communism') in London, a decent wage, we may not be faced with the seeds sown into the world, resulting in "Leninism, Stalinism, revolution and cold war . . . If only" he "had been treated more kindly... History might have been different."

Kennedy contends: "My topic tonight is a **more sobering one** of concern to publishers as well as editors. I want to talk about our common responsibilities in the face of a common danger. The events of recent weeks may have helped to illuminate that challenge for some; but the dimensions **of its threat have loomed large on the horizon for many years**. Whatever our hopes may be for the future, for reducing this threat or living with it, there is no escaping, either the gravity or the totality, of its challenge to our survival and to our security, a challenge that confronts us in unaccustomed ways in every sphere of human activity.

This deadly challenge imposes upon our society two requirements of direct concern, both to the press and to the president—two requirements that may seem almost contradictory in tone, but which must be reconciled and fulfilled, if we are to meet this national peril. I refer, first, to the need for far greater public information, and second, to the need for far greater official secrecy.

The very word 'secrecy' is repugnant in a free and open society, and we are as a people inherently and historically **opposed to secret societies, to secret oaths** and **to secret proceedings.** We decided long ago that the dangers of excessive and unwarranted concealment of pertinent facts, far outweighed the dangers, which are cited to justify it. Even today, there is little value, in opposing the threat of a closed society, by imitating its arbitrary restrictions. **Even today, there is little value in insuring the survival of our nation, if our traditions do not survive with it.** And there is a very grave danger that an announced need, for increased security, will be seized upon by those anxious to expand its meaning, to the very limits of official censorship and concealment. That, I do not intend to permit, to the extent that it is in my control. And no official of my administration, whether his rank is high or low, civilian or military, should interpret my words here tonight, as an excuse to censor the news, to stifle dissent, to cover up our mistakes or to withhold from the press and the public, the facts they deserve to know.

But I do ask every publisher, every editor, and every newsman in the nation, to reexamine his own standards, and to recognize the nature of our country's peril. In time of war, the government and the press have customarily joined in an effort based largely on self-discipline, to prevent unauthorized disclosures to the enemy. In time of **'clear and present danger,'** the courts have held that even the privileged rights of the first amendment, must yield to the public's need for national security. Today no war has been declared and however fierce the struggle may be, it may never be declared in the traditional fashion. **Our way of life is under attack.** Those who make themselves our enemy are advancing around the globe. The survival of our friends is in danger. And yet no war has been declared, no borders have been crossed by marching troops, no missiles have been fired.

If the press is waiting a declaration of war, before it imposes the self-discipline of combat conditions, then I can only say, that no war ever posed a greater threat to our security. If you are awaiting a finding of 'clear and present danger,' then I can only say that the danger has never been more clear, and its presence has never been more imminent.

It requires a change in outlook, a change in tactics, a change in missions by the government, by the people, by every businessman or labor leader, and by every newspaper. For **we are opposed around the world by a monolithic and ruthless conspiracy** that **relies primarily on covert means** for **expanding its sphere of influence**–on infiltration instead of invasion; on subversion instead of elections; on intimidation instead of free choice; on guerrillas by night instead of armies by day. It is a system which has conscripted, vast human and material resources into the building of a tightly knit, highly efficient machine, that combines military, diplomatic, intelligence, economic, scientific, and political operations.

Its preparations are concealed, not published. Its mistakes are buried, not headlined. Its dissenters are silenced, not praised. No expenditure is questioned, no rumor is printed, and no secret is revealed. It conducts the Cold War, in short, with a war-time discipline, no democracy would ever hope of or wish to match..." [6]

It has been said, this speech, motivated in part, his eventual assassination. He knew that the Secret Elite of America controlled the media, and he wanted to pull the troops and end the Vietnam War. There were 16,000 troops in Vietnam during his term but the 'war machine' could be more lucrative with 500,000 troops during Johnson's presidency for another ten years, another reason to take out Kennedy.

Most presidents in the 20th century stayed in line with the thinking of the international banking interest. Kennedy had physically suffered in the World War II. He knew the deception of war and had an awareness of the political machine.

It is now known that 40 billion dollars was loaned to the USSR to finance and provide weaponry to North Vietnam. Thus, the Global Elite ultimately financed both sides of the war. [7]

Kennedy knew of the impending loss of their nation's real freedoms and the threat posed to the free world by those in high places.

CHAPTER 24

FREEMASONRY IN
THE CHURCH

The evidence suggests that members of Freemasonry/Illuminati exist within the Holy Roman Catholic Church, particularly in the latter half of the 20th century. Some of these were and are cardinals, arch-bishops, bishops, and priests working against the Pope. Father Luigi Villa, was encouraged by Padre Pio, the famous stigmatist, to investigate ecclesi-astical Freemasonry in the Church; listing code names and their membership numbers in a book called, '*Paul VI beautified?*' The list of memberships is quite extensive and will not be printed here. I cannot agree with everything in this work, but it is an eye opener. I also stand firm that 'the office' of the Pope is infallible. I believe that Pope Paul VI was a victim of the Secret Sect, not always able to have control of affairs, just as some of the prophecies allude to.

Various goings-on in the '60s and '70s attest to this fact. There were excommunications, by Code of Canon Law, against some of the priests who were members of the secret societies at that time. Catholic saints and visionaries of Marian apparitions prophesied this time clearly, with great concern and warning. It is interesting that the 'vision' of 'ecumenism' was encouraged during the process of Vatican II and into conciliar reforms that followed. Although a legitimate call to recognize our brothers and sisters and respect for their religious beliefs, what became mainstream for a time, was a form of ecumenism that was watering down the Catholic Church's principles of worship and beliefs.

Freemasons have encouraged ecumenism in the 1800s and at the turn of the 20th century in book and written letter. The main objective of this deceptive organization is to dilute the goals of all Christian religions, including the Jewish people, manipulating them into compliance with the purposes of Freemasonry but without the **true faith**. Through their evil schemes, they realize most people on earth gravitate towards some form of religion, so they know that it cannot be taken away from them but can be deceptively replaced.

This was one of the waves of Freemasonry, that the saints, including Anne Catherine Emmerich predicted, who saw the Secret sect infiltrating the Church to a great degree in high places. Insiders inferred irregularities after Vatican II. Mary appearing at Garabandal in the 1960s, verifies a very troubled time of cardinals, bishops, and priests on the road to perdition taking many souls with them.

By 1967-'68, the Italian state was lifting the tax exemption from the Vatican, which posed a huge problem for Vatican Incorporated. Pope Paul VI with possibly poor advice, may have turned to men of less than impeccable character to find 'better ways,' to invest all of the long term investments accumulated over the years.

Pope John Paul I, reigned for thirty-three days and then died. Irregularities were revealed and known before hand, of inside affairs and the stress that caused his premature death[1] at the Vatican during that time. It was known that John Paul I had heart problems. It is stated that Albino Luciani (JPI) clearly understood the irregular financial goings on. The day before he died, he requested any number of resignations from those in positions of authorization that were taking the Vatican's financial affairs into immoral duress. A long list was obtained by John Paul I of cardinals, bishops, and priests that were members of the Freemasons, with their code names and membership numbers. Many were in positions at the Vatican.

John Paul I sent the information to an outside source, a cardinal, that confirmed memberships. Resignations did not take place until John Paul II was investigating, and some were never asked to resign. After John Paul II came on to the scene, the corruption of finances at the Vatican was dealt with, involving the Vatican bank or IOR, Banco Ambrosiano, the P2 Masonic International Lodge, Italian Mafia, Roberto Calvi, Bishop Marcinkus, Cardinals Baggio, Casaroli, and Villot. There were many unanswered questions, with too much to ignore.

Interestingly, Mary said to the visionaries of Medjugorje concerning John Paul II: "This is my Pope, it was difficult for him **to be elected.**" [2] What does that imply?

Communist Infiltration in the Church

Communism is the largest tentacle of Freemasonry/ Illuminati, and often, dangerously, the least detected. For example, Bella Dodd was in the Communist Party in America in the 1930s until 1950. She became a Catholic, assisted by Bishop Fulton Scheen. In the early 1950s, she admitted before the U.S. House Un-American Activities Committee: "In the 1930s we put eleven hundred men into the priesthood, in order to destroy the Church from within...Right now they are in high places in the Church." [3] Dodd also admitted to have: "dealt with no fewer than four cardinals within the Vatican who were working for us." [4]

A revelatory book, AA-1025-The Memoirs of an Anti-Apostle, chronicles the life of an active communist that became a Catholic priest to subvert the Catholic Church. After a car accident, documents recording his evil intentions were found, by a nurse after he died. That information was put together into a book. [5]

Mother Elena Leonardi from Mary (April 10, 1977): "The **Red Lucifer** works in Rome with the strongest infernal legions! The strong (one) is in Rome, infiltrated into the Vatican, marching **amid the ranks of high prelates!** This fight of persecutions against the Catholic Church and the communist front lines to destroy the Church will be terrible!" [6] **She added,** "Continue writing what Jesus and I order you to do...if they do not do penance, the Vatican will be invaded by revolutionary communist. The Holy Father (Paul VI) is in grave danger, the Church persecuted and the people! The evil ones march beside the devil. The sinning youth advance without a pause.... **Politicians** have **taken a mistaken road.**" [7]

Prophecies Connecting the Secret Sect

Let us ponder the prophecies addressing the secret sect in the 20th century: Venerable **Sister Mariana de Jesus Torres** (1600s): "During this epoch the Church will find herself attacked by waves of the **secret sect.**" [8]

Sister Jeanne Le Royer (1731-1798) : "My Father God, has manifested to me the malice of Lucifer, and the perverse and diabolical intentions of his emissaries (secret societies), against the Holy Church of Jesus Christ. At the command of their master these wicked men have traversed the earth like furies, with the intention to prepare the way and a place for the Antichrist, whose reign is approaching; through the corrupted breath of this proud spirit they have poisoned the minds of men. These have succeeded in confounding all sound principles, and spreading everywhere such darkness as to obscure the light both of faith and of reason...."[9]

Blessed Anne Catherine Emmerich: "Again I saw in vision, St. Peter's undermined according to a plan devised by the secret sect, while at the same time, it was damaged by storms..." [10]

Elizabeth Canori-Mora : "God will employ the powers of Hell for the extermination of these impious and heretical persons (secret sects) who desire to overthrow the Church and destroy it to its foundation." [11]

Blessed Anne Catherine Emmerich: "I saw St. Peters. A great crowd of men were trying to pull it down, whilst others constantly built it up again. Lines connected these men, one with another and with others throughout the whole world. I was amazed at their perfect understanding. The **demolishers,** mostly apostates and members of the different sects, broke off whole pieces and worked according to rules and instructions. They wore aprons bound with a blue riband (Freemasonry apparel). In them, were pockets and they had trowels stuck in their belts. The costumes of the others were various."

There were among the demolishers, distinguished men wearing uniforms and crosses. They did not work themselves, but they marked out on the wall with a trowel where and how it should be torn down. To my horror, I saw among them Catholic priests. Whenever the workmen did not know how to go on, they went to a certain one in their party. He had a large book that seemed to contain the whole plan of the building and the way to destroy it. They marked out exactly with a trowel (symbol of freemasonry the parts to be attacked, and they soon came down. They worked quietly and confidently, but slyly, furtively and warily. I saw the Pope praying, surrounded by false friends, who often did the very opposite, to what he had ordered..." [12]

Enzo Alocci from Mary: "The world is all in a fury, as a beast launching towards evil; the sins which are being committed will be washed away with a lot of blood. The devil uses great cunning to infiltrate into good souls, invade the Church, and seize the souls of many priests. He has launched a great battle against the Church, against me, and against all people on earth." [13]

Persecution of Pope Paul VI

Mother Elena Leonardi was a special spiritual daughter of Padre Pio who received messages from Mary and Jesus. In 1947, Padre Pio told her the Virgin was entrusting to her a great mission. She had prophecies and warnings not only for Pope Paul VI but also for Pope John Paul II. The mission was to warn people throughout the world about what was going on at the Vatican, facilitating a response to pray for the popes.

March 2, 1975, the Blessed Virgin said to her: "Never before has the world needed prayer and penance as in these tragic times because the Pope, the Church, the priests are in danger, and if there is no prayer, the powers of evil will break loose, and in the front lines there will be priests. Defend the Church with your example and sanctity of life..." [14]

April 2, 1976: "I see the Heavenly Mother and Father Pio with a dazzling light. With a painful voice, she tells me: My daughter, prepare yourself to suffer the crucifixion. You must defend and **console the Holy Father Paul VI** because of all the sins of infamy committed against him. Unite yourself with his crucifixion..." [15]

February 13, 1977, Mary said: "God will punish the world with greater severity! The time for the great trial will also come for the Church. Cardinals will oppose cardinals, bishops against bishops. Satan will walk amid their ranks like a rabid wolf. There will be many changes in Rome! What is corrupt will fall and will never again rise up...The Church will remain in darkness, and the world will be crazed by the terror. A great war will be unloosed. The good people go on their way without worry; the evil to damnation, accompanied by the devil; kidnappings, murders, bloodshed, abortions, pierce my Heart!" [16]

July 6, 1977: "There will be anarchy within the Vatican City and the communist, like wolves, riot and destroy. The **Holy Father**, My Vicar, is **running great risks**. He is surrounded by **Freemasonry**. Satan stalks among the bishops, the prelates, lay people, and cardinals! Among them, there is a diabolical transformation, and they scandalize the other nations and humanity!" [17]

July 6, 1977: "My Vicar remains faithful to me! He has been calumniated and accused of immorality by those who are nearest to him! They **want him to resign** as Pope!" [18]

August 18, 1977: "Painful days are approaching for the Holy Father. He is threatened **with death**...the vicar is very ill. I protect him with my mantle and help him." [19]

July 22, 1978: "The Holy Father **is very ill** because of serious grief's and I do not want him to be caught in the reprisal they are preparing against him; I will come before the 15th of August **to take him with me**." [20] Pope Paul VI dies unexpectedly on August 6, 1978.

The Smoke of Satan has Entered the Church

In 1972, Pope Paul VI warned: "**From some fissure, the smoke of Satan has entered the temple of God.** There is doubt, uncertainty, problems, restlessness, dissatisfaction, and confrontation. No one trusts the Church and...do not feel...of being masters and teachers. He entered doubt into our minds and came to the windows that were to be opened to light...In the Church this state of uncertainty reigns. It was believed that after the council, there would be a day of sunshine in the history of the Church. It came a day instead, of clouds, storms, darkness, searching, and uncertainties.... And how did this come about? We will confide to you the thought that may be. We ourselves admit in free discussion, that there has been a power, an adversary power. His name is the devil, this mysterious being...something preternatural came into the world, precisely to disturb, **to suffocate the fruits of the ecumenical council,** and to prevent the Church...getting back...to perform the function assigned by God to Peter, to confirm the brethren in the Faith." [21] These words of grave concern reached the ears of the public, confirming this result.

Implementation of Vatican II Gone Awry

The Vatican II documents could have brought positive pastoral change if they were adhered to. However, the changes after Vatican II, the conciliar meetings, and the administration of changes during the late 1960s and 1970s, makes one wonder what took place. Verbal questionings from Paul VI and Cardinal Ratzinger reveal certain factions intercepted the process, and it did not turn out as expected; in fact, some things have gone awry. Here are some comments, confirming concerns of the outcome.

Cardinal Ratzinger said, "But a critical spirit later added, that it was a construction site where the blueprint had been lost, and **everyone continues to build according to his taste**, the result is evident."[22, 23] Comments of other witnesses: "The Council has produced in the Church, the greatest crisis in her history.... Accommodate the rite of the Mass to the doctrinal and liturgical desires of the Protestants... Could appear to be a deliberate attempt to eliminate the sacrificial nature of the Mass. This facilitates, acceptance of the Novus Ordo by Protestants and places grave doubts about transubstantiation on the minds of Catholic clergy and faithful." [24]

These comments reflect the infiltration of the Freemasonry agenda. Most people did not realize their intention, to take the power out of the Mass, to eliminate transubstantiation, and to reduce the Mass towards a mere memorial and not a sacrifice. This would have also eliminated the presence of Christ as He is in the Eucharist. Errors of Freemasonry influenced decisions made during the 1960s and 1970s. Most intended changes were not successful but the intention to subvert was there.

Sister Jeanne La Royer (1731-1798): "One day I heard a voice which said: **The new Constitution** will appear to many, other than what it really is. They will bless it as a gift from Heaven; whereas, it is in fact sent from Hell and permitted by God in His just wrath. It will only be, **by its effects** that people will be led to recognize the Dragon who wanted to destroy all and devour it."

"One night, I saw a number of ecclesiastics. Their haughtiness and air of severity seemed to demand the respect of all. They forced the faithful to follow them. But God commanded me to oppose them. 'They no longer have the right to speak in My name,' Jesus told me, 'It is against My wish a great power rise up in the Church. It plundered, devastated, and threw into confusion and disorder, the vine of the Lord, having it trampled underfoot by the people and holding it up to ridicule by all nations. Having vilified celibacy and oppressed the priesthood, it had the effrontery to confiscate the Church's property and to arrogate for itself the powers of the Holy Father, whose person and laws it held in contempt." [25] "The Church in Council (during the sixth age) shall one day strike with anathemas, pull down, and destroy the evil principles of **that criminal constitution**. What a consolation! What a joy for the truly faithful!" [26]

This prophecy that mentions, 'the new Constitution,' refers not to the Vatican II documents but to the **documents** of the **Freemasonry/ Illuminati Constitution** from the 1700s that brought errors to the conciliar process by the influence of Freemasonry from within the Church.

Afterwards, this persuaded the Catholic world **by its effects** that this was the interpretation of what was declared by Vatican II documents. The Freemasonry/ Illuminati's goal, was and is, to pull down the spiritual power of the Catholic Church a n d destroy it. This prophecy confirms: 'to arrogate for itself,' or assume, or take over, without the right, 'the powers of the Holy Father.' This seemed possible during Pope Paul VI's reign because of the opposition taking place during that time.

Cardinal Ratzinger, 1988: "Certainly there is a mentality of narrow views that isolates Vatican II and which provoked this opposition. There are many accounts of it, which give the impression that from Vatican II onward, everything has been changed, and what preceded it has no value or at best, has value only in the light of Vatican II....The truth is that this particular Council defined no dogma at all, and deliberately chose to remain on a modest level, as a merely pastoral council." [27]

Prophecies of Marie-Julie Jahenny

The prophecies of Marie-Julie Jahenny, who lived from 1850 to 1941 and suffered stigmata, are hard to accept or understand. After reading her prophecies, I decided not to place this information into this work but changed my mind with encouragement from the Holy Spirit. [28] Marie-Julie predicted many future occurrences of Freemasonry influence; of suppression of Catholic crucifixes in hospitals, courts, and schools, to the creation of atheistic teaching establishments. She predicted civil wars and both world wars.

Marie-Julie Jahenny observes Lucifer speaking to Our Lord: "I will attack the Church, I will overthrow the Cross, I will decimate the people, I will deposit a great weakness of faith in hearts. There will also be a great denial of religion. For a time, I will be master of all things, everything will be under my control **even your temple** and all your people." [29] She claimed in 1902 and 1904, Our Lady and Our Lord announce a conspiracy **to invent a 'New Mass'** that infiltrates into the Church by the **secret sect**: "I give you a warning. The disciples who are not of My Gospel are now working hard to remake, according to their ideas and under the influence of the enemy of souls, a Mass that contains **words that are odious in my sight**." [30]

"When **'the fatal hour' arrives,** when the faith of my priests is put to the test, it will be these texts that will be celebrated in this second period. The **first period is of my Priesthood, which exists since me.** The **second is the one of the persecution** when **the enemies** of the faith and of holy religion **will impose their formulas in the book of the second celebration.** Many of My holy Priests will refuse the book, sealed with the words of the abyss.

Unfortunately, amongst them are those who will accept it…these infamous spirits are those who crucified me and are awaiting the kingdom of the new messiah (Antichrist)." [31] During and after the conciliar reforms, the Mass or Celebration was manipulated under the influence of Freemasonry, such that, the new Mass was designed to take away from the presence of the Eucharist. This Mass in the 1960s and onwards does not become invalid, but it signifies **some words that are odious** in the sight of Jesus. The words of the imposed formulas of the second celebration may be referring to odious words placed into the Offertory prayers. According to Marquis de la Franquerie, who recorded prophecies of Marie-Julie Jahenny, these odious words may be from the Jewish Kabbala, deviations from the Word of God.

With the firm direction of Pope Benedict XVI, despite opposition from within at the Vatican, in 2011, the Mass was brought back to its original intent, in meaning, particularly for the English translation. This prophecy above will be fulfilled to it's fullest at **'the fatal hour'** (also called 'fatal event') in the late 2020s. Marie-Julie goes on to say from Mary: "They won't stop on this hateful and sacrilegious road. They will go further to compromise all at once, and **in one blow**, the Holy Church, the clergy, and the faith of my children." [32]

Prophecies at Akita

The prophecies of Mary at Akita, Japan to Sister Agnes Sasagawa in 1973 are very direct to the clergy: "The work of the devil will infiltrate even into the Church, in such a way that **one will see Cardinals opposing Cardinals, Bishops against Bishops.** The priests who venerate me will be scorned and opposed by their confrères. Churches and altars will be sacked. The Church will be full of those who accept compromise, and the demon will press many priests and consecrated souls to leave the service of the Lord… The demon will be especially implacable against the souls consecrated to God. The thought of the loss of so many souls is the cause of my sadness. If sins increase in number and gravity, **there will no longer be pardon for them…** Pray very much the prayers of the Rosary. I alone am able to still save you from the calamities that are approaching. Those who place their confidence in me will be saved." [33]

CHAPTER 25

"THE WICKED SHALL PREVAIL"

I n the 1980s, unknown to most of the population of the globe, was a time of immense spiritual darkness. It was a time when music was at its darkest, the communist leaders were 'rattling their sabers,' with the darkest of intentions, and the heart of America was weakened.

Without the building of a prayer army at Lourdes that has continued quietly throughout the generations and with a devotional response by people, to Mary at Fatima, across the earth, would have brought about total destruction of the world, by a nuclear holocaust at this time. St. Bridget saw this time of the 1960s, '70s, and '80s. She saw the darkness of the 1980s as being of the same intensity, as it will be, during the time of the Antichrist, coming at the beginning of the seventh Church age.

The **prophecy of St. Bridget** states: "The time of the Antichrist well known to me will come when iniquity and impiety shall above measure, abound, when injustice shall have filled the measure to overflowing, and wickedness shall have grown to immeasurable proportions...Before, however, Antichrist arrives, the gates of faith will be opened... **In the year 1980(s) the wicked shall prevail.**" [1]

In the 1980s, two grave situations were coming to a crescendo: the first was, that Pope John Paul II's life hung in the balance; the other was an impending world war that threatened humanity with total annihilation.

Prophecies from Mother Elena Leonardi specify inside information about Pope John Paul II:

Mother Elena Leonardi from Mary on July 22, 1978: "The Eternal Father will give you **another Patriarch** who is humble and good. Love him, and make others love him (JPII)." [2]

January 17, 1979: "There are terrible days in store for the Holy Father: they attack and culminate him, preparing an attack against his dignity in order to do him harm; he is surrounded by dangerous persons and for this reason he must be alert." [3]

March 23, 1979: "(There) are nations which the Pope must unite...the Pope must put order in the Church because of the corruption which plagues the churches...the scandal of the priests and nuns...dress the priests with cassock or collar, neither with unbuttoned collars nor with tie...Put order in the monasteries. There are many offenses and too many Freemasons... they are preparing a trap for him in the Vatican." [4]

April 10, 1979: "Go to see Bishop Paul and tell him that he must translate these books urgently, and he must send them to Russia and Germany." [5]

April 14, 1979: "Pray for the Pope, they are preparing poison for him... how to eliminate him...do penance...these messages (are) to be translated into all languages and everyone must believe...**Russia must be converted**. My voice must reach beyond the iron curtain. I want you to speak to the Pope; he must know everything. I protect him and I will guide him." [6]

March 13, 1980: "Russia will march with her red brigades throughout Italy, sowing death and destruction. Satan wants victory. Treachery comes against the Pope: **Freemasonry hurls itself against the Church**; the Pope will be calumniated; they want to kill him; he will live days of suffering. Pray for him." [7]

On May 13, 1981, **John Paul II was shot in Rome** on the Feast of Fatima, in an open car in St. Peter's Square. He bent down to reach to a little girl, carrying a likeness of Our Lady of Fatima. At that split second, two shots were fired at John Paul II, by an assassin, both missing his head, and a third hitting him in the abdomen. It took him six months to recuperate, and during that time, he realized that Our Lady of Fatima saved him in that moment. He read the secrets of Fatima, including the one that had not been revealed to the world and all the documentation on the events of Fatima. In August of 1981, he experienced the 'dancing of the sun' and allegedly received a vision of future pending events. After these experiences, John Paul II was quoted as saying, " I have come to understand, that the only way to save the world from war, to save it from atheism, **is the conversion of Russia**, according to the message of Fatima." [8]

Since that revelation, he devoted himself to preparing the Church for the future, particularly the youth of the world, holding and attending numerous international youth conferences. He realized that the youth are the future, and he wanted **to prepare them for the storm that is gathering on the horizon**, after he passes from the earth. In addition, he would write vigorously and continue his travels to reach out to those who are willing to listen.

One month after the shooting, Mary starts appearing at Medjugorje in the former Yugoslavia. In her first apparitions, she is pleading for prayer for peace. In the early 1980s, Mary is aware of Russia moving into Afghanistan and possibly into Poland. She is aware of the potential nuclear threat that will engulf the whole world. By the summer of 1981, the tension is building to the brink of self-destruction.

CHAPTER 26

OUR LADY OF MEDJUGORJE

June 24, 1981 to 20–?

This is the last apparitions of Mary, Mother of Jesus to humanity in this fifth Church age, **gathering more prayer warriors** to defeat Satan who wants to destroy the Church in this final decisive victory.

Medjugorje is a village, east of the coast of the Asiatic sea in Bosnia, Herzegovina, surrounded by mountains with indescribable jagged rock, visible everywhere that makes you think that this is an uninhabitable land. Surprisingly within, exists a quiet peaceful plain of gentle valleys, laden with beautiful red soil, that contrasts lush green vineyards, small villages, and farms. Roosters are heard during the early morning dew, as the sun comes up, with the smell of freshly tilled soil on the cool morning air that invites you to stay forever.

In the early part of the 20th century, these lush valleys surrounded by mountains, experienced fierce hailstorms of diabolical proportions, destructive to vineyards, tobacco fields, and lively-hoods. In 1933, Pope Pius XI was instructed in a dream to raise a cross, "on the highest Golgotha in Hercegovina." [1] Mount Krizevac was chosen, where the local people built a large cross, visible throughout the valley. After this time the storms subsided.

On the feast of John the Baptist **June 24, 1981**, that early morning encountered an unusual thunderstorm of intense proportions of wind and rain with hail and lightning that frightened many to remember the day. Considerable damage was reported in the area that morning. In the sunny afternoon, two girls, Ivanka Ivankovic age 15 and Mirjana Dragicevic age 16, were returning home from sheep pastures and were walking on the road, down towards the village of Bijakovici. They looked towards the hill of Podbrdo when Ivanka saw a beautiful, luminous figure, radiating tremendous light on a cloud, with her feet not showing. Ivanka said: "Mirjana, look there is the Gospa!" Mirjana without looking said, "Come on! Would Our Lady appear to us! " [2]

They headed back to the village of Bijakovici and encountered Milka Pavlovic, Marija's sister who wanted help to bring her sheep home. The three went back around six in the evening, walking and talking. Ivanka saw the Lady again, this time holding Jesus in her hands. Ivanka said it again, and when Mirjana found the light, she fell to her knees with Ivanka following. They all saw the Lady holding a child in her hands.

Vicka, awakening from a sleep after an exam, was looking for Ivanka and Mirjana. When she reached the road, she saw them waving their hands to come. Mirjana said: "Look up there, the Madonna! (Our Lady." Vicka said, "What do you mean the Madonna? What is the matter with you?" [3] Vicka did not even look and ran away down the road. She met both Ivan Dragicevic and Ivan Ivankovic. Vicka said to them, "The Madonna, they said that the Madonna has appeared up there. Let's go there, you and me, I'm afraid." Ivan Dragicevic said, "Of course we'll go, but why are you afraid?" Vicka thought, "He's not afraid." [4]

"But when we got there, and I turned towards Ivan and asked, "Do you see anything? He was gone, I saw him running away." [5] Vicka felt she could not move to look, she felt like something was blocking her, then she said, something came out of her heart and soul and then, she could see as the others, the beautiful lady with blue eyes, dark hair and rosy cheeks. She wore a grey dress and white veil with a crown of 12 stars. She was in the air on a grey cloud, above the ground with her left hand reaching outward, and was uncovering and covering something in her left hand. The Lady beckoned them to come closer, but they were all to frighten to do so. The vision of the Lady remained for about 45 minutes.

On the next day, Thursday **June 25, 1981**, most of the visionaries worked in the tobacco fields but finished early so Ivanka, Mirjana, Vicka, and Ivan decided to return to the hill. Three bright flashes like lightning were seen by those on the hill and seen by those in the village. The Lady was seen by Ivanka first, then Mirjana and Vicka. When Vicka Ivankovic 16, saw the Lady, as promised, she ran to get Marija Pavlovic 16, and Jakov Colo who was only 10 years old, abandoned by his father at the age of eight and then would lose his mother at 12. Ivan Dragicevic 16, made it in time to see her. This would be the six visionaries and would be the anniversary date for the apparitions according to our Lady of Medjugorje. On this day Milka Pavlovic's mother stated that her sister Marija was going and one was enough, giving Milka work to do in the field. Ivan Ivankovic at 20 thought that to see this sort of vision was for children. Neither one of these two saw the Lady again. The Lady called to them to come up the hill. Vicka describes, they were taken up the hill effortlessly over the jagged rock and thorn bushes until they were right at her feet. The witnesses who saw them were amazed at the speed of their ascent up the hill, estimated at about two to five minutes that should have taken 12 to 15 minutes. When they reached her feet, they felt thrown down to their knees. Jakov landed in the middle of a prickly bush but afterwards showed no scratches. Jakov exclaimed: "I see Our Lady!" [6] All were afraid and were weeping a little, responding by praying Our Fathers. Ivanka talked to the Lady first, asking about her mother who had died two months earlier. Our Lady confirmed Ivanka's mother was with her and not to worry about her. Mirjana considered the most intelligent, related her fears to 'Gospa,' as she was called in Croatia, meaning 'Our Lady.' "They will not believe us when we go home. They will tell us that we are crazy." [7] Our Lady just smiled. They were on the hill for 10 or 15 minutes, enjoying her presence. Others were reaching the place of apparition. Vicka states: "Then she said to us, "Go in God's peace." Our heads were all turned in the direction where she was leaving, all in the same direction. No one said anything, but everyone was frightened."[8] Afterwards, Ivanka was overcome with emotions at the words of Our Lady and was crying, no one could console her. Her grandmother met her on the road, and Ivanka told her everything.

On the **third day**, Friday June 26, word travelled fast with several thousand sand from the surrounding villages, and those coming from greater distances gathered on the hill. Seeing three brilliant flashes at the village and the entire area, the children ran up the hill. This time, Our Lady appeared 300 meters higher up the hill. When Our Lady arrived, Vicka, on the advice of Marinko who befriended and supported the children, threw holy water on the Blessed Virgin and said to the apparition, "If you are Our Lady stay with us, and if you are not, you better go away." [9] Our Lady smiled with approval as the water dissipated from her dress into the air.

They asked Our Lady why she was coming to them in this place. Our Lady said, "I have come because there are many believers here. I have come to convert and reconcile people." [10] She asked that everyone should be at peace. The heat was intense this day, and the crowd pushing in on them caused Ivanka, Mirjana, and Vicka to faint. They were carried away from the crowd to revive them. Mary asked the children to stand instead of kneeling. After 30 minutes, the Lady was asked if she was coming again. She said she was and then she said, "Go in the peace of God." [11] The three seers were helped down the mountain. As Marija was walking down, she was called by the vision again and went to the left, falling to her knees. She sees in this vision, a cross, made out of colors of the rainbow. It was a cross without the body of Christ. Our Lady was seen in front of the cross and was crying tears running down her cheeks. She called to Marija urging, "Peace, peace, only peace. Reconcile your selves. Peace must take place between God and man and between men. Go in God's peace."[12] Marija's deep experience created urgency in her, to bring peace into hearts, family, and the world.

On Saturday June 27, the **fourth day**, the local communist government caught wind of the events and interrogated the children at the police station, but they remained firm about the apparitions. A local doctor examined them but could find nothing wrong. They were released and went back to the hill. This day, the children were asked to submit to a test. They were asked to split up and be in different places. Ivanka, Mirjana, and Vicka were to be one group; Marija and Jakov paired, and Ivan on his own. Fr. Zrinko Cuvalo, the associate pastor went for the first time with Marija and Jakov to experience this alleged apparition. At the lower part of the hill, Marija saw the light and felt the call. She climbed up the hill in a seemingly rapid supernatural state, seen by the priest and Jakov who could not keep up. Marija was called to a place, 2 meters higher on the hill. The Lady was standing in front of her and then disappeared. Marija did not see the other visionaries because of the crowd but waited for the Lady. Jakov and the priest found the other three visionaries, and together they found Marija. This day Ivan went home from the police station. His parents insisted because they were afraid for Ivan, of the police and the crowd. After Ivan started from his home and walked a way outside the village, to see; the Lady suddenly appeared to him on the road.

Back on the hill, the other children began to pray and then sing. The crowd sang as well and many prayed. The children were confident the Lady would appear. The same flashes of light were seen. The crowd could see the unusual expression on their faces and knew that they were seeing the Lady. The crowd pushed towards the place where the children's eyes were fixed. The crowd had little self-control, as they wanted to experience the presence of the Lady from Heaven. The children could see that the crowd was so close that they were stepping on the Lady's veil. She disappeared. The children said, they would have to stand back. Marinko and some people formed a perimeter around the children. Mary reappeared, but a boy stepped on her veil, again she disappeared. The children asked the crowd to be more considerate and orderly. Finally, Our Lady stayed for a longer time.

When she reappeared, the children asked her many questions. Ivanka asked her, her name and she responded, "**I am the Blessed Virgin Mary.**" [13] Mirjana was greatly concerned about allegations by skeptics. Our Lady replied: "There is always injustice among people, pay no attention to what they say."[14] Father Jozo Zovko, the parish priest, asked the children to ask Our Lady what the Franciscan priests should do? She replied: "The Friars should believe firmly." [15] Vicka asked for proof for the people so that all would believe. Our Lady responded: "Let those who do not see, believe, as if they see." [16] She disappeared again without saying, "Go in God's peace." The children waited for a long time, and finally the crowd started to leave.

This day gave genuine proof that the children were not in control of this apparition. She appeared in several places and decided where the children would meet, in a new place where the other children were not aware of Marija's position. That became obvious to the crowd. The children saw the usual flashes of light that led them to the call of Our Lady, different than going to a particular place. The crowd witnessed the flashes of light again. The veil of Our Lady stepped on, has never been recorded in the history of Marian Apparitions. This day, confirmed several unusual events and gives them some proof of credibility. As they walked down the rocky hill, Marinko and others, help the children down, keeping the crowd back. Suddenly the seers moved to one side and exclaimed, "There she is!" Marinko and the others blocked off an area for the seers. Our Lady said to them in a loving way, "My angels, you are my dear angels." [17] She confirmed a meeting for the next day at the same time and place on the hill, departing with the words, "Go in the peace of God." [18]

By Sunday, June 28, the **fifth day,** more than 15,000, the largest crowd so far, came to the hill. It was a beautiful sunny day. Marija and Jakov along with Fathers Viktor and Zrinko started towards the hill. Marija shouted, "Look, look, look!" Marija and Jakov, "...ran ahead at what seemed incredible speed almost seeming to fly," [19] witnessed Father Zrinko. Both priests saw Marija in her red skirt and white blouse that was easy to see as she ran so quickly. At exactly 6:30 p.m., Our Lady came in the usual way on Mount Podbrdo. The seers asked the people to kneel. They asked Our Lady many questions for themselves and from the crowd that day. "...Dear Blessed Virgin, what do you want of these people here?" "That those here who do not see me, believe like the six of you who see me." "Dear Blessed Virgin, will you leave us some sign here on earth that will convince these people that we are not liars, and that we are not playing games." "Go in peace of God." [20] She then left with a light behind her and was gone. The seers began to sing well-known Croatian religious songs. Right after the apparition, Fr. Zrinko Cuvalo interrogated the children like the communist state police would. He tried to confuse them with questions to distort the truth, but they continued to give sound answers and in the end, he became a firm believer.

On Monday, the **sixth day,** June 29, the children were taken to Citluk and then to the hospital in Mostar, tested for mental sanity by the local authorities, past the tests, and returned to the hill that evening. The Blessed Virgin came at 6:26 p.m. The children's words were recorded. Mary answered similar questions from the day before but stressed to have "firm faith and confidence." [21] They were feeling persecution but Mary said, "You will endure it, my angels." She stated, "There is only one God, one faith. Believe in God with all your might, trust in Him." [22]

Dr. Darinka Glamuzina was sent to follow the children that day from Mostar. She was close by on the hill with the seers. The seers asked Our Lady if the doctor could touch her. Our Lady said, "There have always been unfaithful Judases. Let her come." [23] The doctor touched Our Lady, then our Lady disappeared. As people saw the doctor leave the hill, she seemed in shock over something she experienced there. She had nothing to do with the investigations after that day.

Our Lady reappeared. The seers then pleaded for the healing of a paralyzed boy who could not speak, named Daniel: "Dear Madonna, will this little boy, Daniel, ever be able to speak? Please make a miracle so that everyone will believe us. These people love you so very much. Dear Madonna, make a miracle. She is looking at him. Dear Madonna, say something." The children continue to plead with her just like children with their mom. Our Lady finally gives in, "Let them (parents) believe firmly that he will be healed. Go in God's Peace." [24] Daniel started to speak later that evening. His healing was gradual with prayer and trusting in God from the parents. That evening the seers were taken to the rectory and questioned again. Afterwards, the seers went to Marinko's house and talked to people from the balcony until 11 p.m.

On Tuesday, June 30, the **seventh day,** five of the children were picked up by two social workers from Citluk, with the purpose of keeping the seers from the hill, at Podbrdo that evening. Ivan was not with them. The two social workers drove the seers around the countryside and passed through towns and villages along the way. By late afternoon, they came close to Cerno, only a few kilometers from the Podbrdo hill. The seers wanted the car stopped because of the urge within them to see the Blessed Mother. They pulled off the road in the open country and could see Mount Podbrdo. The seers went to their knees and prayed as usual. They could then see the light flashes on Mount Podbrdo, and Ivanka asked the two social workers whether they could see the light. They said they could. Our Lady appeared to the visionaries. Mirjana felt uncomfortable about how they accepted the social workers plan and ended up having the vision here, instead of the hill. She asked Our Lady if this was acceptable to meet in this place. She said, she did not mind. Mirjana then asked Our Lady, if she would mind if they meet at the church, instead of the Hill. Our Lady was hesitant and said, "I will not (mind, My angels."[25] She looked at the seers for a long time. They asked her if she was leaving a sign. She said nothing, then slowly left, saying again, go in the peace of God. The light could be seen leaving the hill as usual by the visionaries on the hill. Ivan did not experience a vision that day. The two examiners who witnessed the children, as they saw them in ecstasy, became believers.

They arrived in Medjugorje and met for the third time with Father Jozo Zovko, the parish priest. He recorded their conversation. He asked questions and had discussion with the children. Father Jozo thought they were at the hill but heard their experience of that day. Fr. Jozo asked what they said to the people on the hill. They said they did not go to the hill. Vicka and Mirjana were concerned that the crowd did not know what had happened that day. After more discussion, they considered the Madonna's words and decided not to go to the hill. The communist officially banned them off the hill although at that time, they were not aware. In agreement with Fr. Jozo, they would meet in the church, and people would find out soon enough. Everyone who believes would come to the church. It's interesting how the Spirit of God protected the children from the largest crowd ever that day. Unknowingly, it was too dangerous for the children to venture to the hill and back. The events set in motion this day, would change the venue to the safety of the Church for a time.

Father Jozo Zovko

Father Jozo Zovko, the Franciscan parish priest of Medjugorje, had just given an eight-day retreat during June 1981, for sisters in a convent in Zagreb, Croatia and asked them to pray for renewal in his parish. Wednesday, June 24, his last day, he was told excitedly: "Father Jozo, have you heard that Medjugorje was struck by lightning during the night? They say the post office has burned down, and a lot of damage has been done." [26]

Fr. Jozo phoned, but the lines were down. On June 25, Fr. Jozo flew to Split, to stay overnight at the Franciscan monastery, closer to Medjugorje. He was told that Fr. Zrinko had been there, looking withdrawn and distant, looking for him. On June 26, Jozo went to Mostar hospital to see his mother. Another member of his parish was there and exclaimed to him: "...you get over to Medjugorje as fast as you can. Our Lady has been appearing to some children." [27] Fr. Jozo hardly knew this woman, concluding that she must be out of her mind. He hastened back to Medjugorje and no sooner greeted the housekeeper who promptly replied, "People are coming from everywhere. They say Our Lady's been appearing to some children up on the hill." [28] He was astonished. He asked her, "Has Fr. Zrinko spoken to them?" She said, "Yes, he has recorded the conversations." [29] Fr. Zrinko entered the rectory revealing this disturbed look and related his fears of a communist conspiracy or worse. Fr. Jozo interrupted him and asked him if he knew these children. He said he had talked to them but doesn't really know them. Fr. Jozo had the children brought to him but could not recall seeing any of them. He talked to Mirjana who was being accused of drug usage, but Fr. Jozo found her to his surprise, a very normal teenage girl. He started to lean towards the conspiracy so he taped all of their conversations. He suggested to the children that they should pray more and read the Bible. He asked them about their knowledge of other apparitions. Mirjana said, "I'd never heard of any other apparitions. I didn't know about Fatima or Lourdes. I suppose I'd never been interested in that kind of thing. In those days, I only went to church when I had to." [30] Marija was surprised that Mary had ever appeared on earth before. By this time, Fr. Jozo was so disheartened about their lack of awareness, he gave them prayer books, rosaries and a book entitled," The Apparitions of the Blessed Virgin." [31]

By the eighth day of the apparitions, Wednesday, July 1, Fr. Jozo stated: "I was in anguish because of all the events. It was at this time that something began to happen in me which led me to become more than a listener to the children's reports. People from government services, were brought in to put a stop to the events. Those who were believers did not do it happily. The two girls who had experienced the events in Cirno resigned because of their own experience. Sometime in the middle of the day, the police came to find the children and stopped them after the two girls had failed. They wanted to remove them from the hill and from the people. They asked throughout the village where the children are. The people responded in various ways, in the fields, in the village...through the vineyards, towards the church. While all this was going on, I was in the church praying, feeling a great responsibility in front of God as Pastor... No one was in the church with me at that moment. And then something happened that for me was important and decisive. It was both a turning point and a moment of revelation. While I was praying I heard a voice say, "Come out and protect the children." I left my Bible and breviary, genuflected and with no further thought or delay, I left the church. As I was leaving the church through the middle door, with my foot in the air and the door handle in my hand, the children ran toward me from the left side of the church, escaping from the police. They told me, "The police are chasing us, hide us!" They had gathered around me and were crying. Ana, Vicka's sister, was with them, sharing their fate. I embraced the children and took them to the rectory. I locked them in an unoccupied room of the house." [32] Shortly after, Our Lady appeared to them in the room. Fr. Jozo heard banging on the door, and the police asked him if he had seen the children. He said he had, and said that he had them in the church. The police just looked at him and ran towards Bijakovici near apparition hill.

Word was getting out to the people who were going to the hill that a service would be held in the Church. At 5:00 p.m., the associate pastor prayed the rosary and at 6:00 p.m., Fr. Jozo said Mass. Father Jozo saw Our Lady above the congregation in the Church that evening, and preached like he never did before, to become her strongest advocate. The church was so crowded that Fr. Jozo said he could hardly extend his hands when he said, "The Lord be with you." He said, "In the homily, I asked the people to pray and to fast, begging God to help us to understand the events in our parish....In that Mass, I wanted the people to cease being spectators and become participants in the events." [33] The visionaries spoke to the people after Mass and prayers continued until midnight. Father Jozo asked the people to come the next night starting a continual routine of prayer. Rosary and confessions were at six, and a Croatian Mass was held at 7:00 p.m. with Adoration of the Blessed Sacrament afterwards. This routine has continued each night to this present day with millions of pilgrims, including thousands of priests and bishops that have come from all over the world each year. Today, Masses start at 7:00 a.m. each hour in different languages until about 2:00 p.m. Many priests (25-30) con celebrate at an English Mass each day.

The communist government continued to bring a halt to the events. They demanded that St. James Parish be closed down but Father Jozo refused. On August 17, 1981, Father Jozo Zovko was arrested, was tried and convicted of subversion against the state of Yugoslavia and was sentenced to three and a half years to hard labor in prison. He suffered many cruel and horrible tortures. But unusual graces attended Father Jozo, such as light radiating from his cell at night, and the cell door would be unlocked and open. Our Lady showed the children, Father Jozo in prison and he spoke to them directly. She said to the children, "Do not fear for Jozo, he is a saint." [34] The cruelty of the torturers gave way to the devoutness of this man to Christ and Our Lady, and with the pressures from the people and others around the world, he was released after 18 months on condition, not to go back to St. James parish. He also had a vision of a special place where he would preach and bring healing to many. This place was built and used for many years.

Ten Secrets of Medjugorje

The ten secrets of Medjugorje have remained shrouded in mystery. But the children have said one thing that is an absolute give away for serious researchers. The secrets are all in the scriptures. Mary has said to the visionaries, "Everything is there in the Gospels."[35] On June 25, 1991, Mary gave her monthly message to Marija: "There are many people, who do not desire to understand my messages and to accept with seriousness what I am saying... If you pray, God will help you to discover the true reason for my coming. Therefore, little children, pray and read the Sacred Scriptures so that through my coming, you will discover the message in Sacred Scripture" [36] Over the last 39 years, information revealed has been consistent in general, but some details change with parts of messages corrected or better understood. All of the visionaries say, they will receive ten secrets. Whether they receive the same secrets, we do not know, although their information leads us to believe that most have the same secrets. A couple of the seers are receiving personal information for the future.

Mirjana, who lived in Sarajevo, was staying with her grandmother in Medjugorje that first summer of the apparitions. On December 25, 1982, Mirjana received the last or the tenth secret. The secrets are written on a mysterious parchment, hand written by the Blessed Virgin, given to Mirjana. The parchment has been seen by others, and the material is nothing ever seen on earth. Only Mirjana can see what is on the parchment. Mirjana stated: "I know every date of every secret."[37] Mary requested of Mirjana that she choose a priest to announce the first two secrets to the world. Her first two secrets will be announced by a priest, Fr. Petar Ljubicic, who will pray and fast for seven days, and then he will announce it publicly to the world, three days before the secrets are to take place.

Mirjana says, "The first two secrets will come as advanced warnings for the whole world and as proof that the Blessed Mother is here in Medjugorje." [38]

"If people saw the first secret, as it was shown to me, all of them would most certainly be shaken enough to take a new look at themselves and everything around them." [39] The **first secret** will **break the extended power of Satan.** After a short time, on the day of Miracles, the **third secret** unfolding, a **visible sign,** will appear on Apparition Hill, possibly like a column of fire, similar to what the Israelites experienced; a fire by night and a cloud of smoke by day in the desert. The visible sign will call many back to the faith. It will, too, be a sign for atheists. The Miracle sign will be something not seen before on earth. Mary related to the children, a foretaste of this event on October 28, 1981: "The fire seen by the faithful, was of a supernatural character. It is one of the signs, a forerunner of the great sign." [40]

Vicka has stated during Father Livo's interview: "The third secret is about a sign that she will leave here on the mountain of the apparitions. This sign will **remain here forever.**" [41]

Mirjana says: "The third secret will be a visible sign at Medjugorje, permanent, indestructible, and beautiful."[42] Jakov added: "The Blessed Mother said that there **will still be some, who will not believe**, even after the permanent sign comes." [43]

Mary has spoken to all of the seers: "The visible sign will be made manifest. When the sign comes, for many, it will already be too late." [44] According to the seers, those who are still alive, will have little time to convert, before the next five secrets take place, and as the visionaries say, they are nothing good. Mary has disclosed dates on which the different secrets will come to pass. Mirjana stated: "One of the evils that threatened the world in the seventh secret has been averted, thanks to prayer and fasting."[45] Mirjana also related: "The eighth secret is worse than the other seven. I prayed for a long time that it might be less severe… Later, the Madonna told me that she'd been able to have the secret lessened. But then, she told me the ninth secret and it is even worse. The tenth secret is totally bad and cannot be lessened what so ever ." [46] Mirjana reiterates: "**The ninth and tenth secrets are grave matters.**"[47]

When in Portland, Oregon, on February 2, 1990, during a vision with Mary, Mirjana was seen: "…three times it seemed that a great wind came upon you and you swayed back, as if you were blown by this great wind…" She stated: "The Blessed Mother was speaking to me about very serious things." [48] After this vision the message was: "…God the Father is the only way, truth, and life. To…reach eternal life…give good example to your children and to those who do not believe. You will not have happiness on earth; neither will you come to Heaven if you do not have a pure and humble heart and if you do not fulfill the laws of God. I am asking you for your help to join me in praying for those who do not believe…reconcile and purify your souls by going to confession. Take your rosary and pray. Take all your sufferings patiently…remember how patiently Jesus suffered for you…the unbelievers…Show them your example and pray for them…" [49]

Chastisements from God are inevitable and according to the visionaries we cannot expect the whole world to be converted. Mary has revealed many things to Mirjana about the future, more than the rest of the seers. She says the world has never been like this before, and God has not been prayed to, less, than in this time. If people could only see what's ahead of them. After the chastisements (ninth and tenth secrets come to pass: "Life in the world will change. Afterwards, men will believe like in ancient times." [50] That part of mankind who is left on the earth, will go back to the land and will have faith as they did long ago.

Fr. Janko Bubalo, interviewed Vicka who stated, we should not be afraid: **"People should not be afraid**, if they are prepared. If we are afraid of these kinds of things, we don't have confidence in God. Fear of this kind does not come from God. It can only come from Satan who wants to disturb us so that we close ourselves to God and are not able to pray." [51]

In 1982, Mirjana was given a vision of Satan disguised, asking Mirjana to renounce the Madonna, to follow him in happiness and love in life, instead of sorrow and suffering. Strong in her faith, Mirjana sent him away. Mary arrived and explained, "Excuse me for this, but you must realize that Satan exists. One day he appeared before the throne of God and asked permission to submit the Church to a period of trial. God gave him permission to try the Church for one century. **This century is under the power of the devil,** but when the secrets confided to you, come to pass, his power will be destroyed. Even now, he is beginning to lose his power and has become aggressive. He is destroying marriages, creating division among priests and is responsible for obsessions and murder. You must protect yourselves against these things through fasting and prayer, especially community prayer. Carry blessed objects with you. Put them in your house, and restore the use of holy water." [52] This confirms Pope Leo XIII's vision. As the secrets unfold, Satan will lose his power. During the time of the unfolding of the ten secrets, one of the seers will continue to have daily apparitions of the Madonna.

Our Lady wants the parishioners to meet together once a week to pray. This started on March 1, 1984 on Thursdays. She gave a message for the prayer group each week. Mary encourages prayer groups around the world. Marija was given charge of the messages until January 1987. After that, she continued receiving messages on the 25th of the month for the world, starting in January 1987.

Defeat of the Soviet Union

In October 1981, Mary complained of the western world: **"The west has made civilization progress, but without God, as if they were their own creators. Whole regions of the Church would be healed if believers would go to confession once a month!"** She later exclaimed, "You who believe, be converted! Hasten your conversion!" [53] We are all called to fast on bread and water, Wednesdays and Fridays. "Through fasting and prayer one can stop wars; one can suspend the laws of nature." [54] On May 25, 1987, she states: "I call on each one of you, to consciously decide for God and against Satan. I am your Mother, and therefore, I want to lead you all to complete holiness. I want each one of you to be happy here on earth, and to be with me in Heaven." [55]

On March 18, 1989, **Our Lady of Medjugorje** requests: "One more time I beseech all of you to pray, to help by your prayers, the unbelievers...My wish, is just to warn you all as a mother. **I beg you**, for people **who do not know about the secrets**... I want to tell you, how I suffer for all because I am the Mother of all..." [56] Only a few months later, the Berlin Wall came down on November 9, 1989, and the break up of communist nations started to take place.

August 25, 1991, Our Lady of Medjugorje states: "...Satan is strong and wants to sweep away my plans of peace and joy and make you think that my Son is not strong in His decisions...with your help, **everything that I desire to realize through the secrets, that I began in Fatima**, may be fulfilled. I call you dear children to understand now, the importance of my coming and the **seriousness of the situation**...pray that everything I have started, may be completely realized in its fullness..." [57]   In these two messages, Mary clarifies, **the apparitions of Fatima and Medjugorje are connected** and are a continuation of her plans.

Then came this message on September 25, 1992: "I am with you also in these restless days in which Satan wishes to destroy everything which I and my Son, Jesus, are building up. In a special way, he [Satan] wishes to destroy your souls. He wishes to guide you as far away as possible from Christian life as well as from the Commandments... Satan wishes to destroy everything which is holy in you and around you. Therefore, little children, pray, pray, **pray, in order to be able to comprehend all that God is giving you** through my comings." [58] The prayer response to Mary's requests in the 1980s and early 1990s helped to bring down communism in the former Soviet Union, as well as satellite nations such as Yugoslavia.

Heaven, Hell, and Purgatory

All six of the visionaries have been shown Heaven and Purgatory, and four have seen Hell. Mary has said that, "**most** go to Purgatory, **few** go the Heaven, (directly and **many** go to Hell." [59]

Hell was described by Vicka: "We saw many people in Hell. Many are there already, and many more will go there when they die...The Blessed Mother says that those people who are in Hell, are there because they chose to go there. They want to go to Hell.... In the center of this place is a great fire, like an ocean of raging flames. We could see people before they went into the fire, and then we could see them coming out of the fire. Before they go into the fire, they look like normal people. The more they are against God's will, the deeper they enter into the fire, and the deeper they go, the more they rage against Him. When they come out of the fire, they don't have human shape anymore; they are more like grotesque animals, but unlike anything on earth. **It's as if they were never human beings before**...They were horrible. Ugly. Angry. And each was different; no two looked alike...When they came out they were raging, smashing everything around, hissing, gnashing, and screeching." [60]

Marija shares her experience: "Yes, it's a large space with a big sea of fire in the middle. There are many people there. I particularly noticed a beautiful young girl. But when she came near the fire, she was no longer beautiful. She came out of the fire like an animal; she was no longer human...At the moment of death, God gives everyone the grace to see his whole life, to see what he has done, to recognize the results of his choices on earth...The one who lives in sin on earth can see what he has done and recognize himself as he really is. When he sees himself and his life, the only possible place for him is Hell. He chooses Hell because that is what he is. That is where he fits. It is his wish. God does not make the choice. God condemns no one. We condemn ourselves. Every individual has free choice. God gave us freedom." [61]

Mirjana saw Purgatory: "There are several levels in Purgatory. **The more you pray on earth**, the higher your level in Purgatory will be...the lowest level is the closest to Hell, where the suffering is the most intense. The highest level is closest to Heaven, and there the suffering is the least. What level you are on depends on the state of purity of your soul. The lower the level, the people are on, in Purgatory, the less they are able to pray and the more they suffer. The higher a person is in Purgatory the easier it is for him to pray." [62] "I could see the people shivering, thrashing and writhing in pain...The Blessed Mother... explained...**so many people on earth today do not even know about Purgatory**...so many people who die are quite abandoned by their loved ones. They cannot help themselves in Purgatory. They are totally dependent on the prayers and sacrifices of the generous people on earth who remember them.... Those who have died no longer have free will as they had on earth. They no longer have a body." [63]

Vicka herself was greatly affected by her glimpse of Purgatory: "They are so lonely that it is almost sickening to remember those moments I was there."[64] Vicka was in such turmoil and anguish after hearing the sighing, sobbing, and those crying, that in 1982, she asked Our Lady if she could do something special to help souls. Mary stated: "There are many religions on earth now which do not believe in Purgatory–that really exists. People in those faiths have no one to pray for them. They are really alone and abandoned by their loved ones on earth." [65] It should be noted here, that souls in Purgatory are not able to pray for themselves. They can pray for others, but prayers for themselves gives no merit for their release. Only prayers from others, gives merit for release. Mary invited Vicka to suffer and asked her if she knew the seriousness of her request and should talk to her spiritual director and confessor, Fr. Janko Bubalo. He recommended three days of prayer and fasting. Immediately after, Vicka spoke to Our Lady and accepted the suffering, she started suffering pain from a brain tumor, marked by severe headaches, and resulting in comas that lasted for hours. She was taken to Zagreb hospital, where examinations with the latest technology confirmed it was an inoperable brain cyst. Vicka accepted this suffering for the souls in Purgatory for five to six years. It was so debilitating that Our Lady then told her the date that her healing would take place. Six months before, on February 4, 1988, Vicka wrote a letter to Fr. Bubalo. Mary revealed to her that the pain would cease on September 25, 1988. Three priests witnessed the receiving of the letter from Vicka who instructed them to open the letter on September 25, 1988. The three priests and the president of the new commission to study Medjugorje were there to witness the opening of the letter. When the letter was opened the pain ceased for Vicka. This incredible and miraculous event sheds light on the reality of the visionaries with Mary at Medjugorje.

In conclusion: Mirjana's daily apparitions ended on Dec. 25, 1982. After that time, she now knows all ten secrets. Mary stated to Mirjana: "I selected you and told you all that is necessary. I transferred to you, many horrors that you must carry worthily. Think of me, and think about how many tears I have shed because of these horrors. You must be courageous." [66] Our Lady appears to her once a year on March 18; her birthday, for the rest of her life. She was to see Mary only once a year after that. Mirjana was so beside herself that she would break down crying in school. She continued to struggle with what she was given, until Mary, the loving Mother of us all, showed the traits of a real mother and changed her mind. She started visiting Mirjana again on August 2, 1987, and since then on the second of each month, receiving monthly messages. She prays with Mirjana for those who do not know God.

It has been now stated that Our Lady will continue visiting one of the visionaries even after the start of the unfolding of the ten secrets. She is trying to reach out to as many as possible before the tribulation. The ten secrets are serious scriptural prophecies about to unfold. After the ten secrets are fulfilled, there will be a certain period of true peace on this earth.

CHAPTER 27

JOHN PAUL II CONSECRATES RUSSIA

When Mary intervened at Fatima, she requested much prayer from humanity for decades, and chose a Pope who would take up the fight and pray for the consecration, asking for a special blessing and protection of Russia to Mary's Immaculate Heart, thus preventing a third world war in the 20th century.

In 1982, Pope John Paul II consecrated the modern world to Our Lady of Fatima. In 1983, he renewed consecration with the synod of Bishops. Then, on **March 25, 1984**, John Paul II consecrated the world to Mary's Immaculate Heart, together with all the bishops of the world. He does not name Russia specifically but infers nations that need to be entrusted. His words were: "United with all the pastors of the Church in a particular bond whereby we constitute a body and a college…we **entrust and consecrate** to you those individuals and **nations** which **particularly need to be** thus entrusted and **consecrated**." [1] Mary's original request for consecration was announced in 1929. There was no response to her request. Errors of communism spread to many other nations, thus requiring consecration for other nations as well. Sister Lucia said Heaven accepted this consecration, and Russia would be converted. Lucia said the consecration, "Prevented an atomic war that would have occurred in 1985." [2]

St. Lucia said in her own words: "The consecration of the 1984 collegial consecration of the world by Pope John Paul II **will have its effects**, but it is too late…there has been a tidal wave of evil and proliferation of nuclear weapons." [3] **Mary** assured the visionaries at Medjugorje on July 12, 1982, that, "the **third world war will not** take place." [4]

Significance of Marian Feast Days

What is the significance of Mary and the rosary, the **13th day** of the month, the 25th day, and other feast days of Mary? The first day to recall is October 13, 1884, when Pope Leo XIII had visions of Satan and God. Mary appears on May 13, 1917. Then on June 13, July 13, August 13 and 19, September 13 and October 13, to three children at Fatima, Portugal. On the feast of Our Lady of Assumption August 15, 1945, Japan surrendered and the Second World War ended.

On **May 13, 1955**, after seven years during which over one million Austrians were praying the rosary, Russia unexpectedly pulls out of Austria, a strategically vital country.

On **October 13, 1960, one million people prayed at Fatima in the cold, during the 'cold war,' when Russia's top scientists were testing long-range atomic missiles eventually **blowing up,** killing three hundred scientists. [5]

In 1962, six hundred thousand women prayed the rosary on the streets of Brazil to ward off a communist takeover.

In 1974 in Portugal, a communist coup was ousted when the bishops and large numbers of people re-consecrate Mary to their country and prayed the rosary at Fatima.

On **May 13**, 1981, John Paul II is shot in St. Peter's Square, sparking awareness to consecrate Russia to Mary's Immaculate Heart.

On **May 13**, 1982, Mary said to the Visionaries of Medjugorje, "His enemies have wanted to kill him, but I have protected him." [6]

On **March 25, 1984**, Pope John Paul II "...united with all the pastors of the Church in a particular bond whereby we constitute a body and a college," **consecrates** the whole world, especially the peoples for which by reason of their situation you have particular love and solitude." [7] Afterwards Sr. Lucia was assured from Heaven that the Consecration is fulfilled.

On **March 25, 1984,** Mary says to the visionaries at Medjugorje that day: "Rejoice with me and with my angels, because a part of my plan has already been realized." [8]

On March 25, 1984, Maria Esperanza, a mystic, had seven successive apparitions, also witnessed by 108 other people at a site called Betania near Caracas, Venezuela. This is a sign and a confirmation of the Consecration. The Virgin Mary in 1976 who called herself 'Reconciler of Peoples and Nations' had encouraged Maria to that site. Many apparitions to hundreds and then thousands occurred in the days and months that followed.

On **May 13, 1984, one of the largest crowds at Fatima gathered to pray for Russia. That very day, a massive **explosion** occurs at Severomorsk naval base in the Soviet Union and **destroys** two thirds of the Northern Fleet's surface-to-air missiles, killing hundreds of scientists and technicians, and destroying factories and assembly buildings. [9]

On **January 25, 1987,** Mary from Medjugorje: "I want you to comprehended that God has chosen each one of you, in order to use you in a great plan for the salvation of mankind." [10]

On **February 25, 1988**, Mary pleaded at Medjugorje: "Dear children, Satan is very strong, and therefore I ask you to dedicate your prayers to me so that those who are under his influence may be saved." [11]

On May 13, 1988, hope of success was showing after much encouragement from Mary at Medjugorje. That brought about another **explosion that **destroyed** the main factory in the Soviet Union, making SS 24's containing long-range nuclear warhead missiles.[12]

On July 25, 1991, Mary's monthly message at Medjugorje to the world pleaded: "At this time, peace is threatened in a special way, and I am seeking from you to renew fasting and prayer in your families... I desire you to grasp the seriousness of the situation, and that much of what will happen, depends on your prayers.... I am inviting you to begin to pray and fast seriously as in the first days of my coming." [13] By this time the communists where losing their grip in Russia and the former Soviet Union. Between August 15, 1991, Our Lady's Assumption date and August 22, 1991, the Communist tried to take back Moscow, in a coup that ended in five days. President Gorbachev was pushing for an end to the Soviet Union. It was financially in ruins. Stimulation for individuals was non-existent. Incentive for growth in industry or agricultural individual ownership of land or property was non-existent. They were decades behind the West and Gorbachev knew it. He had toured parts of Alberta and Ontario, Canada, as Agricultural Minister of the Soviet Union in the early 1980s and was surprised by the incredible crops and industry of this land. On August 22, 1991, the feast of the Queenship of Mary, Gorbachev shut the doors on Moscow's headquarters of the KGB, the same place that executed untold numbers of people and spread Satan's fear and terror to control people's lives on a daily basis.

On **August 25, 1991**, at Medjugorje, Mary states to the world: "I invite you to renunciation, for nine days, so that with your help, **everything I wanted to realize through the secrets that I began in Fatima may be fulfilled.**" [14]

On **December 8, 1991**, the feast of Our Lady's Immaculate Conception, the Soviet Union was abolished **without a shot being fired**. On December 12, 1991, the Feast of Our Lady of Guadalupe, the Russian Parliament formed a non-communist commonwealth. **The media and the world stood stunned at the impossible**. On **December 25, 1991**, the red flag came down from the Kremlin. On January 1, 1992, the feast of the Mother of God, Russia became an independent country again after 70 to 80 years of Satan's grip of terror.

On **May 13, 1992, on the feast of Fatima more prayer for peace is offered up. The very next day **explosions** take place at Vladivostok **destroying large amounts of weapons**, causing the evacuation of 50,000 people at that navel base. [15] On **September 8, 1992**, Our Lady's celebrated Birthday, the hammer and sickle flag was taken down from the Soviet space station, leaving only the name 'Mir' meaning 'Peace' in Croatian and other Slavic languages.

On **May 13, 1994, the feast of Fatima brought more prayer from around the world for peace. The very next day the storage depot close to Novonezhino for the Soviet Pacific fleet **blew up** shaking the ground 60 miles away. [16]

All **five occurrences were connected to **May 13 and** are pertinent to Russia and the destruction of the Russian armaments. **Some things only moms can do**! Mary told the children at Medjugorje that John Paul was 'her Pope,' the one she handpicked, to accomplish her mission. He continued to witness for Christ in the sufferings he endured from Parkinson's disease. He carried the weight of suffering for the whole world in his body and soul.

Understanding the True Face of Communism

What Mary is fighting against is larger than the defeat of communism in Russia and the former Soviet countries. The battle against the Red Dragon noted in Revelation 12, has continued for many centuries. In this fifth Church age, the Red Dragon has gained power, starting with those in Europe in power positions for 200 plus years, having a conviction to Satan's plan; to control the world, executed through the Illuminati, hidden within the Freemasons' upper fraternity. This is confirmed in many prophecies referring to the **Secret sect**. This governance has also been exposed by those in this organization at the highest levels and documented in literature.

Freemasonry has deceived nations into socialism or to a darker evil called communism working towards Global governance of these nations. This **hidden communism**, the real communism is directed by the Globalists, since its conception with the Rothschild's and other powerful families from Europe. They brought about the French Revolution, the American Revolution with London banking interests, and the Russian Revolution with Wall Street money; all driven to control the world through monetary power.

Mary clearly stated at Garabandal, that communism would be the problem in the latter days. It would cause the break-down of the world.

Most of us today, think that communism has been in 'those countries' and has been lessened, since the break-up of the Soviet Union, when in fact it is the most powerful evil force on this earth at this time. It is seen now in its true stripes in many western economies. Communism has many faces. Unbelievably, it controls the so-called land of the free, the United States of America, with a governing structure above the visible government. This has also taken root in the 27-plus countries of the European Union, which in fact has gone a step further, insidiously controlling the union with little or no input by its member nation-states. This control is growing in many other areas of the world and will continue to grow until the Warning. This **Red Communism** cloaked by the Globalists, is about to illicit grave changes that will affect the western world economies and in fact the whole world. Consider the clues contained in these prophecies:

Marie-Julie Jahenny from Jesus: "The red cloud has reached the earth. Men are coming out of it, supplied with their crimes. These are my most treacherous enemies, and also yours, My children." [17]

Mother Elena Leonardi, Jan 17, 1979: "In Italy, the nation favored by God where the Pope lives, the most Catholic of nations; there exists at this time,... the greatest concentration of communism in the world." [18]

CHAPTER 28

TEARS OF THE VIRGIN MARY

In Luke 19: 36-40, when Jesus was entering triumphantly into Jerusalem: "They spread their cloaks on the roadway as he moved along; and on his approach from the descent of the Mount of Olives, the entire crowd of disciples began to rejoice and praise God loudly for the display of power they had seen... some of the Pharisees in the crowd said to him, 'Teacher rebuke your disciples.' Jesus replied: **"If they were to keep quiet, even the stones would cry out."**

In our day, few people are speaking out for God, and it seems **that the stones are crying out** with blood, tears, and oil running down the eyes of statues of Mary throughout the world. Mary cries out for the sake of her Son and in desperation for souls at the edge of perdition. This phenomenon of tears has continued throughout the last two thousand years. But in the last two hundred years and particularly in the last sixty-five, it has been increasing dramatically.

Could anyone explain seeing a large tall statue of Mary in South Vietnam, with tears running down its cheeks? The eyes of the large statute are 20 feet or so above the people, who are poor farmers that live on the land with their families; there is no sophistication or modern conveniences around them. They are simple people all standing around looking in amazement. Then there are pictures, even photographs that are weeping. Icons weep tears, blood, and oil that miraculously heal. These are signs and wonders for those being saved.

In 1994, Pope John Paul spoke at the dedication of Our Lady of Tears at Syracuse, Sicily, where a plaster figure of Our Lady wept on numerous occasions for four days in 1953, attracting thousands of pilgrims. He said: "The tears of the Madonna belong to the order of signs; they testify to the presence of our Mother in the Church and in the world. A mother weeps when she sees her children threatened by evil, be it spiritual or physical.... Here we guide the mother's tears... tears of sorrow for all those who reject God's love, for the broken families or troubled youth, undermined by the culture of consumption and often misguided...tears of prayer; prayer of a mother who gives strength to any other prayer and stands as a supplicant to those who do not pray...tears of hope, which melt the hardness of hearts and opens them to the encounter with Christ, source of light and peace to individuals, families and society as a whole." [1]

At Roca Corneta, Italy, from 1957 to 1975, tears fell over 100 times and were proven human tears. A Marian statue called Regina Mundi weeps tears of blood over a globe held in her hands. This is in conjunction with a stigmatist, Enzo Alocci, of Porto Santo Stefano, Italy. Messages from Mary started on October 16, 1972. Over one hundred Rosa Mystica statues sent, by request, around the world, have wept tears and some statues weep tears of blood. This started first of all in the spring of 1947, with Mary appearing to Pierina Gillio in Montichairi, Italy with statues shedding tears and have been verified from 1974 continuing into the 1990s. Statues and images of Mary continue to weep human tears and blood. Images and statues of Jesus weep and shed blood as well. These signs continue all over the world in various places.

Blessed Sister Elena Aiello from Our Lord: "Launch forth into the world, a message to make known to all that the scourge is near at hand. The Justice of God is weighing upon the world. Mankind, defiled in the mire, soon will be washed in its own blood; by disease, by famine, by earthquakes, by cloud-bursts, tornadoes, floods, and terrible storms, and by war. But **men ignore all these warnings** and are **unwilling to be convinced** that **my tears, are plain signs to serve notice** that **tragic events are hanging over the world**, and that the hours of great trials are at hand." [2]

Mother Elena Leonardi from Mary July 28, 1976: "The hour of Justice has arrived, and the signs of these times, the most grievous...progressively multiply...tough messages given to extraordinary souls, as also by **so many weeping and bleeding images** of the Virgin and the very Crucifix itself." [3]

Mother Elena Leonardi, Jan 20, 1975: "Sinning humanity does not repent. God's anger is cast down upon this world! The **heavenly Mother sheds tears** of **blood** over all this corruption. The devil is destroying all humanity, and the calamity of evil envelops all of you. The heavenly Mother calls all priests to pray, do penance, and form cenacles for prayers of atonement...humanity is threatened by terrible punishments which it has provoked." [4]

Our Lady of Kibeho, Rwanda

Rwanda is a small country in the east-central heart of the continent of Africa. On November 28, 1981, Mary starts to appear to 17-year-old **Alphonsine** Murmureka, attending a Catholic girls school. Alphonsine described her as wearing a flowing seamless white dress with a white veil that covered her hair. Her hands were clasped in front of her, pointing toward Heaven. Mary introduces herself for the first time saying: "**I am the Mother of the Word.** Of all the things in Heaven, what makes you happy?" Alphonsine replied: "I love God, and I love His mother who gave us their son, Jesus who has saved us!" "Really?" Mary replied very pleased. "Then know, **I have heard your prayers** and **am here to console you.** I want your friends and schoolmates to have your faith, for they do not have enough."[5] She appears to her for exactly eight years till 1989.

Mary appears in January 1982, to **Anathalie** Mukamazimpaka for the next two years. On March 2, 1982, Mary appears to **Marie Claire** Mukangango for the next six months. Many signs and wonders take place, in conversions, prayer meetings, healings, fasts and silences, and other unusual phenomena, requested by Mary, during the years of the apparitions. Others claimed to see Mary and Jesus as well.

The Blessed Virgin took Alphonsine on a mystical journey, and she implored everyone, "Don't bury me; my body will look dead, and you will think that I'm dead, but please don't bury me." [6] For eighteen hours she seemed to lie in a deep sleep, her body very heavy, and they could not separate her hands that were joined together in pray. On this journey, the Blessed Virgin showed her **Heaven and Hell**. Anathalie claimed that Mary affirmed to her the world was in bad shape and people do not love. Young people, **are not only without God but are against God**. She revealed to her, visions of the future; of rampant murder, blood running, fire burning on the hill, mass graves, skulls, and beheaded bodies. She said, Our Lady appeared here to remind us of what we have forgotten and insisted on prayer, conversion, penance, and humility.

On August 19, 1982, all the seers had terrible visions of the future genocide in Rwanda. "I see a river of blood," recounted Alphonsine. "The trees are exploding into flames, the country is burning! Please Mother, you are scaring me...Oh no! No! Why are those people killing each other? Why do they chop each other? I'm not a strong enough person to watch people killing each other." [7]

Nevertheless, Mary continued revealing dreadful images. Alphonsine, frozen in fear, saw a pile of severed human heads, still gushing blood. The scene worsened, as Our Lady expanded the scene to reveal a huge valley filled with headless corpses rotting. This prophecy seemed shocking and repulsive but did not leave the minds of those involved.

In the 1980s, Mary gave other warnings that were not just for Africa. She warned them of disastrous sexual promiscuity just as the world started to discover a new epidemic; Auto-Immune Deficiency Syndrome (AIDS). She made this plea to Maria-Claire who was later killed in the genocide, when she begged for the release of her husband: "When I tell you this, I am not addressing myself strictly to you, child, **but I am making this appeal to the world...the world is in revolt against God...the world is on the edge of catastrophe**." [8] In 1990, Pope John Paul II, visited Rwanda and exhorted the people to listen to the words of the Virgin Mary before it was too late.

On April 6, 1994, after an airplane was shot down, as it was attempting to land, killing both the Rwandan president and the Hutu Burundi President, the

the incident ignited a mass genocide, pitting the Hutus against the Tutsi. This regime of persecution against the Tutsi people had in fact been encouraged and organized since the 1960s. The ethnic cleansing, fueled by violent propaganda and published by the Hutus' 10 commandments, called for the installation of Hutu ideology into schools and governments. In 1990, with a counter invasion of the Tutsi Rebel front, invading into northern Rwanda from Uganda, increased tensions with fears of the Tutsi enslaving Hutus. Large numbers of Hutus were pressured by the rebel Tutsi to flee northern Rwanda forcing them south. The killing of Tutsi living in the south , prevailed, until a cease-fire in 1993.

The genocide took place over the next three months of April, May, and June of 1994, well organized by the Rwandan Hutu militia. It was discussed in cabinet meetings 'to get rid of all the Tutsi'. Mayors, police, government officials, nationwide organized militia with AK47s, grenades and machetes would eliminate all Tutsi people, who were generally lighter in color, than the darker Hutu. Most of the people were forced to comply or be killed. To kill people who were their very neighbors and friends for years in their own villages and towns was pure delirium. Roadblocks were put up to systematically capture and kill all Tutsi. The river of Kagea looked like a river of blood, with bodies floating in it. There were hundreds of thousands of headless corpses rotting in piles with no one to bury the dead.

The Hutus were about 85 % of the population of 7.3 million in Rwanda; the Tutsi comprised about 15%. It is estimated at around 800,000 to 1,071,000 were killed in 100 days, or 10,000 murders every day, the highest rate of killing in recorded military history. It is estimated that 300,000 Tutsi survived and fled to Burundi and Uganda. Hundreds of thousands of women were victims of sexual assault in various hideous forms; in fact, rape was systematic and was used as a weapon, and many are now HIV positive. The visionaries of Our Lady at Kibeho in Rwanda saw the scenarios in advance.

This may be an example or precursor to events that may take place in the future in countries closer to home, but we always pretend that it is not possible in these forms. Let us remind ourselves of our Christian heritage that is being swiftly taken away in this secular world. How will we be seen in the future? We must pray and heed the requests and warnings of Our Mother of the Word.

Our Lady of Peace to Pedro Regis
at Anguera, Brazil

I was encouraged by the Holy Spirit to record many of the prophecies given to **Pedro Regis**. An extensive volume of specific prophecies are given to us from **Our Lady of Peace** to Pedro Regis with surprising details for a major tribulation about to unfold. Our Lady of Peace says, she has been given permission from Heaven **to give details** in the Land of the Cross (Brazil). [9]

On September 29, 1987, Pedro Regis, living in **Anguera, Brazil,** returned home from a school where he was training to be a teacher. He had suffered seizures for 18 months and while walking home, experienced approaching symptoms, so he sat on the ground near an anthill.

A woman appeared to him, of about twenty, dressed in white, with a veil that covered over her face. He thought she was a nun. She said she would help him and lifted him with great ease to a building. He could not remember what happened after that. When he came to, he asked his family where the young woman was. They did not understand whom he was talking about. Many ants were crawling on him, but he was not bitten.

On October 1, 1987, as he was talking to his sisters in their home, the young woman appeared to him and asked that his sisters would leave the room. She talked to him, giving him a message and instructed him to pray the rosary every day. He was to find a priest to assist him on this journey. At first, he was in doubt but soon realized it was an apparition.

On October 3, 1987, Pedro heard a feminine voice outside his home and asked his sisters to check it out. They saw no one, but after another call, Pedro came out and saw a brilliant light on a hill, not far from their house. He walked towards the light but his sisters thought there was something wrong with him. He continued towards the hill, but on reaching the hill, the light disappeared. As he turned around, he saw the young woman surrounded by brilliant light. He instantly fell to his knees in front of her. She said to him: "Don't be afraid. I am the Mother of Jesus. I am here because I need you to help my poor children who need my assistance." [10] She told him that he was cured of his seizures and to return to this place every Saturday. He is asked to write the messages down at the same time as she dictates them to him. The first message recorded was: "I am the Queen of Peace, and I want all my children to be at my side, to fight the great evil that could come to the world. In order for this evil not to happen, you should pray and have faith…. The world is in great danger, and to free you from this danger, you need to pray, to convert, and to believe in the Word of the Creator. By praying, you will find peace for the world. My children, many of you go to Church but do not go with a clean heart or go without faith. Many go to show that they are Catholic. That is a great error. **You need to follow one path; the Truth.** Some **have not learned to forgive**, but you need to forgive your neighbor. Enmity is the work of Satan, and he is happy when he can separate a brother from another. That is the reason that I ask, with all my burning Heart, convert, pray, and learn to forgive your neighbor." [11]

The messages from 1987 to 2004 are generally calling people to spiritual maturity, warning of what may come to pass, if they do not change. The messages from about 2005 have become specific to different regions, countries, cities, towns and villages, warning of impending disasters, disruption, destruction, devastation, desolation, and death, and are bound for these places. This next message specifically informs us of what Mary is commissioned to say from Heaven, for the first time, **speaking publicly and directly about future events.** [12]

Our Lady of Peace to **Pedro Regis,** message # 3328 June 5, 2010, at Anguera, Brazil: "Dear Sons and Daughters, I am your Mom, and I come from Heaven to announce that these are the most sorrowful times for humanity. God has chosen this country and sent me to call you to a sincere conversion. Don't lose heart. Don't back out. God needs you. What you have to do, do for the glory of God, for only He can reward you, for all you do in favor of my plans. There will be no eternal condemnation for those who accept my appeals. Announce to everybody that God is in a hurry, and now is the time of Grace."

"**Never before have I revealed in any of my apparitions in the world, what I have revealed here. Only in this land has God permitted me <u>to speak</u> <u>to you about future events</u>. God has chosen the land of the Holy Cross (Brazil) to announce what is to come to the world.** I still have noble things to reveal to you. Pay attention. Something frightening will happen in the Iberian Peninsula, and death will come to my poor children. Pray. Pray. Pray. I suffer because of what is coming to you. I don't want to oblige you to listen. Listen to me with love. I want to bring you to Him who is your only true Savior. Forward. This is the message I give you today, in the name of the Most Holy Trinity. Thank you for permitting me to reunite you here once more. I bless you in the name of the Father, of the Son, and of the Holy Spirit. Amen. Remain in peace." [13]

This is a typical message of Mary, Our Lady of Peace appearing to Pedro Regis at Anguera, Brazil. They are all dated and numbered chronologically as they were revealed to Pedro Regis since 1987. When Pedro visits other places in Brazil and elsewhere, Mary does appear at those places as well. In this prophecy, she also names a specific region of Europe where something frightening will happen, and death will be the result. The Mohammedans will rise up and will affect first, the area of Portugal, Spain, and Gibraltar affecting many people.

Two major examples of prophecies that came true in our time: The **first,** was about Japan's earthquake warnings with dates on them. God has warned Japan since the early 1970s, at Akita, of impending destruction. Here are parts of the original specific messages of **Our Lady of Peace** to **Pedro Regis** about Japan and the world:

April 28, 2005, message # 2515: "A giant earthquake will befall Japan such as has never been seen in all its history." [14]

August 2, 2005, message # 2556: "Japan will live moments of anguish, but the worst is yet to come." [15]

December 31, 2005, message # 2622: "Japan will drink the bitter cup of suffering." [16]

March 4, 2006, message # 2649: "Japan will drink the bitter cup of pain." [17]

February 5, 2010, message #3275: "It will happen in Japan and will be repeated in Paraiba (Brazil. Shouts of despair will be heard on all sides." [18]

March 16, 2010, message #3293: "Asia will shudder, and there will be great suffering for My poor children." [19]

March 20, 2010, message #3295: "A mega-quake will shake Japan, and My poor children will weep and lament. Greater pain never existed. I suffer because of what is waiting for you." [20]

April 17, 2010, message #3307: "A great destruction will be seen in Japan." [21]

May 29, 2010, message #3325: "Japan will suffer, and the pain will be great for My poor children." [22]

October 28, 2010, message #3392: "Death will pass through Japan and will leave a great trail of destruction." [23]

February 15, 2011, message #3440: "Akita (Japan will drink the bitter cup of pain." [24]

On **March 11, 2011**, a devastating earthquake of 8.9 to 9 struck Japan. [25]

The following was the second realized prophecy. Our Lady of Peace to **Pedro Regis** # 3294, March 18, 2010 from, Anguera, Brazil: "Dear Sons and Daughters… Humanity is sick and needs to be healed. I come from Heaven to show you the way to good and holiness. **Don´t back out. Death will pass on the coast of the Gulf and will leave a great trail of destruction.** I am your sorrowful Mother and I suffer because of your sufferings. Courage. Don´t let the flame of faith fail within you. This is the message I transmit to you to day in the name of the Most Holy Trinity." [26]

Pedro Regis # 3337, June 26, 2010: "Death will pass through the Gulf Coast causing great destruction. There will be a similar destruction in Brazil… You still have a long and spiny road to travel." [27] On April 20, 2010, the oil rig operated by Deepwater Horizon in the Gulf of Mexico exploded, spilling millions of barrels of oil for months and devastating wildlife and livelihoods in fishing, tourism, and other industries. This major disaster will last for decades in that area.

CHAPTER 29

EARTHLY CONCERNS

Most people today are lulled into believing that the problems of our planet will work out, without having to change our lifestyle. We hear many flimsy excuses that seem to leave it to those in the future to be concerned with. We are out of order with God's decrees.

Isaiah 24: 3-6: "The earth is utterly laid to waste, utterly stripped... the earth mourns and fades, the world languishes and fades; both the heavens and earth languish. The **earth is polluted** because of it's inhabitants, who have transgressed laws, violated statutes, broken the ancient covenant... a curse devours the earth, and **its inhabitants pay for their guilt... few men are left.**"

The subjects addressed in this section are a small fraction of the problems confronting people of the earth's fragile ecosystem. Pollution of sea, land, and the atmosphere has been a continual grave concern since the 1950s.

Global Dimming

In the 1950s, Israel developed an agricultural project, to measure amounts of sunlight, reaching the earth's surface, for irrigation purposes. This continues to this day and is measured in many countries around the globe. By the 1980s, researchers were startled to find that the solar radiation or rays of the sun had dropped a staggering 22% in the Middle East. With accumulated research, from all over the earth, a decrease of direct sunlight, is reaching the earth's surface. Dimming appears to be caused by air pollution particles of coal, oil, wood, soot, volcanic ash, Sulphur compounds, airplane fuels, and other visible pollutants rising into the upper atmosphere. Visible air pollutants reflect sunlight back into space, lessening the rays of light reaching the actual surface of the earth. The particles seed the formation of water droplets, increasing larger numbers of water droplets, reflecting the sun's rays back into space. This causes disproportionate rainfall due to the lack of solar rays to evaporate the ocean waters.

Global dimming may also distort the real effects of heating or cooling of the atmosphere by not letting in the sun's rays, to reach the surface of the earth. In the far north, where particle pollution is less, we have seen a significant rise of melting of that polar region. The average earth's temperature has only risen a half of a degree. It is interesting that for three days after 9-11, virtually no airplanes were flying in the skies of the United States. The skies were clear with no aircraft trails. The scientist discovered from 5000 weather stations, an increase in temperature of over one degree, over average, the largest magnitude swing in the last 30 years. This is a clear indication that if particle pollution stops, the temperature may go up. Even though the United States uses more fuel than any other country, the dimming in the United States, is only at about 10%, possibly from car and industry pollution improvements. At this time, the measured drop in solar radiation across the world is at about 10%. If particle pollution continues to increase in the world, the over-all temperature will go down, taking us into colder times. Another possibility could be volcanic ash reaching the upper atmosphere lowering the temperature quickly, decreasing our ability to grow foods abundantly.

Decreased Pan Evaporation

Other interesting long-term observations confirm changes are eminent. The lack of evaporation of water throughout the world is measured. Again, this process of measuring evaporation of water originated for agricultural purposes. In the 1980s and 1990s, significant decreases through pan evaporation were measured. With the average temperature of the surface of the earth warming, it would be expected that evaporation would be increasing. However, the rate of evaporation, on the earth has been steadily dropping for 50 years.

There are two possible explanations: first, the decrease of humidity, over the pans and secondly, reductions in solar radiation to the earth. This is a grave concern, of the lessening of water evaporation over the oceans. The direct sunlight to a water surface is now considered, the fastest evaporation catalyst, on most of the earth. This will bring less moisture and greater upset or imbalance to the earth's weather. These changes to climate may precipitate greater **extremes of weather.**

Global Weather Extremes

As of 2019, we have seen or experienced many extremes of weather. This was and is predicted for the future by those given revelation from Our Lord. International scientists called, Intergovernmental Panel on Climate Change (IPCC) have concluded with 95% certainty that human activities since the 1950s have caused the rises in temperatures from burning fossil fuels.[1] To say that mankind has not affected our planet in these areas would be a farce and a deception.[2, 3]

But from the 1950s and onwards to about 2005, sun spots have had a marked increase in flare ups that also have had an impact on temperature increases. This pattern of solar flareups correlates to increased temperatures. This was called a **Modern Grand Maximum** during the last half of the 20th Century. [4] Heat has accumulated in the oceans causing increase temperatures and melting in the polar regions. Heat from Industrial pollutions has an effect.

NASA is now predicting a **Grand Solar Minimum** that could quickly move temperatures downward.[4] Sunspots are already at a minimum in 2019. Cooler temperatures are mentioned in the prophecies for the 2020s and 2030s during the transpiring of the 10 events, related by visionaries.

Extreme Ocean Changes

An increase in ocean temperature of one degree over the last one hundred years is considered part of the change. Major changes are considered unavoidable with changes to the circulation of ocean currents due to the higher temperatures. The Oscillation of ocean currents such as the El Nino southern oscillation, the Pacific Decadal Oscillation and the North Atlantic Oscillation will see continual changes to these currents increasing or decreasing in temperature. Unusual amounts of Arctic Ocean's old glacial ice has melted off in the last three decades. Islands are appearing suddenly, where once it was not known. The sun is warming the open waters bringing warmer temperatures into the north. This has affected weather patterns throughout northern countries. Greenland has a significant melt off. Warming patterns are rising in the Antarctica. But will these trends continue with a grand solar minimum ?

Ocean Pollution

It's a sight to behold: plastics floating in the Pacific Ocean have concentrated in staggeringly large areas, held by ocean currents and poisoning fish that mistake this garbage for food. Micro-plastic is now found in tiny shellfish in the Arctic ocean.

Areas of the Pacific and the Atlantic have become 'nutrient poor ocean deserts. Oxygen concentrations in areas of the Northwest U.S. coast, the coast of South Africa, and the Gulf of Mexico have dropped dramatically giving way to dead zones and extinction of marine species from these ecosystems.

The place of the most irresponsible shame in this world is the Gulf of Mexico with 27,000 oil wells abandoned, an environmental minefield. Leaking wells continue in spite of the greatest disaster of a continual oil well blowout for close to 3 months in 2010. Another contributor of pollution to the Gulf includes major run off of agricultural chemicals, pesticides, insecticides, and phosphorus and nitrogen fertilizers from the vast Missouri/ Mississippi River water-sheds, which contributes to the dead zone in the Gulf.

Forty percent of the population of the world lives in cities on the oceans, yet we are still dumping man-made polluted wastes into the oceans. Ships still haul garbage out into the oceans, dumping it despite restrictions on this practice. Oceans, normally alkaline are becoming acidic, with less ability to ward off dangerous organisms that affects human and marine life.

Destruction of Coral Reefs and Fisheries

Coral reefs are comprised of living creatures, but a major part of the eco-system that provides fish with food and protection in the great oceans of the world, are dying from increased ocean temperatures and pollution caused from industrial development. Fishing trawlers dragging the bottom of the oceans floors for souvenirs (jewelry) made from coral, continues to destroy this vast precious ecosystem, particularly in equatorial waters.

Indiscriminate practices of the fishing industry means that ocean trawlers vacuum all fish out of the oceans, taking all species used or unused. Blue fin tuna are on the edge of extinction. The Grand Banks of Newfoundland has been shut down for many years to replenish cod fishing and other fish stocks. The countries near the Baltic Sea have placed a ban on fishing just recently. The Japanese take 100's of whales per year out of the Antarctic Ocean, for so-called scientific purposes, is a travesty. At this time about 10% of large fish species, are left in the oceans leaving only the small species of fish. Scientist's predict by the late 2030s, most of the ocean's fish and marine dependent species will be virtually gone. International waters have little surveillance of fishing practices. In the past, the thought of our vast oceans running out of fish was inconceivable.

Industrial Pollution Affecting People, Land, Water, and Air

Effluents from industrial sources containing many chemicals are affecting land, water, and air. The monetary giants have abused the properties of many individuals and peoples. They have taken advantage of land areas, of the poor and the marginalized, building factories and plants where lack of education and understanding to their indiscriminate execution of operations, leaves only silence to their abuse, particularly in third world countries.

Males of certain species are becoming more female. Thousands of chemicals affect reproduction organs, causing males and females to have parts of both species, thus negating production. In an ongoing case of industrial pollution in Sarnia, Ontario, close to a native reserve, 50% fewer boys are born due to the 1000 plus synthetic chemicals made from petroleum. After this observance, at a conference in California, a statement was made, that we are seeing the first signs of extinction.

Agricultural Pollution

Chemical pesticides, herbicides, and fertilizers acidify the soils and poison the land. Overuse of land has depleted soil nutrients, leeching ground water and water runoff carries residues into streams and rivers. In addition, researchers have found that so-called inert herbicide killer, Roundup, has a toxic effect on human cells, particularly on embryonic, placental and umbilical cord cells.

Global Resource Depletion

Shortages in agriculture, fish, metals, wood, and other resources are becoming apparent, but consumption controls are not being addressed. Many of these shortages are a result of political policies that inhibit innovation. Lack of clean water or shortage of water will affect over one half of the population on this planet by the 2030s. The recorded number of declining oil reserves by many nations throughout the world is certainly apparent. As of 2018, the United States has an increase in potential oil reserves from fracking rock. Canada has estimated 400 years of oil in the tar sands slow recovery. Fracturing rock and mining for oil come with a high cost. Recent statistics show that after one year of fracking, most wells are dropping off from 30% to 50%. Additionally, worldwide, easy liquid oil is in decline, and the demand is going up in many countries of the Global South and East. Known oil reserves are expected to pass peak in 2030s.

Wild Mammals and Birds Endangered

Since the 1970s, one half of all mammals of the earth are in decline, reduced by 25% according to the World Wildlife Fund organization. Many smaller species have reached extinction. W.W.F.'s Living Planet Index showed 1477 vertebrate species from 1970 to 2005 showed a 27% decline. The marine salt water Living Planet index had a dramatic drop of 28% in a 10-year period from 1995 to 2005. The freshwater Living Planet index dropped 29% from 1970 to 2003. The International Union for Conservation of Nature that looks at over 44,838 animals and plant species concluded 45% are listed as threatened with extinction. Moreover, 3246 species are critically endangered with a high risk of dying out. The world's largest and popular African parks, including Masai Mara and the Serengeti, have seen population declines of almost 60% from 1970 to 2005. Their 'Red List' of threatened species reveals a bleak future for many wild species of fauna and flora as primary prey and habitat loss continue to encroach on their territory.

Wakeup Call to Genetically Modified Foods

The introduction of Genetically Modified (GM) foods has brought with it, an increase in chronic illnesses and food allergies in America and the UK. Studies with animals, by many research doctors show disorders of vital organ damage, gastrointestinal and immune system problems, accelerated aging, infertility, and dysfunctional regulation of insulin.[1] Some studies reveal, genetically modified corn varieties are causing organ damage in mammals. GM corn contains a toxic pesticide, inserted into the DNA, creating an insect-killing BT-toxin in every cell. GM soy flour fed to female rats, causes most of their babies to die in three weeks, with those surviving notably smaller. Male rats fed GM soy, showed testicle changes in color, from pink to dark blue with damaged sperm cells. Two-dozen US farmers claimed thousands of pigs became sterile after consuming certain GM corn varieties. In South Africa, indigenous chickens with a wild cautious sense in their natural breeding, after feeding on GM maize, refused to eat the grain, sensing the contaminants in the feed. Monsanto's 'Roundup ready' crops can resist Roundup herbicides. Bayer Crop science's 'Liberty link' crops resist liberty herbicides. Most corn and soybeans are now genetically modified. So when GM soybeans and corn are fed to humans, what are the consequences?

Moreover, the claims by the agro, multi-nationals of increased yields, have not been substantiated by the findings of UNESCO, WHO, FAO and World Bank; in fact, yields have deceased. The push to claim, GMO's are the answer to the hungry populations of the world, is not true.

Bees Vanishing

Bees may be affected by electromagnetic waves emitted by mobile phone towers and cell phones. Tests by placing cell phones near beehives have crippled the navigational ability of worker bees to find their way back to the hives and the queen bee, resulting in the collapse of the hive within a short period of 10 days.

More likely, a combination of pesticides, insecticides, and genetically modified plants has weakened the immune systems of bees and their natural ability to ward off viral and bacterial infections. Most research has found the Bt gene in genetically modified crops does not affect the bee by itself, but the combination of exposure to viral, bacterial, and other poisons are contributing to the problem. The findings of researchers, of bees exposed to crops that are genetically modified, having the Bt gene, are ingesting significant quantities of the Bt, a living bacterium whose mode of action is to form a pore or hole in the insect's gut cell membranes. Bt is also shown to produce cognitive impairment in bees' unusual array of complex learning processes.

A new study has finally found that corn seeds coated with **neonicotinoid insecticides**, [2] used widely around the globe, are killing insects by paralyzing their nervous systems. During and just after spring seeding, beekeepers observe large die offs of bees. Research has observed that pneumatic seed drilling machines spray insecticides, coating the seed as it enters the ground, but spray drift in minute particles of insecticide, escape into the air at ground level, as the machine is traveling forward, causing toxic effects on the nervous systems of bees. Some seed drill companies have tried to prevent this but with little success. Honeybees pollinate many plants and are essential; without them, entire ecosystems will be disrupted or destroyed. We have come to a serious juncture.

Blaming Everything but the Sin of Mankind

It is not about global warming or global cooling. It is not about climate changes, or extremes, CO2 emissions, nor the number of sun spots on the sun. Although, it is all of the above, God's word is telling us, it is **the sin of mankind affecting** the **planet earth** most severely. It is a recoil of the planet's eco-systems, from mankind's rebellion and chaotic mindset, against God's order of love for the earth and the universe. If we follow God's order, living within the earth's natural ecosystem for abundant life on this earth, we will **receive our rains** in **proper season** and **our sunshine** in **proper season**. We will have food, clothing, shelter, and peace in safe communities.

God's Instruction for Order on Our Planet

Leviticus 26:3-4, God says, "If you live in accordance with my precepts and are careful to observe my commandments (order) I will give you rain in proper season, so that the land will bear its crops, and the trees their fruit; your threshing will last till harvest time, and your harvest till the time for sowing, and you will have food to eat in abundance, so that you may dwell securely in your land. I will establish peace in the land, that you may lie down to rest without anxiety. I will rid the country of ravenous beasts, and keep the sword of war from sweeping across your land."

Weather Extremes in Various Places

Amos 4: 6-9, "Though I have made your teeth clean of food in all your cities, and have made bread scarce in all your dwellings, Yet, you returned not to me, says the LORD. Though I also withheld the rain from you when the harvest was still three months away; I sent rain upon one city but not upon another; One field was watered by rain, but another without rain dried up; Though two or three cities staggered to one city for water that did not quench their thirst; Yet you returned not to me, says the LORD. I struck you with blight and searing wind; your many gardens and vineyards, your fig trees and olive trees the locust devoured; Yet you returned not to me, says the LORD."

Curses Revoked

2-Chronicles 7 :13-14, "If I close heaven so that there is no rain, if I command the locust to devour the land, if I send pestilence among my people, and **if my people**, upon whom my name has been pronounced, **humble themselves** and pray, and seek my presence and turn from their evil ways, I will hear them from heaven and **pardon their sins** and **revive their land**."

THE WORLD, TEMPTATION, AND THE DEVIL

CHAPTER 30

THE WORLD, TEMPTATION, AND THE DEVIL

The proceeding topics are about **the direction, the world is taking**, without a relationship to God, resulting in the breaking down of the very foundations of this civilization, shifting us towards desolation.

Declining Demographics in the Western World

After World War II, the populations of most countries increased with many discoveries and advances in medicine. Since the 1990s, populations in Canada and the United States as well as in Europe, are in decline from a demographics point of view. In Canada, the births per woman is at 1.56 in 2018 but to sustain our population, 2.2 births per woman are needed. It will now take 60 to 80 years, to regenerate a young population, if we can immediately increase the births per woman rate to 2.8. In the United States, the births per woman is at 1.80 in 2018. A young working force is diminishing in many modern western world countries. Larger families stimulate an economy. Traditionally, young people would get married; need a house, car, and all the amenities of modern living. Many young people live together and do not have children or have them at a later age. Many have fewer children because of unaffordable costs. This decline, poses grave consequences for the future of our developed countries.

In 2018, one out of two Canadians, 15.6%, is 65 years or older. The age group 0 to 16 years is 16.1%. The Canadian working force is 41% of the population. The working force in the 1980s was 63% to 68% of all Canadians.

In the U.S., Americans, 65 and older are 15% of the population. The U.S., age group 0 to 14 population is 18.7%. The U.S. working force is 46% of the population. The working force in the 1980s was 63% to 66%. In 2018, the working force is clearly reduced and those working are of an older age.

One of the agendas lobbied by the Globalists today is to consume the resources as fast as possible by exploiting the rewards of Third World nations. Since the 1960s, the United Nation's constant push of a so-called population explosion has been subtly advanced. The agenda of sterilizing some women in third world countries has taken place, a sinister trend towards eventually euthanizing the elderly and handicapped. This agenda is infiltrating our own countries as well. The young and the strong are still needed, to supply basic necessities, in a manner in which we have obtained basic goods in the past. Even with the immigration of people into our countries, brings an increase on the burden, to supply our basic needs. Many bring their families and come with skills that do not reach the educational requirement levels to place them in the job or skills that they had. It takes time for upgrading. The blue-collar trades have been in short supply for many years. We are getting closer to a point where obtaining the basic resources such as food, clothing, and shelter in the years to come may not be as available as it once was. Major changes are coming to this world.

Same Sins of Civilizations Past

Major changes are coming in the future. What is not calculated into scenarios is **the sin of the world,** about to fall upon all humanity. No civilization in the past, has escaped judgment. This one will not be the first. The study of civilizations past, all resulted in ruin, with evidence of three distinct changes:

-Turning to other gods (all deceptions of Satan)
-Change in sexual practices (homosexual, fornication, LGBTQ)
-Sacrificing of children or the weak (abortion, euthanasia) [1]

This **first** change is a result of people seeking self-centered gratification for themselves, as **their own god, craving everything** to the point of over-whelming greed. Consumerism has become rampant.

This **second** change leads people to be fulfilled through **sexual desires of the carnal person**. The entertainment and advertising media today pervades almost every thought.

The **third** change results from **fear that accumulates from increased sin,** leading to **appeasing the gods** or justifying the addictions. Abortion is justi-fied to excuse self-centered desires of sexual passions. Abortion is unknow-ingly a sacrifice to Satan.

The World Has Become Desolate [2]

Many people are not cognizant of the depth of sinfulness in this world. Living in unjust ways, aside from God and his order, precipitates a negative impact on people's lives, on our immediate surroundings, and on nations, resulting in strife, chaos, wars, famines, disruption of family life, weather disruptions, and upheaval to the planet earth. Disclosures for this time:

St. Columba (?-597) "people will read and write a great deal; but charity and humility will be laughed to scorn, and the common people **will believe in false ideas.**" [3]

Enzo Alocci (stigmata and apparitions of Mary), 1966 to the present, in Italy: "Cry to the world that the sins of men will soon be watered with all kinds of calamities. There will be revolutions, tempests, floods, and earthquakes. Volcanoes will erupt. These days left before the punishments, are given to you by the mercy of the Eternal Father." [4]

Mother Elena Leonardi from Mary: "Men live in the obstinacy of sin, but God's wrath is near, and the world will be tormented by great calamities..."[5]

Blessed Sister Elena Aiello from Our Lord, Good Friday, April 16, 1954: "The world is flooded by a deluge of corruption. The governments of the people **have arisen as demons in human flesh**, and even though they speak of peace, they prepare for war with devastating weapons that can annihilate whole peoples and nations.... So ungrateful have they become towards My Sacred Heart and abusing My graces, they have converted the world into a scene of crimes. Innumerable scandals carry souls to their ruin, especially the souls of the youth. They have given themselves, without restraint, to the pleasures of the world which have degenerated into perversions."

"The bad example of the parents, produces within the families, scandals and infidelities, instead of the practices of virtue and prayer. The home, source of faith and holiness is stained and destroyed."

"The willfulness of men does not change, and they stubbornly continue in their sins. The punishments and afflictions, God sends to make them become reasonable, are severe, but men are enraged as if they were wounded beasts, and harden their hearts against the grace of God." "The world no longer merits pardon but deserves fire, destruction, and death." [6]

Enzo Alocci from Mary, May 8, 1972: "I am obliged to let go the arm of my Son, to restrain the scandals which are affecting many good souls. Wickedness is very great. Or rather I must tell you that many millions of souls **are precipitating into the infernal abyss.**" [7]

Mother Elena Leonardi, Sept. 30, 1976: "**Women** are guilty of this infanticide; creatures are exterminated and flushed down the drain....**Men,** your women are without shame, your children drugged, thieves, lifeless homes, divorced families without God's law, and immorality. Provocative women, repent from your sins, abstain from diversions, devote yourself to prayer, say the holy rosary, meditate in the silence of recollection, and listen to the voice of my mercy and love. [8]

Mother Elena Leonardi, Dec. 12, 1977: "...because of the evil of mankind, unclean spirits have **taken over three parts of mankind**, as God's word has been abandoned, and the devil has taken possession of souls which have deserted the way of the Church." [9]

Marija Pavlovic, July 25, 1991, from Our Lady of Medjugorje: "I invite you all to prayer and renunciation. For now as never before, **Satan wants** to **show** the world **his shameful face** by which **he wants to seduce** as many people as possible **onto the way of death** and sin…help my Immaculate Heart to triumph in the sinful world…. Forget your desires, dear children, and pray for what God desires and not for what you desire."[10]

Blessed Sister Elena Aiello from Blessed Virgin Mary: "People are offending God, too much. Were I to show you all the sins committed on a single day, you would surely die of grief. These are grave times. The world is thoroughly upset because it is in a worse condition than at the deluge." [11]

Our Lady of Peace to **Pedro Regis** #3283: "Humanity has gone far from the truth and my poor children are going spiritually blind. The devil has managed to deceive my poor children, and they no longer accept the divine laws. Each day the number of those who no longer believe increases, and humanity goes towards the abyss of self-destruction." [12]

Pedro Regis #30: "Masonry, (Secret Sect) with its deceiving tactics, works in hidden ways to destroy my Church. Know, my sons, that there is **no salvation for those who take part in masonry**, for they are followers of Lucifer. Persons who desire salvation will gain it by serving only God and not by serving God and the devil." [13]

My Beloved Ones, I Plead With You

Jesus and Mary speak harsh and critical words to their **beloved priests** through many ordinary but spiritually aware people. Most are not priests but have been called by Jesus and Mary to speak out, even if it is not popular to speak out about priests. Some of these chosen ones have suffered much for priests.

Julka (Julia) of Zagreb from Jesus: "I warn you through My chosen ones and prophets, yet, I have but few zealous priests and monks, who call dead souls, with a strong voice, to awake them, **from their deadly sleep**" [14]

Melanie from Our Lady of La Salette: "Woe to the priests and to those dedicated to God who by their infidelity and their wicked lives are crucifying My Son again! **The sins of those consecrated** to God cry out towards Heaven and **call for vengeance.**" [15]

Marie-Julie Jahenny: "When I see the enemies presenting their promises… to many of those who are priests of my Divine Son. When I see those souls allowing themselves to descend to the bottom of the abyss, I tell you this: I am surprised as the Mother of God Almighty, that my Son does not immediately open the Heavens to pour out the **blows of his anger** on His enemies who **insult and outrage Him…**" [16]

Blessed Sister Elena Aiello from Our Lord: "The Church is opposed, and the priests are despised **because of the bad ones** who give scandal. Help

Me, by suffering, to repair for so many offenses, and thus save at least in part, humanity, precipitated in a slough of corruption and death." [17]

Sister Mildred Mary Neuzil (July 18, 1959) in a convent in Fostoria, Ohio, visited by Mary as Our Lady of America from 1956 to 2000: "O my Priests, My religious, what would I not do for you, if you would only let me! I come daily, laden with graces, which you daily refuse...How long will you spurn my approaches?" [18]

Mother Elena Leonardi from Mary April 14, 1979: "Bishops and priests and cardinals doubt my appearances far more than the simple people among the faithful." [19]

Pierina Gilli from Mary, February 2, 1977: "Many people doubt. The bishops and priests doubt the most, without even looking into the event...All those who do not want to believe in and persist in denying these appearances and messages will one day bitterly regret this because they are depriving My people of many sources of grace which we wanted to give them. Yes, they will regret it, but it will then be too late." [20]

Peirina Gilli, April 7, 1977: "I weep...because they do not believe what I say to our chosen souls at my places of appearance. Another reason for my weeping is the attitude of some cardinals, bishops, and priests." [21]

Our Lady of Peace to **Pedro Regis** #42 June 2, 1988: "Jesus is present in the Eucharist to strengthen the spirit of each one of us. Thank God for this. Because of the errors that nowadays burden the Catholic Church, the majority, being the fault of my beloved sons, I myself will correct them, once and for all. And this will happen very soon." [22]

Pedro Regis #52 "Jesus, talking to Peter, said: "What you bind on earth is bound in Heaven, and what you loose on earth will be loosed in Heaven. My loves, with these words Jesus leaves no doubt the Holy Father is infallible. Any Christian who doesn't obey the Holy Father, certainly is not obeying God.... Many errors are being spread within the Holy Church. Shepherds who are not united to the Pope cause these errors...pray much for priests, for many of them will lose the faith. Satan, is the father of lies, priests will be the target of his vengeance." [23]

Marie-Julie Jahenny: "Woe to the priests who do not think about the immense responsibility they will have to render to me! They are the cause of an evil, beyond measure. They are fierce against the good that I operate on the earth, to awaken the Faith, to excite souls to serve Me more faithfully." "Soon, they will be punished terribly." [24]

In Hell, It's Too Late

Blessed Virgin Mary to all the visionaries at Medjugorje (1982): "Today many persons go to Hell. God permits his children to suffer in Hell due to the fact that they have committed grave unpardonable sins. Those who are in Hell, **no longer have a chance to know a better lot.**" [25]

St. Faustina Kowalska relates a horrible experience of Hell: "I was led by an Angel to the chasms of Hell. It is a place of great torture; how awesomely large and extensive it is! The kinds of tortures I saw:

The **first** torture that constitutes Hell is the loss of God.

The **second** is perpetual remorse of conscience.

The **third** is that one's condition will never change.

The **fourth** is the fire will penetrate the soul without destroying it terrible suffering since it is a purely spiritual fire, lit by God' s anger.

The **fifth** torture is continual darkness and a terrible suffocating smell and despite the darkness, the devils and souls of the damned see each other and all the evil, both of others and their own.

The **sixth** torture is the constant company of Satan.

The **seventh** torture is horrible despair, hatred of God, vile words, curses, and blasphemies.

"These are the tortures suffered by all the damned together, but that is not the end of the sufferings. There are special tortures of the senses. Each soul undergoes terrible and indescribable sufferings, related to the manner in which it has sinned. There are caverns and pits of torture where one form of agony differs from another. I would have died at the very sight of these tortures if the omnipotence of God had not supported me. **Let the sinner know that he will be tortured throughout all eternity**, in those senses which he made use of to sin. I am writing this at the command of God, so that no soul may find an excuse to say, there is no Hell, or that nobody has ever been there, (or not know) what it is like."

"I, Sister Faustina, by the order of God, have visited the abysses of Hell so that I might tell souls about it and testify to its existence…the devils were full of hatred for me, but they had to obey me at the command of God. What I have written is but a pale shadow of things I saw. But I noticed one thing; that most of the souls there, are those who disbelieved that there is a Hell. When I came to, I could hardly recover from the fright. How terribly souls suffer there!" [26]

Blessed Sister Elena Aiello from Our Lord: "My daughter, look upon my Heart pierced by the thorns of so many sins; my face, disfigured by sorrow; my eyes, filled with tears. The cause of such great sadness **is the sight of so many souls going to Hell** and because the Church is wounded – inwardly and outwardly." [27]

St. John Bosco was taken to the depths of Hell and saw souls: "They were covered with worms and vermin, gnawing at their vitals, heart, eyes, hands, legs and entire bodies so ferociously, to defy description...they were prey to every kind of torment." [28]

Judith 16: 21: "He will give fire and worms into their flesh that they may feel forever." [29]

Isaiah 66: 24: "Their worm shall not die, and their fire shall not be quenched." [30]

Sister Josefa Menendez (1890-1923) saw and describes horrible realities of Hell : "Many curse their tongues, their eyes...whatever was the occasion of unjust trading and most of the damned are in Hell for these sins.... I saw their sin.... The majority accused themselves of sins of impurity, of stealing, of many worldly people fall into Hell, and no words can render their horrible and terrifying cries: Damned forever...I deceived myself; I am lost.... I am here forever....There is no remedy possible...a curse on me.... Some accused people, others blamed circumstances, and all detested utterly the occasions of their damnation....Today, I saw a vast number of people fall into the fiery pit...they seemed to be worldly people, and a demon cried vociferously: "The world is ripe for me.... I know that the best way to get hold of souls is to rouse their desire for enjoyment...."

"I saw several souls falling into Hell, and among them was a child of fifteen, cursing her parents for not having taught her to fear God nor that there was a Hell. Her life had been a short one but full of sin, for she had given in to all that her body and passions demanded in the way of satisfaction. Especially, she had read bad books.... On one occasion when I was in Hell, I saw a great many priests, religious and nuns, cursing their vows, their order, their Superiors, and everything that could have given them the light and the grace they had lost..." [31]

Blessed Sister Elena Aiello from Our Blessed Lady: "The Madonna then came closer, and with a sad expression, showed me the flames of Hell. She said: Satan reigns and triumphs on earth! See how the souls are falling into Hell. See how high the flames are and the souls who **fall into them, like flakes of snow**, looking like transparent embers! How many sparks! How many cries of hate and of despair! How much pain!"

"See how many priestly souls! Look at the sign of their consecration in their transparent hands! [In the palms of their hands the sign of the cross, in more vivid fire, could clearly be seen!] What torture, my daughter, in my maternal Heart! Great is my sorrow to see that men do not change! The justice of the Father requires reparation; otherwise, many will be lost!" [32]

SECTION IV

THE GREAT TRIBULATION

In 1994, John Paul II, conveyed to the world that we would be *"Crossing the Threshold of Hope,"* in this coming new century, described in a book that he published in an interview format, for those who are willing to listen.

He states: "Every Christian must be keenly aware of the dangers to which man is subject to; in this world, in his temporal future, and in his final eternal, eschatological future. The awareness of these dangers does not generate pessimism, but rather **encourages the struggle** for victory **of good in every realm.**" [1]

John Paul II, acknowledged, he had accomplished the initial defeat of visible communism, with Mary, Our Lady of Fatima. He was known as her chosen Pope according to the children at Medjugorje in the early 1980s. John Paul II, at that time, was aware of **a great storm** on the horizon: "Precisely at the end of the second millennium, there **accumulates on the horizon** of all mankind enormously **threatening** clouds, and **darkness falls upon human souls.**" [2] He received this knowledge, during visions while convalescing, but he knew there would be peace at length in the world. Mary's words contained a promise to the seers of Fatima and Medjugorje, of a certain period of peace.

Cardinal Karol Wojtyla, who was chosen as Pope John Paul II, was quoted at a Eucharistic congress in 1976: "We are now standing in the face of the greatest historical confrontation, humanity has ever experienced. I do not think the wide circle of **American society**, or the wide circle of the Christian community **realizes this fully.**"

"We are now facing the **final confrontation** between Church and anti-church, between the Gospel and the anti-Gospel, between Christ and the Antichrist. This confrontation lies within the plans of Divine Providence. It is therefore **in God's plan**, and it must be a trial, which the Church **must take up** and **face courageously**." [3]

At World Youth Day, in 1993 in Denver, Colorado, Pope John Paul II challenged the youth and all peoples: "**Do not be afraid** to go out on the streets and into public places, like the first apostles who preached Christ and the good news of salvation in the squares of cities, towns, and villages. This is no time to be ashamed of the Gospel.... It is the time to preach it from the rooftops." [4]

John Paul II has made many comments pertinent to our time and potential future, not to be taken lightly: "The tears of the twentieth century have **prepared the ground work for a new springtime** of the human spirit." "God is preparing a great spring time for Christianity," "(a) New Pentecost," "the dawn of a new era of evangelization." "As the new evangelization unfolds, it must include a special emphasis on the family and renewal of Christian marriage (and)...followers of Christ who are unconditionally pro-life," "of building a new civilization, the civilization of love." **"Even if in the world, evil should prevail** over goodness, even if contemporary **humanity should deserve a new 'flood'** on account of its sins."** [5]

CHAPTER 31

FORTY YEARS OF TRIBULATION

2000-2040

There is a gathering "**storm**" on the horizon, and few people are aware of the hour. **Charlie Johnston**, a fundamentalist Christian, from the southern United States, received locutions and visions of Mary and the Angel Gabriel. He then became a Catholic. He also had visions of the future declaring: "I was shown Pope John Paul II and was told that he knew what was coming, and that he had completely devoted himself to preparing the Church for **the storm** to come. I saw him at his desk writing furiously and traveling far and wide, but that everything he was doing, was to prepare the Church so that she would weather **the storm**. That was his mission. I was shown, **the storm** would not break into its fullness until he had passed. This was not a particular grace for him, but the reason was **to completely fulfill his mission**, at which point he would then constantly intercede for the Church in Heaven." [1, 2]

John Paul II stated, that precisely at the end of the twentieth century, darkness would fall upon humanity. From 2000 until 2038, the world will bear unprecedented hardships. Life will take time to rebound from the punishments and chastisements even after 2038. [3]

Mary, Mother of Jesus, stated at Garabandal, in the early 1960s, after the death of Pope John XXIII, there would be three more popes, and then the secrets (events) will take place. Those three popes have since passed on. That took us into Pope Benedict XVI's reign. An unexpected change took place during his pontificate. His resigning has brought us to the edge of this prophecy. Although, Pope Francis I is elected, this promise of Mary at Garabandal, about the Warning, will take place during Pope Emeritus Benedict XVI's lifetime. After the Warning and the Outpouring of the Holy Spirit, and the day of Miracle signs, will come **the great storm**.

Mary, commissioned by her Son, has spoken words of grave concern to visionaries. Prophecies from Anne Catherine Emmerich (1820s) and Mother Mariana de Jesus Torres (1600s) are revealed for the latter part of the 20th and first part of the 21st century. Early Church Fathers and Doctors of the Catholic Church, including Venerable, Blessed, and Canonized saints have given prophecies to awaken us of the impending consequences. In the latter part of the 20th century, the Holy Spirit revealed to members of the Catholic Charismatic Renewal of what is to come.

Billy Graham, Charles Swindoll, David Wilkerson, and other evangelicals, have given powerful messages of what we stand to lose eternally. It has been met with ridicule, complacency, and contempt. Many have fallen into a world of **self-gratification** and **self-contentment** with this life-style being everything, accepting the delusion that the **spiritual realm is non-existent.**

Prophecies of the Great Storm:

Berthe Petit, mystic, stigmatist (1870-1943): "The human race will have to go through **a great storm** that will sharpen divisions among men and reduce their plans to ashes." [4]

Melanie Calvat at La Salette: "God will strike in an unparalleled manner. Woe to the inhabitants of the earth! God will exhaust his anger, and no one will be able to escape so many evils at once. The heads, the leaders of the people of God, have neglected prayer and penance, and the devil has darkened their minds; they have become those wandering stars, which the ancient devil will drag with his tail to destruction. God will permit the ancient serpent to sow divisions among rulers, in all societies, and in all families; both physical and moral punishments will be suffered. **God will abandon men** to themselves and **will send chastisements, one after the other, for over 35 years.**" [5] (starting from about the year 2000)

Blessed Sister Elena Aiello from the Virgin Mary: "Materialism marches on, ever fomenting bloody strife's and fratricidal struggles. Clear signs portend that peace is in danger. That scourge, like the shadow of a dark cloud, is now moving across mankind; **only my power,** as Mother of God, is **preventing the outbreak of the storm.** All is hanging on a slender thread. When that thread shall snap, **Divine Justice** shall pounce upon the world and execute its dreadful purging designs. All the nations shall be punished because sins like a muddy river, are now covering all the earth." [6]

Our Lady of Medjugorje to Mirjana August 2, 2011: "Dear children, today I call you to be born anew in prayer and through the Holy Spirit to become a new people with my Son... despite all sufferings and trials, they are secure and saved....As individuals, my children, **you cannot stop the evil** that **wants to begin to rule in this world** and **to destroy it.**"[7] The time has come that the situations on this earth are beyond our control. All that will happen by those perishing (Globalists), will be countered by Jesus Christ himself at the time of the Warning and the continual unfolding of the ten secrets of Medjugorje. Not all can be seen at this time. "**All will be seen clearly in the rear-view mirror.**"[8]

Prophecies of Saint Malachy

St. Malachy was born in Ireland and became a priest, bishop, and eventually archbishop in Ireland. According to St. Bernard of Clairvaux, he reestablished Christian morals in a barbaric area, restoring the discipline of the Church and introducing Roman Liturgy. His meekness, humility, obedience, modesty, and true diligence defined this worker of the Lord. He journeyed to Rome in 1139; on the way, visited St. Bernard at Clairvaux. St. Malachy set out for Rome, a second time, in 1142. He stopped in Clairvaux where he died in the arms of St. Bernard, on the day and hour that Malachy predicted his own death. He had the gift of prophecy, and numerous miracles are recorded. His life is well documented because of St. Bernard of Clairvaux.

St. Malachy, visited Rome in 1139. He recognized the hardships afflicting Pope Innocent II. The Pope was at the point of believing that the papacy in the Church would not go on. The Holy Spirit gave St. Malachy, visions of all the popes that would reign in difficult times in Rome; from that time on until the end of this 5th Church age (2038). St. Malachy recorded these in a manuscript and gave them to Pope Innocent II who later placed them in the archives and were unread for four centuries. Malachy predicted all the popes from Celestine II, in 1143, to Peter the Roman, the last one recorded. Pope Emeritus Benedict XVI is the second last pope on his list. Pope Francis I, is the last. The list of incredible prophecies is available of the 112 popes, listed by symbolic titles in Latin, each corresponding to something about that person elected. This title was characteristic of the place of birth or where they lived or what noble family they came from; some noticeable character trait or personality; unusual circumstances or something shown on his coat of arms or insignia. This list included ten anti-popes from 1159 to 1447, a troubled period in the fourth Church age; at that point in time, the opposition to the elected pope was countered by a second pope, recognized by many of the people of the time. Some anti-popes were driven out. It should be reflected upon: the Holy Spirit reveals both the anti-pope and the true pope in the vision, obviously giving credibility to the anti-pope.

The popes that are of interest to our time, are the last three, who have struggled against the darkness and prevail with success.

John Paul II: "Of the eclipse of the Sun" or
"From the toil of the Sun" [9] (1978 to 2005)

Karol Wojtyla, was born under a solar eclipse on May 18, 1920. His mother died at an early age. He lived under communism for many years and was very familiar with the tactics of the regime. He toiled in factories, living on one side of the convent where St. Faustina lived. He would pass that convent to go to work. It is said, he would always fall to his knees at noon, to say the Angelus, receiving ridicule from his fellow workers as he prayed. He became a priest and a bishop, consecrating his life to the Blessed Virgin with a personal motto, "completely yours." When he became Pope, his first words were, "Be not afraid." He dealt with the financial scandal at the Vatican and was the most traveled Pope, known as 'the Pilgrim Pope,' in his visits to various nations. He was very popular with the youth of the world and held World Youth Day events. He stayed the course against much opposition. He was instrumental in the breakdown of communism and holding down Freemasonry in the Church. He died on April 2, 2005; his funeral on April 8, coincided with a solar eclipse in the Americas.

Benedict XVI: "Glory of the Olive" [10] (2005 to 2013)

Joseph Ratzinger, John Paul's 'right hand man,' continued the 'body of work,' John Paul II started. The 'body of work' that has persevered and preserved the Church in its true form, is not well recognized at this time, but it will be under stood as time passes. This 'body of work' will be 'shot at' in an organized way, taking down the visible church; reflecting on the third secret of Fatima. This opposition will continue, until a pope is able to place the Church, between the pillars of Holy Eucharist and the Blessed Virgin Mary. St. John Bosco's dreams reaffirm this scenario.

His motto derives from the symbol of the Benedictines, the olive, a symbol of peace. This peace will start to be realized on the day of the Warning or Illumination and the day of Outpouring of the Holy Spirit, taking place in his lifetime. Pope Emeritus Benedict XVI has been retired since 2013 and may still witness the unfolding of the day of the Miracle signs and the third admonition according to the prophecies. The transition to full peace will be reached after the next pope.

Francis I: "Peter The Roman" (2013 to 20-?)

"In extreme persecution, the seat of the Holy Roman Church, will be occupied by 'Peter the Roman', who will feed the sheep **through many tribulations**, at the term of which the city of seven-hills will be destroyed and the formidable Judge will judge the people. The End." [11] This will be the last legitimate true Pope in Rome, nearing the end of this fifth Church age. Pope Francis I, is the last pope on St. Malachy's list, called 'Peter the Roman.'

There is much speculation about the papacy, because of St. Malachy's prophecies **ending with this pope.** In light of the prophecies of Garabandal and Medjugorie, from the prophecies of the early Church Fathers, the Doctors of the Church, the honored Catholic saints, and the book of Revelation, this Pope will take the flock through what the Latin text calls 'persecutione extrema'. It says, Peter the Roman, will feed the sheep through many tribulations. Many want to interpret this as 'final persecution,' but there will be more popes after Peter the Roman.

I believe Pope Francis I, will reign into the 2020s and part of the 2030s, through most of the persecution, calumny, strife, and war according to the prophecies and despite his age.

The statement goes on to say, the city of the seven hills, Rome, will be destroyed, confirming Anne Catherine Emmerich's prophecies. Much of the Vatican and St. Peter's Basilica will be destroyed. According to Anne Catherine Emmerich, only the Sanctuary and the High Altar will remain. After Peter the Roman, no legitimate pope will be in authority for 25 months or more, at the end of this fifth Church age, as stated in the prophecies.

Many have thought, because St. Malachy's prophecies of popes are ending, this will bring an end to the Catholic Church and the end of the world. These prophecies were given to the world, for the sake of the troubled times of the latter part of the fourth Church age in crisis and all of the Fifth Church age of affliction, desolation, humiliation, and poverty ending in 2038. After this time, Satan and his minions will no longer roam freely throughout the world during a time of peace.

"I Did Not Come from Heaven for Your Amusement"

Mary, Mother of Jesus has uttered stark, shocking words in her messages. This is evident at La Salette in 1846 and from Marie-Julie Jahenny in 1901-1904. This language continues during the visitations of Our Lady of Peace to Pedro Regis at Anguera, Brazil, since 1987.

Our Lady of Peace to **Pedro Regis**, July 31, 2011, from, Anguera, Brazil: "I ask you to be defenders of the truth, for the truth will liberate you and carry you to salvation. Humanity is sick, and the moment has come for a great returning to the Lord. Be led by the hands of the Lord, and you will be healed spiritually. Repent, for repentance is the first step to be taken on the path to conversion. I am your Mother, and I love you immensely. Open your hearts, and live my appeals. I did not come from Heaven for your amusement. **The time I predicted in the past, has arrived**. Bend your knees in prayer." [12]

"Behold, now is the time of great trials for mankind. Tell everyone that I don't come from Heaven as a joke...." [13] "You live in a time worse than in the time of the flood. Mankind has challenged the Creator and walks to the abyss of self-destruction."[14] "Humanity is moving toward an abyss of self-destruction that men have prepared with their own hands."[15] "Take my appeals to the world, and God will repay you generously."[16] "God is in a hurry, and the moment of your return has arrived."[17] "I want to lead you to the One who is your only Way, Truth, and Life. You still have ahead of you, long years of hard trials." [18]

CHAPTER 32

THE SECRET SECT'S NEW WORLD ORDER

T he Globalists', or Global Elite as they prefer to be called, chief goal, is to bring the world under a controlled world **society**, taking away all of our freedoms, our property, and our freedom to worship; the rise of a terrifying Orwellian state. In 1900, about 85% of people were self-employed, but now, it is at about 5%. The deceptive **process of consolidation**, that is, larger companies taking over the market share and reducing the competition, reduces the price point for seller and consumers, even in these inflationary times. This takes us away from individual independence, eventually forcing us to rely on outside means of support to maintain a lifestyle. Although, we all continue to think we are getting a better deal at the 'big box stores,' we are falling into the hands of the 'financial few,' who have it all. This is a very dangerous path. We have become 'Dodo birds' to a deceptive process. **"We are losing the rights and privileges that God has given us."** [1]

The signing of the Lisbon treaty in the European Union, which came into effect on Dec 1, 2009, sadly ended national sovereignty for all of the 28 European nations that have formed a European Union. The E.U. still have parliamentary guidance for infrastructure, but it is controlled behind closed doors by a group of financially powerful, unelected elite, turning it into a business without regards for the people. They make all decisions, with the intent to gain more control towards a one-world government, without any reverence to God. There are many quotes by these people, in high places that incriminate them about their goals, but they care not, because they believe, they are on the right path. We do not hear this, in the mainstream media because of ownership and control of the media by these very people. Since 2018, the United Kingdom is considering getting out. The fees in this Union is exorbitant and they feel they are not getting the benefit.

Those who research the intentions of these governing bodies and inter-national agreements, see a merging of the old British and European empires, with the United States shadow power structure, that controls all the financial decisions for the directions of these 'former' democracies. This power structure strongly influences the United Nations, which today is for the most part, a vehicle for this elitist power group, to further their economic schemes and their ideologies without God.

The Bilderberg group is a part of this control, above governments, that has a definite influence on the direction of economic growth and humanist intentions, for the United States, the United Kingdom, and European Union. This has been growing to include Japan, China, India, and other South East Asian interests. South Africa, Central and South American interests have been exploited for some time.

London banking interests, including the branch of the Rothschild Money Trust, since the time of the influence of the Rothschild family in Germany, in the 1770s, have continued in secret, to take control of monetary systems by establishing and **controlling the central bank of each nation** throughout the world. In the 1800s, no one could resist the strength of Mayer Amschel Rothschild's ability, the father of five sons in Europe. He was quoted as saying, "Permit me to issue and control the money of a nation and I care not who makes its laws." [2] This method is used today in various ways throughout all the major nations of the western world, by a more complex financial power structure. Few people know of the control of America's Federal Reserve banks by the London Banking interests that includes the branch of the House of Rothschild. The Federal Reserve Bank of New York establishes all monetary policies, interest rates, the volume and the value of bonds and money exchange in the United States, which affects much of the world. The three major stock holders of this bank have major London banking connections. The Bank of England, still to this day, decides gold prices. The British Empire has declined from a political and military stand-point, but the monetary grip is there. Certain banks have always been owned and controlled in Canada and the USA by the bank of England.

The Rockefeller's have managed to control major areas of financial growth, not only in America but also throughout the world, including special interest, in Southeast Asia. A quote from David Rockefeller is revealing: "Some even believe we are part of a secret cabal **working against the best interests** of the United States, characterizing my family and me as 'internationalists' and of conspiring with others around the world **to build a more integrated, global political and economic structure–one world**, if you will. If that's the charge, I stand guilty, and I am proud of it." [3]

The saddest reality of the financial and political systems in place, is the rejection by people who hear of 'conspiracies or conspiracy theories,' and do not take the time to study the paper trail that exists, but laugh and think that those reading about the conspiracy of world takeover, are absurdly foolish, **accomplishing the very posture that those in high places want people to speak and believe.**

The real conspiracy is from Satan, to control the world and to destroy it, by influencing international organizations that do exist above governments.

The Bilderberg Group

The Bilderberg Group, started in May 1954, in the Netherlands, with the first meeting taking place in Hotel de Bilderberg, with various European and American delegates. The intent was to have discussions, behind closed doors, without the media, to express openly what each participant saw as critically important to a post war economy. They have meetings for one week a year, with 120 to 200 or so of the most powerful global elite, who are **well known generational families** that have been in controlling positions for most of the 20th century. Some families have continued from the 1800s, throughout the European and American economic structures.

The Trilateral Commission

David Rockefeller, formed the Trilateral Commission in 1972, after the Bilderberg group refused to include Japan and Southeast Asia. It has become a triangle commission of Europe, North America, and Southeast Asia. The Trilateral commission was instrumental in forming the European Union, becoming a prototype in Global Governance. They have also taken control of the patent process at a global level.

Barry Goldwater, a former senator of the United States, said of the Trilateral Commission: "What the Trilaterals truly intend, is the creation of a worldwide economic power, superior to the political government of the nation-states involved. As managers and creators of the system, they will rule the world." [4]

Controlling the Media for World Domination

David Rockefeller confirms having control of the media. This also confirms President Kennedy's awareness of this control back in the 1960s. Rockefeller was quoted at a 1991 Bilderberg meeting as saying: "We are grateful to the Washington Post, the New York Times, Time magazine and other great publications whose directors have attended our meetings and respected their promises of discretion for almost forty years. **It would have been impossible for us to develop our plan for the world,** if we had been **subjected to the lights** of **publicity** during those years. But the world is now more sophisticated and prepared to march towards a world government. The supranational sovereignty of an intellectual elite and world bankers, is surely preferable to the national auto–determination practiced in past centuries." [5]

World Bank and International Monetary Fund

In 1944, at the Bretton Woods conference, the World Bank (WB) was created and is managed by American interests, based in Washington D.C. The International Monetary Fund (IMF) was created by European interests, at that same conference and is headquartered in Washington as well. The World Bank ostensibly helps with humanitarian needs and to help, to grow economies of Third World countries. The International Monetary Fund, is an International Fund, to help nations in financial distress. However, these world institutions do not lend money unless the needs of a country are decentralized from the governing bodies, to privatization. Multinational corporations fill in the gap, with so called solutions. At the same time, 'swing deals' are made with the Global Elite, to obtain financial gains, in the said countries, leaving the people on the outside, particularly in the Third World.

The Bohemian Grove

The Bohemian Grove, was established north of San Francisco, in 1872, just after the Civil War, to influence politics in the United States. In 2000, a broadcaster and documentary filmmaker, Alex Jones, snuck in and exposed this property of 2700 acres, in the Redwood forest of northern California, for what it is. Each summer, this exclusive club of good old boys (men only of the elite, presidents, and other world leaders, supposedly get together for relaxation in a non-business environment. The Manhattan Project, the thrust to create the atomic bomb, was apparently conceived here. The ritual practice of worshiping an owl god, Moloch, with a forty-foot statue on the property, is one of the first orders of informal business. This was an ancient practice of worship, including sacrificing children to this owl god, by the Ammonites. This particular get-together, implements the so-called practice of sacrificing a woman in effigy that is yelling and screaming as she is sacrificed. There has been controversy over the years, as to what takes place, during these events. Is this what goes on, in the country of the land of the free?

Major Changes Not Seen

What is written here, is a very small fraction of the information available by credible lifelong researchers, revealing to us, that we are a people caught in a net. Professor of history Carroll Quigley; economics professor and historian Antony C. Sutton; researcher and author, Dr. Stanley Montieth; researcher and author, Gary Allen; researcher and writer, G. Edward Griffin; in the late 1700s John Robison and Abbe Barruel and others, backed up with volumes of information, have exposed what takes place in this so-called free world.

Dr. Quigley, reveals, this network is reaching their goal: "Nothing less, than to create a world system of financial control, in private hands, able to dominate the political system of each country and the economy of the world as a whole. This system...to be controlled, in a feudalistic fashion, by the central banks of the world, acting in concert, by secret agreements, arrived at in frequent private meetings and conferences...." [6]

Yet, such machinations remain dangerously hidden. As time passes, a distinct paper trail of political and economic inconsistencies, expose their agenda, and begs the question: When is humanity going to wake up and look at the truth before us?

The up and coming power structure that is most likely, in-with, the good old boy's power structure, was established in 2009 and is called the BRIC group. It includes countries of Brazil, Russia, India, China, and, with the addition of South Africa in 2010, is now termed the BRICS group. These countries are becoming stronger economically and claim to have had enough of the western greed. The 'Big Five' have formed an agreement, to use their own rival, world money supply or a new currency; not the Federal Reserve note, currently used as the world currency for trade. As of 2018, they are a serious contender, representing 41% of the population with currency reserves of $4.46 trillion, on 30% of the land, gaining a rapidly combined GDP of $40.55 trillion U.S. A so-called caution by the new alliance, seeks to keep the West out, with 'their' old ways; striving to prevent other countries, from driving wedges between them. They want to be partners in development and to share in revenues more evenly. But is this realistic for countries without major oil reserves? To rule out some of the Global elite, in deep, with this southeastern economy would be a mistake.

The Forbes prediction for the 2020s, states that China's economy will surpass the United States' economy in the years to come. India's economy is rising quickly too and is predicted to surpass China in the mid 2020s.

This change in future economic power will not be conducive to the western economy. The western powers, at this time, have considerable access to the oil reserves in the Middle East, through the Global Elite, that allow this present life style to continue by manipulated force, if necessary, as we saw after 9-11. As of 2018, the USA has found longer life by fracking shale and have increased their production. But fracking is high cost, using much more water and sand at high pressure to release the oil or natural gas. It has caused local earthquakes polluting underground water, methane is released causing increased pollution and other concerns. It is considered short term in many locations; one to three years.

But a Globalist plot is in the wind. By their usual (false flag) clandestine procedures, will trigger a war or excuse to go to war, to take down Israel and the USA, and to control all the major oil reserves in the world for the South-eastern economy. Interesting enough, more details of what will really take place is revealed in the prophecies.

Prophecies Pointing to Grave Changes

According to words from Heaven, a world conspiracy does exist to implement grave changes and will ignite an unforeseen revolution. We hear this in these prophecies:

Fr. George Michael Wittman (1760-1833) "**Secret societies** will work great ruin and **exercise a marvelous monetary power**; through that, many will be blinded and infected with most horrible errors...the tempest will be terrible...great confusion will reign, amid the princes and nations. The incredulity of the present day is preparing those horrid evils."[7]

Pope Pius XII (d 1958) "The world is on the **verge of a frightful abyss**. Men must prepare themselves **for suffering**, such as **mankind** has **never seen**."[8]

Blessed Elena Aiello from Blessed Virgin Mary: "The powers of evil are getting ready **to strike furiously in every part of the globe**. Tragic events are in store for the future. For quite a while, and in many, I have warned the world. The nation's rulers do, indeed, understand the gravity of these dangers, but they refuse to acknowledge that it is necessary, for all people, to practice a truly Christian life to counteract that scourge." [9]

Blessed Elena Aiello from Our Lord: "Cry out until the priests of God lend their ears to my voice, **to advise men that the time** is near at hand. If men do not return to God with prayers and penances, the world will be over-turned."[10]

Padre Pio, stigmatist priest (1887-1968) "I can give you only one piece of advice for today: Pray and get others to pray, for the world is **at the threshold** of its perdition."[11]

Mirjana Dragicevic-Soldo, Medjugorje, August 2, 2011: "As individuals, my children...,**you cannot stop the evil** that **wants to begin to rule this world and to destroy it.**"[12] This states the intentions of Satan and the followers of his secret sect who are planning grave changes.

Our Lady of Medjugorje to Mirjana, Sept 2, 2011: "Dear children! With all my heart and soul full of faith and love in the Heavenly Father, I gave my Son to you and am giving Him to you anew. My Son has brought you, the **people of the entire world**, to know the only true God and His love. Therefore... do not wander, do not close your heart before that truth, hope and love. **Everything around you is passing** and **everything is falling apart**, only the glory of God remains. Therefore, renounce everything that distances you from the Lord." [13]

9-11: 'Who Dun It?'

How do we look at Sept 11, 2001 and the destruction of the Twin Towers and other buildings on that day? There is much evidence of a set-up. In fact, the towers could not have gone down, with one airplane and fuel that burned up in three seconds. Over fifteen hundred architects and engineers with expert knowledge, in the construction of tall buildings, have signed a petition, substantiating, overwhelming evidence of an inside job. It has been proven repeatedly that other tall buildings, burning, have never collapsed. Firemen, policemen, medical personal, media in the early hours and hundreds of ordinary people, gave testimony, contrary to the official conclusions. The videos are many, where we see and hear explosions, and see multiple explosions blowing straight out the sides of the building, just below, as the building collapses in a classic-style demolition. [14] It was visible to those who understand thermite and nano-thermite; it was used to blow the towers, thus creating extreme heat that creates distinct pyroclastic flows or clouds that occur in volcanic eruptions, also seen at space shuttle launches, where great heat and energy is exhausted. These distinct clouds were visible.

The explosion from the bottom up of the Customs building, WTC #6, is more than suspect, with video showing the white dust cloud rising upwards, just seconds before the second plane struck the south tower. Explosives are supposedly set up to demolish building number 7, that first evening, because it was now faulty–impossible in such a short time. Later revealed, permission is given by the owner of the building that evening and admits, "The smartest thing to do is pull it," [15] his stated words on television. To believe that it fell, in a classic demolition style on its own, is more than suspect. The inside main frame of the Twin Towers was so extensively built with concrete and rebar that part of the towers, would have stood. This complex, was imploded intentionally, in order to create another 'Pearl Harbor'.

A final report, one year before 9-11, by a group, for the 'Project for the New American Century', P.N.A.C., reveals this intention. It is revealed in this report called, "Rebuilding America's Defenses" in Chapter 5, "Creating Tomorrow's Dominant Force," on pages 51-52. The conclusion (because of the weak economy and need for oil states: "Further, the process of transformation even if it brings **revolutionary change,** is likely to be a long one, absent **(unless) some catastrophic and catalyzing event like a new Pearl Harbor.**"[16] This group, included high-ranking members of President George Bush's staff that were also on Bush Senior's Staff. This was an example of a **false flag operation**, to make it look like the enemy infiltrated a country to do harm.

That country would then have visible, legitimate evidence for retaliation. It could then go to war against that country or countries for their intended purposes. In this case, it gave the United States of America, a pretense to go to war, to secure more oil, for America and the "war machine," which is running out. This would line the pockets of Elitists in the United States and global oil companies, spurring on many other international initiatives around the world It also was an opportunity to gain more control of the people in America, by impinging on constitutional liberties. Since this event, similar control measures are taking hold on a global scale.

Who was flying the planes? As Mark H. Gaffney states: "Is it reasonable to suppose that... four amateur pilots who between them had zero experience flying large Boeing airliners?" could have flown those planes. "There is no certainty that... (they would even be able to locate the buildings, let alone hit them on the first attempt."[17] It was revealed in 2011 that planes as large 747's can be flown by remote control. Drone planes of all sizes are now flown on missions in war zones. In fact, according to an aeronautical engineer, "the U. S. military developed 'Remotely Operated Vehicles' technology as far back as the mid-1970s, in response to a sharp upsurge in terrorist hijacking during this period... to take control of the plane's computerized flight control system through remote channel."[18]

What can an ordinary person do about this kind of treachery, in a nation that has lost control of its own future? This is an example of the changes that will continue to unfold by the powerful Global Elite and their disregard for humanity unless there is intervention.

Prophecies Expose Mohammedans, Tyrants, and Heretics

These prophecies reveal the power stemming from the Freemasonry/Illuminati. What will happen in Europe and in much of the western world, will be similar over most of the earth. Tribulations will 'continue for over 35 years,' starting around 2000 and increasing in intensity. '9-11', was the first event of the Global elite's power grab. Most people do not understand how the European and American elite are breaking down the Muslim nations to take control of their oil and other resources. Iraq is a prime example. Iran will be next. The younger generation of Muslims is cognizant of this exploitation and will rise up.

The Warning or Illumination from God will delay but not prevent some of the goals of the Global Elite. While at the same time, it will spark the Muslims to fight for their rights and cause great destruction to many peoples. Here are prophecies with clues to what is next:

St. Vincent Ferrer 1300s: "In the days of peace that are to come **after** the desolation of revolutions and wars…" [19]

Ven. Holzhauser: "These are evil times, a century full of dangers and calamities. Heresy is everywhere, and the followers of heresy are in power almost everywhere…But God will permit a great evil against his Church: Heretics and Tyrants will come suddenly and unexpectedly…and destroy everything." [20]

Ven. Holzhauser: "Are we not to fear during this period that the **Mohammedans** will come again, working out their sinister schemes against the Latin Church." [21] Holzhauser is referring to radical Muslim peoples or nations.

Our Lady of Peace to **Pedro Regis**: "In the Iberian Peninsula is the nest of the beasts, (Mohammedans) which will bring great suffering to mankind." [22]

St. Hilarion (291-371) "The people of the peninsula of Europe will suffer by unnecessary wars until the Holy man comes." [23] The Great Catholic Monarch will rise up in the 2030s against the Mohammedans.

Monk Johann Friede (1204 to 1257) "**Before** the **powers of destruction** (Secret sect / Global Elite) **will succeed in their design**, the universe (world) will be thrown into disorder, and the age of iron (our civilization) will plunge into nothingness."[24] This prophecy gives hope that the Globalists will not be able to accomplish their one world government. They will not disappear completely, until the Chastisements come directly from God in the 2030s to 2038.

CHAPTER 33

THE SECOND REVOLUTION

2020 or early 2021

"**N**inety-nine point nine percent of the population of the world has no idea what is going down.**"** [1] The newly elected President of the United States has unabashedly changed the way America will do business and is reviving Judeo / Christian values at governmental levels. That will not settle well with the Globalist. They have control of Central Banking in the world, and they decide how business is run with nations. They have subtly infiltrated educational systems, in the last one hundred years, to persuade many against God. A rebellion, against all that is right, pervades nations and is trying to dominate. The Global Elite will orchestrate horrendous events against Israel, the United States and the western financial world.[2] They will use the disguise of a false flag to create another 'Pearl Harbor' or '9-11' **against Israel** first, to create a reason to confiscate the rest of the oil from Middle-eastern countries. Israel, will immediately declare war [3] on those countries who have threatened them over the years particularly Iran.[4] The intention of the Globalists, is to strengthen the growing economies permanently, in favor of China and India and other BRICS nations. These blatant acts of destruction will permanently secure the oil for the BRICS nations. When this **first part** of **their scheme** takes place, immediately after, **God will intervene** with the Warning.

The western economy is failing, due to many negative demographic trends and cannot be reversed. The already visible social, demographical, political, and spiritual breakdown of American society is taking its toll. Although Trump has been successful in stimulating the economy, it is not what the Globalist intended. The Globalists will make vehement and preposterous decisions.

The world is reaching peak oil in the very near future. The Globalists intend on swinging the easy to process oil reserves, for the Southeastern economies, which have reached about 8 to 10 percent growth, although, the growth is slowing down. In the last 200 hundred years, they have created crises, to change power structures and gain monetary control. Observing some of the most financially powerful families on earth, the Rothschild's and the Rockefeller's have joined forces, with the Rothschild's purchasing 37% in the Rockefeller's group's wealth and management business in 2012. This is a significant clue to global changes.

This plan of a **second revolution**, similar to the French Revolution, will change the course of history for their purposes and goals, destroying the western world economy. The **first scheme**, of this second revolution is against Israel and Iran, and has been pending for many years. This is initially due to the fact, that they know the oil is reaching past peak, and those with the most power, want to control the remaining oil and profit from those nations.

At this same time, God's **first two admonitions**, the Warning and the Outpouring of God's Spirit, will intervene into their plans and will thrust the world into an unexpected direction, a more spiritual direction. Many people will not change. Without God's intervention, these revolutionary events just before us, would bring total destruction to the human race. This may bring a few short weeks of standing down and reflecting on what just happened.

The **second scheme** of this revolution will continue unfolding, **after the first two admonitions** but in a different way and time-frame. The next part of the Globalists' plan, will materialize into unprecedented destruction of New York City and surrounding area, causing a declaration of war by the U.S. and on other threatening countries, particularly **North Korea**. [5]

This will cause civil chaos, confusion, and economic devastation, particularly in the United States. After bombing North Korea, according to prophecies, if understood correctly, **China** will challenge America, sending bombs over Alaska and Canada, devastating American cities and infrastructure. They will not invade America. Russia will side with America. Eventually, China will make war with Russia.

At the same time, chaos, fear, and confusion will reign in most countries of the world. This chaos is the result of systematically planned events by the Globalists. To what degree of unfolding chaos in various countries, cities, and towns will depend on the immediate and long-term prayer response, returning to God and His will. This is a very serious breakdown for many countries, if a person reflects on similar events of the French Revolution. The whole world will suffer a similar pandemonium for a time, **until God rescues us again** with **a third admonition**.

The Holy Spirit has been very revealing, about these impending events in the prophecies below. The plan of a second revolution is intended, and the effects of the events will be worldwide, destroying the western world economy. Those who spend much time begging for mercy and direction will have the best chance to bring their children and grandchildren through this unthinkable trial.

Ven. Magdalene Porsat (1843) "There will be no respite between the sixth (universal bankruptcy) and seventh crises; the passage shall be rapid. The year 1789, upset France only ; that, which is coming, shall cause the revolution of the whole world. [6] The seventh crisis shall come to parturition."[7] Realizing the loss of a way of life, will bring panic, confusion, and chaos.

Blessed Sister Elena Aiello from Mary, to 1961: "You cannot possibly imagine what is going to happen. A great revolution shall break out and the streets shall be stained with blood."[8]

Mother Elena Leonardi from Mary, with Padre Pio, July 1973: "Listen to me and be attentive to what I tell you: A world revolution is on the verge of exploding and no human arm can stop it." [9]

Mother Elena Leonardi from Mary, Oct.1977: "The revolution has already begun a long time ago and cannot be stopped by human hands! There is a Satanic power that walks in their midst. They are commanded by a Satanic legion, and they destroy everything that falls into their hands. Deadly weapons are hidden everywhere in all parts of the world. Evil has grown, and God's hand weighs over their heads." [10] This part, " deadly weapons are hidden in all parts of the world," is especially concerning. There is a tremendous need to pray for protection. With scare tactics to cause confusion, panic and chaos, take care not to respond emotionally nor to everything you hear. Sound minds must prevail.

Sister Rosa Columba of Taggia, 1847: "A **great revolution** will spread over all Europe and peace will not be restored until the white Flower (Great Catholic Monarch) the lily, has taken possession of the throne of France." [11]

Blessed Sister Elena Aiello from Mary, 1895-1961: "Raise your voice until priests of God heed my messages; and advise men that the time is near…if they do not repent and turn to God through prayers and sacrifices, the world will be involved in **a new war.**"[12] Involving the Middle East, Israel, Iran, North Korea, U.S.A., Russia, China, and general civil chaos.

"Upheaval of a Region of the World"

2020 or early 2021

In the years before the Warning, an upheaval of a region of the Middle East will develop. For many years, nations have entered into strategic positions, like players on a chessboard, in war-ready postures in the Middle East to defend their oil interests. This will become intense. Russia, China, India, Israel, U.S.A., European Union and other nations are all trying to secure as much liquid oil and gas from the Middle East including Mediterranean areas. Iraq, Iran, Syria, Libya and other Islamic factions are, and have been, the so-called antagonists; even though guilty themselves, there is a planned outcome by the dominating nations. These events have and are unfolding before the Warning.

Our Ladyof Medjugorje's yearly apparition of March 25, 1985 to Mirjana relates of events at the time of the Warning: "It is an upheaval of a region of the world. In the world, there are so many sins. What can I do if you do not help me? Remember that I love you. God does not have a hard heart. Look around you and see what men do, then you will no longer say that God has a hard heart. How many people come to church, to the house of God, with respect, a strong faith, and love God? Very few!" [13]

Jacinta-visionary of Garabandal (1960s): "It is an invasion, well, something **that seemed to me like an invasion; something that was a great evil** in which communism played a great part, but I no longer remember which countries or what region was stricken, the Blessed Virgin insisted in telling us to pray [that it be averted]...These difficult events will take place before the Warning...."[14] Communism exists in the European Union and in America, along with many other countries but is not recognized as such. Communism is in great part, a control of the banking systems and manipulation of the political systems by the Globalists through agreements with the governments of many countries, changing the laws over time, gradually gaining greater control of the economic and political systems, and the people. Exceptionally, Jacinta is seeing an invasion, resembling the start of the French Revolution or Bolshevik Revolution, in the Middle East and affecting other major nations.

Our Lady of Peace to **Pedro Regis**: "Bend your knees in prayer for the peace of the world. Humanity lives strong tensions and walks to **self-destruction**. A proud man (Obama) will **make agreements** with Iran (in 2016). He seems to be a peace-maker, but in truth, will be a thorn in many nations. The men of terror, led by the one with an appearance of prophet (**Iranian leader**), will bring suffering and pain to the nest of the eagle (USA) and the country of the Savior (Israel). Behold, the time has come, what I predicted." [15]

"Humanity needs peace, and you can contribute, so that peace reigns in the hearts of men and women. **Israel won't take long before it encounters a great suffering**. France will grieve the death of its children and Los Angeles will be shaken. Behold the difficult times for humanity. Be converted and return to Him, who is your Way, Truth, and Life. **Terrorists are preparing something painful for mankind. England** will suffer. Georgia will also suffer a heavy cross. Remain firm on the way, I have pointed out for you. Great pain will **come to Alaska**. I am your Mom and I am at your side. **A swift bird shall fall** (An armament?). Don't just cross your arms." [16] "The land of the Queen (England?), will be surprised, and its enemies will cause great destruction. The **land of the Savior** (Israel), must suffer much..." [17]

"When Conditions Are at Their Worst"

2020 or early 2021

This upheaval, will become so intense that nuclear bombs will be detonated, against countries in the Middle East and elsewhere. Then the Warning or Correction of Conscience, from God, will take place.

More clues about the impending world crises are as follows:

Conchita: "When communism comes again, everything will happen.... Yes, when it newly comes again…"[18] When the spirit of communism rises up again, spearheaded by the Globalists, it will bring about another revolution, this time worldwide.

Jacinta: "These difficult events **will take place before the Warning** because the Warning itself will take place when the situation will be at its worst." [19] "The Virgin said that **the Warning** would come, **when conditions were at their worst.**" [20]

Our Lady of Peace to **Pedro Regis:** "Humanity is contaminated with evil, and my poor children pursue the paths of self-destruction. Israel will live the anguish of one condemned because of the surprise by the men of terror." [21]

"Humanity will suffer and men will mourn their life spent without God. The **City of Jerusalem,** will be **destroyed,** and when they go through the tribulation, it will not be recognized. There will be only a great desert. O men, turn to me. Accept the love of God, and turn away from hatred."[22] "**The land of the Savior** (Israel) must suffer much, but when **it feels defeat,** it **will defend** itself with weapons that **spread fire in the sky**.…" [23]

"Peace in the world is threatened. Humanity is heading towards a great abyss, and the moment has come for your return to the Lord. **The Middle East will tremble with a great atomic holocaust.** The moment of pain for humanity is coming. I come from Heaven to call you to conversion. Open your hearts, and accept the will of God for your lives. Don't back out. Go forward on the path I have pointed out." [24] "Humanity is heading towards destruction. The earth will shake and tremble with the **large atomic holocaust. Iran** will be devastated by **Israel.** Behold, the difficult times for humanity. Return to the Lord. Tell everyone that this is the favorable time to conversion. There will come a day when many will repent of life spent without God, **but it will be too late.**" [25]

"**In the Sinai** there will be a great event. Know that men will drink the poison prepared by their own hands. **Before three major events are honored,** (3 admonitions from God) **you will see horrors.** A Friday will be marked forever. Take care of your spiritual life." [26] The Warning will come on the day or just after the predicted atomic holocaust in the Middle East. The Warning, the first major event, will come on a Friday.

"Dear children, I came from Heaven, to reveal to you the major events for these your times. I speak to you because I have the permission of my Lord. Be vigilant. Mankind moves away from the creator and walks into the abyss of destruction. Pray. God wants to save you, but you cannot live outside of his grace. An amazing event will be seen **on a lot** located **in Jerusalem.** O men, where do you want to go?" [27]

CHAPTER 34

DIVINE INTERVENTION

2020 or early 2021

If God does not intervene at this time, no flesh will be left on the earth, just as it states in Matthew 24: 21-22. This is the time! God will intervene and change the direction humanity must take, submitting to God's plan. Divine intervention will take place because humanity will have lost its way. We will have forfeited the freedom to continue, as we have, due to near self-destruction. God's encounter will awaken and test all people on this earth for the next 17 years, from 2020 or 2021 until 2038 on a continual basis, until all people submit their lives to God's will or lose eternally.

Divine Justice Approaches

These prophecies address what is approaching:

St. Faustina Kowalska from our Lord: "Write this: before I come as **Just Judge**, I am coming first as the King of Mercy. **Before the day of justice arrives**, there will be given to people, a sign in the heavens of this sort: All light in the heavens will be extinguished, and there will be great darkness over the whole earth. Then the sign of the cross will be seen in the sky, and from the openings where the hands and the feet of the Savior were nailed, will come forth great lights which will light up the earth for a period of time." [1] This is the Warning or Illumination of Conscience. This is a quiet, still, personal moment with God, where we will see all of our sins throughout our entire life.

St. Faustina Kowalska from Jesus: "While there is still time, let them have recourse to the fount of My Mercy. He who refuses to pass through the door of my mercy, **must pass through the door of my Justice**." [2]

Blessed Sister Elena Aiello from Our Lord, Good Friday, April 16, 1954: "There must be much penance and prayers, by the faithful, to mitigate the deserved chastisement which is now detained by the intervention of My dear Mother, who is Mother of all men. Near at hand is the scourge that will cleanse the earth of evil! **Divine Justice clamors for satisfaction**, for the many offenses and evils that cover the earth. No more can be tolerated. Obstinate men, hardened in their faults, do not turn to God." [3]

Mother Elena Leonardi received a vision of Mary and Padre Pio on April 2, 1976: "If men do not cease offending my Son, **Divine Justice** will be sent to the earth, in the not too distant future, its due punishment. It will be the worse punishment ever seen in human history." [4]

Blessed Sister Elena Aiello from the Blessed Virgin Mary: "How youth lives in perdition! How many innocent souls find themselves enwrapped in a chain of scandals? The world has become as a flooded valley, overflowing with filth and mud. Some of the most difficult trials of **Divine Justice** are yet to come, before the deluge fire." [5]

Three Admonitions from God

Admonitions are good things from God. They may seem like punishment but are correction. God reveals the truth to us and gives us guidance, truly needed in this generation. For the first time in the history of the world, at the unfolding of the first admonition, called the Worldwide Warning or Illumination of Conscience, we will have reached **a point of no return**. The repercussions of our innumerable sins, are going to fall upon us, taking us swiftly **to the point** of **total destruction and annihilation**. Without God intervening, we would all perish. Satan requested of God, 100 years of extended power to destroy the Church and the whole world. Without the "salt of the earth" (Matt 5:13, all would be destroyed. The Church has become weakened. Without God's direct intervention, as it says in Matthew 24:22, "**unless those days** had been **shortened, no flesh would be saved**." [6]

The first and second admonitions, are the first and second secrets of Medjugorje, taking place in tandem. The third secret of Medjugorje, that is, the day of Miracles and Miracle signs, will take place throughout the world, within a year after the first two admonitions. These events will carry us through at the same time as the calamitous events unfold. The first secret and the second secret of Garabandal are the same as the first and third secrets of Medjugorje.

This Divine intervention is Divine Mercy. We see Jesus relating this message to us, through St. Faustina, in the 1930s. His mercy, is to let everyone know that he is giving everyone, a last chance, to find humility or a last stand alone, without His incredible love and patience. The over whelming response of prayer and fasting by humanity, is in response to the humble Woman with her beginnings at Mount Carmel, over 2000 years ago. She is the Mother of Jesus and was sent to Garabandal when the punishments and chastisements were still conditional in the early 1960s. Twenty years later, starting in the early 1980s, Mary, Mother of Jesus visits Medjugorje. By that time, the punishments and chastisements are no longer conditional. She has come to warn us of what is approaching. As Mary said at La Salette in 1846, she could see it all before her; the world is "on the edge of the abyss." After that length of time, Mary has given the children at Medjugorje, the inevitable sequence of ten major events about to unfold. The children of Garabandal were screaming in fear when they saw what is coming, especially to those who will not listen.

The Worldwide Warning

2020 or early 2021

In the 20th century, Mary, Mother of Jesus, has revealed to us, at the very least, at three major apparition sites of Garabandal, Spain; Medjugorje, Bosnia Herzegovina; and Anguera, Brazil; prophecies of the Worldwide Warning, also called a Correction of Conscience or Illumination of Conscience to unfold soon. This will be the first admonition from God.

In this event, we will see Jesus Christ on the cross in His suffering. In that same moment, we will see all of the sins that we have committed in our lifetime. We will realize, the horror of our sins, as God sees our sins. This event, will take place in a split second of time, on earth, from beginning to end. It will seem like a long time, as we are shown everything that has happened in our whole life; all the events good or bad, even the smallest of infractions. We will feel the pain of our offenses against God and others. We will experience bewilderment, confusion, desolation, and devastation, of the truth about ourselves, plunging us into hopelessness, just as the apostles experienced the loss of Christ, at crucifixion and in the tomb. We will feel the absence of God, as though, completely abandoned. There are those who will not survive the severe pain of their great sin and die.

For over two days, we will suffer in mourning; we will know, how we have offended God. This mourning will last "until the third day," referred to, in Hosea 6: 1-6, after the initial encounter with Jesus Christ on the Cross. We will feel so ashamed and not find solace, until God pours out His loving Spirit, upon all mankind. On the third day, we will know that we are loved.

Our Lord confirmed to me: "**After the Warning, nothing will ever be the same again, as we have known it.**" [7] "Some of these prophecies will not be understood until after the Warning:" [8]

Ezekiel 7: 4 : "I will bring your conduct down upon you, and the consequences of your abominations shall be in your midst; then you shall know that I am the Lord."

Hosea 5: 14-15: "For I will be like a lioness to Ephraim, like a lion's whelp to the house of Judah, I..., I will catch, and go, I will take away, and there is none that can rescue. I will go, and return to my place, until you are consumed, and seek my face." [9]

Hosea 6: 1-6: "In their affliction, they shall look for me. Come, let us return to the Lord, for it is **He** who has taken us, but **He** will heal us, **He** has struck us, but **He** will bind our wounds. **He** will revive us after two days; on on the third day, **He** will raise us up, to live in His Presence. Let us know, let us strive to know the Lord; as certain as the dawn is coming, and his judgment shines forth like the light of day! **He** will come to us like a rain, like spring rain that waters the earth. What can I do with you? Your piety is like a morning cloud, like the dew that goes away in the early morning. For this reason, I have slain them... by the words of my mouth.... For it is love that I desire...and knowledge of God." "On the third day" describes the Day of the Outpouring of His Holy Spirit on all mankind. This will unfold on the Sunday after the Warning. This is the second secret of Medjugorje.

Zechariah 12: 9-14: "And it shall come to pass in that day...I will pour out upon the house of David, and upon the inhabitants of Jerusalem, the spirit of grace, and of prayers; and **they shall look upon him**, whom they have pierced; and they shall mourn for him, **as one mourns for an only son**, and they shall grieve over him, as the manner is to grieve for the death of the first born. In that day, there shall be a great lamentation in Jerusalem... and in all the surrounding lands and in all the families." This is paraphrased 11-14 and references the time of the crucifixion but is not only speaking of the time that Jesus died, rather, this is about a future event when all shall mourn. At the time of the Warning, Jesus allows us to experience the same pain and suffering. We shall all mourn as Mary, Mother of Jesus mourned. We will realize and feel her pain, as though losing an only son.

Isaiah 52:13-15: "See, my servant shall prosper, he shall be raised high and greatly exalted. Even as many were amazed at him, so marred was his look beyond that of man, and his appearance beyond that of mortals, so shall **He startle many nations**, because of Him, kings shall stand speechless; for **those who have not been told, shall see,** those who have not heard shall ponder it."

Matthew 24: 22, 27, 34: "Unless those days had been shortened, no flesh would be saved, but for the sake of the elect, those days shall be shortened...as lightning comes out of the east and flashes to the west, so will be **the coming** of the **Son of Man.**" [9] "Be sure of this: If the owner of the house knew when the thief was coming he would keep a watchful eye..." This is the second coming or intervention of Christ in human history but not the final coming.

Thessalonians 5: 2, 4: "You know very well that the day of the Lord is coming like a thief in the night... ruin will fall on them with the suddenness of pains overtaking a woman in labor, and there will be no escape."

Revelation 3: 1-3: "I know your conduct; I know the reputation you have of being alive, when in fact you are dead...If you do not rouse yourself, I will come like a thief, at **a time you cannot know.**" This dire warning pertains to the Church of Sardis, the fifth Church in Revelation that reflects Christ's words for our times. *The Book of Destiny,* by Rev. Kramer, convincingly reveals that the seven churches in Revelation will unfold, as periods of time, in chronological order. This is one kind of interpretation and understanding of the seven churches; for instance, the fifth letter to the Church of Sardis is the fifth Church age that we live in. The sixth letter is to the Church of Philadelphia; the sixth Church age. Holzhauser also confirms this.

Revelation 6: 1-2: "Then I watched while the Lamb broke open the first of the seven seals, and I heard one of the four living creatures cry out in a voice like thunder, 'come and see.' To my surprise, I saw a white horse and its rider had a bow, and He was given a crown. He rode victorious, to conquer yet again." This event of the Warning is the **opening of the first seal** of Revelation.

St. Bernard of Clairvaux , 1090-1153, Doctor of the Church: "We know that there are three comings of the Lord. The third lies between the other two. It is invisible, while the other two are visible… In this **middle coming**, he comes in spirit and in power…as the prophet says,…so that I may not sin against you." [10] This alludes to an intervention of Christ between the first and the **second coming** traditionally understood.

Direct prophecies of the saints, proclaimed since the 1500s:

St. Edmund Campion, 1540-1581, Priest and Martyr: "I pronounce a great day, not where, in any temporal potentate should minister, but where in, the Terrible Judge, should **reveal all men's consciences** and try every man of each kind of religion. This is the day of change…" [11]

Blessed Anna Maria Taigi, 1769-1837: "A great purification (three days of darkness) will come upon the world **preceded** by an "Illumination of conscience" in which everyone will see themselves, as God sees them." [12, 13]

St. John Mary Vianney, 1786-1859: "A time will come when people will believe that the end is near. It will be **a sign** of the **last judgment**." [14]

St. Faustina Kowalska: "Once I was **summoned to the judgment** of God. I stood alone before the Lord. **Jesus appeared, such as we know Him** during **His Passion**. After a moment, His wounds disappeared, except for five, those in His hands, His feet, and His side. Suddenly, I saw the complete condition of my soul, as God sees it. I could clearly see, all that is displeasing to God. **I did not know,** that even **the smallest transgressions**, will have to be accounted for." [15]

Marie-Julie Jahenny, stigmatist: "**One more judgment** will take place before the last one, **a judgment of justice**…altogether with a judgment of glorious resurrection in peace and hope for the friends of God." [16]

Therese Neumann, stigmatist: "Our Lord himself, called it a '**Minor Judgment.**'" [17]

Four Girls at Heede, Germany, Mary appeared November 1, 1937, then later Jesus explained: "I will come with my peace. With a few faithful, I will build up my kingdom. **As a flash of lightning, this kingdom will come**… much faster than mankind will realize. I will give them a special light. For some, this light will be a blessing, for others, darkness. The light will come like the star that showed the way, to the wise men. Mankind will experience my love and my power. I will show them My justice and My mercy. My dearly beloved children, the hour comes closer and closer. Pray without ceasing.... It will be terrible, **a minor judgment**. I will make myself known to man. Every soul shall recognize me as their God." [18] At this moment in time, Jesus is taking over his kingdom, faster than mankind will realize. From this moment on, His decrees of punishment and chastisement, will bring the fulfillment of many exceptional promises.

Conchita at Garabandal says: "**like two stars.** .that crash and make a lot of noise, and a lot of light…but they don't fall. It's not going to hurt us, but we are going to see our consciences. The Warning will not kill, but some people, may die from shock. When it comes, you will know, we have opened up the end of time." Conchita said the Virgin announced this event: "by a word beginning with the letter 'A' (Admonition). It will be, "**like a punishment, for the just and the wicked alike.** For the just, to bring them closer to God and **for the wicked, to announce to them,** that **time is running out,** and that these **are the last warnings.** Nobody could prevent **the Warning** from coming. It's a certainty, although, I do not know the day or anything about the date."[19] When this event starts, we may see the light of God, come like two stars crashing, before seeing Jesus on the cross. When Conchita speaks of the end of time, she is referring to the end of Satan's extended reign in the world and the coming end of this fifth Church age.

Mirjana at Medjugorje says: "**It is a warning;** it has to be seen…this has to shake us up, so the world will start thinking…but to prove there is a God…the first Warning will be self-explanatory." It will last "a short time…" The first secret "was the worst… it shocked me really." [20]

Our Lady of Peace to **Pedro Regis**: "The **prophets who have gone,** will return to announce the day of the great Warning. God will give you a chance to repent." [21] "The **Calvary of humanity** will begin **on a Friday**, but the **victory of God** will **come afterwards…**" [22] "Know that the Lord will act in your favor. He will manifest his goodness to you. It will allow you, to see all your life. **Everything** will be **shown, as in a mirror.** God will give you, the chance of repentance. He wants to save you. Courage. An extraordinary phenomenon from heaven, will be experienced on this earth. It is a warning from God. Pray. Only **through prayer,** will you **understand the thoughts of God,** for yourselves." [23] "The day will come when people will receive a great grace. A great miracle of God will transform hardened hearts. Each one will see his errors and will receive the grace of repentance. It will be a great opportunity that the Lord will give to His wayward children."[24] "The day is coming **when mankind** will have **a great chance to repent.** God will show a great sign, and mankind will have no explanation." [25]

The **Calvary of humanity** will start on a Friday. I have often thought on a Good Friday but not necessarily. Those who hate the Judeo/Christian way, want to destroy it to the foundations.

Maria Esperanza (1928-2004) Stigmatist, interviewed in 2003: "It is very **different than what people think.** He's going to come in silence.... People will realize, He is among us, little by little.... His **first presentation,** will be like this, because in those days, an innocent person, whom He (Jesus loves a lot) will die, an innocent person (Benedict XVI) will pass on, around this time."[26] "This (the Warning) will shock the world, will move the world. Many people will believe. **He will disappear for some days...**"[27] During this first part of Jesus' intervention, He will come in silence on the Cross. It will take time for people to realize what has happened to them. This prophecy, is alluding to, another intervention of Jesus Christ. The rest of this prophecy is continued under the title: "The Rescue By Our Lady of the Immaculate Conception." The "three popes"" prophecy that Conchita of Garabandal states, also confirms the Warning taking place during the lifetime of Pope Benedict.

Enlightenment from God's Admonitions

There are **two scenarios** of Christ's coming, described in Matthew 24. He will **come like lightning from east to west,** and he will be coming on the clouds. It also warns: "If the owner of the house knew when the thief was coming, he would keep a watchful eye." This reiterates what Revelation 3:3 says to the 5th Church, Sardis: "If you do not rouse yourselves, I **will come** upon you, **like a thief.**" This is a coming of Christ but not what we thought. The Warning will transpire in a nanosecond, from the east to the west, all over the world, even though, it will seem to take a long time, in the assessment of our lives. If you are driving a car or a plane, you will still be driving, when it is over. How well you will be driving afterwards, that is another question!

Christ is taking over, more of His kingdom on earth; all that has been given to Him. Nothing will ever be the same again. His Kingdom is coming, His will, will be done, on this earth, more completely, as it is in Heaven. After the time, of **the expiation of our sins** passes, that is, after the unfolding of the ten secrets (events) of Medjugorje, inescapable by Divine Providence, His kingdom will then bring a visible full reign, of the Sacred Heart of Jesus and the Immaculate Heart of Mary, on this earth, during the sixth Church age.

According to saints' prophecies, this will bring a Catholic age of peace to fruition, during the sixth Church age, after 2038. As Mary has said, after the ten secrets unfold and are completed, there will be a certain period of peace on the earth. The early Church Fathers spoke of a time of real peace, for the ages to come."

Satan's **reign will be** broken, with little time left. Mirjana, one of the seers of Medjugorje stated, after the first secret takes place, Satan's power will begin to wane. Mary is defeating Satan, in the ultimate battle, on this earth, as Revelation 12 reveals, although, she will protect the Church, at the beginning of seventh Church age, during the time of the Antichrist, as well. Again, this is the unfolding of events of Revelation, unfolding like birth pangs.

This is a time of **welcomed justice** for many. It will lead to the end of abortion and many similar sins, rampant on this earth. This will be a gift of equal justice for Mary, from God the Father, for what Satan did to her Son. Satan will have **lost the greatest and ultimate battle**, not being able to destroy the Church in this fifth Church age. After the seven Church ages have past, he will be condemned forever to a place of ruin.

This is the **opening** of the First Seal of Revelation. John Paul II, a mystic, very in tune with the Holy Spirit, was aware of the unfolding of the decrees in Revelation. He stated in 2004, in the future tense: Jesus Christ is the only one, who can open the seals of Revelation. [28]

The opening of the First Seal, will **begin** on a **Friday**, and continues, until the third day, on Sunday. The first two events must take place during the life time of Pope Benedict Emeritus who will be 94 years in 2021. The victories of the first seal will continue with the Day of the Miracle and Miracle signs in 2021.

Jesus rides forward, **victorious**, to further His victories with more events unfolding later. These first three admonitions, begin a renewal process for those in the Church and for all those who will come into the Church, during the breakdown of our world civilization. This breakdown will continue for approximately 17 years until 2038.

Interestingly, the visionaries at Medjugorje, heard from Mary that all of the secrets are in the Scriptures. **The secrets are events** that are going to take place on this earth and are the **same as** some of the remaining **unfulfilled prophecies** of future events found **in the Bible**. All prophecies of the Bible **are predestined** and are going to be **fulfilled literally**. This means, these prophecies cannot be changed. Prayer cannot change these events. The visionaries have said so as well.

When researching the prophecies, nine of the events are in Revelation. The **seventh** is not. The seventh is a rebellion and apostasy against God in the late 2020s. Interestingly, the seventh was able to be mitigated by prayer from the visionaries and pilgrims but not eliminated.

This means, nine secrets of Medjugorje are predestined. Once the events start, they will unfold according to the word of God. We have come to that point of specific Biblical prophecies unfolding, for the continual grace of salvation and protection for the Church.[29]

John Paul II the Mystical

Pope John Paul II, was called: the great, the actor, the prayerful, the defeater of communism, and his motto, "totus tuus," Latin for, "totally yours," was to Mary, Mother of Jesus. The least recognized was, the mystical, dimension of his life.

In 2004, **one year** before **John Paul II died**, he spoke in Vatican square, on the canticles (hymns of praise, found in Chapters 4 and 5, from the book of Revelation. He said, it offers a "glorious heavenly scene" that exalts the Creator God and the Lamb, a symbol of Christ. Pope John Paul, talked about the Lamb, who is the only one, able to open up the seven seals: "**That scroll** contains the whole series of divine decrees that must be accomplished in human history, to make perfect justice prevail. **If the scroll remains sealed**, these **decrees can be neither known** nor implemented, and **wickedness will continue** to spread, **oppressing believers**. Hence, the need for **authoritative intervention**; it would be made by the slain and risen Lamb...to take the scroll and to open its seals." [30]

What a statement from Pope John Paul II, who could see the truth and the urgency of this intervention; another part of Revelation unfolding! Revelation 5: 2, 6, 9, states: "Then, I saw a mighty angel who proclaimed in a loud voice: "Who is worthy, to open the scroll and break its seals... I saw a Lamb standing, a Lamb that had been slain... Worthy are you, to receive the scroll and break open its seals."

The opening of the seven seals, is the first intervention of major changes and unfolding punishments, revealed from Revelation, at the end of this fifth Church age. There are three interventions of punishments, in Revelation. The second intervention, will not take place, until the time of the Antichrist, at the beginning of the seventh Church age. The third and last intervention, of punishments will take place, after the end of the seventh Church age. John Paul II, was aware of future events, about to unfold, after receiving revelations, during his convalescence.

Opening of the First Seal of Revelation

2020 or early 2021

The **first Secret** of Medjugorje and first Secret of Garabandal, revealed as the Warning, will take place on a Friday. This is also the opening of the First Seal of Revelation. This is calculable, by reading the pertinent prophecies. Heaven does not keep the truth from us; rather, the Holy Spirit always gives us, wisdom and knowledge, for guidance and direction.

Revelation 6: 1-2: "Then I watched, while the Lamb broke open the first of the seven seals, and I heard one of the four living creatures cry out in a voice like thunder, 'come and see.' To my surprise, I saw a white horse, and its rider had a bow, and he was given a crown. He rode victorious, to conquer yet again."

Father Herman B. Kramer, a well-known author, priest, and theologian, who wrote, *The Book of Destiny,*[31] spent over 30 years, studying the scriptures particularly Revelation, considering the various interpretations of its words. It includes, the meaning of the symbols of the first Seal that have been discussed, since the early days of the Church:

Verse 1: The Lamb who was slain, became worthy to open the first of the seven seals. One of the four living creatures, calls on John, in a voice like thunder, to come and see, who is a voice of one with the appearance of the lion. Early Church Fathers, envisioned the lion as the emblem of St. Mark, secretary of St. Peter. St. Mark's gospel was the first gospel written. The four living creatures are the episcopate: who share prerogatives and powers that God has conferred on them, comprised of the Episcopal office, dignity and authority in the Church. The lion signifies the emblem of royalty, representing the papacy, with the voice of authority, reverberating around the world. The supreme bishop commands all people, to receive these revelations.

Verse 2 says: "I saw a white horse and the rider had a bow, and he was given a crown...He rode forth victorious, to conquer yet again." In Roman times, the white horse was the symbol of victory, of domination, of triumphs, of sacred color, and color associated with the divine deity.

But who is the rider? There are three competing interpretations:

The **first** interpretation: **the rider** represents **Jesus Christ. . .** Among the Early Church Fathers, St. Irenaeus (-202), had many writings that helped form the early Church. He was a disciple of Polycarp who was a disciple of St. John. St. John's great love for Jesus, opened his mind to a greater understanding, than most, to interpret the events he witnessed. St. Irenaeus, in his writings clarifies: "to this end was the Lord born..." of whom, also, John says in the apocalypse: "He went forth conquering that He should conquer."[32] St. Victorinus and St. Andreas supported this understanding. Pope Pius the XII, also commented, the rider was Jesus Christ.

The **second** interpretation: **the rider** is an enemy of the Church who deceives and destroys the Church. Father Kramer leans towards this, which has certainly been the view of many evangelical interpreters of modern times.

The **third** interpretation: **the rider** represents the preachers of the gospel throughout the world.

The bow is seen as a means of **inflicting wounds, one at a time,** and may have been used for a long time, also seen, as inflicting wounds on the Church. The bow is seen **as far reaching** and can only **single out individuals for death. The Crown** signifies a long and continuous victory.

St. Bridget's prophecies, early Church Fathers, Doctors of the Church, Catholic saints and the Marian prophecies lead us to believe that we are about to endure the **greatest tribulation** that humanity has ever seen. The Marian and Catholic saints' prophecies certainly parallel the writings in the 2nd, 3rd, 4th, 5th, and the 6th seals in **a literal context.**

That brings us back to the first seal, begging the question: **who is the rider?** I agree with the Early Church Fathers and believe the unpopular belief of sacred tradition, passed on down to our day. I believe the Holy Spirit is telling us that the rider **is Jesus Christ,** riding on that horse in a symbolic way, to translate to us, first of all, the Lamb is worthy to open up the seals and he rides **from Victory to Victory.** This is revealed to us, not only symbolically but literally, too, confirming the information that Mary conveys at Medjugorje, Garabandal, and at Anguera. These first three secrets or admonitions are victories that ignite a temporal and eternal change, in a heartbeat to all of mankind.

In the unfolding of the **first Seal of Revelation,** that is, the first secret of Medjugorje and Garabandal, **is the revelation of Jesus Christ in victory,** riding on a white horse, with His bow drawn, having placed an arrow into everyone's heart, one at a time, individually and personally, inflicting a wound that will have far reaching and lasting effects, into the depths of every person, surrendering our lives to die to self, executing a spiritual change. **Jesus Christ has been given the victory !**

In a surprise moment that few are aware of, the day of the Warning or Illumination of Conscience is taking place by Jesus Christ, intervening in human history. Jesus is coming like lightning, from east to west, in a split second. Jesus' Kingdom will come into everyone's hearts over the whole earth, and Satan's reign will be broken. Jesus Christ is riding **from victory to victory.**

Isaiah 42:13 reiterates: "The Lord goes forth like a hero, **like a warrior,** he stirs up his ardor, he shouts out his battle cry, against his enemies, he shows his might."

Psalm 38: 1-5 (Prayer of an Afflicted Sinner) "O Lord, in your anger punish me not, in your wrath chastise me not, for **your arrows** have sunk deep in me, and your hand, has come down upon me. There is no health in my flesh because of your indignation, there is no wholeness in my bones because of my sin, for my iniquities have overwhelmed me, they are like a heavy burden, beyond my strength."

He will inflict in us or renew within us, the '**Fear of the Lord,**' the first step to wisdom. In this generation, God is going to impose His love upon us, quickly, like lightning, and intervene in our free will, because he loves us and does not want us to perish. He is giving us every chance to be with him, through His Divine Mercy. He is intervening because we have come to **a point of no return**.

Our Lord has confirmed, "All that God has given to us, **all our rights** and **privileges, as Christians** and **as peoples, in developed nations, are subtly** and **swiftly being taken away from us,**" [33] and the majority do not recognize it. As the first of the seven seals is broken open, as John Paul II states, a **set of decrees** will be set in motion.

Outpouring of the Holy Spirit Upon All Mankind

2020 or early 2021

This will be **the second secret of Medjugorje unfolding**. Revelation 6: 1-2 continues: "He was given a Crown, He rode victorious..." This is the continual unfolding of the first seal of Revelation. Jesus has been crowned and has all the victory, and will crush Satan, by pouring out His Holy Spirit **upon all mankind**. On the third day after the Warning, this **Outpouring of the Holy Spirit** may be revealed on a **Sunday** in late 2020 or early **2021**. This is the **second admonition** from God.

There are clues to understanding this day. The first and the second secrets are the first and second admonitions that happen in tandem. Mirjana states: "Ten days before the **first** secret and the **second** secret, I will notify Father Petar Ljubicic. He will pray and fast for seven days, and then he will **announce these** to the world." [34] These prophecies describe this outpouring.

Joel 3: 1-5: "I will pour out my Spirit upon **all** mankind...even upon the servants and the handmaids, in those days, I will pour out my Spirit."

Hosea 6: 1-6: "**In their affliction,** they look for me. Come, let us return to the Lord, for it is He, who has taken us, but **He will heal us**, He has struck us, but **He will bind our wounds**. He will revive us after two days, **on the third day,** He will raise us up, to live in His Presence. Let us know, let us strive to know the Lord; as certain as the dawn is coming, and his judgment shines forth like the light of day! **He will come to us like a rain, like a spring rain** that **waters the earth**." This prophecy is a future event. 'On the third day,' describes the Day of Outpouring of His Holy Spirit, on **all mankind**, on **a Sunday**; after the Friday of the Illumination of Conscience or Warning .

Revelation 6: 2: "He was given a Crown. He rode victorious, to conquer yet again." This outpouring, is a continuing of the victories, of the opening of the First Seal of Revelation.

Prophecies were revealed at the High Altar of St. Peter's Basilica in 1975 at the International Catholic Charismatic Conference in Rome. A participant recounts what the Holy Spirit spoke to him: "I speak to you of the dawn of a new age (sixth Church Age) for my Church. I speak to you of a day that **has not been seen before**...prepare yourselves for the action that I begin now, because things that you see around you, will change; the combat that you enter now, is different; it is new. **You need wisdom** from me that you do not yet have. **You need the power** of my Holy Spirit, in a way that you have not possessed it; you **need an understanding** of my will and of the ways that I work, that you do not yet, have. Open your eyes, open your hearts, to prepare yourselves for me and for the day that I have begun." [35] This is the day that people will experience God. They will know the very **Presence of God** into their life; as it says in Psalm 27, "your presence O Lord I seek." They will be comforted, as St. Paul says, he is the comforter, referring to the Holy Spirit. People will feel God's love, **like a warm rain upon themselves and within themselves**. They will start to realize their greater gifts, and those gifts will become manifest, just like it was with the early apostles, and all through the ages, by those who truly responded to God's Holy Spirit. They will realize their vast potential and will initiate a change in their lives.

The prophecies of this tandem event combine the Warning and the Outpouring of the Holy Spirit confirming God's word on **two separate days** within three days. This will be **a spiritual event** for each and every one of us, on an individual basis, as we accept the Lord, into our individual lives, in a new way or renewed way. This **will be fulfilled in a literal way**, on the day of His **Outpouring upon all of humanity**, [36] on that Sunday. No one will be left out. On that day, God is taking us even further, than the apostles on that day, by **experiencing Pentecost**, that is, to experience the outpouring of His Holy Spirit upon us. This sobering reality **will not be easily understood at first**. In this Divine Mercy, during these admonitions, He is letting all of mankind know that Jesus Christ has paid the price and that all can come freely. On that Sunday, many will turn to him, and receive **His outpouring of love**.

Mirjana states: "The first two secrets will be warnings to the world, events that will occur before a visible sign is given to humanity." [37]

CHAPTER 35

DECREES OF PUNISHMENT

2020 or early 2021 to 2038

Pope John Paul II stated, the **decrees** of the seals must unfold, or wickedness will increase and oppress believers. The time has come. The opening of the first seal of Revelation, reveals Jesus Christ on a white horse, with a bow and a crown, riding forth victoriously, to conquer yet again. There is no defeat. Jesus the Lamb, is worthy **to open all of the seals**. God's will, will be done on this earth, because all humanity would be lost in the near future, if He did not intervene at this time. That gives Him the right to do so, so that His kingdom of human souls, the Church Militant on this earth, will continue, until the completion of His Kingdom, in the generations to come. If Jesus does not intervene, the earth will become void and desolate, accomplishing Satan's goal. Jesus will intervene, setting in motion, on this earth, the unfolding of the remaining seals, that is, **decrees of punishments;** with reasonable consideration, include the fourth, fifth, sixth, and eighth secrets of Medjugorje unfolding. Not the seventh. (explained Chptr. 40) This is also the unfolding of the second, third, fourth, and fifth seals of Revelation.

The accumulation of the sin of mankind, brings wars, famines, sickness, disease, persecution, and death. Spending time in prayer, can mitigate the consequences for individuals and communities alike. God has a plan; to preserve a part of his Church, so it will continue on this earth. God has an order to His universe, based in love, and when mankind deviates from that order, there will be repercussions. The hand of God's protection will be withdrawn to a greater degree. Without the decrees of punishments taking place, the alternative would be greater than the decrees; a loss of all humanity. The **true punishments**, due to mankind, **cannot be levied out**. The punishments will not exceed the decrees. The unveiling of the decrees of punishment is Divine Mercy.

The denial of these next events happening, will be a major contributor, to a greater loss of life, as the decrees unfold. This statement is not new, reflecting on the history of the 20th century and the denial of the truth about events during that time. Old Testament scriptures, clarify a similar order of events that the Lord set in motion when people fell away from His protection in various lands of the Middle East.

In Ezekiel 14:12-23: "Thus, the word of the Lord came to me: Son of man, **when a land sins** against me, **by breaking faith, I stretch out my hand** against it and **break its staff** of bread. I let famine loose upon it and cut off from it, both man and beast; and even if these three men were in it, Noah, Daniel, and Job, they could save only themselves, by their virtue, says the Lord God. If I were to cause **wild beasts** to prowl the land, **depopulating it**, so that it became a waste, traversed by none because of the wild beasts, and these three men were in it, as I live, says the Lord God, I swear they could save neither sons or daughters; they alone would be saved and the land would be a waste. Or if I brought the **sword**…to pass through the land cutting off from it, man and beast, and these three men were in it, as I live, says the Lord God, they would be unable, to save either sons or daughters; they alone would be saved. Or if I were to **send pestilence** into this land, pouring out upon it, my blood-thirsty fury, cutting off from it, man and beast, even if Noah, Daniel, and Job were in it, as I live, says the Lord God, I swear that they could save neither son nor daughter; they would save only themselves by their virtue.

Thus say the Lord God: even though I sent Jerusalem, my four cruel punishments, **the sword, famine, wild beasts, and pestilence**, to cut off from it, man and beast, still **some survivors shall be left in it**, who will bring out sons and daughters; when they come out to you, you shall see their conduct and their actions and be consoled, regarding the evil I have brought on Jerusalem [all that I have brought upon it]. They shall console you, when you see their conduct and actions, for you shall then know that **it was not without reason, that I did do it**, what I did, says the Lord God."

These punishments of the Old Testament are not new and are similar to the punishments of the seals of Revelation. We must reflect, on what this means for the future. Will the righteous only survive, while some members of our families, particularly our children, who have been exposed to the world of television, Internet, Facebook, and the wayward thinking of the world, succumb to the trials awaiting us?

A young American mother, experienced a vision of Mary on August 22, 1983, during which Our Lady stated: "Know that it is not possible to escape God's hands. The angels must do what has been told." She was told, to relate the messages of the Five Angels that she saw. Jesus explained to her, how the **Five Angels** were poised to carry out this assignment. The first Angel will unleash, **"War**…to cause great disturbances in all places." The Second Angel will, "cause **great division** in the Church…that judgment, will begin with God's own people, before the purification. This judgment will divide many."

She was shown how the angels worshiped Jesus, and said, He is appealing to everyone to love Him, as He is being rejected by so many; and many, "don't give Him the true worship and adoration that He deserves." The third angel caused, **"Famine**...have been ordered to strike the fields and the crops; the reason given was that God wants all to share." The fourth Angel, **"Persecution**...there would be much suffering for those who stand on the side of God. **This will come about because of the division in the Church**." To be on the right side will be wrong, and to be on the wrong side, will be right, or so, the world will perceive it." The fifth Angel, "carried the **diseases and plagues** that will come upon this earth...will come without cures; that the doctors and all people, will be confused by, all that will come. They will not hold the answers...the only ones we can turn to, are Our Lord and His Mother." [1]

After the first and second secrets, "there will continue to be divisions in relationships in families and Christian communities."[2] Wounds and divisions will heal, as they turn back to God and to His truth. Some of the divisions are Christian differences, in understanding of teachings and so called end times events. The misunderstandings by people in different Christian denominations, including the Catholic Church, sow confusion, about end time's events. In the Catholic Church, many teachers of our day, allegorize the prophetic word; instead of taking it literally which includes understanding the symbolism in a prophecy. The Lord's word says: "My word is straight-forward; it is not there to confuse nor confound." The prophetic word is not taken seriously, as God's direct word to His People. Many of the **teachers of our day**, have not been taught what the Catholic Church has traditionally taught throughout the ages or disregard it as not credible. A literal fulfillment is indicated by the early Church Fathers, Doctors of the Church, canonized saints, and Marian prophecies that confirm the Biblical prophetic scriptures yet to be fulfilled. Not all Biblical prophecies will be fulfilled at this time.

The various beliefs of the other Christian churches regarding imminent fulfillment of prophecies such as the Rapture or the taking up of the Bride, the Antichrist's arrival, and the Second coming of Christ, literally fulfilled at this time will continue. This is a monumental example of error and conflicting stress, placed on Christian unity, when these 'end times' or more correctly, 'end of an age' events, unfold in the near future. There will be stress placed on the differences of opinion by Jewish and Muslim peoples as well. Moreover, there will continue to be a mix of false claims and false apparitions, influenced by the dark side, such as the arrival of aliens and distorted persuasions created on television and the Internet, causing confusion and deception. Liberalism in the latter part of the 20th century in the Catholic Church is a major problem, of people unknowingly responding to the dark spirit of Freemasonry, Communism, secular humanism, modern media, and secular education, placing constant contradiction towards God's will for humanity.

God's hand of protection and immediate blessings are being pulled back from the world. That means **God's blessings will be held back** because of our complacency towards God, since the latter part of the 20th century. We must be aware of God's intention, to make changes to this world and to this earth. God intends to preserve a remnant of His Church. **God is preparing a people.**

The **opening** of **the seven seals** will **take place,** [3] over this whole civilization that **has become desolate.** For "the sake of flesh", **worldwide events** will unfold, not upon one or two nations but on all nations. These again, are the waves of the birth pangs, of the lessening of evil in the world and **the increase** of the **victorious kingdom** of God, over this world and on this earth, just as it is in Heaven. [4]

Mirjana from Medjugorje uses an analogy to explain how God is going 'to clean house': "Women will understand me better with the following example: when we want to do our spring cleaning, we first turn our homes upside down. We move our sofas, cupboards, tables, chairs; nothing remains in its place. To someone it may seem like a mess, but when we put everything back into its place, everything is spic and span. Therefore, if we wish to make some order, we first, need to make a big mess. I can see the signs of this." [5]

As Venerable Holzhauser saw in his visions, we are coming to an end of an age, the fifth Church age; the end of conflict and opposition to the Church of Jesus Christ. He is asserting His kingdom of peace, to triumph, into the sixth Church age. This will not be accomplished by nations, only by Jesus Christ.

Opening of the Second Seal of Revelation

2020 or early 2021

The Second Seal of Revelation is the fourth secret of Medjugorje. 6 Revelation 6 : 3-4 states: "When the Lamb broke open the second seal, I heard the second living creature cry out, 'Come forward.' Another horse came forth, a red one. Its rider was given power to rob the earth of peace, by allowing men to slaughter one another. For this, he was given a huge sword." War, civil chaos, and upheaval, in every city and town will unfold at a level that has never been seen on the face of the earth before. It will be triggered by fear and panic, of realizing the loss of our life-style, in a single hour. It will expand rapidly to major war in some areas.

Venerable Magdalene Porsat, 1843: "I announce to you, the seven crises, the seven wounds, and sorrows of Mary, which should have to precede her triumph and our cure, namely: Inclemency's of seasons and inundations; diseases to animals and plants; cholera over men; revolutions; war; **a universal**

bankruptcy; (then) confusion... Behold now the sixth calamity, the commercial crisis; Commerce marches to its ruin, because the axle, confidence, is shattered. There will be **no respite** between the sixth and **seventh crises; the passage shall be rapid.** The year **1789,** upset France only; that which is coming, **shall cause the revolution of the whole world.** The crisis shall come to parturition." [7] The French Revolution began in 1789 and proceeded in three phases. A similar, nefarious plan is already in motion.

New York, New York

2021

We **will have little time to convert** before destruction and civil chaos set in. A sad day is coming. In 2007, I first read contemporary prophecies of New York's destruction by a nuclear bomb, but the Holy Spirit did not confirm it. I asked Our Lord if this event was true. Later on, while I was reading a blog and people were talking about the wind direction of the fallout, drifting westward from the nuclear explosion, onto New Jersey and Pennsylvania or going eastward towards Connecticut, Rhode Island and the ocean. I was not going to read it, but the Lord's presence came to me, a strong anointing, convincing me about the reality of the fallout and the possible directions of the wind drift. I then knew it was coming. I felt like I was in shock. I had to walk around. [8]

David Wilkerson was a well-known Christian minister in New York who passed on in 2011. He was a country preacher in Pittsburgh, who in 1958, decided to sell his television and pray for two hours a night instead. He heard the Lord speak to him, to reach out to killer gangs, prostitutes, run-aways, and drug-addicted people, on the streets of New York City, and went there to start a ministry. In 1973, he had **visions of five calamities,** coming to New York and the Untied States. He wrote a book called, "The Vision," describing what was destined for all of America, if they did not change. Since 1999, he has warned New York about **a thousand fires coming to the city.** On March 7, 2009, he wrote this, to whomever will hear: "I am compelled by the Holy Spirit, to send out an urgent message to all our mailing list and to friends and to bishops, we have met all over the world. **An earth-shattering calamity is about to happen.** It is going to be frightening, we are all going to tremble, even the godliest among us. For ten years, I have been warning about a thousand fires, coming to New York City. It will engulf the whole megaplex, including areas of New Jersey and Connecticut. Major cities all across America will experience riots and blazing fires, such as we saw in Watts, Los Angeles, years ago. **There will be riots and fires in cities, world-wide.** There will be looting, including Times Square. What we are experiencing now, is not recession, not a depression. We are under God's Wrath. In Psalm 11: 3 it is written: "If the foundations are destroyed, what can the righteous do?" [9]

Thomas Merton, was a well-known contemplative priest who studied for years in the New York area. He saw this for the future and wrote a poem in 1947, while in a monastery in Kentucky:

"Oh, how quiet it is after the black night, When flames out of the clouds burned down your carinated teeth, And when those lightnings, Lancing the black boils of Harlem and the Bronx Spilled the remaining prisoners, [The ten and twenties of the living] Into the trees of Jersey, to the green farms, to find their Liberty. How are they down, how have they fallen down, Those great strong towers of ice and steel. And melted by what terror and what miracle? What fires and lights tore down, With the white anger of their sudden accusation, Those towers of silver and of steel? ...The ashes of the leveled towers still curl with tufts of smoke, Veiling your obsequies in their incinerating haze,

They write, in embers, this your epitaph: "This was a city, That dressed herself in paper money. She lived four hundred years, With nickels in her veins. She loved the waters of the seven purple seas, And burned on her own green harbor, Higher and whiter than ever any Tyre. She was as callous as a taxi; Her high-heeled eyes were sometimes blue as gin, And she nailed them, all the days of her life, Through the hearts of her six million poor. Now she has died in the terrors of a sudden contemplation. Drowned in the waters of her own, her poisoned well. Can we console you, stars, For the so long survival of such wickedness?"

Tomorrow and the day after, Grasses and flowers will grow, Upon the bosom of Manhattan. And soon the branches of the hickory and the sycamore, Will wave where all those dirty windows were—Ivy and the wild grapevine, Will tear those weak walls down, Burying the brownstone fronts in freshness and fragrant flowers; And the wild rose and the crab-apple tree, Will bloom in all those silent mid-town dells. [10] There shall be doves' nests, and hives of bees, In the cliffs of the ancient apartments, And birds shall sing in the sunny hawthorns, Where was once Park Avenue. And where Grand Central was, shall be a little hill, Clustered with sweet, dark pine."[11] The city of New York in the future.

Our Lady of Peace to **Pedro Regis** at Anguera, Brazil: **"The danger for people will come, by means of their own hands.** People will construct weapons that will take humanity to Calvary. The **cross of suffering** for mankind **will come from Europe.** Don't get away from prayer. I am your Mom, and I want to help you. Listen to me, and you will be victorious. In these difficult times, always call on Jesus. Embrace true doctrine, and don' t let the devil deceive you. Only Jesus is the absolute Truth of the Father and without Him, you cannot attain salvation."[12]

This cross of suffering (plot) will come from Europe, most likely through the Rothschild dynasty and associates (Bilderberg group) who control the central banking systems of the world. They have control of the Bank of International Settlements at Basel, Switzerland, the Bank of England, and the European Central Bank. In addition, they hold strong connections to the Federal Reserve, the International Monetary Fund, and the World Bank. They own much of the gold in the world via the London Gold Exchange. They dictate the price of gold on a daily basis. This is where the plot, 'will come from Europe,' to destroy a country that is not measuring up anymore, to economic progress and to so called modern thinking, as they see it. These mad men, will instigate the plot, of the second revolution, of change, at any cost.

Our Lady of Peace to **Pedro Regis**: "Satan will place in their minds, to launch fire, on the children of the Eagle (USA), causing great destruction, to much of their nest."[12] "Dear children, nuclear and biological weapons, will be used by men of beard, and terror will spread, to many nations. The devil, managed to lure large numbers of poor children, away from the grace of My Divine Son. Unfortunate are those, who live attached to material goods. Know that there will be a great chaos in the world economy, and only the meek and humble of heart will survive."[13] "Men with beards, will act in a great city. A weapon of great destruction will be prepared in a laboratory."[14] 'Men of beard' is a reference to the Mohammedans, in terrorist organizations.

"**The West shall tremble** with the adverse events caused by the invisible enemy."[15] "Know, all of you that **now is a good time for your conversion**. Don't cross your arms. God is in a hurry. Get closer to prayer. Don't stay stuck in sin. My Lord hopes much from you. **Enemies will enter Manhattan**, and My poor children will carry a heavy cross. Don't back out. I will speak to My Jesus, for you."[16] Mary is speaking to New York, the United States, and the world.

"**Dear Sons and Daughters**, I am your Mom and I love you. I thank you for all that you do (praying & fasting) for the plans of God. Tell everybody that God is in a hurry, and there is no time to be lost. Return to Him who is your one and true Savior. Don't cross your arms... Don't leave, what you have to do, for tomorrow. I know each one of you by name, and I know what you need. Courage. Even in your trials, don't lose heart. You need to carry your cross with joy; for that is the only way, you will experience victory. I am at your side. Be docile. Accept my appeals and don't stray from the path I have pointed out. **Humanity** will yet, **experience great trials**. People get away from God and do not know where to go. I suffer because of what is coming to you. The **nest of the eagle will be invaded**, and there will be great destruction. Terror will spread, and my poor children will weep and lament. Seek strength in Jesus. Listen to His words and go to meet Him in the Eucharist. I will speak to my Jesus for you. Go forward without fear." [17]

The very heart of the nest of the eagle is New York, **the heart of the financial beast,** of the United States of America and the world. After this, the economy of the western world will be devastated into ruin.

"Those who dwell in **Philadelphia,** will live moments of great difficulties. Terror will come. **Poison will spread** and **will contaminate many** of my poor children. I suffer, for what is coming to you. Pray. Pray. Pray."[18]
"Don't get away from prayer. It will be on the east coast. A **giant wave** will cause great destruction. The eagle will **suffer again.**"[19] The nuclear fallout will reach areas around New York, such as New Jersey, Connecticut, and Pennsylvania, part of upstate New York, Massachusetts, Delaware, and the ocean. The atomic force of air displacement will affect the ocean, pushing the water away from the New York area, only to return because of the void of the ocean water level, causing large tsunami waves, back towards shore. The air displacement could reach many miles in all directions.

Chapter 18 of Revelation, taken literally, strongly reflects the prophecies of New York described above. After reading Father Kramer's 'Book of Destiny,' Chapters 17 and 18 in Revelation, includes all five major kingdoms of the world, (Babylon the Great, influenced by Satan), that have been conquered and destroyed by Christ. This sixth kingdom, the Roman kingdom that we live in, is losing strength. This is explained later in this work.

Here are some of chapter 18's verses: "Fallen, Fallen is **Babylon the Great!** She has become a dwelling place for demons...The kings of the earth, committed fornication with her, and the world's merchants grew rich from her wealth and wantonness...Depart from her, my people, for fear of sinning with her and sharing the plagues inflicted on her. For her sins have piled up as high as heaven...committed fornication with her and wallowed in her sensuality, will weep and lament over her, when they see the smoke arise, as she burns. They will keep their distance, for fear of the punishment inflicted on her...The merchants of the world will weep and mourn...for there will be no more market for their imports, their cargo of gold and silver, precious stones and pearls; fine linens and purple garments, silk and scarlet cloth; fragrant wood of every kind, ivory, expensive wooden furniture, bronze, iron, and marble; cinnamon, amomum, perfume myrrh, frankincense; wine, olive oil, fine flour and grain; cattle and sheep, horses and carriages; slaves and human lives..."

"In a single hour this great wealth had been destroyed...what great city could have compared with this great one... this great city, in which all ship owners grew rich from their profitable trade with her. **In a single hour** her destruction has come about!"

Major War and Worldwide Civil Chaos

2021

This surprise detonation of a nuclear bomb or two, on New York City, will be incomprehensible. The world as a whole, will never be the same, again. It will bring down the heart of the beast in the financial world and generate mass chaos. This will be a direct and visible repercussion of the sins of America upon itself.

What happens when a nuclear bomb falls on a city or area? The famous TEAK Nuclear Test explosion, with 3.8 megatons over Johnston Island, in 1958, produced a nuclear fireball that expanded for 200 miles in diameter, lasting six minutes, and disturbing the local magnetic field for about 15 minutes. A visible red shock wave reached 6 miles in diameter. This was a high level test, at 76.8 km above sea level. At ground level, Hiroshima or Nagasaki experienced only about .16 and .21 megatons. The average American warhead today is .3 megatons. In a city like New York, buildings would be leveled. The electrical grid destroyed for miles around. Trees, buildings and infrastructure flattened for miles, from the movement of air displacement. Radiation will contaminate all living things, in all directions and continue with the wind drift, carrying this poison, in a farther direction. Fires for some distance will occur. Shock waves of air displacement will cause tsunami waves on the ocean.

Our Lord has confirmed, the stock markets, the banks, and the insurance companies will fail to recover in the United States.[20] The breakdown of the financial system including savings, mutual funds, retirement pensions, and medical funds will reverberate around the world. The western financial stock markets will cease to exist. The real estate markets will plummet. The price of food and gasoline will sky rocket, with the possibility of not obtaining these necessities for a time. Credit and debit systems will shut down. Cash in hand, may have value, if you are able to get product. This will bring about much panic and chaos. People will start to hoard supplies of food, gasoline, and money, if they can get any from the banks, and other necessary supplies. The shelves at the grocery stores will be empty. Gasoline may not reach the gas stations by semi-truck on a regular basis. **Howard Storm's vision,** revealed, **people killing people, over a cup of gasoline.** Stores may be pilfered of all belongings. When people cannot get to their jobs, this will result in delays of necessary products to the customers. I believe the United States will be devastated from sea to sea and will never recover, to its former glory. The chaos and the strife will be unprecedented in America. Howard Storm discloses: "that the world will watch in horror as your country (USA) is obliterated by strife."[21] All other countries will be affected to varying degrees, but the financial collapse will hurt everyone.

Hope During the Great Storm

Charlie Johnston, grew up in a fundamentalist family, in the southern United States. He claims since his earliest childhood memories, he has known his guardian angel. He was told, "there was going to come a time, in the world, in my lifetime, **when a grave crisis would happen**, in fact, the gravest crisis in the history of civilization; that there would be work for me, if I was willing to accept it." [22] He has become Catholic and received spiritual direction from three Catholic priests for more than 22 years.

Charlie was shown, in visions, the intensity of "the Storm." "It would feel like the end, to a lot of people, but that it was not. It was God's cleansing of people." [22] Charlie states a message of hope: "My purpose is to reassure people, of **God's loving intention** for them, **in the trials** that are now breaking; to help to strengthen them, to endure, until the time of deliverance."[23]

Charlie's job is to: "Defend the Faith; Hearten the Faithful; and Defend the Faithful."[23] Going forward, he encourages everyone to: "**Acknowledge God; take the Next Right Step,** and **be a Sign of Hope to those around** us." [23]

Charlie advises: "Do not pray to avoid the Storm; the Storm is the act of mercy. If we continue to go down the path we are, then it is over. All you have to look forward to, is impoverishment and chains. If you had terminal cancer, and you were given chemo-therapy that you knew, with certainty, would not only cure you but would leave you healthier and stronger than you were to begin with, you would be an udder fool, to pray to get out of the therapy, because if you don't have the chemo-therapy, you die. Spiritually, we have a terrible cancer on the world. "The Storm" is the instrument, by which God renews the world. So if you get rid of the Storm…it all comes to a halt. So, that's why I say, people talk about mitigating this… the storm is part of God's mitigation."[24]

Charlie is only allowed to reveal a brief summary of events, from the visions. Events stated, are generally: "I see the world, in disastrous straits, economy collapsing, global civil war fought along cultural lines."You have the obligation, to defend yourself and your neighbor. We have the right to: "Faith, Family, and Freedom."[24]" When the crash comes…, 2 to 4 months of chaos, the greatest killer will be panic. It is the beginning of the most desperate and furious part of the Storm.., a new interim situation must emerge…, several upheavals in leadership. Once some vestigial stability is reached… to restore some confidence." [24]

"Once that has been done, **Islam** must be confronted and defeated. The surprise will be, how quickly it falls, once it is confronted. Helping, will be Our Lady of Tepeyac, the Mother of Conversion. There will be a mass conversion, in Islam, largely driven by its women... But it will not begin to happen, until we take it seriously and confront it directly. But the west must take care, to wage war against Islam, while recognizing the longing of most Muslims for God (pray for them) If... the west alienates Muslims, their culture may well fall..." [25]

"The great challenge which is **China**, will rise before us, revealing Islam, to have been merely, a cub of a challenge. That is when things get really rough. The battle with China, is where Christianity ill functionally be re-unified, and people will get a firm idea, of how small we are, and how hopeless every thing is, without reliance on God. At some point, Russia and America will become steadfast allies, in the fight against China. That will ultimately contribute dramatically, to the reunification of Christianity. The global war will get more and more desperate...stalemated to a certain extent, like the trench warfare of WWI. The struggle, will become so desperate that all will lose hope, that peace, order and stability can ever be restored to the world. The battle is not winnable. At every juncture, new terrors will be unveiled. And at every new terror, new graces will be poured forth, if we keep to our post, with stead-fast resolve." [25] Praying and showing leadership.

"Throughout the Storm, Satan's agents will be felt, in political and religious spheres. He would destroy the whole thing from within, were it possible. But it is not. While we are busy congratulating ourselves, on the victory [against Islam], we will see how powerful and determined, to take world-control, China has become. That is the final battle of this period. We will not win it. Rather, we must fight with fortitude and endure." [26]

War Will Take Place

2021

Whatever the scenario is, after New York's destruction, "**war will take place.**"[27] **Our Lady of Peace** to **Pedro Regis**: "Humanity is going towards an abyss of destruction that people have prepared with their own hands. Bend your knees in prayer and God will save you. I am your Mom, and I know what awaits you. Take my appeals to all. Don't keep silent. God needs your witness. Those who make my messages known, will not experience eternal death. Fully trust in the goodness of the Lord, and follow me on the path, I have pointed out... Behold, **mankind is heading towards** a great **transformation,** and **people will not have an explication**. The times have come which I have announced in the past."[28]

Charlie Johnston states, after visions of Mary, Mother of Jesus, and Archangel Gabriel: "**North Korea** is the dragon's tail... China is a very bad actor. You will know for certain that "the storm" **has broken in its fullness** when it comes through North Korea."[29] "The Storm...will break through North Korea, but will not be centered in North Korea."[30]

Our Lady of Peace to **Pedro Regis**: "The eagle (U.S.) will not fly tranquilly. Its nest will tremble, and there will be great fear. Bend your knees in prayer. Humanity is very tense, and **the moment has come for its return to the Lord**."[31, 32] "Know that humanity will live moments of great difficulties. This fire (Nuclear bomb) will dim the light, and there will be a big bang. Pray to be winners. A great tragedy will occur in **Korea.** Men bring destruction by their own hands. Listen to my appeals. I don't want to force you, but listen with love to what I tell you. The **leader** of a great nation (USA) **will suffer an attack**. The danger of a third world war becomes real. Bend your knees in prayer."[33]

"**Russia** will make an agreement, and this agreement will appear as, something painful for men."[34] "China and Russia are heavy stones to humanity."[35] "Russia will stumble and face a heavy cross."[36]

"Dear children, this is the time of your return. Do not remain on the sidelines. The day will come when the sun and the moon will no longer fulfill their travel, as in your days. Your eyes will see the signs, announced by my Son, Jesus. Bend your knees in prayer, asking the Lord's mercy for all of you. The dragon (**China**) will meet the eagle (**USA**) and launch fire on their children, causing the destruction of a large part of its nest."[37] "Dear children, bend your knees in prayer. **World peace is threatened**. I suffer for what awaits you. The day will come when the furious dragon (**China**) will launch fire on the nest of the bear (**Russia** and great suffering will be experienced, my poor children. Behold, the time has come, for me predicting it. The evil penetrates many hearts, and many of my poor children, go blind, spiritually."[38]

Charlie Johnston: "China is the real center and the real implacable enemy of western civilization. China may already be the most militarily strong nation in the world. It will be the challenge posed by China, once she is fully unmasked, that drives Russia into the west and common cause with America." [39]

"It is the decisive battle between good and evil. It will be followed by a great period of Christian unity, peace, and authentic prosperity. That is what will come..., after we have been through the greatest crisis in the history of Western Civilization. Governments will fall, including our own (USA), and nations will be transformed, as the **global civil war** that will mark this period, sets in. The first wave will be the struggle with **Islamic Jihad**. The surprise, will be how easily it topples, once we take the challenge seriously–and prayerfully go to Our Lady of Tepeyac [Guadalupe], praying for the conversion of the Muslims....

While we are busy congratulating ourselves on our decisive victory, the real challenge will rise. **China will seek to conquer the world**–and many will be stunned, at how carefully and completely it has prepared its assault. We (USA) will not prevail over that one. Rather, Russia, will ultimately become our most steadfast ally, and in our weakened state, all we can accomplish, is to endure until rescue comes.." [40]

The Globalists, are encouraging other nations, particularly China, to gain control economically and militarily, and to surge ahead of the Western economy in all ways possible. China is considered more powerful, because America is imploding and the Globalists are letting go of the western economy.

"Remain Where God has Placed Us"

"Remain where God has placed us" is the advice of Father Nectou (1700s) during the frightful crisis. He relates to persevere in prayer. Many will panic, but the frightful crisis will be of short duration. Though, this will not be the case for the whole area around New York. Millions will die after New York is leveled; those left, will leave that area. Strategically, the best place for most on the planet is to remain where God has placed them. The prayers of many people, allow the Holy Spirit's presence. This does not mean, there won't be panic where we are at, but if people are prepared with food and water in their homes, they will be able to get through, by persevering in prayer.

Father Nectou, S. J. (1760s) states: "When those things come to pass... then will **such confusion reign upon the earth** that people will think God has permitted them to have their own contrary will, and that the providence of

God, is not concerned about the world. The confusion will be so general that men will not be able to think aright, as if God had withheld His Providence from mankind. During the worst crisis, the best that can be done would be to **remain where God has placed us**, and **persevere in fervent prayers**... This disaster will come to pass shortly after the power of England, begins to wane." [41]

This prophecy from **Fr. Nectou** is very important. This **initial crisis** will continue for **about one or two months** of an **incomparable worldwide cataclysmic break-down**, so the best place, for most people, is to stay where you live. The crises will bring hardships in obtaining basic necessities. Many will leave to safer places, but in general, most should stay where they are. Hopefully, people will show leadership and take proper direction, with God in mind. As this time passes, God will intervene again, and things will settle down.

Stock Up Food, Water, and Other Necessities

Our Mormon neighbors have been wise enough to store supplies of whole grains and dried foods in their homes, to last for as long as seven years traditionally, in anticipation of periods of drought or tribulation, in years past. Today, supplies of food stored, are recommended to last three months, one year, and two years if you can afford it and have the space. An amount of cash on hand is recommended as well, but when the shelves are empty, it will have little value. It is also amazing, in Mormon oriented areas and states such as Utah, warehouses of food are stockpiled for emergency use. This tradition is part of their normal lives.

FEMA in the USA, recommends emergency long-term stored foods, for three months to one year. They give recommended food volumes to store, per person, per year, with different package sizes, depending on age and weight of a person. A simple supply of four basic survival foods includes: .5–5.4 kilograms of salt, 16–45 kilograms of honey or sugar, 27–45 kilograms of powdered milk, and 91–166 kilograms of whole grain wheat for one year, for one person. Dried foods have a longer shelf-life than canned foods, and is the safer, long-term choice. [42]

Clean water is the number one necessity. Yes, you would need greens and other vegetables, before that year has passed, to maintain health. There are many natural greens available from the earth, but the awareness of this knowledge is limited, to the few who have researched it. Many weeds, yes weeds and other native plants can be eaten that provide nutritional health, found around cities and in the country.

In fact, look at *www.eattheweeds.com.* and *www.northernbushcraft.com*

are pertinent to U.S.A. and Canadian natural edible plants.[43] There are many books on wild edible plants.[44] Greens and other vegetables can be dehydrated, or dried in the sun, or in a warm upstairs room, then stored in a dry/low moisture room. These can be stored in food grade sacks, bags, wooden boxes, food grade plastics, or glass containers in a cool dry place. Salt, honey, and whole grains, will keep indefinitely, if stored at room temperature. Whole grains and honey can be purchased from neighboring farmers such as Hutterite Brethren Colonies. Whole grains and honey found in the Egyptian pyramids kept for over 3000 to 4500 years in dry conditions. Keep it simple, as possible. Sugar needs to be dry and bug-proof. Gardens must be grown in the future. Obtain seeds, and learn how to reproduce seed. You can start now.[45]

Growing up in the 1950s and 1960s on a farm and hearing the stories of grandparents, in the early 20th century, brings historical memories of a self-sustaining living. Many lived on the land and grew gardens, storing all their produce, for the whole year. Grains, eggs, and animal meats, were available on the farm, with no real reason to go to town, except, for salt or sugar and other imported necessities at intervals. [45]

According to the prophecies, when New York goes down, a mass panic will unfold in the United States and will trigger a similar response in other neighboring countries, and the rest of the world. For **the first few months**, there will be, no guarantee that anything will be normal when it comes to food supply and other basic needs. **This break-down will affect many nations**, forcing us to become more self-sufficient.

Canada relies heavily on the U.S.A., for much of its produce, processed foods, and other products made, particularly during the winter. If the USA is going to be obliterated by strife, will Canada be able to import all the necessary produce, foods, and other products, normally transported to Canada, to supply their needs?

Growing fruits and vegetables on plots of land, possibly rented or share cropped from neighboring farms, will become available. In Canada, having hot-houses will be necessary, for growing above ground produce. Root vegetables will grow outside. **Knowing how to grow vegetable gardens**, will be the most important knowledge and resource management to have in the future years. Community cooperation will be very important, using the local maximum potential of your local area, for growing foods. The most important needs will be food, clothing, shelter and warmth, particularly in the northern climates.[46]

The United States will suffer first and foremost, but with bank systems and the whole economy collapsing, it will affect its neighbors first, and then, the rest of the world. The Lord has confirmed to me that money will not be obtained for a time. [47] What that will look like for Canada and Mexico, until stability returns, are unknown but cannot be ignored. Most cities will be places of riots, destruction, and discontent at a massive local level, not seen before because of the lack of food and other basic necessities, causing a self-preservation mode of survival kicking in. This will lead to dangerous situations that should be avoided. The loss of life savings, in different investments, will be devastating. The banking systems will surely shut down, until banking institutions know where they stand. That could take time.

Julian Assange of Wikileaks states: "We all think of the Internet, as some kind of Platonic realm where we can throw out ideas, and communications, and web pages, and books, and they **exist somewhere out there**. Actually, they exist on web servers in New York, or Nairobi, or Beijing, and information comes to us, through satellite connections or through fiber-optic cables."[48] Only **three** major memory banks in the world? What happens when New York is destroyed? What will governments do when this system or part of this system goes down? Banks are connected everywhere on this Internet highway.

We already see mass protests and dissatisfaction with the lack of government response, to people's needs because of Globalists' decisions. Scenarios of hardship and breakdown have taken place in Venezuela. Maria Esperanza lived in the 1990s in Venezuela. Major companies closed their doors and moved employees out of the country. Schools closed down. Oil supplies were not exported. Venezuela continues to degrade, as a nation. Maria stated that what happened there, **is a precursor** to **what will happen in America**. It will be felt in surrounding countries. To what intensity, only God knows. **Do not feel embarrassed** or foolish, **stocking up foods**. Go to the bank, and **ask for your money** in cash. It may take a week to get it. I believe if the government of a country is still stable, cash will still have value. This is about wisdom. In Proverbs, it says: "The ant prepares for the storm" by gathering up many sticks, so his home is not washed away. In Matthew 25, Jesus talks about the five wise virgins who filled their lamps, and the five foolish virgins who went without and were left out. Will it be too late to get supplies? It is time to pray about these decisions.

Charlie Johnston reveals: "Many ask what to do as the storm gets more violent. Do not come up with some grandiose human scheme. That sort of thing is what brought us to this point. God loves simplicity. Simply take the next right step and be a sign of hope to those around you. There will be much panic and chaos, particularly as the technology, we so rely on, fails. Be prudent, but do not take excessive precautions, thinking you can exempt yourself from the consequences of the storm. The main reason we have brought this on ourselves, is, because we think we are sufficient to ourselves. If you try to out-maneuver God, he will show you, who is the Creator and who is the created."[49]

"Grow a garden, put in some fruit trees and learn how to can fruits and vegetables, get a supply of wood, and a place to burn it. Things like that are sufficient. Help your neighbor, reach out to him. Form little communities that work together to help each other. If a stranger comes to you, earnestly seeking help, **do not turn him away**, for God will provide. But if one comes to assault you, your family, your neighbors, **use sufficient force** to turn him away, and **defend yourselves**. Jesus told his disciples, in Luke 22: 36-38 that it was time for them to arm themselves. He knows. You have a dual obligation, neither to initiate violence nor to sit idly by and allow those around you, to suffer it." [49]

A Step–Down Decree

At the opening of each seal of Revelation, God will decree, a continual step down, step down, transition of our society, returning to God and to the land. This stepping down will continue until people on earth, are living in a sustainable harmony, at equilibrium with our earth's natural ecosystem.[50] This physical earth cannot take any more pollution, degradation, and pillage; of the land, sea, and air; from the agricultural, maritime, and industrial production abuses. The natural resources of the land will be exhausted for our children, grandchildren, and great grandchildren. God is taking action.

The world system breaking down, will cause a stepping down to a simpler way of living, during the unfolding of the events of the seals, until 2038. This will be a long painful process for many, and many will lose their lives. This is why it is important to be aware and prepare. Denial of these inevitable events will bring about a greater loss of life.

God knows, it cannot be a sudden change. It will take time. God allows us to still have free will, and the Holy Spirit will work with us through that freedom. This is one reason for the step down process, allowing people time to consider negotiating the changes; with time to prepare and adjust to a different lifestyle, similar to our grandparent's and great-grandparent's experience. For most of us, it will be a very difficult change because of the lack of under-standing of agricultural knowledge needed for this change; in learning how to use the resources and to have the land, to implement these changes. There is still a volume of resource information and resource knowledge out there. With the desire for healthy organic foods, many have taken interest, in self-produced gardens and other means of production, such as having a few chickens, even in the cities. This is encouraging.

We also, must remind ourselves, in distant lands, people still live close to the land, particularly in warmer climates. People still live on the land in Northern Canada and northern Asian climates. In northern, semi-colder climates like Canada and the northern United States will bring the greater challenge, for those who have lived the good life.

Prophecies of Worldwide Chaos

The war and chaos, will bring death and destruction, particularly, to individuals who fear and panic, demanding a self-centered satisfaction, for themselves. Many will suddenly realize, they have lost the good life and all their dreams of a life, like the last generation. Life will change. According to saints' prophecies, **deadly weapons** are **hidden** in **different parts** of the world. This is part of the Globalists' scheme, to provoke panic, and to direct their plots of change, obtaining greater control of society.

Father Nectou S. J. : "**A great multitude** of persons **shall perish** in these calamitous times, but the wicked shall never prevail. They indeed, shall conspire for the destruction of the Church, but time shall not be allowed them because this frightful crisis, shall be of short duration. When all will be considered lost, all will be found safe." [51]

Our Lady of Peace to **Pedro Regis**: "Humanity is heading towards destruction that men have prepared with their own hands. **Millions** of people will carry a heavy cross, and millions **will die**. Death will cross most continents, and parts of the earth will be destroyed. No greater pain has existed. Bend your knees in prayer." [52]

Charlie Johnston for the USA: "This war, will take place all over. It will **involve terrorism**...but goes beyond that and will **include persecution**... is a definitive struggle, between the values of Christian Western civilization and forces that want to destroy that. It is a battle for the soul of the world..." [53]

Mother Elena Leonardi from Padre Pio, 1975: "...a revolution, **many bombs exploding** causing great destruction."[54] "**Terrible anarchy** will break loose because of what will happen...Italy will be purified in blood...a great revolution will break out, and the streets will be streaming with blood."[55]

Mother Elena Leonardi from Jesus 1977: "The revolution will make havoc in Rome, and the other nations and provinces. It will be worse than Babylon. The damnation of souls!" [56]

Mother Elena Leonardi from Mary, 1977: "The revolution has already begun...and cannot be stopped by human hands! There is a satanic power which walks in their midst....Deadly weapons are hidden everywhere, in all parts of the world. Evil has grown. God's hand, weighs over their heads."[57]

Sister Rosa Columba (Asdenti) of Taggia (d1847)"A great revolution will spread over all of Europe. A lawless democratic spirit of disorder shall reign supreme throughout all Europe. There will be a general over-throw, and there shall be a great confusion of people against people, and nations against nations, with clashing of arms and beating of drums..." [58]

Charlie Johnston: "This is not the end, and good will come of it. There will be a moment of sheer desperation." [59]

The Mohammedans Will Rise Up

The Globalists, have been in the process of stealthily, infiltrating Muslim countries, for their purposes, by changing government regimes, to take control of their resources, particularly the oil, and forcing these nations, to submit to using Globalists' central banks. We see and hear of the uprising of the Muslim people, to defeat the 'great Satan' (America) and the 'small Satan' (Israel) as they see it; **non-Muslim's are the infidels that must be exterminated**. Christians and non-Christians, alike, will suffer tremendous punishments, by the Muslim people in some areas, particularly in Europe, and in the Middle East, as they did from the seventh century, until about the seventeenth century. God is going to **use this for His purposes**.

Ven. Holzhauser: " The Mohammedans are to come again, working out their sinister schemes... " [60]

Our Lady of Peace to **Pedro Regis**: "The day will come when the **furious** Lion (Mohammedans) will lay at the feet of the dragon. A union of beasts will bring great suffering to my poor children."[61] "Bearded men (Mohammedans) **are greatly betrayed**, and their great fury will rise against many nations. **The one** who spreads terror **will be caught**, and that nation looked up to (USA), will be **terribly struck**." [62]

"A wicked man will appear because its believers will experience great suffering. Sana'a is the capital of this country (Yemen). Bend your knees in prayer."[63] The 'bearded men', are Muslim's of many Middle Eastern countries who have been taken advantage of, by America and the Globalists, for their oil, and used **as scapegoats**, for their plots of destruction, in America and the world, giving the Elite, more monetary and political control of all nations. Mary, Mother of Jesus sees the truth.

"**It will begin on the coast of Portugal**. It will be repeated in the Holy land. An army will march across Europe, leaving a trail of destruction and death."[64] "A **frightening event** will happen in Spain and will spread to various countries of Europe.

France will drink a cup, bitter with pain, which I announced in the past."[65] "A devastating force will cross Europe, causing destruction and death."[66] "The **men of terror**, will cause destruction and death, in various parts of the world. A famous statue is broken (Liberty?)." [67] "The malevolent action of men will cause death and destruction in various nations. Return to the Lord. Answer to his call, to be saved. A wicked man will command a large invasion. Anger and the desire for death, are in the hearts of men."[68] "A **large army** will **depart from Mecca**, and wherever they go, they will leave a trail of destruction and death. The wickedness of men will be so great, on the land; the Lord will anticipate the Day of Judgment."[69] "The men of terror will come to the Vatican. The square will be filled with corpses. Mankind will see the evil actions of the men of beard. The Coliseum falls to the ground. Know that the

Lord is grieved because of the sins of men." [70] "The furious lion will attack the Church and will cause great suffering to my poor children. The heads will unite and will plan a major attack. I suffer, for what you do not expect."[71]

Charlie Johnston: "In the early years, Jihad, **will seem** the great battle. Certainly, it is the most showy and determined, but it will collapse more quickly and easily than people can imagine. Once we understand, it is a battle that **we can't negotiate** our way out of." [72]

Chaos in the Church

Some prophecies are certain; the secret sect will still be at work to destroy. There will be enemies that will continue to rise up against the Church, inside the Church, and outside the Church, until the chastisements come, from God, destroying those "tyrants and heretics." After the Warning, many members of other churches will see the real connection, through witnessing of the first three admonitions, **announced by Mary** in the 20th century, **to the Catholic Church** and **to the world**. With the return of Anglicans, already taking place, many members of other church denominations will come back to the original Church. Jesus, the Creator of the Universe, is going to chastise His Church, until it is in poverty and humility, becoming One Church.

Blessed Sister Elena Aiello: "You cannot possibly imagine what is going to happen. A great revolution shall breakout, and the streets shall be stained with blood. The Pope's sufferings on this occasion, may well be compared to the agony that will shorten his pilgrimage on earth. **His successor shall pilot the boat during the storm**. And so, the wicked shall perish, according to the inexorably severity of Divine Justice. If possible, publish this message throughout the world, and admonish all the people, to do penance and to return right away to God."[73] From Our Lady who tells us that Pope Benedict, may pass on during the months of World Revolution or may pass on, just shortly after this time. His successor, Pope Francis I, who is Peter the Roman and is the last Pope of this Fifth Church age who takes the boat (Church) through many trials and tribulations.

Our Lady of Peace to **Pedro Regis:** Wise men will announce new discoveries about the life of **my Son, Jesus**. Take care. Do not let the Devil deceive you. Do not let your faith be shaken. The **truth of my Jesus is in the Gospel**. Listen to what He teaches us, the true teaching of the Church, of My Jesus. Accept the teachings of the Pope. The demon will cause great confusion, but I urge you, to stay with the truth. A big tree will be cut, and its bad fruit shall not multiply. **The truth is kept fully, only in the Catholic Church.**" [74]

CHAPTER 36

SORROWFUL EVENTS UPON THE EARTH

S ome of these prophecies below, may include the chaos erupting in the first round of world break-down. Many other events may unfold, such as, stronger earthquakes, increased volcanic activity and other natural disasters, between now and 2038. This is only a small portion of the prophecies that are available, recorded here from Our Lady of Peace to Pedro Regis in Anguera, Bahia, Brazil. When Our Lady of Peace, mentions a town or city, and there are many towns or cities of the same name, she may be referring to one or more than one of the locations.

Canada

Our Lady of Peace to **Pedro Regis**: "**Chilliwack** (only one) will be in ruins. Do not stand idly by. This is the time of grace. I am your Mother, and I want your conversion."[1] Is an earthquake going to affect the Harrison lake dam? "**Vancouver** (2 others) will carry a heavy cross. Now are difficult times for humanity." [2]"I did not come from Heaven as a joke. What you have to do, is not leave it for tomorrow. God is in a hurry. **Kelowna** (only one city) will live moments of great affliction and my poor children will weep and lament. I grieve for what is coming to you. Do not retreat." [3] Will earthquakes affect this area?

"Courage, you will yet, to see horrors on this earth. **The sons of Regina** (only one city) **will weep because of the suffering of Aurora** (many places). This is the time of your return. Do not leave what you have to do, for tomorrow."[4] **Aurora**, Ontario has the largest auto and truck parts manufacturing in North America, called Magna International. Magna has stated grave concerns about decisions made at Canada's political levels. Regina is the largest central area of grain production on the prairies in Canada. Parts may not be available in the future.

"**Hamilton** (12 others) will see the death of its people, and people will weep and lament." [5] "Bend your knees in prayer. **When you are separated from prayer, you become the target of the enemy.** I am your Mother, and I came from Heaven to help you. Your lack of faithfulness takes you into slavery. You belong to the Lord. It was for you that my Jesus died on the cross.

Listen to me. Now is the time for your decision. Go forward without fear. A painful event will occur in **Montreal** (or Montreal, France)."[6]

"Fill yourselves with the love of the Lord, for love is stronger than death and more powerful than sin. Don't get away from prayer. Only by prayer will you attain peace. Accept the Gospel of My Son Jesus. Let the words of My Son transform you. Your full happiness is in Jesus. Don't back out. The **heart of the North** will shake (Canada). Pay attention. Pray." [7]

Our Lord confirmed to me: "Nuclear Power Plants in **Ontario** will have fracturing and meltdown." [8] (from earthquakes in that region?) Our Lord also confirmed to me: "The mountains to the west, in **Alberta**, will be there for a thousand years." (A long time) [9]

United States of America

"Your true liberation is in Jesus. Return to Him, who sees what is hidden and knows you by name. Bend your knees in prayer. The **famous Los Angeles** will live moments of dread. Oh men and women be converted. **Where do you want to go?**" [10] "Humanity has gone away from its Creator and is heading on the path of destruction. Return quickly. The famous Los Angeles will mourn the death of its sons. China will stumble, and a great punishment will come. Oh, men and women, where do you want to go to?" [11]

"Those who live in the **land of riches** will experience a heavy cross. The earth will shake, and death will be present. They will drink the bitter cup of sorrow. In the west, near the Pacific, shouts and wailing will be heard." [12] "**Washington** residents will drink the bitter cup of suffering." [13] "Those who live in **Santa Bárbara** will shout for help."[14] "**California** will need help. Bend your knees in prayer for its inhabitants." [15]

"The **great and famous river** that crosses the nest of the eagle (USA) will be contaminated (Mississippi). My poor children will carry a heavy cross. Suffering will also come for **Three Falls** (Niagara)" [16] "A great city by the side of the Potomac (Nuclear power plant) will live moments of great affliction."[17] "Those on the **Columbia River** will experience an accident (Nuclear Power Plant) and drink the cup of pain. The river will lose its brightness." [18]

"In the Valley of the moon (**Sonoma**, California) will come great suffering. Entire regions of the land will disappear."[19] "**Yakima** will experience a heavy cross. Bend your knees in prayer. What you have to do, do not put off until tomorrow." [20]

The Land of Santa Cruz (USA?)

Mary speaks of the land of Santa Cruz. There are many places called Santa Cruz. I do feel strongly, she is referring to the land of the United States of America, using Santa Cruz as a symbolic name. It is strongly inferred, in this next prophecy where Santa Cruz is on the famous fault, in California. Santa Cruz means 'Holy Cross', which can refer to Brazil, as well as many other places, called Santa Cruz.

"In a region of **the Land** of **Santa Cruz**, in the past, many men were successful and many impoverished. Because of a famous fault (San Andres?) will come a great catastrophe that will call the world's attention. No longer will it experience the 'smell of the fruit'. Life without God loses its value and effectiveness. God does not forsake the poor. The rich will have regret. Your strength lies in prayer."[21] "The suffering also reaches the land of Santa Cruz. In many regions, the land will tear and large cracks will appear. Many places that you contemplate today will cease to exist."[22] "A great tragedy will happen in the land of Santa Cruz. Higher pain does not exist."[23] "The men of terror will cause great destruction, in the land of Santa Cruz."[24] "A painful event will be in the Church, and the faithful will weep and lament. It will be in the land of Santa Cruz." [25]

Central America

"**Mexico** will experience moments of great distress."[26]"Your cross will be heavy, but trust in My Maternal protection. I am always close to you. Mexico: the moments of pain for many are approaching."[27] "Something frightening will happen in land of the Holy Cross and will be repeated in Guatemala."[28]

South America

"Know that the deep waters of the ocean that bathes your **Brazil** will bring suffering and pain. Tell everyone that God is in a hurry, and that you can no longer live in sin. Brazil will be at war. Pray. Bend your knees in prayer." [29] "Requests for relief will be heard by souls in **Buenos Aires**. The cross will be heavy." [30] "Entire nations will cease to exist. The city of Salvador (Brazil) will disappear, but the men of faith will be spared. Repent quickly." [31]

"Humanity is on the track to the abyss of destruction which men have prepared with their own hands. The earth will pass through great trans-formations, and many places will no longer exist. Famous **islands of** your **Brazil** will be destroyed. **A giant** (meteor or comet?) will come **from the north** to torment my poor children." [32] Great suffering will come for the inhabit-ants of **Chile**."[33] "A great happening will shake the faith of many people. It will be in the land of the Holy Cross (Brazil)."[34]

"A frightening event will happen in Uruguay and be repeated in **Esprito Santo**. Death will pass through **three states** in Brazil, accompanied by great destruction." [35]

"**Belém** (Brazil) will live the anxiety of one condemned. The destruction will be great and my poor children will experience a heavy cross." [36] "The water will rise with great fury and cause great destruction. The land of the Holy Cross (Brazil) will drink the bitter cup of suffering." [37] "Difficult times are coming for **Brazil**. Frightening things will happen, and many of my poor children will carry a heavy cross. Cities will be hit by strong winds, causing great destruction."[38] "A sorrowful event will happen in the Land of the Holy Cross (Brazil). Men try to escape the Tubarão (Shark), but find death."[39] "Those who dwell in a great city in **Brazil** will live moments of great tribulations. Scientists will give the warning, and everybody will flee. The discovery of a great gap will get the attention of the whole world." [40]

England

"Terror will come to England, particularly the South Hamptons. The pain will be great for my poor children."[41] "Don´t let the devil deceive you. Flee from wickedness, and return to the Lord to be saved. I am your Mom, and I come from heaven to point out to you the way of goodness and holiness. I ask you to be men and women of prayer. Mankind has fled from the Creator because people have gotten away from prayer. **Something sorrowful** will happen in the **land of the Queen** (England?)." [42] "Those who dwell in the land of the Queen will live moments of great tribulation. It will be on a Friday, and men will weep and wail. Pray. Pray. Pray." [43]

Europe

"**Berlin** will be in ruins."[44] "Humanity lives in the darkness of paganism, and my poor children go to a great abyss. **Athens** stumbles and loses their fame. The strong arm of God will act. The inhabitants of Denmark, Belgium, and Germany will experience great suffering."[45] "The Netherlands will drink the bitter cup of pain. Death will pass and my poor children will live moments of anguish."[46] "Something frightening will happen in Europe, and three countries will be struck at the same time."[47] "A shocking event will happen in Germany. Death will pass through, and my poor children will experience a heavy cross."[48] "A frightening event will happen in Geneva... Geneva will live moments of great tribulation. The fury of an invisible enemy will attack my poor children." [49] "A devastating force will cross Europe causing destruction and death."[50] "Something frightening will happen in Rome and be repeated in the north of France."[51]

"Something frightening will happen in Spain and my poor children will carry a heavy cross. Terror will spread and people will tremble."[52] The capital of Spain (Madrid) will tremble. Men cause terror, destruction, and death."[53] The land of San Sebastian (northern Spain) will be jolted. A giant will rise and will bring suffering to many." [54] Suffering will come for those who dwell in Lisbon."[55] The Island of Madeira will live moments of great tribulations. Death will come and people will weep and lament."[56]"Those living in the city of **Santander** will call for help."[57] "A painful event will take place at **Fatima** (Portugal), and my poor children will weep and lament." [58]

Eastern Europe

"Bulgaria will see greater destruction than ever before in its history."[59] "**Poland** walks like the blind. The Treasury will be lost (Banks collapse). Pray. Pray a lot."[60] "**Kosovo** will be in ruins and great will be their suffering."[61] Terror will be spread by **Lithuania** bringing great losses. Screams and wailing will be heard on all sides."[62] "The suffering will come to **Cyprus**, and **Malta** will shed tears for their children. Pray."[63] "Something very sad will happen in **Yugo-slavia**, and many people will have their faith shaken."[64] "You will yet, to see horrors on earth. Turkey will have to weep and lament the death of its children."[65]

Middle East

"Great Terror will come to the **Sinai**." [66] "**Saudi Arabia** will live moments of pain, never experienced before in its time."[67] "The **Holy Land** will be shaken. Great horrors come to men."[68] "The idolatry of **Egypt** will fall apart."[69] "A warning will come to Palestine before it will be struck and my poor children will suffer in the Holy Land. I am your Mother, and I have come from Heaven to assist you."[70] A frightening phenomenon will happen on the **Sea of Galilee**, and no one will have an explanation. I am your Mom, and I never get tired."[71]

"A frightening event will happen to **Iran**, and in **Pakistan**…The happenings will be in different times but will be alike." [72] "Death will come to Yemen, and there will be great destruction. I suffer because of what is coming to you."[73] "The earth will shake in **Iran**."[74] "You are heading towards a future of great difficulties. The earth will shake, and **Egypt** will drink the bitter chalice of pain. Pray. Pray. Pray. The **Middle East** will experience a heavy cross, and My poor children will shout for help. These beautiful countries will be in tears for the death of their children. Bend your knees in prayer. Your victory is in the Lord. Don't cross your arms." [75]

Africa

"Pray for my poor Ethiopian children. **Ethiopia** will bear a heavy cross. I am your Mother, and I'm very close to you. Do not allow the demon to try you with questions about what will happen in Ethiopia." [76] Pray.

"**Kenya** will need help."[77] "**Libya** will stumble."[78] "I don't want to force you, but what I say should be taken seriously. Valparaiso hotels, **Gold Coast** (Ghana)…will live moments of great affliction. Weeping and wailing will be heard on all sides. Know that God has haste."[79] "There will be a great massacre in **Egypt**, and my poor children will experience a heavy cross."[80] "Those who dwell in **Morocco** will shout with sorrow. Its beauty will no longer exist, for it will be devastated."[81] "In Algeria, death will come, and there will be great destruction. I suffer because of what is coming to you." [82]

Southeast Asia

"Nature will be transformed and men confounded. **China** will go through great trials. Here, the land will shake, killing millions of innocents. The land is full of wickedness." [83] "**Mongolia** shall drink the bitter cup of pain."[84] "The country of large islands (**Indonesia**) will be battered, and my poor children will live moments of anguish. The Earth will shake. Stand not far from God's grace. Repent quickly. The great terror approaches. What I have said in the past will hold. I suffer for what you will experience."[85] "Death will go through Asia, and My poor children will weep and lament."[86] "Humanity is going towards an abyss of destruction that men have prepared with their own hands. A sleeping giant (volcano) will arise in **Indonesia**...No greater tragedy existed."[87] "The earth will shake in **Tangshen** (China)."[88] "**India** will shout for help, and My poor children will carry a heavy cross." [89] "Difficult days will come to India and **Pakistan**." [90]

Unusually Interesting

"The great sign of God will leave wise men confused. **Seawater** will lose its natural flavor. **God wants to be heard**. A major crisis is facing humanity. O men turn fast. What I say is not to make you afraid, but that you may be prepared. I am your sorrowful Mother, and I know what awaits you." [91] "The tree top famous Garden (in the Amazon) has **a root** that will spread (be used) through out the world."[92] "**From Egypt** there will come news that will permeate the world, and many men will have their faith shaken. Do not forget my appeals. Stand firm on the path that I have mentioned." [93]

"A great discovery will be made in the land of Santa Cruz. It will be for the good of humanity, and the scientists will rejoice. Know that the Lord does not leave. Trust in him, and you will be great in faith."[94] "From the depths of the earth there will be a great mystery. Science does not explain, and the inhabitants of the land of Santa Cruz fear."[95] "A science discovery will cause great confusion to men. Do not turn away from the truth." [96]

"Mankind moves away from God and walks into the abyss of self destruction. Keep yourselves from evil, and seek the Lord, to be saved. Men embrace all kinds of immorality and challenge the creator. Indeed, to all of you, the righteousness of the Lord will come. The **angels of the Sodom** come to the earth, and **woe to those living in immorality** and disobedience to the Lord. I suffer for what awaits you." [97]

"You are heading towards a future of great trials. The death of a great leader will cause great confusion. The **fall of a prophet** will be necessary for the good of many souls. You cannot understand the mysteries of God. Bend your knees in prayer. Seek strength in the Eucharist and in the words of My Son, Jesus. The Church will encounter a great problem in the **revolt** of a **famous congregation**." [98]

"The world is experiencing strong tensions and walks to a great chasm. A treasure will be found **in Israel**, but because of it, there will be many deaths."[99] "A great earthquake will **shake Iran**, and a hidden secret will be revealed."[100] "The Discovery of a great gap will get the attention of the whole world."[101] "An archaeological **discovery** will be made in Rome and will cause great confusion for the Church. Stand firm in the faith."[102] "The devil works to create destruction, but you can defeat him with prayer and by faithfully hearing the Word of God. An extraordinary discovery will bring suffering and pain to My poor children. The **valley of Sidim**: this is the place (South end of the Dead Sea). Stay on the path I have pointed out, and you will be victorious." [103] "Humanity runs great dangers. Now is the time for your return. A **hidden treasure** will be discovered in Transjordan; joy and pain for My poor children. Pray. Pray. Pray."[104]

CHAPTER 37

THE RESCUE BY OUR LADY OF THE IMMACULATE CONCEPTION

I t is understood, **Satan's extended reign and power** have **come to an end** as **of October of 2017.** The time request from Satan, of an unrecognized power grip is over, but the adverse effects are still here. Satan still tempts and influences humanity, leaving humanity on the road to annihilation. When the first nuclear event unfolds, God will intervene with the Warning and an Outpouring of His Holy Spirit. **After** a frightful crisis of incredible destruction, Our Lady of the Immaculate Conception will rescue us.

Nasreen Jouni, a stigmatist who had visions of Mary, but Our Lord said to her, on February 17, 2012: "My daughter, I know you are weak and I know without me, you are always imperfect, unable to move…My Chalice of Mercy has overflowed. Daughter, when My Mother appeared in Fatima, on May 1917…the devil asked the Divine Throne, to tempt the world for a hundred years. This is going to end in 2017. He will no longer reign on earth because I will come with my peace. I will cover the world with my peace. I am peace and passion. My call is to the whole world." [1] The extended time frame is over but the adverse effects are still here. Every person can feel it at this time. Sin is rampant. Ironically, by October 2017, many are exposed publicly; exposing sexual abuse, exposing the truth about people's lives in the media, in government and politics, and in the Catholic Church.

Increasingly, the Holy Spirit is now exposing many. But many still refuse to acknowledge the other's needs; only acknowledging their own self-centered interests. Many live their lives, pretending all is well.

Marija Pavlovic Lunetti, Medjugorje visionary, October 24, 2017: "I believe that this year (2017), the Immaculate Heart of Mary will triumph." [2] Mary, Mother of Jesus will intercede more effectively and more completely, now that Satan's extended power is diminished.

The Rescue from the Storm

A time will come when the chaos will have to stop, or no one will be left on earth. In these unprecedented spectacular prophecies, it is understood that Mary will appear to everyone in their homes, manifesting her presence. This Rescue will take place on a worldwide basis.

This will bring peace at this time, and people will realize, it is time to accept what God has in store for us and surrender to His will. This gives us hope that life on earth will be restored back to Christian values.

Charlie Johnston, after visions of the Blessed Virgin and Archangel Gabriel: "Then the Blessed Mother will be allowed to rescue us. It will result in a fundamental re-unification of Christianity. "The Storm" is not God's punishment. "The Storm" is God letting us suffer the consequences of our actions. Even with the Storm, He is still holding back the full consequences." [3] "The sequence of ever deepening chaos will continue until... the world will be miraculously, utterly, and visibly delivered from the terror by the intercession of Our Lady of the Immaculate Conception."[4] "The Lord will send **Our Lady to rescue us visibly**.... Rescue will not come, until all including me, have lost hope. When that time comes, pretend to have hope, remembering, that faith is an act of the will, until Our Lady comes."[4] "It is the decisive battle between good and evil. It will be followed by a great period of Christian unity, peace, and authentic prosperity. " [5]

Medjugorje visionaries ask Mary in 1982: "People are surprised that you are appearing in so many places." Our Blessed Mother responded, "If it is necessary, **I will appear in each home**." [6] In this Rescue, Jesus continues to unfold the first Seal of Revelation 6: 1-2 "He rode victorious, to conquer yet again." Jesus is intervening again, to calm us and help us realize that we must begin to prepare for change.

Maria Esperanza, stigmatist, interviewed by Michael H. Brown in 2003: "He (Jesus after the Warning) will disappear for some days and appear again. And when he disappears, people will go back again, to the mess, to the crazed things. He will bi-locate. **He will multiply himself**, to assist everyone, **in their homes**, because this will be a definite thing. He will come and knock on every door. And then people will realize it is truly Him. He will let himself be seen for a little while and then will disappear, until God **decrees, what has to be done**. And then people will understand what is happening and begin preparing themselves. There is not much time for that. I will say from ten to twenty years." [7]

The Triumph of Mary's Immaculate Heart

Mary's proclamation, "In the end, My Immaculate Heart will Triumph," was first heard at the Fatima apparitions. The challenge from Satan to destroy the Church in 100 years is defeated, by Mary and her prayer armies. This **decisive victory was won by Mary, in October 2017**. All of a sudden, many sins are publicly exposed. Sexual abuse in the Catholic Church, in other churches, in schools, with politicians, media reporters, broadcasters, Hollywood moguls, actors and the sexual abuse of women, who have been silent for too long, are all coming to light at the same time, through different media platforms. Many other areas, such as the economic breakdown of nations, the disregard of our earth and its natural ecosystems. The recoil of **the sinfulness of mankind**, according to the word of God, is causing an increase in natural disasters; don't blame global weather extremes. Our **self-centred sin** will bring more suffering than ever before. Although, this 100 years of extended reign is over, the fight is not over. The fallout of man's sins falling upon us **will continue until 2038**. Satan will lose much power and influence over mankind, as the decrees continue to unfold. The early Church Fathers and other saints, talk about a time of genuine peace coming to the earth. After 2038, the victory of the Triumph of Mary's Immaculate Heart over Satan and his followers will be accomplished.

Lady of Peace to **Pedro Regis:** Difficult days are coming, but the Lord will be with you. The earth will pass through great trials, but in the end, will come, a great victory of God with the 'Final Triumph' of My Immaculate Heart. Be just. **Only those who are just**, will contemplate the transformation of the world." [8] Although, this will be the major and decisive victory of removing power away from Satan at this time, the complete victory will only come after the tenth secret of Medjugorje has unfolded in 2038. The repercussions of our sin, on this world will play out until 2038. It is a winding down. The decrees will continue. **There will be one more uprising in the late 2020s** and distinctly continuing into the 2030s, according to the prophecies. [9] God's chastisements in the 2030s to 2038 will end all the evil, and then will begin the age of Peace. This will be Mary's '**Definitive Triumph**', starting in 2038.

After the Rescue, the opportunity for much evangelization and a turning back to God, particularly in North, Central, and South America will be witnessed. But **the decrees of God's seals of Revelation will continue to unfold.** In the last part of the message to Nasreen Jouni, Jesus states, "My call is to the whole world." Those who have decided against God, may subtly continue to follow the darkness that influences them. However, this still gives us an opportunity to awaken many to conversion during the 2020s.

Optimistic Messages of Medjugorje

In spite of all the tragedy that will fall upon the world, people should look to the future with confidence. Humanity will continue, within God's predestined plan, with renewed generations of families. Children will be an essential part of a family, working together, to survive and thrive going forward.

Marija Pavlovic, Medjugorje: "I have an optimistic view of the future. If we all begin to live these, messages, a new world will be born." [10, 11]

Mirjana from Mary: "**Do not be afraid to have children.** You should rather fear not to have any! **The more children you have, the better!**" Mirjana confirms this in an interview with Sr. Emmanuel Maillard: "Yes, she did say that, and she knows why she said it. I know, too... but I can't tell you more...When the secrets are revealed, people will understand why it was so important for them, to have many children. **We are all waiting for the Triumph of the Immaculate Heart of Mary.** " [12]

Living on the land, like our grandparents and great grandparents did, will take many hands, to make light work.

Our Lady as Co-Redemptrix,
Mediatrix, and Advocate

A fifth Marian dogma is encouraged from Heaven and reputably will be the last. Mary, Mother of Jesus has a continual role as Co-Redemptrix, Mediatrix, and Advocate, exhibited in the first five Church ages, as she has labored for souls. This role of Co-Redemptrix is to guide many souls to eternal redemption.[13] John Paul II clarifies: "Mary's role as **Co-Redemptrix** did not cease with the glorification of her Son." [14]

A dogma is a truth revealed by the Holy Spirit, to the teaching magisterium of the Catholic Church and announced to the people. This may come about by encouragement, given to saints, through visions or locutions, and then reaches the highest levels of authority for consideration. It may be revealed directly by the Holy Spirit, to the popes as well. With consultation of the episcopate, it is then proclaimed by the Pope and is considered infallible.

There have been four Marian Dogmas proclaimed in the last 2000 years. At the council of Ephesus in 431 A.D., Mary is declared, the Mother of God. In 649, the Lateran Synod proclaims, Mary's Perpetual Virginity, in light of Mary's virginal conception of Jesus and giving birth to Jesus, remaining a virgin. In 1854, Pope Pius IX, declared Mary, as the Immaculate Conception. This meant, when Mary herself was conceived, she was conceived without sin, not having original sin in her life, contrary to the rest of mankind. This was confirmed during apparitions of Our Lady of Lourdes. In 1950, Pope Pius XII, proclaims the Assumption of Mary into Heaven, body and soul. These four dogmas were proclaimed, reflecting her unique role while on earth, encouraged by Heaven, through the Holy Spirit.

She is **Mediatrix of all Grace**, who mediates as a mother, at the throne of God for many souls, especially those otherwise lost. She also intercedes as **Advocate,** in human history, in difficult times, to defend, comfort, and guide. Hints for the encouragement of this definitive title, for this Woman in redemptive battle, is first recognized, at Rue De Bac in Paris, France in 1830. During the apparitions of Mary, concerning the Miraculous Metal, the words to be inscribed, are shown to Catherine Laboure in repeated visions. The words "O Mary, conceived without sin, pray for us **who have recourse to you.**" [15] confirms from Heaven, her involvement in the co-redeeming participation of salvation. These words oblige us, to highly esteem the salvific favor.

Other apparitions of Mary, at La Salette and Pontmain, France, and Knock, Ireland reflect this continual role. Marie-Julie Jahenny at La Fraudais, France hears from Jesus, "My Mother is untiringly imploring me, and together with her, (for) a great number of penitent and atoning souls. I cannot deny her anything. Therefore, it is thanks to My Mother, and because of my elect that those days are going to be shortened."[16] Berthe Petit, a stigmatist from Belgium, heard Jesus: "It is in Co-Redemption, that My Mother was above- all great. That is why I ask, that the invocation, as I have inspired it, should be approved and diffused throughout the whole Church.... It has already obtained grace. It will obtain more, until the hour comes, when by Consecration to the Sorrowful and Immaculate Heart of My Mother, the Church, shall be uplifted and the world renewed." [17]

At Fatima, the image of the thorn-encircled heart, appeals to the sorrows that Mary experienced at the same time as Christ in redemption.

By the 1940s, Mary's words become plainly clear. She is the "**Mediatrix of All Graces**,"[18] at apparitions to Sister Mary of the Trinity, a victim soul at Jerusalem; Barbara Ruess of Marienfried, Germany; Peirina Gilli at Montichiari, Italy, requesting devotion to Rosa Mystica; and Carmelite Sister Teresita at Lipa, Philippines.

Ida Perlman's 56 apparitions of Mary, from 1945 to 1959, in Amsterdam, Holland, clearly defines, repeatedly, this request from Our Lady of All Nations. On **April 29, 1951**, she reiterates: "I stand here as the Co-Redemptrix and Advocate. Everything should be concentrated on that... The **new dogma** will be the **dogma of the Co-Redemptrix**. Notice I lay the special emphasis on Co. I have said, that this will arouse much controversy. Once again, I tell you that the Church, Rome, will carry it through and silence all objections. The Church, Rome, will incur opposition and overcome it... my purpose and my commission to you is...to urge the Church, the theologians, to wage this battle...this time is our time. By this, I mean... the world is caught up in degeneration and superficiality. It is at a loss...The Father sends me, to be Advocate; **to implore the Holy Spirit to come**. For the world is not saved by force. The Holy Spirit will save the world. It is only ideas that rule the world... It is the wish of the Father and the Son to send me into the world, in these times, as Co-Redemptrix, Mediatrix, and Advocate. This will constitute **a new** and **last Marian dogma**... This picture will go before it. This dogma will be much disputed; and yet it will prevail." [19]

On November 15, 1951, Mary appeared to Ida, "standing on the earth with a cross at her back. There were rays streaming from her hands and a multitude of sheep gathered around the globe." [20]

On April 4, 1954, Mary states: "Listen well, from the outset, the Handmaid of the Lord was chosen to be the Co-Redemptrix; Tell your theologians they can find it in all their books.... I am not bringing a new doctrine. I am now bringing old ideas...because the Lady is Co-Redemptrix, She is also Mediatrix and Advocate not only because she is the Mother of the Lord Jesus

Christ, but–and mark this well–because she is the Immaculate conception... Do fight and ask for this dogma: it is the crowning of your Lady..."[21]

On May 31, 1955, Mary continues: "The Lady of all Nations, is permitted to come, in order **to banish Satan**.... She comes to announce the Holy Spirit. The Holy Spirit **will only now descend over this earth**...Know well, that the Holy Spirit is nearer than ever. The Holy Spirit will come now; you pray for His coming. He has always been ready; now, however, the time has come.... Once the dogma **has been pronounced**, the Lady of All Nations, will give her **blessings...**"[22]

Our Lady of Medjugorje, Mirjana, March 18, 2012: "I am coming among you because I desire to be your mother–your intercessor. I desire to be the bond between you and the heavenly Father–**your Mediatrix**. I desire to take you by the hand and to walk with you in battle against the impure spirit. My children, consecrate yourselves to me completely. I will take your lives into my motherly hands..."[23]

The Pope may be pronouncing this dogma, sometime before the Church event. After this, the Holy Spirit will descend upon the whole earth. A rare and singular, worldwide Church event, may take place, of the celebration of the feast of Our Lady as **Co-Redemptrix, Mediatrix, and Advocate.**

"I Will Pour Out My Spirit Upon All Mankind"

Mary's prophecy of May 31, 1955, is astounding and confirms what is revealed in Joel 3:1: "**Then**, I will pour out **my Spirit upon all mankind.** " Although, the Holy Spirit has entered individual's lives in His Church, and has worked in His Church for two thousand years, a unique full coming of the Holy Spirit will take place **upon the whole earth**, literally. Mary, as Our Lady of All Nations, also speaks clearly of this unique event, taking place at this time in history. This Outpouring of the Holy Spirit confirms Joel 3:1-3, and parallels the first two secrets of Garabandal and first three secrets of Medjugorje unfolding.

The Holy Spirit will descend, at this time, all over this earth, in a unique way, especially at the places of Miracle signs. The Holy Spirit is rightfully bringing more of God's kingdom upon the earth, as it is in Heaven.

The time has come. This will destroy Satan's extended influence over people on this earth. This is **in conjunction with the proclamation** of the **Marian** Dogma. This is in the statement of April 29, 1951, above. Mary states that the head of the Church, that is in Rome, will carry this out, at this time, just before the Outpouring of the Holy Spirit. **One depends** on the other, but **the dogma must be proclaimed.** The Pope and the episcopate of the Church will agree upon this dogma in advance of the proclamation.

The events of the literal reading of Biblical verses from Joel 3: 1-4, reflect and parallel the three secrets of Garabandal. The ten secrets of Medjugorje contain the same three secrets of Garabandal. The ten secrets of Medjugorje include: three admonishments from God, five punishments from the accumulation of mankind's sins, and two chastisements that are not conditional anymore, and are coming directly from God. Joel 3: 1-4 speaks of three major events all directly from God.

Joel 3: 1-4

First: "Then afterward, I will pour out my Spirit on all mankind. Your sons and daughters shall prophesy, Your old men shall dream dreams; your young men shall see visions, Even upon the servants and the hand maids. In those days I will pour out my spirit."

Second: **"And I will work wonders in the heavens and on the earth, blood, fire and columns of smoke,"**

Third: "The sun will be turned to darkness, and the moon to blood before the coming of the great and terrible day of the Lord."

Mary at Garabandal, Spain, 1960-1965

First: A Warning/ Illumination of Conscience

Second: **Miracle signs at the nine pines will unfold on a Thursday evening at 8:30 near Garabandal.**

Third: God's Chastisement. (Conditional in the 1960s)

Mary At Medjugorie, Bosnia Herzegovina, 1981 to 20-?

First: 1 A Warning: Correction of Conscience, awakening our Spirit to God.
         2 Day of Outpouring of the Holy Spirit with God consoling us.

Second: 3 **Miracle Signs on the earth.** Day of physical healing, but may not be everyone. **A Visible Sign seen on Apparition Hill.**
         4 War and civil chaos caused by nuclear events; Western Economy crashes.
         5 Famines.
         6 Spiritual-abandonment reflects catastrophic events, plagues and death.
         7 The Church crisis and confusion. The "Fatal Event".
         8 Persecutions and martyrdom of Christians in the 2020s and 2030s.
         9 Collision of two stars and other celestial events in 2030s will bring cleansing, purification, and restructuring of the earth.

Third: 10 The Comet and Three days of Darkness, God's Chastisements– not conditional in 2030s to 2038, annihilating the evil people.

Day of the Miracle and Miracle Signs

2021

This is the 3rd secret of Medjugorje and also the 2nd secret of Garabandal. Jesus will reach out farther to humanity through the first Seal of Revelation: "He rode victorious, to conquer yet again," will be revealed as a day of Miracles and Miracle signs unfolding upon the earth. This day will fall on a Thursday, in March, April or May. This is the **third admonition** from God.

There are riddles given by Our Lady of Garabandal, for this particular day of Miracle signs and Miracle healing and are listed from comments by Mari-Loli and Conchita:

–There will be "three popes" [24] after John XXIII, and then it will happen during Benedict XVI's reign or his lifetime.
–"It will take place within a year after the Warning." [25]
–"It will take place either during March, April, or May." [26]
–"It will take place on or between the eighth and the sixteenth." [27]
–It will be on a "feast of a saint, martyr of the Eucharist." [28]
–It will take place **on a Thursday** at 8:30 p.m. at the nine pines by Garabandal. [29]
–It will coincide with a great event in the Church.
–"It is a singular event, that happens very rarely, and has never happened in my lifetime. It is not new or stupendous, only rare, like a definition of a dogma.
–It will affect the entire Church. It will happen on the same day as the Miracle, not as a consequence of the Miracle, only coincidentally." [30]
–The great event in the Church, the celebration of the 5th Marian Dogma; "Our Lady as Co-Redemptrix, Mediatrix, and Advocate."

The Miracle sign will be seen by everyone, who are present at the nine pines and the surrounding mountains. "**It will last about fifteen minutes**." [31] All those who are sick or need physical healing, who are present, will be cured in the first fifteen minutes.

The Permanent sign will be **at the Nine Pines,** near Garabandal, and will be **like** a column of **fire.** It will be possible to film or televise, but you will not be able to touch it, and it will **remain "forever** at the pines." [32] The **Pope will see it** from wherever he is on that day.

This day of a Miracle sign, will also take place at Medjugorje, although specified time parameters have not been revealed. It will most likely take place on the same day, as at Garabandal. Mirjana will announce it before hand. Mirjana has said: "The third secret will be a visible sign at Medjugorje, permanent, indestructible, and beautiful." [33] In 1981, hundreds of people saw flames rising up on Podbrdo Hill, as a probable forerunner, of the great sign. Mirjana states of the third secret of Medjugorje about the Miracle sign: "This sign will be given for atheists. You faithful already have signs, and you have become the sign for the atheists... This time is, for deepening your faith and for your conversion. When the sign comes, it will be too late for many." [34]

Conchita at Garabandal, was told in a locution from Jesus that the purpose of the Miracle was: "to convert the whole world." Conchita asked if Russia would be converted: "Yes, she will be converted, and thus everybody will love our hearts. Russia will be converted, as a consequence of the Miracle." [35]

Our Lady of Peace to **Pedro Regis:** "An extraordinary phenomenon will be seen in various countries of Europe. It is a call from God, to men and women who go away from His Grace. I come from Heaven, to reclaim what belongs to God... I don't want to obligate you, but listen to Me. I want to help you, but what I can do, depends on you. Put all your confidence and hope in Jesus. Your liberation is coming. Don't back out." [36]

Miracle Signs at Credible Marian Apparition Sites

Little known visionaries of Mary, claim similar Miracle signs at places such as Cuenca, Ecuador; Betania, Venezuela; and Anguera, Brazil. Other sites that Mary has truly appeared at over the centuries such as Rue de Bac, La Salette, Lourdes, and Fatima, will experience these signs.

Patricia (Pachi) Talbot Borrero, at 16, claimed to have seen the Blessed Virgin from the late 1980s until March 3, 1990, in a high mountain valley called El Cajas, 12,000 feet above sea level near Cuenca, Ecuador. Pachi was told, "At the end of the apparitions in the world, I will **leave a great sign** in **this** place and in all those where I have been."[37, 38] Pachi's experiences seem to parallel information and experiences of other seers, claiming Miracle signs around the world where Mary has appeared. This is an astounding and wonderful revelation of what awaits us.

Maria Esperanza, a mystic of Venezuela, was guided to a special location at Betania, where a pillar of fire had been seen for a short time and is considered a Miracle site. [39]

Our Lady of Peace to **Pedro Regis** at Anguera: "Do not forget: to whom much is given, much will be charged. Men need to take the message of salvation that my Jesus has left you. Do not cross your arms. God needs a lot from you. God sent me here to talk to you and call you to conversion. Know that this place will be **a grand haven** for many believers. God will leave great wonders here. I have noble **things to accomplish here**... The plans of the Lord will never be destroyed." [40]

St. Hildegard, Doctor of the Church: "Then within the Christian people, the Holy Godhead will accomplish signs and wonders, as accomplished, at the time of Moses with **the pillar of cloud,** and as Michael the archangel did when he fought the heathen for the sake of the Christians." [41]

The pillar of cloud is a similar sign, corresponding to descriptions of the third secret of Medjugorje and second secret of Garabandal. This will bring atheist to God. The children of Garabandal stated, the Pope would see the Miracle, "wherever he will be." [42]

Miracle Sign on "Martyr of the Eucharist" Feast Day

The only considered "Martyr's of the Eucharist," on the day of the Miracle sign, falling in the three month time-frame on a Thursday, are St. Imelda, May 13th; St. Hermenegild, April 13; and Our Lord Jesus, on the feast of Ascension, on any day in May between the 8th to the 16th.

St. Imelda has been a favorite over the years, since the 1960s, because of the unique circumstances of her martyrdom. Imelda Lambertini, born in 1322, as a child, she spent much time in prayer, arranging flowers and pictures in a special place of devotion, in her home. At nine, she entered into a Dominican convent. She was especially attracted to the presence of the Lord in the Eucharist and at the Tabernacle. Her all-consuming desire was to receive Our Lord in Holy Communion. She was known to ask: "Tell me, can any one receive Jesus into his heart and not die?"

On the evening of the vigil of Ascension Thursday at Mass, when she was eleven years old, she was the only one not allowed to receive communion because, a child had to be 12 years old. At the end of Mass, Imelda knelt near the tabernacle and as the other nuns were leaving, they noticed a Sacred Host hovering in the air above Imelda. The priest was alerted and he placed the Eucharist on a paten. Contemplating the design of Heaven to give Imelda her first communion, he placed the Host in her mouth. She smiled, and seemed to be euphoric, then fell into an unconscious state to the floor. When they lifted her up again, she had died in rapture of her first communion with Our Lord. The date was May 12, 1333. The traditional feast day is the day a saint dies, but her official feast day has been **May 13**. Her body is incorruptible and lies in the church of San Sigismondo, in Bologna, Italy. She is called, "Patroness of fervent First Holy Communion." [43]

The next time that St. Imelda's feast day falls on the Thursday, will be on May 13, 2021. St. Hermenegild's feast day, falling on a Thursday, will only transpire on April 13, 2023. [44]

Consider the times we live in and the way President **Trump** is not backing down from the Globalists' Communism or the New World Order, the Islamic aggression in the world, China and North Korea, and the Liberal left in America. He is standing up for Israel. **Trump** is moving America away from globalism and back to nationalism. It won't be long before the Globalist take action and these prophetic events start to occur.

The year 2020 will bring the last months of Trump's first term. Charlie Johnston a U. S. visionary has stated, the angel told him: "the President would not finish his term." Charlie Johnston thought it would be Obama but that did not happen. The continued opposition to Trump could shorten his term in traumatic ways causing chaos and confusion for the country and the world.

A crucial clue here, currently, is the feast of St. Imelda, falling on a Thursday and is due on the 13th of May, 2021, when possibly the third event of the 10 secrets or events is to unfold in human history. I believe after Trump is stopped, the USA and the world will go through the "Storm." The third secret/event would bring a halt to the war and chaos by or before May 13, 2021.

The riddle pertinent for the day of the Miracle sign, will likely unfold in 2021 for the Martyr of the Eucharist: The Miracle sign will take place after the Warning but within a year after the Warning. It must take place on the feast day of a "Martyr of the Eucharist" that falls on a Thursday. It must occur on or between the 8th and the 16th of the month and only during one of the months of either March, April, or May. In 2021, the Thursday will be May 13. This is the feast day of St. Imelda Lambertini and is also the feast of the Ascension of Jesus Christ. He was and is the true martyr of the Eucharist.

Restoration from God's Three Admonitions

Revelation 6:2 says: "He rode victorious, to conquer yet again." In these first three admonitions, He is giving us the tools or graces to survive the rest of the seven Seals of Revelation that are unfolding. Those graces are to build us 'Body, Soul and Spirit.'

First, on the day of the Warning or Correction of conscience, God will get our attention, and awaken **our spirit** to **His Spirit** on that **Friday**.

Secondly, on the day of the Outpouring of His Holy Spirit, on the **Sunday**, He will **let us know the goodness** of **our soul**, that is, who we are. Our soul is comprised of our intellect, our free will, and our emotions. It is our eternal personality, whom we are. He will let us know that He loves us, and this will increase our faith to trust in Him. We will know who we are, as God sees us. We may receive major gifts of the Holy Spirit, along with many blessings, including healing for our inner woundedness, on that Sunday. Physical healing could take place on this day as well.

Thirdly, on the day of Miracles, particularly at Garabandal, all who are there will receive healing of their sickness and physical debilitation.

At Medjugorje in 1992 : "Reports from pilgrims in Medjugorje, describe how they experienced an illumination of conscience, seeing their entire life pass before their eyes, as in a film." They could see their entire life in front of them, passing by, moment by moment," with the shadows of sin and the light of love which they had given...They felt a profound repentance...

They all received at the same moment, a great healing, physical and spiritual."[45] At Garabandal, Mary said to Conchita, the sick and the physically impaired that are present, at that time, would be cured.

Yet, important questions remain: Will future physical healing promised by Mary, only take place at Garabandal and possibly Medjugorje? Or will physical healing of the sick and physically impaired, occur at all Marian apparition sites all over the world that day? Will physical healing of the sick or impaired take place for all those who are open to the Holy Spirit on the day of the Miracle signs and Miracle healing ?

A Time for Evangelization

After the Rescue, many will give in to God with a new trust in mankind, but many will still not understand the ways and knowledge of God. This will be a time of hunger, not only for physical needs, because famine will be a decree increasing at that time. The hunger will be for God and what His word says to us. His word, includes a plan for this earth and His Church. Words of prophecy from the High Altar at St. Peter's Basilica, in 1975 state: "A time of glory is coming for my Church, a time of glory is coming for my people. I will pour out, on you, all the gifts of my Spirit. I will prepare you for a spiritual combat. I will prepare you for a time of evangelization that the world has never seen." [46]

Our Lady of Peace to **Pedro Regis** at Anguera, Brazil, states the continual unfolding of signs of God and his love for us: "A grand event will happen in Brazil and draw the attention of the world. God will allow men to see into heaven." [47] "Something marvelous will happen in the land of the Holy Cross (Brazil). During Holy Mass in the shade of a Brazil tree, the first and **only** **Eucharistic miracle** in Brazil will happen. Because of this miracle, many who have left the Church will return...I don't come from Heaven to obligate you, but what I say must be taken seriously." [48]

"An extraordinary phenomenon will happen in the Land of the Holy Cross (Brazil). In the presence of various Church authorities, the Lord will permit this grace that will be for the good of the Church in your nation. The phenomenon will happen by means of an image of Saint Peter. It will happen in a monastery and will get the attention of the world." [49]

"The day will come when, with the permission of God, a great miracle will happen in Brazil. It will happen with a priest and will be motive for conversion, for many men and women who have strayed." [50]

"The day will come when a great event will happen in a religious house of Carmelite nuns. An image will weep in the presence of a bishop and three priests. It will be the first and only happening in your Brazil. The phenomenon will be repeated three times and will be a motive for the conversion of many wandering souls. Pay attention. The signs of God cannot be ignored. I come from Heaven to announce the truth to you." [51]

"**Minnesota**: the grace of God will come upon his people, and **a great joy** will come **to its inhabitants**. I encourage you to assume your true role as Christians. I am your Mom, and I come from Heaven to bless you and tell you that you are important for the realization of my plans."[52] "The city of Ventura (California) will rejoice. Men will see **great wonders** of the Lord."[53] "A grandiose event will occur in **Poland** and men will marvel." [54] "In celebration of a great saint, will be **a great sign** in the sky of Europe. Mankind will have no explanation. Be attentive to the signs of God. Do not be troubled. Who is with the Lord will never be defeated." [55]

Spiritual Direction

God gives us free will and does not want us to be lost eternally. He instructs us in the ways to go, directly through the Bible and through many of His followers who have heard the Holy Spirit, in the last 2000 years. This includes Mary, Mother of Jesus, who comes from Heaven to guide us.

Our Lady of Peace to **Pedro Regis**: "You must be **in this world, without belonging to the world**. You must desire paradise while living on earth. Belong to the Lord. It was exactly for this that My Son, Jesus, gave Himself for our salvation, with total dedication. **Only in love, can you understand the mysteries of God.** Fill yourselves with Love of the Lord, and you will easily encounter holiness. The **spiritual poverty of humanity** is the fruit of a **lack of love**. Don't forget. Love wants to be loved. I want to lead you to victory, but what I can do, depends on you." [56]

"When I ask you to pray, you must understand that **prayer contributes to your spiritual progress. Prayer is** the **secure resource** (the life line) to God **for you, in these difficult times**…large cities will disappear. Its large buildings will fall as dry leaves in large areas. This is the time of great trials for men." [57]

"I am your Mother, and I know what awaits you. **I am not forcing you**, but I ask you, **not to separate yourselves** from the **path that I have mentioned**. The **line will be broken**. The pain will be great. I ask you to keep alive the flame of faith. What you do not do, is let yourselves be for tomorrow."[58] "Your strength is in Him, that sees the hidden and knows each one of you by name…God sent me before you, to warn you about everything that is to come. What I say, is not to cause you fear. **I prepare you** for **the weight of the cross**. If you pray, you will understand that my calls are not of fear but of alert, that leads you to hope. Continue firm. The designers against my plans will achieve nothing. Those who belong to me, understand my call." [59] "In the **great tribulation** for mankind, **God will send prophets to guide** the chosen. Difficult days will come to humanity." [60]

Mother Elena Leonardi from Mary: "If humanity wants to be saved, it must do penance and receive Holy Communion in atonement for all the offenses, curses, and blasphemy against God and the heavenly Mother. Do Penance!" [61]

"Will Have Little Time to Convert"

After the three admonitions transpire, the visionaries at Medjugorje claim: "After the visible sign, those that are still alive, will have little time for conversion." [62] Afterwards, **"it will be too late,"** [63] responds Ivan, after the permanent sign is visible at Medjugorje. Saying yes, to the three admonitions from God, positions us for strength of body, soul, and spirit.

Even though a respite of peace and evangelization will take place, at this time, a **tribulation** of events **will continue** from the past accumulation of our apathy towards God, and our resignation to the ways of the world around us. In other words, the temporal punishment of our sins will fall upon us. An example, is the weather extremes experienced, are the consequences of our sinfulness upon us, not climate change. These events will sink us into this spiritual reality, unprecedented in the history of the world, since Adam and Eve. The next events to unfold, will severely affect most of us, in this so-called modern world, on this earth.

Our Lady of Peace to **Pedro Regis:** "Power-seeking will result in a great war between religious, and the successor of Peter (Pope Francis I) will see the death of many of his priests. The kidnapping of a religious leader will divide the Church, but the Lord will take care of His people." [64] "I ask you to keep on praying for the Church. The **fury of the enemies** (secret sect) **will affect the Church**, and many who were fervent in faith will become indifferent. The Church will be taken to Calvary, and the faithful will see the death of many consecrated persons. I am your Sorrowful Mother, and I suffer because of what is in store for you. Be strong and firm in the faith." [65]

"The devil wants to cause confusion in the Church and in your nation; he will continue sowing discord, between the sons of God, deceiving with scandals, false signs and false apparitions. A great number of my poor children will be victims of snares of the devil... The devil will continue to make false signs in your Brazil, with false stigmata's and tearful images. I am your sorrowful Mother, and I suffer because of those who will give themselves to the devil, causing confusion in my poor children. God will charge those who deceive and contribute to the withdrawal of many of my poor children, from the path of truth." [66]

"Pray also for Pope Benedict XVI. (Emeritus) **Dark days are coming**, and **great will be the pain of the faithful**. I am your Mother, and I came from Heaven to lead you to the truth. Hold fast to the Gospel, and defend the true doctrine. **You still have ahead of you, long years of trials**, but in the end my Immaculate Heart will Triumph. Go forward without fear." [67]

CHAPTER 38

DECREES OF PUNISHMENTS WILL CONTINUE

After some time, humanity will have calmed down after the reality of the visitation of Mary and Jesus into every home. There will be a turning back to God, but the seals of revelation will unfold decrees of punishments. Humanity will suffer the consequences of their falling away from God, and as the words from Heaven have clarified: the fullness of the decrees does not equal the true punishment.

Opening of the Third Seal of Revelation

Fifth Secret of Medjugorje?

The opening of the third Seal of Revelation is **famine,** which will come after the war and chaos, as, has often happened in such circumstances in the past. Revelation 6: 5-6 states: "When the Lamb broke open the third seal...This time I saw a black horse, the rider held a pair of scales in his hand. I heard what seemed to be a voice coming from the four living creatures... **A day's wages** for **a ration of wheat,** and **the same** for **three of barley,** but spare the olive oil and the wine."

The price of a bushel of wheat has been around $1.00 to $2.00 for most of the 20th century. The first signs of significant change came in 2011, when the price shot up to $8.50 per bushel and has remained higher than historical prices. **Rationing** of essential foods, verifies **famine** of unprecedented proportions. It will be used as payment. In the days to come, food will be the most important concern worldwide.

The reasons for famines or shortages of food have varied over the centuries. Droughts, frost, cold weather, snow in summer, open winters, hail, winds, floods, and volcanic eruptions, all constitute reasons for eventual famines, from a natural point of view. Historical records show, warfare, often preceded the onslaught of famines in the earlier centuries. We can observe other reasons why mankind could be responsible. We have certainly heard from spiritual guidance that **the sin of mankind** can bring famines. Mary, Mother of Jesus, predicted at La Salette, the coming famine, to Scotland and

Ireland, the great potato famine in the late 1840s.

In the 20th century, more people have died from a sinister twist that we call famines, but are really a withholding of resources, by regimes, to advance their schemes; in turn, destroying an agricultural land base of food production that was sustainable for a people, for hundreds of years. Russia was a glaring example of a net exporter of grains to the world, until communism took hold in the 20th century.

After World War II, the World Bank (WB) and the International Monetary Fund (IMF) were formed to rebuild Europe. As time passed into the 1960s and 1970s, this available credit was used for domestic purposes, in the United States and other countries. By the 1980s, the WB and IMF were lending to poor Third World countries; leveraged loans, on the condition that the countries privatize their economies, away from national government control; to allow western international conglomerates, access to their raw materials and agricultural land base.

In developing countries, many agricultural peasants have lost their lands, due to the increased input costs in agriculture. They have no choice but to sell the land to agricultural conglomerates and to move to the cities, becoming landless plantation workers, with only part time work, while agricultural monopolies, through private conglomerates, have taken over the land, for their own enrichment. The earnings of poor farmers are marginal at best, and in fact, leave them with meager food rations. Those who still own their land, are pitilessly charged maximum affordable costs, for farm inputs, such as seed grain, that now, has plant breeder's rights. Roundup-ready herbicides, which destroy all plants, where it is sprayed, leave the smaller farmer on adjacent plots of land, with a lesser harvest of grains, due to harmful spray drift.

The deception of increased yields for small farmers is a financial farce and has been questioned by many international organizations that have researched specific yields. Many Third World countries have lost control of a self-sufficient means, to have food on the table, and actually have less, than in the past, when they owned their small farms, before intervention by corporate business. The people have no other means to fall back on. They have been forced to live in cities, with little or no means to obtain income. In fact, many shantytowns such as in South America and in India have become the norm. This is a travesty, in much of the so-called developing third-world. These countries had their own sources of food, produced by individuals, for hundreds and thousands of years. In the 21th century, with many lobbyist deceptions, maximum profits have been placed as the ultimate goal.

In Canada and the USA, agricultural conglomerates are squeezing the family farms through government deregulation, and monopolizing by increasing costs, thus having greater control of the industry. Companies like Cargill Inc., have a large share of all grain markets and have breeder's rights to newer seed varieties. They own the seed, even if, there is cross-pollination from winds onto other farmer's fields. They have become ruthless, against American farmers, by taking court action for financial gain, destroying their businesses.

What will happen, after the Warning comes to the world and shortly after New York is destroyed? Will there be food in the years to come? After New York is destroyed, there will be war that brings about mass shortages of necessary goods. How will people obtain food, if there is a breakdown of our modern transport systems and large agricultural farms cannot get parts, particularly, fragile computer parts, or fuel for machinery. What will be the alternatives?

Machinery and machinery parts, 50 years ago, were available from one factory that distributed all parts easily. Today parts are made and come from all over the world, including computer parts for combines and tractors, from China, Japan, Europe, India, Australia and many other places. What if just one of the component parts can't reach its destination, or if production companies fail to continue production of machinery parts? **Our Lady of Peace** states to Pedro Regis: "**Humanity is heading** towards an **abyss** of **destruction** that men have **prepared with their own hands.**" [1]

The quandary of purchasing equipment parts from around the world instead of producing it at home, will bring sorrow, not ever seen on earth. This may bring areas of the agricultural industry to a standstill. Food production will have to return to localization and on a manual level, eventually using animals as labor for production of food.

Moreover, the existence of Genetically Modified Seed (GMO's) is an abomination to God's creation. Research in Europe and Russia has led to the ban of GMO's. In the Western hemisphere, many are oblivious to the health risks, although scientist and doctors continue to speak out. The elite have strong marketing schemes and have governmental persuasion over most of the agricultural industry.

Prophecies of Famine

Here are a few saints' forewarnings:

St. Senanus: "The earth will not produce its fruits, for the race of people to whom I allude; full mansions will be deserted, and unpleasant will be the tidings concerning them. Dreadful plagues will come upon all the race of Adam." [2]

St. Columbkille (d 597) "People oppressed **for want of food**, shall pine to death. Dreadful storms and hurricanes shall afflict them. Numberless diseases shall then prevail. **Fortifications shall be built narrow,** during those times of dreadful danger. " [3]

St. Hildergard (1100s) Doctor of the Church: "Before the Comet comes, many nations, the good excepted, will be scourged **by want and famine.**" 4

Venerable Fr. Bartholomew Holzhauser: "Jesus Christ will purify His people through cruel wars, famines, plagues, epidemics, and other horrible calamities. Those Christians who survive the sword, plague, and famines, will be few on earth." 5

Father Laurence Ricci, S. J. (d 1770 "After the rule of Napoleon, a time will come **when people will become poor**, and the world will be punished in three ways; wars, famines, and pestilences. At a time when the world seems doomed, God will intervene..." 6

The **Ecstatic of Tours**–French nun, 1800s: "Before the war breaks out again (2030s) **food will be scarce** and expensive. There will be little work for the workers, and **fathers** will hear **their children crying for food**..." 7

Marie-Julie Jahenny: "The famine will be great... **Everything** will be **thrown into confusion**... the punishments will be shared by all and will succeed one another, without interruption..." 8

Jacinta of Fatima: "Can't you see all those highways, and roads, and fields full of people, who are crying with hunger and **have nothing to eat**? And the Holy Father is in a church, praying before the Immaculate Heart of Mary? And so many people praying with him?" 9, 10

Opening of the Fourth Seal of Revelation

Sixth Secret of Medjugorje?

The decree of the fourth Seal of Revelation, will bring **death over one quarter of the earth.** Revelation 6:7-8: "When the Lamb broke open the fourth seal... I saw a horse, sickly green in color. Its rider was given the name of **Death**, and the nether world was in his train. These four (living creatures) were given authority **over one quarter of the earth**, to kill with sword, and famine, and plague, and the wild beasts of the earth."

This fourth seal, immediately unfolds death. The consequences from the second and third seal opening, will bring death, but the fourth seal will also be a separate result on its own, as it is **a decree**, to bring about a result of Death. The earth will be given over to cataclysmic events, from **magnetic polar shifts, shift of the earth's axis, earthquakes, volcano's erupting, fires, storms, and pestilence;** resulting in **chaos, war, famine, injuries of all kinds causing infections, malnutrition, sickness, disease, plague, and death.** Some of these events, have already started, since 2000, but some of the prophecies may only take place during the time of the comet, collision of two stars and related events. The Blessed Virgin, continues to encourage prayer and fasting: "You have forgotten that **through prayer and fasting,** you can **avert** war **and suspend the laws of nature.**"11 How many are connecting to God in prayer and fasting? Not many. This is what is coming and why.

Spiritual Abandonment Reflects Catastrophic Events

All of the catastrophes at this time, are, and will be, the consequences of our sins. These are what, the seals opening, are all about. It is a set of decrees unfolding, by a Merciful God, to give us a lesser sentence, that offsets the plan of Satan, whose intention was to annihilate humanity completely from the earth.

These cataclysmic events will take place because of the consequences of people, turning away from God, over the last half of the 20th century and into the first part of the 21st century. These events unfolding will cause many deaths. Mary, **Our Lady of Peace,** announces some of these events, very specifically, to Pedro Regis at Anguera, Brazil.

Shift of the Magnetic Field

The north magnetic pole has moved towards Russia, at a rate of five miles per year, for decades, in the 20th century. Since 2000-2001, it is suddenly moving at a rate of 40 miles per year, an 800% increase. Scientists have found 'cracks' or magnetic fluctuations, affecting the protective ionosphere, troposphere winds, and moisture levels. Scientists have issued warnings of mammoth super-storms in the future. Super-storms could cause long term damage to agricultural land bases, basic manufacturing, and infrastructures causing countries and cultures to collapse. The magnetic field, shields the earth from excess solar radiation.

Our Lady of Peace to **Pedro Regis:** "The poles **will switch** and the earth will undergo major transformations. All living beings will suffer. I would ask you to be strong and in all things, imitate My son Jesus. You are not alone. Bend your knees, and seek your strength in the Lord." [12] "Great sufferings for My poor children will come from water and fire. **There will be gaps in the magnetic field of the earth**, and this will **cause disequilibria in the life of humans and animals.**"[13] "A **sudden displacement of the Poles** will bring suffering on **the Earth, the Sun, and its surroundings**. I ask you to do the will of God, and stay far from sin…what I say should be taken seriously."[14] "**The moving of the poles, will change life on Earth,** and my poor children will live moments of distress… I love you, and I come from Heaven to help you. Listen to me. Do not let the devil, take you away from the truth."[15] "The earth will shake, and abysses will appear. My poor children will carry a heavy cross. The earth will lose its equilibrium, and frightening phenomena will appear. I suffer because of what awaits you."[16]

Earthquakes

Earthquakes in many parts of the world will increase. Some scientists claim that earthquakes have not increased in this time, but other information shows earthquakes have increased, with higher Richter scale intensity and in new areas. Earthquakes will likely take place in more populated areas in the future. Contrary to popular belief, the sin of the world, does affect the natural eco-system of the earth. On March 11, 2011, an earthquake hit Japan with an 8.9-9.0 Richter scale intensity, damaging the nuclear reactors and causing a tsunami. More than 28,000 were dead or missing and 500,000 displaced. This happened, in spite of being directly warned to pray, by Mary, at Akita, in 1973; a warning they did not heed.

David Wilkerson's 1973 book, *"The Vision"* speaks of a severe earthquake that he sees in the future for America: "I believe it is going to take place where it is least expected. This terrible quake may happen in an area that's not known as an earthquake belt. It will be so high on the Richter scale that it will trigger two other major earthquakes." He claims that before this major quake in America there will be another strong quake: "possibly in Japan, and may precede the one that I see coming here. There is not the slightest doubt in my mind, about this forth-coming, massive earthquake, on our continent. I believe it will be many times more severe…" [17]

Blessed Sister Elena Aiello from Mary: "Great calamities will come upon the world which will bring confusion, tears, struggles, and pain. Great **earthquakes** will **swallow up entire cities** and **countries**; bringing epidemics, famine, and terrible destruction, especially where the sons of darkness (Pagan or anti-God nations) are." [18]

Cardinal La Roque (1800s): "Devastating storms and earthquakes will frighten the inhabitants of Switzerland and remind them of their frailty." [19]

Our Lady of Peace to **Pedro Regis**: "Humanity will experience great suffering when the earth is shaken by an earthquake which **will drag many regions, now inhabited, into the sea.** Remain firm on the path I have indicated to you." [20] "**Continents will be moved,** and **the land will split into various pieces.** Whoever is faithful to the end, will live to give witness to the love of God. **I don't want to make you afraid,** but **you need to know about all this**"[21] "An earthquake will raise the earth. Men will see something similar to ocean waves." [22]

"Humanity will drink the bitter cup of suffering. The continental **plates** will be shaken with **the great earthquake**, which has not been, **since** the time of **Adam**."[23] "Humanity is heading towards an abyss of self-destruction that men have prepared by their own hands. Terrible earthquakes will **swallow** mountain ranges and cities, and My poor children will experience a heavy cross. Pray. Pray. Pray." [24] "The earth's plates will shift, and **nations will** disappear... As creature, **you challenged the Creator**... now you drink your own poison..."[25] "The crust of the earth will split in many regions of the earth. **Energy coming from the interior** of the earth will bring suffering to many of my poor children. Listen to what I am saying. Humanity is on the eve of the most terrible suffering and punishment. What I have already announced, is going to happen."[26]

"Those **who live in the land of riches** (USA) will experience a heavy cross. The earth **will shake**, and death will be present. They will drink the bitter cup of sorrow. In the west, **near the Pacific**, shouts and wailing will be heard." [27] "Shouts for help will be heard **in San Francisco**, and the same sorrowful things will be heard in **Pakistan... I am your Mom,** and I know what awaits you. I love you as you are, but I need your sincere and courageous yes, for this is the only way that I can transform you and lead you to him." [28]

"Many populated regions will be deserted. You will yet, in the future, **see the earth shaking,** like fruit on **a tree that moves with the wind**. I suffer because of what is coming to you. Bend your knees in prayer." 29

Shift of the Earth's Axis

Our Lady of Peace to **Pedro Regis**: "There will be **a large tilt of the axis,** which will affect the lives of men and animals. The pain will be great. I am your Mother, and I want to help you."[30] "**Sleeping giants** will awake, and there will be great suffering for many nations. The **axis of the earth** will change, and my poor children will live moments of great tribulations... Return to Jesus. Only in Him, will you find strength to support the weight of the trials **that must come.** Courage. I will speak to My Jesus for you." [31]

Gravitational Changes

Our Lady of Peace to **Pedro Regis**: "You will see great suffering on earth. Men go to destruction prepared by their own hands. The day will come when nature will confuse men. The **gravitational force** of the earth will **bring great suffering** and pain. The birds will cry, and the pain will be great for my poor children." [32]

Changes in Nature

Our Lady of Peace to **Pedro Regis**: "The creature is valued more than the Creator, and the time has come to say, enough. There will be signs in the sun, moon, and stars. Nature will be transformed, and men and women will be confused. China will go through great tests. There will be an earthquake causing the death of millions of innocents. The world is full of wickedness. Return now, if you want to be saved." [33]

"Remain firm on the path I have pointed out to you. Know, there **will be great changes in nature.** In many poor regions of Brazil, the Lord will make great wealth appear. The poor will live well." [34]

Fire

Our Lady of Peace to **Pedro Regis:** "The land beloved by the Mother (India) who lived to help the poor, will live moments of profound affliction. I am your sorrowful Mother, and I suffer because of what awaits you. **A fire will fall in Arizona.**" [35]

"Wise men will be surprised: a devastating **fire** will take place **inside the Earth,** and many will experience a heavy cross. Suffer for what you   expect." [36] "Rivers of fire will flow on the earth. The waters will be contaminated in many regions of the world."[37] "When the giant boulders melt, mysterious things will appear. Don't flee from the truth." [38]

"**A fire will cause great destruction in the land of ice** (Iceland, Greenland, Antarctica?).   From the depths will come great destruction to people."[39] Ice on the land that melts, will raise the ocean levels. Ice in the ocean that melts, has displacement value already, not affecting the ocean levels. Volcanoes will bring greater global dimming and cooler temperatures.

"**Rivers of fire will run over the land**, and many places will disappear. Rivers will change their course, and lakes will appear. The day will come when man will desire death but will have to experience the weight of the cross. Bend your knees in prayer. You will yet, to see horrors on earth." [40] "Don't be deceived by false wisdom... Humanity, by its knowledge, has made great conquests, but wants to be like God...A **destructive fire coming from the depths of the earth** will provoke great changes in nature. Many regions of the earth will become desert. Death will travel **in the interior of the earth** and **cause destruction** in many countries."[41] "A frightening event will happen in a famous national park (Yellowstone ?). A destructive fire will start, and people will weep and lament. I suffer because of your suffering. Pray, pray, pray." [42]

Severe Weather Extremes

The recent patterns of extreme weather will continue until the spring of 2038. Extreme warm temperatures will cause droughts, disease, pestilence, and wild fires. Extremes of cold will cause frost damage to crops and shorten growing seasons. The extremes of rain and snow will continue, to cause flooding, destroying crops and property on a continual basis. Many will have to move to higher ground.

Our Lady of Peace to   **Pedro Regis:** "Men and women will live moments of anguish, and many will say, 'this is another deluge'. Many regions of the earth will be hit with great storms. People will run to high ground because many places will be flooded." [43] "Know that destructive tornadoes will come to Brazil, and men will suffer great loses." [44]

Our Lord confirmed to me: "Don't be surprised to see **snow storms** in the **middle of summer in Canada.**" [45]

Mountains

Our Lady of Peace to **Pedro Regis**: "The **Andes chain of mountains will descend**, and many nations will carry a heavy cross. The earth will pass through great transformations, but in the end, victory will come to men and women of faith." [46] The Andes Mountains run along the west coast of South America, for 4500 miles / 7242 km, connected to seven countries of Venezuela, Colombia, Ecuador, Peru, Bolivia, Chile and Argentina.

Something frightening will happen in China and will be repeated in Chile. **A famous mountain range will descend**, and my poor children will weep and lament." [47] "California will face a heavy cross. The ground will rise and the **mountains will descend**. I suffer because of what will come to my poor children. Pray. Pray. Pray." [48] "In the **Twelve Mountains**, will experience a heavy cross (Himalayan and Karakoram range)." [49]

"A destructive force will arise from the depths of the earth, and many **regions** that are **now visible, will no longer exist**. Bend your knees in prayer. I suffer because of what is coming to you." [50]

"**Jura** (mountain range of Switzerland) **will descend** and many regions of the world will carry a heavy cross." [51]"Switzerland also pours tears. It will be in Basel. O men, where do you want to go? The Lord loves you and awaits you."[52] I believe this will be the Jura mountain range of Switzerland. The corruption of world financial affairs at Basel, Zurich, and Geneva, Switzerland will recoil on this region. This will destroy the base of most of the hidden financial affairs of the world. Earthquakes and moving tectonic plates may swallow up that whole region.

Volcanoes

Volcanoes can increase particle pollution in the upper atmosphere, blocking out the sun's rays. This has occurred in the past, when summer did not take place, in 1816, causing the loss of crops, hunger, and starvation in Europe, Asia, China, and India. Increases in intensity of these kinds of events will contribute to a greater loss of life. The Pacific Ring of Fire shows a significant increase in volcanic activity that is affecting a record increase in earthquakes.

Our Lady of Peace to **Pedro Regis**: "**Unexpected volcanic eruptions** will occur when the earth is shaken by a great earthquake, which will make the mountains crumble." [53]

"Humanity is heading towards the abyss of destruction that men prepare by their own hands. **A toxic smoke** coming **from** the **interior of the earth** will bring suffering to men. Do not stray from prayer. The Lord awaits you with open arms."[54] "**Volcanoes arise** with great power, and many will experience **great suffering**. Men challenge the Creator and now go to the abyss of destruction. I ask you to remain steadfast in prayer. God is in a hurry. **What you need to do today, leave it not for tomorrow.**"[55]

"A sleeping giant will bring suffering and death to Africa." [56] "A sleeping giant will arise in Indonesia."[57] "The earth will shake and immense rivers of fire will rise from the depths. Sleeping giants will awake and there will be great suffering for many nations."[58] "Asia will shake, and **a giant, sleeping for centuries,** will cause great destruction…Humanity will live the anguish of one condemned, but in the end there will be the definitive Triumph of My Immaculate Heart." [59]

Extreme Explosions

Our Lady of Peace to **Pedro Regis:** "A large explosion will cause terrible disasters and earthquakes and will destroy many regions of the earth." [60]

Tsunamis

Our Lady of Peace to **Pedro Regis:** "A **giant will fall** and in the **encounter with the waters** will cause great destruction. Regions of the earth will suffer, but those who are with the Lord will receive comfort and peace."[61] "**A giant mountain** (part of comet or large meteor?) **will travel across the Pacific at high speed and cause great destruction in many regions**… Only through prayer, will you find the strength to support the weight of the trials that await you."[62] "When fresh water is invaded by salt water, my poor children will weep and lament. Extensive, will be the destruction. I ask you to intensify your prayers." [63]

Stones and Boulders

Our Lady of Peace to **Pedro Regis:** "Large stones will fall on men. The suffering will be great. I am your sorrowful mother and know what you will encounter." [64] "**A giant** will fall on **Mexico** and the terror will mirror every where. My poor children will carry a heavy cross. Pray. This is the message that today I offer you…"[65] "The force of nature will provoke phenomenon never seen before. Objects will be thrown from the earth by a force that no one can explain. Forces will arise from the depths of the earth that leave men preoccupied, but I want to tell you that God will not abandon His people. Pray. You will yet to see things that human eyes have never seen. Keep to the path that I have pointed out." [66]

Genetic and Technological Destruction

Our Lady of Peace to **Pedro Regis:** "An error caused by genetic modification will cause great destruction and suffering for humanity…"[67] "The **unbridled research** for technological advances will lead men to their own destruction. The day will come when many, will repent of life without God, but it will be too late. Men will seek death from the realization of what they have done."[68] "Mankind is headed for destruction prepared by their own hands. Men are **led into the interior of the earth**. That will be the reason for the destruction of many regions." [69]"What men construct in the depths, will cause great destruction."[70] "Science will advance and **create a manner of transportation** frightening to the eyes of man. What is visible will become invisible to human eyes. Behold difficult times for humanity. Return to Jesus. Let Him be your light, for this is the only way you won't be contaminated by the darkness of the devil." [71]

Plagues Without a Solution

Today, for the first time in history, dangerous bacteria, viruses, spores, and other forms of infection are studied in high security laboratories producing biological pathogens and toxins for research, including for biological warfare as weapons of mass destruction. This could lead to a pandemic or epidemic with no solutions to contain it. Pathogens could escape if research facilities are damaged from various breakdowns of our society. New pathogens will arise.

Marie-Julie Jahenny: "From the time when **the rage of the impious will stop** for a **short respite**, there will come a great disease, **almost suddenly**. This chastisement will leave its victims, as those without life; they will still breathe with the ability to speak; the flesh, raw like, after a deep burn. This malady will be very contagious, and nothing will stop it. It is a punishment from God to **bring many [souls] back**." [72]

This prophecy above divulges that after the chaos, (2 to 4 months in 2021 ?) and after very few years of respite, (?) from the rage of the impious; the **onslaught of this grave disease**, with no known remedy, **will come suddenly**. Marie-Julie Jahenny speaks of **brewing and steeping hawthorn leaves**, to stop a disease with an unknown cure.

Marie-Julie Jahenny instructed by Mary on August 5, 1880: "There will be a grave illness which human science will not be able to alleviate. This illness will attack firstly, the heart, then the spirit, and at the same time, the tongue. It will be horrible. The heat accompanying it, will be a devouring fire, insupportable and so intense that the members of the body affected, will be red; an unendurable fiery red. At the end of seven days this disease, sown like a seed in the field, will spread everywhere rapidly and make great progress. This disease will produce continual vomiting and nausea. If the remedy is taken too late, that part of the body affected, will become black, and in the black, there will be seen a sort of pale, yellow streak."

"My children, here is the only remedy which could save you. You are familiar with **the Hawthorn** that grows practically in all hedges. The **leaves** of the Hawthorn, not the wood, can arrest the progress of this disease. You will gather **the leaves**, not the wood. **Even dry**, they will keep their efficacy. You will put them into boiling water, and leave them there for 14 minutes, covering the receptacle, **so** that **the steam remains therein**. At the onset of this disease, one must use this remedy, **three times a day**." [73]

There is an account of Mary, appearing in extremely, bright light, above a huge **Hawthorn tree** in 1399 in Spain. Those who came to the place of apparition, to honor Mary's requests, would have special grace, and would "**ward off pestilence** and **all disease**." Maternally, she explains, "I was sent in the Hawthorn, **for the good of souls** and **bodies of the faithful**, of the human race."[74] Great devotion to Mary, honoring her requests, will bring remission of sins. Using the leaves of the Hawthorn, will stop the plague from spreading throughout the body. There are many varieties of hawthorn trees or bushes; all are efficacious.

Painful prophecies to behold:

St. Senanus: "The earth will not produce its fruits for the race of people to to whom I allude… **Dreadful plagues will come upon all the race of Adam.**"[75]

Cardinal La Roque: "**Plagues** amongst humans and **beasts** will accompany the earthquakes. The sickle of death will harvest in Prussia, in palaces, as well as in houses of the poor, many will flee to England, but to no avail, for even there, death will over take them." [76]

Our Lady of Peace to **Pedro Regis:** "The **most painful event** of the **fifteenth century will be repeated** (Bubonic plague. Humanity is heading towards self-destruction which men have prepared with their own hands…"[77, 78] Bubonic plague can be treated today, if diagnosed early. There are ongoing cases of Bubonic plague in the United States every year. Know one knows if treatment will be available when the system starts breaking down.

"You who are infected with the plague will not recognize yourselves. Those that are not contaminated will not be able to think. Bend your knees in prayer. I am your mother, and I suffer because of **what you do not expect.**"[79, 80] These words from Heaven to Marie-Julie Jahenny and Pedro Regis, are about a **new plague** not yet known to science. **Our Lord has confirmed to me twice, these plagues will come.** Most likely to Canada and the United States and many other places, after a few short years of respite.

"Science stumbles and error committed by men will be born, a giant will kill many innocent. The search for scientific progress will lead men to madness." [81] "Smallpox will be used as a weapon, against a nation, by men of beard. The suffering will be great for many." [82]

"The blood tree, will lose its root (traditional medicine. Angola, weep for your children. The disease that resembles a huge field of green grams (beans) will torment men. Corpses are scattered everywhere. Terrorists are the culprits. I suffer for what will come to you. Repent." [83]

"**An epidemic** will spread to various nations, and my poor children will experience a heavy cross." [84] "A disease will come and **will be worse than all those that have already existed.** Men will be contaminated and millions of dead are scattered everywhere. I suffer for what awaits you." [85]

Maria Esperanza (1929-2004) from Jesus, to alleviate **the plague**: " I am going to give you **a remedy for the illness of infants and small children**. You must take the leaves from the hawthorn plant, and steep them into a tea for 8 minutes. Then, administer the tea orally to the infant or child, 1/4 cup at a time, continually, throughout the day and night, until the ravages of the illness subside. The symptoms will be flu-like, with high fever, purple-blackened color to the lips, jerking and flailing like convulsions." [86]

Death

Our Lady of Peace to **Pedro Regis:** "Dear children who live in wealth, will not see the wonder, the rich land, and will miss the happy smile. This will happen in Brazil, and men will experience a heavy cross. This will include Sweden, England, the West Coast, and the South Coast; death will pass." [87]

"**Death** will pass by Argentina, and my poor children will live moments of dread." [88] "People will flee in terror from **Lima**, and many will meet with death. Now is a time of sorrows for humanity. Suvo (Fiji islands) and Marajo (Amazon delta) are where it will happen." [89]

"**Death** will cross various countries of Europe, and there will be great destruction. Now is the time of great tribulations for humanity."[90] "Death will pass through the South of France, and my poor children will carry a heavy cross." [91] "Death will pass through northern France, and my poor children will carry a heavy cross. There will be great destruction." [92]

Isaiah 24: 3-6: "The earth is utterly laid waste, utterly stripped. For the Lord has decreed this thing. The earth mourns and fades, the world languishes and fades; both heaven and earth languish. The **earth is polluted** because of **its inhabitants, who** have **transgressed laws, violated statues,** and **broken** the **ancient covenant.** Therefore, a curse devours the earth and its inhabitants pay for their guilt; therefore, they who dwell on earth, turn pale, and few men are left."

Abbess Maria Steiner (d-1862): "I see the Lord, as he will be scourging the world and chastising it in a fearful manner, so that **few men and women will remain.** The monks will have to leave their monasteries, and the nuns will be driven from their convents, especially in Italy..." [93]

Mother Elena Leonardi from Mary, March 6, 1977: "Great persecution will come over the Roman Empire and over the persecuting powers... **millions** and **millions of dead, godless men.**" [94]

CHAPTER 39

BACK TO THE FUTURE

2020s and 2030s

At the beginning of the 20th century, about 63% of the population in Canada and 60% in the USA, lived on the land in a self-sustaining lifestyle. Only about 37% to 40% of the population lived in towns or cities. Today, over 80% of people live in cities or large towns or in small towns that are dwindling or turn into growing cities.

People think they are getting away from it all, though remaining close to outside work, but are constantly dependent on supplies, brought in from all over the world; including foods from distant countries. Many of those foods could be produced locally. All necessities are being shipped onto our little plots of land with barely enough room to place a house on, using paper money, debit, or credit card to obtain it. **We need to wakeup!** Are we going to have enough food when supply lines change or are cut off?

The major world oil producing companies are in the process of reducing drilling and exploration costs, due to the fact, they know the potential is not there anymore. The only way to continue to retrieve oil, is to use new and more expensive technology, to push the oil out of the ground.

Uniquely, since 2012, in North America, 'fracking the ground' has increased production in the USA and Canada. The Northern Alberta oil/tar sands, is a prime example of high retrieval costs for oil at $85 to $100 per barrel as of 2018 to extract oil out of the sand and using an upgrader. In 2018, the oil price was at average $64.90 per barrel. In the past 10 years, Global initiatives have suppressed the Canadian markets for oil. From 2015 to 2019, the governments in Canada have stalled the expansion of export pipelines and transport by oil tankers. The demographics of our countries, show, we are increasingly of older age populations. This will tend to keep the price of oil on the lower side. A large increase in a young population is needed to stimulate an economy.

For many years, it has been understood, with **the known global reserves**, that peak oil has been estimated in the early 2030s, diminishing over the next 50 years, if we can still obtain it, considering the rise of China, India, and south-eastern nations demanding more of it.

With the United States supplies at 12.08 million barrels/day in 2019 with fracking and Canada with 400 years in the tar sands, there appears to be an over abundance in North America; **but worldwide**, it is a different story.

After Oil

A book called, *"The Long Emergency: Surviving the End of Oil, Climate Change, and other Converging Catastrophes of the Twenty-First Century"* by James Howard Kunstler received my attention, after the Holy Spirit urged me to read it.[1]Kunstler's words call attention to the imminent crisis, of which many, remain unaware.

Kunstler says we are sleep walking into the future and are not looking at the reality of the dilemma of our most critical resource that is running out faster than we are being told. That resource is oil, and the fact remains that our lifestyle is dependent exclusively on the continued usage of liquid fossil fuels. He looks at an in-depth study of all the possible alternatives to using oil and is convinced that those sources will not rescue us, after so many years of promised alternatives. None of the options have come to fruition to replace oil. Yes, there is wind energy and solar for electricity but it will not replace the transportation industry. Nuclear energy has many dangers.

Other possible sources such as grains for fuel, have not been refined enough with fossil fuels and are not economical or feasible because of many other problems that arise using them. To use alternatives still leaves us dependent on the use of oil products and oil operated equipment, to run the operations, to maintain new forms of energy. It costs more to produce the corn and now Canola oils, used in alternative fuels and oils, and at the same time, is using up more of the oil, with tractors running on diesel in the fields, to produce this new fuel. The immoral aspect is using grains for fuel, while people starve in various parts of the world. We are reaching a time where food will be the first concern.

It costs more to produce the electricity with fossil fuels than the value obtained to run the vehicle with electricity. We could use sunlight and store energy to have electricity for cars, but no one has been able to improve batteries to any significant amount to store the electricity. The horsepower is just not there, for equipment of any size, to run on electricity from the sun. Most of the decisions made, are political, **"to suit the fossil fuel fiesta."** [2] Kunstler talks about, how we are destroying the planet with the abuse of fossil fuels and how it is affecting the whole earth and our lives. But in the last chapter, he discusses the changes that are coming and will lead us back to a simpler way of life, a life that is local, not global.

A documentary called: *A Crude Awakening: The Oil Crash* by Basil Gelpke and Ray McCormack, was also confirmed to me, by Our Lord, as reliable information, addressing the need to change.[3] As of 2008, 58 countries were already past peak oil. This means their production will continue to decline. According to these guys, the last major oil finds were Alaska North Slope oil in 1967, Siberian oil in 1968, and the North Sea in 1969. It is old news that since 1985, major oil nations, fudged their numbers. Countries like Qatar added 50%

to reserves. Venezuela doubled its reserves in 1987, and Saudi Arabia increased their reserves to incredible amounts overnight. This increase in reported reserves, allowed them to sell more oil proportionally. But this has left deceptive information as to accurate reserves. It is becoming clear that production is leveling out. World production stands at about 97 million barrels per day. However, with the continued expansion of the economies of China and India, world oil production will need to increase to 120 million barrels per day by 2030.

According to the experts in this documentary, it will be virtually impossible to meet that demand. The glass is half empty, as these new economies try to become like the West. The experts say, 200 million barrels per day will be needed of new oil finds, to compensate for the continual decrease of old and declining oilfields over the next 20 years. **This demand on a daily basis is just not there.**

According to the experts, by 2030 the Middle East will have to increase production to 50 million barrels per day. Iran is only at 3.2 million per day, Kuwait struggles at 3.2 million per day. Saudi Arabia states they can produce 12.39 million per day in 2017. Saudi Arabia produced 10.2 in 2018 and 9.95 million barrels per day in 2019. They clearly stated, **if Saudi Arabia has peaked, then the world has peaked.** Iraq is producing 4.5 million barrels per day, and projecting 6 million barrels by 2030. The United Arab Emirates is at 2.89. This is far from adding up to 50 million barrels per day, **not to mention** the **total world demand of 120 million barrels** per day by 2030.

The United States uses 25% of the world's oil at about 20.5 million barrels per day and has now increased production with fracking to 12.08 million barrels per day, in 2019. Russia has increased to 11.16 million and uses about half, for their use. China is down at 3.8 million per day. India is down at 695,619 barrels per day. Venezuela has dropped to 1.36 million barrels in 2019, but due to governmental failure. About five or six other countries produce 2-3 million barrels per day, with smaller amounts from many other countries.

Canada is at 4.6 million barrels per day. Canada has the oil sands. Shell Canada estimates the oil sands hold about 2 trillion barrels. It is a surface mining operation of the first 75 meters with high costs in natural gas and water usage. Recovery of this oil emits three times the pollution, with water pollution affecting pristine lands of Northern Alberta and Saskatchewan.

About 2.91 million barrels per day were recovered in the oil sands in 2018. In 2025, estimates are only at 3.5 million barrels per day according to the Canadian Association of Petroleum Producers (CAPP). The "In Situ" method of pulling oil out of the sand, deeper than 75 meters is now used.

As of January 2020, mandatory curtailment of oil has reduced production to 3.81 million barrels due to the Canadian Federal government stalling on production initiatives. This has been created by Globalist initiatives to stall production for their purposes. This **leaves a grave short-fall**, leaving the world in a near future crises, in order to continue our lifestyle. The other possibility, is to prepare for changes to alternatives. What are the chances of a smooth transition to that, when funds and research have continued to be hampered by the Global lobbyists?

The need to diversify, stands before us in a new and pronounced way. The sooner we realize, what God is calling us back to, the easier it will be in the future, for those who are listening. I am referring to a self-sustainable land based living, growing our own gardens of vegetables, fruit crops, and grains. To have localization, not globalization, is the future reality. The only stock options, we will have to consider in the future, is our own livestock for meat and milk, chickens for meat and eggs, pigs for meat, sheep for wool and meat, and bees for honey, which will lead us towards self-sufficiency.

Oddly enough, future prophecies in the Bible predict this very way of life, where people will not build for others. They will not build for profit. This also means living in smaller, supportable, family-oriented communities, or Christian-based communities, sharing effective ways, but staying within the natural, non-waste environment, and using equipment that is reusable and long-term repairable. As the large farms cease productivity, due to a lack of input resources for productivity, the opportunity to rent or buy small portions of land will be available from large farmers, to produce our own vegetables, grains, and produce. Much property may be available because of financial ruin and the loss of people on the earth. Those who live in towns and cities will have to walk out to the perimeter of the urban sprawl to access available land. **"Eventually the cities and towns will be empty."** [4] After 2038, most people, will live on the land. Only a few of the old, will still live in the cities, refusing to leave. The prophecies say so.

Look to the Amish

James Howard Kunstler, maintains, the economy of the future, "will center on farming, not high tech... To put it simply, Americans have been eating oil and natural gas for the past century, at an ever-accelerating pace. Without the massive inputs of cheap gasoline and diesel fuel for machines, irrigation, and trucking, as well as, the use of petroleum-based herbicides and pesticides, and fertilizers made out of natural gas, Americans will be compelled to radically reorganize the way food is produced, or starve." [5]

He goes on: "I don't believe that working animals will replace all the things done by engines, all of a sudden, but they are sure to be an increasing presence in our lives; and a time may come when we live with far fewer engines, indeed, and **many more working animals.**" [6]

He argues: "We will just have to do farming differently, on a smaller scale, locally, the hard way. An **obvious model** for this kind of agriculture, already exists in the American **Amish community,** which has stubbornly resisted the blandishments of high-tech, through the entire oil drunk extravaganza of the twentieth century." [7]

Proof in productivity: "Amish farming practices today are impressively productive and efficient, even carried on **without electricity** or **motor vehicles.** Wendell Berry has compared their operations favorably with industrial farming in several books." [8] Wendell Berry is an author, poet, activist, and farmer for natural traditional ways of farming verses Industrial Agricultural.

Kunstler explains: "The models are there, and the knowledge is there, but it is not in general circulation…There are plenty of non-Amish people practicing small-scale organic agriculture, and organizations supporting them…which assists small scale farmers with local marketing; with preservation of traditional knowledge and technical help, and with political activism, to prepare the public for inevitable change. There is also a wide spread secular subculture of people, working commercially, in a diverse range of 'obsolete' farm-related crafts, harness makers, smiths, farriers, makers of horse drawn tilling machinery, breeders of draft horses, mules, and oxen … These crafts, people manage to keep alive, skills that Americans will need desperately, when no more trips to the Walmart are possible. The existing literature on small–scale organic farming is vast. Making a transition out of complex systems, on a local basis, including systems of social organization, once common in America but surrendered in recent decades. The difficulties of this transition, will depend on how rapid the onset of the Long Emergency actually is. I believe the disorders and instabilities of the post-peak oil, singularity, will assert themselves rather quickly, long before the world runs out of oil. The quicker they come on, the harsher they will be." [9]

He again reiterates his statements about the **end of suburbia** and all large cities: "The future is now here, for **a living arrangement that has no future**. We spent all our wealth in the twentieth century, building an infrastructure of daily life that will not work very long in the twenty-first century. It's worth repeating **that suburbia is best understood, as the greatest mis-allocation of resources in the history of the world."** [10]

By the 2030s, the breakdown will be quite visible, and gas and oil will be scarce. That does not mean there won't be petroleum in the ground, but the breakdown of supply lines will inhibit the distribution of many resources. The **electrical grid will not be functioning**. Civil chaos will take root, as people try to control food and necessary resources. But with God's intervention at the beginning of this tribulation, we should hope and pray that in North America, we would use common sense and hard work, if everyone is to survive.

In saying that, Our Lord has conveyed to me: "**there will be people who will not submit to God and will continue to be an aggravating threat.**"[11] People may be desperate for food in those days, stealing at night, for what can be obtained. There will be loosely organized rise-ups, of those who will blame the Christians for all the hardships of that time. Only God knows what is in store for us.

CHAPTER 40

THE "FATAL EVENT," CONFUSION, AND CHAOS IN THE CHURCH

Seventh Secret of Medjugorje?

Late 2020s

T his Fatal Event will take place, but **is not part** of God's Seals of Revelation unfolding. This may be the seventh secret of Medjugorje. It is an event by those in the Church turning away from Christ into error. This will start in the late 2020s.[1] Our Lord has confirmed this to me. The incubation of the 'Fatal Event' within the Church that Marie-Julie Jahenny describes, started in the 1700s with the infiltration of Freemasonry, Enlightenment thinkers and continued through the French Revolution. According to Anne Catherine Emmerich, from the 1820s, waves of secular doctrines **from the secret sects** will continue to infiltrate the Church. This continues to sway some priests, bishops, cardinals, theologians, religious and laypeople into a subtle thought process, farther away from the truth. This is leading many, to individualism and liberalism that props up spiritual ideas, contrary to the governing process that Jesus Christ established for two thousand years. A major crisis in the Church existed in the latter part of the 20th century, although, subsided with Pope John Paul II and Pope Benedict XVI; still, it has not disappeared. This infiltration of sinister rebellion of 'insiders' from within the Church will expand the Church's suffering in the late 2020s. Mirjana says: "One of the evils that threatened the world, the one contained in the seventh secret, has been averted, thanks to prayer and fasting."[2] Thanks be to God, one of the calamities will not materialize.

The Vengeance of Hell Against the Church

Marie-Julie Jahenny announces many difficulties, coming in the late 2020s. These prophecies are disheartening and inconceivable:

Marie-Julie Jahenny from St. Michael: "After the standard of hell has prevailed a few months (in 2021), the banner of the Lord will rise in turn, to also win, but again it will fall. And **in the second round** (late 2020s), the effect will be so great that most of the **people will live as before** without priests, without Masses, without receiving the Adorable Divine Heart." [3] The year 2021 will constitute the **first round**; the second, the **fatal round,** will start in the late 2020s.

Marie-Julie Jahenny: "You are about to see **those who govern the Church**...giving their lives and their strength to those who will establish **a fatal government**... They will close the sanctuaries...and surrender to the disorders of hell." [4] "At the time of the **fatal event**...It **will be the ministers of God**, who **will be the first to begin**, not all of them...but **woe to the pastors who abandon the flock**" [5]

Marie-Julie Jahenny from Our Lady: "The time of crimes has begun... the devil will appear in the form of living apparitions... **woe to those who dare to make pacts** with these personages, who appear in diabolical visions... My victim, many souls will be possessed a few months before (the fatal event)...the world will be mad with fear and in this madness, the devil who is everywhere on earth, will make them deny their baptism and the cross." [6]

Marie-Julie Jahenny from St. Michael: "All the demons will come and assemble: **there are many in the form of man** and who after a long time would like to throw brightness [i.e., make seeming miracles?] but they have held something back so far. Consequently, freedom will open [to them] and this brightness will run up and down through the entire kingdom... **All these men are under the habit worn by even the true servants of God**: they are fierce demons, they have a strange hunger to feed and to be fed, they need victims, they need the flesh of the ministers of the Lord, the flesh of His Christian children, the blood of their veins where the faith is flourishing." [7]

Marie-Julie Jahenny from Our Lord: "When the fatal hour arrives, when the faith of my priests is put to the test, it will be these texts that will be celebrated in this second period. The first period is of my Priesthood, which exists since me. The second, is the one of the persecution; when the enemies of the faith and of holy religion will impose their formulas, in the book of the second celebration. Many of My holy Priests will refuse the book, sealed with the words of the abyss. Unfortunately, amongst them, are those who will accept it...these infamous spirits, are those who crucified me and are awaiting the kingdom of the new messiah (Antichrist)."[8] These formulas from the second book, of the second celebration, were in part, attempted during and after the conciliar reforms, but will be placed on the altars during the fatal event. These formulas are words that will be placed into a different mass that are odious and from the pits of hell.

Marie-Julie Jahenny from Our Lord, describes how Lucifer will proceed: "He will address priests: "You will dress in a large red cloak... We will give you a piece of bread and a few drops of water. You can do everything that you did when you belonged to Christ..." "But, says Our Lord, "they do not add, Consecration and Communion." And Hell had added: "We will permit you to say it in all houses and even under the firmament. There will not remain any vestige of the Holy Sacrifice, no apparent trace of faith. Confusion will be everywhere..." [9]

Marie-Julie Jahenny from Our Lord: "My deepest pain, it is owing to this kind of joy in Christian hearts–who were Christians, but who have lost grace–it is seeing this joy...(and then seeing) the power of mortal men who will order throughout the kingdom, **a horrible religion**, as opposed to that which exists today and that makes the happiness of My people." [10]

Marie-Julie Jahenny from Our Lady: "They will not stop at this hateful and sacrilegious road. They will go further, to compromise, all at once, and in one go, the Holy Church, the clergy, and faith of my children... She announces the "dispersion of the pastors" (and bishops) by the Church itself; **real pastors** who will be replaced by others, formed by hell, initiated in all vices, all iniquities, perfidious, who will cover souls with filth...New preachers of new sacraments, new temples, new baptisms, new confraternities..." [11]

Marie-Julie Jahenny: "All of the works approved by the infallible Church will cease to exist, as they are today, for a time. In this sorrowful annihilation, brilliant signs will be manifested on earth. If because of men, the Holy Church will be in darkness, the Lord will also send darkness that will stop the wicked in their search of wickedness..." [12]

Marie-Julie Jahenny from St. Michael: "I affirm that there **has never been** a **like epoch** despite the many anxieties that have passed on earth, so many victims have succumbed; but never has there been a time so cruel, as that which is commencing; that follows slowly to the end, his terrible revenge." [13]

Marie-Julie Jahenny from Our Lord: "I am inconsolable. I see running there, to escape from death and rouse themselves from imposed suffering, multitudes of Christians. [i.e., Christians no longer want to do penance, they avoid all prescribed penances of the Church, **for** a religion that is all 'happy' and does not reflect on serious issues of the soul.] I see them **embrace the religion of a merry heart**, without thinking about Me, on the Church, of their baptism, and all that is good for the Christian soul... by manifesting these signs to My people [i.e., the warnings], I want to bring back My people, before the punishment, because I love them. I see, eagerly entering this guilty, sacrilegious, infamous, in a word, a similar [religion] to that of Mahomet [Because Islam, refutes the godhead of Jesus Christ], there I see Bishops entering. By seeing these Bishops, many, so many, and their (followers), and without hesitation rush into damnation and Hell; My Heart is wounded to death, as at the time of My Passion. I am going to become **an object of horror,**

for the most part, of my people [i.e., His pure, suffering life will become an object of horror]. All youth will be spoiled and soon will fall inputrefaction; the smell of which will be unbearable."[14]

Marie- Julie Jahenny:"St. Michael says, all will descend into the tomb of deep mourning. Satan and his own, will triumph joyfully... the buried Church, the ruined cross, prayers seemingly disappeared, all the people appalled by the empire of massacres, but the Lord will bring forth the sun to console after it has been obscured."[15]

Schism

Schism is the rupture of the union from the ecclesiastical body of the Holy Church. It will occur most likely because of the influence of the French Church, possibly the former Archbishop Lefebvre left wing grievances; to practice the old traditions, contrary to Rome.

Marie-Julie Jahenny: " The Lord announced a **schism** of the Church in France with Rome: The heart of the diocese of [...] will revolt and will not be pacified. Its cries and menacing words will make the strong tremble. In the days when the gloom of the great vengeance will surround the people with struggles and conflicts, this pastor [The Bishop of...], like the others **will not** submit to orders of the Roman Pontiff... When the power of mortal men-soiled, corrupt men who are threatened with a terrible death–when this power will order a frightful religion in the whole Kingdom... I see only **a small number** enter this religion that will **make the whole world tremble.** ... From the height of My glory, I see, joining with alacrity, this guilty, infamous, sacrilegious religion. I see bishops joining... On seeing this many, many bishops... Ah! My Heart is wounded to death–and the whole flock following them, all of it, without hesitation, hastening to damnation and hell... Others will follow these French bishops... If I tell you that, to found this infamous and accursed religion, the bishops and priests will not let off, at the second call. You may be sure, my children, that the bishops and priests will not be in favor of the one, I have destined to raise up your country, there will be very, very few in favor of him... They will be against the King..." [16] The Lord is speaking of the Great Catholic Monarch.

Our Lady of Peace to **Pedro Regis** "A nation will **challenge the Church** (France?), and great will be the suffering, for a successor of Peter (Peter the Roman." [17] "I would ask you to intensify your prayers, in favor of the Church of My Jesus. An order will be given to a cardinal. **Obedience to the enemies** will cause great confusion. This will surprise, causing shock, pain, and destruction."[18] "**One who opposes Christ** will gain an ally and together will cause serious conflicts in the Church of My Jesus." [19] "**An order** shall be given by an order. There is falsehood in its promise, and the throne of Peter will be shaken. Now live the times of great spiritual confusion."[20] "The opponent will find in the Vatican, the key that will open the door to act in the world.

He, with his cunning, will involve men and women of great wisdom. His project will involve men of science and religion. This poisonous project will attract project leaders from the whole world; people famous and simple people." [21]

"The revolt of many consecrated persons will cause great suffering for the Church. A wound will open at the heart of the Church because of the Great Schism. The action of the devil will make many devoted, to deviate from the truth. Pray for the Church. " [22] "The revolt is the fruit of disobedience." [23]

"The action of the demon will lead many theologians to deny great dogmas of the Church. This will cause divisions in the house of God." [24] "Many will turn against the successor of Peter, and there will be a great crisis of faith. A successor of Peter will carry a heavy cross and will see the death of many consecrated persons." [25]

An Apostasy

Apostasy is the abandonment of a defined lifelong spiritual commitment to a contrary position. The final great apostasy that St. Paul speaks about will take place after the beginning of the seventh Church age. The birth pangs continue at this time, in this fifth Church age. The satanic spirit of the secret sect will push the Church to the brink of collapse. Apostasies will occur, from the secret sect that has influenced education by monetary support, in countries of the western world. Contempt for the sacred will include, trying to eliminate consecration of the bread and the wine from the Holy Mass. This is still an ultimate goal of the Freemasonry/ Illuminati.

Marie-Julie Jahenny: "Later on, the Lord showed me **the number of apostasies** at the time of the **fatal event**... It **will be the ministers of God**, who will be the first to begin, not all of them...This punishment (beginning of the unfolding of the Sixth Seal) will open the heavens, and the God of vengeance will appear, with a display of justice. Never had I seen from so close the anger of God... But **woe to the pastors who abandon the flock**." [26]

Our Lady of Peace to **Pedro Regis:** "Do not let yourselves be deceived by the false ideologies and by false prophets. **Know that the truth is kept fully only in the Catholic Church**... A **great apostasy** will lead many of my poor children to move away from God. Take care. What I say should be taken seriously. Those who do not walk in the truth of the Church, will be lost in the confusion of the false religions." [27]

"In many parts, the heresies will win. Apparently it will be a defeat for the Church, but the final victory will be my child Jesus." [28] "Europe will rise up against the Church. It will reject the truth and cause great suffering to a successor of Peter." [29] "The great apostasy will reach the Church in the land of Santa Cruz (USA?) The devil will cause great spiritual blindness in many consecrated." [30]

"There will be a man, apparently full of virtues, but in truth will be one sent by the devil, who will be mistaken, for thinking that much of his doctrine is true, but will find a great barrier, in the strength and loyalty of My devotees and chosen ones." [31]

"Mankind lives in the darkness of sin, and my poor children are lost in the darkness of spiritual blindness. The action of the demon will lead many to lose true faith. You will see horrors on Earth. The Church will be persecuted. Peter's throne will fall, but the righteous will win. Listen to my pleas. **I do not come from Heaven for the fun of it**. A great religious war will rise, and the believers will be thrown out. Love the truth and defend it." [32] This prophecy is typical, of persecution in the history of the Church. It comes from within, from those who have abandoned the truth and the side of Jesus.

Antichrists Will Rise Up

The time of the Antichrist that St. Paul, early Church Fathers, Doctors of the Church and Catholic saints speak about **will not appear** until **after** the end of the sixth Church age of peace. However, there have always been antichrists; they rise up when nations are unable to solve the basic problems of sustaining themselves. Attractive, charismatic leaders, appear, promising the world to the people, while often blaming the religious leaders for problems. This will be an exceptional time. We are warned.

Marie-Julie Jahenny: " The temples of God, where Hell has taken up residence, has placed its field of action. It is time to raise one's eyes to Heaven because **in all corners of the world,** there will be Antichrists, **as at the time** of the last Judgment, who will travel through the whole world to pervert... " [33]

Our Lady of Peace to **Pedro Regis**: "One who opposes Christ, will manifest and will seduce many of my poor children into error. You are given awareness. It is a **false messiah** that will seduce even many consecrated." [34] "Whatever happens, do not allow the flame of faith to go out, within you. Do not flee from prayer... The precious food will be seen and desired, but men will fear. An **antichrist will act with great fury** to destroy the Church of My Jesus. Its major thrust will cause the greatest spiritual damage, which men have **not witnessed since the time of Adam.** O children, I suffer for what comes to you. I am your Mother, and I will be near you." [35]

"Mankind will be surprised by the presentation of **a man with good appear ance**, and this will entice many to their mistakes, because their actions come from the evil one. Many will **see him as the Savior**, and he will be able **to gather around him**, a large number of people. You are warned."[36] "One that will be welcomed as the light, will in fact, be the terror of nations. **His plan will be only one** but will bring serious consequences for my poor children. Pray. Stand firm on the path that I pointed out. Love the truth."[37] "A man **who seems to be good** and just will come, but he will be a traitor, and lead mankind to suffering." [38]

"The day will come when an apparently good and just man will appear. He will deceive many people, for he will perform great prodigies. He will come from the southern hemisphere and many people will consider him as a savior. Pay attention and don't be deceived. Listen to My appeals." [39]

Visible Break Down of the Church

At Medjugorje, the visionaries in the early years voiced their concern of a break down of the visible Church. The Roman Catholic Church will suffer, but it will succeed into the sixth Church age of peace.

St. John Bosco is a priest well known for prophetic dreams. In 'The Two Columns in the Sea,' a part of the vision is summarized: "There will be an Ecumenical Council (Vatican II) in the next century (20th century), after which there will be **chaos in the Church**. Tranquility will not return, until the pope succeeds in anchoring the boat of Peter between the Twin Pillars of Eucharistic Devotion and Devotion to Our Lady."[40] This will not be accomplished fully, until the Angelic Pastor with the stigmata cross on his forehead, becomes Pope; after Peter the Roman and the empty papal chair. In order to survive this time, true Church members must be anchored in Eucharistic Devotion and Devotion to Our Lady.

Ven. Holzhauser: "But God will **permit a great evil against His Church;** heretics and tyrants will come suddenly and unexpectedly; they will break into the Church, while bishops, prelates, and priests are asleep. They will enter Italy and lay Rome waste; they will burn down the churches and destroy everything." [41]

Our Lady of Peace to **Pedro Regis:** "Pray. The action of the demon will lead many to disbelieve the faith. A terrible plan will be put into practice with the goal of destroying the Church of my Jesus. Many will recede away, and the Pope will feel alone."[42] "Because of the bad shepherds, who deny the great dogmas of the faith, the faithful will become cold and full of doubts. The Church will be tormented by major storms, and few will remain steadfast in the faith." [43]

"The Lord is in control of everything, but **for the good of men**, will allow major trials to His Church. The day will come when in the Church you will see few pious men and defenders of the truth. **Many will be contaminated by the false doctrines, applied by bad theologians,** and **many hearts will be hardened and will not accept the truth**. I suffer for what awaits you. Listen to the voice of the Lord, and accept the teachings of the successor of Peter." [44, 45]

"A **discovery on the Vatican grid** will cause confusion. Bend your knees in prayer in favor of the Church."[46] "The Sacred laws will be weakened, and few will have respect for the sacred. The clerics of the Holy Church will turn their backs on truth, and large numbers will kiss false doctrines. This will bring great spiritual confusion in the house of God…" [47]

"A great crowd marches and in their hearts there will be a great desire for revenge, bringing suffering and pain for faithful men. They shall pollute the sanctuary, and the pain will be great for the Church of My Jesus." [48] "An attack will draw the attention of the world, and for men and women of faith, it will be a time of great pain. The action of the enemy will cause damage, and the Church will be divided." [49]

How Many Popes?

In the time of this last Pope, on St. Malachy's list, we are moved to reflect on the unfulfilled prophecies, of possible tribulations before us. It seems many in Europe will not be happy with 'Peter the Roman,' and these prophecies relate, possible unlawful popes as well.

St. Francis of Assisi: "There will be very few Christians who will obey the true Sovereign Pontiff and the Roman Church with loyal hearts and perfect charity. At the time of this tribulation, a man, not canonically elected, will be raised to the pontificate, who by his cunning, will endeavor to draw many into error and death. Then scandals will be multiplied, our Order will be divided, and many others will be destroyed, because they will consent to error, instead of opposing it. There will be such diversity of opinions and schisms among the people, the religious, and the clergy, that, except those days were shortened, according to the words of the Gospel, even the elect would be led into error, were they not specially guided, amid such great confusion, by the immense mercy of God." [50]

Our Lady of Peace to Pedro Regis: "A well dressed man will enter into the house of God and will take a special place. The enemies of God will join him and will do great damage to all humanity. He will seem like a good man and will seduce many people. The rock will not be overcome because God is faithful to His promises." [51] "The one who could have been Peter (Cardinal) will become Judas. He will open the doors for the enemy and will make men and women of faith suffer..." [52] "The day will come when there will be two thrones, but only on one, will be the true successor of Peter. It will be a time of pronounced spiritual confusion for the Church...."[53] "Astonishing events will shake the Church. The uprising of a great religious leader will cause suffering and pain for my children..."[54] "Frightening things will happen and wise men will be confused. You live in a time of great spiritual confusion. When a man presents himself with three names, there will be great confusion in the house of God. Pray, pray, pray..." [55]

A Franciscan Capuchin Friar, Genzano, Italy (1700s): "During these sad calamities, the Pope shall die. Through the death of the supreme pontiff, the Church will be reduced to the most painful anarchy, because from three hostile powers [through their influence] three pope will be contemporaneously elected: one Italian, another German, the third Greek, This, by force of arms, shall be placed on the throne..."[56]

CHAPTER 41

OPENING OF THE FIFTH SEAL OF REVELATION

Eighth Secret of Medjugorje?

The fifth Seal of Revelation will unfold with decrees of persecution and martyrdom. Persecution and martyrdom have been continual in the 20th and 21st century, since the rise of communist regimes throughout the world. This is most likely the eighth secret of Medjugorje.

Revelation 6 :9-11 states: when the lamb broke open the fifth seal, I saw under the altar, the spirits of **those who had been martyred** because of the witness they bore to the word of God. They cried out at the top of their voices: How long will it be, O Master, holy and true, before you judge our cause and avenge our blood among the inhabitants of the earth? Each of the martyrs was given a long white robe, and they were told to **be patient a little while longer, until the quota was filled** of their fellow servants and brothers **to be slain**, as they had been." 'Until the quota was filled,' is a prophecy fulfilled at the beginning of the seventh Church age.

At the end of this fifth Church age, the fifth seal, decrees martyrdom of a portion of humanity, mainly the Christian people, killed by those against God. This will happen mostly in the nations that will have been over-come **by Muslims**, mostly European, Mediterranean, Middle East countries, African, the Philippines, and countries south of Russia. [1]

Those who have continued to **reject God**, will rise up against Christian society. This has been apparent in the latter part of the 20th century and continues on. This will include all those who apostatize and turn on those still in the Church. This will include governments still in power, backed and encouraged by the secret sect, that is, those who are in Freemasonry/Illuminati and still have control by deception, fear, and chaos. This will exist in the western countries until 2038. The heightened persecution and martyrdom will take place during the very late 2020s and the early 2030s.

Prophecies of Persecution and Martyrdom

St. Hildegard of Bingen (Doctor of the Church): "Toward the end of the world, **mankind will be purified** through sufferings. This will be true, especially of the clergy, who will be robbed of all property. When the clergy has adopted **a simple manner of living**, conditions will improve." [2]

Blessed Abbot Merlin Joachim of Fiore: "After many prolonged sufferings endured by Christians, and **after a too great effusion of innocent blood**, the Lord shall give peace and happiness to the desolate nations." [3]

Abbess Maria Steiner (?-1862): "...The monks will have to leave their monasteries, and the nuns will be driven from their convents, especially in Italy... **The Holy Church will be persecuted**... Unless people obtain pardon through their prayers, the time will come when they will see the sword and death, and Rome will be without a shepherd. The Lord showed me how beautiful the world will be after this awful chastisement. The people will be like the Christians of the primitive Church." [4]

Prophecies at the High Altar of **St. Peter's Basilica,** 1975, at the International Catholic Charismatic Conference in Rome (continued): "My Church will be different; difficulties and trials will come upon you. The comfort that you know now, will be far from you, but the comfort that you will have is the comfort of my Holy Spirit. **They will send for you, to take your life**, but I will support you. Come to me. Band yourselves together around me. Prepare, for I proclaim a new day, a day of victory and triumph for your God." [5]

Mirjana was frightened about **the eighth secret** of Medjugorje and prays to Our Lady for mercy on mankind (Nov. 6, 1982): "I have prayed; the punishment has been softened. Repeated prayers and fasting reduce punishments from God, but it is not possible to avoid entirely the chastisement. Go on the streets of the city; count those who glorify God, and those who offend Him. God can no longer endure that." [6]

A Franciscan Capuchin Friar (1700s): "**All the ecclesiastics,** both secular and regular, shall be stripped of all their possessions, and of every kind of property; obliged to beg from lay persons; their food and everything nec-essary for their support, and for the worship of God. All **religious orders will be abolished, except one** having the rules of the most rigid and most severe institute of the ancient monks." [7]

Sister Rosa Columba (Asdente) of Taggia (d 1847): "Many terrible calamities impend over Italy. Priests and religious shall be butchered like cattle in the shambles, and the earth, especially in Italy, shall be watered with their blood. The persecution in Italy, is to begin by the suppression of **the Jesuits;** they shall be called back again; then a third time, they will be suppressed and never more **be revived.** During a frightful storm against the Church, **all religious orders will be abolished except two,** namely, the Capuchins (St. Francis) and the Dominicans (St. Dominic), together with the Hospitallers (serving the infirm since 1100s) who shall receive the pious pilgrims who, in great numbers, shall go to visit and venerate the many martyrs in Italy, killed during the impending persecution." [8] "A cruel and bloody persecution shall rage against religion…through **the malice of wicked children of the Church.**" [9]

Our Lady of Peace to **Pedro Regis**: "I ask you to **have the courage of John the Baptist.** Defend without fear the true doctrine. Whatever happens, do not allow the flame of your faith to be extinguished within you. My Jesus will not, abandon His Church. The cross will be heavy, and **many consecrated persons will suffer death,** but by the grace of my Jesus, **a man of faith will come forth** who will take the Church to her final great victory." [10]

"**Many will be persecuted and many will be martyred.** Great will be the suffering of those who love the truth. Be courageous…Seek strength in the Eucharist with fasting and prayer. I am your Mother and walk at your side." [11] "Many devoted, will live the anguish of one condemned. The blood of many devoted will **race through the streets** and **squares as rain water.** The Church will suffer major attacks." [12]

"The day will come when the cross will be heavy for the men and women of faith. **The opponent will prevent Christians joining to pray in public places,** many will be martyred, and others will deny the faith. I ask you not to separate yourselves from prayer." [13] "The strength of the opposing party will cause great suffering for my poor children… churches will be destroyed. **Famous shrines will be attacked,** and death will be present within the Church. I suffer for what awaits you." [14]

"The day will come when men **will be forced to deny the real presence of Jesus in the Eucharist.** The faithful will be threatened and placed on trial… This is the greatest pain for the faithful. Many overcome by fear will flee. In many places, the enemies will win, but the final victory will be the Lords." [15] "The Tabernacles will be removed, and **only those in secret will worship the Lord…**Like the early Christians, you will be prosecuted and brought to trial. Suffer for what you expect. Pray." [16]

"The great persecution will reach, above all, the men and women of faith. The faithful priests will be beaten and taken to prisons. In the land of Santa Cruz (U.S.A?), will create laws to separate you from God. Do not shrink back."[17] "**A movement will rise** and will spread throughout the world. **It will work openly against the Church** and dispel many men and women of God's grace."[18] "As well as the first Christians…the good will be pursued and **left in prison.**" [19] "In the land of Santa Cruz (USA?) was born a movement that will give strength to **the sects** and will bring suffering to the Church of My Son Jesus."[20]

"The great suffering to the Church will come **in the form of political power.** Laws will be created to stop the action of the Church. In many places, churches will be destroyed and the Christians will weep and lament." [21]

"**A movement was born** and will spread around the world. **Women will coordinate it,** and it will bring great suffering to the Church of My Jesus. I suffer for what awaits you. Bend your knees in prayer. Love the truth and defend it. Flee from false ideologies, and embrace the Gospel of My Jesus..." [22] "The devil wants to separate you from the truth. Close your eyes **to the false seductions of the world,** for you belong to the Lord. I want you to be good to all. Love. In the love of the Lord, you will discover the great treasures that are within you. Be prudent in the use of your liberty." [23]

Marie-Julie Jahenny: "The vengeance of hell will rise to the altars; the most infamous of all men [those possessed]. They will take the place of the true servants of the Lord. Everything will be against the Faith and against the holy laws in their sacred ceremonies. The law will oblige parents to leave their children, to pervert them. These sacrileges **will last 44 days.** Many Christians will suffer martyrdom. These crimes will be followed closely, [by] the vengeance of the Lord." [24] The Chastisements from God, will take place not long after the 44 days of sacrileges in 2038.

Chapter 42

Opening of the Sixth Seal of Revelation

Very late-2020s to 2038

The opening of the sixth Seal of Revelation, is the opening of the **ninth secret of Medjugorje,** starting with a collision/explosion in the universe igniting other events, before, eventually culminating with the **tenth secret** of Medjugorje or the **third secret** of Garabandal. These events are chastisements directly from God. Revelation 6: 12-13 states: "When I saw the Lamb break open the **sixth seal** there was a violent earthquake, and the **sun** became **black as** goat's-hair **(sackcloth)** tent cloth, and the **moon grew red as blood**. The **stars…** **fell** like figs, shaken loose by a mighty wind." This is the passage of the nucleus and coma of the comet, coming close to the earth, that cause three days of darkness.

According to Mirjana of Medjugorje: "The **ninth** and **tenth** secrets are **grave matters…**The punishment is inevitable because we cannot expect the conversion of the entire world. The chastisement **cannot be mitigated** by prayers and penance. It cannot be suppressed." [1] These **two chastisements,** achieve God's purposes: to clean up the earth, restoring the earth to a balanced ecosystem and to destroy the evil people, leaving a remnant Church on the earth. Many places, countries, and continents will be changed, leaving the physical composition of the earth, almost unrecognizable.

Pope John Paul II did speak about the opening of the seven Seals of Revelation. Jesus Christ Himself, will set these decrees in motion, to bring a transformation of God's will on the earth. This **sixth seal begins with** a collision in the universe that will transpire years before the final chastisement. Reflecting on the sixth seal, it describes the darkness of the sun and the moon as blood red, mirroring these prophecies:

Joel 3: 4: "The sun will be turned into darkness, and the moon to blood, at the coming of the day of the Lord."

Matthew 24: 29: "And immediately **after the tribulation of those days,** the **sun** shall be darkened, and the **moon** shall not give her light."

Luke 21: "There will be **signs** in the sun, moon, and the stars. On the earth, **nations will be in anguish,** distraught at the roaring of the sea and the waves. Men will die in fright, in anticipation of what is coming upon the earth."

'The day of the Lord' is understood as a day or days of chastisement and not His actual coming. The opening of the sixth seal, in its full description, will not be completed at this time, at the end of this fifth Church age. The rest of the sixth seal unfolding, will be accomplished after the end of the seventh Church age. These events taking place at the end of this fifth Church age, will destroy a large portion of mankind, during the time of the comet and the three days of darkness, just before Easter, in the year 2038.

Our Lady of Peace to **Pedro Regis:** "Dear children, this is the time of your return. Do not remain on the sidelines. The day will come when **the sun and the moon** will no longer fulfill their travel as in your days. Your eyes will **see the signs,** announced by My Son Jesus." [2]

A Collision in the Universe
Very late 2020s or early 2030s

An unforeseen scenario, of a collision of 'two giants,' deep in the universe, starts the final Chastisements from God. The collision is the beginning of the ninth secret of Medjugorje. This collision, "like two stars…that crash and make a lot of noise, and a lot of light…," may have begun during the moment of the Warning. Conchita at Garabandal alludes to this. The light, the shock waves and rock debris from the explosion could take years to reach the earth.

Our Lady of Peace to **Pedro Regis:** "The **great light will be visible** in the **southern hemisphere**. If men do not repent, fire shall fall from heaven, and a large part of humanity will be destroyed. What I gave to you in the past will hold true." [3]

"A collision **between two giants** in the universe will provoke great damage on earth. **Fire will fall from heaven,** and many regions of the earth will be stricken." [4] "Bend your knees in prayer. I am your Mom, and I love you. I ask you to always belong to the Lord. Seek the things from above, and fill yourselves with the love of God. I desire your spiritual good. Open your hearts, and help me. I need your sincere and courageous yes. Don't back out. Now is the time I told you about, in the past. Tell everyone that God is truth, and that God exists. He loves you with the immense love of a Father. Courage. Go forward." [5] "A **southern star will lose its brightness** and men will fear major events. In a short time, will come great destruction." [6]

Our Lady of Peace to **Pedro Regis:** "Amazing events will draw the attention of men. An **explosion in the universe** will cause great astonishment to wise men. The earth will suffer." [7] The heat energy from the great flash of light or explosion in the universe, is God's swift action, to end the continual evil intentions of destroying God's name, on the earth. This will be the end of all the electrical systems on earth, at that time. In order to preserve a remnant of his Church on earth, God will intervene. As Our Lady of Peace says to **Pedro Regis: "God is in a hurry…"** [8]

Worldwide Destruction of the Electrical Grids
Very late-2020s or early 2030s

The cessation of a functional electrical grid in the years ahead is a disturbing prophecy. One possibility that could arise, is from the failure to maintain power grid systems amidst a lack of resources. A second possibility could be large solar bursts from the sun. Scientists now state that solar flares could take out electrical power grids across nations. The third is undeniable; a collision deep in the universe will bring with it, the destruction of the electrical grids.

Johann Friede (1204 to 1257) an Austrian monk from the Order of St. John who foresaw the comet coming to earth, states: "The great time will come in which mankind will face its last, hard trial... **When even your artificial light will cease to give service, the great event** of the firmament **will be near.**" [9] If **artificial light will cease to exist,** obviously **electricity will no longer be available.**

Our Lady of Peace to **Pedro Regis**: "I am your Mother and come from Heaven, to show you the way to salvation. Don't cross your arms. Return to God as quickly as possible. Pray. Pray for yourselves and for others. Pray for the conversion of everybody. Renounce everything that takes you away from God and live my messages. **If there is no conversion, the wrath of God** will **come upon you,** so be converted, be converted, be converted. **All the means** of **communication** that work **to destroy the plans of God**, will be **laid waste** by the wrath of God, which will come **like a great bolt of lightning** and everything will be destroyed. Be converted. The destiny of your Brazil and of the world, depends on your conversion." [10]

Mari Loli, a visionary at Garabandal, revealed to Father Gustavo Morelos: "In spite of seeing the Virgin, we began to see a great multitude of people who were suffering intensely and screaming with tremendous fear...There will come a time when **all motors and machines will stop**; a **terrible wave of heat** will strike the earth, and men will begin to feel a great thirst. In desperation, they will seek water, but this will evaporate from the heat... Then, almost everyone will despair, and they will seek to kill one another... They will lose their strength and fall to the earth. Then it will be understood, it is God alone, who has permitted this. Then, we saw a crowd in the midst of flames.. The people ran to hurl themselves into the lakes and sea. But, the water seemed to boil and in place of putting out the flames, it seemed to enkindle them, even more..." [11]

The **collision/explosion** in the universe will transmit tremendous heat energy in all directions, including towards planet earth. The great flash of light will get here first, like a great bolt of lightning. It will get here before the audible sound of the explosion. Afterwards will come the rock and debris. This bolt of heat **will bring a swift and sudden end to communication systems on**

this planet. This means television, radio, Internet, phones, cell phones, GPS, satellites and all communications that transmit the flood of filth and deception that is taking people away from God, will cease. If humanity does not give it up intelligently, God is going to break down all electrical power systems, on this planet, by some swift unknown, 'like a bolt of lightning' that will leave us 'in the dark' as this next prophecy states: "The displacement of poles will change life on earth, and my poor children will live moments of distress. The day will come that the sophisticated means of **communication will collapse.** Men will be left deaf and blind. Pray. Beseech the Lord's mercy for you. I love you, and I come from Heaven to help you. Listen to me. Do not let the devil take you away from the truth."[12] Ultimately, the deep freezers and coolers to store food will cease to work, as will the rest of the electrical appliances in our homes. Our Lord has confirmed to me that I should learn how to **dry foods** on drying racks.[13] All modern industrial, agricultural, and maritime production will come to a halt. **This is the day of change** on earth, not for the better in the short term, but **to a great retrogression** of our lives; **back to the land,** and a simpler way of life. Our Lord has confirmed to me, to obtain **wood stoves** for heating. Wax candles will help for light in winter months. Many will lose their lives, in northern climates. This will bring a great wave of chaos and strife; humanity will not ever face such traumatic change. Many will not take heed before hand.

Warfare at this time will not be as high tech, dependent on electrical and computers. The use of older mechanical methods may be used in warfare. This is in part, God's intention to stop nuclear disaster at that time; in fact, this will be the end for nuclear. Oil will not be obtainable, with the electrical breakdown of all industrial processing. Driving trucks for maintenance and the whole process of sustaining systems will come to a halt, according to Mari Loli's prophecy. The shocking truth to future changes is going to be hard to accept.

The Trumpets
Early 2030s

The seventh seal of Revelation reveals the opening of the seven Trumpets. The first four angels' Trumpets, announce literal events unfolding, after the collision/explosion in the universe. The angels are directly involved here. The first Trumpet reveals physical matter coming from the collision /explosion. Months or even years may pass, after the collision/explosion before the flash of light, the sound wave, and rocks and particle debris reaches the earth's atmosphere, igniting on fire and heating up the earth for a time. The next two Trumpets follow sometime in between, and before the comet. The fourth Trumpet is related to the visible comet. The fifth Trumpet is a direct woe; then the sixth Trumpet is part of the last major chastisement from God. The collision/explosion causing the events of the first angel's Trumpet may take place, some years before the actual comet's approach to the earth in 2037 and 2038.

Revelation 8: 3-5: "And I saw that the seven angels who stood before God, were given seven trumpets. Another angel came and stood at the altar, holding a gold censer. He was given a great quantity of incense to offer, along with **the prayers of all the holy ones**, on the gold altar that was before the throne. The smoke of the incense along with the prayers of the holy ones went up before God from the hand of the angel. Then the angel took the censer, filled it with burning coals from the altar, and hurled it down to the earth. There were peals of thunder, rumblings, flashes of lightning, and an earthquake. "

This Revelation prophecy is confirmed by **Blessed Elena Aiello:** "Before my eyes, there extended an immense field, covered with flames and smoke, in which souls were submerged, as if in a sea of fire." The Blessed Virgin Mary states: "And **all this fire, is not** that, which will fall **from the hands of men,** but **will be hurled directly from the Angels.**" [14] This prophecy confirms the opening of the Trumpets of Revelation 8: 3-5, of the angel with the gold censer, filled with live coals, hurled down to the earth. At the beginning of God's chastisements, the angels are assigned, to execute these predestined universal mass events.

The First Angel's Trumpet
Fire from the sky

Revelation 8: 7: "When the **first angel** blew his trumpet, there came hail and then **fire** mixed with blood, which was hurled down to the earth. A third of the land **was scorched**, along with a third of the trees and every green plant."

Isaiah 66: 15-16: "Lo, the Lord shall come in fire, his chariots like the whirlwind, to wreak his wrath with burning heat and his punishment with fiery flames. For the Lord shall judge all mankind by fire and sword. And many shall be slain by the Lord."

Marie-Julie Jahenny: "A rainfall of fire, thunder, and flames and fire and hail…shall proceed to the earth. The heat from the sky will be so scorching as to be unbearable, even within your closed homes." [15]

Mother Elena Leonardi (1976 visionary) An unforeseen fire will descend over the whole earth, and a great part of humanity will be destroyed."[16]

Josyp Terelya (1987) Ukrainian visionary: "fields aflame, even the air and water burning, smoke and fire everywhere…rivers of blood." [17]

Blessed Elena Aiello from the **Blessed Virgin Mary:** "See how **Russia** will burn! Before my eyes, there extended an immense field covered with flames and smoke, in which souls were submerged as if in a sea of fire." [18] "Clouds with lightning, flashes of fire in the sky, and a tempest of fire shall fall upon the world." [19]

Mother Elena Leonardi (1970) "Sometimes right before my eyes, I see rainfall of blood and fire which seems to come from Heaven. I see an endless sea and atomic bombs exploding. But I do not succeed in understanding such visions, and I cannot grasp their exact meaning."[20]

Mother Elena Leonardi (1974) : "My daughter, I am the Lady of Sorrows, with My gaze on heaven to implore the Heavenly Father because of the great cataclysm, which will simultaneously convulse the earth. It will be terrible frightful, as if it were the end of the world! But the end of the world has not arrived yet..." [21] "**An unforeseen fire will descend** over the whole earth, and a great part of humanity will be destroyed. This will be a time of despair for the impious: with shouts and satanic blasphemy, they will beg to be covered by the mountains, and they will try to seek refuge in caverns, but to no avail. Those who remain, will find God's mercy in my power and protection, while all who refuse to repent of their sins will perish in a sea of fire...Russia will be almost completely burned." [22]

Blessed Elena Aiello from the Blessed Virgin Mary: "I will manifest my partiality for **Italy**, which will be **preserved from the fire**, but the skies will be covered with dense darkness, and the earth will be shaken by fearful **earthquakes which will open deep abysses. Provinces and cities** will be destroyed, and all will cry out that the end of the world has come! Even Rome will be punished according to justice, for its many and serious sins because here, sin has reached its peak." [23]

Sister Agnes, the Stigmatic Nun of Akita, Japan (Oct 13,1973): "If men do not repent and better themselves, the Father will inflict a terrible punishment on all humanity. It will be a punishment greater than the deluge, such as one, will never have seen before. **Fire will fall from the sky** and will **wipe out a great portion of humanity**, the good, as well as the bad, sparing neither priests nor faithful. The only arms, which will remain, will be the Rosary and the Sign, left by My Son. Each day recite the prayers of the Rosary. With the rosary, pray for the Pope, the bishops, and the priests." [24]

Marie-Julie Jahenny: "My children, for **three days the sky will be on fire**, furrowed by fear of Divine wrath. What saddens me, is that this anger will not stop the forces of hell. They are neither afraid of my Son nor hell. It needs be that these times pass."[25]

Our Lady of Peace to **Pedro Regis:** "A rapid fire will cross the heavens of the various countries of Europe, falling on a famous temple, and men will weep and lament."[26]**An immense ball of fire will come leaving a great desert.** On all sides will be heard screams and lamentations. It's the hour of the Lord. Worldly things are temporary, but the Lord is forever. Repent." [27]

Mari Loli, at Garabandal, gave short detailed comments of the event of the fire from the sky: "That was horrible to see. We were frightened. I know no words that will explain it. We saw rivers change into blood...**Fire fell down from the sky**...And **something worse still, which I am not able to reveal now**... we don't expect the Chastisement, but without expecting it, it will come..." [28]

Rapid Melting of Polar Caps and Glaciers

During these fiery events in the sky and onto the earth, the polar caps and glaciers will ultimately melt, raising the ocean levels. NASA and other scientific calculations state that if all the ice from the polar caps, glaciers and land ice were to melt, the sea levels would rise 192 to 230 feet. Many low areas of continents will be underwater. About 40 % of the population of the world lives in cities on coastal lands near the oceans. Just how much melting will take place is not known during these events.

Our Lady of Peace to **Pedro Regis** reiterates, many people will have to move to higher ground. "The waters will rise with great fury, and many regions of the earth will disappear." [29]

Sunlight Will Become Perceptibly Weaker

Particle pollution will continue to build up, despite scientists' warnings. With the chaos of the spiritual battle, volcanoes will be more active. Evaporation of water in the North Polar Region, could cause more cloud-cover as well. There may be many other reasons for the sunlight becoming perceptibly weaker.

Johann Friede (1204-1257) who sees the comet coming to earth states: "When the nights will be filled with more intense cold, and the day with heat, a new life will begin in nature. The heat (also) means radiation from the earth, the cold, the **waning light of the sun**. Only a few more years, and you will become aware **that sunlight has become perceptibly weaker**. When even your artificial light will cease to give service, the great event of the firmament will be near." [30] This is certainly sobering when we hear scientist telling us today, of the evidence of **global dimming**, from a lack of sun's rays; meaning less sunlight reaches the earth's surface, because of particle pollution in the upper atmosphere. Volcanoes and other repercussions will bring a cloudy and smoky appearance to the sky. A **grand solar Minimum** is forecast for the 2020s and 2030s moving our planet to cooler temperatures.

Our Lady of Peace to **Pedro Regis**: "Dear children, what I reveal to you **is** not to cause you fear; but to warn you about everything of what is to come. Bend your knees in prayer. If you are converted, I will ask my Jesus to beg his mercy in your favor. Two neighbors will **look to the blue sky** that then will be cloudy and they will miss, in discussion, all the times in which they had the good earth. Live my appeals." [31] "The sun in the middle of the day will be more valuable than the evening sun." [32]

Sister Jane La Royer: "**The thick vapors** that I have seen rising from the earth and **obscuring the light of the sun**, are the false maxims of irreligion and license, which are **confounding all sound principals**, and spreading everywhere, such darkness, as **to obscure both faith and reason**." [33] She is not only speaking spiritually; but literally as well. This confirms, all kinds of **pollution**, obscures sunlight; but was first of all, brought about, by sinful irreverence to God and his order to the natural ecosystem.

Four Years of War Before the Comet

2033-June 2037

Before the comet arrives, four years of war will transpire at that time. The breakdown of civilization and the lack of necessary resources, particularly food, will spur this war.

The Ecstatic of Tours–French nun: "**Before the war breaks out again** (2030s) food will be scarce and expensive. There will be little work for the workers, and fathers will hear their children crying for food. There will be earthquakes and signs in the sun. Towards the end, darkness will cover the earth (Comet)." [34]

Abbot Werdin D' Otrante: "The nations will be **at war for four years**, and a great part of the world will be destroyed. All the (secret) sects will vanish. The capital of the world (Rome) will fall…and after the victory of the Angelic Pope and the Great Catholic Monarch, peace will reign on earth." [35]

The End of an Age

God will close this age by 2038. At that time, the chastisements will leave only a remnant of His Church to continue on this earth. God will destroy the evil people, just as he did in Noah's day, in Lot's day and in Egypt at the Red Sea. He will cleanse and adjust the physical earth, including, halting the desolation of mankind. We hear many prophecies stating, the end of an age at this time.

Another age will come. Two pillars of Christ, born into this age, are about to rise up and are seen now, but recognized by few. Ven. Fr. Bartholomew Holzhauser gives us an unusual description of the fifth Church age, beginning with Pope "Leo X" but ending with "a Strong Ruler and Holy Pope." There are many prophecies of a great **Catholic Monarch** to rise up that St. Hippolytus, St. Methodius, and St. Augustine speak of.

St. Augustine : "**A Frankish king** will one day rule over the entire Roman Empire." [36] The Holy Roman Empire is continuing. St. Cataldus and St. Ceasar had similar information. In 1997, this Great Catholic Monarch was born. He will take charge over the earth as a Catholic Monarch, near the end of this age, bringing about great changes both spiritually and temporally.

Holzhauser's prophecies also describe, "**a Holy Pope.**" [37] This Holy Man was born in 1971, and is destined to continue as Pope, at the beginning of the sixth Church age.

CHAPTER 43

THE GREAT CATHOLIC MONARCH

2030s

Going back to kings and to a monarchical system, is hard for any person to imagine, when we think of the democracies we have lived in, have been the answer to our way of life. Or have they? In our future, in our children's and grandchildren's future, it is predicted, other kings will rule after the great Catholic Monarch's reign, foretold by the saints and in the scriptures. Prophecies talk about ten kings and kingdoms, during the age of genuine peace, in the sixth Church Age.

Sometime in the 2030s, the great Catholic Monarch will battle in war, against the Mohammedans and other tyrants to take back Europe, and eventually most of the earth. It says: "The Empire of the Mohammedans will be broken up, and this Monarch will reign in the east and as well as the west." [1]

This future Monarch comes from a long line of royalty, extending back more than 1400 years. This lineage started from the Frankish kingdom in western Germany, at the time of Clovis I, the first King of the Franks of old Roman Gaul, in about 481. Clovis became a Christian because of influence from his wife who was spreading Christianity among the Franks. Descendants continued throughout the Merovingian dynasty, Carolingian Empire, Pepin, Charlemagne, continuing onwards in royal lineages of the House of Habsburg, and the House of Lorraine, to the 'end' of the Holy Roman Empire, lasting until 1806 with Francis II. He became the emperor of the Austrian Empire, becoming Francis I of Austria, and it lasted until the last emperor, Charles I, in 1918. This ongoing Monarchical kingship, ended with Charles I of Austria, but it is not over. Many Catholic saints prophesy, a great king rising up, from the lineage of the last King Charles of Austria. The events of this monarch, King Charles, **gives rise to the unusual**, and **must be pondered on.**

Charles I of Austria to the Great Catholic Monarch

Charles Von Habsburg-Lothringen was born August 17, 1887, in lower Austria. Known as Karl I, or Kroly, was raised a devout Catholic, received a Catholic education and developed a strong devotion to the Eucharist and the Sacred Heart of Jesus. In 1911, he married Zeta of Bourbon–Parma, and on their wedding day, he said to Zeta, "Darling, now we have to help each other on the stairway to heaven." [2] In the next ten years, Zita gave birth to eight children.

In 1914, with the assassination of Archduke Francis Ferdinand, in Sarajevo, triggering the First World War, nephew Charles, became heir presumptive to Austria and Hungary. He was a General Field Marshall in the army and became the Supreme Commander of the whole army, in 1916. The father of Pope John Paul II, was a soldier in this army. This father, called his son Karol, after Charles known as Karol. In 1916, the king's titles were Charles I, Emperor of Austria and Charles IV, King of Hungary, and the last Monarch of the Habsburg dynasty to 1918. Charles had many struggles to keep the different ethnic groups together. He tried to have a confederation with each, of a self-determined national interest, but they were determined to have separate nations. On November 11, 1918, Charles reluctantly recognized, the independence of the individual countries but never abdicated officially, hoping to be called back as leader of Austria and Hungary. By late November, Charles and his family fled to Switzerland, banished from Austria. In 1921, he tried to gain the throne of Hungary but was imprisoned with Zita, and all their family wealth and property was seized. They were exiled with their children to Madeira, an Island of Portugal. Charles knew that the will of God was to rule by monarchs, but the darkness of the 19th and 20th century brought a forceful change towards republics and to self-determination; encouraged by lobby groups of the secret sects, subtly turning away from God, to self-governing, becoming the consensus among many nations.

When Charles was sworn in as Emperor, he experienced an **anointing from God**. After the ceremonies, he offered his life to God, for the good of the people. It is said that he could not give up **the anointing** that God had given Him. He was given direction from God, to follow that path and knew it in his soul. He spent many hours before the Blessed Sacrament, having a great love for the Sacred Heart of Jesus. John Paul II said, **he is an example to be followed by all politicians**. Reviews by writers and novelists considered Charles a great leader, a statesman, and fearless king who loved his people but was despised by many. He was considered a saint and the only decent man who came out of the war, who believed in peace. They lived on Madeira from donations. In 1922, on his deathbed, suffering from chronic pneumonia, Charles stated, "My whole aspiration in life has always been **to discern as clearly as possible**

God's will for me, and to carry it out to the best of my ability." [3, 4] His final words were "Jesus, Thy will be done." [5] He was only 34 years old and at the time, Zita was pregnant with their eighth child at 29 years.

In 1972, Archduke Rudolf, the youngest son of Charles, had been present when the body of his father, Charles, was exhumed at Maderia and confirmed that **the body of his father was incorrupt.** This brought about the beatification of Blessed Emperor Charles, by Pope John Paul II, with Anne Catherine Emmerich's beatification on that same day in 2003. Since Charles I, the lineage of the eldest, in line to the throne, as the future Monarch: **Otto von Habsburg** was born November 20, 1912, and died July 4, 2011, who was crown prince of Austria and was the oldest son of Charles I.

Karl von Habsburg–Lothringen, born January 11, 1961, archduke and Prince of Austria, Prince of Hungary, Croatia, and Bohemia. He is the oldest son of Otto and current pretender to the throne.

Ferdinand Zvonimir von Habsburg–Lothringen was born June 21, 1997,[6] and is the only son of Karl This **is the great Catholic Monarch,** who will rise up in the 2030s. In 2021, Ferdinand will be 24 years old. This is the same year that he will experience the outpouring of the Holy Spirit, when the awareness of his calling may become very apparent.

Prophecies of the Great Catholic Monarch

How do we know that this is the great Catholic Monarch to rule the Holy Roman Empire again, according to many saint's prophecies? How do we know the dates? We discover this, in the scriptures in Daniel 9: 1-27, where God decrees seventy weeks of years, as a time decreed, for the Jewish people. The prophecy states: "Seventy weeks are decreed for your people and for your holy city: then transgression will stop, and sin will end; guilt will be expiated, everlasting justice will be introduced, vision and prophecy ratified, and a most holy will be anointed."

In this part of the prophecy, the Angel Gabriel explains the whole time frame as '70 weeks of years'; that is, 70 is times weeks, weeks is clearly defined as 7 times, that equals 490 years, starting in 1948 at "the utterance of the word that Jerusalem was to be rebuilt." In 1948, Israel became a nation, never to leave their homeland again. Only a remnant is left, likely a tested, tried and true people, a highly intelligent people, for the Father in Heaven, to fulfill His word for the Jewish people who will become like the sands of the sea, in numbers, in future prophecies.

This next verse expands on the first part, in more detail, and is connecting Bible verses to the great Catholic Monarch: **"Know** and **understand this: From the utterance of the word,** that Jerusalem was to be rebuilt, **until one who is anointed and a leader, there shall be seven weeks."**

This takes place from 'the utterance of the word,' the time that Israel became a nation, again. It says from this time, there will be 7 weeks of years that equals 49 years, until 'one who is anointed and a leader,' will rise up, as the saint's prophecies predict of the great Catholic Monarch. This prophecy starts from May 14, 1948, to June 21, 1997, a time of (49 years, 1 month, 8 days) 49 years. In 1997, Ferdinand Zvonimir von Habsburg was born on June 21, 1997, a descendant of the Frankish Kings of old. These Kings were part of the Holy Roman Empire. He was baptized (anointed) on September 20, 1997. (49 years, 4 months, 7 days)

The last parts of Daniel 9, will be explained later in this work. When we look at Venerable Holzhauser's prophecies of what he sees, at the end of the fifth Church age, of **the great Catholic Monarch** and **the Angelic Pastor** or **Holy Pope, who has a cross of redemption on His forehead,** it is undeniable of what is coming. **There are too many clues** that **are extra-ordinary. The signs of these two outstanding pillars** of God, **are rising up before us now.**

Prophecies of the Great Catholic Monarch's lineage integrity:

St. Hippolytus: "The Great French Monarch who shall subject all the East, shall come around the end of the world." [7]

St. Methodius: "A Roman Emperor will rise in great fury against them drawing his sword, he will fall upon the foes of Christianity and crush them." [8]

St. Augustine states: "A **Frankish king** will one day rule over the entire Roman Empire." [9]

St. Caesar of Arles: "When the entire world and in a special way, France, especially the provinces of the north, of the east, and above all, that of Lorraine and Champagne, shall have been prey to the greatest miseries and trials, then the provinces shall be comforted by a prince who had been in exile in his youth, and who **shall recover the crown of the lilies.**" [10]

St. Catald(us) of Toranto or Tarentino (?-685)"... **a king of the House of Lily** (France, he will assemble great armies and hurl back the tyrants out of his Empire." [11]

Blessed Bishop Rabanus Maurus (780?-856) "Our principal doctors agree in announcing to us towards the end...one of the **descendants of the kings of France** shall reign over all the Roman Empire, and he shall be the greatest of French monarchs, and the last of his race." [12]

Monk Adso, Chronicler of many saints' prophecies, (d-992) "Some of our teachers say that **a king of the Franks** will possess the entire Roman Empire. This king will be the greatest and last of all monarchs, (of Frankish kings), and after having prosperously governed his kingdom, he will come in the end to Jerusalem, and he will lay down his scepter and his crown upon the Mount of Olives." [13]

St. Hildegard: "The **White Flower** (French Monarch) will **take possession** of the Throne of France." [14]

St. Bridget of Sweden: "An **emperor of Spanish origin** will be elected, who in a wonderful manner will be victorious through the sign of the cross."[15]

Bishop Christianos Ageda: "He shall **inherit the crown** of the fleur-de-lis."[16]

David Poreaus (? -1622): "The Great Monarch will be of **French descent**, large forehead, large dark eyes, light brown wavy hair, and an eagle nose." [17]

Blessed Anna-Katerina Emmerich (July 26, 1820): "I have had a vision of **the Holy Emperor Henry**. I saw him last night in a beautiful church, kneeling alone before the main altar...as he knelt and prayed, a light shone above the altar, and the Blessed Virgin appeared alone. She wore a robe of bluish white that shot forth rays. She carried something in her hand. She covered the altar with a red cloth, over which she spread a white one. She lay upon the altar, a magnificent luminous book, inlaid with precious stones. She lit the candles from the sanctuary-lamp...She took her stand at the right of the altar. Now came the Savior Himself, clad in priestly vestments carrying the chalice and the veil. Two Angels were serving Him, and two others accompanied Him... His chasuble was full and heavy; red and white mantle shining with light and precious stones...there was **no altar bell**, but the cruets were there. The wine was as red as blood, and there was, also some water. **The Mass was short.** The **Gospel of St. John was not read** at the end. When the Mass had ended, Mary came up to Henry, and she extended her right hand towards him, saying that it was in recognition of his purity. Then, she urged him not to falter. Thereupon, I saw an angel, and he touched the sinew of his hip, like Jacob. He (Henry) was in great pain; and from that day on he walked with a limp." [18]

Anne Catherine Emmerich describes the short Mass that we use today after the Tridentine Mass ceased to be said generally, after the 1960s. The altar bell was not rung, and the Gospel of St. John was not read, revealing to us that this Mass, is the Mass that is said now, although the altar bell is rung again in some places. The usage of the name, "**the Holy Emperor Henry**" described above, is a reflective contemplation, by Anne Catherine Emmerich, of an earlier Emperor, who was canonized a saint, Henry II, who lived from 972 to 1024, although married, reportedly remained a virgin, who honored God all his life. The wife given to him, continued the same kind of holy life, as a chaste spouse, who was canonized a saint in the Church.

Henry prayed for assistance, **in pushing invaders back out of the Holy Roman Empire**, and faithfully prayed on the first night when entering another town, in a church, dedicated to our Blessed Lady. When he prayed at Saint Mary Major's in Rome, he experienced a vision of "the Sovereign and Eternal Priest-Child Jesus" entering to say Mass. Two saints assisted and countless saints and angels were in the church. After the Gospel was read, an Angel was sent by Our Lady to give Henry the sacred book to kiss. The Angel touched him at the same time on the thigh and said, "Accept this sign of God's love for your chastity and your justice,"and from that time on, the Emperor Henry, walked with a limp. It's interesting this similar occurrence will take place for the Catholic Monarch as well, but that experience must give many graces of anointing, of protection and guidance. Jacob in the Old Testament received this similar blessing. Anne Catherine Emmerich is relating to the future great Catholic Monarch who has a similar anointing as Henry II, in reclaiming the Holy Roman Empire for Christ, and it will be worldwide. [19]

The Counter-Revolution Begins

The great Catholic Monarch will hear the call from God and gather armies in the name of God to bring a change towards living in the true doctrine of Jesus Christ on this earth.

Father Nectou: "A reaction will follow, which shall be taken for a **counter-revolution**; this shall last **for some years**, but this shall only be a patch sewed together. There will be no schism; but the Church shall not yet triumph in France; there will be more trouble. A man disliked by France will be placed on the throne; **a man of the house of Orleans shall be made king.** It is only after this event that the **counter-revolution** shall begin. It shall not be affected by foreign powers; but two parties will be formed in France, which shall fight unto death. The party of evil will at first be stronger; the good side shall be weaker. At that time, there shall be such a terrible crisis, that people, frightened by events, shall believe that the end of the world is come. Blood shall flow in several large cities. The very elements (of the earth) shall be convulsed. It will be like a little general judgment. A great multitude of persons shall perish in these calamitous times. But the wicked shall never prevail. They indeed shall conspire for the destruction of the Church; but time shall not be allowed them, because this frightful crisis shall be but of a short duration. When all will be considered lost, all shall be found safe. During **this revolution**, this very likely will not be confined to France. **Paris will be destroyed so completely** that twenty years afterwards, fathers will walk over its ruins as their children ask them, 'What kind of place was this?' to which they will answer: 'My child, this was a great city which God has **destroyed on account of her crimes.**" [20]

St. John Vianney: "After this victory, their enemy [the Prussians] shall not quit entirely, the occupied country. They (the Prussians) shall come back (for a second invasion of France); but this time, our army shall fight well everywhere. For during the first war our men would not combat well, but in the second war, they will fight. O, how they will fight! The enemy (the Prussians) will allow the burning of Paris, and they will rejoice at it, but they shall be beaten; they shall be driven entirely from France."

"Our enemies shall return and will destroy everything in their march. They shall arrive near Poitiers without meeting with any [serious] resistance they shall be crushed by the defenders of the West who shall pursue them. [Here the Papal soldiers of Cathelineau and of Charette will cover themselves with immortal glory. **This shall be the beginning** of the successive triumphs of virtue and justice.] From other directions, their provisions shall be cut off, and they shall suffer very serious losses. They will attempt to retire towards their country, but very few of them shall ever reach it. All they took from us, shall be returned and a great deal more." [21]

Bug De Milhaus–saintly man living in the Pyrenees (d. 1848): "A war, in Europe, is announced by name and their **prophecies will be fulfilled**. That war will ravage all places. Pestilence and many other plagues will scatter terror everywhere. The fanaticism of false beliefs and of intolerant parties will fill many countries with victims. Iberia [Spain and Portugal] will be the asylum of all the refugees. Catholics fleeing from the fury of their enemies will seek refuge in Spain." [22]

St. Hildegard of Bingen: "At this time, as a punishment for their sins, Christians especially will **attempt armed resistance**, to those who at that time are persecuting them, sensing no concern for the death of their bodies." [23]

Battles of the Great Catholic Monarch

2033 to 2037?

Europe will see **battles** with the Monarch, riding on a horse, **against the Muslims** and **the pagan sects**, first. The Russians will have entered Europe in about this same time. Electricity will cease to work in the 2030s before the comet comes. The breakdown of our modern world will be apparent in those years. The conflicts will be limited to older ballistic armaments not of any great size, leaving man against man, horse and rider against horse and rider. That is why the blood will flow like rainwater.

St. Methodius: "A day will come when the enemies of Christ will boast of having conquered the whole world. They will say: "Christians cannot escape now!" But **a Great king will arise** to fight the enemies of God. He will defeat them, and peace will be given to the world, and **the Church will be freed from her anxieties**." [24]

Blessed Anne Catherine Emmerich: "Then, I saw in the great distance, great legions approaching. In the foreground, I saw **a man on a white horse**. Prisoners were set free and joined them. **All the enemies were pursued**." [25]

Sister Bertina Bouquillon (1800-1830?): "Once again, the mad men seem to gain the upper hand! They laughed God to scorn. Now, the churches are closed; the pastors run away; the Holy Sacrifice ceases. The wicked try to destroy everything; their books and **their doctrines are swamping the world**. But the day of justice is come. **Here is your king;** he comes forward amidst **the confusion of those stormy days**. Horrible times! The just and wicked fall!

There was **also a great battle**, the likes of which, has never been seen before. **Blood was flowing like water after a heavy rain.** The wicked were trying to slaughter all the servants of the religion of Jesus Christ. After they had killed a large number, they raised a cry of victory, but suddenly the just received help from above." [26]

Blessed Anne Catherine Emmerich (October 22, 1822): "**I saw the battle** also. The enemies were far more numerous, but the small army of the faithful cut down whole rows [enemy soldiers]. During the battle, the **Blessed Virgin stood** on a hill, **wearing a suit of armor.** It was a terrible war. At the end, only a few fighters for the just cause survived, but the victory was theirs." [27]

St. Thomas a'Becket: "**A knight** shall come from the West. He shall capture Milan, Lombardy, and the three Crowns. He shall then sail to Cyprus and Famagoste and land at Jaffa, and reach Christ's grave, where **he will fight. Wars** and **wonders shall befall,** till the people believe in Christ toward the end of the world." [28]

St. Cataldus: "The **Great Monarch will wage war** until he is forty years of age (June 2037)…He will conquer England and other island empires. Greece, he will invade and be made a king there. Of Clochis, Cyprus, the Turks, and barbarians he will subdue and have all men to worship the Crucified One. He will at length lay down his crown in Jerusalem." [29]

He Will Push Back the Mohammedans

Rudolph Gekner (1675) Chronicler: "A great prince of the North **with a most powerful army** will traverse all Europe, **uproot all the Republics**, and defeat all the rebels. **His sword moved by Divine power** and will most valiantly defend the Church of Jesus Christ. He will combat on behalf of the true orthodox faith and shall subdue to his dominion, the Mohammedan Empire." [30]

Bug De Milhaus: "Then the region of the river Tajo [Spain and Portugal] will produce **a valiant warrior** similar to the Cid, and he will be as religious as Ferdinand III who, planting the standard of the faith, will unite around himself innumerable armies. With his army, he will go out to **meet a formidable giant** who, with his ferocious soldiers, will advance towards the conquest of the Peninsula. The Pyrenees will witness the cruelest combat ever seen throughout the centuries. The battle will last three days. In vain, the fearsome giant will try to encourage his own to continue the fight, but the finger of God, will already show him the end of his reign, and his army will fall under the sword of the new Cid. Then the victorious army, protected by their Supreme Creator, will cross provinces and seas and will carry the standard of the cross, even to the banks of the River Neva [in the heart of Russia]. The Catholic religion will triumph everywhere." [31] The formidable giant is the Mohammedans.

Birch Tree Country Prophecies

This battle in the Birch tree country is in the **area of Westphalia**, Germany. Uniquely, many seers such as peasants, farmers, and other ordinary people have experienced future visions about this area. This will be the last battle of the **great Catholic Monarch**, sometime just before June of 2037.

Blessed Bernhardt Rembordt (1689-1793): "Cologne will be the site of a terrible battle. Many foreigners will be slaughtered there; both men and women will fight for their faith. It will be impossible to prevent this horrible devastation. People will wade up to their ankles in blood. At last, a foreign king (Catholic Monarch) will appear and win a victory for the cause of the righteous. The remaining enemy will retreat into **the Birch tree country**. There **the last battle will be fought** for the just cause…"[32]

Old German Prophecy: "A terrible war will find the North fighting the South. The South will be **led by a Prince wearing a white coat with a cross on the front; he will be lame afoot.** He will gather his forces at Bremen for Mass. Then he will lead them into battle beyond Woerl near the **Birch tree country**. After a terrible battle at a brook, running eastwards near Berdberg and Sondern, the South will be victorious."[33]

Peter Schlinkert was born in 1730 and had a vision of Duke Clemens of Westphalia – a vision that saved a life. He wrote this prophecy of the Birch Tree Country: "Near **the Birch tree** [Westphalia], the army of the West will fight a terrible battle against the army of the East, and after many bloody sacrifices will be victorious. The soldiers of the East will retreat over the Haar (Germany), and when the villagers see Werler and Haar on fire, they must quickly flee into the Armsberger Wood.

Another battle will be fought near the Ruhr Bridge near Obenheimer, but here only with artillery. A few days later, the last great battle will be fought on German soil by the village Schmerleck on the so-called Lusebrink. The armies of the East will almost entirely be annihilated, and only a few will be left to bring the news home. After these days of mishap and misery, happiness and peace will return to Germany, even though in the first year, women will have to do the farm work."[34]

Brother Anthony of Aix-la-Chapelle (Aachen, Germany) in 1871 recorded his vision of the final battle near Cologne: "Someday, war will break out again in Alsace. I saw the French in Alsace with Strasbourg at their rear, and I saw Italians fighting with them. Suddenly, great transports of troops arrived from the French side. A two-day battle ended with the defeat of the Prussian army. The French pursued the Prussians over the Rhine in many directions. In a second battle at Frankfurt, the Prussians lost again and retired as far as Siegburg, where they joined a Russian army. **The Russians made common cause with the Prussians.** It seemed to me as if the Austrians were aiding the French. The battle at Siegburg was more horrible than any before, and its like will never occur again. After some days, the Prussians and Russians retreated and crossed below Bonn, to the left bank of the Rhine. Steadily pressed by their opponents, they retired to Cologne, which had been bombarded so much, that only one-fourth of the city remained intact. Constantly in retreat, the remainder of the Prussian army **moved to Westphalia** (Birch tree country), where the last battle went against them. The people greatly rejoiced because they were freed from the Prussians."

"Then a new emperor, about 40 years old (GCM), was elected in Germany, and he met the Pope. Meanwhile, an epidemic broke out in the region devastated by the war, and many people died... In the following year, the Russians will war with the Turks, driving the latter out of Europe and seizing Constantinople. The new German Emperor will mobilize for war, but the Germans will not go beyond their border. When afterwards, I was shown France and Germany, I shuddered at the depopulation that had taken place. Soon after the Russo-Turkish War, England also will be visited by war." [35]

The Prophecy of Mayence (Mainz, Germany) is dated to 1854, and gives a detailed description of the Battle of the Birch Tree: "Woe to thee, great city; woe to thee, city of vice! Fire and sword shall succeed fire and famine. Courage, faithful souls! The reign of the dark shadow shall not have time to execute all its schemes. But the time of mercy approaches. A prince of the nation is in your midst. It is the man of salvation, the wise, the invincible; he shall count his enterprises by his victories. He shall drive the enemy out of France; **he shall march from victory to victory,** until the day of **Divine Justice**. That day he shall command seven kinds of soldiers against three, to the quarter of Bouleaus, between Hamm, Woerl, and Padenborn. Woe to the people of the East, thou shalt spread afar the cries of affliction and innocent blood. Never shall such an army be seen. Three days the sun shall rise upwards, on the heads of the combatants, **without being seen through the clouds of smoke**. Then the commander shall get the victory; two of his enemies shall be annihilated; the remainder of the three shall fly toward the extreme East." [36]

** **Note:** After reading these prophecies, many will be wondering what is happening, meanwhile, back in North and South America. Many of the prophecies refer to Europe and the Middle East because prophecies of Christianity have been most prevalent in these regions for centuries. However, the general devastation described will unfold everywhere. Prophecies from Our Lady of Peace to Pedro Regis at Anguera, Brazil give us a better understanding of coming events in the Western hemisphere.

CHAPTER 44

THE GATES OF HELL SHALL NOT PREVAIL AGAINST HIS CHURCH

B y this time, it will be very hard to believe that the Church will prevail, but Jesus Christ will intervene with His Chastisements, very soon after the Pope, the Vatican and Rome have succumbed to the powerful treacheries of the evil one.

Blessed Sister Elena Aiello asked Our Blessed Mother: "What will become of Italy? Will Rome be saved?" The Madonna answered: "**In part, by the Pope. The Church will be in travail, but the forces of Hell cannot prevail!** You must suffer for the Pope and Christ, and thus Christ will be safe on earth; and the Pope, with his redemptive word, will, in part, save the world." [1]

Our Lady of Peace to **Pedro Regis**: "The true Church of My Jesus will be victorious. The **false church that penetrated into the Church** of My Jesus will be defeated. God will separate the wheat from the chaff. The day will come when all that is false will fall to the earth. God will separate you from evil, and those who listen to the true teachings of the Church will experience a great victory."[2] "The enemies will unite against the Church, and the faithful will carry a heavy cross. God will manifest Himself with great signs and prodigies. After all the tribulation that the Church will experience, triumph will come. Nothing will prevail against the plans of God."[3] "The enemies will try to destroy the Church. You will achieve great things, but many will be against those who truly love the truth. In the great and final persecution of the Church, the enemies will be surprised. Christ will come in defense of his Church. Do not separate yourselves from the path that I have mentioned." [4]

Imminent Invasion of the Vatican

Our Lady of Peace to **Pedro Regis**: "The Vatican will be surprised by a furious and bloody invasion by men with big beards (Russians)." [5] "A swift fire will come upon the Vatican, but the rock will not be broken." [6]

Our Lady of Garabandal to **Mari Loli:** " A time would arrive when the Church would give the impression of being on the point of perishing…It would pass through a terrible test. We asked the Virgin what this great test was called, and she told us that it was Communism." [7]

The Russians Are Coming

The Russians are the only country on earth boasting a formidable military cavalry. After the electrical grids are destroyed, and before the comet comes, they will ride on horses into Europe, particularly into Italy. Historically, they have come out of Russia over the centuries to look for food in difficult times. This is most likely one of the major reasons for invading other southern countries after Russia is burned out severely after the first trumpet..

Sister Rosa Columba (Asdente) of Taggia, Italy (died 1847): "The Russians and Prussians (Eastern Germany) shall come to make war in Italy. They shall profane many churches and turn them into **stables for their horses**. Some bishops shall fall from the faith, but many more will remain steadfast and suffer much for the Church. There will be a great persecution of the Church, begun by her own children." [8]

Blessed Elena Aiello: "If we do not pray, Russia will march upon all the nations of Europe and particularly upon Italy…and will **raise her flag over the dome of St. Peter's**. Italy will be severely tried by a great revolution, and Rome will be purified in blood for its many sins, especially those of impurity! The flock is about to be dispersed, and the Pope must suffer greatly." [9]

Our Lady of Peace to **Pedro Regis:** "Dear children, three large rocks (meteors?) will fall on eastern countries causing destruction and death. The bear (Russia) will invaded various nations and **arrive in Rome**. They will leave their marks, and blood will run through the land. In various places, churches will be burned, but do not forget, God is not far from you."[10] "Small and great cities will cease to exist. One who is opposed to Christ, marches with his army and reaches the big city (Rome). The throne of Peter shall tremble. I suffer for what awaits you. In many places, the heretics will occupy privileged space (Churches and sanctuaries). **When the Lord loses his place of honor**, (Vatican) **the great chastisement will come**. Few will remain steadfast in the faith. I ask you to live my appeals. I revere by safe ways. I ask you to do your part in my army victorious. **Take the rosary. It is the weapon for the big fight**." [11] In this passage, the earthly place of Christ, is through the Popes at Rome.

"The fierce bear (Russia) attacks and leads to suffering and pain against the house of God. The **seed of evil** (communism) **still exists** and the fierce bear is nourished by it." [12]

Pope Flees Rome and is Martyred

2033-2035?

The exact timing and sequence of events are difficult to pinpoint, but by the late 2020s and into the beginning of the 2030s, the last Pope on St. Malachy's list, in this fifth Church age, will go through difficult times. St. Malachy states that despite severe persecution, 'Peter the Roman' will take the Church **through many tribulations**. This means the Pope may be in Rome until the Russians come.

Sister Ludmilla of Prague (1250): "Hardly three generations will pass after the world war, when one will endeavor to prevent the pope from exercising his sacred office, which will be a sign that the fall of Rome and the end of the world is near." [13]

Blessed Anne Catherine Emmerich: "I see the Holy Father in great distress. He **lives in another palace** and receives only a few to his presence...I fear, the Holy Father will suffer many tribulations before his death." [14]

Jacinta of Fatima: "I don't know how it happened, but I saw the Holy Father in a very big house, kneeling by a table, with his head buried in his hands, and he was weeping. Outside the house, there were many people. Some of them were throwing stones, others were cursing him and Poor Holy Father, we must pray very much for him."[15]

Pope Pius X (1835-1914) in 1909, during an audience with the Franciscan order, Pius X experienced a vision and then cried out: "What I see is terrifying! Will it be myself? Will it be my successor? What is certain is that the **Pope will quit Rome**, and in leaving the Vatican, he will have to walk over the dead bodies of his priests..." [16]

On August 20, 1914, just before his death, he received more in another vision: "I have seen one of my successors, ...**fleeing over the bodies of his brethren**. He will take refuge in some hiding place; but after a brief respite, he will **die a cruel death**. Respect for God has disappeared from human hearts. They wish to efface even God's memory..." [17]

Helen Wallraff (1755-1801) Stigmatist: "Some day a pope will flee Rome in the company of four cardinals... and they will come to Cologne (Germany)."[18]

Bishop George Michael Wittman (1760-1833) "Sad days are at hand for the Holy Church of Jesus Christ. The passion of Jesus will be renewed in the most dolorous manner in the Church and in her Supreme head. Violent hands will be laid on the Supreme head of the Catholic Church." [19]

Pope Pius IX (1792-1878): "The Church will **suffer exceedingly**. Her servants and her chieftain will be mocked, scourged, and martyred."[20]

Our Lady of Peace to **Pedro Regis** : "Walk in the truth. Accept the Gospel and live my appeals. The Church of My Jesus will walk on difficult paths and suffer much. When it looks like all is lost, **the Lord will send a just man,** and **he will contribute to the spiritual growth of the Church** (Peter the Roman). After all the good he will do for the Church, **he will be assassinated,** but the Church will remain firm, and its enemies will be defeated." [21] "Here are the times in which I announced in the past. Coming to the Church, is the time of **her greatest agony.** The Church of my Jesus will live the pain of Calvary. A man dressed in white (Pope) will be pursued and led to death. In celebration of this **great Martyr,** the believers will cry and moan. Pray. Only in prayer will you find the strength to walk on." [22] "The Church will suffer and lose but will be victorious. After all tribulation, the Lord will wipe away your tears. The triumph of the Church will be with, the help **of a great man of faith** (Peter the Roman). He will not see [the triumph of the Church], but **the seed planted** (martyrdom) will give great fruits to the Church of my Jesus." [23]

Lucia of Fatima relating the **Third secret of Fatima**: "We saw in an immense light that is God...**a bishop dressed in white**...that, was **the Holy Father.** Other bishops, priests, men and women religious going up a steep mountain, at the top of which there was a big Cross... he prayed for the souls of the corpses, he met on the way, having reached the top of the mountain, he **was killed by a group** of soldiers who fired bullets and arrows at him." [24] This figurative account displays a time when the "bishop in white" includes **the work,** started by John Paul II, and continued with Benedict XVI, will be "killed." It will include the work of the last Pope, 'Peter the Roman' or Francis I in this fifth Church age of affliction. He will be literally, martyred in the end. The visible Catholic Church will experience chaos and will be tested, and many others will suffer martyrdom as well. In the years just before 2038, the Church will seem to be visibly destroyed.

No Pope in Rome

2035-2038

At this time, Italy will be in shambles, amidst four years of continuous war.

Mother Mariana de Jesus Torres from Our Lady of Good Success: "The secular clergy will be far removed from its ideal, because the priests will become careless in their sacred duties. Lacking the Divine compass (Holy Spirit), they will stray from the road traced by God for the priestly ministry, and they will become attached to wealth and riches, which they will unduly strive to obtain. How the Church will suffer on that occasion, the **dark night, of the lack of a Prelate and Father** to watch over them with paternal love, gentleness, strength, discernment, and prudence. Many priests will lose their spirit, placing their souls in great danger." [25]

Abbess Maria Steiner (?-1862): "I see the Lord, as He will be scourging the world and chastising it in a fearful manner, so that few men and women will remain. The monks will have to leave their monasteries, and the nuns will be driven from their convents, especially in Italy. The Holy Church will be persecuted, and Rome will be without a shepherd." [26]

Bishop Christanos Ageda: "The pope will change his residence, and the Church will not be defended **for 25 months** or more because during all that time, there **will be no pope in Rome**...After many tribulations, a pope shall be elected, out of those who survive the persecutions." [27]

Marie-Julie Jahenny: "The abandoned Church will be **without its supreme head** who governs and directs it. For quite a long time, the Church must be deprived of all prayer, all offices, exiled from God, and the saints. They also intend to remove all crucifixes and statues of saints, from all the shrines and throw them in a profane place, to break them with joy" [28]

John of Vatiguerro: "Spoilage, pillaging, and devastation of that most famous city which is the capital and mistress of France (Paris) will take place when the Church and the world are grievously troubled. The pope will change his residence, and the Church will **not be defended for 25 months** or more because during all that time, there will be no Pope in Rome, no emperor, and no ruler in France...After many tribulations, a Pope shall be elected out of those who survived the persecutions. By his sanctity, he will reform the clergy, and the whole world shall venerate the Church for her sanctity, virtue, and perfection." [29]

Our Lady of Peace to **Pedro Regis**: "War will explode on Rome, and there will be few survivors. He who opposes Christ will bring suffering and sorrow to all Europe. **The throne of Peter will be empty.** Tears of pain, and weeping of lamentations will be seen in the Church." [30] "The day will come when there will be few men and women of faith. **The Church will be without Peter**, and many will follow their own thoughts." [31]

Rome and the Vatican Destroyed

This will be the last and final straw. God will take His vengeance against mankind who will not stop or repent. They continue to erase the name of God and His Church from the face of the earth. They will destroy the Vatican and Rome. Chastisements directly from God will come against all those who remain in wickedness. This will follow without hesitation.

St. Malachy: "In extreme persecution, the seat of the Holy Roman Church shall be occupied by Peter the Roman, who will feed the sheep through many tribulations, at the term of which **the city of the seven hills will be destroyed** and the dreadful Judge shall judge the people..." [32]

Our Lady of Peace to **Pedro Regis**: "Friends of the Pope unite against him, but God will severely punish them for their betrayal because they opened the door for the assassins to enter. The city of the seven hills will fall. The day will come when the Pope will leave his home to dwell in another country." [33] "An astounding incident will happen at the Vatican. The Vatican will need to be rebuilt." [34] "Fury and death wishes, will be in the hearts of men. The city of seven hills will be destroyed." [35] "A large invasion will occur against the Vatican, bringing great destruction. A great relic will appear, and there will be a war between the religious." [36] "You have reached the moment of **her greatest ordeal**. An army will depart and **move furiously towards Rome**. Churches will be set on fire, and many holy places will be destroyed." [37] The Mohammedans may still bring destruction as well.

Blessed Anne Catherine Emmerich: "I saw the Church of St. Peter; it has been destroyed but for the sanctuary and the main altar. St. Michael came down into the church, clad in his suit of armor, and he paused, threatening with his sword the number of unworthy pastors who wanted to enter. That part of the church that had been destroyed was promptly fenced in with light timber, so that the Divine office might be celebrated, as it should... Then, (then in 6th Church age)from all over the world came priests and laymen, and they rebuilt the stone walls, since the wreckers had been unable to move the heavy foundation stones..." [38]

Blessed Sister Elena Aiello: Our Blessed Mother speaks again on Good Friday, 1961: "My daughter, Rome will not be saved, because the Italian rulers have forsaken the Divine Light and because only a few people really love the Church. But the day is not far off when all the wicked shall perish, under the tremendous blows of Divine Justice." [39]

CHAPTER 45

GOD'S CHASTISEMENTS

2030- 2038

The fallout of the collision/explosion and the approach of the Comet towards earth, will take many months, according to prophecies. Humanity will suffer from the fallout, and as the comet nears, **three days of complete darkness by Divine decree** will take place. During those three days of complete darkness, Divine justice will release all the demons out of hell to destroy the evil people who will not turn to God; who continue to persecute and to destroy His Church, all good people and the earth. These are **God's Chastisements** coming to the earth! This is **His wrath!** This is the ninth and tenth secrets of Medjugorje and third secret of Garabandal.

Mary of Agreda: "An unusual chastisement of the human race will take place, towards the end of the world." [1]

Blessed Sister Elena Aiello: "Near at hand is the scourge that will cleanse the earth of evil." [2]

Mari Loli at Garabandal to Fr. Gustavo Morelos : "Then she showed how **the great Chastisement** for all mankind **would come,** and that it would come directly from God..." [3]

"The Whole World Shall Cry, Woe"

St. Bridget of Sweden remarks: "When the feast of St. Mark shall fall on Easter, April 25, 2038; the feast of St. Anthony on Pentecost, June 13, 2038; and that of St. John the Baptist on the feast of Corpus Christi, June 24, 2038; the whole world shall cry, Woe!" [4] The spring of 2038.

Catholic saints' prophecies reveal two events unfolding in tandem. We hear St. Bridget exclaiming: **"The whole world shall cry, Woe"** when certain **Saint's feast days** fall on certain **Church feast days** culminating in 2038. According to the visionaries of Medjugorje, the ten secrets are events that are all in the scriptures. Upon examination of the visionaries' fears and tears, it becomes clear that what they are seeing is not allegorical. When reading a lengthy book on an interpretation of Revelation, it concludes for an allegorical, historical unfolding of events, taking place in the Church's long history.

In contrast, other works also look at the undeniable literal manifestation of events of Revelation, understanding the consistent symbolic content of some of the words, from Old and New Testament. Prophecies have always been fulfilled literally, though, sometimes revealed in symbolic language. This literal interpretation of prophecies also reflects early Church Fathers' viewpoints. It cannot be denied. After hearing John Paul II speak, of the seven seals of Revelation to be opened, **in the future tense**, it makes sense to take the words at face value. God says: "My word is straightforward, it is not there, to confuse nor to confound."

The first six seals will be continual. Being reminded of the prophetic scriptures unfolding like birth pangs, the remaining part in the fifth seal of persecution will be completed at the beginning of the seventh Church age. The Trumpets are events of direct woes and chastisements from God. The Trumpets start unfolding shortly after the beginning and during the sixth seal. They will overlap.

The Great Catholic Monarch stops fighting in battles, according to the prophecies, when he is forty years old, in June of 2037.[5] By July of 2037, the comet will become visible in its approach towards earth, appearing for nine or ten months before it reaches the earth. Yet, those who have not turned to God will continue aggravating people in their basic lives and persecuting the Christian Church.

The first four Trumpets literally describe worldwide repercussions from this collision /explosion in the universe. They **will be spread out** from, after the collision/explosion, to the time of the visible comet. Next, in Revelation, a voice cries out: **"Woe,** woe, and again woe **to the inhabitants of the earth** from the Trumpet blasts that the other three angels are about to blow." St. Bridget proclaims **woe** to the world in the spring of 2038 but does not speak, specifically, of the event of the first woe written in the Trumpets. Only one woe from Revelation will take place at this time. The next woe is in Revelation 11 and will take place during the time of the Antichrist, at the beginning of the seventh Church age. The woes in Revelation seem to dispense Divine Mercy to the unrepentant, a final chance to change, before eternal loss.

The Fifth Trumpet or first woe in Revelation 9:1-12, in this case, is a highly figurative description and is a painful warning to the unrepentant, through a foretaste of the depths of hell, permitted by God. This again is Divine Mercy. This first woe clarifies that the unrepentant will be tortured for five months, with pain inflicted upon them, like that from a scorpion. They will yearn for death, but it will evade them.

Those who have the seal of God on their foreheads, stated in Revelation 7:3 will not suffer this trial or torment. This seal most likely is that given to those when they were baptized and are sealed with the Holy Spirit.

Father Zlatko Sudac has a visible sign of the cross on his forehead, and it may be something like that but not visible. It procures at the very least, special protection for a distinct number.

Marie-Julie Jahenny confirms **three events** or three parts to this Biblical prophecy, giving us precise details of God's Woe and Chastisements stating: "The last crisis will be **divided into three parts.**"

"**The first part**: will be long and painful, when Divine vengeance will be manifested, during which **the guiltiest** will be destroyed. But, this blow of justice will only irritate them." [6] **Marie-Julie Jahenny** from the Blessed Virgin Mary explains: "The first blow of Heaven will be the destruction of these **wretched souls** (Globalist/Secret Sect/Deep State/Liberal left) who intend to be victorious, who intend to govern, as they wish, by laws more infamous than ever before; **do not be frightened by these maternal words**. This murdering enemy that has so destroyed many poor people, allied itself, with a multitude of human reinforcements, drawn from across all the realms; the world. They send their circulars soliciting for aid around the world, asking aid and force, aid and strength [said 2 times]. If you saw how this populace was [corrupted by] human blood; but they themselves will suffer the punishment first, the early rigors of justice." [7] This first woe of 5 months of affliction will take place sometime between 2033 and 2038. At this time, demons will inflict a cruel punishment, only on those who are unrepentant. This is the fifth Trumpet and first woe of Revelation.

Revelation 9: 1-12 : "Then the fifth angel blew his trumpet, and I saw a star that had fallen from the sky to the earth. It was given the key for the passage to the abyss... smoke came up out of the passage like smoke from a huge furnace. The sun and the air were darkened by the smoke from the passage. Locusts came out of the smoke onto the land, and they were given the same power as scorpions of the earth. They were told not to harm the grass of the earth or any plant or any tree, but only those people who did not have the seal of God on their foreheads. They were not allowed to kill them but only to **torment them for five months**; the torment they inflicted was like that of a scorpion when it stings a person. During that time these people will seek death but will not find it, and they will long to die but death will escape them. The appearance of the locusts was like that of horses ready for battle. On their heads they wore what looked like crowns of gold; their faces were like human faces, and they had hair like women's hair. Their teeth were like lions' teeth,and they had chests like iron breastplates. The sound of their wings was like the sound of many horse-drawn chariots racing into battle. They had tails like scorpions, with stingers; with their tails they had power to harm people for five months... The first woe has past."

Marie-Julie Jahenny continues: "The second part: will be shorter but more formidable, more sinister: My Divine Son, seeing that all these blows cannot bring back His people to pardon and mercy–lost souls–will strike again more fearfully..." [8]

The Second Angel's Trumpet

The second Trumpet describes a huge mountain cast into the sea. This may be many months before the actual comet enters part of the earth's atmosphere.

Revelation 8: 8-9: "When the **second angel** blew his trumpet, something **like a huge mountain**, all in flames was cast into the sea. A third of the sea turned to blood, a third of the creatures living in the sea died, and a third of the ships were wreaked."

Our Lady of Peace to **Pedro Regis**: "Dear children, **a giant mountain will travel across the Pacific at high speed** and **cause great destruction in many regions.** Bend your knees in prayer. Only through prayer will you find the strength to support the weight of the trials that await you..."[9] "Men and women have turned away from the Creator, and His law is no longer honored... A great mountain **will fall into the deep waters** and will bring **great destruction** to mankind. Waters above water (tsunami?) All will be victorious in the Lord." [10]

The Third Angel's Trumpet

At the third Trumpet, a 'huge star' on fire spreads poison on a portion of the waters, **on the earth**, and many will die. This will be like a huge meteor on fire, spreading over a portion of water sources.

Revelation 8: 10-11: "When the **third angel** blew his trumpet. A huge star **burning like a torch** crashed down from the sky. It fell on a third of the rivers and the springs. The stars name was wormwood, because a third part of all the water turned to **wormwood**. Many people died from this polluted water."

Our Lady of Peace to **Pedro Regis**: "Behold, many will die because, those chosen to defend the truth, will deny it. I grieve for what awaits you. That pain will be repeated in November (Fall of 2037?) The Tagus River (Spain and Portugal) is on your side. **A great mountain will fall to the earth.** Pray. Pray. Pray." [11] "In the past many innocent lives were snuffed out because of much greed. Many innocent children were sold as mere objects, and greed was the major reason. The wrath of God will come. Its **name was derived from a plant** [wormwood?] coming **from far away**. God is merciful, but also fair. Repent of your sins. Return to God quickly. He awaits you with open arms. Your answer will come. The bloodshed has not been forgotten... No prayer can stop the trials to come. This is the message that I convey on behalf of the Trinity." [12]

Just Before the Comet Comes

July 2037- April 2038

There will be many visible signs of impending, turbulent events:

Brother Anthony of **Aachen** : "Then a new Emperor (Great Catholic Monarch) about forty years old, was elected in Germany, and he met the Pope. Meanwhile, an epidemic broke out in the regions, devastated by war, and many people died. After the battle of Westphalia, the French returned to their country, and from then on, there was peace between the French and the Germans. All exiles returned to their homes. When I begged God to take the terrible vision away, I heard a voice saying: 'Prussia must be humiliated in such a manner that it will never again bring sorrow to the Church."[13] Prussia consists of eastern and part of northern Germany. Their punishment is still to come during the Darkness.

St. Hildegard of Bingen, Doctor of the Church: "At this time, as a punishment for their sins, Christians especially, will attempt armed resistance sensing no concern about the death of their bodies. A **powerful wind** will rise **in the north**, carrying heavy fog and the densest cloud of dust, by **Divine command**, and it will rage against them and it will fill their throats and eyes, so that they will cease their savagery and be stricken with great amazement." [14]

Our Lady of Peace to **Pedro Regis:** "Dear children, be attentive to **the signs of God.** The day will come when **the Earth** will lose its natural movement; **the Sun** will become dark, and nothing will be as before. Hear the voice of the Lord. Flee from sin, and desire Holiness with immense love. Have courage."[15] "At the height of the great persecution, **the Lord will show a great sign.** The heretics, if converted, will witness to the love of God. This will be the time of the final triumph of My Immaculate Heart." [16] "The day will come when men shall cry for help, and they will wish for death. A fast moving fire and destroyer will reach the earth that is coming from very far away, and men will not prevent its destructive action. I suffer for what comes to you. Continents will cease to exist, and the land shall not be the same. Everything will be different." [17]

"A large sign will be given to humanity, but if men do not repent, God's wrath will fall on humanity. Men will see something like a sun that is visible in the sky for long hours. All eyes will be on it in the summer. God is in a hurry. Pray. Intensify your prayers for greater support, for when the trials come."[18] In June of 2037, the Great Catholic Monarch will stop fighting. This message from Mary states, the comet will be visible in the summer. This is the summer of 2037, about nine months before the comet reaches the earth in April of 2038. This cataclysmic event will affect the weather and all aspects of life on earth.

The Fourth Angel's Trumpet

The fourth Trumpet will bring the shortening of the day, possibly by **the earth going off its axis** for three days, as Marian apparitions received by Patricia Talbot of Cuenca, Ecuador and Pedro Regis state. The earth may turn faster after the 'huge star' crashes down to the earth, possibly losing a third of day and a third of night. This event may be hard to accept but seems tenable.

Revelation 8: 12: "When the **fourth angel** blew his trumpet, a third of the sun, a third of the moon, and a third of the stars were hit hard enough to be plunged into darkness. The day lost a third of its light, as did the night."

Our Lady of Peace to **Pedro Regis:** "Rejoice, for your names are already written in heaven. Be converted and assume your true role as Christians. Bend your knees in prayer. Humanity will carry a heavy cross. **The earth will incline** (tilt) **when the great object comes nearer.** Time will be lost. People will be confused by what the Lord will permit. True wisdom is what comes from God. This is the message that I transmit to you, in the name of the Most Holy Trinity." [19]

"Humanity will carry a heavy cross when the earth loses its normal movement. There will be **a change in the gravitational force** of the earth, which **will attract a distant giant.** Don't flee from prayer. God wants to save you, but you have to do your part. The **geography** of the world **will change.** The day will come when the **lives** of men **will no longer be the same.** Don't be frightened. Those who are with the Lord will experience victory." [20]

"Pay attention to the signs of God. The day will come when **the earth** loses **its natural movement**; the sun will become dark and nothing will be like it was before. Hear the voice of the Lord. Flee from sin, and seek holiness with immense love. Be courageous. I am with you." [21] "Know that humanity will live moments of great tribulations. There will be a great **change in the angle** of the **orbit of the earth**, which will affect the lives of humans and animals. It will cause great pain. I am your Mom, and I want to help you. Return quickly. Tomorrow could be late." [22]

Marie-Julie Jahenny: "The earth will shake from (its) place... the space of six days. A day of rest and [on] the eighth day, **the trembling** will begin **again**. The land will shake so hard that the people will be thrown up to 300 paces..." [23]

Isaiah 24:18-20, 23: "For the windows on high will be opened, and the foundations of the earth will shake. The earth will burst asunder, the earth will be shaken apart, **and the earth will be convulsed.** The earth **will reel like a drunkard**, and it **will sway like a hut.** It's rebellion will weigh it down...On that day, the Lord will punish the host of the heavens in the heavens, and the kings of the earth on the earth... then the moon will blush and the sun grow pale."

Answering the Cry of the Poor

For 2000 years, prayers have been lifted up to God pleading, 'Your Kingdom come' in a real, visible, and victorious way, accumulating an assurance, His will, will be done on this earth, as it is in Heaven. The time has finally arrived, to further the Kingdom of Christ, when God answers the prayers of **the cry of the poor,** throughout all the afflicted Church ages, **at the altar of gold,** before the throne of God.

"Marie-Julie Jahenny continues with **the third part:** "Everything must be lost from top to bottom. That, my dear children, is when Saint Michael the Archangel, who is awaiting orders from Heaven, will descend with his armies, to fight with my good children, the true and good children of victory... Justice will pass everywhere. During this time, you will not have the Bread of the Strong... No apostles, you will have only your faith as food, my Divine Son as Sovereign Priest, to forgive you... My dear children, all the souls living in His Divine Heart will run no danger. They will only have a faint knowledge of His anger. They will be enclosed in this immense sea of prodigies and power, during **these great blows of Divine Justice."** [24]

This **third part,** is the **combination** of **the Sixth Seal,** when **the Comet,** consisting of the nucleus and coma, come close to the earth; causing **three days of darkness** by Divine Decree. **The Sixth Trumpet** describes four angels bound up, to release 200,000,000 demon minions, in figurative imagery, to kill a third of mankind. This will take place in the three days of Darkness.

Revelation 9: 13-19 : "Then the **sixth angel** blew his trumpet, and I heard a voice coming from between the horns of the Altar of gold in God's presence. It said to the sixth angel who was still holding his trumpet, "Release the four angels who are bound up on the banks of the great river Euphrates." So the four angels were released; this was precisely the hour, day, month, and year to kill a third of mankind. Their cavalry troops, whose count I heard, were two hundred million in number; a number I heard myself."

"Now in my vision, this is how I saw the horses and their riders. The breastplates they wore were fiery red, deep blue, and pale yellow. The horses' heads were like heads of lions, and out of their mouths came fire, and sulfur and smoke. By these three plagues; the smoke, the sulfur, and the fire that shot out of their mouths; a third of the mankind was slain. The deadly power of the horses is in their mouths and in their tails; for their tails were like snakes, with heads poised to strike."

This is the major Chastisement from God and is the last event, the tenth secret of Medjugorje or third secret of Garabandal in this fifth Church age. This is **the Three Days** of **Darkness,** during which **a third of mankind** will be **destroyed.**

Two Days of Darkness Before
the Three Days of Darkness

March 2038

Prophecies of two days of darkness reveal a similar, lesser experience before the preeminent three days of darkness.

Marie-Julie Jahenny: "The sun shall be darkened before…, the real darkness that will **arrive 37 days after**; the signs of the darkening of the sun, of signs of the earth, and the announced storm."[25] "…The Flame [of the Holy Spirit] says that in the designs of the Lord, there will be two days of horrible darkness, **separate from** the three days that many souls have announced. The sky will be purple and red; it will be so low that a clump of tall trees will be lost within it, up to a quarter of the tallest trees. These two days will tell [or foretell] and be as a genuine cachet of goodness, [i.e., they remind us the Three Days of Darkness are coming]; but will also be the descent of God in His wrath on the earth. You will not be free from the darkness…**During these two days,** the trees will be burned and will not produce any fruit the following year, because the sap will be burned and stopped. The rain that falls from the sky, will have a foul odor, and wherever it falls, it will be as a big hailstone of fire that pierces, that which is most solid and will leave a visible mark of burning. Your homes will be preserved. Only that which is covered lightly will suffer [i.e., of weak construction]. The water that will be poured on the earth will be black, a frightening black, and most of the land will bear it equally everywhere, but it will not hurt that which serves as food to the Christians."

"The Flame said in Brittany, France, in these two days of darkness, under the lowering sky, it will seem light, but no one will be able to see, because they cannot put out their face, by day, when opening a door; there will be an envoy of God, in the form of a hot flash, which will obscure the human eye… The Lord is urging me to pass on His words… The day of this darkness will still be bearable, despite the darkness… but if the day is calm, the night will be violent, and during the two nights, cries will come out, where they know not…at night, **the blessed candle** should not be put out. During the day, they will be able to go without it, a grace that comes from beyond the Heart of God." [26]

The Comet

April 2038

What will take place when a comet comes near the earth? Comets are composed of rock emitting fine dust, sand, gravel, small particles of rock, large rocks, ice, water, frozen gases and poisonous gases. They can reflect very little light in deep space and are very hard to detect. They have eccentric orbits that can take from a few years to even thousands of years before passing by the earth. We cannot be aware of all the comets that will pass through our solar system. That has become apparent, with the introduction of new comets seen in the last 40 years.

Comets are distinguished by a coma, a phenomenon whereby the sun heats up the gases, and matter explodes in all directions. The nucleus of a comet is generally less than 50 km across, but the coma may be larger than the sun and generate tails over 150 million kilometers or more; always in the opposite direction of the sun, caused by the solar winds or radiation, no matter which direction, the comet is moving. The coma may also have a lesser secondary tail, from its orbital path. Some comets may pass only once through the solar system, and then, are thrown out, never to return. There are documents found throughout the ancient world, over 3000 years ago, of the passing of a comet with a significant impact on the earth, as recorded on "an Egyptian Papyrus, a Mexican manuscript, a Finnish narration, and many others." Some of the plagues detailed in Exodus may have been the result of the comet passing over Pharaoh's kingdom when God was to take His people out of Egypt. A layer of fine red dust fell around that time and is recorded in documents but has not been found visibly. [27]

God allows spectacular natural events on the earth, in showing His presence and power, for His purposes, in reclaiming His Kingdom on earth. Natural events, as well as supernatural events, occurred at the time of the crucifixion. Looking at this future comet from the description of the prophecies and from a scientific point of view, gives us a set of events that are more than the result of a comet alone.

A collision between two giants in the universe will thrust matter in every direction, including towards Earth. This whole event will affect the earth for years, intensifying, as it gets closer. The visible journey of the comet predicted, will be seen for months, before entering our atmosphere. It will affect the weather, such as extreme heat causing droughts or extreme cold causing crop failures. It will also have physical effects on the earth, as it gets closer affecting the magnetic field, gravity, and change of the tilt of the earth on its axis.

The nucleus, including the density of the coma itself, will block the light of the sun, for three consecutive days, giving intense blackness all over the earth. Prophecies substantiate this comet as a monster in size. It will be seen at quite a distance as it is coming, for about nine months. As it is getting closer, the push and /or pull of this monstrous celestial body will affect the earth as it is precariously flailing towards us at a tremendous speed.

Normally, comets swing around the sun from gravitational pull. The explosion in the universe may have a different effect on this comet. Prophecies speak of the collision seen in the southern hemisphere, with matter thrust towards an encounter with Jupiter, then possibly deflecting towards the nebula of the Greater Bear. Our Lady of Peace to Pedro Regis: "**There will be a change in the gravitational force of the earth, which will attract a distant giant.**" [28] This may be why the comet will come from the nebula of the Greater Bear in the north, (just below the Big Dipper, as the supposed direction of the comet. Prophecies speak of what looks **like two suns in the sky**, asserting the comet's close proximity to the sun and its size. The tail or the coma will be ahead of the comet, with particles of rock, gravel sludge, rocks, and large rocks coming before the actual comet. [29] The unfolding of the first three events of the Trumpets will reach the earth, sometime earlier, before the actual comet arrives. The large rocks and slush of rocks on fire, mentioned in the Trumpets, is directly from the collision in the universe.

According to the prophecies, after the collision/explosion, a bright flash of light takes place in the southern sky near the constellation of Orion, taking out the power grids some years before the comet, with particle matter affecting Jupiter as years pass, and then possibly affecting the nebula of the Greater Bear constellation, in the north; nonetheless, the earth's gravitational change will attract the comet.

Just before the comet enters the earth's atmosphere, it will be a very cold night. As it gets closer, a powerful wind will rise from the north, carrying heavy fog, the densest cloud of dust, the roaring of the wind, possibly carrying poisonous gases. Thunderbolts from violent lightning will be heard, as outer particles of the coma create static in the atmosphere. The frozen ice, water particles, and dust containing hydrogen gas, mixed with the oxygen in the air, will ignite parts of the sky on fire. The color from the reaction of the oxygen and hydrogen, combined with other particle pollution, such as arsenic (from scientific observances), is the color of blood red; resulting in what looks like a **blood red moon,** as well as the blood red clouds and fire that appears to be blood red.

According to the saints, loose particles of rocks, the densest dust, and rocks, entering the atmosphere, will look like **the stars are falling out of the sky,** with the gases and molten rocks igniting the forests, grasslands, and houses creating a fire storm. The air will be depleted from the burning skies. The lack of oxygen will create a vacuum, with a rapid return of air from other areas, creating incredible hurricane winds. Combustion of hydrogen and oxygen will form dense clouds of water vapor, releasing torrential rains, unleashing flash flooding.

From the prophecies of the saints, high magnitude earthquakes from the magnetic push and pull of the comet will change the face of the earth. Large tall buildings will cease to stand, lying in piles of rubble. The topography of the land will change and in many places not recognizable. Roads and highways will be broken up. Bridges will collapse, railways twisted and heaved, dams torn open, pipelines severed, electrical lines destroyed, flood damage from the torrential rains, the ground rippled as in waves and torn up as though a cultivator ploughed the fields. After this time, all the satellites and all the space junk floating around the earth will not exist. The Hand of God will somehow rectify the ozone layer, particle pollution, greenhouse gases, pollution in the oceans, plants and animals in foreign ecosystems, and all other irregularities. God's Divine Decrees will be completed, having had enough of mankind's wayward ways.

Some areas may not be as damaged. In fact, some places will be protected, for those who pray, and who plead for mercy. Our Lord to Julia of Zagreb states: "If only they had fasted for one day a week or made some atonement. I would have spared this region!"[30] The immediate devastation to mankind will take a whole generation to rebuild, according to the prophecies. We will not go back to this so-called 'former glory.' We will live on the land and from the land, as God intended.

Prophecies of the Comet

These extreme prophecies are self-explanatory:

St. Hilarion of Czenstochau (291 to 371): "One day before the comet shines, a lot of people from need and misery will be in want of a home. The Great Empire in the sea who are of different folk stock and origin, will be devastated by earthquake, storm and flood." [31] This is about the United States of America. The seer would have seen the USA as the great power before the time of the comet. The USA has been called the melting pot of different nationalities, a reflection of this prophecy.

St. Hildegard-Doctor of the Church (1098-1179): "Before the comet comes, many nations, the good excepted, will be scourged with want and famine. The great nation in the ocean that is inhabited by people of different tribes and descent (USA), by earthquake, storm, and tidal waves will be devastated. It will be divided and in great part submerged. That nation will also have many misfortunes at sea and lose its colonies in the east through a tiger and a lion. The comet, by its tremendous pressure, will force much out of the ocean and flood many countries, causing much want and many plagues. The ocean will also flood many other countries, so that all coastal cities will be fearful, and many of them will be destroyed by tidal waves. Most living creatures will be killed, and even those who escape will die from a horrible disease." [32]

Contemporary prophecies speak about the United States breaking up and being partly submerged, particularly from the Mississippi and eastward. We hear about Los Angeles, San Francisco, and various parts of the western shore, sliding into the ocean. Modern day contemporary prophets are not always reliable. Pedro Regis gives information, for South America,Central America, the U.S. of A., and Canada.

Abbot Merlin Joachim of Fiore:"After many prolonged sufferings endured by Christians, and after a too great effusion of innocent blood… **a monster shall appear in the sky** (Comet." [33]

Our Lady of Peace to **Pedro Regis**: "I am your Mom, and I come from Heaven to call you to a sincere conversion… Humanity is heading towards a great abyss, and my poor children will carry a heavy cross…An extraordinary phenomenon will happen in Europe. People will not be able to explain it. When people **see the appearance of a great light,** know that the great final battle is near…People will call the light, **a Second Sun.** What I have forecast in the past will happen. Courage. I will speak to My Jesus for you. Go forward without fear." [34] "Something larger than the earth will be seen that will make men wake up and think. They will not find any solution, but God will come to the rescue of His people. **In the universe is one that science does not yet know,** but with the Lord's permission will discover…God wants to save you, but you cannot cross your arms. The earth is in danger because the creature wants to be more than the Creator. Repent. There is still a chance that everyone can be saved."[35]"The **great comet will come** and cause great destruction." [36]

"**A giant will come,** and when **men announce** that **it is near,** humanity will live moments of **great difficulties.** The earth will go through an **immense transformation.** Know that all of this must happen, but in the end, the faithful will win. God will transform the earth, and those who are just will live happily. **Rivers and lakes will appear. There will be riches and abundance.** Courage. Don't lose heart. Behold the times I announced to you in the past. I am your Mom, and I want your wellbeing. Forward on the path I have pointed out." [37] "Humanity is on track, to the abyss of destruction which men have prepared with their own hands. The earth will pass through great transformations, and many places will no longer exist. Famous **islands of your Brazil** will be destroyed. **A giant (comet)** will come **from the north,** to torment my poor children." [38]

Johann Friede (1204 -1257 an Austrian monk of the order of St. John: "When the nights will be filled with more intensive cold and the day with heat, a new life will begin in nature. The heat means radiation from the earth, the cold, the waning light of the sun. Only a few more years and you will become aware that **sunlight has become perceptibly weaker.** When even the artificial light will cease to give service, **the great event of the firmament will be near.** The Nebula of the Greater Bear will arrive in the vicinity of earth… and will fill the space of **five hundred suns** at the horizon. It will more and more cover up the light of the sun, until the **days will be like nights** at full moon. The illumination will not come from the moon, but from Orion, which constellation by the light of Jupiter, will send forth its rays on the greater Bear and will dissolve its nebula with the force of light."[39]

"**By this time**, mankind will be stricken with terror. In the abodes of the children of light, the Book of Revelations will be read, and in the palaces of the Church, as they await the arrival of **the great comet**. Birds will be like reptiles and will not use their wings. Animals of the ground, in fear and alarm, will raise such clamor, that it will make human hearts tremble. Men will flee their abodes, in order not to see the weird occurrence. Finally, complete darkness will set in and **last for three days and three nights**. During this time, men, deprived of the power of light, will fall into slumber-like sleep, from which many will not awaken, especially those who have no spark of spiritual life. When the sun will again rise and emerge, earth will be covered with a blanket of ashes, like snow in winter, except that the ashes will have the color of sulfur. Damp fog will ascend from the ground, illuminated by igneous gases." [39]

This is a very sobering prophecy. Some of the words are hard to understand and with imperfect translations still leave questions. It attests to a colder time with less sun and our heat coming from the earth. If it becomes cold each night, firewood, coal, and other fuels will be needed. Pondering other possibilities, we must consider what events unknown, will rise up on this earth that will increase particle pollution. Most likely volcanic eruptions, the fire from the skies, the burning of cities and towns, forests, grasslands, during the chaos and wars that spread dense clouds across much of the earth.

In this prophecy, the comet will come from the Nebula of the Greater Bear. This nebula may be the owl nebula, located near the lower part of the Big Dipper. It is part of the Greater Bear constellation, in the north. Mary speaking to Pedro Regis, also verifies a collision/explosion in the southern sky. It confirms prophecies that speak of **a great fertility of the earth** after this event. Orion is in the far south at night and speaks of a reference to Christ. He mentions the millennium but is referring to the time of peace for the sixth Church age. These events, will bring a time of genuine peace and the end to our industrial civilization.

Isaiah 50 : 3 : "I will clothe the heavens with darkness and will make sack-cloth their covering." [40]

Our Lady of Peace to **Pedro Regis**: "Dear children, **the Earth** will be **covered by darkness**. The darkness will come out of immense light. A mystery, when the big bright light will be revealed. Here are the tougher times for humanity. Give your best in this mission that the Lord has entrusted to you. Do not stand still. Humanity is heading for destruction..."[41]This 'immense light' is the comet that **will fill the space of five hundreds suns** on the horizon. The comet will hide the sun for three days as it comes close to the earth.

The Three Days of Darkness
April 2038

This event will coincide during the time of **the Comet** passing the earth, causing three days of darkness, on Holy Thursday, April 22; Good Friday, April 23; and Holy Saturday, April 24 in 2038.

St. Bridget states, "the whole world shall cry, **woe!**" during a certain year when certain saints feast days fall on certain Church feast days. Review p.302.

Marie-Julie Jahenny states, the Three Days of Darkness will come on a Holy Thursday, Good Friday, and Holy Saturday. Combining these prophecies of the visionaries, defaults to April 22, 23, and 24 of 2038.

Marie-Julie Jahenny discloses from Our Lord: "The Three Days of Darkness will be on a Thursday, Friday, and Saturday, days of the most Holy Sacrament, of the Cross, and Our Lady (**Easter**)... three days less one night. The earth will be covered in darkness, and **hell will be loosed on earth.**"

"Thunder and lightning will cause those who have no faith, or trust in my power, to die of fear. During these three days of darkness, no windows must be open, because no one will be able to see the earth and the terrible color it will have in those days of punishment without dying at once. The sky will be on fire, the earth will split. During these three days of darkness, let the blessed candle be lit everywhere, no other light will shine. **No one outside a shelter will survive.** The earth will shake, as at the judgment, and fear will be great."

"Yes, we will listen to the prayers of your friends, not one will perish. We will need them to publish the glory of the cross. The **candles of blessed wax**, alone, will give light during this horrible darkness. One candle alone will be enough for the duration of this night of hell... In the homes of the wicked and blasphemers, these candles will give no light." [42]

Our Lady warns: "Everything will shake except the piece of furniture on which the blessed candle is burning. This will not shake. You will all gather around the crucifix and my blessed picture. This is what will keep away this terror. During this darkness, the devils and the wicked will **take on the most hideous shapes**... **Red clouds like blood** will move across the sky. The crash of the thunder will shake the earth, and sinister lightning will streak the heavens out of season. The earth will be shaken to its foundations. The sea will rise, its roaring waves will spread over the continent...the earth will become like a vast cemetery. The bodies of the wicked and the just will cover the ground. Three quarters of the population of the globe will disappear. Half the population of France will be destroyed." [42] This event with the red atmosphere, along with the demons, and the wicked taking on hideous forms are mentioned in the same event. Satan **will take as many as he can with him**, before he is bound up again.

The Angels Will Help

Our Lady of Peace to **Pedro Regis**: "God is in a hurry, and now is the time for your sincere and loving return to the God of salvation and peace. **I am your mom,** and I am very close to you… Now is the time of great spiritual trials. Seek strength in prayer and the Eucharist… Great and sorrowful happenings will come to you, but don't lose heart. **The angels of the Lord will come from Heaven,** and His chosen ones will not experience physical pains. In the great and final tribulation, people will see the powerful hand of God in action." [43] "In this time, the righteous will receive the protection of the angels of the Lord, and no evil will reach them. Those who dedicate themselves to me will experience a joy without end. These will contemplate what human eyes have never see ." [44]

Prophecies of the Three Days of Darkness

A period of total darkness is revealed in the scriptures, revealing God's Chastisement; including figurative descriptions of demon spirits and the wicked released from Hell, to destroy that part of unrepentant mankind.

Amos 8: 9-10: "On that day, says the Lord God, I will make the sun set at midday and cover the earth with darkness, in broad daylight. I will turn your feasts into mourning and all your songs into lamentations."

Joel 2: 1-8,10: "Blow the trumpet (Revelation…Let all who dwell in the land tremble, for the **Day of the Lord** is coming; Yes, it is near ; a day of darkness and of gloom, **Like**… a people numerous and mighty! **The like** has not been (seen from of old, nor will it be after them, even in the years of distant generations. Before them, a fire devours, and after them, a flame enkindles; … **from them** there is no escape. **Their appearance** is that **of horses** (Revelation/ **Trumpets** like steeds they run… Like a mighty people arrayed for battle. Before them peoples are in torment, every face blanches… The sun and the moon are darkened, and the stars withhold their brightness." This prophecy has similar language as in Revelation, chapter nine of the fifth and sixth trumpets that relates to a similar description.

Isaiah 13: 6-13: "Howl, for the day of the Lord is near, as destruction from the Almighty comes. Therefore, all hands fall helpless, the bows of the young men fall from their hands. Every man's heart melts in terror. Pangs and sorrows take hold of them, like a woman in labor they writhe; they look aghast at each other, their faces aflame. Lo, **the day of the Lord** comes cruel, with wrath and burning anger. To lay waste the land and **destroy the sinners within it**. The stars and constellations of the heavens send forth no light. The **sun is dark** when it rises, and the light of the **moon does not shine**. Thus, I will punish the world for its evil and the wicked for their guilt. I will put an end to the pride of the arrogant, the insolence of tyrants, I will humble. I will make **mortals more rare than pure gold**, men, than gold of Ophir. For this, I will make the heavens tremble, and the earth shall be moved out of her place, for the indignation of the Lord of hosts, and for the day of His fierce wrath." 'The day of the Lord' is a day of punishment and not the second coming.

Isaiah 26 : 20-21: "Go my people, enter your chambers, and close your doors behind yourselves for a brief moment, until the wrath is past. See, the Lord goes forth from his place to punish the wickedness of the earth's inhabitants. The earth will reveal the blood upon her, and no longer conceal her slain."

Revelation 9 : 13-19: "The **sixth angel** blew his **trumpet**... Cavalry troops, whose count I heard, were two hundred million in number... I saw the horses and their riders... The horses' heads were like heads of lions, and out of their mouths came fire, and sulfur and smoke. By these three plagues; the smoke, the sulfur, and the fire that shot out of their mouths; **a third of the mankind** was slain. The **deadly power of the horses** is in their mouths and in their tails; for their tails were like snakes, with heads poised to strike."

Marie-Julie Jahenny states, during this darkness, the devils and the wicked will take on the most hideous shapes. They will have power and strength to destroy many structures that were used for evil, on the earth and will have the power to destroy evil people who refuse to turn to the truth of Jesus Christ.

Prophecies of the Three Days of Darkness, from **Catholic saints**, reveal a **more practical understanding** of what will take place and what we must do before hand to prepare and during that time:

St. Anna-Maria Taigi (1769-1837: "God will ordain two punishments: one, in the form of wars, revolutions and other evils will originate on earth; **the other will be sent from Heaven.** (Comet) There will come over all the earth an intense darkness, lasting three days and three nights. Nothing will be visible, and the air will be **laden with pestilence**, which will claim principally but not exclusively, the enemies of religion. During those three days of darkness, artificial light will be impossible; only blessed candles will burn and will afford illumination. He, who out of curiosity, opens his window to look out or leaves his house, will fall dead on the spot. During those three days of darkness, the people should remain in their homes; pray the Rosary and asking God for mercy. On this terrible occasion, so many of these wicked men, enemies of His Church and of their God, shall be killed by Divine scourge; that their corpses around Rome will be as numerous as the fish which a recent inundation of the Tiber had carried into the city. All the enemies of the Church, secret as well as known, will perish over the whole earth, during that universal darkness, with the exception of some few, whom God will convert. The air shall be infected with demons, which will appear under all sorts of hideous forms."[45]

Amidst the wrath of God, the hideous demons coming out of hell, cannot be looked at or a person will drop dead. There are many comments about **blessed** wax candles, as the only light, miraculously continuing in the houses of the saved. Crucifixes and pictures of Mary are mentioned and meditated upon.

Blessed Sr. Elena Aiello from Our Lady (Good Friday, April 16, 1954): "Clouds with lightning-rays of fire and tempest of fire will pass over the whole world, and **the punishment will be the most terrible**, ever known, **in the history of mankind**. It will last 70 hours. The wicked will be crushed and eliminated. Many will be lost because they will **have stubbornly remained** in **their sins**. Then, they will feel the force of light over the darkness. The hours of darkness are near... some **nations** will be purified while others **will disappear** entirely."[46] This confirms what Mary at Fatima stated when she pleaded with people to take heed, or nations will disappear, meaning that whole nations of certain peoples who refuse to turn to God will disappear. This was often thought about because of the nuclear possibility, but God Himself will annihilate these nations because of their unrepentant hearts.

Blessed Sr. Elena Aiello continues: "Be not silent, my daughter, because the hours of darkness, of abandonment, are near. I am bending over the world, holding in suspension, the justice of God. Otherwise, these things would already have now come to pass. Prayers and penances are necessary because men must return to God, and to My Immaculate Heart—the Mediatrix of men to God, and thus the world will be at least in part saved. Cry out these things to all, like the very echo of my voice. Let this be known to all because it will help save many souls, and prevent much destruction in the Church and in the world." [47]

Our Lady of Peace to **Pedro Regis**: "Soon, there will be **three consecutive days** of darkness that not even science will know how to explain. All of you will suffer much in these days. I promise to all who are at my side that they will not lack light. I ask you to **always keep candles, blessed by a priest**, in your house. Don't be afraid. Do what I tell you to do. Continue to pray for priests. Pray for vocations to the priesthood. Pray for the Holy Father. Pray that Satan doesn't manage to destroy my plans. I bless you in the name of the Father, and of the Son, and of the Holy Spirit." [48] "The day will come when the earth will be involved in thick darkness. Men cry for help and do not know where to go."[49]

St. Casper (Jasper) **del Bufalo** (1786-1837) : "The death of the impenitent persecutors of the Church will take place during the three days of darkness." [50]

Blessed Mary of Jesus Crucified of Pau (1846 -1878): "All states will be shaken by civil war and conflict. During darkness lasting three days, people **given to evil will perish**, so that, only one fourth of mankind will survive. The clergy, too, will be greatly reduced in number, as most of them will die in defense of the faith or their country." [51]

Palma Maria d' Oria (1825-1863): "There shall be three days of darkness. Not one demon shall be left in hell. They shall all come out, either to excite the wicked murderers, or to dishearten the just. This shall be Frightful! Frightful!"[52] "There shall be three days of darkness, during which the atmosphere will be infected by innumerable devils, who shall cause the death of large multitudes of unbelievers and wicked men. Blessed candles alone shall be able to give light and preserve the faithful Catholics from this impending dreadful scourge. Supernatural prodigies shall appear in the heavens." [53]

Father Bernard Maria Clausi, OFM (d-1849): "Before the triumph of the Church comes, God will first take vengeance on the wicked, especially against the godless. It will be a new judgment, the like, that has not been seen before, and it will be so terrible that those who outlive it, will imagine that they are the only ones spared. All people will then be good and contrite. The judgment will come suddenly and be of short duration. Then comes the triumph of the Church and the reign of brotherly love." [54]

Julka (Julia) of Zagreb: "A strong warm wind will come from the south. It will seize upon the whole globe and cause dreadful storms. After this, about ten claps of thunder, at once, will strike the earth with such force that it will shudder throughout. This is the sign that the great tribulation and the black darkness are beginning. These will last three days and three nights. On this account, people should go into their houses, close them up well, darken the windows, bless themselves and the house with holy water, and light blessed candles. Outside, such dreadful things will be happening that those who venture to look will die. All the devils will be let loose on earth, so that they can destroy their prey, themselves."

"The demons will howl upon the earth and call many, in order to destroy them....They will imitate the voices of relatives and acquaintances who have not reached a safer place. Once the horror commences, do not open your door, to anyone at all." "In many places, several people will gather in fear. From the same group, some will perish, others remain alive for this day and moment, and for that darkness, many will have prepared the blessed candles, but they will not burn, if the people have not lived in accordance with My Commandments; others will even be unable to light them for fear. But, for those who believe, although they have but a stub of the blessed candle, it will burn for these three days and nights without going out. Some people will fall into a deep sleep granted by me, so as not to see what is happening on the earth (children?)." [55]

Padre Pio (1887-1968): "Pray! Make reparation! Be fervent and practice mortifications. Great things are at stake! Pray...Men are running towards the abyss of Hell in great rejoicing and merry-making, as though they were going to a masquerade ball or the wedding feast of the devil himself! Assist me in the salvation of souls. The measure of sin is filled! The day of revenge, with its terrifying happenings is near – nearer than you can imagine! And the world is sleeping in false security! The Divine Judgment shall strike them like a thunderbolt! These godless and wicked people shall be destroyed without mercy, as were the inhabitants of Sodom and Gomorrah of old. Yes, I tell you, their wickedness was not as great as that of our human race today." [56]

This part is from the Holy Spirit to **Padre Pio**: "Keep your windows well covered. Do not look out. Light a blessed candle, which will suffice for many days. Pray the rosary. Read spiritual books. Make acts of Spiritual Communion, also acts of love, are so pleasing to us. Pray with outstretched arms, prostrate on the ground, in order that many souls may be saved. Do not go outside during these hours. Provide yourself with sufficient food. The powers of nature shall be moved, and a rain of fire shall make people tremble with fear, have courage. I am in the midst of you." [57]

"Take care of the animals during these days. I am the creator and preserver of animals as well as man. I shall give you a few signs before hand, at which time you should place more food before them. **I will preserve the property of the elect**, including the animals, for they shall be in need of sustenance, afterwards as well. Cover your windows carefully. **My elect shall not see my wrath.** Have confidence in me, and I will be your protection."

"**Hurricanes of fire** will pour from the clouds and spread over the entire earth! Storms, bad weather, thunderbolts, and earthquakes will cover the earth for two days. An uninterrupted rain of fire will take place! It will begin during a very cold night. All this is to prove that God is the Master of Creation. Those who hope in me and believe in my words have nothing to fear because I will not forsake them **or those who spread my message**. No harm will come to those who are in the state of grace and who seek my Mother's protection."

"That you may be prepared for these visitations, I will give you the following signs and instructions: The night will be very cold. The wind will roar. After a time, thunderbolts will be heard. Lock all the doors and windows. Talk to no one outside. Kneel down before a crucifix, be sorry for your sins, and beg my Mother's protection. **Do not look during the earthquake** because the anger of God is Holy! Jesus does not want us to behold the anger of God because God's anger must be contemplated with fear and trembling."

"Those who disregard this advice will be killed instantly. The wind will carry with it, poisonous gases, which will be diffused over the entire earth. Those who suffer and die innocently, will be martyrs and they will be with me in My Kingdom. Satan will triumph! But in three nights, the earthquake and fire will cease."

"On the following day the sun will shine again, angels will descend from Heaven and will spread the spirit of peace over the earth. A feeling of immeasurable gratitude will take possession of those who survive this most terrible ordeal, the impending punishment, with which God will visit the earth since creation."

"How unconcerned men are regarding these things! This shall so soon come upon them, contrary to all expectations. How indifferent they are in preparing themselves for these unheard of events, through which they will have to pass so shortly. The weight of Divine balance has reached the earth. The wrath of my Father shall be poured out over the entire world. I am again warning the world through your instrumentality, as I have so often done here before."

"This catastrophe shall come upon the earth like a flash of lightning. At which moment, the light in the morning sun shall be replaced by black darkness! No one shall leave the house or look out a window from that moment on. I myself shall come amidst thunder and lightning. The wicked shall behold My Divine Heart. There shall be great confusion because of this utter darkness. In which the entire earth shall be enveloped, and many, many shall die from fear and despair."

"On that day, as soon as complete darkness has set in, no one shall leave the house or to look from out of the window. The darkness shall last a day and night, another day and night, and another day–but on the night following, the stars will shine again, and on the next morning, the sun shall rise again, and it will be spring time."

"In the days of darkness, my elect shall not sleep, as did the disciples in the garden. They shall pray incessantly, and they shall not be disappointed in me. I shall gather my elect. Hell will believe itself to be in possession of the entire earth, but I shall reclaim it."

"Again and again, I have warned men, and often, I have given them special opportunities to return to the right path but now wickedness has reached its climax, and the punishment can no longer be delayed. Tell all, that the time has come, in which these things shall be." [56, 57]

Marie-Julie Jahenny from Mary (Stigmatist): "Those who have served me well and have invoked me, who have my blessed picture in their house, who carry my rosary on them and say it often, **I will keep intact all that belongs to them**...The heat from heaven will be unbearably hot, even in the closed homes. The whole sky will be on fire, but the lightning will not penetrate into the houses where there will be the light of the blessed candle. This light is the only thing that will protect you." [58]

Blessed Isabel (Elizabeth) **Canori-Mora** (1774-1825): "As soon as St. Peter, the prince of the Apostles, had gathered the flock of Jesus Christ in a place of safety, he reascended into heaven, accompanied by legions of angels. Scarcely had they disappeared, when the sky was covered with clouds so dense and dismal that it was impossible to look at them without dismay. All of a sudden, there burst out such a terrible and violent wind that its noise sounded like the roar of furious lions. The sound of the furious hurricane was heard over the whole earth. Fear and terror struck not only men but also the very beasts."

"God will employ the powers of hell for the extermination of these impious and heretical persons who desire to overthrow the Church and destroy it to its very foundation. These presumptuous men in their mad impiety, believe that they can overthrow God from His Throne; but the Lord will despise these artifices, and through an effect of His Mighty Hand, He will punish these impious blasphemers by giving permission to the infernal spirits to come out from Hell. Innumerable legions of demons will overrun the earth, and they shall execute the orders of Divine Justice, by causing terrible calamities and disasters; they will attack everything; they shall injure individual persons and entire families; they shall devastate property and alimentary productions, cities and villages. Nothing on earth shall be spared. God will allow the demons to strike with death, those impious men, because they gave themselves up to the infernal powers, and **have formed with them a pact against the Catholic Church.**"

"Being desirous of more fully penetrating my spirit with a deeper sentiment of His Divine Justice, God showed to me the awful abyss; I saw in the bowels of the earth a dark and frightening cavern, whence **an infinite number of demons were issuing forth**, who **under the form of men and beasts**, came to ravage the earth, leaving everywhere ruins and blood. Happy will be, all true and faithful Catholics! They shall experience the powerful protection of the Holy Apostles, St. Peter and St. Paul, who will watch over them, lest they be injured, either in their persons or their property. Those spirits shall plunder every place where God has been outraged, despised, and blasphemed; the edifices they profaned will be pulled down and destroyed, and nothing but ruins shall remain of them." [59]

Martha Robins (1902-1981) a stigmatist who lived on Holy Eucharist for many years, relates words from Jesus during a vision: "**I play with the plans of men**. My right hand prepares miracles, and My Name shall be glorified in the entire world. I shall be pleased to break the pride of the wicked. Much more admirable and extraordinary will be **the event that will come out of our encounter...** Then it will be understood that neither human power, nor demons, nor industry, will end the conflict, but that it will end only when **reparation has been consummated.**" [60]

CHAPTER 46

THE AFTERMATH ON EARTH

S t. Bridget clearly stipulates that Easter Sunday, April 25, 2038, the Feast of St. Mark, will open a time of great change to the planet earth and to humanity. It will take time to adjust to the changes to the earth and to radically different way of life. Many visionaries have spoken of the aftermath.

Blessed Elizabeth Canori-Mora: "Great legions of devils shall roam the whole earth, **leaving a trail of ruins** and executing the commands of Divine Justice. These evil spirits shall devastate, in a special manner, all the places in which God has been outraged most, blasphemed against, or treated sacrilegiously. Nothing shall be left in these places." [1]

Blessed Sister Elena Aiello: "I will manifest my partiality to Italy which will be preserved from the fire, but the skies will be covered with dense darkness, and the earth will be shaken by fearful **earthquakes which will open deep abysses. Provinces and cities will be destroyed**, and all will cry out that the end of the world has come. Even **Rome will be punished** according to justice, for its many and serious sins because here, sin has reached its peak." [2]

Julka (Julia of Zagreb, Croatia from Jesus: "My servant [Jonah] I hurled into the depth of the ocean, because he did not obey My Word…The earth has turned completely deaf to the voice of the creator…I shall destroy cities and mountains, valleys and fields. I shall gather the little flock of my faithful sheep. The earth will burst into tears, but then it will be too late because at that moment, it cannot serve me anymore. I shall make the earth into a graveyard and shall adorn it with the dead bodies of men. In the days of disaster and misery, I shall watch carefully over my sheep. I came into the world to save all people, but too many did not want to accept me." [3] "I discovered myself in a small plain between high mountains. This place seemed familiar, but it was quite devastated. I could nowhere see a house or a human being. [4] The ground was so thoroughly turned up that it looked **like a gigantic plough had ploughed it up.** As I walked over these huge furrows, I got so exhausted that I almost fell down. While I stumbled weeping through this vast wasteland, I suddenly spotted a man who was coming from a high mountain. I was delighted and went after him, but he too was quite beside himself, on account of the affliction he had experienced. He gave a painful sigh, looked at the sky and thanked the Lord for his survival. He was a priest, dressed in blue with a collar. After him, a young mother with two or three small children emerged from a cave. She looked like the priest's sister. She was quite crushed, and she sighed uninterruptedly, and her children clung closely to her."

"When the priest noticed a broad high stump, he went up to it. He took from the ground a few small sticks, which he set up on the stump like candles. He also made a cross and laid it in the middle. Then, he began to offer the holy Mass under the bright sky with great reverence. He faced eastwards. Although he had no mass vestment, no sacred vessels, and no missal, he acted as though he had them all. When at the end he imparted the blessing, he was so moved that he noticed no one about him. The mother and her children stood on the Epistle side, and I stood on the Gospel side. The children had laid their little head on their mother's lap. The dear Savior said later, that is how it will be. Many priests will perish in this great distress. Those who survive are poor because **many of this world's goods will be lost.**" [5]

Julka (Julia) of Zagreb: "The earth will remain **waste and empty**, and one man will go in search for another, when they have found one another, they will love one another so much that they will be one in heart and mind. A small town was badly punished. About ten persons remained alive...Later some women came from the monastery. When they saw the church and monastery in ruins, they groaned aloud, they wrung their hands and wailed. A young tall priest suddenly turned up from somewhere. I expressed my feelings to him, 'Look now we have no church, no priest, no Holy Mass, nothing at all!' But he answered, 'We shall now live in the way we read in the Sacred Scriptures and in the Holy Gospel...' The Lord later said: 'As you have seen, it will indeed be like this in this village because of the disobedience of my servants who were unwilling to do penance. **If only they had fasted for one day a week** or made some atonement. **I would have spared this region!**'" [6]

Mother Elena Leonardi: "In this sacrilegious struggle, much of which has been created by man, will be demolished, due to both savage impulse and enraged resistance." [7]

A Remnant Shall Be Saved

These prophecies predict that God will bring a quarter to a third of the population of mankind through the severe test of the tribulation. Two thirds to three quarters will perish. Some countries will be left uninhabited, and yet, a remnant of His Church will continue on this earth. Afterwards, mankind will be very limited in resources. Neighbors will be far and few, but the promise of His Church will continue.

Isaiah 13: 12: "I will make mortals more rare than pure gold, men than gold of Ophir."

Jeremiah 25:32-38 "Thus says the Lord of hosts: Lo! Calamity stalks from nation to nation. A great storm is unleashed from the ends of the earth. On that day, those the Lord has slain, **will be strewn from one end of the earth to the other**. None will mourn them, **they shall lay like dung on the field**. Howl you shepherds and wail... The **time for your slaughter has come**... there is no flight for the shepherds...by the sweeping sword, by the burning wrath of the Lord."

Zechariah 13: 8,9 "In all the land, says the Lord, **two-thirds** of them **shall be cut off** and perish, and one third shall be left. I will bring the **one-third through fire**, and I will refine them as silver is refined, and **I will test them as gold** is tested. They shall call upon my name, and I will hear them. I will say, they are my people, and they shall say, 'The Lord is my God.'"

Blessed Casper Del Bufalo (1837: "He who out lives the darkness and the three days, it will seem to him **as if he were alone** on earth because of the fact that the world will be covered **everywhere with carcasses**." [8]

Sister Mary of Jesus Crucified at Pau, France, Stigmatist (1846-1878): "During a darkness lasting three days, the people given to evil will perish, so that **only one-fourth of mankind** will survive." [9]

Marie-Julie Jahenny: "The earth will be like a vast cemetery. The bodies of the wicked and the just will cover the ground...**Three quarters of the population** of the globe will disappear in the last crisis...Half the population of France will be destroyed. After the punishments, there will be villages left without a soul." [10]

St. Lucia of Fatima from Our Lord (1939): "The time is coming when the rigor of my Justice will punish the crimes of various **nations**. Some of them **will be annihilated**." [11]

Blessed Sister Elena Aiello from Our Lord (April 8, 1955): 'If men do not amend their ways, a terrifying scourge of fire will come down from Heaven, upon all the nations of the world, and men will be punished according to the debts contracted with Divine justice. There will be frightful moments for all, because Heaven will be joined with the earth, and all the un-Godly people will be destroyed, **some nations** will be purified, while **others will disappear entirely**." [12]

Enzo Alocci, stigmatist, from Mary (1966): "Man will soon realize his nothingness and will be hurled down to his knees. The day is not far off when the whole earth will be covered with fire, and the world will abound with corpses. Only **one quarter of mankind** will survive." [13]

(Fr) Pere John Lamy: "The state of the early Christians will come back again, but there **will be few men on earth then**." [14]

Our Lady of Peace to **Pedro Regis**: "You live in a time worse than the time of the flood. Humanity has become contaminated by sin and needs to be cured. I come from Heaven to call you to conversion... **Entire nations will disappear,** and **humanity will drink a bitter cup of pain**. I suffer because of what is waiting for you. Don't stray from the way I have pointed out. Behold, the time I have forecast has come." [15] "After the great tribulation, the Lord will send His angels to guide His chosen ones. I ask you, to not be afraid. Don't forget God is on your side." [16]

Julka (Julia) of Zagreb from Jesus (1973-1975): "The people will realize in the end, who it is, they have disobeyed. Retain my instructions for the days, when there is only **a small flock left**. They will hunger to hear my words." [17]

The Comet Fertilizes the Earth

In 2038, the comet will fertilize the earth; even the deserts over which it passes, will receive astounding increases in the fertility of the soil, across this planet.

Johann Friede: "When the sun will again rise and emerge, the earth will be covered with a blanket of ashes like snow in winter, except that the ashes will have **the color of sulfur**...Earth will absorb these ashes and **form such fertility** as has not been experienced ever before." [18] The color of hot liquid sulfur has a dark or blood red appearance but solid (dry) sulfur is yellow.

Abbe Souffrand: "During the reign of the Great King, the noblest virtues will be practiced throughout the world, and the land **will yield abundant crops**." [19]

St. Bridget: "People without intelligence shall glorify me, and **deserts shall be inhabited**." [20]

St. Hildegard: "During this period of Peace, people will be forbidden to carry weapons, and iron will be used only for making agricultural implements and tools. Also during this period, **the land will be very productive**, and many Jews, heathens, and heretics will join the Church." [21]

St. Methodius: "In the last period... the great grace of God...provided a Monarch, a long duration of peace, and **a splendid fertility of the earth**." [22]

A Great Sign Appears in the Sky

This great 'Sign of the Cross' will be the sign of the victorious Jesus over His enemies, similar to the time of Noah when the rainbow in the sky was the sign of reconciliation of God the Father with future mankind.

Blessed Elizabeth Canori-Mora: "After the frightful punishment, I saw the heavens opening... **a great light appeared upon the earth, which was the sign of reconciliation of God with men**. All men shall become Catholics, and they shall acknowledge the Pope as vicar of Jesus Christ." [23]

Johann Friede: "Of mankind there will be more that are dead than there have been casualties in all wars. On the seventh day after the return of light, earth will have absorbed the ashes and formed such fertility as has not been experienced ever before. But **Orion will cast its ray on the earth** and show a path, toward the last resting place, of the greatest and most eminent man, who had ever lived on the earth. The survivors will proclaim His ancient doctrine in peace and will institute the millennium (after the 6th Church age of peace), announced by **the Messiah**, in the light of true brotherly and sisterly love, for the glory of the Creator and for the blessedness of all mankind."[24]

Thomas a Kempis from Our Lord: "This sign **of the Cross** will appear in the heavens when the Lord comes to judge." [25]

Palma Maria d' Oria: "There shall be three days of darkness... But (after), **a grand cross shall appear**, and the triumphs of the Church will make people quickly forget all evils." [26]

Pope Pius IX: "There will **come a great sign** which will fill the world with awe. But this will occur only **after the triumph** of a revolution, during which the Church will undergo ordeals that are beyond description." [27]

Our Lady of Peace to **Pedro Regis**: "A great sign from God will appear, and mankind will be astonished. Those separated, will be led to the truth, and great faith will possess the elect of the Lord." [28]

"When you get to the big day, in which **the Lord will give men the chance to return to his love**, the Angel of the Lord will touch the sky, and this will change color. The mountains descend, and the men will accommodate an infinite beauty... **This will be the day of the great sign.** The Earth will be at peace. The Lord will wipe away your tears, and you will see the mighty hand of God act." [29]

Definitive Triumph of Mary's Immaculate Heart

This is the final triumph of Mary's Immaculate Heart; promised since her apparitions at Fatima. The battle will cease with the defeat of Satan, after which true peace will begin on the earth.

Our Lady of Peace to **Pedro Regis**: "**Three days after**, the great miracle will happen; **the definitive triumph of My Immaculate Heart**, and peace will reign forever. Courage. I am your Mother, and I come from Heaven to call you to conversion."[30] "In the great triumph of my Immaculate Heart, the heavens will open, and **the angels of the Lord will come to help my chosen ones**. Those who remain faithful to the end will contemplate that which **human eyes** have never seen." [31] "All darkness will be gone and the light of God will shine in the hearts of men and women of faith. Joy will reign in the hearts of those chosen by God, and there will be only one flock and one shepherd. The victory of God over the forces of evil will come with **the final triumph of my Immaculate Heart.**" [32]

"After the great final tribulation, you will see a new Earth. **That will be the time of the definitive triumph of my Immaculate Heart.** Humanity will find peace, and men and women of faith will live in happiness." [33] "The day is coming when **only the just will inhabit the earth.** It will be a time of full grace for the elect of God. That will be the time of the **definitive triumph of my Immaculate Heart**. The Lord will do great things for those who hear His voice and accept His call."

Section V

The Sixth Church Age

The sixth Church age is the time of the sixth Church referenced in Revelation 3: 7-14, called the Church of Philadelphia, of which Jesus Christ has nothing critical to say against, at that time. He states: "I have left an open door before you that no one can close...you have held fast to my word and have not denied my name." This will be an era of unprecedented peace on earth.

CHAPTER 47

AGE OF PEACE

2038 to 2383?

Many are unaware of this age of peace for the Catholic Church, which will last approximately 345 years, according to the calculations of Daniel 9: 24-27, until the actual birth of Antichrist. There are many prophecies to be considered. Many unheard of, auspicious changes await humanity during this era.

Satan Will Be Bound

Satan will be **bound again** at the very end of this fifth Church age or beginning of this sixth Church age, but this is not the last time. He will be unloosed at the beginning of the seventh Church age, for the deceptive time of the Antichrist. At the end of Antichrist's life on earth, Satan will be bound for the thousand years, until the conclusion of the seventh Church age with the Jewish people. Then he will be loosed again to deceive the nations **for the last time**, at the end of the seventh Church age. For the beginning of this sixth Church age:

Fr. Bartholomew Holzhauser: "There will raise a valiant king anointed by God...He will rule supreme in temporal matters. The Pope will rule supreme in spiritual matters, at the same time... He will root out false doctrines...All nations will adore God, their Lord, according to Catholic teaching...People will love justice, and peace will reign over the whole earth; for **Divine Power will bind Satan for many years,** until the **coming of the Son of Perdition...**" [1]

Our Lady of Good Success to **Mother Mariana:** "This, then, will mark the arrival of my hour, when I, in a marvelous way, will **dethrone** the proud and cursed **Satan, trampling him** under my feet and fettering him in the infernal abyss." [2]

Blessed Isabel (Elizabeth) Canori-Mora: "After this frightful punishment, I saw the heavens opening, and St. Peter came down again upon the earth; he was vested in his pontifical robes and surrounded by a great number of angels, who were chanting hymns in his honor, They proclaimed him as sovereign of the earth. I saw St. Paul descending upon the earth. By God's command, he traversed the earth and **chained the demons** that he brought before St. Peter, who commanded them to return to hell, whence they had come." [3]

Our Lady of Peace to **Pedro Regis**: "When the great day comes, **humanity will be liberated**, and my poor children will be free. The **devil will be chained**, and mankind will again, have peace. It will be a time of glory for the just, and all will live only to serve My Son Jesus." [4]

Reign of the Sacred Heart of Jesus and the Immaculate Heart of Mary

This reign of the two Hearts of Jesus and Mary [5] will influence humanity in this age, bringing grace for blessings, not expected or seen before; peace not ever experienced before and spiritual revival with enthusiasm. An ease of domestic life on earth, including new discoveries in science and medicine, not ever realized before.

Sister Lucia from Our Lady at Fatima: "God wishes to establish in the world a devotion to my Immaculate Heart…to bring peace to the world." [6]

St. Louis-Marie Grignion De Montfort: "The power of Mary over all devils will be particularly outstanding in the last period of time. She will extend the Kingdom of the Christ over the idolaters and Muslims, and there will come **a glorious era** when Mary is the Ruler and **Queen of Hearts**." [7]

Marie-Julie Jahenny: "It will come; the reign of My Sacred Heart. They do not ask of me, this great wonder, especially at the foot of the Holy Altar…" [8]

Marthe Robins: "In place of the throne of the beast, two glorious thrones will arise; one of **My Sacred Heart** and the other of the **Immaculate Heart of Mary**." [9]

"A Period of Peace"
2038 - 2383?

Since 1917, at Fatima, Mary has promised this victory for the world and continues to speak of peace at Medjugorje. Mirjana confirms: "The Blessed Virgin Mary is preparing us for everything that is going to take place…She will finish in Medjugorje what she has started in Fatima and that Her Heart would prevail." [10]

Our Lady of Fatima: "In the end my Immaculate Heart will triumph… and a period of peace will be granted to the world." [11]

Our Lady of Medjugorie to Marija: "Pray for peace, so that as soon as possible, a time of peace which my heart waits impatiently for, may reign." [12]

Fr. Bartholomew Holzhauser: "Men will live in peace, and this will be granted because people will make their peace with God. They will live under the protection of the great Monarch **and his successors.**" [13]

Sr. Jeanne Le Royer had many visions and was commanded by God to write them down. She described: "the knowledge of these things shall contribute to the salvation of many souls and form a treasure for the faithful of the last age of the world... I see in God that the Church will enjoy a profound peace over a period, which seems to me, to be of a fairly, long duration. This respite will be the longest of all that will occur between the revolutions, from now till the General Judgment."

"One day I found myself in a vast plain alone with God. Jesus appeared to me, and from the top of a small hill, showed to me a beautiful sun on the horizon. He said dolefully, 'The world is passing away, and the time of My Second Coming draws near. When the sun is about to set, one knows that the day is nearly over, then the night will soon fall. Centuries are like days for me. Look at this sun, see how much it still has to travel, and estimate the time that is left to the world.' I looked intently, and it seemed to me that the sun would set in two hours. Jesus said: 'Do not forget that these are not millenaries, but **only centuries,** and they are **few in number.**' But I understood that Jesus reserved to Himself, the knowledge of the exact number, and I did not wish to ask Him more. It sufficed me to know that the peace of the Church, and the restoration of discipline were to last a reasonably long time." [14]

Our Lady of La Salette to Melanie Calvat: "After a frightful war, a great king will arise, and his reign will be marked by a wonderful peace and a great religious revival." [15]

St. Methodius: "In the last period, the great grace of God who provided a Great Monarch, a long duration of peace, and a splendid fertility of the earth." [16]

A Transformed Earth

People will live on the land and from the land, in a return to basic historical forms of agricultural. This may be hard to comprehend, but "the use of horses will be the only way to get around and will serve to work the land, growing food, needed to replenish the earth's population during the sixth Church age." [17] "People will only need small plots of land considering the nutrient rich land after the comet." [18] There are people on this earth who still use livestock to work the land and have a self-sustainable living, in balance with the earth's ecosystem.

Fr. Pere Lamy (1855-1931) "The working class will be bound to turn to the land. Land work will receive great impetus. Land will again be very dear." [19]

Our Lady of Peace to **Pedro Regis**: "The day will come when men and women will live in full happiness, for the Lord will reign in all hearts. **You will**

walk in an earthly paradise, and there will be no more suffering. Know that the Lord has prepared for His own, that which **human eyes have never seen...** When all the tribulations have passed, new heavens and **a new earth will arise.** There will be an extraordinary sign in the heavens. Men will seek an answer, but will not find it, for the secret comes from God." [20]

"**The day will come when people will dwell in a new land...the earth will be transformed.** All that you see today will be different." [21] "He will dry your tears, and the earth **will be...a new paradise.** The Creator **will restore the earth**, and you will see what human eyes have never seen." [22] "The things that you contemplate today, **will cease to exist.** Everything will be new. **Transformed**, men and women will just inhabit the earth." [23]

Like a Garden

Our Lady of Peace to **Pedro Regis**: "The Lord will transform the earth, and peace will reign among men. God **will give rise to rivers in the deserts, with great abundance**, in the poorest regions of the earth. The wonders of the Lord will be great. Men will understand the call of the Lord, and all will serve with love and loyalty. Happiness will reign among men for a long time." [24] "The earth will go through major changes. Humanity will be totally transformed, and God will **transform many deserted places** into beauty that human eyes have never seen. Men will contemplate wonders hidden now. The righteous shall inherit a new earth, and no one will experience suffering. All this will come after the great purification." [25]

"A great victory of God, for you, will appear. The earth will be transformed, and men will see the powerful hand of God in action. The signs of death, present in the world, will no longer exist. This will be the definitive triumph of My Immaculate Heart. The chosen ones of God will see **a new heavens and a new earth**." [26] The collision in the universe may splatter matter and stars, giving a new view of the universe. The comet will transform earth into a lush plentiful garden because of the fertilization across the earth, from the comet. We will experience a renewed heavens and earth, not ever seen before.

CHAPTER 48

THE POWERFUL MONARCH
AND THE HOLY POPE

Fr. Bartholomew Holzhauser gives the most complete description of general events of the future in the sixth Church age. He speaks of the beginning and the end of this age, and is the only one who sees **seccessors** of the Catholic Monarch, but they will **not be his descendants**. The Great Catholic Monarch will be the last of his lineage. The Angelic pastor or Holy Pope with the stigmata of a cross on his forehead, will guide the Church.

Fr. Bartholomew Holzhauser states: "The sixth period of the Church **will begin** with the powerful Monarch and the Holy Pontiff...and it **will last until** the revelation of Antichrist. In this period, God **will console** his Holy Church for the affliction and great tribulation, which she has endured during the fifth period. All nations will become Catholic. Vocations will be abundant as never before, and all men will seek only the kingdom of God and His justice. Men will live in peace, and this will be granted because people will make their peace with God. They will live under the protection of the great Monarch and his successors."

"During the fifth period, we saw only calamities and devastation; oppression of Catholics by tyrants and heretics; executions of kings and conspiracies to set up republics. But by the Hand of God Almighty, there occurs so wondrous a change during the sixth period that **no one can humanly visualize it.**"

"The **Powerful Monarch**, who will be sent by God, will **uproot every republic**. He will submit everything to his authority, and he will show great zeal for the true Church of Christ. The empire of the Mohammedans will be broken up, and this Monarch will reign in the east as well as the west. All nations will come to worship God in the true Catholic and Roman faith. There will be many Saints and Doctors of the Church on earth. Peace will reign over the whole earth because **God will bind Satan** for a number of years until the days of the Son of Perdition." [1]

The Holy Pope and the Cross-on His Forehead

2038 -?

The **Angelic Pastor** or Holy Pope with the **sign of the cross**-on his forehead is present on this earth today. Zlatko Sudac, a priest in Croatia, will become pope in the late 2030s, according to the prophecies by Venerable Holzhauser and Abbot Werdin D'Otrante. This **sign** in blood on his forehead is an unusual form of stigmata. In fact, it is the only known case of this sign in the history of the Church.

Zlatko Sudac (pronounced 'Sue-dots') was born on January 24, 1971, in Vrbnik, on the northern Adriatic island of Krk, part of Croatia. His parents still live there. He has one sister who is married and has three chil-dren. As a young child, he had visited Medjugorie. Later he served in the Yugoslavian military and had religious doubts, but had a strong conversion after attending a seminar given by a charismatic priest, Emilio Tardiff, in Slovenia.

In 1993, he entered studies into the priesthood, and on June 29, 1998, he was ordained a diocesan priest. Less than one year later, on the next Friday, after Padre Pio's beatification, Father Sudac, who was at a friendly get together, at a friend's home, received a stigmata of a cross on his forehead, an unprecedented event in Church history. On certain days, such as first Fridays, it bleeds and is painful, or he feels it pulsing when he prays. He has the gift of Tongues, the gifts of Healing, the gift of Counsel, and the gift of Knowledge. These are supernatural gifts of the Holy Spirit, not ordinary natural gifts.

On the feast of St. Francis, on October 4, 2000, when he was studying at a convent in Italy, a strange happening occurred. He could not find the chapel; he searched every door and then finally found it, where he immediately went to the Blessed Sacrament, opened the tabernacle, took the monstrance in his hands and kneeling, gazed at the presence. Eventually he fell asleep. When he woke up, he was bloody, bleeding from his wrists, his feet, and his side.

Since this experience, he has the gift of 'fear of the Lord', the gift of bi-location, gift of prophecy, the gift of levitation, gift of reading souls, gift of illumination, and knowledge of the near future, **especially about future dangers**. Fr. Suduc's awareness of future events has not been available.

He says: "We must look at the giver not the gift. I experience myself as sandals which God puts on, and which, He will tread upon, so that through them, He may come to those people whom He intends to reach." He says he feels a tremendous 'fear of the Lord'. "God surpasses any and all thoughts about Him. The only way to communicate with God is to love God. We have to sink into God so that I no longer exit. When I do this I don't lose myself but find myself in God." [2]

Prophecies of the Holy Pope

Rudolph Gekner: "A new pastor of the universal Church (Pope) will come from the shore of Dalmatia (on the Adriatic Sea near Croatia), through a celestial prodigy (comet) and in a simplicity of heart, adorned with the doctrines of Jesus Christ. Peace will be restored to the world." [3]

Fr. Bartholomew Holzhauser: "The fifth period of the Church, which began circa 1520, will end with the arrival of **the Holy Pope** and of the powerful Monarch who is called,"Help from God" because he will restore everything (in Christ)…No one will be able to pervert the word of God, since, **during the sixth period**…By the grace of God, by the **power of the Great Monarch**, by the **authority of the Holy Pope**, and by the union of all the most devout princes, atheism and every heresy will be banished from the earth. The council will **define the true sense of the Holy Scriptures**, and this will be believed and accepted by everyone." [4]

Abbot Werdin D'Otrante (1200's): "The Great Monarch and the **great Pope** will precede Antichrist. The nations will be at war for four years (2030s) and a great part of the world will be destroyed. The Pope will go over the sea, carrying the **sign of Redemption on his forehead**. The Great Monarch will come to restore peace, and the Pope will share in the victory. Peace will reign on earth." "The Pope will cross the sea **in a year when** the Feast of St. George (April 23) falls on Good Friday, and St. Mark's feast (April 25) falls on Easter Sunday…"[5] The four years of war from about 2034 to 2037 will be a trying time for this man who becomes pope in 2038. He will cross the sea with the sign of the Cross on his forehead, is alluding to the priest, Father Zlatko Suduc, who is the only person that will fulfill this prophecy.

St. Anna-Maria Taigi: "After the three days of darkness, St. Peter and St. Paul, having come down from heaven, will **preach in the whole world** and **designate a new Pope**. A great light will flash from their bodies and will settle upon the cardinal, **the future Pontiff**. Then, Christianity will spread throughout the world. He is the Holy Pontiff, chosen by God, **to withstand the storm**. At the end, he will have the gift of miracles, and his name shall be praised over the whole earth. Whole nations will come back to the Church, and the face of the earth will be renewed. Russia, England, and China will come into the Church." [6]

Sister Bertina Bouquillon: "Suddenly, the just received help from above. A saint raises his arms to heaven; he allays the wrath of God. He ascends the throne of Peter. At the same time, the Great Monarch ascends the throne of his ancestors. All is quiet now." [7]

St. Caesar of Arles (470-543): "At the same time, there will be a great Pope, who will be the most eminent in sanctity and most perfect in every quality. **This Pope** will have with him the Great Monarch, a most virtuous man, who shall be a scion of the holy race of French Kings. This Great Monarch will assist the Pope in the reformation of the whole earth. Many princes and their nations that are living in error and impiety shall be converted, and an admirable peace shall reign among men during many years, because the wrath of God shall be appeased, through their repentance, penance, and good works. There will be one common law, only one faith, one baptism, and one religion. All nations shall recognize the Holy See of Rome and shall pay homage to the Pope." [8]

Blessed Abbot Merlin Joachim of Fiore (1130-1202): "A remarkable Pope will be seated on the pontifical throne, under the special protection of the angels. Holy and full of gentleness, he shall undo all wrong; he shall recover the estate of the Church, and reunite the exiled temporal powers. He shall be revered by all people and shall recover the kingdom of Jerusalem. He shall reunite the Eastern and the Western Churches. The sanctity of this beneficent pontiff will be so great that the highest potentates shall bow down before his presence. This holy man shall crush the arrogance of holy religious schism and heresy. All men will return to the primitive Church, and there shall be only one pastor, one law, and one master; humble, modest, and fearing God. The true God of the Jews, our Lord Jesus Christ, will make everything prosper, beyond all human hope, because God alone, can and will pour down on the wounds of humanity, the oily balm of sweetness...At that time a handsome monarch, a scion of King Pepin, will come as a pilgrim, to witness the splendor of this glorious Pontiff, whose name shall begin with R... A temporal throne becoming vacant, the Pope shall place on it, this king whose assistance he shall ask...there will be two heads, one in the east, and the other in the west. This Pope shall break the weapons, and scatter the fighting hordes. He will be the joy of God's elect. This Angelic Pope will preach the gospel in every country. Through his zeal and solitude, the Greek Church shall be forever reunited to the Catholic Church. The power of this Pontiff's holiness will be so great, as to be able to check fury and impetuosity of threatening waves. Mountains shall be lowered before him, the sea shall be dried up, the dead shall be raised, the churches shall be reopened, and altars erected. After nine years he shall render his soul to God."

"This Holy pope (next pope?) shall be both pastor and reformer. Through him, the east and west shall be in everlasting concord. The city of Babylon shall then be the head and guide of the world. Rome, weakened in temporal power, shall enjoy great peace. During these happy days, the Angelic Pope shall be able to address to Heaven, prayers full of sweetness. The dispersed nation (Jews) shall also enjoy tranquility. Six and a half years after this time, the pope will render his soul to God. The end of his days shall arrive in an arid province, situated between a river and a lake near the mountains…"

"A man of remarkable sanctity will be **his successor** in the Pontifical chair. Through him, God will work so many prodigies that all shall revere him, and no person will dare to oppose his precepts. He shall not allow the clergy to have many benefices. He will induce them to live by the tithes and offerings of the faithful. He shall interdict pomp in dress, and all immorality in dances and songs. He will preach the gospel in person, and exhort all honest ladies to appear in public without any ornament of gold or precious stones. After having occupied the Holy See for **a long time**, he shall happily return to the Lord."

"**His three successors** shall be men of exemplary holiness. One after the other will be models of virtue, and shall work miracles, confirming the teaching of their predecessors. Under their government the Church shall spread, and these popes shall be called **the Angelic pastors.**" [9] The city of Babylon is mentioned as a central city of the world. Reference is also made to possibly five successors of angelic pastors or popes.

Our Lady of Peace to **Pedro Regis**: "A man will contribute to the return of my poor children, and the truth will reign in the House of God. The day will come when the throne of Peter will have seated, one that will **change forever**, the direction of the Church." [10]

Revival of the Holy Roman Empire

St. Ephraem (306-373): "Then the Lord, from His Glorious Heaven shall **set up His peace.** And the **kingdom of the Romans, shall rise in place** of this latter **people** and establish its dominion upon the earth, even to its ends, and there shall be no one who will resist it." [11] Early Church Fathers affirm a period of peace that will precede Antichrist.

The interpretation of the dream of Nebuchadnezzar recorded in Daniel 2: 31-45, explains four major kingdoms to exist during and after the time of Nebuchadnezzar. The Egyptians and the Assyrians already perished as world powers. Daniel explains that Nebuchadnezzar's Kingdom of Babylon was the first shown in his dream. The Medo-Persian was next, followed by the Greek empire. In the Roman kingdom, Daniel explains: "God of Heaven will set up a kingdom that shall never be destroyed or delivered up to another people, rather, it shall break in pieces, all these kingdoms and put an end to them, and it shall stand forever."

Daniel explains earlier in the reading, about the 'stone', a reference to Jesus Christ breaking to pieces, these kingdoms, as fine as chaff, blown "away without leaving a trace." The 'stone' or 'cornerstone' does not destroy this Roman Kingdom but rather builds His kingdom during the time of it. King Constantine, Emperor of the Roman Empire, allowed reforms that included supporting Christianity by the year 312. From that time, the Roman Empire was shaping into a holy empire and by 380 was declared Christian by Emperor Theodosius. After this, the Romans let the Franks settle in Belgium. Clovis I, of the Merovingian dynasty is the first King, in 481. Clovis I, converts to Christianity along with all the Franks. This lineage continues to this day through Carolingian, Ottonian, Saxon, Salian, Luxembourg, Habsburg, and Habsburg-Lorraine. The great Catholic Monarch will continue this Holy Roman Empire.

Our Lady of Peace to **Pedro Regis**: "Dear children, God allows, and wise men will announce: 'Existed, does not exist and will exist.' The answer will come. Know that large are the mysteries of the Lord."[12] Mary speaks of the Holy Roman Empire existing again.

Reign of the Powerful Monarch
2038- ?

The Great Catholic Monarch will reign solely over the earth at that time.

Melanie Calvat: After a frightful war, a Great King will arise, and his reign will be marked by a wonderful peace and a great religious revival." [13]

Blessed Ignatius of Santhia: "A scion of the Carolingian race, by all considered extinct, will come to Rome, to behold and admire the piety and clemency of this Pontiff, who will crown him, and declare him **to be the legitimate Emperor of the Romans**. From the chair of St. Peter, the Pope will lift up the standard, the crucifix; and will give it to the new emperor. This new Emperor with the robust Italian and French people, and with those of other nations, will form a most mighty host, called the Church Army, through which he shall destroy the Ottoman Empire and all heresies. The new emperor, with the assistance of God and the Pope, will cooperate in the reformation of abuses; he will assume the direction of temporal governments; he will assign a decent pension to the Supreme Pontiff, and also to the bishops and clergy. And they all, being detached from every earthly covetousness, will live in peace..." [14]

St. Vincent Ferrer: "The Eagle (the Great Monarch) shall capture the false king, and all things shall be made obedient unto him, and there shall be a new reformation in the world." [15]

John of Vatiguerro: "But after this, a young, captive Prince shall recover the Crown of the Lilies and shall extend his dominions all over the world." [16]

St. Methodius: "a Great king will arise...and peace will be given to the world, and the Church will be freed from her anxieties." [17]

St. John Vianney: "The good shall triumph when the return of the king shall be announced." [18]

Fr. Lawrence Ricci S. J. (1775): "This great ruler will restore stolen Church property. **Protestantism will cease**. This duke will be the **most powerful** monarch on earth. At a gathering of men noted for piety and wisdom, he will, with the aid of the pope, introduce new rules, and **ban the spirit of confusion**. Everywhere, there will be one fold and one shepherd." [19]

Sister Marianne (Ursuline): "It is then, that **the Prince shall reign,** whom the people did not esteem before, but whom they shall then seek. The triumph of religion will be so great that no one has ever seen the equal. All injustices will be made good; civil laws will be made in harmony with the laws of God and of the Church. Education in the schools will be most Christian, and **the workers guilds** will flourish again." [20]

Our Lady of Peace to **Pedro Regis**: "After all tribulation, God will **arise a great man** of **faith**. Through him, the Church will be restored, and a new time of grace will arrive for the faithful." [21] "Through him, the doors will open and **my appeals will be scattered throughout the world**." [22]

CHAPTER 49

TIME OF FAITH AND ORDER

The Church of Philadelphia will flourish at this time. The Lord says nothing critical against this Church. It is a time of grace and tranquility. At this time, only one Church, the Holy Roman Catholic Church will exist. Revelation 3:8 reveals the character of the (Sixth) Church of Philadelphia: "I know your deeds; that is why I have left an open door before you, which no one can close. I know your strength is limited; yet you have not denied my name."

St. Francis of Paola (1416-1507): "**A new order will then be founded,** that of the Cruciferi (Cross-bearers) because their members will have the cross on their banners. This order will be comprised of three groups – the first group will be armed horsemen; the second group, priests, and the third, nurses. These Knights of the Cross (Crusaders) will convert Mohammedans, heretics, and fallen-away Christians to Christ." [1]

Sister Mechtilde of Helfta (1200s): "They will be **clad in double garment,** the undergarment white and the outer one red and fastened with a girdle. Their beards and hair will be unshorn. They will go barefooted, except in winter when they will wear red sandals with white thongs. They will have no possessions and will not be allowed to have gold or silver. Each of them will bear at all times, a staff which will be painted white and red, and which will have a crook, a span long. On one side of the staff will be portrayed the Passion of Christ, and on the other side, His Ascension into Heaven. No member of this order shall be younger than 24 years old. They will be priests, confessors, and good preachers." [2]

St. Francis of Paola, in letters to Simeon de Limena, Count of Montalto: "One of your posterity shall achieve greater deeds than your lordship. That man, will be a great sinner in his youth, but like St. Paul, he shall be drawn and converted to God. He shall be the founder of a **new religious order,** different from all others. He will divide it into three strata, namely military knights, solitary priests, and most pious **hospitallers.** This shall be **the last religious order** in the Church, and it will do more good for our holy religion than all other religious institutions…" [3]

Blessed Anne Catherine Emmerich: "After many tribulations, peace will restored, and religion and charity, reign once more among men. Then convents will flourish in the true sense of the Lord. I saw a picture of this future time that be I cannot describe, but in which I saw the whole earth, arising from darkness, and light and love awakening. I had also, numerous pictures of the restoration of Religious Orders. The time of Antichrist is not so near, as some imagine..." [4]

Sister Jeanne le Royer (1731-1798) : "I see in God, a **large assembly of pastors** who will uphold the rights of the Church and of her Head. They will restore the former disciplines. I see, in particular, **two servants of the Lord** who will distinguish themselves in this glorious struggle, and who, by grace of the Holy Ghost, will fill with ardent zeal, the hearts of this illustrious assembly...All the false cults will be abolished; all the abuses of the revolution will be destroyed; and the **altars of the true God restored**. The former practices will be put into force again, and our religion.... will flourish more than ever." [5]

Fr. Pere Lamy: "The monasteries will flourish again, and the convents will once more be filled. After these calamities, many souls will come and dwell in them." [6]

Sister Bertina Bouquillon: "All is quiet now. Altars are set up again; religion comes to life again. What I see now is so wonderful that I am unable to express it." [7]

St. John Vianney: "This shall re-establish a peace and prosperity without example. Religion shall flourish again better than ever before." [8]

Fr. Bartholomew Holzhauser: "Peace will be restored and England will return to the Catholic faith with greater fervor than ever before..." [9]

Father Nectou: "Order will be restored everywhere. Justice will reign throughout the whole world, and the counter-revolution will be accomplished. The triumph of the Church will then be so complete that nothing like it has ever been seen before. Those Christians who are fortunate enough to survive, will thank God for preserving them and giving them the privilege of beholding this glorious triumph of the Church." [10]

Blessed Anne Catherine Emmerich: "Then, I saw that the Church was being promptly rebuilt, and she was more magnificent than ever before." [11]

Unusual Prophecies During the Sixth Church Age

These prophecies tell us of odd but true occurrences taking place in this age of peace.

St. Hildegard, Doctor of the Church: "After, there will be so **few men left** on earth that **seven women will fight for one man**, that they will say to the man: 'Marry me, to take the disgrace from me.' For in those days it will be a disgrace, for a woman, to be without a child, as it was by the Jews in the Old Testament." [12]

Isaiah 4:1: "Seven women will take hold of one man, on that day, saying, "We will eat our own food and wear our own clothing. Only let your name be given us, put an end to our disgrace."

(Fr.) Pere Lamy: "Peace will be given back to the world…the manufacturers of airplanes, the exploitation of the mines, the ironworks, **all this will dwindle.** There will be no more of these great factories, where morality withers and disappears…When peace is given back to the world, big business will shrink to smaller proportions and will stay there…when peace is given back to the world, plots of [farm] land will rise to more value than they are now. **Even if the old workmen will insist on dying in the towns,** it will come to pass…The world will have to be re-evangelized over again, and that will be work for a whole generation. A **great effort** will have to be made for the conversion of man. There will be quite a lot of **difficulties.** The spiritual state of the first Christian will come back; moreover, there will be so **few men on earth.**" [13]

St. Hildegard: "Peace will return to the world when the white flower, again, takes possession of the throne of France. During this period of peace, **people will be forbidden to carry weapons,** and iron will be used only for making **agricultural** implements and tools." [14]

Our Lady of Peace to **Pedro Regis:** "The day will come when Europe will stretch out its hand to the world, as a beggar who needs aid. **Russia will be a cornerstone** for many nations…" [15]

Visionaries of Medjugorje said that after the ten secrets have unfolded: "With the realization of the secrets entrusted to them by Our Lady, life in the world will change. Afterwards, **men will believe like in ancient times.**" [16]

A Spiritual Transformation

Fr. Bartholomew Holzhauser: "It is in that age that the relation of the sixth Spirit of the Lord will be known, that is to say the Spirit of Wisdom, that God diffuses over all surfaces of the globe in those times. For men will fear the Lord their God, they will observe the law, and serve it with all their heart. The sciences will be multiplied and complete on the earth. The **Holy Scriptures** will be **unanimously understood**, without controversy and without the errors of heresies. Men will be enlightened, so much, as in the natural sciences and in the celestial sciences."

"Finally, the sixth Church, the Church of Philadelphia, is the type of this sixth age, for Philadelphia signifies **friendship of brothers,** and again, guarding the heritage in union with the Lord. Now all these characters convene perfectly in the sixth age, in which they will have love, concord, and perfect peace, and in which the powerful Monarch will have to consider almost the entire world as his heritage. He will deliver up the earth, with the aid of the Lord, his God, from all his enemies, of ruin and of all evil." [17]

Maria Esperanza stated: "I feel that here on earth, like a reflection of heaven, we will have beautiful things in the future that **will resemble the things of heaven.** Here on earth we are going to see beautiful cities that are going to be built in resemblance of heaven, **like** the coming of God's King-dom–a new world. There will be like communities all over the world. We will live in communities…Rivers of supernatural light are waiting us; sur-prises, beautiful surprises. Each of us will encounter ourselves, and beauti-ful ideas will come to our minds, beautiful talents, and more than anything else, we will achieve the simplicity of an innocent child. And that's the most important thing: We will be able to achieve the innocence of a child." [18]

Our Lady of Peace to **Pedro Regis**: "**The future has reserved for you extraordinary discoveries, awaited by mankind.** Rejoice because the Lord is at your side, and you will find salvation only in His grace." [19] "The day will come when you will **see the great wonders of the Lord**, and He shall be called by the name 'All Chosen'. The earth will be rich, and nothing will be lacking for men. The faithful will live happily, and no evil will reach the children of God." [20]

Ecumenical Council in the Sixth Church Age

This will be the greatest council in the Church ages that will verify the scriptures and abolish heresies. [21]

Jeanne le Royer: "But the **Church in Council** assembled, shall one day strike with anathemas, pull down, and destroy the evil principles **of that criminal constitution**. What a consolation! What joy for all the truly faith-ful!" [22] The constitution referred to here, is the Illuminati's 'Novus Ordo Seclorum,' which brought about communism and its detrimental effects on countless people and on the Church.

Ecstatic of Tours, nun in France: "The **Council will meet again** after the victory. But, this time, men will be obliged to obey; there will be only one flock and one shepherd. All men will acknowledge the Pope as the Universal Father, the King of all peoples. Thus, mankind will be regenerated." [23]

Fr. Bartholomew Holzhauser: "No one will be able to pervert the word of God, since, during the sixth period, there will be **an ecumenical council** which will be the **greatest of all councils**. By the grace of God, by the power of the Great Monarch, by the authority of the Holy Pontiff, and by the union of all the most devout princes, atheism and every heresy will be banished from the earth. The Council will **define the true sense of Holy Scripture,** and this will be believed and accepted by everyone." [24]

Revelation 10: 4-7: "I was about to start writing when the seven thun-ders spoke, but I heard a voice from heaven say, "Seal up what the seven thunders have spoken, and do not write it down!" Then the angel whom I saw standing on the sea and on the land, raised his right hand to heaven and took an oath by the One who lives forever and ever, who created heaven and earth and sea, along with everything in them: "There shall be no more delay.

When the time comes for the seventh angel to blow his trumpet, the mysterious plan of God, which he announced to his servants the prophets, shall be accomplished in full." The seventh trumpet is accomplished during the beginning of the 6th Church age.

St. Bridget of Sweden: "The gates of faith will be opened... and the scriptures shall be verified." [25]

All Nations Will Become Catholic

These prophecies confirm other monumental changes:

Fr. Bartholomew Holzhauser: "In this period...all nations will become Catholic...and adore the Lord their God, in the true Catholic and Roman faith." [26]

St. Caesar of Arles: "All nations shall recognized the Holy See of Rome, and shall pay homage to the Pope." [27]

Blessed Abbot Merlin Joachim of Fiore: "A remarkable Pope will be seated on the pontifical throne. He shall...recover the estate of the Church and reunite the exiled temporal powers...He shall re-unit the Eastern and the Western Churches. All men will return to the Primitive church, and there shall be only one pastor, one law, one master – humble, modest, and fearing God... This Angelic Pope will preach the gospel in every country. Through his zeal and solitude, the Greek Church shall be forever reunited to the Catholic Church." [28]

Blessed Father Joseph Freinademetz (1852-1908): "During this period, nearly the whole of China, shall return to Christianity." [29]

CHAPTER 50

THE END OF THE
SIXTH CHURCH AGE

D iscouraging prophecies come into view at the very end of the sixth Church age. **St. Caesar of Arles** states: "But after some considerable time, **fervor shall cool**, iniquity shall abound, and moral corruption shall become worse than ever, which **shall bring upon** mankind, **the last** and **worst** persecution of **Antichrist and the end of the world**." [1]

Revelation 3:10-11 to the (6th) Church of Philadelphia: "Because you have kept my plea to stand fast, I will keep you safe **in the time of trial** which is coming to the whole world, to test all men on earth. **I am coming soon.** Hold fast to what you have, lest someone rob you of your crown."

As the Sixth Church Age Progresses

The **ten kings and kingdoms** explained in the book of Daniel 7 and Revelation 17, disclose, that the latter part of the Roman civilization will be destroyed by the Antichrist. Daniel 7: 24 describes the ten kings during Antichrist, that shall rise out of "the Roman civilization" and "another kingdom shall rise up after them" that will be the last king or kingdom of Babylonian worldly influence, that is referred to in Revelation 17:9; and will last for only a short time, of seven years, including three and one-half years of total power for the Antichrist. Without explaining this in any more detail, the scriptures and saints give knowledge of kings and kingdoms, developing throughout the world, towards the end of the age of Peace.

St. John Chrysostom, Doctor of the Church: "In the same way as these kingdoms, which existed before the Roman Empire, were destroyed [the Babylonian by the Persian, the Persian by the Greek, the Greek by the Roman], **so will the Roman Empire be destroyed by Antichrist**. This will happen when the Roman Empire shall have been divided into ten kingdoms."[2]

St. Jerome, Doctor of the Church: "Therefore, let us state what all the ecclesiastical writers have passed down: At the consummation of the world **when the Kingdom of the Romans has been destroyed**, when ten kings shall have divided the territory of the Romans between themselves, an eleventh [man] shall rise to [the kingship of] a small kingdom, who when he shall have over come three of the ten kings, i.e., the kings of the Egyptians, of the Africans, and the Ethiopians, and consequently, as we learn more manifestly – whom he shall have killed, the other seven kings shall submit their necks to the victor [the eleventh king, Antichrist]." [3]

Daniel 7: 24: "The ten horns shall be ten kings rising out of that kingdom (Roman (6th kingdom; another (Antichrist, of the (7th kingdom shall rise up after them, different from those before him, who shall lay low three kings. He shall speak against the most High and oppress the holy ones of the most High."

Seventy-Weeks of Years

What is the **70 weeks of years** all about? In Daniel 9:2: "**I Daniel** tried to understand in the scripture, the counting of the years, of which the Lord spoke to the **prophet Jeremiah**; that for the ruins of Jerusalem, seventy years must be fulfilled." Daniel prayed in earnest, in sackcloth and ashes and fasted. The angel Gabriel was sent to him in rapid flight, to explain the prophecy of the seventy years of the Babylonian captivity. Daniel saw that the 70 years of exile were over, and that the Jewish people were back in their homeland; still being persecuted by other nations, and he wondered why it had not stopped. This prophecy of the 70 years gave hope to the Jewish people for the end of persecution in Babylon at that time. Daniel **was given more information than he asked for,** from the angel Gabriel.

In fact, **the Angel Gabriel** gave Daniel an overview for the entire future for the Jewish people, until continual peace would reign, recorded in 9: 24-27: "Seventy weeks (of years are decreed for your people and for your holy city, then transgression will stop and sin will end, guilt will be expiated, ever-lasting justice will be introduced, vision and prophecy will be ratified, and **a most holy will be anointed.**"(Jesus Christ will be recognized as the Messiah. This is a complete overview of the 70 weeks of years, that is, 70 years x 7 (a week is 7 = 490 years. This starts when the Jewish people have suffered long enough for their sins and are finally diminished and humbled, submitting to God, allowing them to return to their homeland. This started in 1948 and will continue for 490 years until the end of the Antichrist, at about 2438 when Jesus Christ is recognized as the Messiah.

Now, **the Angel Gabriel** details knowledge of the future, in different time frames: [4] "Know and understand this: From the **utterance of the word** that Jerusalem was to be rebuilt, **until** one who is **anointed and leader, (Great Monarch)** there shall be seven weeks." This is the time when the Jewish people had finally suffered the expiation of their sins, and the nations of the world, the United Nations, began negotiations to give back the Jewish people their homeland back in 1947. This 'utterance of the word' is confirmed by Israel, by declaring it so and taking back some of their lands in 1948. Then, 7 weeks of years (7 x 7= 49 years) pass until 1997, and one who is anointed is born; that is the great Catholic Monarch.

The **Angel Gabriel** continues: "During 62 weeks it shall be rebuilt, with streets and trenches, in time of affliction." Over the next 62 weeks of years or 62 x 7 = 434 years (1997 to 2431, the Jewish people continue to live in Israel according to God's word. This is a time of rebuilding and retribution, but with the destruction of Jerusalem and other places, in a time of affliction, as they rebuild their nation.

The **Angel Gabriel** then states: "After the 62 weeks an anointed (a Catholic Monarch) shall be cut down when he does not possess the city (Jerusalem); and **the people** of **a leader** (Antichrist) who will come, shall **destroy** the **sanctuary**. Then the end shall come like a torrent; until the end, there shall be war, the desolation that is decreed." One of the great Catholic Monarch's **successors** will be slain by the Antichrist, during the time of the 10 kings and 10 kingdoms. By this time, a Catholic Monarch is one of the 10 kings of the 10 kingdoms, who has a smaller kingdom, and it is snatched up by the Antichrist, after he kills the Monarch.

After "a period of peace," this "leader" of the people, will be the Antichrist, and the people with the Antichrist shall destroy the sanctuary. Similar events happened at the time of Antiochus Epiphanes, but the sanctuary was not destroyed at that time, only desecrated. The second temple sanctuary was still intact at the time of Jesus on earth. Jesus Christ referred to the similar characteristics of Antiochus Epiphanes, to the one who is to come; the Antichrist. In Matthew 24, Jesus mentions decreed punishments to the people on earth at that time. Again, this is more birth pangs related to the increase of Christ's kingdom, on this earth, and the vanquishing of evil, as detailed in Revelation Chapter 11, Chapter 12 verse 14-17, Chapter 13, Chapter 15, and particularly in Chapter 16.

At the beginning of the seventh Church age, the greatest persecution and surrendering of Christians' lives will commence. The Antichrist will convince the Jewish people that he is the Messiah, provoking furious punishments from God, through the Two Witnesses spoken of in Revelation 11.

Lastly, **the Angel Gabriel** confirms: "For **one week** or 1 x 7 =7 years, he (Antichrist) shall make a firm compact with many; **half the week** (three and a half years) he shall abolished sacrifice and oblation; On the temple wing (he), shall be the horrible abomination, until the ruin that is decreed, is poured out upon the horror." This is the Antichrist; the Man of Iniquity, whom St. Paul, and St. John and other Catholic saints speak about. Three and a half years or half a week is the clue; connecting this to the saints' prophecies, confirming this as future prophecy. [5] This part of the prophecy describes the extent of the abomination, abolishing the sacrifice of the Mass for Christians. The worst possible abomination is the Antichrist himself, desires to be worshiped as God in the Jewish temple in Jerusalem, claiming to be the Messiah.

The Antichrist, with the power of the devil, deceives the Jewish people, and not only desecrates the sanctuary of the temple (third temple), but it is destroyed by the Gentile people of that time. He deceives and martyrs more Christians, than has taken place, in any other time in the history of the world.

Some believe that this prophecy in Daniel, was for the time of Cyrus (the most holy will be anointed), who built the second temple. Also, the 62 weeks or 434 years are considered, as the time of the rebuilding of Jerusalem, after the exile from Babylon. Antiochus Epiphanes was seen as the leader desecrating the temple, but the clue here is, the sanctuary of the temple was not destroyed at that time, as this prophecy clarifies.

The False Prophet

Revelation describes prophecies of the False Prophet: the second beast or a second part of the diabolical trinity of Satan. He is the precursor of Antichrist, who will be given power, to promote the diabolical workings of the Antichrist. This mysterious leader is rumored to lead troops, forcing people through fear, to turn away from Christ, most likely abolishing the sacrament of Holy Eucharist in deceptive ways.

Revelation 13:11-15 states: "Then I saw **another wild beast** (False Prophet) come up out of the earth; it had two horns like a ram and it spoke like a dragon. It used the authority of the first beast (Antichrist) to promote its interests, by **making the world** and all its inhabitants, **to worship the first beast**, whose mortal wound had been healed. It performed great prodigies; it could even make fire come down from heaven to the earth, as men looked on. Because of the prodigies, it was allowed to perform by authority of the first beast; **it led astray the earth's inhabitants**, telling them to make an idol, in honor of the beast that had been wounded by the sword; and yet lived. The second wild beast was then permitted to give life to the beast's image, so that the image had the power of speech and of putting to death, anyone who refused to worship it."

Revelation 16: 13-14 confirms: "I saw **three unclean spirits,** like frogs, come from the mouth **of the dragon**, from the mouth **of the beast**, and from the mouth of **the false prophet**; these spirits were devils who worked prodigies. They went out to assemble all the kings of the earth, for battle, on the great day of God the Almighty." This **diabolical triune force,** imitating the true Trinity of God, is preparing to battle against God, the Almighty, at the valley of Armageddon, in another attempt to destroy the Church.

St. Vincent Ferrer: "In the days of peace that are to come after the desolation of revolutions and wars, before the end of the world, Christians will become so lax in their religion that they will refuse the sacrament of Confirmation, saying that "it is an unnecessary sacrament," and **when the false prophet**, the **precursor of Antichrist** comes, all who are not confirmed, will apostatize, while those who are confirmed, will stand fast in their faith; only a few will renounce Christ." [6]

Melanie Calvat, according to Our Lady of La Salette: "A **precursor** of the Antichrist, with his troops, drawn from many nations, will wage war against the true Christ, sole Savior of the world; he will shed much blood and will seek to annihilate the cult of God, so as to be regarded as a god.

"The earth will be struck with calamities of all kinds; there will be wars up to the last war, which will then be waged by the ten kings of the Antichrist; kings who will all have a common design and will be the sole rulers of the world. Before this happens, there will be **a sort of false peace** in the world. People will think only of amusing themselves, the wicked will indulge in all kinds of sin; but the children of Holy Church, children of the true faith, my true imitators, will grow in the love of God and in the virtues dearest to me. Happy the humble souls, led by the Holy Ghost! **I shall battle along with** them, until they reach the fullness of maturity." [7] This description is similar to the prophecies of the Catholic saints. These words, given to us in the fifth Church age, by Mary, Mother of Jesus, reach, unusually far out into the future and are discussed again, later. Mary, Mother of Jesus, will do battle again for the Church, at the beginning of the seventh Church age.

The Antichrist

Catholics often misunderstand the subject of Antichrist. As an individual searching for understanding in the 1970s and the 1980s, I first discovered the meaning of the Antichrist through evangelical and other Church interpretations. It wasn't until after St. Bridget appeared to me that I understood, what is really going to take place.

We live at a time when the spirit of Antichrist is at its strongest, as St. Bridget alludes to, in her prophecy, mentioned at the beginning of this work. 1-John 2:22, explains in simple terms, who Antichrist is : "He who denies that Jesus is the Christ (Messiah). He is the Antichrist, denying the Father and the Son."

At this point, it is imperative to understand where all this 'Antichrist' jargon which we hear about, these days, began. From the 'Catechism of Perseverance,' written by Abbe Gaume (1850), it states: "All the Angels were created in the state of innocence and justice, but, they were no more impeccable than man. Being free, they had, like men, to undergo a trial. The beatific vision and immutability in good, were the recompense, which they should gain by the proper use, with the assistance of grace, of their free will. God, therefore, subjected them to a trial. Every trial to be meritorious, must be essentially costly and painful."

"What was the trial of the angels? " [8] It was the Son of God, Jesus, who was to become man, lower than the angels. There was no way that Lucifer and a third of the angels were going to bow down to a man, the Son of God, lower than himself. According to Mary of Agreda, Lucifer is heard: "He (Jesus) not only commanded us to adore Him, but also, to recognize as our superior a Woman, his mother, a mere earthly creature." [9]

Unrighteousness was found in Him. The explanation continues: "At this revelation, the pride of Lucifer, one of the highest angels, rebelled. He cried out: 'I protest. Is my throne to be lowered? I will raise it above the stars... It is I and no other, that shall be like the most High!' One third of the angels of various hierarchies answered: 'We also protest.' At these words an archangel, (Michael) no less brilliant than Lucifer, cried out: 'Who is like unto God? Who can refuse to believe and adore, that which He proposes for the faith and adoration of His creatures, I believe and I adore.' Two thirds of the angels answered: 'We believe and adore.'" [10]

Revelation 12:7 states: "Then war broke out in Heaven, Michael and his angels battled against the dragon." As soon as their guilt was realized, they precipitated into unrecognizable demon entities that fought back. The huge dragon to be known as Satan was driven out, "with one-third of the stars" (demon minions) who were hurled down to the earth. Satan is the one, who is the anti-Christ, the one against-Christ.

There are two aspects of Antichrist. St. John the evangelist states, in 1-John 4:3, "the spirit of antichrist, that is to come, in fact, is already at work." Since the beginning, the spirit of antichrist has been at work, deceiving people in every age, in the world and in the Church to varying degrees.

But St. John speaks of Antichrist's arrival in the future, as recorded in 1-John 2:18: "As you have heard that Antichrist cometh (the man of iniquity is coming)." [11]

St. Paul says, the "man of iniquity" recorded in 2-Thessalonians 2:3-7 is coming in the future: "Let no man deceive you, by any means, for unless the apostasy comes first, and the man of sin be revealed, the son of perdition, who opposes and is lifted up as God, and is worshipped, who sits in the Temple (before the Jewish people) showing himself as God. Do you not remember when I was with you, I told you about these things?" This man will be born on the earth, possessed by Satan, in his final attempt to deceive and destroy the Gentile Christian nations. He will deceive the Jewish people into believing that he is the Messiah.

The scripture goes on: "For now, you know what holds him back, so that he can be revealed, in his own time. For the mystery of iniquity is already at work, but there is one who holds him back, until that one is taken from our midst." The Antichrist will not be born until the beginning of the seventh Church age, according to Venerable Holzhauser.

I also believe that the one that holds back the Antichrist is **the presence of Christ in the Blessed Sacrament** and **the Presence in** the Holy Mass. According to prophecies, the Antichrist will not only abolish the sacrifice of the Jews, at that time, but also, the False Prophet beforehand, will abolish the presence of Christ, in the Sacrifice of the Mass, in a deceptive way. Some claim, it is the Roman Empire, that holds Antichrist back, but the prophecies of the saints state, Antichrist himself destroys the Roman Empire. It is the Presence of Christ in Holy Eucharist, in the tabernacles, protecting the Church, holding back Antichrist.

The conspiracy, to eliminate His Presence has been subtly prevalent in the last few hundred years, amidst the incursion of Freemasonry and Protestantism. This conspiracy, was strongest in the 20th century, as Freemasonry tried to change the Mass, during and after the conciliar reforms. At the beginning of the seventh Church age, the prophecies reveal, abolishing the consecration of the bread and wine.

A precursor to Antichrist was the Syrian King Antiochus IV Epiphanes. In Daniel 11: 21-39, it relates the brutal authority of Antiochus IV Epiphanes desecrating the temple of the Jews by sacrificing a sow pig before an image of Zeus. This is a foretaste of what the Antichrist will be like. Daniel's prophecy 8:23-27 speaks of the small horn that refers to the Antichrist to come.

Jesus reiterates this warning in Matthew 24:15: that a similar event will take place in the future and much more. Nero Caesar was the example of Antichrist in John's time, described in 1-John 2:18 when the persecutions of Christians began. John states, it will be sometime in the future, when the man who is **Antichrist**, will come and deceive, even though John acknowledges the **presence of Antichrist** or **spirit of Antichrist** at his time. There have been many Antichrist personages over the centuries: Nero, Domitian, Marx, Lenin, Stalin, Hitler and many more.

The Antichrist Will Be Coming

Antichrist is coming according to these saints' prophecies.

St. Ephraem, Doctor of the Church: "Then the Lord from his glorious Heaven shall set up his peace...there shall be no one who will resist it. After iniquity shall have subsequently multiplied...coming forth from perdition, the **man of iniquity** shall be revealed upon the earth. The seducer of men, and the disturber of the whole earth." [12]

Venerable Holzhauser: "Peace will reign over the whole earth because God will bind Satan for many years until the **coming** of the 'Son of Perdition'." [13]

St. Bridget: "**Before the Antichrist comes**, the portals of the Faith will be opened to great numbers of pagans." [14]

St. Paul in 2-Thessalonians 2:1-12: "Let no one seduce you... the mass apostasy has not yet occurred, nor the man of lawlessness been revealed; that son of perdition and adversary who exalts himself above every so called god... who seats himself in God's temple and even declares himself to be God... The secret force of lawlessness is already at work... but there is one who holds him (Antichrist) back, until that restrainer shall be taken from the scene...This lawless one will appear as part of the workings of Satan, accompanied by all the power, and signs, and wonders at the disposal of falsehood....And the Lord Jesus will destroy him, with the breath of His mouth and annihilate him, by manifesting His own presence." The restrainer is the Presence of Jesus Christ in the Holy Eucharist.

St. Cyril of Jerusalem, Doctor of the Church: "This one shall seize the power of the Roman Empire, and shall falsely style himself (as) Christ. By the name of Christ he shall deceive the Jews, **who are expecting the Anointed;** and he shall seduce the Gentiles by his magical illusions." [15]

SECTION VI

THE SEVENTH CHURCH AGE

2383? -3383 or longer?

CHAPTER 51

THE FINAL TRIBULATION
OF THE GENTILE CHURCH

Accounting to Venerable Holzhauser, the seventh Church age will endure from **"the Birth of Antichrist till the end of the world."** [1, 2] The seventh Church age will start about the year 2383 based on the prophecies of Holzhauser about Antichrist, who will live 55 and a half years. The coming of Christ on the clouds, for His Gentile, **Bride** Church, will be about 2438, according to the prophecies from Daniel 9: 24-27. Christ will come on the clouds and destroy the Antichrist. That is about 55 and half years into the seventh Church age. We will not know the day or the hour but we will know the season. This will be the time of the taking up of Christ's Bride or the Gentile Church. The Gentile (Bride) Church will continue for the first six Church ages.

This seventh Church age is designated for the Jewish people and the promises of God will be fulfilled for them. The end of the world is not the end of the existence of the earth. **The end of the world is the end of Satan and his influence on nations in the seven world civilizations.** The definition of 'world', from reading scripture, is the 'people of this world' and 'the civilization that exists' who are influenced by God, Satan, and an influence by people with varying degrees of good and evil, around us. The world is the dilution of good by evil forces in newly deceptive ways. The world is Babylon the great, as stated in Revelation. God so loved that world, as it says in John 3:16, in order to save its people.

When this influence of evil ends, so will the world end. Nations will continue on this earth, as God had intended after he created Adam and Eve, and before Satan interfered. In Acts 3: 21, 'Universal Restoration' will take place after the thousand years; that is, after the seventh Church Age is completed, and after Satan has been done away with, justly.

Many other events must unfold simultaneously with this coming of Christ at the beginning of the seventh Church Age, but this is not the final or complete return of Christ, which will occur only after the seven Church ages are completed and death is done away with. As God the Father has stated, Jesus is to stay at the right hand of the Father until all his enemies are done away with. The last enemy is death. That will take place at the final White Throne Judgment. That will be the time of Christ's final return after the seventh Church age.

The Birth of Antichrist

References for the place of Antichrist's birth, conflict, but it will either be within northern Israel or east in the desert. Jesus references, woe to Bethsaida, Chorazin, and Capernaum, which are in Northern Israel.

St. Hippolytus (d 236): "The patriarch Jacob, expresses himself **regarding Antichrist**...as he prophesied respecting Judah, he also did with respect to his son Dan...'Let Dan be a serpent, sitting by the way, that bites the horse's heel.' And what other serpent is there, but the deceiver who was in the beginning... Jeremiah, as well, speaks in this manner: 'From Dan we will hear the sound of the sharpness of his horses, at the sound of the neighing of his horses, the whole land trembled' (Jeremiah 8:16). Furthermore, Moses says: 'Dan is a lion's whelp, and he will leap from Bashan'(Deut.33:22)....He is naming the tribe of Dan as the one where the accuser is destined to come forth." [3]

St. Methodius (d 311): "When the **Son of Perdition** appears, he will be of the tribe of Dan, according to the prophecy of Jacob... he will be an ordinary man of the tribe of Dan to which Judas Iscariot also belonged." [4] "He will be born in Chorazin, nourished in Bethsaida, and reign in Capernaum. **Chorazin** will rejoice because **he was born in her**, and Capernaum because he will have reigned in her. For this reason in the third Gospel, the Lord gave the following statement: 'Woe to you, Chorazin, Woe to you, Bethsaida, woe to you, Capernaum–if you have risen up to heaven, you will descend to hell.'" [5]

St. Jerome (340-420), Doctor of the Church: "**Antichrist** will be **born** near **Babylon**. He will win the support of many with gifts and money. He will sell himself to the devil, and thereafter will have no guardian angel or conscience." [6]

Pope St. Gregory the Great (540-604): "Before the birth of her child, the **mother of the Antichrist** will announce the advent of Messiah, who (she claims) will restore great prosperity to mankind." [7]

St. Bridget: "As Christ was born from the highest type of womanhood [Virgin] so **Antichrist** will **be born from the lowest** [prostitute]. He will be a child-wonder at birth. His mother will be an accursed woman, who will pretend to be well informed in spiritual things, and his father will be an accursed man, from the seed of whom the devil shall form his work." [8]

Fr. Bartholomew Holzhauser: "**Antichrist** will come as the Messiah, from a land **between two seas** in the East...He will be born in the desert; his mother being a prostitute to the Jews and Hindus; he will be a lying and false prophet... He will begin work in the east as a soldier and a preacher of religion when 30 years old." [9]

Melanie Calvat according to Our Lady of La Salette: "It will be at this time that the Antichrist will be **born to a Hebrew nun**, a false virgin who will communicate with the old serpent, the master of impurity; his father will be a bishop. At birth, he will vomit blasphemy, he will have teeth, in a word, this will be the devil incarnate. He will scream horribly, he will perform wonders; he will feed on nothing but impurity. He will have brothers who, although not devils incarnate (possessed) like him, will be children of evil. At the age of twelve, they will draw attention to themselves by valiant victories they will have won; soon they will each lead armies, aided by the legions from hell." [10]

He Will Be Possessed by Satan

Doctors of the Catholic Church confirm Antichrist will be possessed by Satan. Satan will have great control over the body and soul of this man of iniquity.

St. Jerome: "Nor do we think him to be the devil or a demon as some others do, but one of mankind, in whom Satan shall dwell totally.... his mouth uttering boasts, for he is the man of sin, the son of perdition, such that he will seat himself in the Temple, as if he were God." [11]

St. Jerome: "Satan shall exercise his influence over all the powers of Antichrist, both over those of his body and his soul, namely over his will, his intellect, and his memory." [12]

St. John Chrysostom: "Antichrist will be **possessed by Satan** and will be the illegitimate son of a Jewish woman from the east." [13]

St. Hilary (315- 386): "Antichrist will teach that Jesus Christ is not the Son of God, but is the wickedest of all criminals." [14]

He Will Deceive the Jewish People

Antichrist will be the most cunning and deceptive creature:

Daniel 9:27: "For one week he shall make **a firm compact** with many, **half the week**, he shall abolish sacrifice and oblation..."

St. Irenaeus (d 202): "The Antichrist will **deceive the Jews** to such an extent that they will accept him as the Messiah and worship him." [15]

St. Anselm (1033-1109), Doctor of the Church: "Towards the end of the world, Antichrist **will draw the hearts of the Jews to him** by his great generosity and sympathetic attitude, so much so, that they will praise him as a demi-god. The Jews will say to one another: 'there is not a more virtuous, just, and wise man than he, to be found in our entire generation. Of all men, he certainly will be able to rescue us from all our miseries." [16]

Fr. Bartholomew Holzhauser: "Antichrist and his army will conquer Rome, kill the Pope, and take the throne. He will restore the Turkish regime (Muslims), destroyed by the great Monarch. The Jews, knowing from the Bible that Jerusalem will be the seat of the Messiah, will come from everywhere and accept Antichrist as the Messiah..." [17]

St. Irenaeus (125-202): "By means of the events which shall occur in the time of Antichrist, it is shown that he, being an apostate and a robber, is anxious to be **adored as God**; and that, although **a mere slave**, he wishes himself to be proclaimed as a king." [18]

Rebuilding of the Jewish Temple (3rd)

A third temple will be built, although it is not necessary. Christ is the living temple.

St. Hippolytus: "The Savior raised up and showed his holy flesh like a temple, and he [Antichrist] **will raise a temple** of stone in Jerusalem." [19]

St. Irenaeus: "At the time of his reign, Antichrist will command that **Jerusalem be rebuilt** in splendor, and will make it a great and populous city, second to none in the world and will order his palace to be built there." [20]

St. Anselm: "For **the Temple** which Solomon built, having been destroyed, in its place, he (Antichrist) **shall restore it**, he shall circumcise himself, and he shall give forth the lie that he is the son of the omnipotent God." [21]

2-Thessalonians 2: 4: "That son of perdition and adversary who exalts himself above every so-called god, proposed for worship, he, who seats himself in God's temple, and even declares himself to be God."

He Will Deceive Christians

St. Vincent Ferrer: "Again Antichrist will direct his attacks against simple folk, who because their hearts are turned to Him (Christ) in rectitude of intention, are so pleasing to God. He will make use of magic and produce lifelike apparitions, which are, after all, the merest trickery. He will bring down fire from heaven, and make images speak, for the demon can cause their lips to move. To all appearance, he will recall the dead spirit of your father, the phantom infants will seem to **speak.**

Those in the third category, whom he will try to seduce are learned folk, sure as masters and doctors of civil and canon law, who can argue and grasp proofs of things. Against these, Antichrist will weave spells of enchantment, bringing out the most-subtle arguments, the most seductive reasoning, to render these learned men tongue-tied and incapable of answering. It is not difficult to understand how this is done since the demon already holds their souls in the chains of sin; for the greater their knowledge, the more heavily burdened will be their consciences if they do not live up to it. If he can hold their souls in chains, it is easy for him to bind a morsel of flesh like the tongue so that they cannot speak, except what he chooses. The temporal lords and the ecclesiastical prelates, for fear of losing power or position, will be on his side, since there will exist neither king nor prelate unless he wills it." [22]

Melanie Calvat, according to Our Lady of La Salette: "The seasons will be altered, the earth will produce only bad fruit, the stars will lose their regular motion, the moon will reflect only a faint reddish glow. Water and fire will give the earth's globe convulsions, and terrible earthquakes will swallow up mountains, cities, etc... Rome will lose the Faith and become the seat of Antichrist... The demons of the air, together with the Antichrist, will **perform great wonders** on the earth and in the (air), and men will become more and more perverted." [23]

The Abomination of Desolation

Through **the False Prophet**, the abomination of desolation will begin just before the rise of the Antichrist. That means **the consecration of the bread and wine will not take place.** It will deceivingly be removed from the altars, before the Antichrist will have complete power for three and a half years. This will bring desolation, emptiness, devastation, and sorrow to the earth and the people of God.

Sister Jeanne Le Royer: "Many precursors, false prophets, and members of infernal secret societies, worshippers of Satan, shall impugn the most sacred dogmas and doctrines of our holy religion, shall persecute the faithful, and shall commit abominable actions; **but the real extreme abomination of desolation, shall more fully, be accomplished during the reign of Antichrist, which will last about three years and a half...** When the time of the reign of Antichrist is near, a false religion will appear, which will be opposed to the unity of God and His Church. This will cause the greatest schism, the world has ever known. The nearer the time of the end, the more the darkness of Satan will spread on earth, the greater will be the number of children of corruption, and the number of the just will correspondingly diminish." [24]

St. Alphonsus de Liguori: "The devil has always managed to get rid of the Mass by means of the heretics, making them the precursors of the Antichrist who, above all else, **will manage to abolish,** and in fact, will succeed in abolishing, as a punishment for the sins of men, the Holy Sacrifice of the Altar, precisely as Daniel predicted." [25]

Daniel 9:27: "half the week, he shall abolish sacrifice and **oblation."** The Antichrist himself will also be the ultimate abomination of desolation residing in the Temple claiming to be Messiah.

The Image of the Beast

Revelation 13: 15: "The second beast was then permitted to give life to the beast's image, so that **the image had the power** of speech and of putting to death anyone who refused to worship it."

St. Vincent Ferrer: "For **he will cause images** and babes of a month old to speak. The followers of Antichrist will question these statues or babies, and they will give answer, concerning this lord who has come in the latter times, affirming that he is the savior. The devil will move their lips and form the words they utter, then they will declare Antichrist to be the true savior of the world; and in this way he will cause the destruction of many souls." [26]

The Mark of the Beast

Many comments are heard at the end of this fifth Church age about the "mark of the Beast" and "666." The prophesied mark will be imprinted on followers of Antichrist at the beginning of the seventh Church age.

St. Hildegard of Bingen: "When the great ruler (Great Catholic Monarch) exterminates the Turks almost entirely, one of the remaining Mohammedans will be converted, become a priest, bishop and cardinal, and when the new Pope is elected [immediately before Antichrist] this cardinal will kill the pope before he is crowned, through jealousy, he wishing to be pope himself; then when the other cardinals elect the next pope, this cardinal will proclaim himself Anti-Pope, and two-thirds of the Christians will go with him. He, as well as Antichrist, are descendants of the Tribe of Dan. [Some say that the Turks are of the Tribe of Dan]... The **mark** [of Antichrist] (or **of the Beast)** will be **a hellish symbol of Baptism**, because thereby a person will be stamped, as an adherent of Antichrist and of the Devil, (as) that person gives himself over to the influence of Satan. Whoever, does not have this mark of Antichrist, can neither buy nor sell anything and will be beheaded... He will win over to himself the rulers, the mighty, and the wealthy, who will bring about the destruction of those who do not accept his faith and finally will subjugate the entire earth." [27]

St. Cyril of Jerusalem: "He will oblige all his followers to bear, **impressed upon their foreheads or right hands** the mark of the beast, and will starve to death, all those who refuse to receive it." [28]

Three and One-Half Years

Bible prophecies of three and one-half years or half a week, mirror prophecies of the Catholic saints. They point to the time of the reign of Antichrist, and the events surrounding the end of the Gentile (Bride) Church, and the awakening of the Jewish people to Jesus Christ. It is a length of time decreed for the power of the Antichrist and for the power of the two witnesses, Elijah and Enoch.

Daniel 9: 26, 27: "After 62 weeks (of years, after the age of peace), an anointed (Catholic Monarch) shall be cut down, when he does not possess the city (Jerusalem); and the people (Gentiles) of a leader (Antichrist) who will come, shall **destroy** the sanctuary, then the end will come... for one week he (Antichrist) shall make a **firm compact** with the many. **Half the week,** he shall abolish sacrifice and oblation..."

Daniel 12: 1-7: "At that time, there shall arise Michael, the great prince (Archangel), guardian of your people. It shall be a time unsurpassed in distress, since nations began until that time... and I heard him swear by him who lives forever that it should be for **a year, two years, and a half year;** and that, when the power of the destroyer of the holy people was brought to an end, all these things should end."

Revelation 11: 3 : "I will commission my two witnesses to prophesy for **twelve hundred and sixty days** (three and a half years), dressed in sack cloth."

Revelation 12:14: "The woman was given the wings of a gigantic eagle so that she could fly off to her place into the desert, where, far from the serpent, she could be taken care of for **a year and for two and a half years** more."

St. Hippolytus: "When Daniel says, I shall make my covenant for one week, **he indicates years;** and **the one-half** of the week, is for the preaching of the prophets, and for **the other half** of the week, that is to say, for three years and a half, Antichrist will reign upon the earth. And after this, his kingdom and his glory shall be taken away. Behold, those who love God, what manner of tribulation there shall rise in those days, such as has not been, from the foundation of the world." [29] The Jewish year is based on 360 days, **times,** three and a half years, or 1260 days, or half a week. The Antichrist abolishes the daily sacrifice and sets up the horrible abomination for 1290 days. Elijah and Enoch come from Paradise and open the seven bowls of plagues, recorded in Revelation, upon the Antichrist and his kingdom, for 1260 days or three and one-half years; the Antichrist then kills Elijah and Enoch. After three and one-half days, they will rise from the dead and are called up to Heaven.

Wondering Where The Lions Are?

This will be **the greatest persecution and mass slaughter of Christians** that the world will ever experience; it will **fill the cup of Martyrdom, completely,** presaged in Revelation 6:11: "Each of the martyrs was given a long white robe, and they were told to be patient a little while longer/**until the quota was filled of their fellow servants and brothers to be slain, as they had been.**" The last part of this prophecy will be fulfilled during the time of Antichrist, at the end of the Gentile (Bride) Church.

St. Cyril of Jerusalem: "Antichrist will exceed in malice, perversity, lust, wickedness, impiety, and heartless cruelty and barbarity of all men that have ever disgraced human nature…he shall, through his great power, deceit, and malice succeed in decoying or **forcing** to his worship, **two thirds of mankind**; the remaining third part of men will most steadfastly continue, true to the faith and worship of Jesus Christ… In his satanic rage and fury, Antichrist will persecute these brave and devoted Christians during **three years and a half,** and **torture them with such an extremity of barbarity, with all the old and new invented instruments of pain, as to exceed all past persecutors of the Church combined.**" [30]

The Two Witnesses

This is the fullest account in the Bible of the two witnesses, Elijah and Enoch, sent by God to restore His people of Israel.

Rev 11:1-14: Someone gave me a measuring rod and said: "Come and take the measurements of God's temple and altar, and count those who worship there. Exclude the outer court of the temple, however; do not measure it, for it has been handed over to the Gentiles, who will crush the holy city for forty-two months (three and a half years). I will commission my **two witnesses** to prophecy for **those** twelve hundred and sixty days dressed in sackcloth."

"These are the two olive trees and the two lamp stands which stand in the presence of the Lord of the earth. If anyone tries to harm them, fire will come out of the mouths of these witnesses, to devour their enemies. Anyone attempting to harm them will surely be slain in this way. These witnesses have power to close up the sky, so that no rain will fall, during the time of their mission. They also have power to turn water into blood and to afflict the earth, at will, with any kind of plague."

"When they have finished giving their testimony, the wild beast that comes up from the abyss will wage war against them. Their corpses will lie in the streets of the great city, which has the symbolic name "Sodom" or "Egypt," where also their Lord was crucified. Men from every people and race, language and nation, will stare at their corpses for three days, but refuse to bury them. The earth's inhabitants gloat over them and in their merriment, exchange gifts, because these two prophets harassed everyone on earth. But after the three days, the breath of life, which comes from God, returned to them. When they stood on their feet, sheer terror gripped those who saw them. The two prophets heard a loud voice from Heaven say to them, 'Come up here!' So, they went up to Heaven in a cloud, as their enemies looked on. At that moment, there was a violent earthquake and a tenth of the city fell in ruins. Seven thousand persons were killed during the earthquake, the rest, were so terrified that they worshiped the God of Heaven…The **second woe** is past…"

Who are these two witnesses, and what is God's purpose for them? These two men were seen in the days of the Old Testament. Neither has died, but rather they were taken up to Paradise where Adam and Eve lived before they were cast out. The Old Testament reveals that **Enoch** was the seventh son (of good stock) of Adam. Genesis 5: 24 records that Enoch, walked so close with God that God took him into Paradise. This is reiterated in Sirach or Ecclesiasticus 44:16: "Enoch walked with the Lord and was taken up, **that he may give repentance to the nations.**" St. Paul says in Hebrews 11:5, "Enoch was taken away without dying..." **Elijah** the prophet is taken up to Paradise, as recorded in 2 Kings 2: 11: "As they (Elisha and Elijah) walked on conversing, a flaming chariot and flaming horses came between them, and Elijah went up to Heaven in a whirlwind." In Malachi 4: 5 (3:23 in newer versions of the Bible): "Lo, I will send you Elijah, the prophet, before the coming of the great and terrible day of the Lord."

In Mark 9:13, where Jesus says: "Let me assure you, Elijah has already come. They did entirely, as they pleased with him, as the scriptures say of him." But John the Baptist clearly states, when the Pharisees asked him, whether he was Elijah, he said, "I am not," in John 1:21. We also hear in Mark 9:11, Jesus clearly states, "Elijah will indeed come first and restore everything," before His coming. St. Gregory the Great (540- 604) explains this seemingly contradiction, by saying that Our Lord spoke of John, with the 'office' of Elijah, as the angel had explained to Zachariah in Luke 1:17: "God himself will go before him, in the spirit and power of Elijah..." More-over, John the Baptist did not come **before** the great and terrible Day of the Lord, but Elijah will come before the 'bowls of wrath' are poured out on the kingdom of Antichrist, described in Revelation.

The early Church Fathers, St. Jerome and Hippolytus, understood the literal return of Elijah. These prophecies clear up who is coming from comments of the early Church Fathers, Doctors of the Church and other saints:

St. Irenaeus states: "The disciples of the apostles say, that they (**Elias and Enoch**) whose bodies were taken up from this world, have been **placed in an earthly paradise**, where they will remain until the end of the world." [31]

St. Hippolytus: "For this is what the prophets **Enoch and Elias** will preach: Believe not the enemy who is to come and be seen; for he is an adversary and corrupter and son of Perdition, and deceives you; and for this reason, he will kill you, and smite them with the sword." [32]

St. Hippolytus explains Daniel's words: "Daniel says: 'And one week (he) will make a covenant with many, and it shall be, that **in the midst** (half) of the week sacrifice and oblation shall cease.' By one week, therefore, he meant the last week, which is to be at the end of the whole world; of which week, the two prophets **Enoch and Elias** will take up the half. For they will preach 1260 days clothed in sackcloth, proclaiming repentance to the people and to all the nations." [33, 34]

St. Hildegard: "**Enoch and Elias** will be instructed by God, in a most secret manner in Paradise. God reveals to them the actions and condition of men, that they may regard them, with eyes of compassion. Because of this special reparation, these two holy men, are wiser than all the wise men, on the earth, taken together. God will give them the task of opposing Antichrist and of bringing back, those, who have strayed from the way of salvation. Both of these men will say to the people: 'This accursed one (Antichrist) has been sent by the devil, to lead men astray and into error; we have been preserved by God in a hidden place, where we did not experience the sorrows of men, but God has now sent us to combat the heresy, of the son of perdition.' They will go into all cities and villages, where previously Antichrist had broadcasted his heresies and by the power of the Holy Spirit will perform wonderful miracles, so that all nations will greatly marvel, at them. Thus, as to a wedding feast, Christians will hasten to death, by martyrdom, which the son of perdition, will have prepared for them, in such numbers, that those murderers will be unable, even to count the slain; then the blood of these martyrs will flow like rivers." [35]

St. Mechtilde: "Both are in Paradise, living in blessed happiness. An angel will lead **Enoch and Elias** out of Paradise. The transparency and bliss which their bodies possessed there, will then disappear... As soon as they behold the earth, they will become afraid, just as people do, who, when they first behold the sea, do not know how they will be able to traverse it. They will appear as preachers **when the majority of the good have died as martyrs** and for a long time will comfort the people... Enoch and Elias will force Antichrist to a showdown; they will tell men who he is and through whose power (Satan) he is working miracles. Then many men and women who had previously followed Antichrist will be converted." [36]

St. John Damascene: "**Enoch and Elias** the Thesbite, will be sent, and they shall 'turn the heart of the fathers to the children' that is to say, turn the synagogue to our Lord Jesus Christ and the preaching of the Apostles. And they will be destroyed by him (Antichrist)." [37]

St. Robert Bellarmine: "For it must be known that in the divine letters [Scripture], the Holy Spirit has given to us, six sure signs, concerning the coming of Antichrist: two, which proceed Antichrist himself, namely the preaching of the Gospel in the whole world, and the devastation of the Roman Empire; the two contemporaneous men, which, it is to be seen prophesied as **Enoch and Elias;** the greatest and last persecution, and also, the **public sacrifice** [of the Mass] **shall completely cease**; the two following [signs] surely, the death of Antichrist after three and a half years [after his rise to power] and the end of the world; none of which signs, we have seen at this time."

"The third demonstration arises from the coming of Enoch and Elias, who live now and shall live until they shall come to oppose Antichrist himself, and to preserve the elect in the faith of Christ, and **in the end shall** convert the Jews, and it is certain that this has not yet been fulfilled."

"But it is easily seen that by us [Catholics], truly this is not a childish fantasy, but a most true concept, that Enoch and Elias shall personally return; and it is also seen that the contrary concept [that they will not personally return] is either absolutely heretical, or a serious error very close to heretical." [38]

St. Benedict of Nursia: "During the **three and a half years** of Antichrist's reign, God will send Henoch and Elias to help the Christians." [39]

Blessed Dionysius of Leutzenburg: "Enoch and Elias will be borne with the speed of lightning in a fiery chariot **from Paradise to Jerusalem**. There they will hasten into the temple and announce that this godless being who is being honored in the Temple, is he, whom, the prophets have foretold is the Antichrist. The two prophets will publicly denounce him. They will reveal their appearance on earth as promised by God. Elias will preach principally to the Jews and Enoch to the Mohammedans and other nations." [40]

Our Lady of La Salette to **Melanie Calvat:** "The Church will be in eclipse, the world will be in consternation. **Enoch and Elias** will come. They will preach with the power of God, and men of good will, will believe in God, and many souls will be comforted; they will have great progress by virtue of the Holy Ghost and **will condemn the diabolical errors of the Antichrist**."

"Woe to the inhabitants of the earth. There will be bloody wars, and famines; plagues and contagious diseases; there will be frightful showers of animals; thunders which will demolish cities; earthquakes which will engulf countries, voices will be heard in the air; men will beat their heads against the walls; they will call on death, yet death will constitute their torment; blood will flow on all sides. Who could overcome, if God doesn't shorten the time of trial?"

"At the blood, tears, and prayers of the righteous, God will relent; Enoch and Elias will be put to death; Pagan Rome will disappear; the fire of Heaven will fall and consume three cities; the whole universe will be struck with terror, and many will allow themselves to be seduced because they didn't adore the true Christ living in their midst. It is time; the sun is darkening; Faith alone will survive." [41]

Sirach 48:10 (of Elijah): "You are destined, it is written, in time to come, to put an end to wrath, before the day of the Lord, to turn back the hearts of fathers toward their sons, and **to re-establish** the **tribes of Jacob**." The tribes of Israel after Elijah, tells us, the seventh Church age will be for the Jewish people.

Malachi 3: 22-24 or **4: 4-6:** "Remember the law of Moses my servant, which I enjoined him on Horeb, the statutes and ordinances for all Israel. Lo, I will **send you Elijah, the prophet**, before the day of the Lord comes, the great and terrible day, to turn the hearts of the fathers to their children, and the hearts of the children to their fathers, **lest I** come and **strike the land with a curse**."

THE FINAL TRIBULATION OF THE GENTILE CHURCH

The Ark of the Covenant Revealed
by the Two Witnesses

In 2-Maccabees 2, the Prophet Jeremiah is warned by God to take the tent and the Ark of the Covenant to the mountain where Moses saw God's inheritance for the Israelites. Jeremiah also said, "the place is to remain unknown until God gathers his people together again, and show them Mercy. Then, the Lord will disclose these things, and **the glory of the Lord will be seen in the cloud**, just as it appeared in the time of Moses..."

Blessed Dionysius of Luetzenburg: "After the discovery of the Ark of the Covenant, Enoch and Elias will restore **the Holy Sacrament of the Altar;** because of the fact that the Ark of the Covenant will be in the possession of the two holy prophets and not in Antichrist's hands, the Jews will recognize that Jesus Christ is the true Messiah. A great throng of Jews from all lands will then make their way to Mount Nebo." [42] Enoch and Elijah will restore and awaken the Jews to the Holy Eucharist. The sacraments will continue into the seventh Church age.

Conversion of the Jews to the
Messiah–Jesus Christ

In the Old Testament, the Jewish people were a stubborn and hard-hearted people that have refused to recognize Jesus Christ as the Messiah, which raises the following question: Is this the way that God the Father convinces the Jewish people, by allowing them to experience the opposite of Christ, an impostor, claiming to be the Messiah, before they recognize the truth?

Blessed Ann Catherine Emmerich: "The Jews shall return to Palestine, and become Christians towards the end of the world." [43] The seventh Church age is for the Jewish people as Christians.

The Seven Bowls of Plagues

Deeper in Revelation, in Chapter 15 and 16, the **second set of punishments** takes place, which will transpire at the beginning of the seventh Church age. They will be activated by the words of the two witnesses, Elijah and Enoch to punish the Antichrist and his followers. Revelation 11:6 states, the two witnesses, "have the power to close up the sky...turn water into blood and to afflict the earth at will with any kind of plague." In Revelation 15 and 16, the seven angels hold the seven plagues, which are contained in the seven bowels and are destined for the Gentiles of the ten kingdoms of Antichrist, that trample Jerusalem at that time. Two thirds who do not believe in God anymore, have become worse sinners than those at the end of the fifth Church age.

These decrees are to be issued during the time of the Antichrist. These decreed plagues will unfold **by the power given to the two witnesses**. The decrees literally speak of all the wrath that God will unleash on the people: the **first bowl**, on those who have accepted the mark of the beast (Antichrist); **second bowl**, the sea turned to blood; the **third bowl**, on rivers and springs with the angel crying out, "They deserve it"; the **fourth bowl**, out on the sun with scorching heat, and "still they did not repent"; the **fifth bowl** on the throne of the beast (Antichrist), plunged into darkness, they bit their tongues and blasphemed the God of Heaven. The **sixth bowl**, the river Euphrates, is dried up to prepare the way for the Kings of the East.

Three unclean spirits will persuade these kings to oppose God in a place called in Hebrew, **"Armageddon."** This is the great valley of Jezreel or Megiddo. If you go to the land of Israel today and ask about the valley of Armageddon, people will point to the valley of Megiddo. There are tours, for the many who take interest in Biblical prophecy, that will be fulfilled literally in the future. John uses the literal Hebrew name, Armageddon, because at **his time**, that was the pronunciation of that valley. The name Armageddon, according to etymologists, probably came from Megiddo, **transliterated** from the original Hebrew, "Har Megiddon" into Greek, with a rough breathing accent for the "H" sound to "ar" –Megiddon to Armageddon. It is **the place of the last great battle on earth** that God, the Almighty will allow, where they will turn on each other until the blood is up to the horse's bridle.

A similar battle took place at the time of the battle of Jezreel, in that same valley where God confused their minds, to turn on each other and destroy each other in their delusion. This area is located in the northwest part of the valley of the river Jordon that is located in a huge fertile plain, considered the largest valley on earth, where hundreds of millions of people, from many nations, will perish in this last battle on earth.

The **seventh bowl** is poured out, "…upon the empty air. From the throne of the sanctuary, came a loud voice exclaiming: "It is finished!" There followed: lightning, thunder, then **a violent earthquake** on all the Gentile cities and the **plague of giant hailstones**, on all those who blasphemed God. This will end the seven kings or kingdoms or civilizations of the world. This will be the final destruction of 'Babylon the Great.'

The End of Antichrist

The early Church Fathers', Doctors' of the Church and other Catholic saints' prophecies disclose Elijah and Enoch rising up to Heaven. After 30 days, Antichrist will try to follow them up to Heaven. Jesus Christ will appear on the clouds, visible to everyone, and will annihilate the Antichrist. Some prophecies speak of St. Michael, the Archangel taking him down and hurling him into the abyss. After the taking up of His Bride, and the Resurrection of the living, Jesus will remain in Heaven **until** the completion of the seventh Church age. This will be part of the birth pangs at the beginning of the seventh Church age, awakening the Jewish people to the Messiah, or Christ.

Fr. Bartholomew Holzhauser: "Antichrist **will live fifty-five and one-half years; that is, 666 months.**" [44]

St. Mechtilde: "Enoch and Elijah will expose the devilish trickery of Antichrist to the people. Consequently, he will put them to death. For three and one-half days, their bodies will be exposed to insults, and the followers of Antichrist will presume that all danger is now past, but suddenly the bodies of the two prophets will move, rise, and gaze on the crowd and begin to praise God. A great earthquake, similar to that, at Christ's crucifixion will take place: Jerusalem will be partially destroyed and thousands killed. Then a voice from Heaven will call out, 'Ascend!' Where upon the prophets will ascend into Heaven, resulting in the conversion of many. **Antichrist will reign thirty days after their ascension.**" [45]

St. Zenobius (-285): "Then the son of God, our Lord Jesus Christ, **shall come in person. He shall appear on the clouds** of Heaven surrounded by legions of angels, and shining with glory. He will put to death, Antichrist, the beast, the enemy, the seducer, and all his followers. This shall be… the beginning of the general judgment." [46]

Daniel 7:13: "One like the Son of Man coming on the clouds of Heaven."

Matthew 26:64: "You will see the Son of Man, **seated at the right hand of the power** and **coming on the clouds** of Heaven." At this time, Jesus Christ will be seen coming on the clouds **but will remain at the right hand of God.**

Blessed Dionysius of Luetzenburg: "The Antichrist will kill Enoch and Elijah and leave them unburied. These, however will be resurrected after three and one-half days and ascend into Heaven, in a cloud, in the presence of their enemy. This miraculous event will actually confuse Antichrist. In order that the nations will not abandon him, he will lift himself up with great majesty into space on Mt. Olivet, with the purported intention to cast down the prophets who ascended into Heaven. But in this moment, Christ will strike him down. The earth will open and swallow him and his prophet alive. Then a large part of Jerusalem will fall into ruins from the earthquake." [47]

St. Augustine: "Where with Christ in His coming, is to strike those perse-cutors of the Church, whom He shall find alive upon earth, when He shall kill

Antichrist, with the breath of his mouth, then even **this is not the last judgment** of the wicked." [48] St. Augustine sees this as **not the last judgment** of the wicked, even though this is the end of the Gentile (Bride) Church and the second coming of Christ, for the Bride Church of six Church ages. This is not the final coming of Christ.

Our Lady of La Salette to **Melanie Calvat:** "The time is at hand; the abyss is opening. Here is the king of kings of darkness. Here is the beast with its subjects, calling itself, the savior of the world. In pride he will rise skyward to go to Heaven, he will be stifled by the breath of St. Michael, the Archangel. He will fall, and the earth, which for three days, will be in con-stant change, will open its fiery bosom; he will be plunged forever, with all his followers into hell's eternal chasms. Then water and fire will purify the earth and consume all the works of men's pride, and everything will be renewed. God will be served and glorified." [49]

Revelation 19:20: "**The beast** was captured along with **the false prophet** who performed in its presence the prodigies, that led men astray, making them accept the mark of the beast and worship his image. **Both are hurled alive into the fiery pool of burning sulfur.**"

The Two Harvests of God

At the beginning of the seventh Church age and at the end of Antichrist's reign, **two harvests of God will take place.** [50]

Revelation 14:14-16 states: "Then as I watched, a white cloud appeared, and on the cloud sat one like a Son of Man, wearing a gold crown on His head and holding a sharp sickle in His hand. **Another angel** came out of the temple and in a loud voice, cried out to him who sat on the cloud, 'Use your sickle and **cut down the harvest**, for now is the time to reap; the earth's harvest is fully ripe.' So the one sitting on the cloud wielded his sickle over all the earth and **reaped the earth's harvest.**" This is the **harvest of the Gentile nations;** that will mark the **end of the Gentile (Bride)Church; filling the cup to completion,** at the beginning of the seventh Church age.

The passage goes on to say: "Then out of the temple in Heaven came another angel, who likewise held a sharp sickle. A **second angel** who was in charge of the fire, at the altar of incense, cried out in a loud voice, to the one who held the sharp sickle, 'Use your sharp sickle and **gather the grapes** from the vines of the earth, for the clusters are ripe.' So, the angel wielded his sickle over the earth and gathered the grapes of the earth. **He threw them into the wine press of God's wrath.**" This takes place during **the pouring out of the seven bowls** on the nations of the world and includes **the great battle of Armageddon,** after the beginning of the seventh Church age, towards **the end of** the Antichrist's reign.

CHAPTER 52

CHRIST COMES AGAIN

The timing of the actual **Final Coming** of Christ is the subject of numerous theological opinions. The knowledge of time frames for the seven Church ages helps reveal 'comings' of Christ or interventions of Christ, like the waves of birth pangs, at the end of the fifth Church age, at the beginning of the seventh Church age, and at the end of the seventh Church age.

All the scenarios in scripture, of Christ's coming, are **not a one-time event.** His Kingdom is coming like birth pangs, becoming more visible on the earth, as the fullness of His intentions for the salvation of all mankind is accomplished, through the seven Church ages. We all experience **His coming** when we die. This is why there is a strong theme in the New Testament to always be ready. In Hebrews 9:28, St. Paul says: "So Christ... will appear a second time, not to take away sin, but to bring salvation to those who eagerly await him."

There are several postulates of this event in the Catholic Church and the other Christian churches. **Christ's literal final coming** goes hand in hand with the definition of **a literal** thousand years **or allegorical** thousand years, bearing in mind that even the traditional beliefs of the Church in eschatology are not written in stone, nor are they infallible teachings. They are educated opinions based upon the information available. [1] Only the basic message of salvation through Jesus Christ, extolled in the scriptures, from Genesis to Revelation, is an infallible teaching in the Catholic Church. This does not include the prophecies that have not been fulfilled. Christ fulfilled between 325 and 365 prophecies in His First Coming, based on different opinions of interpretation.

The unfolding of Revelation in a chronological order with interludes and digressions in some parts, as it appears to take place in light of Holzhauser's prophecies, concludes, **Jesus' final coming is placed at the end** of the 1000 years or the seventh Church age. Here is the clue. St. Paul repeats God's words in Hebrews 1:13: "Sit at My right hand, till I make your enemies your footstool." Matthew 22: 44 reiterates: "The Lord said to my Lord, sit at my right hand, until I humble your enemies beneath your feet." In 1-Corinthians 15:26, "the last enemy to be destroyed is death." The **last enemy** is **death,** and that does not take place until after the 1000 years or seven Church ages are completed. This is also after the white throne judgment where death is thrown into the pool of fire, meaning there will be no more death. There will be comings of Christ, which includes the Final Coming.

First: We will have experienced **a coming of Christ** or intervention during **the Warning** that is revealed in Matthew 24:27 at the end of this fifth Church age and is mentioned first of all by St. Bernard of Clairvaux. This coming will come upon us swiftly. "As lightning from the east flashes to the west, so will the coming of the Son of Man be." It also says in 1-Thessalonians 5:2, "You know very well that the day of the Lord is coming like a thief in the night." In Revelation 3:3, He speaks to the fifth Church Sardis: "If you do not rouse yourselves, I will come upon you like a thief, at a time you cannot know." These are references to a coming of Christ **at the end** of the fifth Church age fulfilled in the Warning. This is the opening of the first seal of Revelation.

Second: The word of God goes on to say in Matthew 24:30: "All the clans of the earth will strike their breasts as they see the **Son of Man coming on the Clouds** of Heaven with power and great glory." Matthew 26:64: "You will see the Son of Man (Christ) **seated at the right hand** of the Power and **is coming on the clouds** of Heaven. Rev 1:7 also says, "He comes on the clouds," where we will see him from a distance, first, before he acts accordingly. A reference in the Old Testament speaks to the Jewish people in Daniel 7:13-14 of the same event: "One like the son of man coming on the clouds of Heaven... received dominion, glory, and kingship; nations and peoples of every language serve him... that shall not be taken away..." This event takes place **at the beginning** of the seventh Church age when Jesus comes for **all of His Bride Church**. It will be considered the Second Coming for the Gentile (Bride Church. At this time, Christ will remain at the right hand of God the Father. The Jewish people finally awaken, and see Jesus, their Messiah on the clouds. This will occur at the beginning of the seventh Church age and at the end of Antichrist.

Third: In Acts of the Apostles 1: 9,10,11, right after Jesus ascended to Heaven from the Mount of Olives, "He was lifted up before their eyes in a cloud which took Him from their sight. They were still gazing up into the heavens, when two men dressed in white, stood beside them. "Men of Galilee," they said, "Why do you stand there looking up at the skies? This Jesus who has been taken from you, **will return, just as you saw Him go up** into the heavens." Now, Heaven sends two angels to tell the apostles and all of mankind, that Jesus will come **back to the earth, at the same place** on the Mount of Olives, in the same way, visibly landing, in the same manner just as He left. It is clear from heavenly angels that he is coming back to the earth and standing on it. This event is **His Final Coming**, after the 1000 years, at the end of the seventh Church age. This scenario is described further in Zechariah 14: 4-5 of the visible return of the Lord to the Mount of Olives.

The Fullness of the Gentile (Bride) Church

St. Paul relates a "mystery" about the full number of Gentiles who will enter in, before the conversion of the Jewish people can take place. In Romans 11:25-26, St. Paul says: "I do not want you to be ignorant in this mystery, lest you be conceited; blindness has come upon Israel; **until the full number of Gentiles enter in,** and **then** all Israel will be saved."

After the fallen angels were cast out of Heaven, God wanted **to replace the numbers in attendance,** by offering it to those who commit their lives to Christ, as revealed to Mary of Agreda: "Having lost the right to the places, which had been reserved for them...it passed over to mankind."[2] Those who fall in love with Christ, characterize the uniqueness of the Bride Church. This was and is being accomplished by the gathering of the unique Bride of Christ, for the last two thousand years, and will continue until the beginning of the seventh Church age. This is considered the time when the full number of Gentiles decreed, will have entered in. The members of the Bride of Christ will be given the places that were originally for the angels that subsequently rebelled.

In the Jewish tradition, at a wedding, the bridegroom does not know when he is to go with his bride to the bridal chamber. Instead, the father is to make the announcement of the day and the hour. In other words, **they do not know the day or the hour.** This is why Jesus states, no one knows the day or the hour, not even the Son, except the Father in Heaven, when Christ will come for His Bride.

This is a clue as to what will happen. The day and the hour are more about a joining of the complete bride and the bridegroom. **This is what is important to Jesus on that day.** It is about the celebration of a full love relationship, as related in Revelation Chapter 19: 7-9: "Let us rejoice and be glad and give him glory, for this is the wedding day of the Lamb; His Bride has prepared herself for the wedding. She has been given a dress to wear, made of finest linen, brilliant white. The linen dress is the virtuous deeds of God's saints. The angel, then said to me: Write this down: Happy are they who have been invited to the wedding feast of the Lamb." It is a unique privilege to be part of the Bride.

This event of the fullness in numbers, will take place at the beginning of the seventh Church age, just at the end of the final martyrdom and tribulation of the Gentile (Bride Church. This will bring about the coming of the Lord and the taking up of his Bride to **meet Jesus on the clouds,** and to enter into the banquet, for the Bride (Gentile Church) and Bridegroom (Jesus).

Prayer: "St. Bridget pray for us, for wisdom and knowledge, guidance and direction, health and protection, from the Antichrist and Antichrist spirits, now and throughout the generations to come, until the completion of the Gentile, Bride Church, when the full number have entered in."[3] Recite: "Prayer to the Sacred Head."

In the Twinkling of an Eye

The day will come (beginning of seventh Church age) when **in the twinkling of an eye**, as **Christ comes on the clouds,** He will take up, from the earth, the remainder of His Church into Heaven at that time. The physical bodies of Christians will be changed from corruptible to incorruptible, or transfigured in the twinkling of an eye, to meet Christ in the air. A portion of mankind (Gentiles) will be left on the earth, at that time. The Jewish people will also be left, to begin the thousand years during the seventh Church age. Many non-Catholic Christians call this event the 'Rapture,' and many, including Catholics, believe this event will take place, at this time (fifth Church age).

Scriptures reveal a miraculous transfiguration of the physical body. St. Paul says: "Not all will die but be transformed in the twinkling of an eye." Matthew and Luke also describe the taking up of His Church, surrounded by the reality, of a time of God's punishment upon the evil people. At the beginning of the seventh Church age, this transfiguration will unfold, after 'the cup is filled with the blood of the martyred saints' (Revelation), along with those who survive the time of the Antichrist, who are Gentile Christians. They will be taken up in a twinkling of an eye, thus the fullness of the Gentile (Bride) Church, will be lifted up with Christ, to the Bridle chamber in Heaven.

Consider these New Testament scriptures about this event:

St. Paul–1-Corinthians 15:51-52: "Now, I am going to tell you a mystery. Not all of us shall fall asleep, but all of us are to be changed, in an instant, in the twinkling of an eye, at the sound of the last trumpet. The trumpet will sound and the dead will be raised incorruptible, and we shall be changed."

St. Paul–1-Thessalonians 4:11-17: "We would have you clear, about those who sleep in death; otherwise, you might yield to grief, like those who have no hope. For if we believe that Jesus died and rose, God will bring forth with Him from the dead, those also, who have fallen asleep, **believing in Him**. We say to you, as if the Lord himself had said it, that we who live, **who survive** until his coming, will in no way have an advantage over those who have fallen asleep. Know, the Lord himself, will come down from Heaven, at the word of command, at the sound of the Archangel's voice and God's trumpet; and those who have died in Christ will rise first. We the living, the survivors, **will be caught up with them, in the clouds to meet the Lord in the air.** Thenceforth, we shall be with the Lord unceasingly. Console one another with this message."

Matthew 24:39-41: "So will it be at the coming of the Son of Man. Two men will be out in the field, **one will be taken and one will be left**. Two women will be grinding meal, one will be taken, and one will be left."

Luke 17:26-36: "As it was in the days of Noah, so will it be in the days of the Son of Man. They ate and drank, they took wives, right up to the day Noah entered the ark, and when the flood came, it destroyed them all... It will be like that, on the day, the Son of Man is revealed... on that night there will be two in bed, **one will be taken, and the other will be left**. Two women will be grinding grain together; one will be taken and the other left." The last two prophecies clarify; **people will be left** on the earth, after Jesus takes up His Bride.

The First Resurrection

St. Paul teaches of the first Resurrection in 1-Thessalonians 4:16: "Those who have died in Christ will rise first," at the beginning of the seventh Church age; at the end of the time of the Antichrist, at the same time as the taking up of the Christians in a twinkling of an eye, and just at the beginning of the thousand years, for the Jewish people.

Revelation 20:4-6 states: "They came to life again and reigned with Christ for a thousand years. The **others, who were dead**, did not come to life, until the thousand years were over. This is the first resurrection; **happy and holy are they who share in the first resurrection**! The second death will have no claim on them, they shall serve God and Christ as priests, and shall reign with him for a thousand years." Those who came to life again, in the first resurrection, will be with Christ at the wedding banquet in Heaven, for the thousand years. The "others who were dead" are those going to eternal ruin, and will resurrect and are judged after the thousand years, at the final white throne judgment.

The Messiah is Coming

Catholics and other Christians should realize that we are not the only ones being saved; that God has a plan for all. God has a purpose for His people, the Jewish people. They have been waiting for thousands of years, for God's promises, about the coming Messiah, to be fulfilled, according to the Old Testament prophecies. In the Old Testament, we see two scenarios relating to the Messiah: for Christians, a **Suffering Messiah** on the earth in Isaiah 53; and for the Jewish people, a **Reigning Messiah** on the earth in Isaiah 9 and 11. Christians have recognized the Suffering Messiah on the earth, but the Jewish people have not. The **Jewish people have recognized** and are waiting for the Reigning Messiah, coming to the earth, but it seems Christians **have not**.

In Daniel 7:13-14 it states: "As the visions during the night continued, **I saw One like the Son of Man** coming **on the clouds of heaven**;When he reached the Ancient One and was presented before him, He received dominion, glory, and kingship; nations and peoples of every language serve him. His dominion is an everlasting dominion that shall not be taken away, his kingship shall not be destroyed." This is the Reigning Messiah that the Jewish people are waiting for and see Him coming on the clouds, at the same time as Catholic Christians see Him, coming on the clouds, at the beginning of the seventh Church age.

This is the time of the end of the Gentile Church, and the beginning of the seventh Church age for Jewish people. There are six Church ages for the Gentile Church. The last Church age is given to the Jewish people and will include all Gentile peoples, even in that time, that still remain on the earth. This does not mean that Jesus will sit on the earthly throne of David, at this time, in the seventh Church age. People will still die in this age; thus, Jesus is still at the right hand of the Father.

God the Father will fulfill His promises to Abraham about **living in their land forever.** He is a Father that keeps his Word. In Genesis 13:15, God said to Abraham, to **look in all directions,** at, "**all the land that you see**, I will give to you and your descendants **forever.**" And in Genesis 17:8, "I will give to you and **your descendants,** the whole land ...as a **permanent possession.**" A 'permanent possession' and 'forever' from God's perspective **is forever.** God does not give this kind of promise to the Gentile Church nor to any other people or nation living on earth.

Understanding the Differences

The distinction between Gentile Christians and Jews is the way they come into God. The Gentiles enter in by making a decision to fall in love with Christ. This is an understanding of who the Bride is. It is a relationship brought about by a free decision. In contrast, the Jewish people originally entered in by birth, a descendant of the Jewish race, the chosen people of God.

The **visible coming of Christ on the clouds** at the beginning of the seventh Church age has a **two-fold purpose.** The Gentile (Bride) Church ends at that time. This means the fullness of the Bride has been completed, or the full number of Gentiles has entered in. This is the **Final** (Second) **Coming** of Christ **for** the Gentile (**Bride**) **Church,** who has entered into Christ through Baptism of Water and of Spirit.

At the same time, this is for the Jewish people, the **coming of the Messiah,** who will come with power, and glory, and might, the one whom they have been waiting, many thousands of years for. But this is not the end of the earth. One more Church age, the seventh Church age is decreed for the Jewish people. Other nations will continue to exist alongside the Jewish nation or Jewish peoples.

The Seven Kingdoms of
Daniel 7 & Revelation 17

Six major worldly kingdoms have existed throughout time and are described in the prophecies of Daniel and in Revelation, called kings or kingdoms. One last kingdom (seventh of Antichrist is yet to come for a limited time. In Revelation 17, Babylon the great, refers to all the major worldly kingdoms that have existed or will exist on this earth. The underlying reality of these kingdoms is severely influenced by the beast and the harlot. Revelation explains in a straightforward way: the beast is Satan himself, and the harlot is the large numbers of peoples, and nations, and tongues seduced by the beast to varying degrees. We as people on this earth, and as individuals, are seduced to varying degrees, by Satan, and by people seduced by Satan, in subtle ways and by pervading thought; that developed these worldly kingdoms, deceived by Satan. That is the symbol of the harlot. We are called to resist that harlotry or the worldly life.

John says in Rev. 17: "I saw a woman, seated on a scarlet beast, which was covered with blasphemous names. **This beast had seven heads and ten horns.** The woman was dressed in purple, scarlet, and adorned with gold and pearls and other jewels. In her hand, she held a gold cup that was filled with the abominable and sordid deeds of her lewdness. On her forehead was written a symbolic name, 'Babylon the great, mother of harlots and all the world's abominations.' I saw that the woman was drunk with the blood of **God's holy ones** and the blood of the martyred, for their faith in Jesus…The beast (Satan you saw…it existed once, and now exists no longer, and it will exist again... **the seven heads** are seven hills, on which the woman sits enthroned. They are **also seven kings**: five have already fallen, **one lives now**, and **the last** has not yet come; but when he does come, he will remain **only for a short while**."

According to John, the sixth kingdom, the **one that lives now** is the **Roman kingdom** that Jesus Christ overcomes. This Roman kingdom has persisted in different governing forms and at different strengths for 2600-plus years and will continue, even into the sixth Church age of peace, until the coming of Antichrist. It is during the time of the Roman Kingdom, when Jesus Christ **is establishing His kingdom** that will remain forever. The seventh king who is Antichrist, and his kingdom, will destroy the Roman kingdom, but Antichrist's kingdom will remain only for a short time.

The last kingdom, the time of Antichrist's power, who will rule at the beginning of the seventh Church age, will be seven years long. His kingdom will include the 'ten horns,' meaning ten earthly kingdoms, with ten kings on the earth. This will be **the last worldly (king) kingdom** on the earth, influenced by the beast (Satan) **and** the harlot or worldly peoples influenced by the beast.

376 AFTER THE WARNING TO 2038

We all know that since Noah, Abraham, Isaac, and Jacob, Egypt is the **first** kingdom that existed on the earth. It exploited God's people but fell from power over time. Although, the Babylonian kingdom existed before the Assyrians, the **Assyrians** were the **second to fall.** In Daniel 2, the interpretation of Nebuchadnezzar's dream tells us of **the next four kingdoms** that would fall. The first one is Nebuchadnezzar's kingdom of **Babylon**, then the **Medo-Persian** empire, which does not last that long. The third is the **Greek** (Hellenistic) empire that would last until the **Romans**.

Daniel then records: "God of Heaven sets up a Kingdom **that shall never be destroyed** or delivered up to another people; rather, it shall break in pieces all these kingdoms and put an end to them." In Revelation, John explains the first five kingdoms have fallen. In Daniel, it explains **the characteristics** of the Greek kingdom that divides into four different parts, continuing in part, into of the **Roman kingdom,** the fourth kingdom of Nebuchadnezzar's dream and **continues to this day**. The Roman kingdom continues to exist but Jesus Christ is **uniquely establishing His Kingdom** during the Roman Kingdom. The Greek kingdom still influences us with acquired forms of philosophy, arts, languages, politics, educational systems, science, literature, theatre, and architecture. This Greek influence, continues during the Roman kingdom but will perish as well. The Roman Kingdom will be destroyed by Antichrist who reigns in the last kingdom of the Beast, which only lasts seven years. Christ brings about **an end** to all the seven kingdoms, spoken of in Daniel and Revelation. This will be the end of **worldly** influence by the Beast. This will **in fact be the end of the world** but not the end of the earth. The remaining kingdom that shall never be destroyed will be Christ's Kingdom.

CHAPTER 53

THE THOUSAND YEARS

The 1000 years or the seventh Church age **is not part of the kingdoms of the world** but rather becomes **a distinct Church age of peace.** Satan will be bound for the thousand years.

Revelation 20:1-3: "Then I saw an angel come down from heaven, holding the key to the abyss and a huge chain in his hand. He seized the dragon, the ancient serpent, which is the devil or Satan, and chained him up for a thousand years. The angel hurled him into the abyss, which he closed and sealed over him. He did this, **so that the dragon might not lead the nations astray,** until the thousand years are over."

A Utopia During the Seventh Church Age

When we look at the scriptures of the Old Testament from a Jewish point of view, there are too many clues on the table, to ignore the reality of a literal utopia, promised to the Jewish people. No worldly civilization has lasted more than five hundred years. Rome in its original existence came close but Jesus' reign will last far longer than that. These scriptures are still to be fulfilled:

Isaiah 32:15-20: "Then will the desert become an orchard, and the orchard be regarded as a forest. Right will dwell in the desert, and justice will bring about peace...My people will live in peaceful country, in secure dwellings, and quiet resting places."

Isaiah 32:15-20:"Then will **the desert become an orchard,** and the orchard be regarded as a forest. Right will dwell in the desert, and justice will bring about peace...My people will live **in peaceful country**, in secure dwellings, and quiet resting places."

Isaiah 65:17-25: "Lo, **I am about to** create new heavens and a new earth. The things of the past shall not be remembered or come to mind. Instead, there shall always be rejoicing and happiness in what I create; for I create Jerusalem to be a joy, and it's people to be a delight. I will rejoice in Jerusalem and exult in my people. No longer shall the sound of weeping be heard there. Or the sound of crying; No longer shall there be in it, an infant who lives but a few days, or an old man who does not round out his full lifetime; **he who dies a mere youth who reaches but a hundred years,** and he who fails of a hundred, shall be thought accursed. They shall live in houses they build, and eat the fruit of the vineyards they plant. They shall not build houses for others to live in, or plant for others to eat. As the years of a tree, so the years of people, and my chosen ones, shall long enjoy the produce of their hands. They shall not toil in vain nor beget children for sudden destruction. For **a race blessed by the Lord**, are they and their offspring. Before they call, I will answer, while they are yet speaking, I will hearken to them. The wolf and the lamb shall graze alike, and the lion shall eat hay like the ox, but the serpent's food shall be dust. None shall hurt or destroy **on all my holy mountain**, says the Lord."

Zechariah 8:1-23: "Thus says the Lord of hosts: I am intensely jealous for Zion, stirred to jealous wrath for her, **Thus says the Lord. I will return to Zion,** and **I will dwell within Jerusalem**; Jerusalem shall be called the faithful city and the mountain of the Lord of hosts, the holy mountain…Old men and old women, each with staff in hand because of old age, **shall again sit in the streets of Jerusalem.** The city shall be **filled with boys and girls playing in her streets**…Even if this should seem impossible in the eyes of the remnant of this people, shall it in those days be impossible in my eyes also…**I will rescue my people from the land of the setting sun** (Americas), and I will bring them back to dwell within Jerusalem. They shall be my people, and I will be their God, with faithfulness and justice…There shall yet come peoples, the inhabitants of many cities, and the inhabitants of one city shall approach those of another, and say, Come! Let us go to implore the favor of the Lord, and I too, will go to seek the Lord. Many peoples and **strong nations shall come to seek the Lord of hosts in Jerusalem** and to implore the favor of the Lord. In those days **ten men of every nationality,** speaking different tongues, **shall take hold of every Jew by the edge of his garment and say, "Let us go with you for we have heard that God is with you."**

From the time of Adam, until the time of the flood, mankind lived hundreds of years in a life span, but according to Genesis 6:3, when God saw the wickedness, he said: "His days shall comprise one hundred and twenty years," instead of the long lives, they lived before the flood. God made a decreed to change the length of time for man on the earth. When the thousand years takes place, people will live hundreds of years again, **but there will still be death.**

Like the Sands of the Sea

Around 1900, 11.6 million Jewish people existed in the world. They grew to 17 million by 1939; after the World War II, they were reduced to a mere 11 million. As of 2009, the global Jewish population is around 13.3 million, just 0.195% of a percent of the population of the world. God says he will make them like sands of the sea. This has not happened so far, but look at what is recorded in these verses, about the Jewish people and the great increase in numbers of people in Israel and the earth.

Exodus: 32:13: "How you swore to them by your own self, saying, I will make your descendants **as numerous as the stars** of the sky, and all this land that I promised, I will give your descendants as **a perpetual heritage**."

Daniel 3: 36: "To whom you promised to multiply their offspring, **like the stars** of heaven, or **the sands** on the shore of the sea."

Hosea 1:10-11: "And the number of the children of Israel, shall be **like the sands of the sea**, that is, without measure, and shall not be numbered… And the children of Judah, and the children of Israel shall be gathered together, and **they shall appoint themselves, one head**, and they shall rise up (from) out of the land, for great is the day of Jezreel."

Jeremiah 3:14: "I will appoint over you shepherds after my own heart, who will shepherd you wisely and prudently. **When you multiply and become fruitful in the land**, says the Lord, they will in those days, no longer say, 'The ark of the Covenant of the Lord.' They will no longer think of it, or remember it, or miss it or make another." The Jewish people shall have leaders after Gods own heart.

Section VII

His Reign
Will be Forever

CHAPTER 54

AFTER THE THOUSAND YEARS

After the end of the thousand years of peace, Satan will be released for a short time, to seduce the nations all over the earth, **for the last time.** Revelation 20 states: "When the thousand years are over, **Satan** will be released from his prison. He will go out **to deceive the nations,** in all four corners of the earth, and muster for war the troops of Gog and Magog, numerous as the sands of the sea. They invaded the whole country and surrounded the beloved city where God's people were encamped; but fire came down from heaven and devoured them."

For the third time, without warning this time, **punishments** are cast down upon the people who became deceived and rebellious.

St. Augustine (354-430) Doctor of the Church: "And when the thousand years are finished, Satan shall be loosed from his prison, and shall go out to seduce the nations…" [1]

Zechariah 14: 1-21: "Lo, a day (after the end of the seventh Church age) shall come for the Lord, when the spoils shall be divided in your midst. And **I will gather all the nations against Jerusalem** for battle; the city shall be taken, houses plundered, women ravished, half of the city shall go into exile, but the rest of the people shall not be removed from the city. Then the Lord shall go forth and fight against those nations, fighting as on a day of battle. **That day his feet shall rest upon the Mount of Olives,** which is opposite Jerusalem to the east. **The Mount of Olives shall be cleft in two, from east to west, by a very, deep valley,** and **half of the mountain shall move to the north and half of it to the south,** and be filled up by the earthquake, as in the days of King Uzziah of Judah. Then, the Lord my God, shall come, and **all his holy ones with Him."**

"On that day, there shall no longer be cold or frost. There shall be one continuous day, known to the Lord, not day and night, for in the evening time there shall be light. On that day, living waters shall flow from Jerusalem, half to the eastern sea, and half to the western sea, and it shall be so in summer and in winter. The Lord shall become king over the whole earth; **on that day, the Lord shall be the only one, and his name the only one."**

"And from Geba to Rimmon in the Negab, all the land shall turn into a plain, but Jerusalem shall remain exalted, in its place. From the Gate of Benjamin to the place of the First Gate, to the corner Gate; and from the Tower of Hananel, to the kings wine presses, they shall occupy her, never again shall she be doomed; Jerusalem shall abide in security."

"...**this shall be the plague,** with which the Lord shall strike all the nations that have fought against Jerusalem; their flesh shall rot while they stand upon their feet, and their eyes shall rot in their sockets, and their tongues shall rot in their mouths. On that day, there shall be among them, a great tumult from the Lord; every man, shall seize the hand of his neighbor, and the hand of each, shall be raised against that of his neighbor. Judah, also shall fight against Jerusalem. The riches of all the surrounding nations, shall be gathered; gold, silver, and garments, in great abundance. Similar to this plague, shall be the plague upon the horses, mules, camels, and asses; upon all the beasts that are in those camps."

"**All who are left of all the nations** that came against Jerusalem, **shall come up year after year to worship the King,** the Lord of hosts, and to celebrate the feast of Booths. If any of the families of the earth, does not come up to Jerusalem to worship the King, the Lord of hosts, no rain shall fall upon them. And if the family of Egypt does not come up, or enter ; upon them, shall fall the plague which the Lord will inflict upon all the nations that do not **come up to celebrate the feast of Booths**. This shall be the punishment of Egypt, and the punishment of all the nations that do not come up to celebrate the feast of Booths."

"On that day, there shall be upon the bells of the horses, "Holy to the Lord." The pots in the House of the Lord shall be as the libation bowls before the altar. And every pot in Jerusalem and Judah shall be holy to the Lord of hosts, and all who come to sacrifice shall take them and cook in them. On that day, there shall no longer be any merchant in the house of the Lord of hosts."

The Last Judgment

Rev. 20:10: "The devil (Satan) that led them astray was hurled into the pool of burning sulfur, where the beast and the false prophet had also been thrown. There, they will be tortured day and night, forever and ever."

1-Corinthians 15: 24-26 says: "Just as in Adam, all die, so in Christ, **all will come to life again**, but **in proper order;** Christ, the first fruits, and then at his coming, all those who belong to him. When after having destroyed every sovereignty, and power, he will hand over the kingdom to God the Father. Christ must reign until God has put all enemies under his feet, **and "the last enemy to be destroyed is death."**

Rev. 20:11: "Next, I saw a large white throne and the one who sat on it… I saw the dead, the great and the lowly, standing before the throne… Among the scrolls, the book of the living was opened. The dead were judged…the sea gave up its dead…death and the nether world gave up their dead…**then death and the nether world were hurled into the pool of fire,** which is the second death; anyone…not found in the Book of the Living, was hurled into this pool of fire." The wicked, will resurrect bodily and are judged at this time, but are sent to the second death for eternity.

A New Heavens and a New Earth

Revelation 21: 1-6: "Then, I saw new heavens and a new earth. [2] The former heavens, and the former earth had passed away, and **the sea was no longer** (**oceans**). I also saw a New Jerusalem, the holy city, **coming down out of heaven** from God, beautiful as a bride, prepared to meet her husband. I heard a loud voice cry out: This is God's dwelling among men. He shall dwell with them, they shall be his people, and he shall be their God who is always with them. He shall wipe every tear from their eyes, and there shall be **no more death** or mourning, crying out or pain, for **the former world** has passed away. The One who sat on the throne said to me, "See I make all things new!" Then He said, "Write these matters down, for the words are trust worthy and true… To anyone who thirsts, I will give to drink, without cost from the spring of life-giving water."

Heaven and earth as we experience, will pass away, and God will bring about a new heavens and new earth. The earth's oceans will cease to exist. There will be only day, no more night. The land around Jerusalem, the Promised Land, will remain the same.

In the **Acts of the Apostles 3:13**, Peter and John go up to the temple, and at the gate called, 'the Beautiful', a crippled man is begging for alms. He sees Peter and John and gets their attention. They gave all their attention to the beggar. Peter says to him: "I have neither silver nor gold, but what I have, I give to you! In the name of Jesus Christ, the Nazorean, walk!" The man walked and jumped for joy, thus getting the attention of the crowd. When Peter saw the Jewish people staring at them, he gave a discourse on who Jesus was, and is, **for the Jewish people**. Peter speaks out:

"The God of Abraham, of Isaac, and Jacob, the God of our Fathers, has glorified his Servant Jesus, whom you handed over and disowned in Pilate's presence, when Pilate was ready to release him. You disowned the Holy and Just One, and preferred instead to be granted the release of a murderer. You put to death, the Author of Life, but God raised him from the dead, and we are his witnesses. "

It is **His name** and trust in **this name** that has strengthened the limbs of this man, whom you see and know well. **Such faith** has given him perfect health, as all of you can observe. Yet, I know, my brothers **that you acted out of ignorance, just as your leaders did**. God has brought to fulfillment, by this means, what he announced long ago, through His prophets; that His Messiah would suffer."

"Therefore, reform your lives! Turn to God, that your sins may be wiped away! Thus may **a season of refreshment**, be granted to you, by the Lord when He sends you Jesus, already designated as your Messiah. **Jesus must remain in heaven, until the time of universal restoration**, which God spoke of long ago, through His prophets…"

What does Peter mean by this, 'universal restoration' when Jesus returns from Heaven to the earth? It says in Acts 1:6, "While they were with Him, they asked, Lord, are you going **to restore the rule in Israel now?**" His answer was: **"The exact time is not yours to know.** The Father has reserved that to himself. You will receive power when the Holy Spirit comes down on you; then you are to be my witnesses… to the ends of the earth. No sooner had he said this, than he was lifted up, before their eyes in a cloud, which took him from their sight." This strongly points to a restoration of Israel that Jesus himself is destined to complete.

Psalm 132: 11 -14: "The Lord has sworn truth to David, and he will not make it void; of his offspring, I will set on his throne. If your sons keep my covenants and decrees which I shall teach them… For the Lord has chosen Zion, **He has chosen it for his dwelling**. This is **my rest, forever** and ever, here will I dwell, **for I have chosen it**."

Luke 1:32 (Angel Gabriel) "Great will be His dignity, and He will be called Son of the Most High. **The Lord God will give him the throne of David**, his Father. He will rule over the house of Jacob forever and his reign will be forever."

2-Peter 3: 13-15: "What we await are **new heavens** and a **new earth** where, according to his promise, the justice of God will reside. So beloved, while waiting for this, make every effort to be found without stain or defilement and at peace in his sight."

Ezekiel 43: 1-7: "Then he led me to the gate which faces the east, and there I saw the Glory of the God of Israel, coming from the east. I heard the sound of many waters, and **the earth** shone with his glory… and I saw that the temple was filled with the Glory of the Lord. Then, I heard someone speaking to me from the temple, while the man stood beside me. The voice said to me: **Son of Man, this is where my throne shall be, this is where I will set the soles of my feet; here I will dwell among the Israelites forever.**"

EPILOGUE

After many trials and hardship in my life, St. Therese of Lisieux appeared to me on July 30, 2010. That morning, after spending time in prayer and after some breakfast, I sat on the couch. To my surprise, I saw a young, beautiful woman, quite tall about twelve years, standing near the table where I sat and prayed each morning. Her dark brown hair was pulled back on the sides and had a curly wave to it. She wore a long, cream colored coat and was standing at the right of the chair, and was looking at the table. I exclaimed out loud, "Who is that?" I was surprised to hear a chorus of voices, say, "It's Therese." She then turned to me, and just looked at me very seriously and intently for a moment... Then, she was gone. This I believe, would not have taken place without persevering in prayer and attending many daily Masses and receiving healing and deliverance in my life, leading to further awakening and understanding into what God intends for my life. I realized from an earlier age that prayer or connecting with God could make a difference in my life, and I knew I could receive personal experiences from the Holy Spirit. But I resisted for so many years, from making the commitment to discipline my life, giving part of my daily routine to the Lord. A **person has to take the time it takes,** each day. It is easier said than done, but by committing to a routine, I started to see results, until the 'wow' experiences started to happen.

A bit of advice for prayer: Just be there, and do it anyway, even when you do not feel like it! Without increased prayer, connecting to God, and finding deeper conversion into Christ going forward, it will be impossible to sustain ourselves, through the events about to unfold. We have been on party time since the sixties, and the mitigating prayer for us, from our grandparents and great grandparents has been used up. Believing in Christ, is **obeying all of His word** and the directives through His Church. His Church has been the longest standing entity on this planet for the last 2000 years.

Bibliography

AA-1025-The Memoirs of an Anti-Apostle, Marie Carré, 1991, Tan Books and Publishers, Inc., Rockford, Illinois.

Admirable Life of Mother Mariana (The), Volumes I & II, Fr. Manuel Sousa Pereira 1790, translated by Marian T. Horvat, PH.D., 1999; Tradition in Action, Inc., 2006, Los Angeles, CA.

Age of Enlightenment (The), Sir Isaiah Berlin, 1956, Mentor Books, The New American Library, New York.

Air Waves From Hell, Father Frank Poncelet, 1991, The Neumann Press, Long Prairie, Minnesota.

A Key to Charismatic Renewal in the Catholic Church, Rev. Vincent M. Walsh, 1976, Abbey Press, St. Meinrad, Indiana.

An Exorcist Tells His Story, Fr. Gabriele Amorth, 1999, Ignatius Press, San Francisco, California.

Apparitions of Our Lady at Medjugorje (The), Svetozar Kraljevic O.F.M., 1984, Franciscan Herald Press, Chicago, Illinois.

Athanasius and the Church of Our Time, Dr. Rudolf Graber, Bishop of Regensburg, 1974, Christian Book Club of America, Hawthorne, California.

Baptized in the Spirit and Spiritual Gifts, Steve Clark, 1976, Servant Books, Ann Arbor, Michigan.

Begone Satan, Rev. Carl Vogal, 2010, Tan Books, Charlotte, North Carolina.

Bernadette Speaks, Fr. Rene Laurentin, 1999, Pauline Books, Boston, MA.

Bernadette Soubirous (Saint), Abbe Francois Trochu, translated by John Joyce S. J., 1985, Tan Books Publishers, Inc., Rockford, Illinois.

Bleeding Hands, Weeping Stone, Elizabeth Ficocelli, 2010, Saint Benedict Press, Charlotte, North Carolina.

Bohemian Grove: Cult of Conspiracy, Mike Hanson, 2012, Rivercrest Publishing, Austin, Texas.

Book of Destiny (The), Rev. Herman Bernard Kramer, 1975, Tan Books and Publishers, Inc. Rockford, Illinois.

Bridge to Heaven: Interviews with Maria Esperanza of Betania (The), Michael H. Brown, 2003, Queenship Publishing Company, Goleta, California.

Brigitta Of Sweden: Life and Selected Revelations, translated by Albert Ryle Kezel, 1990, Paulist Press, New Jersey.

Brotherhood of Darkness, Dr. Stanley Monteith, 2000, Hearthstone Publishing, Oklahoma City, Oklahoma.

Butler's Lives of the Saints, (4 volumes), Father Herbert Thurston, S.J. and Donald Attwater, 1956, Christian Classics, Notre Dame, Indiana.

Catherine Laboure-Visionary of the Miraculous Medal, Fr. Rene Laurentin, 2006, Pauline Books, Boston, Massachusetts.

Catherine Laboure of the Miraculous Medal(Saint), Father Joseph I. Dirvin, C.M., 1984, Tan Books and Publishers, Inc., Rockford, Illinois.

Catholic Prophecy-The Coming Chastisement, Yves Dupont, 1973, Tan Books Publishers, Inc., Rockford Illinois.

Charisms and Charismatic Renewal: A Biblical and Theological Study, Francis A. Sullivan S. J., 1982, Servant Books, Ann Arbor, Michigan.

Christian Trumpet (The), complied by Fr. Gaudentius Rossi Pellegrino, 1873, Thos. B. Noonand & Co., 17, 19, and 21 Boylston St., Boston, Massachusetts

Code of the Illuminati, ('Memoirs Illustrating the History of Jacobinism'-original title) Part III, 1798,Abbe Augustin Barruel, 2008 republished by Forgotten Books.

Creature From Jekyll Island (The), 5th edition, G. Edward Griffin, 2010, American Media, Westlake Village, California.

Crossing the Threshold of Hope, His Holiness John Paul II, 1994, Alfred A. Knopf, Toronto Canada.

Day Will Come (The) , Michael H. Brown, 1996, Servant Publications, Ann Arbor, Michigan.

Days of the French Revolution (The), Christopher Hibbert,1980, HarperCollins Publishers, Inc., New York, New York.

Death by Government, R.J. Rummel, 1994, Transaction Publishers, New Brunswick, New Jersey.

Divine Mercy in My Soul-Diary of Saint Maria Faustina Kowalska, 1987, Marian Press, Stockbridge, Massachusetts.

Elizabeth Ann Seton: a Self Portrait, Sister Marie Celeste, S. C, 1986, Franciscan Marytown Press, Libertyville, Illinois.

Encountering Mary, Sandra Zimdars-Swartz, 1992, Princeton University Press, Princeton, New Jersey.

Facts About Luther (The), Msgr. Patrick F. O'Hare, LL.D., 1916, originally by Fredrick Pustet Co., 1987, Tan Books Publishers, Inc., Rockford Illinois.

Fatima Prophecies: At the Doorstep of the World (The), Dr. Thomas W. Petrisko, 1998, St. Andrew's Productions, McKees Rocks, PA.

Fatima, Russia & Pope John Paul II, Timothy Tindal-Robertson, 1992, The Ravengate Press, Still River, Massachusetts.

Fatima in Lucia's Own Words, Sister Lucia's Memoirs, 1976, The Ravengate Press, Cambridge, Massachusetts.

Federal Reserve Conspiracy (The), Antony C. Sutton, 1995, CPA Book Publishers, Boring, Oregon.

Final Hour (The), Michael H. Brown, 1992, Faith Publishing Company, Milford, Ohio.

Final Warning: A History of the New World Order, David Allen Rivera, 2010, Progressive Press.

Forty Dreams of St. John Bosco, complied by Fr. J. Bacchiarello, S.D.B., 2012, Tan Books, Charlotte, North Carolina.

Freemasonry: Mankind's Hidden Enemy, Bro. Charles Madden, O.F.M.conv, 1995, Tan Books Publishers, Inc., Rockford, Illinois.

Gift of Prophecy (The), Rev. Robert DeGrandis S.S. J. 1984.

Great Encyclical Letters of Pope Leo XIII (The), Benziger Brothers, 1995, Tan Books Publishers, Inc., Rockford, Illinois.

Habsburgs-Embodying Empire (The), Andrew Wheatcroft, 1995, Penguin Books Ltd, London, England.

Holy Bible (The), Douay Rheims Version, Translated from the Latin Vulgate, Revised by Bishop Richard Challoner, 1749-1752, 1972, Tan Books.

Holy Shroud and Four Visions (The) , Rev. Patrick O' Connell, B.D.& Rev. Charles Carty, 1974, Tan Books Publishers, Inc., Rockford, Illinois.

House of Rothschild-Money's Prophets (The), Niall Ferguson, 1998, Penguin Books , New York, New York.

How the World Really Works, Alan B. Jones, 1996, ABJ Press, Paradise, California.

I See Far, A Friend of Medjugorje, 2004, Caritas of Birmingham, Sterrett, Alabama, St. James Publishing.

Life and Revelations of Anne Catherine Emmerich(The), (2 Volumes),Very Reverend Carl E. Schmoger, C.SS.R. , 1867, 1885, 1976, Tan Books and Publishers, Inc. Rockford, Illinois.

Life of Jesus Christ and Biblical Revelations (The), of Anne Catherine Emmerich, (4 volumes), Clemens Brentano, Very Reverend Carl E. Schmoger, C.SS.R. , 1986, Tan Books and Publishers, Inc. Rockford, Illinois.

Long Emergency (The): Surviving the End of Oil, Climate Change, and Other Converging Catastrophes of the Twenty-First Century, James Howard Kunstler, 2005, Grove Press, New York.

Marie-Julie Jahenny-The Breton Stigmatist, Marquis de La Franquerie, 1975, www. todayscatholicworld.com

Marx & Satan, Richard Wurmbrand, 1986, Living Sacrifice Book Company, Bartsville, Oklahoma.

Maria of Agreda–Mystical Lady in Blue, Marilyn H. Fedewa, 2009, University of New Mexico Press, Albuquerque, New Mexico.

Mary of the Americas: Our Lady of Guadalupe, Christopher Rengers, OFM Cap, 1989, Alba House, New York.

Mary's Triumph, Revelations to Mother Elena Patriarca Leonardi, (1983) House of the Kingdom of God and Reconciliation of Souls, Rome, Italy.

Masonry Unmasked: An Insider Reveals The Secrets of The Lodge, John Salza, 2006, Our Sunday Visitor Publishing Division, Huntington, Indiana.

Melanie and the Story of Our Lady of La Salette, Mary Alice Dennis, 1995, Tan Books Publishers, Inc., Rockford, Illinois.

Memoirs Illustrating the History of Jacobinsim, 1741-1818, Abbe Barruel, 1995, American Council on Economics and Society, Fraser, Michigan.

Miracle of the Illumination of all Consciences (The), Thomas W. Petrisko, 2000, St. Andrews Productions, McKees Rocks, PA.

More About Fatima, Rev J. Da Cruz C.S. Sp, 1975, U.S.A.

My Descent into Hell, Howard Storm, 2005, Doubleday, New York.

Mystical City of God (The), (4 Volumes), Mary of Agreda, 1914, translated by Rev. George J. Blatter, 2006 Tan Books. Rockford, Illinois

Mysteries, Marvels, Miracles in the Lives of the Saints, Joan Carroll Cruz, 1997, Tan Books Publishers, Inc., Rockford, Illinois.

Naked Capitalist (The), W. Cleon Skousen, 1970, Buccaneer Books, Cutchogue, New York.

Napoleon Bonaparte: An Intimate Biography, Vincent Cronin, 1972, William Morrow& company, Inc., New York.

New American Bible, Catholic Publishers Inc., 1971, Thomas Nelson Publishers, New York.

New Pearl Harbor, David Ray Griffin, 2004, Olive Branch Press, Northampton, Massachusetts.

New Pearl Harbor Revisited: 911, The Cover-up, and the Expose', David Ray Griffin, 2008, Olive Branch Press, Northampton, Massachusetts.

9/11 Mystery Plane and the Vanishing of America, Mark H. Gaffney, 2008, Trine Day LLC, Walterville, Oregon.

None Dare Call It Conspiracy, Gary Allen, and Larry Abraham, 1971, Buccaneer Books, Cutchogue, New York.

Our Lady Comes to Garabandal–Including Conchita's Diary, Father Joseph A. Pelletier, A.A., 1979, Assumption Publication, Worcester, Massachusetts.

Our Lady of America, Sister Mildred Mary, 1993, Our Lady of America Center, Fostoria, Ohio.

Our Lady of Good Success, Marian Therese Horvat, Ph. D., 2009, Tradition In Action, Inc., Los Angeles, CA.

Our Lady of Guadalupe and Saint Juan Diego-The Historical Evidence, Eduardo Chavez, 2006, Rowman & Littlefield Publishers, Inc.

Our Lady of Guadalupe and the Conquest of Darkness, Warren H. Carroll, 1983, Christendom Press, Front Royal, Virginia.

Our Lady of Kibeho, Immaculee Ilibagiza with Steve Erwin, 2010, Hay House, Inc., New York, City.

Queen of Peace Visits Medugorje (The), Joseph A. Pelletier, A. A., 1985, Assumption Publication, Worcester, MA.

Queen of the Cosmos, Jan Connell, 1990, Revised 2004, Paraclete Press, Brewster, Massachusetts.

Paul VI Beatified?, Fr. Luigi Villa, 2009, The Apostolate of Our Lady of Good Success, Oconomowoc, WI.

Pere Lamy, Comte Paul Biver, 1973, Tan Books Publishers, Inc., Rockford, Illinois.

Perfectibilists: The 18th Century Bavarian Order of the Illuminati, Terry Melanson, 2009, Trine Day, Walterville, Oregon.

Prophecies: The Chastisement and Purification, Reverend Albert J. Hebert S. M., 1986, Paulina, La.

Prophecies of Saint Malachy (The), Colin Smyth, 1969, commentary Peter Bander, 1973, Tan Books Publishers, Inc., Rockford, Illinois.

Prophecy for Today, Edward Connor, 1984, Tan Books and Publishers, Inc. Rockford, Illinois.

Prophets and Our Times (The), Rev. R. Gerald Culleton, 1941,1943, 1974, Tan Books Publishers, Inc., Rockford, Illinois.

Ratzinger Report (The), Cardinal Joseph Ratzinger with Vittorio Messori, 1985, Ignatius Press, San Francisco, California.

Reign of Antichrist (The), Rev. R. Gerald Culleton, 1974, Tan Books Publishers, Inc., Rockford, Illinois.

Renewal and the Powers of Darkness, Cardinal Leo-Joseph Suenens, 1983, Servant Books, Ann Arbor, Michigan.

Revelations of St. Bridget, excerpts from the 1611 Antwerp edition, 1965, Academy Library Guild, 1984, Tan Books Publishers, Inc., Rockford, Illinois.

Rule by Secrecy, Jim Marrs, 2001, Harper Collins, New York, New York.

School of Darkness, Bella V. Dodd, Ex-Communist, 1954, http://genis.cogia.net

Secret of the Rosary (The), St. Louis Mary De Montfort, 1995, Montfort Publications, Bay Shore, New York.

Secrets, Chastisement, and Triumph-Of the Two Hearts of Jesus and Mary (The), Kelly Bowring, 2010, Two Hearts Press, LLC Cumming, GA.

Secrets of the Federal Reserve-The London Connection (The), Eustace Mullins, 1991, Bridger House Publishers, Carson City, Nevada.

She Went in Haste to the Mountain, 2003, Eusebio Garcia de Pesquera O.F.M. (3 volumes) St. Joseph Publications, Cleveland, Ohio.

Sister Mary of the Cross-Shepherdess of La Salette, Fr. Paul Gouin, The 101 Foundation, Asbury, New Jersey.

Spark From Heaven, Mary Craig, 1991, Ave Maria Press, Notre Dame, Indiana.

Spear of Destiny (The), Trevor Ravenscroft, 1973, Weiser Books, San Francisco, California.

St. Michael and the Angels, 1983, by approved Sources, Tan Books and Publishers, Inc., Rockford, Illinois.

Sun Danced at Fatima (The), Joseph A. Pelletier, A. A., 1983, Image Books, Garden City, New York.

Therese Neumann-Mystic and Stigmatist, Adalbert Albert Vogl, 1987, Tan Books Publishers, Inc., Rockford, Illinois.

Thunder of Justice-the Warning, the Miracle, the Chastisement, the Era of Peace (The), Ted & Maureen Flynn, 1993, MaxKol Communications, Inc.

Thunder of Justice-the Warning, the Miracle, the Chastisement, the Era of Peace (The), Ted & Maureen Flynn, 2010, MaxKol Communications, Inc.

Tragedy & Hope, Carroll Quigley, 1966, The Macmillan Company, New York.

Trial, Tribulation & Triumph-Before, During, and After Antichrist, Desmond A. Birch, 1996, Queenship Publishing, Santa Barbara, California.

True Story of the Bilderberg Group (The), Daniel Estulin, 2009, Trine Day, Walterville, Oregon.

Unseen Hand (The), A. Ralph Epperson, 2010, Publius Press, Tucson, Arizona.

Vision (The), David Wilkerson, 1974, Pyramid Publications, Dallas, Texas.

Visionaries, Mystics and Stigmatists, Bob and Penny Lord, 1995, www.bobandpennylord.com.

Visions of the Children (The), Janice T. Connell, 2007, St. Martin's Griffin. New York.

Voices, Visions and Apparitions, Michael Freze, S.F.O., 1993, Our Sunday Visitor Publishing Division, Huntington, Indiana.

Wall Street and the Bolshevik Revolution, Antony Sutton, 1974, Buccaneer Books, Inc.,Cutchogue, New York.

Wall Street and the Rise of Hitler, Antony Sutton, 1976, Buccaneer Books, Inc.,Cutchogue, New York.

We Are Warned: The Prophecies of Marie-Julie Jahenny, complied, translated, and edited by E. A. Bucchianeri, 2011, www.scribd.com

Words from Heaven, A Friend of Medjugorje, 2006, Caritas of Birmingham, Sterrett, Alabama.

Works of the Seraphic Father St. Francis of Assisi, St. Francis of Assisi, 1882, R. Washbourne.

World Revolution: The Plot Against Civilization, Nesta H. Webster, 1921, Constable and Company Ltd, London, England.

Acknowledgements & References

Note: All biblical quotes are from: **The New American Bible (1970), Catholic Publishers Inc. 1971, Thomas Nelson Publishers, New York, and will be used unless otherwise stated.
**Note: The Douay Rheims Version of the Holy Bible translated from the Latin Vulgate and revised by Bishop Richard Challoner, 1749-1752, (1972) Tan Books, will be referred to occasionally.
** Note: There are many points of knowledge or information confirmed by the Holy Spirit, to the author, in this work. The author considers this knowledge or information from the Holy Spirit as a reference. It will be noted as 'Author anointed' and then the statement will follow.
** Note: Brackets like this one [...] are used by the original authors in quotes. Brackets like this one (...) by the author of this work.

Section I
An Awakening

Chapter 1---Beginnings---
Author's information

Chapter 2---Saint Bridget of Sweden---
Author's information
The Final Hour by Michael H. Brown
The Holy Shroud and Four Visions by Tan
    Books and Publishers.

Chapter 3---Prophecies of Saint Bridget---
Revelations of St. Bridget, excerpts from
    Antwerp edition 1611
www.spiritdaily.net/Prophecy-seers/bridget.htm
1, 2, Birgitta of Sweden-Life and Selected
    Revelations by Albert Ryle Kezel, p 72, 78-
    79
3 Butler's Lives of the Saints by Father Herbert
    Thurston, S. J. and Donald Attwater, vol.
    4, p 56
4 The Reign of Antichrist by Rev. R. Gerald
    Culleton, p 138-139
5 Author anointed; the Holy Spirit confirms to
    me Mary, Mother of Jesus accomplishing
    a victory against this Iniquity of Evil that
    brings Satan's influence on this earth to a
    standstill.
6 The Christian Trumpet by Fr. Gaudentius
    Rossi Pellegrino, p 23

Chapter 4---Prophecies of Catholic Saints---
1 Catholic Prophecy by Yves Dupont p 36
2, 3, The Prophets and Our Times by Rev. R.
    Gerald Culleton, p 127-128, 128-130
4, 5, 6, Catholic Prophecy by Yves Dupont, p
    16, 114, 23

7, 8, 9, Trial, Tribulation & Triumph by
    Desmond A. Birch, p 327, 326, 326
10 Catholic Prophecy by Yves Dupont, p 113

**Chapter 5---Holzhauser's Prophecies and the
    Seven Church Ages---**
1 Author anointed; Our Lord confirms the
    summary of the seven periods of the history
    of the Church.
2 Bartholomew Holzhauser–Catholic
    Encyclopedia Vol. 7, 1910–www.newadvent.
    org/cathen/07439b.htm
**Seven Church Ages-Venerable Holzhauser
    (summary)**
3 Bartholomew Holzhauser–Catholic
    Encyclopedia Vol. 7, 1910–www.newadvent.
    org/cathen/07439b.htm
4 Author anointed; Our Lord confirms this
    summary to me in two places. The Holy
    Spirit is a direct reference for information in
    this work.
Holzhauser's Prophecies
5 The Prophets and Our Times by Rev. R.
    Gerald Culleton, p 172
6 "Interpretatio Apocalypsis" from
    Bartholomew Holzhauser, 1850, p 68-69/
    Trial, Tribulation & Triumph by Desmond A.
    Birch, p 331,332, 337
7 Venerable Bartholomew Holzhauser Visions
    1646/ www.catholicrevelations.org
8 Prophecy for Today by Edward Connor, p 35
9 Catholic Prophecy, p 40
10 Bartholomew Holzhauser Visions 1646/
    http://www.catholicrevelations.org/PR/
    ven%20bartholomew%20holzhauser.htm
11 Bartholomew Holzhauser–Catholic
    Encyclopedia Vol. 7, 1910–www.newadvent.
    org/cathen/07439b.htm

Chapter 6---Birth Pangs---
1 This explanation of the birth pangs of the Church ages was confirmed by the Holy Spirit several times as I worked on it, on May 9, 2009.

Chapter 7---The Fifth Church Age--- (1520 to 2038)
Catholic Encyclopedia 1910
www.thelatinlibrary.com
1 www.medjugorje.ws/en/apparitions/docs-medjugorje-apparitions/
Marian Apparitions
The Last Secret by Michael H. Brown
2 The Secret of the Rosary by St. Louis De Montfort, p 18
3 The Fatima Prophecies: At the Doorstep of the World by Thomas W. Petrisko, Fr. Rene Laurentin, Michael J. Fontecchio, Introduction, p xvii
4 The Ratzinger Report by Vittorio Messori, p 111-112
5 Author anointed; these messages bring us to a fuller understanding of what is going to take place in the near future.
Marian Apparitions (summary)
6 www.catholic.org/clife/mary/app.php?id=13
7 Our Lady Comes to Garabandal by Fr. Joseph A. Pelletier, A. A., p 176
8 www.pedroregis.com/english/mensagens_ing.php
Mystery of Iniquity
9 Douay Rhiems Bible revised by Bishop Richard Challoner

Section II
The Fifth Church Age Begins

Chapter 8 ---The Downward Spiral---
Pope Leo X
Catholic Encyclopedia, Vol. 9, 1910- www.newadvent.org/cathen/09162a.htm
Reign of Charles V
www.1911catholicencyclopedia.org/Charles_V_of_the_Holy_Roman_Empire
Martin Luther
The Facts About Luther by Msgr. Patrick F. O'Hare
'Martin Luther', Catholic Encyclopedia Vol. 9, 1910- www.newadvent.org/cathen/09438b.htm
'History of the Printing Press'- www.ideafinder.com/history/inventions/printpress
www.staycatholic.com/indulgences
www.italyheaven.co.uk/rome/scalasanta.html

1, 2, 3, Martin Luther, Catholic Encyclopedia vol. 9, 1910
4 Ender, Briefwechsel, III p 208, Martin Luther, Catholic Encyclopedia vol. 9, 1910
5, 6, from: The Facts About Luther by MSGR. Patrick F. O'Hare, LLD, p 71,72
7 Schreckenbach,"Luther u. der Bauernkrieg", p 44, / Catholic Encyclopedia vol. 9, 1910
8 Martin Luther, Catholic Encyclopedia vol. 9, 1910
9 Author anointed; the reformation brought a triumph of the temporal power over the spiritual.
10, 11, 12, 13, 14, 15, 16, 17, Martin Luther, Catholic Encyclopedia vol. 9, 1910
King Henry VIII
'Henry VIII', Catholic Encyclopedia Vol. 7, 1910, www.newadvent.org/cathen/07222a.htm
'The Life of King Henry VIII', 11th edition, vol. XIII Cambridge University, 1910
Encyclopedia Britannia/www.luminarium.org/renlit/tudorbio.htm
Council of Trent
Catholic Encyclopedia, http://www.newadvent.org/cathen/15030c.htm

Chapter 9---The Woman Clothed with the Sun---
Our Lady of Guadalupe and the Conquest of Darkness by Warren H. Carroll
Our Lady of Guadalupe
Our Lady of Guadalupe and Saint Juan Diego by Eduardo Chavez, p 9-30
Mary of the Americas-Our Lady of Guadalupe by Christopher Rengers, O.F.M. Cap, p 83-94

1, 2, "Our Lady of Guadalupe and the Conquest of Darkness" by Warren H. Carroll, p 99-100, 101
3 Mother of Death, Mother of Rebirth, The Virgin of Guadalupe-Journal of the American Academy of Religion, 1988, Vol. 56, issue 1, p 25-50
4 www.sancta.org
Battle of Lepanto
www.ewtn.com/library/mary/olislam.htm
5 www.aquinaandmore.com/catholic-articles/About-the-Battle-of-Lepanto/article/137
Our Lady of Good Success
www.spiritdaily.com/goodsuccess1.htm
6 Author anointed; Our Lord confirms Mariana dies twice before the final time.
7, 8, Our Lady of Good Success-Prophecies for Our Times Marian Therese Horvat, Ph. D p 33, 33

9, 10, The Admirable Life of Mother Mariana Vol. 2 by Fr. Manuel Sousa Pereira, p 21-22, 22-23

11 The Admirable Life of Mother Mariana, Vol. 2 by Fr. Manuel Sousa Pereira, p 23, 39

12 The Admirable Life of Mother Mariana Vol. 2 by Fr. Manuel Sousa Pereira, p 210, 211, 212, 213

13 Our Lady of Good Success-Prophecies for Our Times by Marian Therese Horvat, Ph. D p 63

Mary of Agreda

The Mystical City of God by Mary of Agreda

Maria of Agreda: Mystical Lady in Blue by Marilyn H. Fedewa, www.newmexicohistory.org/filedetails.php?fileID=485

Margaret Mary Alacoque

St. Margaret Mary Alacoque-Catholic Encyclopedia-www.newadvent.org/cathen/09653a.htm

www.ewtn.com/library/mary/margmary.htm

14 Visionaries, Mystics and Stigmatists by Bob & Penny Lord, p 208

Chapter 10---Secret Sects–Freemasonry and Conspiracies---

Code of the Illuminati by Abbe Augustin Barruel

Freemasonry: Mankind's Hidden Enemy by Bro. Charles Madden O. F. M. http://www.thirdorderofsaintdominic.org/Freemasonry.html

Encyclicals on Freemasonry, www.Vatican.va

Proofs of a Conspiracy by John Robinson

University of Ingolstadt/Catholic Encyclopedia

House of Rothschild-Money's Prophets by Niall Ferguson

Freemasonry Unmasked by John Salza

The Deadly Deception by Jim Shaw

1 Catholic Encyclopedia, www.newadvent.org/cathen/09771a.htm/ Masonry [Freemasonry]

2, 3, 4, World Revolution: The Plot Against Civilization by Nesta H. Webster, p 6, 22, 23

5 Memoirs Illustrating the History of Jacobinism by Abbe Augustin Barruel, p 588

6, 7, 8, World Revolution: The Plot Against Civilization by Nesta H. Webster, p 17, 17, 17-18

9 Edinburg Review-Illuminism and the French Revolution, p 57 (July 1906)

10 Perfectibilists: The 18th Century Bavarian Order of the Illuminati by Terry Melanson, p 22-23

11, 12, 13, Final Warning-A History of the New World Order by David Allen Rivera, p 25, 25-26, 25

14 Anointed Oct 20, 2011; Our Lord confirmed to me the connection of Illuminati taking advantage of the lower level Freemasons. This quote confirms the connection between Freemasonry and Illuminati.

15, 16, World Revolution: The Plot Against Civilization by Nesta H. Webster, p 15, 20

17 Catholic Prophecy by Yves Dupont, p 59

Age of Enlightenment

The Age of Enlightenment: the Eighteenth Century Philosophers by Isaiah Berlin

The French Revolution (1789-1802)

The Days of the French Revolution by Christopher Hebert

Perfectibilists-The 18th Century Bavarian Order of the Illuminati by Terry Melanson

18 http://europeanhistory.about.com/od/thefrenchrevolution/a/hfr3_2.htm

19 Secret societies now called Globalist

20, 21, 22, Rule of Secrecy by Jim Marrs, p 222, 227, 222

23, 24, World Revolution: The Plot Against Civilization by Nesta H. Webster, p 31, 31

25 Author anointed Feb. 26, 2014; they (Globalists) have a plan in operation, carried on right up to the present moment–the **systematic attempt** to create grievances in order to exploit the people.

26 Rule by Secrecy by Jim Marrs, p 224

27, 28, World Revolution: The Plot Against Civilization by Nesta H. Webster, p 31, 32

29 Rule by Secrecy by Jim Marrs, p 225

30 Final Warning–A History of the New World Order by David Allen Rivera, p 51

31 Rule by Secrecy by Jim Marrs, p 224

32 World Revolution: The Plot Against Civilization by Nesta H. Webster, p 41- 42

33 Rule by Secrecy by Jim Marrs, p 227

34 Final Warning–A History of the New World Order by David Allen Rivera, p 51

35, 36, 37, 38, World Revolution: The Plot Against Civilization by Nesta H. Webster, p 47-48, 48-49, 49, 49

39, 40, Catholic Prophecy by Yves Dupont, p 40, 53

41 The Prophets and Our Times by Rev. R. Gerald Culleton, p 204

Napoleon and the Republic

Napoleon Bonaparte-An Intimate Biography by Vincent Cronin

Encyclopedia Britannica
1911-www.1911encyclopedia.org
Napoleon-I
http://www.eupedia.com/europe/frankish_
influence_modern_europe.shtml
42 Final Warning–A History of the New World
Order by David Allen Rivera, p 68

Chapter 11---Our Lady's Call for Prayer
Warriors---
1 The Prophets and our Times by Rev. R.
Gerald Culleton, p 173
St. Louis De Montfort
The Secret of the Rosary by St. Louis De
Montfort
2 Catholic Prophecy by Yves Dupont, p 33
Anne Catherine Emmerich
The Life and Revelations of Anne Catherine
Emmerich, arranged and edited by the Very
Rev. Carl E. Schmoger, C.SS.R (2 Volumes)
3 The Life of Jesus Christ and Biblical
Revelations from visions of Anne Catherine
Emmerich recorded by Clemens Brentano,
edited by the Very Rev. Carl E. Schmoger,
C.SS.R., Vol. 4, p 354
Our Lady of the Miraculous Medal
4 Catherine Laboure: Visionary of the
Miraculous Medal by Fr. Rene Laurentin, p
16-17
5, 6, 7, 8, Saint Catherine Laboure of the
Miraculous Medal by Fr. Joseph I. Dirvin,
C.M., p 50, 82, 83, 84-85
9, 10, 11, Saint Catherine Laboure of the
Miraculous Medal by Fr. Joseph I. Dirvin,
C.M., p 86, 94, 94
Our Lady of La Salette
Encountering Mary by Sandra L. Zimdars-
Swartz, p 165-189
The Day Will Come by Michael H. Brown, p
343
www.catholicapologetics.info/catholicteaching/
privaterevelation/lasalet.html;
www.sspxasia.com/Newsletters/2003/Jul-dec/
Secret_of_La_Salette.htm
12, 13, Sister Mary of the Cross–Shepherdess
of La Salette, by Fr. Paul Gouin, p 63, 63-64
14 Author anointed February 15, 2011; Our
Lord confirms the authenticity of this
edition.
15 The 1879 edition of the message of Our
Lady of La Salette by Melanie Calvat with
imprimatur by Mgr. Bishop of Lecce, France
/ Sister Mary of the Cross–Shepherdess of La
Salette by Fr. Paul Gouin, p 64-67

16 http://www.catholicapologetics.info/
catholicteaching/privaterevelation/lasalet.
html
17 Melanie and the Story of La Salette by Mary
Alice Dennis, p 65
18 World Revolution: The Plot Against
Civilization by Nesta H. Webster, p 157

Chapter 12---The Illusion of Karl Marx---
1, 2, 3, 4, 5, 6, Marx & Satan by Richard
Wurmbrand, p 11, 12, 12, 13, 16, 16
7, 8, 9, 10, 11, 12, Marx & Satan by Richard
Wurmbrand, p 18, 19, 20, 20, 20-21, 21
13 Final Warning–A History of the New World
Order by David Allen Rivera, p 211
14 Marx & Satan by Richard Wurmbrand, p
37
15, 16, 17, Final Warning–A History of the
New World Order by David Allen Rivera, p
211, 212, 213

Chapter 13---Our Lady of Lourdes --- (1858)
1, 2, 3, 4, 5, 6, Saint Bernadette Soubirous
1844-1879 by Abbe Francois Trochu p 45,
47, 54, 54, 57, 59
7 Bernadette Speaks: A Life of St. Bernadette
Soubirous in her Own Words by Fr. Rene
Laurentin, p 34
8 Saint Bernadette Soubirous 1844-1879 by
Abbe Francois Trochu, p 59
9, 10, www.catholic.org/clife/mary/app.
php?id=13
11 Saint Bernadette Soubirous 1844-1879 by
Abbe Francois Trochu, p 69
12 www.catholic.org/clife/mary/app.php?id=13
13, 14, 15, St. Bernadette Soubirous 1844-
1879 by Abbe Francois Trochu, p 96-97,
103, 105
16 www.catholic.org/clife/mary/app.php?id=13,
conversation between the priest and
Bernadette.
17 St. Bernadette Soubirous 1844-1879 by
Abbe Francois Trochu, p 126
18, 19, www.catholic.org/clife/mary/app.
php?id=13, conversation between the priest
and Bernadette.
20, 21, 22, 23, 24, St. Bernadette Soubirous
1844-1879 by Abbe Francois Trochu, p 130,
135, 135, 140, 156
25 www.catholic.org/clife/mary/app.php?id=13,
conversation between Our Lady and
Bernadette.
26 St. Bernadette Soubirous 1844-1879 by
Abbe Francois Trochu, p 158

Chapter 14---Demons Unloosed From Hell---
Marx and Satan by Richard Wurmbrand
1 Sister Mary of the Cross–Shepherdess of La
  Salette by Fr. Paul Gouin, p 65
2 The Life of Jesus Christ and Biblical
  Revelations from Anne Catherine Emmerich
  by Clemens Brentano, edited by Very Rev.
  Carl E. Schmoger, C.SS.R.,vol. 4, p 354
3 http://www.traditioninaction.org/SOD/
  j141sdQueenofAngels_8-02.htm
Pope Leo XIII–Vision of God and Satan
4 The Secrets, Chastisement, and Triumph by
  Kelly Bowring, p 27-28
5 Begone Satan by Carl Vogal, p 23
6 St. Michael and the Angels by Approved
  Sources, p 104
7 An Exorcist Tells His Story by Gabriele
  Amorth, p 39

Section III
Satan's Extended Reign

Chapter 15---The Twentieth Century Begins---
Death by Government by R. J. Rummel
1 Tragedy and Hope by Dr. Carroll Quigley,
  p 950
2 The Naked Capitalist by W. Cleon Skousen,
  p 6
  The Deception of Communism
3, 4, Marie-Julie Jahenny-the Breton Stigmatist
by Marquis de la Franquerie, p 26-27, 28-29 5
The Admirable Life of Mother Mariana vol.
  II by Father Manuel Sousa Pereira, p 269
6 www.essan.org/Prophecy/catholic%20
  Prophecy/zukunft.htm
7 The Prophets and Our Times by Rev. R.
  Gerald Culleton, p 148-149
  Shadow Government Above Governments
How the World Really Works by Alan B. Jones
  Council on Foreign Relations
  Brotherhood of Darkness by Dr. Stanley
  Monteith
  None Dare Call it Conspiracy by Gary Allen
  and Larry Abraham
8, 9, www.sweetliberty.org/issues/shadow /
  cfrintro.htm/, (73), (1)
10 Rule by Secrecy by Jim Marrs, p 90
  The Federal Reserve
11 The Secrets of the Federal Reserve by
  Eustace Mullins, p 119
12 The Creature from Jekyll Island by G.
  Edward Griffin, p 23
13 Brotherhood of Darkness by Dr. Stanley
  Monteith, p 63
14 The Federal Reserve Conspiracy by Antony
  Sutton, p 113

World War I
The Unseen Hand by A. Ralph Epperson

Chapter 16---Our Lady of Fatima--- (1917)
Fatima, Russia & Pope John Paul by Timothy
  Tindal-Robertson,
The Fatima Prophecies–At the Doorstep of the
  World by Dr. Thomas W. Petrisko
More About Fatima by Rev. J. Da Cruz C. S.
  Sp.
1, 2, 3, The Sun Danced at Fatima by Fr.
  Joseph A. Pelletier A. A., p 18, 20, 22
4, 5, 6, All quotes from Fatima in Lucia's Own
  Words by Sister Lucia, p 159-161, 163-165,
  165-169
7 The Sun Danced at Fatima by Fr. Joseph A.
  Pelletier A. A., p 96-97, Note: p 227-228
8, 9, The Sun Danced at Fatima by Fr. Joseph
  A. Pelletier A. A., p 107, 108-109
10 Fatima in Lucia's Own Words by Sister
  Lucia, p 172
11 The Sun Danced at Fatima by Fr. Joseph A.
  Pelletier A. A., p 120-123
12, 13, from: Fatima in Lucia's Own Words by
  Sister Lucia, p 176, 167
14 Encountering Mary by Sandra Zimdars-
  Swartz, p 197
15 The Final Hour by Michael Brown, p 69
16 Fatima in Lucia's Own Words by Sister
  Lucia, p 167
17 wwvatican.va/roman_curia/congregations/
  cfaith/documents/rc_con_cfaith_doc_
  20000626_message-fatima_en.html
18 www.spiritdaily.net/johnston.htm
19 www.vatican.va/roman_curia/congregations/
  cfaith/documents/rc_con_cfaith_
  doc_20000626_message-fatima_en.html

Chapter 17---Fruit of the Federal Reserve and
  Wall Street---
Brotherhood of Darkness by Dr. Stanley
  Monteith
Who Financed the Rise of Communism?
Wall Street and the Bolshevik Revolution by
  Antony Sutton
None Dare Call It Conspiracy by Gary Allen
  and Larry Abraham, p 67-87, p 121
1 The Naked Capitalist by W. Cleon Skousen,
  p 1
2, 3, Brotherhood of Darkness by Dr. Stanley
  Monteith, p 69-70, 70
4, 5, Brotherhood of Darkness by Dr. Stanley
  Monteith, p 45, 46
Roaring '20s, Crash of '29, and Dirty '30s
Depression

6, 7, How the World Really Works by Alan B. Jones, p 8, 8
8 The Creature from Jekyll Island by G. Edward Griffin, p 495-496

Chapter 18----Divine Mercy----
Saint Faustina Kowalska
1, 2, Divine Mercy in My Soul by Sister Maria Faustina, p 19, 24
3 www.ewtn.com/library/papaldoc/jp2faust. htm
4, 5, 6, 7, 8, Divine Mercy in My Soul by Sister Maria Faustina, p 564, 424, 374, 420, 333
Therese Neumann
Therese Neumann–Mystic and Stigmatist by Adalbert Albert Vogl

Chapter 19--- War is Big Business---
1 The Prophets and Our Times by Rev. R. Gerald Culleton, p 225
2 Pere Lamy by Comte Paul Biver, p 142
World War II
Wall Street and the Rise of Hitler by Antony Sutton
Hitler
3 Author anointed March 17, 2011; Hitler believed the legend, the spear gives power to rule, for the one who possesses it.
4, 5, Spear of Destiny by Trevor Ravenscroft, p 7, 64

Chapter 20--- The Great Deception--- (1945-2016)
"Fifty or Sixty Years Before the Year 2000"
1 The Life of Jesus Christ and Biblical Revelations recorded by Clemens Brentano for Anne Catherine Emmerich, edited by the very Rev. Carl E. Schmoger, C. SS. R., p 353-354
2 www.fatima.ageofmary.com/apostasy/
3 The Admirable Life of Mother Mariana, vol. 2, by Fr. Manuel Sousa Pereira, p 21-22
United Nations
4, 5, 6, www.spiritdaily.org/singer.htm
Literal Fulfillment of Old Testament Prophecies
7 Prophecy for Today by Edward Connor, p 64
Rise of Suburbia
8 The End of Suburbia (video) by Barrie Zwicker, James Howard Kunstler, Peter Calthorpe and Gregory Green, at www. endofsuburbia.com
The Seton Prophecy
Elizabeth Ann Seton: a Self-Portrait by Sister Marie Celeste, S. C.

9 Air Waves from Hell by Father Frank Poncelet, p 93
The Deception of Television
10 Author anointed; going straight to the right side (alpha), which contains all the feelings and sensations.
11 I See Far by A Friend of Medjugorie, p 80-81
12, 13, 14, I See Far by A Friend of Medjugorie, p 63, 67-68, 69
15 www.medjugorje.com/medjugorje-messages/ search-essages/?q=Television&mainform=1

Chapter 21---Our Lady of Garabandal---(1961-1965)
Mary's First Message to the World
1 Our Lady Comes to Garabandal (including Conchita's Diary) by Fr. Joseph A. Pelletier, A. A., p 51
The Warning
2 The Miracle of the Illumination of All Consciences by Thomas W. Petrisko, p 35
3 Our Lady Comes to Garabandal by Fr. Joseph A. Pelletier A. A., p 148
4, 5, 6, The Final Hour by Michael H. Brown, p 135, 135-136, 135
7 Our Lady Comes to Garabandal by Fr. Joseph A. Pelletier A. A., p 147-150
8 The Thunder of Justice by Ted and Maureen Flynn, p 161
9 Garabandal Journal, July- September 1983, p 18
The Miracle Sign
10 Garabandal (Journal), January-March 1983
11, 12, Our Lady Comes to Garabandal by Fr. Joseph A. Pelletier A. A., p 160, 151
13 Garabandal (Journal), January-March 1983
14, 15, 16, Our Lady Comes to Garabandal by Fr. Joseph A. Pelletier A. A., p 151, 160, 160
All Those Present Will be Healed
17 Our Lady Comes to Garabandal by Fr. Joseph A. Pelletier A. A., p 151
The Chastisement
18, 19, Our Lady Comes to Garabandal by Fr. Joseph A. Pelletier A. A., p 162-163, 169
20, 21, 22, She Went in Haste to the Mountain by Eusebio Garcia de Pesquera, O. F. M., Part 2, p 405, 406-408, 410
Three More Popes Prophecy
23, 24, She Went in Haste to the Mountain by Eusebio Garcia de Pesquera, O. F. M., Part 3, p 564, 564
Unusual Blessings
25 Our Lady Comes to Garabandal by Fr. Joseph A. Pelletier A. A., p 70, 75

The Second Message to the World
26 Our Lady Comes to Garabandal by Fr.
  Joseph A. Pelletier A. A., p 176

Chapter 22---A Changing Church---
  Vatican II
www.ewtn.com/library/councils/v2all.htm
www.vatican.va/archive/hist_councils/
  ii_vatican_council/
The Charismatic Renewal
Charismatic Renewal in the Catholic Church
  by Rev. Vincent M. Walsh
Charisms and Charismatic Renewal: A biblical
  and theological Study by Francis A. Sullivan
  S. J.
Baptized in the Spirit and Spiritual gifts by
  Steve Clark
The Gift of Prophecy by Rev. Robert
  DeGrandis S.S.J.
1 www.catholiccharismatic.us/ccc/articles/
  Foster/Foster_011.html.
2 http://www.vatican.va/holy_father/john_
  paul_ii/speeches/1998/may/documents/hf-jp-
  ii_spe_19980530_riflessioni_en.html.
3 Renewal and the Powers of Darkness by
  Cardinal Leon-Joseph Suenens p xi
4 http://www.medjugorje.ws/en/messages/
  monthly/2000
5 http://www.medjugorje.ws/en/messages/
  monthly/2004
6 Author's info

Chapter 23---1960's Revolution and Rebellion

Holzhauser's Prophecies
1 Bartholomew Holzhauser 'Visions' 1646/
  http://www.catholicrevelations.org/
  PR/ven%20bartholomew%20holzhauser.htm
2, 3, Catholic Prophecy by Yves Dupont, p 39,
  39
4 Trial, Tribulation & Triumph by Desmond A.
  Birch, p 333
Politics and Greed
5 Presidential Inaugural Address January
  20,1961:
http://www.jfklibrary.org/Research/Research-
  Aids/Ready-Reference/JFK-Quotations/
  Inaugural-Address.aspx
6 Presidential Address before the American
  Newspaper Publishers Association, April
  27, 1961 from http://www.jfklibrary.org/
  Research/Research-Aids/JFK-Speeches/
  The-President-and-the-Press-Address-
  before-the-American-Newspaper-Publishers-
  Association.aspx

7 Author anointed; Our Lord confirming the
  work of the Globalists.

Chapter 24---Freemasonry in the Church---
Athanasius and the Church of our Time by Dr.
  Rudolf Graber
Paul VI Beatified? by Fr. Luigi Villa
1 Author anointed, March 24, 2014; the stress
  caused his premature death.
2 www.medjugorje.com
Communist Infiltration in the Church
AA-1025-The Memoirs of an Anti-Apostle by
  Marie Carre
School of Darkness by Bella Dodd
3 Christian Order Magazine (November 2000)
  http://www.christianorder.com/
  editorials/editorials_2000/editorials_nov00.
  html
4 The Latin Mass Magazine-summer 2001
  http://www.latinmassmagazine.com/
  articles/articles_2001_SU_Hildebran.html
5 Author anointed; an active communist
  became a Catholic priest.
6, 7, Mary's Triumph by Mother Elena
  Leonardi, p 110, 113
Prophecies Connecting the Secret Sect
8 Trial, Tribulation & Triumph by Desmond A.
  Birch, p 326
9 The Prophecies and Our Times by Rev. R.
  Gerald Culleton, p 179
10 The Life and the Revelations of Anne
  Catherine Emmerich by the Very Rev. Carl
  E. Schmoger, C.SS.R., vol. 2, p 281
11 The Christian Trumpet by Fr. Gaudentius
  Rossi Pellegrino, p 128
12 The Life and the Revelations of Anne
  Catherine Emmerich by the Very Rev. Carl
  E. Schmoger, C.SS.R., vol. 1, p 565
13 Prophecies: the Chastisement and
  Purification by Rev. Albert J. Hebert, S. M.,
  p 154
Persecution of Pope Paul VI
14, 15, Mary's Triumph by Mother Elena
  Leonardi, p 65, 77
16 Prophecies: the Chastisement and
  Purification by Rev. Albert J. Hebert, S. M.,
  p 131
17, 18, 19, 20, Mary's Triumph by Mother
  Elena Leonardi, p 119, 120, 124, 139
The Smoke of Satan has Entered the Church
21 http://www.vatican.va/holy_father/
  paul_vi/homilies/1972/documents/hf_p-vi_
  hom_19720629_it.html Note: The Italian
  translation is correct, the English is not
  complete on the Vatican web site.

The Implementation of Vatican II Gone Awry
22 Author anointed; Our Lord confirmed Ratzinger's words.
23 www.spiritdaily.com/ratzinger2.htm
24 In the Murky Waters of Vatican II by Atila Sinke Guimaraes, p 174, 177, 295
25, 26, Catholic Prophecy by Yves Dupont, p 53-54, 59
27 www.romancatholicism.org/vatican-ii.htm Address to the Chilean Episcopal Conference, 1988
Prophecies of Marie-Julie Jahenny
28 Author anointed March 16, 2010; to place prophecies of Marie-Julie Jahenny into this work.
29, 30, 31, 32, Marie-Julie Jahenny by Marquis de la Franquerie, p 34, 36, 36, 40
Prophecies at Akita
33 Trial, Tribulation & Triumph by Desmond A. Birch, p 397, 398

Chapter 25---"The Wicked Shall Prevail" ---
1 The Reign of Antichrist by Rev. R. Gerald Culleton, p 138-139
2, 3, 4, 5, 6, 7, Mary's Triumph by Mother Elena Leonardi, p 139, 152, 156, 157, 159, 161
8 Fatima, Russia & Pope John Paul II by Timothy Tindal-Robertson, p 11

Chapter 26 ---Our Lady of Medjugorje--- (June 24, 1981- 2016?)
1 Spark from Heaven by Mary Craig, p 13
2 The Queen of Peace visits Medugorje by Fr. Joseph A. Pelletier A. A., p 13
3, 4, 5, The Apparitions of Our Lady at Medjugorje by Fr. Svetozar Kraljevic O.F.M., p 8, 8, 8
6 The Queen of Peace visits Medugorje by Fr. Joseph A. Pelletier A. A., p 15
7, 8, 9, 10, The Apparitions of Our Lady at Medjugorje by Fr. Svetozar Kraljevic O.F.M., p 13, 13, 16, 17,
11 The Queen of Peace visits Medugorje by Fr. Joseph A. Pelletier A. A. O.F.M., p 20
12, 13, 14, The Apparitions of Our Lady at Medjugorje by Fr. Svetozar Kraljevic O.F.M., p 18, 24, 24
15 The Queen of Peace visits Medjugorje by Fr. Joseph A. Pelletier A. A., p 25
16 Apparitions of Our Lady at Medjugorje by Fr. Svetozar Kraljevic O.F.M., p 24
17, 18, 19, 20, 21, The Queen of Peace visits Medugorje by Fr. Joseph A. Pelletier A. A., p 25, 25, 28, 28-29, 32

22, 23 Spark From Heaven by Mary Craig, p 46, 47
24, 25, The Queen of Peace visits Medugorje by Fr. Joseph A. Pelletier A. A., p 32, 36
Father Jozo Zovko
26, 27, 28, 29, 30, 31, Spark From Heaven by Mary Craig, p 39, 39, 40, 40, 41, 41
32, 33, The Apparitions of Our Lady at Medjugorje by Fr. Svetozar Kraljevic O.F.M., p 41-42, 43
34 www.medjugorje.org/msg81.htm
Ten Secrets of Medjugorje
35 The Final Hour by Michael Brown, p 217
36 www.medjugorje.com
37 The Apparitions of Our Lady at Medjugorje by Fr. Svetozar Kraljevic O.F.M., p 127
38 www.medjugorje.com
39 The Day Will Come by Michael H. Brown, p 223
40 www medjugorje.org/msg81.htm
41, 42, 43, 44, www.medjugorje.com
45 The Thunder of Justice by Ted & Maureen Flynn, p 208
46 The Apparitions of Our Lady at Medjugorje by Fr. Svetozar Kraljevic O.F.M., p 128
47 The Queen of Peace Visits Medugorje by Fr. Joseph A. Pelletier A. A., p 139
48, 49, The Visions of the Children by Janice Connell, p 49, 49-50
50 The Queen of Peace visits Medugorje by Fr. Joseph A. Pelletier A. A., p 139
51, 52, www.medjugorje.com/ medjugorje/the10secrets
Defeat of the Soviet Union
53 The Thunder of Justice by Ted & Maureen Flynn, p 198
54 The Final Hour by Michael H. Brown, p 217
55, 56, 57, 58, Words from Heaven by A Friend of Medjugorje, p 263, 191, 281, 287
Heaven, Hell, and Purgatory
59 The Final Hour by Michael H. Brown, p 217
60, 61, 62, Queen of the Cosmos by Janice Connell, p 67-68, 130, 29
63, 64, The Visions of the Children by Janice Connell, p 79-80, 126
65 Queen of the Cosmos by Janice Connell, p 71
66 The Visions of the Children by Janice Connell, p 48

Chapter 27---John Paul II Consecrates Russia---
Fatima, Russia & Pope John Paul II by Timothy Tindal-Robertson

Fatima in Lucia's Own Words by Sister Lucia's Memoirs.
1 www.ewtn.com//library/papaldoc/consecra. htm#john%20paul%2011,%201984
2 www.spiritdaily.net/fatimasecretrussia.htm
3 The Fatima Prophecies: At the Doorstep of the World by Dr. Thomas W. Petrisko, p 318
4 www.medjugorje.org/msg82.ht
Significance of Marian Feast Days
http://news.nationalpost.com/2013/03/17/ the-walk-that-changed-the-world/, for Gorbachev.
www.miraclehunter.com/marian_apparitions/ approved_apparitions/betania/7,
www.medjugorje.com /John Paul II
5 www.medjugorje.com /20 years of Apparitions
6 Words from Heaven by A Friend of Medjugorje, p 134
7 www.ewtn.com/expert/answers/ FatimaConsecreation.htm
8 Words from Heaven by A Friend of Medjugorje, p 160
9 www.medjugorje.com /20 years of Apparitions
10, 11, Words from Heaven by A Friend of Medjugorje, p 261, 226
12 www.medjugorje.com /20 years of Apparitions
13, 14, Words from Heaven by A Friend of Medjugorje, p 281, 281
15,16, www.medjugorje.com /20 years of Apparitions
Understanding the True Face of Communism
17, 18, Prophecies: the Chastisement and Purification by Rev. Albert J. Hebert, S. M., p 119, 122

Chapter 28---Tears of the Virgin Mary---
Bleeding Hands and Weeping Stone by Elizabeth Ficocelli.
www.visionsofjesuschrist.com/weeping149.htm
1 www.vatican.va/holy_father/john_paul_ii/ speeches/1994/november/index.htm
2 www.mysticsofthechurch.com/2011/09/ blessed-elena-aiello-mystic-stigmatic.html
3 Mary's Triumph by Mother Elena Leonardi p 83
4 Prophecies–the Chastisement and Purification by Rev. Albert J. Hebert, S. M., p 85
Our Lady of Kibeho, Rwanda
The Thunder of Justice by Ted & Maureen Flynn, revised and updated
5, 6, 7, Our Lady of Kibeho by Immaculee Ilibagiza with Steve Erwin, p 36, 132, 148-149

8 Journal of 'Michael'/ www.michaeljournal. org/kibeho.htm
Our Lady of Peace to Pedro Regis at Anguera, Brazil
http://www.pedroregis.com/english/historico. php for history and prophecies in English.
http://www.apelosurgentes.com.br/mensagens_ por.php. Many prophecies were translated from Portuguese to English.
9 Author anointed Dec. 23, 2010; legitimate prophecies from Our Lady of Peace to Pedro Regis at Anguera, Brazil.
10, 11, www.pedroregis.com/english/historico. php
12 Author anointed June 9, 2012; Our Lady of Peace at Anguera, Brazil is speaking about future events.
13 http://www.pedroregis.com/english/ mensagens_ing.php
14, 15, 16, http://www.apelosurgentes.com.br/ arquivos/mensagens/2005.pdf
17 http://www.apelosurgentes.com.br/arquivos/ mensagens/2006.pdf
18, 19, 20, 21, 22, 23, 24, http://www. pedroregis.com/english/mensagens_ing.php
25 Author anointed June 2012; messages were transmitted from 2005 until 2011 about the earthquake that occurred in Japan.
26, 27, http://www.pedroregis.com/english/ mensagens_ing.php

Chapter 29--- Earthly Concerns---
Global Dimming
http://www.collapsenet.com/free-resources/ essential-voices/item/8096 (Global-dimming BBC-horizon-documentary) http://www. youtube.com/watch?v=nmywf7a9OII
www.guardian.couk/science/2003/dec/18/ science.research.1
http://www.guardian.co.uk/environment/2012/ may/11/global-dimming-pollution
http://news.bbc.co.uk/2/hi/science/ nature/4171591.stm
Decreased Pan Evaporation
www.sciencemag.org (Decreased pan evaporation)
http://journals.ametsoc.org/doi/pdf/10.1175/ JCLI4181.1 (American Meteorological Society, 'The Dominant Factor Affecting Pan Evaporation Trends in Australia')
Global Weather Extremes
1 https://report.ipcc.ch/sr15/pdf/ r15_spm_final.pdf
1 https://climate.nasa.gov/causes/

1 https://www.climate4you.com/Sun.htm

2 https://co2coalition.org/

2 https://co2coalition.org/2017/04/10/a-swelling-volume-of-scientific-papers-now-forecasting-global-cooling-in-the-coming-decades/

Extreme Ocean Changes
http://nsidc.org/arcticseaicenews/
https://phys.org/news/2019-07-arctic-ice-loss-giant-south.html
http://nsidc.org/greenland-today/2019/07/a-record-melt-event-in-mid-june/

Ocean Pollution
https://science2017.globalchange.gov/chapter/13/
https://www.desmoinesregister.com/story/money/agriculture/2018/06/22/iowa-water-pollution-gulf-mexico-dead-zone-nitrogren-missouri-mississippi-river-quality-nirtate/697370002/https://www.cbc.ca/news/technology/billions-of-bits-of-plastic-in-arctic-waters-1.4079765
https://www.mpg.de/13655324/0702-mbio-064278-remote-but-remarkable-illuminating-the-smallest-inhabitants-of-the-largest-ocean-desert
Destruction of Coral Reefs and Fisheries http://abcnews.go.com/Technology/wirestory?id=10201140;
http://www.terradaily.com/reports/Oceans_On_

http://news.nationalgeographic.com/news/2003/05/0515_030515_fishdecline.html

Industrial Pollution Affecting People, Land, Water, and Air
http://www.sciencedaily.com/
The_Precipice_Of_Mass_Extinctionsan_And_Rise_Of_Slime_999html
releases/2007/11/071110081909.htm;
mercola.com
http://articles.mercola.com/sites/articles/archive/2009/01/01/males-of-all-species-are-becoming-more-female.aspx
http://www.theatlanticwire.com/
national/2013/03/half-all-us-rivers-are-too-polluted-our-health/63579/

Global Resource Depletion
Science alert.com.au/opinions-global-food-crisis/20101401-20498.html;
http://makewealthhistory.org/2010/10/12/peak-everything-global-resource-depletion- rates/
http://lifeofearth.org/environment/natural-resource-depletion
http://www.frackcheckwv.net/2013/02/21/new-reports-fracking-is-a-risky-short-term-bubble/
Wild Mammals and Birds Endangered
www.terradaily.com/2007080516103326.ngez8iq.html; www.breitart.com/article.php?id=081006114428.v3nn78li
www.msnbc.msn.com/id/26979274/ns/world_news-world_environment
http://www.sciencedaily.com/releases/2010/07/100712141851.htm
Agricultural Pollution
www.twilightearth.com/environment/report-monsanto-corn-causes-organ-damage-in-mammals/
http://www.environmentalhealthnews.org/ehs/news/roundup-weed-killer-is-toxic-to-human-cells.-study-intensifies-debate-over-inert-ingredients
http://www.huffingtonpost.com/2013/04/25/roundup-herbicide-health-issues-disease_n_3156575.html
Wakeup Call to Genetically Modified Foods
1 Author anointed March 8, 2010; GM grains and food products are causing disorders to the physical bodies of animals in labs and in the field.
http://www.foodconsumer.org/newsite/Safety/biotech/050920090819_chickens_not_fooled_by_GM_Crops
http://www.fourwinds10.com/siterun_data/science_technology/dna_gmo/news.php?q=1267294540
http://fwfarmonline.com.au/news/state/agribusiness-and-general/general/chefs-warn-of-gm-backlash.html
Bees Vanishing
http://earthhopenetwork.net/forum/showthread.php?tid=1201
www.wnd.com/index.php?fa=Page.printable&pageID=143737
www.fourwinds10.com/siterun_data/science_technology/dna_gmo/news.php?q=1269701013
http://www.clevelandleader.com/node/18301
www.nytimes.com/2013/03/29/science/earth/soaring-bee-deaths-in-2012-sound-alarm-on-malady.html?pagewanted=all&_r=0

2 Author anointed April 6, 2013;
Neonicotinoid insecticides are destroying
bee populations when pneumatic drills are
used at seeding time.

Blaming Everything but the sin of Mankind

Chapter 30----The World, Temptation, and the
Devil----
Declining Demographics in the Western World
http://www.dailymail.co.uk/news/
article-2179243/US-birthrate-plummets-
lowest-25-years.html
http://www.timescolonist.com/news/dwindling-
birth-rate-will-hurt-economy-expert-
says-1.3729
Same Sins of Civilizations Past
http://skipper59.blogspot.ca/2010/01/out-of-
control-consumerism-is-chief.html
http://www.guardian.co.uk/environment/2010/
jan/12/climate-change-greed-environment-
threat
http://www.lifesitenews.com/news/1.72-billion-
abortions-worldwide-in-the-last-40-years
1 Author anointed April 9, 2013; confirmed the
same patterns of change, when people turn
away from God.
The World Has Become Desolate
2 Author anointed May 9, 2012; our world
has become desolate, far from God, with no
future.
3 Voices, Visions, and Apparitions by Michael
Freze, S. F. O., p 173
4, 5, Prophecies: the Chastisement and
Purification by Rev. Albert J. Hebert, S. M.,
p 116, 117
6 Trial, Tribulation & Triumph by Desmond A.
Birch, p 389, 390
7 Prophecies: the Chastisement and Purification
by Rev. Albert J. Hebert, S. M., p 93
8, 9, Mary's Triumph by Mother Elena
Leonardi, p 87, 130, 131
10 www.medjugorje.com/medjugorje-
messages/25th-messages/?year=1991.
11 www.mysticsofthechurch.com/2011/09/
blessed-elena-aiello-mystic-stigmatic.html
12 http://www.pedroregis.com/english/
mensagens_ing.php
13 http://www.pedroregis.com/arquivos/
mensagens/ingles/Messages_of_1987_
and_1996.pdf
My Beloved Ones, I Plead With You
14 Prophecies: the Chastisement and
Purification by Rev. Albert J. Hebert, S. M.,
p 34, 35
15 Sister Mary of the Cross–Shepherdess of La
Salette by Fr. Paul Gouin, p 64

16 Marie-Julie Jahenny by Marquis de la
Franquerie, p 26-27
17 www.mysticsofthechurch.com/2011/09/
blessed-elena-aiello-mystic-stigmatic.html
18 Our Lady of America by Sister Mildred
Mary, p 33
19, 20, 21, Prophecies: the Chastisement and
Purification by Rev. Albert J. Hebert, S. M.,
p 27, 39, 39
22, 23, www.pedroregis.com/arquivos/
mensagens/ingles/Messages_of_1987_
and_1996.pdf
24 We Are Warned: The Prophecies of Marie-
Julie Jahenny by E. A. Bucchianeri, p 296
In Hell, It's Too Late
25 Voices, Visions and Apparitions by Michael
Freze, S.F. O., p 181
26 Divine Mercy in My Soul by Saint Maria
Faustina Kowalska, p 296-297
27 www.mysticsofthechurch.com/2011/09/
blessed-elena-aiello-mystic-stigmatic.html
28 Forty Dreams of St. John Bosco by St. John
Bosco, p 160
29, 30, Challoner Douay Rheims Bible
31 Voices, Visions and Apparitions by Michael
Freze, S.F. O. p 225
32 www.mysticsofthechurch.com/2011/09/
blessed-elena-aiello-mystic-stigmatic.html

Section IV
The Great Tribulation

The Great Tribulation
1 Crossing the Threshold of Hope by His
Holiness John Paul II, p 23
2 Prophecies: the Chastisement and Purification
by Rev. Albert J. Hebert, S. M., p 186
3 Farewell address, August 1976, of Cardinal
Karol Wojtyla, Eucharistic Congress,
Philadelphia, PA.
4 The Secrets, Chastisement, and Triumph of
the Two Hearts of Jesus and Mary by Kelly
Bowring, p 32-33
5 The Secrets, Chastisement, and Triumph of
the Two Hearts of Jesus and Mary by Kelly
Bowring, p 33

Chapter 31---Forty Years of Tribulation---
(2000-2040)

1 Author anointed May 12, 2003; Our Lord
confirmed to me, Charlie Johnston's
prophecies.
2 www.spiritdaily.net/johnston3.htm
3 Author anointed August 20, 2002; a very
difficult 40-year period has begun, starting
in 2000.

4 Voices, Visions, and Apparitions by Michael
  Freze, S.F.O., p 180
5 Sister Mary of the Cross–Shepherdess of La
  Salette by Fr. Paul Gouin, p 64, 65
6 www.mysticsofthechurch.com/2011/09/
  blessed-elena-aiello-mystic-stigmatic.html
7 www.medjugorjetoday.tv
8 Author anointed December 2012; All will be
  seen clearly in the rearview mirror.
Prophecies of Saint Malachy
Catholic Encyclopedia / Newadvent, 1913,
  Volume IX, p 473-474, 565
9, 10, The Prophecies of St. Malachy by Peter
  Bander, p 95-96
11 www.catholic-pages.com/grabbag/malachy.
  asp Prophecies in Latin and English.
**"I Did Not Come from Heaven for Your
Amusement"**
12 (3518), 13 (2842), http://www.pedroregis.
  com/english/mensagens_ing.php
14 (3207) http://www.apelosurgentes.com.br/
  arquivos/mensagens/2009.pdf
15 (3731) http://www.apelosurgentes.com.br/
  mensagens_ing.php?_pagi_pg=2
16 (3574), 17 (3256), 18 (3588), http://www.
  pedroregis.com/english/mensagens_ing.php

Chapter 32---The Secret Sect's New World Order---

None Dare Call It Conspiracy by Gary Allen
  and Larry Abraham
The Secrets of the Federal Reserve by Eustace
  Mullins
The Creature From Jekyll Island by G. Edward
  Griffin
http://ec.europa.eu/news/eu_explained/091201_
  en.htm
1 Author anointed; we are losing the rights and
  privileges that God has given us.
2 Final Warning: A History of the New World
  Order by David Allen Rivera, p 30
  3 Memoirs of David Rockefeller by David
  Rockefeller, p 405
The Bilderberg Group
The True Story of the Bilderberg Group by
  Daniel Estulin.
The Trilateral Commission
The Unseen Hand by A. Ralph Epperson p
  231-248
The True Story of The Bilderberg Group by
  Daniel Estulin, p 129-183
4 With No Apologies/ The Unseen Hand by A.
  Ralph Epperson, p 232

Controlling the Media for World Domination
5 www.newswithviews.com/Monteith/
  stanley107.htm/The New American
  (journal) of the John Birch Society February
  10, 2003, p 5
World Bank and International Monetary Fund
http://www.imf.org/external/np/exr/facts/
  imfwb.htm
http://www.globalexchange.org/resources/
  wbimf/facts
The Bohemian Grove
Bohemian Grove: Cult of Conspiracy by Mike
  Hanson
Dark Secrets: Inside the Bohemian Grove
  (video) by Alex Jones
www.thenewamerican.com/usnews/politics/
  item/9468-bohemian-grove-where-the-elite-
  meet-to-eat-and-conspire
www.ucsc.edu/whorulesamerica/power/
  bohemian_grove.html
The New Compact Bible Dictionary by
  Zondervan, p 372
Major Changes Not Seen
The Naked Capitalist by W. Cleon Skousen
https://www.forbes.com/sites/panosmour
  doukoutas/2018/04/21/indias-economy-on-track-
  to-beat-china/#5e3ba0525136
BRICS: https://ged-project.de/ged-blog/
  improving-public-understanding-of-economic-
  globalisation/globalization-report-2018-what-
  about-the-brics-countries/
http://rt.com/business/bank-rival-imf-
  world-852/(BRICS rival Bank)
6 Tragedy & Hope by Carroll Quigley, p 324
Prophecies Pointing to Grave Changes
7 The Christian Trumpet by Fr. Gaudentius
  Rossi Pellegrino, p 38,39
8 The Fatima Prophecies: At the Doorstep of
  the World by Dr. Thomas W. Petrisko, p 321
9, 10, www.mysticsofthechurch.com/2011/09/
  blessed-elena-aiello-mystic-stigmatic.html
11 The Fatima Prophecies: At the Doorstep of
  the World by Dr. Thomas W. Petrisko, p 319
12, 13, www.medjugorjetoday.tv//messages,
  2011-08-02, 2011-09-02
9/11: 'Who Dun It?'
The New Pearl Harbor Revisited: 9/11, The
  Cover-up, and the Expose by David Ray
  Griffin
http://www.informationclearinghouse.info/
  articale1665.htm for information on
  P.N.A.C.

http://www2.ae911truth.org/signpetition.php for 1500-plus signatures of architects and engineers, etc.
http://patriotsquestion911.com/engineers.html
http://articles.latimes.com/2011/jan/11/business/la-fi-drone-warfare-20110111 (drones)
14 Author anointed May 13, 2012; Our Lord confirmed, the tall buildings were blown floor by floor demolition style.
15 The New Pearl Harbor-Disturbing Questions about the Bush Administration and 9/11 by David Ray Griffin, p 175-176
16 Project for the New American Century "Rebuilding America's Defenses" in Chapter 5 "Creating Tomorrows Dominant Force." p 51, 52
17, 18, The 9/11 Mystery Plane and the Vanishing of America by Mark H. Gaffney, p 207-208, 218

Prophecies Expose Mohammedans, Tyrants, and Heretics

19, 20, Catholic Prophecy by Yves Dupont, p 29, 39-40
21 Trial, Tribulation & Triumph by Desmond A. Birch, p 332
22 (2693) http://www.apelosurgentes.com.br/arquivos/mensagens/2006.pdf
23 Catholic Prophecy by Yves Dupont, p 20 25
24 www.essan.org/Prophecy/Catholic%20Prophecy/johannes%20friede.htm

Chapter 33---The Second Revolution---
http://www.foxnews.com/politics/2011/04/25/imf-predicts-chinese-economy-surpass-2016/
http://ezinearticles.com/?Rich-Dads-Prophecy,-by-Robert-Kiyosaki---Review&id=6798153
http://www.independent.co.uk/news/business/news/transatlantic-alliance-between-rothschilds-and-rockefellers-for-wealth-management-7805035.html

** Note: Without our Lord's direct anointing's (confirmations) by the Holy Spirit for this chapter, I would not have been able to bring this together.

1 Author anointed April 14, 2012; Ninety-nine point nine percent of the population of the world has no idea what is going down.
2 Author anointed 2012; They will orchestrate horrendous events against the United States and the western financial world.

3 Author anointed April 20, 2012; America's 'war machine' will be used to obtain access to all the oil in the Middle east by declaring war.
4 Author anointed June 29, 2013; on those countries particularly Iran.
5 Author anointed June 30, 2012; another false flag will take place in America, causing a declaration of war by America on other threatening countries, particularly North Korea.
6 Author anointed April 25, 2012; that which is coming shall cause the revolution of the whole world.
7 Christian Trumpet by Fr. Gaudentius Rossi Pellegrino, p 134
8 www.mysticsofthechurch.com/2011/09/blessed-elena-aiello-mystic-stigmatic.html
9 Prophecies: the Chastisement and the Purification by Rev. Albert J. Hebert, S. M., p 121
10 Mary's Triumph by Mother Elena Leonardi, p 127
11 The Prophets and Our Times by Rev. R. Gerald Culleton, p 197
12 Prophecies: the Chastisement and the Purification by Rev. Albert J. Herbert, S. M. p 35

"Upheaval of a Region of the World"
http://www.telegraph.co.uk/news/worldnews/middleeast/iran/9545597/Armada-of-international-naval-power-massing-in-the-Gulf-as-Israel-prepares-an-Iran-strike.html
13 Words From Heaven 10th Edition by A Friend of Medjugorje, p 178
14 Garabandal Journal, July-Sept 1982,
15 (2516), 16 (2616), 17 (2501), http://www.apelosurgentes.com.br/arquivos/mensagens/2005.pdf

"When Conditions Are at Their Worst"
18 Garabandal–The Finger of God by Albrecht Weber
19, 20, Garabandal Journal, July-Sept 1982, July-Sept 1983
21 (2544), 22 (2514), 23 (2501), http://www.apelosurgentes.com.br/arquivos/mensagens/2005.pdf
24 (3272) http://www.pedroregis.com/english/mensagens_ing.php
25 (2557) http://www.apelosurgentes.com.br/arquivos/mensagens/2005.pdf
26 (2569), 27 (2695), http://www.apelosurgentes.com.br/arquivos/mensagens/2006.pdf

Chapter 34----Divine Intervention--- Divine Justice Approaches

1, 2, Divine Mercy in My Soul by Saint Maria Faustina Kowalska, p 42, 333-420

3 Trial, Tribulation & Triumph by Desmond A. Birch, p 390

4 Prophecies: the Chastisement and the Purification by Rev. Albert J. Hebert, S. M., p 90

5 www.mysticsofthechurch.com/2011/09/blessed-elena-aiello-mystic-stigmatic.html

Three Admonitions from God

6 Challoner Douay Rhiems version of Bible www.mgr.org/garabandal.html Garabandal Journal-July-Sept 1983

The Worldwide Warning

Our Lady Comes to Garabandal by Fr. Joseph A. Pelletier, A. A.

The Queen of Peace Visits Medugorje by Fr. Joseph A. Pelletier, A. A.

Liturgy of the Hours 1975 by Catholic Book Publishing Company

7 Author anointed June 25, 2003; Nothing will ever be the same again as we have known it.

8 Author anointed; Some of the prophecies will only be understood after the Warning.

9 Challoner Douay Rhiems version of the Bible (3 quots includes New American)

10 Sermon by St. Bernard of Clairvaux, Liturgy of the Hours, p 169

11, 12, The Miracle of the Illumination of All Consciences by Thomas W. Petrisko, p 23, 29

13 Author anointed October 23, 2006; confirming Anna Marie Taigi and her visions.

14 The Miracle of the Illumination of All Consciences by Thomas W. Petrisko, p 30

15 Divine Mercy in my Soul–Diary of Maria Faustina Kowalska by Sister Maria Faustina, p 19

16, 17, 18, The Miracle of the Illumination of All Consciences by Thomas W. Petrisko, p 30, 30, 31

19, 20, The Final Hour by Michael H. Brown, p 135, 246-247

21 (3252), 22 (3279), http://www.pedroregis.com/english/mensagens_ing.php

23 (2852) http://www.apelosurgentes.com.br/arquivos/mensagens/2007.pdf

24 (3250), 25 (3525), http://www.pedroregis.com/english/mensagens_ing.php

26 Author anointed; the innocent person refers to Benedict XVI. This again confirms the Garabandal prophecy of three more popes after Pope John XXIII, after which, the Warning will take place, during Pope Benedict's time on earth, who is still honored in Heaven. After the Warning, and first admonitions he will die at that time..

27 The Bridge to Heaven–Interview with Maria Esperanza by Michael H. Brown, p164

Enlightenment from God's Admonitions

28 Author's information

29 Author's information

John Paul II the Mystical

30 www.vatican.va/holy_father/john_paul_ii/audiences/2004/documents/hf_jp-ii_ aul

Opening of the First Seal of Revelation 31

The Book of Destiny by Rev. Herman Bernard Kramer

32 Against Hereses, Book IV, Ch 21:3, Catholic Encyclopedia

33 Author anointed June 25, 2003; All that God has given to us, all our rights and privileges, as Christians and as people in developed nations, are subtly and swiftly being taken away from us.

Outpouring of the Holy Spirit Upon All Mankind

34 The Visions of the Children by Jan Connell, p 66

35 Prophecies: the Chastisement and Purification by Rev. Albert J. Hebert, S. M., p 245

36 Author anointed July 16, 2012; an outpouring of the Holy Spirit will take place upon all humanity; no one will be left out.

37 The Visions of the Children by Jan Connell, p 66

Chapter 35---Decrees of Punishment---

1 Prophecies: the Chastisements and Purification by Rev. Albert J. Hebert S. M., p 162-164 for all the quotes of the young mother's vision of the Angels.

2 Author anointed May 7, 2009; divisions will continue in Christian families and communities with different beliefs.

3 Author anointed March 2012; the opening of the seven seals will take place.

4 Author anointed; confirming the increase of the victorious kingdom of God over this world and on this earth, just as it is in Heaven.

5 http://www.spiritdaily.net/weatherchange.htm

Opening of the Second Seal of
Revelation http://www.encyclopedia.com/
topic/French_Revolution.aspx
6 Author anointed March 26, 2012; the
4th secret of Medjugorje is the 2nd Seal of
Revelation.
7 Christian Trumpet by Fr. Gaudentius Rossi
Pellegrino, p 134

New York, New York
The Vision by David Wilkerson
The Book of Destiny by Rev. Herman Bernard
Kramer
8 Author anointed March 15, 2007; this was the
most disturbing awakening to me of what will
happen to New York and the United States.
9 www.davidwilkersontoday.blogspot.
com/2009/03/urgent-message.html
10 Author anointed; Our Lord confirms to me
the future streets of New York, years after this
event.
11 www.spiritdaily.com/merton.htm
12 (3422) http://www.pedroregis.com/english/
mensagens_ing.php
13 (2492), 14 (2518), 15 (2575), http://
www.apelosurgentes.com.br/ arquivos/
mensagens/2005.pdf
16(2923), 17 (2924), http://
www.apelosurgentes.com.br/arquivos/
mensagens/2007.pdf
18 (3347) http://www.pedroregis.com/english/
mensagens_ing.php
19 (2821) http://www.apelosurgentes. com.br/
arquivos/mensagens/2007.pdf 19(2573) http://
www.apelosurgentes.com.br/
arquivos/mensagens/2005.pdf
Major War and Worldwide Civil Chaos
20Author anointed March 25, 2008; the stock
markets, the banks and the insurance
companies will fail and not recover in the
United States.
21 My Descent into Death by Howard Storm,p
47, 48
Hope During The Great Storm
22 http://charliej373.wordpress.com
23www.mystics of the Church/2014/12/charlie
Johnston-alleged-prophet-
with.html
24 www.getFocus.TV Interview
with Charlie Johnston by Lisa Flood

called, "Weathering The Storm"
25 http://charliej373.wordpress.com
26 http://blessed hope.yuku.com/
Topic/244/ Preferred-Print-Version-
Overview- Of- The- Great- Storm#.Vxv2ha
MrJ2-

War Will Take Place.
27 Author anointed October 27, 2009; War will
take place.
28 (3278http://www.pedroregis.com/english/
mensagens_ing.php
29 www.spiritdaily.com/johnston2.htm
30www.spiritdaily.net/
prophecyupdatejohnston.htm
31 Author anointed June 21, 2012; the moment has
come for the United States to return to the Lord.
32(3280http://www.pedroregis.com/english/
mensagens_ing.php
33(2540, 34 (2520, 35 (2550, http://
www.apelosurgentes.com.br/arquivos/
mensagens/2005.pdf
36(2717http://
www.apelosurgentes.com.br/
arquivos/mensagens/2006.pdf
37 (2492 http://
www.apelosurgentes.com.br/
arquivos/mensagens/2005.pdf
38 (2930http://
www.apelosurgentes.com.br/
arquivos/mensagens/2007.pdf
39 www.spiritdaily.net/
prophecyupdatejohnston.htm
40 http://www.spiritdaily.com/
johnstoncommentary.htm
"Remain Where God has Placed Us"
41 Catholic Prophecy by Yves Dupont, p 47
Stock Up Food, Water, and Other Necessities
42 http://www.aaoobfoods.com/FEMAunits.htm
43 www.eattheweeds.com
44 www.northernbushcraft.com
45 http://familysurvivors.com /lds-food-
storage.htm
46 http://americanpreppersnetwork.net/
viewtopic.php?f=223&t=28927
47Author anointed June 2012; money will not be
obtained for a time.
48 http://rt.com/news/assange-internet-control-
totalitarian-943/

49 http://ww.spiritdaily.com/
johnstoncommentary.htm

A Step Down Decree

50Author anointed June 8, 2012; stepping down will continue until people on earth are living in a sustainable harmony at equilibrium with our earth's natural ecosystem.

Prophecies of Worldwide Chaos

51 Catholic Prophecy by Yves Dupont, p 48
52 (3437) http://www.apelosurgentes.com.br/arquivos/mensagens/2011.pdf
53 www.spiritdaily.net/johnston2.htm
54, 55, 56, Prophecies: the Chastisement and the Purification by Rev. Albert J. Hebert, S. M., p 117, 117, 117
57 Mary's Triumph by Revelations of Mother Elena Leonardi, p 127
58 The Prophets and Our Times by Rev. R. Gerald Culleton, p 197
59 http://www.spiritdaily.net/prophecyupdatejohnston.htm

The Mohammedans Will Rise Up

60 Trial, Tribulation & Triumph by Desmond Birch, p 332
61 (3281) http://www.pedroregis.com/english/mensagens_ing.php
62 (2536), 63 (2579), http://www.apelosurgentes.com.br/arquivos/mensagens/2005.pdf
64 (2708) http://www.apelosurgentes.com.br/arquivos/mensagens/2006.pdf
65(3282), 66 (3303), http://www.pedroregis.com/english/mensagens_ing.php
67(2562), 68 (2592), http://www.apelosurgentes. com.br/arquivos/mensagens/2005.pdf
69(2722) http://www.apelosurgentes.com.br/arquivos/mensagens/2006.pdf
70 (2553) http://www.apelosurgentes.com.br/arquivos/mensagens/2005.pdf
71 (3030) http://www.pedroregis.com/english/mensagens_ing.php
72 http://www.spiritdaily.net/prophecyupdatejohnston.htm

Chaos in the Church

73 www.mysticsofthechurch.com/2011/09/blessed-elena-aiello-mystic-stigmatic.html
74 (2489), http://www.apelosurgentes.com.br/arquivos/mensagens/2005.pdf

Chapter 36---Sorrowful Events Upon the Earth---

Canada

1 (2662) http://www.apelosurgentes.com.br/arquivos/mensagens/2006.pdf
2 (3466), 3(3471), 4(3436), 5(3373), 6(3539), 7(3439),http://www.pedroregis.com/english/mensagens_ing.php
8 Author anointed November 16, 2012;
Nuclear Power Plants in Ontario will have fracturing and meltdown.
9 Author anointed December 10, 2002; Mountains to the west in Alberta will be there for a thousand years.

United States of America

10 (2567) www.apelosurgentes.com.br/arquivos/mensagens/2005.pdf
11 (2624) http://www.apelosurgentes.com.br/arquivos/mensagens/2006.pdf
12 (3306), 13 (3339), 14 (3483), 15 (3400), 16 (3427), 17 (3428), http://www.pedroregis. com/english/mensagens_ing.php
18 (2602)http://www.apelosurgentes.com.br/arquivos/mensagens/2005.pdf
19 (2653) http://www.apelosurgentes.com.br/arquivos/mensagens/2006.pdf
20 (3573) http://www.pedroregis.com/english/mensagens_ing.php

The Land of Santa Cruz (USA?) 21

(2473) http://www.apelosurgentes.com.br/arquivos/mensagens/2005.pdf
22 (3147), 23 (3159), 24 (3169), 25 (3208), http://www.apelosurgentes.com.br/arquivos/mensagens/2009.pdf

Central America

26 (2551), 27 (2564), http://www.apelosurgentes.com.br/mensagens_por.php 28 (3335) http://www.pedroregis.com/english/mensagens_ing.php

South America

29 (2500), 30 (2631), 31 (2636), 32 (3017), http://www.apelosurgentes.com.br/mensagens_por.php
33 (3267), 34 (3236) 35 (3286) 36 (3331), http://www.pedroregis.com/english/mensagens_ing.php
37 (3343) 38 (3353) 39 (3354) http://www.pedroregis.com/english/mensagens_ing.php
40 (3289) http://www.apelosurgentes.com.br/mensagens_por.php

England

41 (2752) http://www.apelosurgentes.com.br/arquivos/mensagens/2006.pdf
42 (3258), 43 (3290), http://www.pedroregis.com/english/mensagens_ing.php

Europe

44 (2521), 45 (2660), 46 (2720), 47 (3246), 48 (3301), http://www.apelosurgentes.com.br/mensagens_por.php
49 (3302), 50 (3303), 51 (3323), 52 (3341), http://www.pedroregis.com/english/mensagens_ing.php
53 (2555) http://www.pedroregis.com/english/mensagens_ing.php3303
54 (2655), 55 (3267), 56 (3464), 57 (3488), 58 (3493), http://www.pedroregis.com/english/mensagens_ing.php

Eastern Europe

59 (2597), 60 (2591), 61 (2605), 62 (2610), 63 (2617), http://www.apelosurgentes. com.br/mensagens_por.php

64 (3231), 65 (3386), http://ww.pedroregis. com/english/mensagens_ing.php

Middle East

66 (2596), 67 (2604), 68 (2627), 69 (2670), 70 (2685), http://www.apelosurgentes. com.br/mensagens_por.php

71 (3314), 72 (3305), 73 (3314), 74 (3387), 75 (3393), http://www.pedroregis.com/english/mensagens_ing.php

Africa

76 (2565), 77 (2594), 78 (2595), 79 (2645), 80 (2706), http://www.apelosurgentes.com.br/mensagens_por.php

81 (3312, 82 (3312), http://www.pedroregis. com/english/mensagens_ing.php

Southeast Asia

83 (2485), 84 (2587), 85 (2639), http://www.apelosurgentes.com.br/mensagens_por.php 86 (3274), 87 (3307), 88 (3387), 89 (3388), 90 (3451) http://www.pedroregis.com/english/mensagens_ing.php

Unusually Interesting

91 (2476), 92 (2504), 93 (2527), http://www.apelosurgentes.com.br/arquivos/mensagens/2005.pdf

94 (2874) http://www.apelosurgentes. com.br/arquivos/mensagens/2006.pdf

95 (2866), 96 (2871), 97 (2872), http://www.apelosurgentes.com.br/arquivos/mensagens/2007.pdf

98 (3260) http://www.pedroregis.com/english/mensagens_ing.php

99 2561) http://www.apelosurgentes.com.br/arquivos/mensagens/2005.pdf

100 (2848) http://www.apelosurgentes. com.br/arquivos/mensagens/2007.pdf

101 (3289) http://www.pedroregis.com/english/mensagens_ing.php

102 (2948) http://www.apelosurgentes. com.br/arquivos/mensagens/2008.pdf

103 (3394), 104 (3395), http://www.pedroregis.com/english/mensagens_ing.php 104 (3395) http://www.pedroregis.com/english/mensagens_ing.php

Chapter 37---The Rescue by Our Lady of the Immaculate Conception

1 www.spiritdaily.org/stimaticsprophecy.htm

2 https://mysticpost.com/2017/11/wow-mary-tv-reports-medjugorje-visionary-says-year-triumph-immaculate-heart-will-happen/

The Rescue from the Storm

3 http://www.spiritdaily.net/prophecyupdatejohnston.htm

4 www.spiritdaily.org/johnston2.htm

4a spiritdaily.org/johnston2.htm

5 http://www.spiritdaily.com/johnstoncommentary.htm

6 The Thunder of Justice by Ted and Maureen Flynn, 1993, p 591

7 The Bridge to Heaven– Interview with Maria Esperanza by Michael H. Brown, p 164, 165 **The Triumph of Mary's Immaculate Heart**

8 (3254) http://www.pedroregis.com/english/mensagens_ing.php

9 Author anointed May 22, 2013; there will be one more uprising in the late 2020s

Optimistic Messages of Medjugorje

10 Author anointed October 27, 2012; to live these (the Virgin Mary's) messages, a new world will be born.

11 http://www.medjugorjetoday.tv/background-7/the-10-secrets-2/mary-will-triumph-bring-on-era-of-peace/

12 http://www.medjugorjetoday.tv/background-7/the-10-secrets-2/mary-will-triumph-bring-on-era-of-peace/

Our Lady as Co-Redemptrix, Mediatrix, and Advocate

13 Author anointed spring 2012; this role of Co-Redemptrix is to guide souls to eternal redemption.

14 The Fatima Prophecies: At the Doorstep of the World by Thomas W. Petrisko, p 351 15 Saint Catherine Laboure of the Miraculous Medal by Fr. Joseph I. Dirvin C. M., p 94 16, 17, 18, The Fatima Prophecies:At the Doorstep of the World by Thomas W. Petrisko, p 353, 354, 357

19 The Thunder of Justice by Ted and Maureen Flynn, revised and updated, p 190, 191,

20 The Fatima Prophecies: At the Doorstep of the World by Thomas W. Petrisko, p 358

21, 22, The Thunder of Justice by Ted and Maureen Flynn, (revised and updated) p 192, 192-193

23 www.medjugorjetoday.tv

"I Will Pour Out My Spirit on All Mankind" The New American Bible 1970

"Day of the Miracle and Miracle Signs"
24 She Went in Haste to the Mountain by Eusebio Garcia de Pesquera, O.F.M., Book 3, p 564"
25 Needles Magazine, July-September 1977,"
"Mari Loli, February 1977,"
26, 27, 28, 29 Our Lady Comes to Garabandal by Fr. Joseph A. Pelletier, p 160, 160, 151, 151
30 Needles Magazine Spring, 1974, Conchita p 28, 31, 32, Our Lady of Garabandal by Fr. Joseph A. Pelletier, A. A., p 151, 151
33 www.medjugorje.com/ 10 secrets.
34 www.medjugorje.org/overview.htm
35 Our Lady of Garabandal by Fr. Joseph A. Pelletier, A. A., p 157
36 (3386) http://www.pedroregis.com/english/mensagens_ing.php

Miracle Signs at Credible Marian Apparitions Sites
37 Author anointed March 2012; will leave a great sign in this place and in all those where Mary has been.
38 www.spiritdaily.net/secretslinked.htm
39 The Bridge to Heaven–Interview with Maria Esperanza by Michael H. Brown, p 108
40 (2739) http://www.apelosurgentes.com.br/arquivos/mensagens/2006.pdf
41 Trial, Tribulation & Triumph by Desmond A. Birch, p 311
42 She Went in Haste up the Mountain by Eusebio Garcia De pesquera,O.F.M. CAP., p496

Miracle Sign on "Martyr of the Eucharist" Feast Day
43 Butler's Lives of the saints, vol. 2, by Alban Butler, p 301,
44 www.ewtn.com/library/MARY/

Restoration from God's Three Admonitions
45 The Thunder of Justice by Ted & Maureen Flynn, revised & updated, p 145

A Time for Evangelization
46 Prophecies: the Chastisement and Purification by Rev. Albert J. Hebert, S. M., p 245
47 (2581) http://www.apelosurgentes.com.br/arquivos/mensagens/2005.pdf
48 www.pedroregis.com/english/mensagens_ing.php 49 (3298), 50 (3318), 51 (3326), 52 (3329), http://www.pedroregis.com/english/mensagens_ing.php 53 (3475), 54 (3481), 55 (3505), http://www. pedroregis.com/english/mensagens_ing.php
(3111) http://www.apelosurgentes.com.br/arquivos/mensagens/2009.pdf

Spiritual Direction
56 (3235) http://www.pedroregis.com/english/mensagens_ing.php57 (2843),
58 (2908), http://w.apelosurgentes.com.br/arquivos/mensagens/2007.pdf

59 (2578) http://www.apelosurgentes.com.br/arquivos/mensagens/2005.pdf
60 (3177) http://www.pedroregis.com/english/mensagens_ing.php
61 Mary's Triumph, Mother Elena Leonardi, p 64
"Will Have Little Time to Convert"
62 The Queen of Peace Visits Medugorje by Fr. Joseph Pelletier A. A., p 163
63 Medjugorje.com
64, (2530), http://www.apelosurgentes.com.br/arquivos/mensagens/2005.pdf
65 (3300), 66 (3321), 67 (3502), http://www.pedroregis.com/english/mensagens_ing.php

Chapter 38---Decrees of Punishments Will Continue---

Opening of the Third Seal of Revelation

1 (3432) http://www.apelosurgentes.com.br/arquivos/mensagens/2011.pdf
Prophecies of Famine
2, 3, The Prophets and Our Times by Rev. R. Gerald Culleton, p 128, 130
4 Catholic Prophecy by Yves Dupont, p 16
5 Trial, Tribulation & Triumph by Desmond A.
  Birch, p 271
6 The Prophets and Our Time Rev. R. Gerald Culleton, p 177
7 Catholic Prophecy by Yves Dupont, p 37,
8 Marie-Julie Jahenny-The Breton Stigmatist by Marquis de la Franquerie, p 44
9 Fatima in Lucia's Own Words, Third Memoir
  by Sister Lucia, p 112, 113
10 Author anointed May 25, 2013; Our Lord confirms the intensity of famines in the near future.Opening of the Fourth Seal of Revelation
11 www.Medjugorje.com
Spiritual Abandonment Reflects Catastrophic Events
Shift of the Magnetic Field
12 (2696), 13 (2713), 14 (2751), http://www.apelosurgentes.com.br/arquivos/mensagens/2006.pdf
15 (2790) http://www.apelosurgentes.com.br/arquivos/mensagens/2007.pdf
16 (3297) http://www.pedroregis.com/english/mensagens_ing.php
Earthquakes
www.endoftheamericandream.com/archives/major-earth-changes-coming-earthquakes-are-becoming-much-more-frequent-and-much-more-powerful

17 The Vision by David Wilkerson, p 32, 33

18 www.mysticsofthechurch.com/2011/09/
blessed-elena-aiello-mystic-stigmatic.html

19 The Prophets and Our Times by Rev. R.
Gerald Culleton, p 193

20 (2529), 21 (2530), 22 (2554), http://
www.apelosurgentes.com.br/arquivos/
mensagens/2005.pdf

23 (2701), 24 (2702), http://www.
apelosurgentes.com.br/arquivos/
mensagens/2006.pdf

25 (2796) http://www.apelosurgentes.com.br/
arquivos/mensagens/2007.pdf

26 (3259), 27 (3306), http://www.pedroregis.
com/english/mensagens_ing.php

28 (2886) http://www.apelosurgentes.com.br/
arquivos/mensagens/2007.pdf

29 (3425) http://www.pedroregis.com/english/
mensagens_ing.php

Shift of the Earth's Axis

30 (2707) http://www.apelosurgentes.com.br/
arquivos/mensagens/2006.pdf

31 (3310) http://www.pedroregis.com/english/
mensagens_ing.php

Gravitational Changes

32 (3168) http://www.apelosurgentes.com.br/
arquivos/mensagens/2007.pdf

Changes in Nature

33 (2485), 34 (2529), http://www.
apelosurgentes.com.br/arquivos/
mensagens/2005.pdf

Fire

35 (2541) http://www.apelosurgentes.com.br/
arquivos/mensagens/2005.pdf

36 (3112), 37 (3244), 38 (3251), 39 (3342),
http://www.pedroregis.com/english/
mensagens_ing.php

40 (3404), 41 (3421), 42 (3397), http://www.
pedroregis.com/english/mensagens_ing.php

Severe Weather Extremes

43 (2534), 44 (2538), www.
apelosurgentes.com.br/arquivos/
mensagens/2005.pdf

45 Author anointed July 1, 2012; we'll see
snowstorms in the middle of summer in
Canada.

Mountains

46 (3243), 47(3398), 48 (3274), http://www.
pedroregis.com/english/mensagens_ing.php

49 (2651) http://www.apelosurgentes.com.br/
arquivos/mensagens/2006.pdf

50 (3435), 51 (3445), http://www.pedroregis.
com/english/mensagens_ing.php

52 (2593) http://www.apelosurgentes.com.br/
arquivos/mensagens/2005.pdf

Volcanos

53 (2538), 54 (2657), http://www.
apelosurgentes.com.br/arquivos/
mensagens/2005.pdf

55 (2704) http://www.apelosurgentes.com.br/
arquivos/mensagens/2006.pdf

56 (3285), 57(3307), 58 (3310), 59 (3391),
http://www.pedroregis.com/english/
mensagens_ing.php

Extreme Explosions

60 (2601) http://www.apelosurgentes.com.br/
arquivos/mensagens/2005.pdf

Tsunamis

61 (2525) http://www.apelosurgentes.com.br/
arquivos/mensagens/2005.pdf

62 (2641) http://www.apelosurgentes.com.br/
arquivos/mensagens/2006.pdf

63 (2845) http://www.apelosurgentes.com.br/
arquivos/mensagens/2007.pdf

Stones and Boulders

64 (2633) http://www.apelosurgentes.com.br/
arquivos/mensagens/2005.pdf

65 (3182) http://www.apelosurgentes.com.br/
arquivos/mensagens/2009.pdf

66(3234) http://www.pedroregis.com/english/
mensagens_ing.php

Genetic and Technological Destruction

67(2538) http://www.apelosurgentes.com.br/
arquivos/mensagens/2005.pdf

68 (2760) http://www.apelosurgentes.com.br/
arquivos/mensagens/2006.pdf

69 (3107) http://www.apelosurgentes.com.br/
arquivos/mensagens/2009.pdf

70 (3110), 71 (3257), http://www.
apelosurgentes.com.br/arquivos/
mensagens/2009.pdf

Plagues Without a Solution

72 We Are Warned–The Prophecies of Marie-
Julie Jahenny by E. A. Bucchianeri, p 245

73 http://ourlady3.tripod.com/marie_julie.htm

74 www.spiritdaily.com/apparitionplague.htm

75, 76, The Prophets and Our Times by Rev. R.
Gerald Culleton, p 128, 193

77 Author anointed June 18, 2012; most
painful event of the fifteenth century will be
repeated.

78 (2483) http://www.apelosurgentes.com.br/
arquivos/mensagens/2005.pdf

79 Author anointed July 27, 2012 a second

time; I feel strongly that it is coming to
Canada and that we would experience it.
80 (2520), 81 (2522), 82(2531), 83(2607),
http://www.apelosurgentes.com.br/arquivos/

mensagens/2005.pdf
84(2626), 85 (2719), http://www.apelosurg
entes.com.br/arquivos/mensagens/2006.pdf
86http://www.heraldguide.com/details.php?
id=245 Esperanza
Death
87 (2665) http://www.apelosurgentes.com.br/
arquivos/mensagens/2006.pdf
88 (3155) http://www.apelosurgentes.com.br/
arquivos/mensagens/2009.pdf
89 (3366), 90 (3450), 91(3602), http://www.
pedroregis.com/english/mensagens_ing.php
92 (3188)   http://www.apelosurgentes.com.br/
arquivos/mensagens/2009.pdf
93 The Prophets and Our Times by Rev. R.
Gerald Culleton, p 200
94 Mary's Triumph by Mother Elena Leonardi,
p 104

Chapter 39---Back to the Future---
(2020s and 2030s)
http://www.shell.com/global/aboutshell/media/
news-and-media-releases/2011/scenarios-
signals-signposts-14022011.html
http://www.rawstory.com/rs/2011/02/15/

shell-report-predicts-peak-oil-now-or-soon-
ponders-depression-2-0/
http://www.theoildrum.com/node/7772
http://www.economist.com/node/17959688
After Oil
1 Author anointed Dec 14, 2010; this book
by James Howard Kunstler called, "The
Long Emergency: Surviving the End of Oil,
Climate Change, and other Converging
Catastrophes of the Twenty-First Century"
is surprisingly true information.
2 The Long Emergency: Surviving the End of
Oil, Climate Change, and other Converging
Catastrophes of the Twenty-First Century"
by James Howard Kunstler p 141
3 Author anointed Nov 22, 2011 & Sept 6, 2019; A
Crude Awakening: The Oil Crash by Basil Gelpke
& Ray McCormack (Documentary) is
also confirmed by the Holy Spirit as
reliable information.
4 Author anointed February 25, 2004;
eventually the cities and towns will be empty.

Look to the Amish
5, 6, 7, 8, 9, 10, The Long Emergency:
Surviving the End of Oil, Climate Change,
and other Converging Catastrophes of the
Twenty-First Century by James Howard
Kunstler, p 239, 246, 246, 246, 247, 248,

11 Author anointed; there will be people who
will not submit to God and will continue to
be an aggravating threat.

**Chapter 40---The "Fatal Event," Confusion
and Chaos in the Church---** (Seventh secret
of Medjugorje?)(Late 2020s)
1 Author anointed May 22, 2013; The Fatal
Event will start in the late 2020s.
2 www.medjugorje.com
The Vengeance of Hell Against the Church
3 We Are Warned: The Prophecies of Marie-
Julie Jahenny by E. A. Bucchianeri, p 252
4, 5, 6, Marie-Julie Jahenny-The Breton
Stigmatist by Marquis de la Franquerie, p
34, 32, 31
7 We Are Warned: The Prophecies of Marie-
Julie Jahenny by E. A. Bucchianeri, p 253
8, 9, Marie-Julie Jahenny-The Breton Stigmatist
by Marquis de la Franquerie, p 36, 39
10 We Are Warned: The Prophecies of Marie-
Julie Jahenny by E. A. Bucchianeri, p 280
11, 12 Marie-Julie Jahenny-The Breton
Stigmatist by Marquis de la Franquerie, p
40, 40
13 We Are Warned: The Prophecies of Marie-
Julie Jahenny by E. A. Bucchianeri, p 253
14, 15, We Are Warned: The Prophecies of
Marie-Julie Jahenny by E. A. Bucchianeri, p
281, 251
Schism
16 Marie-Julie Jahenny-The Breton Stigmatist
by Marquis de la Franquerie, p 35
17 (3040) http://www.apelosurgentes.com.br/
arquivos/mensagens/2008.pdf
18 (2566) http://www.apelosurgentes.com.br/
arquivos/mensagens/2005.pdf
19 (2942), 20 (2952), 21 (2953), 22 (3014),
http://www.apelosurgentes.com.br/arquivos/
mensagens/2008.pdf
23 (3036), 24 (3049), http://www.
apelosurgentes.com.br/arquivos/
mensagens/2008.pdf
25 (3409) http://www.pedroregis.com/english/
mensagens_ing.php
An Apostasy
26 Marie-Julie Jahenny-The Breton Stigmatist
by Marquis de la Franquerie, p 32
27 (3017), 28 (3021), 29 (3051), 30 (3094),
http://www.apelosurgentes.com.br/arquivos/
mensagens/2008.pdf
31 (3202) http://www.apelosurgentes.com.br/
arquivos/mensagens/2009.pdf
32 (2759) http://www.apelosurgentes.com.br/
arquivos/mensagens/2006.pdf

Antichrists Will Rise Up
33 Marie-Julie Jahenny-The Breton Stigmatist by Marquis de la Franquerie, p 32, 33
34 (2554) http://www.apelosurgentes.com.br/arquivos/mensagens/2005.pdf
35 2628) http://www.apelosurgentes.com.br/arquivos/mensagens/2006.pdf
36 (2822), 37 (2826), http://www.apelosurgentes.com.br/arquivos/mensagens/2007.pdf
38 (3255), 39 (3276), http://www.pedroregis.com/english/mensagens_ing.php

Visible Break Down of the Church
40 Forty Dreams of John Bosco by St. John Bosco, p 207-212
41 Catholic Prophecy by Yves Dupont, p 39, 40
42 (2828) http://www.apelosurgentes.com.br/arquivos/mensagens/2007.pdf
43 (2947) http://www.apelosurgentes.com.br/arquivos/mensagens/2008.pdf
44 Anointed August 15, 2012; many will be contaminated by the false doctrines applied by bad theologians and many hearts will be hardened and will not accept the truth.
45 (2955), 46 (2957), 47 (2976), 48 (2979), 49 (2985), http://www.apelosurgentes.com.br/arquivos/mensagens/2008.pdf

How Many Popes?
50 Works of the Seraphic Father St. Francis of Assisi, by R. Washbourne 1882, p 248-249
51 (2472) http://www.apelosurgentes.com.br/arquivos/mensagens/2005.pdf
52 (3046), 53 (3098), 54 (3204), 55 (3452), http://www.pedroregis.com/english/mensagens_ing.php
56 Christian Trumpet by Fr. Gaudentius Rossi Pellegrino, p 36-37

Chapter 41---Opening the Fifth Seal of Revelation--- (eighth secret of Medjugorje?)
1 Author anointed; nations that will be overcome by the Moslems for a time.

Prophecies of Persecution and Martyrdom
2 The Prophets and Our Times by Rev. R. Gerald Culleton, p 139
3 The Christian Trumpet by Fr. Guadentius Rossi Pellegrino, p 142
4 The Prophets and Our Times by Rev. R. Gerald Culleton, p 200
5 Prophecies: the Chastisement and Purification by Rev. Albert J. Hebert, S. M., p 245
6 www.medjugorje.org/msg82.htm
7, 8, 9, Christian Trumpet by Fr. Gaudentius Rossi Pellegrino, p 36-37, 71, 70-71

10 (3500), http://www.pedroregis.com/english/mensagens_ing.php
11 (2837), http://www.apelosurgentes.com.br/arquivos/mensagens/2007.pdf
12 (2941), 13 (2967), 14 (2986), 15 (3000), 16 (3008), http://www.apelosurgentes.com.br/arquivos/mensagens/2008.pdf
17 (3033), 18 (3043), 19(3058), 20 (3078), 21 (3126), http://www.apelosurgentes.com.br/arquivos/mensagens/2008.pdf
22 (3130), 23 (3641) http://www.pedroregis.com/english/mensagens_ing.php
24 We Are Warned: The Prophecies of Marie-Julie Jahenny by E. A. Bucchianeri, p 239

Chapter 42---Opening of the Sixth Seal of Revelation--- (very late-2020s to 2038)
1 Queen of Peace Visits Medugorje by Fr. Joseph A. Pelletier A. A. p 139, Note p 215.
2 (2492) http://www.apelosurgentes.com.br/arquivos/mensagens/2005.pdf

A Collision in the Universe (Very late 2020s or very early 2030s)
3 (3106) http://www.apelosurgentes.com.br/arquivos/mensagens/2009.pdf
4 (3013) http://www.apelosurgentes.com.br/arquivos/mensagens/2008.pdf
5 (3113) http://www.apelosurgentes.com.br/arquivos/mensagens/2009.pdf
6 (2663) http://www.apelosurgentes.com.br/arquivos/mensagens/2006.pdf
7 (3197) http://www.apelosurgentes.com.br/arquivos/mensagens/2009.pdf
8 (2510) http://www.apelosurgentes.com.br/arquivos/mensagens/2005.pdf

Worldwide Destruction of the Electrical Grids (Very late 2020s or early 2030s)
9 www.essan.org/Prophecy/catholic%20Prophecy/johannes%20friede.htm
10 (612) http://www.pedroregis.com/arquivos/mensagens/ingles/Messages_of_1987_and_1996.pdf
11 She Went in Haste to the Mountain by Eusebio Garcia De Pesquera, O.F.M. CAP., p 413
12 (2790) http://www.apelosurgentes.com.br/arquivos/mensagens/2007.pdf
13 Author anointed spring of 1995; I should learn how to dry foods on drying racks.

The Trumpets
14 www.mysticsofthechurch.com/2011/09/blessed-elena-aiello-mystic-stigmatic.html

The First Angel's Trumpet -Fire from/Sky
15, The Fatima Prophecies: At the Doorstep of the World by Dr. Thomas W. Petrisko, p 301
16, Mary's Triumph by Mother Elena Leonardi, p 79

17 The Fatima Prophecies: At the Doorstep of the World by Dr. Thomas W. Petrisko, p 301-302

18, 19, www.mysticsofthechurch.com/2011/09/blessed-elena-aiello-mystic-stigmatic.html

20, 21, Prophecies: the Chastisement and Purification by Rev. Albert J. Hebert, S.M p 88, 89

22, Mary's Triumph by Mother Elena Leonardi, p 79

23, www.mysticsofthechurch.com/2011/09/blessed-elena-aiello-mystic-stigmatic.html

24 ,Trial, Tribulation & Triumph by Desmond A. Birch, p 397-398

25, We Are Warned: The Prophecies of Marie-Julie Jahenny by E. A. Bucchianeri, p 274

26, (3189) http://www.apelosurgentes.com.br/arquivos/mensagens/2009.pdf

27, (2470) http://www.apelosurgentes.com.br/arquivos/mensagens/2005.pdf

28, She Went in Haste to the Mountain by Eusebio Garcia De Pesquera, O.F.M. CAP., p 411
Rapid Melting of Polar Caps and Glaciers 29 (2598), www.apelosurgentes.com.br/arquivos/mensagens/2005.pdf

Rapid Melting of Polar Caps and Glaciers

29 www.apelosurgentes.com.br/arquivos/mensagens/2005.pdf

Sunlight Will Become Perceptibly Weaker (2030s)

30 www.essan.org/Prophecy/catholic%20Prophecy/johannes%20friede.htm

31 (2671) http://www.apelosurgentes.com.br/arquivos/mensagens/2006.pdf

32 (2539) http://www.apelosurgentes.com.br/arquivos/mensagens/2005.pdf

33 Catholic Prophecy by Yves Dupont, p 52

Four Years of War Before the Comet (2033-June 2037)

34 Catholic Prophecy by Yves Dupont, p 37
35 The Prophets and Our Times by Rev. R. Gerald Culleton, p 149

The End of an Age

36 World Trends #41, August 1974, www.catholicrevealtions.org/PR/st%20augustine. htm
37 Catholic Prophecy by Yves Dupont, p 40

Chapter 43---Great Catholic Monarch---(2030s)

1 Trial, Tribulation & Triumph by Desmond A. Birch, p 338

Charles of Austria to the Great Catholic Monarch

The Habsburgs Embodying Empire by Andrew Wheatcroft

www.catholicnewsagency.com/utiles/myprint/print.php

www.remnantnewspaper.com/archives/archives-2005-1015-beatification_of europe.htm-

2 Interview with granddaughter Archduchess Catharina-Maria/Messenger of Saint Anthony April 2009

3 Author anointed December 23, 2009; his

whole aspiration in life has always been to discern as clearly as possible God's will.

4 Interview with granddaughter Archduchess Catharina-Maria/Messenger of Saint Anthony April 2009

5 www.remnantnewspaper.com/archives 2005

6. Author anointed April 1, 2012; this is the Great Catholic Monarch to rise up in the 2030s.

Prophecies of the Great Catholic Monarch

www.christusrex.org/www1/apparitions/http:/pr00063.htm;
http://stateofisrael.com/declaration/

7, 8, The Prophets and Our Times by Rev. R. Gerald Culleton, p 107, 110

9 World Trends #41, August, 1974, www.catholicrevealtions.org/PR/st%20augustine.htm

10, 11, 12, 13 Prophecy for Today by Edward Connor, p 30, 30, 30-31, 31

14, 15, The Prophets and Our Times by Rev. R. Gerald Culleton, p 140, 153

16 World Trends #41, www.catholicrevelatons.org/PRbishops%20christianos%20agreda. htm

17 Prophecy for Today by Edward Connor, p35

18 The Life and the Revelations of Anne Catherine Emmerich by the Very Rev. Carl E. Schmoger, C.SS.R., vol. 2, p 284, 285

19 Little Pictorial Lives of the Saints by Msgr. Paul Guerin, 1882, vol. 8 /www.magnificat.ca/cal/engl/07-15.htm

The Counter-Revolution Begins

20, 21 Christian Trumpet by Fr. Gaudentius Rossi Pellegrino, p 30, 59

22, 23, Trial, Tribulation & Triumph by

Battles of the Great Catholic Monarch

Desmond A. Birch, p 374, 311

to 2037?)24, 25, Catholic Prophecy by Yves Dupont, p 13, 63   26 Trial, Tribulation & Triumph by Desmond A. Birch, p 216
27, 28, Catholic Prophecy by Yves Dupont, p 71, 16
29 Prophecy for Today by Edward Connor, p 30
He Will Push Back the Mohammedans
30 The Prophets and Our Times by Rev. R. Gerald Culleton, p 173 31 Last Times by Fr. Sanchez'/ Trial, Tribulation & Triumph by Desmond A. Birch, p 374

Birch Tree Country Prophecies
32, 33, Catholic Prophecy by Yves Dupont, p 34, 24
34 The Prophets and Our Times by Rev. R. Gerald Culleton, p 143-144
35 Trial, Tribulation & Triumph by Desmond A. Birch, p 347
36 www.rexresearch.com/prophist/ phf3.htm#phf354

Chapter 44---The Gates of Hell Shall Not Prevail Against His Church---
1 http://www.mysticsofthechurch.com/2011/09/ blessed-elena-aiello-mystic-stigmatic.html
2 (3315), 3 (3316), http://www.pedroregis.com/ english/mensagens_ing.php
4 (3073) http://www.apelosurgentes.com.br/ arquivos/mensagens/2008.pdf
Imminent Invasion of the Vatican
5 (2529), 6 (2537), http://www.apelosurgentes. com.br/arquivos/mensagens/2005.pdf 7 She Went in Haste up the Mountain by Eusebio Garcia de Pesuera O.F.M., p 413
The Russians Are Coming
8 Christian Trumpet by Fr. Gaudentius Rossi Pellegrino, p 70-71
9 http://www.mysticsofthechurch.com/2011/09/ blessed-elena-aiello-mystic-stigmatic.html
10 (2498) http://www.apelosurgentes.com.br/ arquivos/mensagens/2005.pdf
11 (2937), 12 (3065), http://www. apelosurgentes.com.br/arquivos/ mensagens/2008.pdf
Pope Flees Rome and is Martyred (2033-2035)
13 The Reign of Antichrist by Rev. R. Gerald Culleton, p 131
14 The Life and Revelations of Anne Catherine Emmerich, Volume II, Very Rev. Carl E. Schmoger, C.SS.R., p 292
15 Fatima in Lucia's Own Words, Third Memoir by Sister Lucia, p 112-113
16 Author anointed January 27, 2010; the vision of Pius X is terrifying and is confirmed by the Holy Spirit.
17 www.spiritdaily.org/prophecyof popes.htm
18 Catholic Prophecy by Yves Dupont, p 78
19, 20, Prophecy for Today by Edward Connor,p 39, 39

21 (3241) http://www.pedroregis.com/english/ mensagens_ing.php
22 (2996), 23(3012), http://www. apelosurgentes.com.br/arquivos/mensagens/2008.pdf
24 www.vatican.va/roman_curia/congregations/ cfaith/documents/rc_con_cfaith_ doc_20000626_message-fatima-en.html
No Pope in Rome (2036-2038)
25 Our Lady of Good Success by Marian Therese Horvat, PhD. p 57
26, 27, Catholic Prophecy by Yves Dupont, p 73-74, 28
28 Marie-Julie Jahenny-The Breton Stigmatist by Marquis de la Franquerie, p 33
29 (2940), 30 (2939), 31 (3096), http:// www.apelosurgentes.com.br/arquivos/ mensagens/2008.pdf
Rome and the Vatican Destroyed
32 www.catholic-pages.com/grabbag/malachy. asp / Catholic Encyclopedia 1913 edition
33(2502), 34 (2561), 35 (2592), http:// www.apelosurgentes.com.br/arquivos/ mensagens/2005.pdf
36 (2997), 37 (3007), http://www. apelosurgentes.com.br/arquivos/ mensagens/2008.pdf
38 Catholic Prophecy by Yves Dupont, p 65
39 http://www.mysticsofthechurch. com/2011/09/blessed-elena-aiello-mystic-stigmatic.html

Chapter 45---God's Chastisements--- (2038)
1 Prophecy for Today by Edward Connor, p 21
2 Prophecies: the Chastisement and the Purification by Rev. Albert J. Hebert, S. M., p 80
3 She Went in Haste to the Mountain by Eusebio Garcia De Pesquera, O.F.M. CAP. , p 413
"The Whole World Shall Cry, Woe"
4 The Christian Trumpet by Fr. Gaudentius Rossi Pellegrino, p 23
5 Author anointed March 2012; according to the prophecies, the Great Catholic Monarch stops fighting in battles when he is 40 years old in June of 2037.
6 Marie-Julie Jahenny-The Breton Stigmatist by Marquis de La Franquerie, p 43
7 We Are Warned: The Prophecies of Marie-Julie Jahenny by E. A. Bucchianeri, p 387-388
8 Marie-Julie Jahenny–The Breton Stigmatist by Marquis de La Franquerie, p 43

The Second Angel's Trumpet:
9 (2641), 10 (2656), http://www.
apelosurgentes.com.br/arquivos/
mensagens/2006.pdf
The Third Angel's Trumpet:
11 (2570), 12 (2482), http://www.
apelosurgentes.com.br/arquivos/
mensagens/2005.pdf
Just Before the Comet Comes (July 2037-
April 2038)
13, 14, Trial, Tribulation & Triumph by
Desmond A. Birch, p 347, 341, 311
15 (2787) http://www.apelosurgentes.com.br/
arquivos/mensagens/2007.pdf
16 (3163), 17 (3201), http://www.
apelosurgentes.com.br/arquivos/
mensagens/2009.pdf
18 (2510) http://www.apelosurgentes.com.br/
arquivos/mensagens/2005.pdf
The Fourth Angel's Trumpet:
19 (2832), 20 (2807), 21 (2787), http://
www.apelosurgentes.com.br/arquivos/
mensagens/2007.pdf
22 (2707) http://www.apelosurgentes.com.br/
arquivos/mensagens/2006.pdf
23 We Are Warned: The Prophecies of
Marie-Julie Jahenny by E. A. Bucchianeri, p 278

Answering the Cry of the Poor
24 Marie-Julie Jahenny-The Breton
Stigmatistby Marquis de La Franquerie, p 43

Two Days of Darkness Before the Three Days
of Darkness (March 2038)
25, 26, We Are Warned: The Prophecies of
Marie-Julie Jahenny by E. A. Bucchianeri, p
301, 246-247
The Comet (April 2038)
27 Catholic Prophecy by Yves Dupont, p 84
28 (2807), http://www.apelosurgentes.com.br/
arquivos/mensagens/2007.pdf
29 Author anointed May 27, 2013; Our Lord
confirmed the tail or the coma, will be ahead
of the comet with particles of rock or gravel,
rocks, and large rocks coming before the
actual comet.
30 Jesus Calls Us, Volume 1 from Julka of
Zagreb / Prophecies: the Chastisement and
Purification by
Rev. Albert J. Hebert, S. M., p 20
Prophecies of the Comet
31 www.catholicrevelations.org/PR/st%20
hilarion.htm
32 Catholic Prophecy by Yves Dupont, p16
33 The Christian Trumpet by Fr. Guadentius
Rossi Pellegrino, p 142-143

34 (3199), 35 (3103), 36 (3109), http://
www.apelosurgentes.com.br/arquivos/
mensagens/2009.pdf
37 (2794) http://www.apelosurgentes.com.br/
arquivos/mensagens/2007.pdf
38 (3017) http://www.apelosurgentes.com.br/
arquivos/mensagens/2008.pdf
39 www.essan.org/prophecy/catholic%20
prophecy/St%20JohannFriede
40 The Holy Bible, Douay Rheims Version,
Revised by Bishop Richard Challoner
41 (2793) http://www.apelosurgentes.com.br/
arquivos/mensagens/2007.pdf
Three Days of Darkness (2038)
42 Marie-Julie Jahenny-The Breton Stigmatist
by Marquis de La Franquerie, p 43-45
The Angels Will Help
43 (3309) http://www.pedroregis.com/english/
mensagens_ing.php
44 (3198) http://www.apelosurgentes.com.br/
arquivos/mensagens/2009.pdf
Prophecies of Three Days of Darkness
45 The Prophets and Our Times by Rev. R.
Gerald Culleton p 193-194
46 Trial, Tribulation & Triumph by Desmond
A. Birch, p 391
47 www.mysticsofthechurch.com/2011/09/
blessed-elena-aiello-mystic-stigmatic.html
48 (110) www.pedroregis.com/arquivos/
mensagens/ingles/Messages_of_1987_
and_1996.pdf
49 (3186) http://www.apelosurgentes.com.br/
arquivos/mensagens/2009.pdf
50 Trial, Tribulation & Triumph by Desmond
A. Birch, p 286
51 Prophecy for Today by Edward Connor, p
27
52 Trial, Tribulation & Triumph by Desmond
A. Birch, p 286-287
53 The Prophets and Our Times by Rev. R.
Gerald Culleton p 200
54 The Prophets and Our Times by Rev. R.
Gerald Culleton p 198
55 The Thunder of Justice (revised & updated)
by Ted and Maureen Flynn. p 295-296
56 Author anointed 3 different times that this is
a credible prophecy of Padre Pio.
57 www.catholicrevelations.org/PR/padre%20
pio.htm
58 Marie-Julie Jahenny-the Breton Stigmatist by
Marquis de La Franquerie, p 44
59 The Prophets and Our Time by Rev. R.
Gerald Culleton, p 189-191
60 Prophecies: the Chastisement and
Purification by Rev Albert J. Hebert, S.M.,
p 87-89

Chapter 46--- The Aftermath on Earth
1, 2, Prophecies: the Chastisement and
Purification by Rev. Albert J. Hebert, S. M.,
p 154, 16
3 Jesus Calls Us, Volume 1 from Julka of
Zagreb / Prophecies: the Chastisement and
Purification by Rev. Albert J. Hebert, S.M.,
p 118
4 Author anointed May 18, 2012; "this place
seemed familiar, but it was quite devastated.
I could nowhere see a house or a human
being."
5, 6, 7, Prophecies: the Chastisement and
Purification by Rev. Albert J. Hebert, S.M.,
p 171, 20, 169
A Remnant Shall Be Saved
8 The Prophets and Our Times by Rev. R.
Gerald Culleton, p 193
9 Thunder of Justice by Ted and Maureen
Flynn, revised and updated, p 294
10 Marie-Julie Jahenny-the Breton Stigmatist
by Marquis de La Franquerie p 43, 44, 50
11 The Fatima Prophecies: At the Doorstep
of the World by Dr. Thomas W. Petrisko p
316-317
12 www.mysticsofthechurch.com/2011/09/
blessed-elena-aiello-mystic-stigmatic.html
13 Prophecies: the Chastisement and the
Purification by Rev. Albert J. Hebert, S. M.,
p 90
14 Voices, Visions, and Apparitions by Michael
Freze, S.F.O., p 175
15 (3287), 16 (2525) http://www.pedroregis.
com/english/mensagens_ing.php
17 Prophecies–the Chastisement and the
Purification by Rev. Albert J. Hebert, S. M.,
p 118
The Comet Fertilizes the Earth
Catholic Prophecy by Yves Dupont has a
commentary on comets.
18 www.essan.org/Prophecy/Catholic%20
Prophecy/johannes%20friede.htm.
19 Catholic Prophecy by Yves Dupont, p 14 20
The Christian Trumpet by Fr. Gaudentius
Rossi Pellegrino, p 24
21 Trial, Tribulation & Triumph by Desmond
A. Birch, p 312-313
22 The Prophets and Our Times by Rev. R.
Gerald Culleton, p 110
A Great Sign Appears in the Sky
23 The Prophets and Our Times by Rev. R.
Gerald Culleton, p 191
24 www.essan.org/Prophecy/Catholic%20
Prophecy/johannes%20friede.htm.
25 Imitation of Christ by Thomas a Kempis,p 41

26 Trial, Tribulation & Triumph by Desmond
A. Birch, p 287
27 The Thunder of Justice by Ted and Maureen
Flynn, revised & updated, p 111
28 (3586) http://www.pedroregis.com/english/
mensagens_ing.php
29 (2861) http://www.apelosurgentes.com.br/
arquivos/mensagens/2007.pdf
Definitive Triumph of Mary's Immaculate
Heart
30 (3101) http://www.apelosurgentes.com.br/
arquivos/mensagens/2008.pdf
31 (3249), 32 (3344), 33 (3558), 34 (3640),
http://www.pedroregis.com/english/
mensagens_ing.php

Section V
The Sixth Church Age

Chapter 47 ---Age of Peace--- (2038- 2438?)
New American Bible 1970
Satan Will Be Bound
1 Catholic Prophecy by Yves Dupont, p 43-44
2 The Admirable Life of Mother Mariana vol.
2 by Fr. Manuel Sousa Pereira p 213-214
3 The Prophets and Our Time by Rev. R.
Gerald Culleton, p 191
4 (3248) http://www.pedroregis.com/english/
mensagens_ing.php
Reign of the Sacred Heart of Jesus and the
Immaculate Heart of Mary
5 Author anointed; the future reign of the
Sacred Heart of Jesus and the Immaculate
Heart of Mary.
6 Fatima in Lucia's Own Words by Sister Lucia,
p 167
7 Catholic Prophecy by Yves Dupont, p 33
8 We Are Warned: The Prophecies of Marie-
Julie Jahenny by E. A. Bucchianeri, p 374
9 Prophecies: the Chastisement and Purification
by Rev. Albert J. Hebert, S. M., p 87
"A Period of Peace" (2038 until 2383?)
10 Spiritdaily.net/weatherchange.htm
11 Fatima in Lucia's Own Words by Sister
Lucia, p 167
12 Words from Heaven by A Friend of
Medjugorje, p 298
13 Trial, Tribulation & Triumph by Desmond
A. Birch p 337
14, 15, Catholic Prophecy by Yves Dupont, p
57-59, 13
16 The Prophets and Our Times by Rev. R.
Gerald Culleton, p 110

A Transformed Earth
17 Author anointed June 25, 2014; the use of horses will be the only way to get around and will serve to work the land growing food, needed to replenish the earth's population during the sixth Church age.
18 Author anointed April 17, 2009; People will only need small plots of land considering the nutrient rich land after the comet.
19 Pere Lamy by Comte Paul Biver p 142
20 (2528) http://www.apelosurgentes.com.br/arquivos/mensagens/2005.pdf
21 (3379), 22 (3268), http://www.pedroregis.com/english/mensagens_ing.php
23 (3149) http://www.apelosurgentes.com.br/arquivos/mensagens/2009.pdf
Like a Garden
24 (2716) http://www.apelosurgentes.com.br/arquivos/mensagens/2006.pdf
25 (3192) http://www.apelosurgentes.com.br/arquivos/mensagens/2009.pdf
26 (3424) http://www.pedroregis.com/english/mensagens_ing.php
Chapter 48---The Powerful Monarch and the Holy Pope---
1 Catholic Prophecy by Yves Dupont p 40
The Holy Pope with the Cross-on His Forehead (2038-?)
www.medjugorjeusa.org/sudac.htm
2 www.stjeromecroatian.org/eng/frsudac.htm
Prophecies of the Holy Pope
3 The Christian Trumpet by Fr. Gaudentius Rossi Pellegrino p 132
4 Catholic Prophecy by Yves Dupont p 38, 40
5, 6, Prophecy for Today by Edward Connor p 33, 26-27
7 Trial, Tribulation & Triumph by Desmond A. Birch p 216
8 Prophets and Our Times by Rev. R. Gerald Culleton p 126-127
9 The Christian Trumpet by Fr. Gaudentius Rossi Pellegrino p 142-144
10 (3093) http://www.apelosurgentes.com.br/arquivos/mensagens/2008.pdf
Revival of the Holy Roman Empire
11 The Sunday Sermons of the Great Fathers Vol. 4 p 335, 352
12 (2809) http://www.apelosurgentes.com.br/arquivos/mensagens/2007.pdf
Reign of the Powerful Monarch (2038-?)
13 Catholic Prophecy by Yves Dupont p 13
14 The Christian Trumpet by Fr. Gaudentius Rossi Pellegrino p 37
15, 16, Catholic Prophecy by Yves Dupont p 29, 28

17 Trial, Tribulation & Triumph by Desmond A. Birch p 244
18 The Prophets and Our Times by Rev. R. Gerald Culleton p 199
19 Voices, Visions, and Apparitions by Michael Freze, S.F.O. p 198
20 Catholic Prophecy by Yves Dupont p 50
21 (3019) http://www.apelosurgentes.com.br/arquivos/mensagens/2008.pdf
22 (3153) http://www.apelosurgentes.com.br/arquivos/mensagens/2009.pdf

Chapter 49---Time of Faith and Order---
1, 2, 3, Trial, Tribulation & Triumph by Desmond A. Birch p 412-413, 414, 268-269
4 The Life and the Revelations of Anne Catherine Emmerich by the Very Rev. Carl E. Schmoger, C.SS.R. vol. 2 p 152-153
5 Catholic Prophecy by Yves Dupont p 56
6 The Prophets and Our Times by Rev. R. Gerald Culleton p 224
7 Catholic Prophecy by Yves Dupont p 51
8 The Prophets and Our Times by Rev. R. Gerald Culleton p 199
9 Trial, Tribulation & Triumph by Desmond A. Birch p 342
10, 11, Catholic Prophecy by Yves Dupont p 48, 63
Unusual Prophecies During the Sixth Church Age
12 www.catholicrevelations.org/PR/st%20hildegard.htm
13 Pere Lamy by Comte Paul Biver p 142
14 Catholic Prophecy by Yves Dupont p 16
15 (3207) http://www.apelosurgentes.com.br/arquivos/mensagens/2009.pdf
16 The Queen of Peace Visits Medugorje by Fr. Joseph A. Pelletier A. A., p 139
A Spiritual Transformation
17 Holzhauser 'Visions' 1646/ www.catholicrevelations.org/PR/ven%20bartholomew%20holzhauser.htm
18 http://www.spiritdaily.net/Prophecy-seers/Esperanza/eperanzaprophecylast.htm
19 (3419) http://www.pedroregis.com/english/mensagens_ing.php
20 (3158) http://www.apelosurgentes.com.br/arquivos/mensagens/2009.pdf
Ecumenical Council in the Sixth Church Age
21 Author anointed Oct 23, 2013; this will be the greatest council in the Church ages.
22, 23, Catholic Prophecy by Yves Dupont p 59, 37-38
24 Trial, Tribulation & Triumph by Desmond A. Birch p 338

25 The Christian Trumpet by Fr. Gaudentius Rossi Pellegrino p 24
All Nations Will Become Catholic
26 Catholic Prophecy by Yves Dupont p 40
27 The Prophets and Our Times by Rev. R. Gerald Culleton p 127
28 The Christian Trumpet by Fr. Guadentius Rossi Pellegrino p 142-143
29 Voices, Visions, and Apparitions by Michael Freze p 175

Chapter 50--- The End of the Sixth Church Age---
1 The Prophets and Our Times by Rev. R. Gerald Culleton p 127
As the Sixth Church Age Progresses
2, 3, Trial, Tribulation & Triumph by Desmond A. Birch p 228, 229-230
Seventy-Weeks of Years
4 Author anointed January 15, 2014; Angel Gabriel details knowledge of the future, in different time frames.
5 Author anointed Nov 22, 2011; three and a half years or half a week is the clue, connecting this to the Saint's prophecies confirming this as future prophecy.
The False Prophet
6 The Prophets and Our Times by Rev. R. Gerald Culleton p 155
7 www.catholicapologetics.info/ catholicteaching/privaterevelation/lasalet. html
The Antichrist
Catechism of Perseverance by Abbe Gaume 1850
The Reign of Antichrist by Rev. R. Gerald Culleton
Trial, Tribulation & Triumph by Desmond A. Birch
8 St. Michael and the Angels by Tan books and publishers p 42
9 The Mystical City of God by Mary of Agreda translated by Rev. George J. Blatter, vol. 3, p 204
10 St. Michael and the Angels by Tan Books and Publishers p 42
11 The Douay Rheims Version of the Bible, revised by Bishop Challoner, 1749-1752.
The Antichrist Will Be Coming
The Reign of Antichrist by Rev. R. Gerald Culleton
12, 13, 14, 15, Trial, Tribulation & Triumph by Desmond A. Birch p 411-412, 338, 449, 227

Section VI
The Seventh Church Age
(2383? -3383 or longer?)
Chapter 51--- The Final Tribulation of the Gentile Church---
1 Author anointed; the seventh Church age begins with the Birth of Antichrist.
2 Catholic Encyclopedia, 1913, Vol. 7
The Birth of Antichrist
The Reign of Antichrist by Rev. R. Gerald Culleton
3 www.catholicrevelations.org/PR/hippolytus. htm, chapters 18, 19
4, 5, www.catholicrevelations.org/PR/st%20 methodius.htm
6 The Reign of Antichrist by Rev. R. Gerald Culleton p 116
7 Trial, Tribulation & Triumph by Desmond A. Birch p 459
8, 9, The Reign of Antichrist by Rev. R. Gerald Culleton p 138, 148
10 Sister Mary of the Cross-Shepherdess of La Salette by Fr. Paul Gouin p 67-68
He Will Be Possessed by Satan
The Reign of Antichrist by Rev. R. Gerald Culleton
11 Trial, Tribulation & Triumph by Desmond A. Birch p 230
12 www.catholicrevelations.org/PR/st%20 jerome.htm
13 The Reign of Antichrist by Rev. R. Gerald Culleton p 116
14 Trial, Tribulation & Triumph by Desmond A. Birch p 453
He Will Deceive the Jewish People
The Reign of Antichrist by Rev. R. Gerald Culleton
15, 16, Trial, Tribulation & Triumph by Desmond A. Birch p 455, 456
17 www.catholicrevelations.org/PR/ven%20 bartholomew%20holzhauser.htm
18 The Reign of Antichrist by Rev. R. Gerald Culleton p 79
Rebuilding of the Jewish Temple (3rd)
19, 20, 21, Trial, Tribulation and Triumph by Desmond Birch p 497, 497, 497
He Will Deceive Christians
22 Trial, Tribulation & Triumph by Desmond A. Birch p 461- 463
23 Sister Mary of the Cross-Shepherdess of La Salette by Fr. Paul Gouin p 68
The Abomination of Desolation
24 Thunder of Justice by Ted and Maureen Flynn, (1993) p 262

25 Alphonsus Liguori La Message 'Officio Strapazzati in Opere Ascetiche' as quoted by Father V. Miceli, The Antichrist (Roman Catholic Books, 1981) p 276

The Image of the Beast
26 Trial, Tribulation & Triumph by Desmond A. Birch p 461

The Mark of the Beast
27, 28, The Reign of Antichrist by Rev. R. Gerald Culleton p 128-129, 114

Three and One-Half Years
29 The Reign of Antichrist by Rev. R. Gerald Culleton p 101

Wondering Where The Lions Are?
30 The Reign of Antichrist by Rev. R. Gerald Culleton p 114

The Two Witnesses
31 Against Heresies, Bk 4, Chp 30; MIGNE,P.G.VII,1206, /www.catholicrevelations.org/PR/st%20irenaeus.htm
32 The Reign of Antichrist by Rev. R. Gerald Culleton p 94
33 Author Anointed; the two prophets **Enoch and Elias** will take up the half-week (three and a half years). They will preach 1260 days clothed in sackcloth, proclaiming repentance to all people.
34 The Reign of Antichrist by Rev. R. Gerald Culleton p 97
35, 36, 37, 38, Trial, Tribulation & Triumph by Desmond A. Birch p 471- 472, 473, 442, 474-476
39 www.catholicrevelations.org/PR/st%20benedict.htm
40 Trial, Tribulation & Triumph by Desmond A. Birch p 472
41 www.catholicapologetics.info/catholicteaching/privaterevelation/lasalet.html

The Ark of the Covenant Revealed by the Two Witnesses
42 Trial, Tribulation & Triumph by Desmond A. Birch p 509

Conversion of the Jews to the Messiah–Jesus Christ
43 The Prophets and Our Times by Rev. R. Gerald Culleton p 207

The Seven Bowls Of Plagues
http://rickhoover.wordpress.com/2009/06/22/a-trip-to-israel/ Information on valley of Megiddo

The End of Antichrist
44, 45, 46, 47, 48, The Reign of Antichrist by Rev. R. Gerald Culleton p 148, 135, 111, 152, 117
49 Sister Mary of the Cross-Shepherdess of La Salette by Fr. Paul Gouin p 64-69

The Two Harvests of God
50 Author anointed; two harvests of God will take place.

Chapter 52---Christ Comes Again---
City of God book XX by St. Augustine
1 Author anointed; traditional beliefs of the Church in eschatology are educated opinions with the information that has been available.

The Fullness of the Gentile (Bride) Church
2 The Mystical City of God by Mary of Agreda, vol. 1, p 107
3 Author anointed; Prayer to St. Bridget, asking for wisdom & protection.

In the Twinkling of an Eye The New American Bible 1970

The First Resurrection
The New American Bible 1970

The Messiah is Coming
The New American Bible 1970

Understanding the Differences The New American Bible 1970

The Seven Kingdoms of Daniel 7 & Revelation 17
The New American Bible 1970

Chapter 53---The Thousand Years---
New American Bible 1970

A Utopia During the Seventh Church Age
New American Bible 1970

Like the Sands of the Sea
New American Bible 1970

Section VII
His Reign Will be Forever

Chapter 54--- After the Thousand Years---
1 The Reign of Antichrist by Rev. R. Gerald Culleton p 116

The Last Judgment
New American Bible 1970

A New Heavens and a New Earth
2 Author anointed; there will be a new heavens and a new earth.

Epilogue
St. Therese of Lisieux

Made in the USA
Columbia, SC
20 November 2020